# THE
# TRANSFER OF POWER
# IN INDIA

By the same author:

THE STORY OF THE INTEGRATION OF THE INDIAN STATES

# THE
# TRANSFER OF POWER
# IN INDIA

---

### V. P. MENON

PRINCETON, NEW JERSEY
PRINCETON UNIVERSITY PRESS
1957

TO MY WIFE

# PREFACE

IT was Sardar Vallabhbhai Patel's desire that I should write two books, one narrating the events leading to the transfer of power in India, and the other dealing with the integration of the Indian States. *The Story of the Integration of the Indian States* has already been published. With the publication of this book, which I call THE TRANSFER OF POWER IN INDIA, I shall have fulfilled my promise to our revered Sardar.

My story starts with the outbreak of World War II in September 1939. I chose this date because, with the outbreak of the war, the world as we knew it came to an end and an entirely new situation was created. From this date up to the transfer of power on 15 August 1947, I have given a detailed narration of events as I witnessed them. In one capacity or other, from 1917 I was continuously associated with the constitutional developments in India. From 1942 till the transfer of power in August 1947 I was the Constitutional Adviser to the Governor-General.

In writing this book, I have endeavoured to adhere to a factual narration, avoiding the expression of personal opinions as far as possible. The first two chapters give a historical background, from the transfer of government by the East India Company to the British Crown, so as to enable the reader to appreciate more clearly the events which followed. In those chapters I have endeavoured to describe in brief the important stages of constitutional progress in this country. If I have dealt with some of those constitutional changes (e.g. the Government of India Act of 1919 and the rules made thereunder, and the Government of India Act of 1935) in what might appear rather dreary detail, I have done so in the belief that my book will provide to the student of constitutional history, material not readily available to him from other sources.

I acknowledge most gratefully the generous help given to me by the Rockefeller Foundation, Humanities Division, through the

*Preface*

Indian Council of World Affairs, for the preparation of this book and the book on the integration of the Indian States. No responsibility, however, attaches to the Foundation (or to anyone else) in regard to either the contents or the views expressed.

I am also thankful to the Indian Council of World Affairs.

My special thanks are due to E. C. Gaynor and R. P. Aiyar for the assistance given to me in writing this book, and also to the stenographers, S. Gopalakrishnan and K. Thankappan Nair and the typist, M. Balakrishnan, all of whom discharged their duties with remarkable diligence and efficiency.

Bangalore,
26 January 1957.                                          V. P. MENON

# CONTENTS

## APPENDIXES

# Contents

# THE
# TRANSFER OF POWER
# IN INDIA

Alas, my Brother ! Mighty Kings and lords,
   Proud princes, courtiers, loveliest maidens gay,
Bards, and their tales of ancient chivalry
   Homage to Time ! all these have passed away.

from BHARTRIHARI's Vairagya Satakam

# I

# THE GOAL OF BRITISH POLICY

## I

ON 15 August 1947 India stepped on to a new road of freedom and endeavour, no longer a dependency of the British Crown but a Dominion and a member of the British Commonwealth of Nations. The day marked the close of over a century and a half of British rule in India. It was during the first World War, in 1917, that the goal of British policy was for the first time authoritatively defined. It was after the conclusion of the second World War that Britain decided to hand over power to Indian hands and to withdraw. This was indeed Britain's finest hour.

Speaking of the achievements of Clive a historian has remarked: 'He was the founder of the glory and greatness of an empire of which a little island in the Atlantic is the parent trunk and Hindustan the noblest branch.' A succession of Governors-General — both distinguished and undistinguished — from Warren Hastings to Dalhousie completed the task so well begun by Clive. After 1857, when the Crown assumed the governance of India, on another series of Viceroys and Governors-General fell the task of consolidating the gains of the preceding century. But throughout, the policy of the British Government in India was evolved more by the exigencies of time and circumstance than as the result of deliberate planning.

It was in the heyday of the Victorian age when, in the wake of industrial revolution and the growth of democracy, a wave of idealism swept over the little island, that there flourished statesmen and thinkers of vision, who could find time and thought for their acquired dependencies and who began to formulate concepts and aims in the true Liberal tradition. To this small set of men belonged the great leader W. E. Gladstone. In an article which he contributed in 1878 and which was published in the *Patriot* of the veteran Indian journalist, Kristo Das Pal, Gladstone wrote:

Here is tutelage unexampled in history. It embraces from one-fifth to one-sixth of the human race: the latest German reckonings of the population of the globe carrying it beyond fourteen hundred millions. Over this population and the vast territory it inhabits, we hold a dominion entirely uncontrolled, save by duty and by prudence, measured as we may choose to measure them. This dominion is *de jure* in the hands of a nation whose numbers as compared with those of its Indian subjects are one to seven, and whose seat is at the other end of the world; *de facto*, it is wielded by a handful of their agents, military and civil, who are not as one to three thousand of the peoples spread, as an ocean, in passive obedience around them.... Of the seventy thousand Anglo-Indians, not one except waifs and strays strikes root in the country and all but a handful have their stay limited to a very brief term of years. At home still less provision is made for the adequate discharge of a gigantic duty. It depends upon a Cabinet which dreads nothing so much as the mention of an Indian question at its meetings; on a minister who knows that the less his colleagues hear of his proceedings, the better they will be pleased; on a Council, which is not allowed to enter into his highest deliberations; and on a Parliament, supreme over them all, which cannot in its two Houses jointly muster one single score of persons, who have either a practical experience in the government of India or a tolerable knowledge of its people or its history.... The truth as to India cannot too soon be understood. There are two policies, fundamentally different; and it is the wrong one that is now in favour. One of them treats India as a child treats a doll, and defends it against other children; the other places all its hopes for the permanence of our Indian rule in our good government of India. Sound finance and moderate establishments, liberal extension of native privileges, and, not least of all, an unfailing regard to the sacredness of the pledge implied in privilege already given, these acts of government will secure the way to prosperity, to contentment, and to confidence in India. Let us only make common cause with her people: let them feel that we are there to give more than we receive; that their interests are not traversed and frustrated by selfish aims of ours; that, if we are defending ourselves upon the line of the Hindoo Coosh, it is them and their interests that we are defending even more and far more than our own. Unless we can produce this conviction in the mind of India, in vain shall we lavish our thoughts and our resources upon a merely material defence.... Between the two methods of procedure there could be no competition, were we as people free to give to the affairs of India anything like the attention which they demand, and which it may some day cost us many a fruitless pang never to have given.

In retrospect, these words strike me as the quintessence of wisdom and statesmanship, though for the men of that generation, cast in Disraeli mould, they might have seemed the outpourings of a vain and garrulous idealist. No words, it seems to me, could describe better the system of government which ruled India almost up to the date of the transfer of power, or the ideals which should have guided Britain's policy in this country.

But we are anticipating. Let us review broadly the position from 1857, when the great Indian Mutiny (as it was then called) brought to an end the East India Company's rule in India.

By the Act of 1858, the powers previously wielded by the Court of Directors of the Company and by the Parliamentary Board of Control passed to the British Crown. The Act charged the Secretary of State for India with the 'superintendence, direction and control of all acts, operations and concerns which relate to the government or revenues of India, and all grants... and other payments and charges out of or on the revenues of India;' and the Government of India and each of the provincial governments (of which there were five) were severally 'required to pay due obedience to all such orders as they may receive from the Secretary of State.' The entire system was thus centred in Whitehall.

The events of 1857 left lasting impressions on the minds of the Indian people. They had experienced enough of the miseries of anarchy and disorder; they now but yearned for an era of peace and stable government. British administrators in India, for their part, realized the consequences of attempting to govern a vast country without in the least knowing the wishes of the people. Sir Bartle Frere, for instance, in a minute recorded in 1860, emphasized the dangers of 'continuing to legislate for millions of people with few means of knowing, except by a rebellion, whether the law suits them or not.'

Such views and sentiments led to the passing of the Indian Councils Act of 1861, which introduced important changes in the administration of the country. The strength of the Governor-General's Executive Council was raised from four to five. The Governor-General was empowered to make rules for the transaction of business in his Executive Council. Lord Canning utilized this power to introduce what is known as the 'portfolio system'. Till then the Executive Council had worked together as a board and decided all questions by a majority vote. Henceforward, the ordinary work of the departments was distributed among the members and only the more important cases were submitted to the Governor-General or were dealt with collectively. The Governors of Madras and Bombay had similar executive councils.

For purposes of legislation, the Governor-General's Executive Council was reinforced by 'additional' members, nominated for two years. There were to be not less than six and not more than twelve additional members, of whom not less than half were to be non-officials. Their business was limited strictly to legislation; the Act expressly forbade transaction of any other business. In 1862, Lord Canning nominated three Indians to his 'Legislative Council'.

The Act also restored to the Governments of Bombay and Madras the power, subject to certain restrictions, of making laws and regulations for the peace and good government of those presidencies, a power which had been taken away by the Charter Act of 1833. For purposes of legislation, each of the Governors' executive councils was enlarged by the addition of the Advocate-General and 'not less than four nor more than eight members' nominated by the Governor. Of this number at least half were to be non-officials. The Governor-General in Council was authorized to create similar legislative councils in the remaining provinces of Bengal, the North-West Provinces and the Punjab, as well as in the new provinces which the Act was empowered to constitute.

The Governor-General's Legislative Council could legislate for the whole of India, while the provincial council could legislate for the whole of the province. In certain specified matters the previous sanction of the Governor-General was necessary, while all bills required the assent, not only of the Governor, but also of the Governor-General.

These councils, however, were not deliberative bodies where subjects could be freely discussed, where grievances could be ventilated, information elicited by interpellation, or acts of administration impugned or defended. They were no more than law-making committees, whose sole purpose was to advise and assist the executive in their legislation and through whom, incidentally, full publicity at every law-making process was ensured.

The two decades following upon the Indian Councils Act of 1861 saw the emergence of an intelligentsia with an increasing interest in the administration of the country. These educated classes became more critical of the acts of Government. The Vernacular Press Act, which was passed in 1878 during the viceroyalty of Lord Lytton (and repealed four years later), lighted a spark that set in motion a whole battery of public criticism. Local political organizations began to spring up in Calcutta, Bombay and Madras. A retired British I.C.S. official, Allan Octavian Hume, alarmed by the tide of discontent, set about to find a means of directing popular impulse into constructive channels. Having enlisted official support, and with the approval of the Governor-General (Lord Dufferin), he addressed a stirring letter to the graduates of the Calcutta University urging them to organize an association for the cultural, moral, social and political regeneration of the people of India. The result was the first session of the Indian National Congress held on 27 December 1885,[1] at the Gokuldas Tejpal Sanskrit College in Bombay, where seventy-two delegates from all over India met under the presidentship of W. C. Bonnerji, a Bengali Christian barrister. The Congress resolutions, modest in tone and character, aimed at the enlargement of the legislative councils and their powers, simultaneous examinations for the I.C.S. in India and in Britain, and certain other administrative reforms. Henceforth the Congress held its annual meeting round about Christmas and its resolutions were duly forwarded to the Government of India and to the Secretary of State.

Lord Dufferin felt that it was time some positive policy was drawn up to meet Indian aspirations and he decided to appoint a committee of his Executive Council to elaborate a scheme. The Committee's report was forwarded to the Secretary of State in November 1888, along with a minute by Lord Dufferin. Lord Dufferin's view is contained in the following noteworthy passage:

It now appears to my colleagues and to myself that the time has come for us to take another step in the development of the same liberal policy, and to give, to quote my own words, 'a still wider share in the administration of public affairs to such Indian gentlemen as by their influence, their acquirements, and the confidence they inspire in their fellow-countrymen are marked out as fitted to assist with their counsels the responsible rulers of the country.' But it is necessary that there should be no mistake as to the nature of our aims, or of the real direction in which we propose to move. Our scheme may be briefly described as a plan for the enlargement of our provincial councils, for the enhancement of their status, the multiplication of their functions, the partial introduction into them of the elective principle, and the liberalisation of their general character as political

---

[1] A significant date in the history of Indian politics.

institutions. From this it might be concluded that we were contemplating an approach, at all events as far as the provinces are concerned, to English parliamentary government, and an English constitutional system. Such a conclusion would be very wide of the mark. . . .

Lord Dufferin left India in December 1888, but his successor, Lord Lansdowne, continued to carry out his policy which ultimately found its expression in the Indian Councils Act of 1892. This Act increased the strength of the legislative councils, both Indian and provincial, and empowered the Governor-General in Council to frame regulations as to the conditions of nomination of the 'additional' members. The regulations prescribed, *inter alia,* that the majority of the non-official seats should be filled on the recommendation of such bodies as municipalities, district boards, chambers of commerce, universities, etc. The term 'election' was sedulously eschewed; but nominations by recommending bodies came to be accepted as a matter of course, and the fact of election to an appreciable proportion of the non-official seats was thus firmly established.

The Act also gave to the councils, in pursuance of the recommendations of Lord Dufferin's Committee, the right of asking questions and of discussing, though not of voting upon, the budget. And thus the councils came to be recognized as more than merely legislative or advisory bodies.

In 1899 Lord Curzon came to India as Governor-General. He certainly did not share the belief expressed by Gladstone that 'the capital agent in determining finally the question whether our power in India is or is not to continue will be the will of the 240 millions of people who inhabit India.' He was on the contrary imbued with a sense of his Imperial mission. Under his regime the administration reached new levels of efficiency. No Viceroy, before or after, initiated administrative measures so numerous and far-reaching. Some of these measures roused great resentment and opposition. The partition of Bengal in particular was vehemently resisted. Lord Curzon sought to justify the measure on the ground that the province was too unwieldy for a single charge and that its partition was necessary in the interests of better administrative efficiency. But the dividing line was so crudely drawn that it meant the splitting of the province into two communal blocs — the one in which the Hindus were in the majority, and the other in which the Muslims predominated. The measure was construed as an attempt on the part of Lord Curzon to cripple the new renaissance in Bengal; and, for the first time, agitation went beyond the accepted methods, namely of prayer, petition and protest. A new programme of resistance was launched which included the boycott of British goods.

World factors also contributed to rouse the enthusiasm of the Indian nationalists. In particular, the defeat of Russia by an Asiatic power — Japan — created a profound and stirring impression.

Within the Congress there were those of the old school, like Dadabhoy Naoroji (the first Indian to become a member of the British House of Commons), Gopal Krishna Gokhale, Surendranath Banerjea and Sir Pherozshah Mehta, who subscribed to the view that the association of Indians in the governance of their country should be a gradual process. But there rose a new school of thought, deriving its inspiration from Bal Gangadhar Tilak, who insisted on *swaraj* (self-rule) as the goal of Indian aspirations. This great Maharashtrian leader had a considerable following in the country, notably in Bombay.

When Lord Curzon (who had been appointed to a second term of office) resigned in 1905, he left behind much ill-feeling and discontent. He was succeeded by Lord Minto; and in December 1905 Lord Morley became the Secretary of State for India. One of Lord Minto's first considerations was to allay the general unrest in the country. He hoped by a policy of concessions to bring round at least the moderate sections. To this end he appointed, with the approval of Lord Morley, a committee drawn from his Executive Council to inquire into the means of associating Indians more closely with the administration. To quote Lord Minto's own words:

We the Government of India cannot shut our eyes to present conditions. The political atmosphere is full of change; questions are before us which we cannot afford to ignore, and which we must attempt to answer; and to me it would appear all-important that the initiative should emanate from us, that the Government of India should not be put in the position of appearing to have its hands forced by agitation in this country or by pressure from Home — that we should be the first to recognise surrounding conditions and to place before His Majesty's Government the opinions which personal experience and a close touch with the everyday life of India entitle us to hold.

In their examination of the Committee's report, the Government of India set themselves the task of considering how they could liberalize their power while still retaining control. What they planned to produce was a sort of 'constitutional autocracy' which would use its predominant power only after listening fully to Indian views. Their hope was to create a constitution which would be regarded as a precious possession and which conservative sentiment at any rate would defend against further change.

Lord Morley was in fact equally clear in repudiating any sort of representative government for India in the western sense of the term. In his view the real object of the changes should be not merely to seek to satisfy Indian aspirations, but to fortify authority. To quote his own words: 'In Indian government there is no grace worth having in what is praised as a concession, and no particular virtue in satisfying an aspiration, unless your measures at the same time fortify the basis of authority on which peace and order and all the elements of the public good in India depend.'

A year later, however, in their specific proposals for the enlargement of the legislative councils which they submitted to the Secretary of State in October 1908, the Government of India showed less disposition to insist on official majorities. Lord Morley, while agreeing with the Government of India in regard to the provincial councils, insisted on a permanent substantial majority in the Imperial Council, so as to 'outweigh the grave disadvantages that induce us to dispense with it in the provincial councils.' The Government of India, he said, must in its legislative as well as in its executive character continue to be so constituted as to ensure its constant and uninterrupted power to fulfil the obligations that it owes and must always owe to His Majesty's Government and to the Imperial Parliament. He declined, in short, to contemplate such a popularization of the system of the government in India as would lead to relaxation of control by Parliament.

We must here digress for a moment in order to trace the development of Muslim and Congress politics in India. British resentment immediately after the Mutiny was — at least in Delhi and Upper India — more against the Muslims than the Hindus; for it was the Muslims who had led the revolt in Upper India. British feeling towards the Muslims was expressed in the following words by Sir Syed Ahmad Khan: 'There was no prickly plant in those awful times respecting which it was not said that it was planted by Mahomedans.' Sir Syed Ahmad Khan is perhaps best remembered as the founder of the Mahomedan Anglo-Oriental College at Aligarh, which later developed into the Aligarh University. But he was noted also for other achievements. Anxious at the time to put the Muslims back into favour with the British, Sir Syed Ahmad Khan made it his special endeavour to persuade his co-religionists to keep aloof from the Congress, which was showing growing signs of opposition towards British policy and administration. In 1888 Sir Syed Ahmad established the United Patriotic Association, which included Muslims as well as Hindu members, all of whom were opposed to the Congress. In 1893 he formed the Mahomedan Anglo-Oriental Defence Association of Upper India, confining its membership to Muslims and Englishmen!

There had always been a weighty consensus of official opinion that in a country like India communal and class electorates were inevitable. It was a view supported strongly by Lord Dufferin and pursued later, in 1892, by Lord Lansdowne's Government. An exception to the general opinion was Sir Dennis Fitzpatrick, who, speaking for the Punjab, said that he doubted 'whether in a province where the antagonism of different races and sects is so intense, it would be expedient to form any scheme expressly based on the idea of choosing class representatives.' A spirited plea for territorial electorates was also put forward by Gokhale, who was then the Secretary of the Sarvajanik Sabha. It appealed to practical experience all the world over to show that a fair representation of the larger interests of a great community could only be secured by the territorial principle. 'The principle of recognizing races and creeds,' said Gokhale, 'stands in no need of encouragement from Government, as the division of interests caused by it has already been the bane of this country.'

In October 1906 a deputation of Muslims, headed by His Highness the Aga Khan, waited on the Viceroy at Simla and presented an address to him. Their request for separate representation was based on the value of their contribution to the defence of the Empire, and on their traditions of past political greatness. Lord Minto replied that he realized that their claim was not merely that they should be represented 'as a community', but that their position should be estimated not merely on their numerical strength but in respect to the political importance of their community and the service it had rendered to the Empire. 'I am entirely in accord with you,' he said. 'I am as firmly convinced, as I believe you to be, that any electoral representation in India would be doomed to mischievous failure which aimed at granting a personal enfranchisement, regardless of the beliefs and traditions of the communities composing the population of this Continent.'

Lord Minto's reply to the deputation was characterized by Lady Minto (in her diary) as 'nothing less than the pulling back of sixty-two millions of people from joining the ranks of the seditious opposition.' The All-India Muslim League was established almost as a direct result of the assurances given by him. The League held its first session in December 1906.[1]

In their official communication to the Secretary of State in October 1908, the Government of India recommended that the Muslims should be granted separate electorates. 'The Indian Muhammadans,' they averred, 'are much more than a religious body. They form in fact an absolutely separate community, distinct by marriage, food and custom, and claiming in many cases to belong to a different race from the Hindus.' Lord Morley was at first opposed to the principle of separate electorates, but ultimately gave in.

The reason for giving the Muslims reserved seats and also separate electorates was that the Muslims feared that in territorial constituencies they would not secure the representation to which their numbers entitled them. Unless seats were actually reserved, they would, whether in single or many-seated constituencies, secure very few seats against the Hindus; and without separate voting, the richer and better-organized Hindus would arrange to put up Muslim candidates who would serve their interests and not those of Muslims. Both lines of defence were therefore held to be necessary. But the Muslims advanced and obtained yet a third demand, namely, that the scale of their representation should be not their wealth or their numbers, but their 'political importance', a qualification not susceptible of exact assessment.

Turning now to the Congress, the radical wing had formulated a policy of the boycott of British goods as a protest against the partition of Bengal. In 1906, the veteran Dadabhoy Naoroji was persuaded to come all the way back from England to preside over the Calcutta session of the Congress, where for the first time the word *swaraj* found a place in the Congress presidential address. The session of the Congress held at Surat in 1907 brought about a parting of the ways between the extremists and the moderates; the former

---

[1] It is an interesting fact that the Hindu Mahasabha was established in the same year.

were keen on passing resolutions on *swaraj*, boycott and national education, while the latter were for watering them down. No agreement could be reached between them and the session broke up in confusion.

At a convention of moderate Congressmen held in Allahabad in 1908 a constitution was drawn up which practically excluded the extremists. The first article to which every member had to subscribe was as follows:

The objects of the Indian National Congress are the attainment by the people of India of a system of government similar to that enjoyed by the self-governing members of the British Empire and a participation by them in the rights and responsibilities of the Empire on equal terms with those members. These objects are to be achieved by constitutional means by bringing about a steady reform of the existing system of administration and by promoting national unity, fostering public spirit and developing and organising the intellectual, moral, economic and industrial resources of the country.

It was in this atmosphere that the Minto-Morley reforms were launched. The Indian Councils Act of 1909 made important changes in the composition and functions of the legislative councils. The number of 'additional' members of the Imperial Legislative Council was raised to a maximum of 60, of whom not more than 28 were to be officials. The Governor-General was empowered to nominate three non-officials to represent certain specified communities; he also had at his disposal two other seats to be filled by nomination. Of the remaining 27 seats, 14 were to be filled by elected members representing certain special constituencies (landowners in seven provinces, Muslims in five provinces and chambers of commerce in Calcutta and Bombay), while thirteen were to be elected by the non-official members of the nine provincial legislative councils.

In the provincial legislative councils the number of 'additional' members was raised to a maximum of 50 in all provinces, except the Punjab and Burma, where the number was fixed at 30; and it was so arranged that a combination of officials and nominated non-official members would secure a small majority over the elected members. The exception was Bengal, where there was a clear elected majority; but this elected majority was more nominal than real, since four of the elected members were representatives of the European community. The greater part of the non-official members was to be elected by groups of local bodies, landholders, trade associations and universities. The Muslims were conceded separate representation in Madras, Bombay, Bengal, the United Provinces and in East Bengal and Assam.

The Act empowered the councils to discuss the budget and, before it was finally settled, to propose resolutions and divide upon them. On all matters of general public importance resolutions could be moved by members and divisions taken. The right to ask questions of the Government was enlarged by allowing the member who asked the original question to put a supplementary one. Resolutions were to be expressed, and to be operative, as recommendations to the executive Government, and any of them might be disallowed by the Governor-General, or Governor, acting as President of the Council, at his discretion. Resolutions were barred on certain specified matters, e.g. those concerning the Army and the Indian States.

In the wake of the Minto-Morley Reforms came the appointment of the first Indian to the Governor-General's Executive Council; he was Sir S. P. (later Lord) Sinha. An Indian was also appointed to each of the provincial executive councils.

These reforms, when they were announced, were hailed with enthusiasm. Seven years later they were denounced by the Congress at Lucknow as the merest moonshine!

The inauguration of the Minto-Morley Reforms was followed by the visit, in 1911, of the King and Queen to India. His Majesty (King George V) made two important announcements. One was the transfer of the capital from Calcutta to Delhi, and the other the annulment of the partition of Bengal. There was no particular enthusiasm about the transfer of the capital; but the annulment of the partition of Bengal was received (except by a section of Muslims) with popular acclamation.

In the despatch[1] of Lord Hardinge's Government to the Secretary of State dated 25 August 1911, recommending the changes mentioned above, there is the following significant paragraph:

The maintenance of British rule in India depends on the ultimate supremacy of the Governor-General in Council, and the Indian Councils Act of 1909 itself bears testimony to the impossibility of allowing matters of vital concern to be decided by a majority of non-official votes in the Imperial Legislative Council. Nevertheless it is certain that, in the course of time,

[1] Commonly known as the 'Delhi Despatch'.

the just demands of Indians for a larger share in the government of the country will have to be satisfied, and the question will be how this devolution of power can be conceded without impairing the supreme authority of the Governor-General in Council. The only possible solution of the difficulty would appear to be gradually to give the provinces a larger measure of self-government, until at last India would consist of a number of administrations, autonomous in all provincial affairs, with the Government of India above them all, and possessing power to interfere in case of misgovernment but ordinarily restricting their functions to matters of Imperial concern.

Politicians in India viewed this as a declaration in the direction of self-government and as defining the lines of British policy in India and they hoped that early measures would be taken to give effect to it. E. S. Montagu, then Under Secretary of State for India, speaking at Cambridge, interpreted the paragraph in the same sense. But the interpretation was challenged in Parliament by Lord Curzon; while the Secretary of State, Lord Crewe, specifically disavowed it. The latter remarked that a political school in India looked forward 'to the inception in India of something approaching the self-government enjoyed by those colonies which have of late years received the name of Dominion. It is in vain to deny the existence of such a school. I say quite frankly that I see no future for India on those lines. I do not believe that the experiment—for it would be an experiment quite new, so far as my knowledge of history goes, in the wide world—of attempting to confer a real measure of self-government with practical freedom from Parliamentary control, upon a race which is not our own...is one which could be tried.... It is certainly my duty to repudiate altogether that reading of the despatch.' Lord Curzon, welcoming the statement of the Secretary of State, added: 'That repudiation we acknowledge: we shall remember it, and I have no doubt we shall often have good occasion to use it in the future.'

The position in 1914 was that, so far as His Majesty's Government's policy towards India was concerned, the fundamentals on which the Minto-Morley Reforms were based continued to hold the field. These reforms had carried to the furthest practicable point the previous line of constitutional development. They had enlarged the legislative councils and the sphere of their deliberations. They had admitted the need for increased representation and the desirability of generally securing non-official approval to Government legislation; and by conceding the important right of discussing administrative matters and of cross-examining Government on its replies to questions, they had done much to make the councils serve the purpose of an inquest into the doings of Government. But the responsibility for the administration remained undivided. The conception of a responsible executive, wholly or partially amenable to elected councils, was not admitted. Power remained with the official Governments, and in consequence there was no loosening of the bonds which subjected local Governments to the Government of India, and the latter to the Secretary of State and Parliament. The people were given increased opportunities of influencing the Government, but the principle of autocracy was retained.

The declaration of war in 1914 evoked expressions of loyalty and support from the Congress as well as the Muslim League. But there were some disturbing factors in the situation, such as the *émeute* of part of the 5th Light Infantry at Singapore, the *Ghadr* (Mutiny) movement in the Punjab and the terrorist movement in Bengal. The entry of Turkey into the war against Britain also caused a serious strain upon the loyalty of the Muslims.

The enemy certainly regarded India as one of the most vulnerable parts of the empire and laid their plans accordingly. Any expectations that India would prove a burden and a source of weakness were falsified; India in fact proved a source of strength from both the military and the economic point of view, and as the struggle deepened, so the extent to which her resources were drawn upon increased.

In December 1915 the Congress and the All-India Muslim League held their respective annual sessions in Bombay. The former authorized the All-India Congress Committee to prepare a scheme of reforms and to confer with the Committee of the All-India Muslim League for that purpose. The two Committees met during the year and prepared a scheme. In 1916 the Congress and the League held their annual sessions simultaneously in Lucknow. The breach in the Congress between the extremists and the moderates had by now been bridged and an agreement was reached between the Congress and the League in regard to the representation of Muslims in the various legislative councils. This agreement, known as the 'Lucknow Pact', was embodied in the scheme of reforms prepared by the Indian National Congress and the All-India Muslim League. It provided for the representation of Muslims through separate electorates in the following proportions:

| Punjab | .. | One-half | |
|---|---|---|---|
| United Provinces | .. | 30 per cent | |
| Bengal | .. | 40 ,, ,, | |
| Bihar | .. | 25 ,, ,, | of the elected |
| Central Provinces | .. | 15 ,, ,, | Indian members |
| Madras | .. | 15 ,, ,, | |
| Bombay | .. | One-third | |

For the Imperial Legislative Council, provision was made that one-third of the Indian elected members should be Muslims elected by separate Muslim electorates in the several provinces in the proportion, as nearly as might be, in which they were represented in the provincial legislative councils by separate electorates. This was subject to two conditions, namely (1) that no Muslim should participate in any of the other elections to the Imperial or provincial legislative councils, save and except those by electorates representing special interests like landholders, universities etc.; and (2) that no bill, nor any clause thereof, nor a resolution introduced by a non-official member affecting one or the other community (which question would be determined by the members of that community in the legislative council concerned) should be proceeded with if it were opposed by three-fourths of the members of that community in the particular council, Imperial or provincial.

In November 1916, when the general outlook had been profoundly affected by the war, Lord Chelmsford's Government again set themselves to formulate proposals for constitutional advance. In their despatch to the Secretary of State they accepted self-government (in a form suited to India) as the goal. They did not look to colonial democratic federations as the inevitable model. As an immediate step, they proposed to enlarge the powers of provincial councils by extending the electorate and increasing the elective element. Their recommendations, in effect, amounted to the giving of legislative control to provincial councils without conceding anything in the nature of direct financial or administrative control. In the Imperial Legislative Council they proposed practically no change. Nor did they discuss any relaxation of the Secretary of State's control over the Government of India.

In 1917 the war entered an acute phase. The political situation in India was far from satisfactory. The 'Home Rule' agitation started by Tilak and Mrs Annie Besant had gained considerable support in the country. In July 1917 Edwin Samuel Montagu succeeded Sir

Austen Chamberlain[1] as the Secretary of State for India. Montagu was convinced that the Indian peoples, by the part played by them in the war, had established their claim to be regarded henceforth as an integral part of the British empire, entitled to share in its common affairs. The claim involved the corollary that all matters within the empire in which their feelings of self-respect had been wounded, or their special or peculiar interests overlooked, should be carefully and sympathetically reconsidered. A great war, he observed, inevitably produced unrest, giving birth to new thoughts and ambitions and creating an atmosphere of expectation. The consciousness that India had played a great part in the struggle of nations had permeated into many quarters where questions of political rights or status had formerly been little thought of, and this had led men of all degrees to reflect on the position of their country with respect to other countries, and the nature of their status in their own country.

On the main proposal of the Government of India, the Secretary of State felt that merely to enlarge the legislative councils and to concede legislative control, without at the same time giving them a share in matters of finance and administration, would only result in discontent and friction and tempt members to resort to obstructive tactics.

Montagu was convinced of the necessity of a new approach to the Indian problem. Within a month of his taking office, he had persuaded his colleagues in the Cabinet (including Lord Curzon) to agree to a policy which he announced in the House of Commons on 20 August 1917 in the following terms:

The policy of His Majesty's Government, with which the Government of India are in complete accord, is that of the increasing association of Indians in every branch of the administration and the gradual development of self-governing institutions with a view to the progressive realisation of responsible government in India as an integral part of the British Empire. They have decided that substantial steps in this direction should be taken as soon as possible, and that it is of the highest importance as a preliminary to considering what these steps should be that there should be a free and informal exchange of opinion between those in authority at Home and in India. His Majesty's Government have accordingly decided, with His Majesty's approval, that I should accept the Viceroy's invitation to proceed to India to discuss these matters with the Viceroy and the Government

[1] Sir Austen Chamberlain resigned his office in consequence of strictures passed on the Government of India by the Mesopotamian Commission with regard to the conduct of the war in the Middle East.

of India, to consider with the Viceroy the views of local Governments, and to receive with him the suggestions of representative bodies and others.

I would add that progress in this policy can only be achieved by successive stages. The British Government and the Government of India, on whom the responsibility lies for the welfare and advancement of the Indian peoples, must be judges of the time and measure of each advance, and they must be guided by the co-operation received from those upon whom new opportunities of service will thus be conferred and by the extent to which it is found that confidence can be reposed in their sense of responsibility.

The support of the Government of India to the new policy was not without reservations. The following views expressed by a distinguished official who was intimately connected with the discussions in those days aptly describe the dilemma that faced them:

Past papers are full of impressive opinion, recorded by generations of the wisest Indian administrators, as to the impossibility of setting up parliamentary institutions in India. I need not repeat them. They dwell upon the infinite divisions of the country; the distrust between creeds and races; the smallness of the intellectual class; their lack of experience in affairs and the narrowness of their interests; the inertia of the natural leaders of what is still an aristocratic society; their timidness in coming forward to contest the position with the politicians; the indifference of the great mass of the people to politics, and their preference for and disposition to rely upon an impartial non-political government. These are the official views that have hitherto held the field unchallenged; and those who held them disbelieved profoundly in the possibility of forming anything but a tiny electorate; they believed that even if formed the electorate will be at the mercy of a small coterie of politicians who will use their power to exalt themselves; and they turned instinctively to plans for constructing an elaborate balance of power between all classes of interests in the country, which necessarily means that the Government will still remain the arbiter of the situation.

On the one hand though we admit the entire accuracy of this picture and the tremendous difficulties which it involves, we seem to be now committed by the trend of world events, and now by the Secretary of State's declaration, to the proposition that the supreme need to which everything else must give way is to develop the natural character of India in the one way that official government can never develop it; that is to say, by leaving Indians to try to set things right for themselves, and to learn by suffering from their own mistakes. It means a prolonged period of discomfort for the country and possibly intervals of disorder; a state of things at which it will be very difficult, and may from time to time become impossible, for the diminishing official government to stand by and look on. It means indeed the exercise of an enormous effort of faith and great political self-control; our being resolved to search for electorates where none exist and to construct them out of the most unpromising materials; being prepared to see minorities unrepresented and majorities tyrannical; to abstain from attempting to secure each class in its just rights, and to leave inequalities and injustices as far as possible to right themselves by being the means of gradually teaching those who are backward or are oppressed a political education.

In the announcement of the Secretary of State, the term 'responsible government' was used for the first time. 'Responsible government' could admit of only one meaning, namely, executives removable at the will of the elected legislatures and electorates in India. The goal was identical with that already achieved by the self-governing dominions. Thus, what was considered as unthinkable by Lord Morley in 1908 and as outside the realm of practical politics by Lord Crewe and Lord Curzon as late as 1912, became possible in 1917, due as much to the exigencies of the war situation as to the increasing growth of political consciousness in India.

## II

The announcement of August 1917, in the words of the authors of the Montagu-Chelmsford report, 'marks the end of one epoch, and the beginning of a new one.' Soon after the announcement, Montagu came out to India and visited the principal towns, receiving deputations of representatives of the various associations and political, communal and commercial bodies. Associated with his inquiries was the Viceroy, Lord Chelmsford. A joint report was signed by them in April 1918 and published in July 1918, shortly after Montagu's return to England. Three months later the war with Germany was over.

The publication of the Montagu-Chelmsford Report was followed by the appointment of two committees, one known as the Franchise Committee to deal with matters relating to the franchise and the composition of the new legislatures, the other as the Functions Committee to consider and recommend the allocation of subjects between the Centre and the provinces. These two committees toured India between November 1918 and March 1919. There ensued some preliminary inquiries and discussions between the Government of India, the provincial governments and the Secretary of State. Eventually, in the summer of 1919, a Bill was introduced in the House of

Commons. This Bill was referred to a Joint Select Committee of Parliament, before whom a large number of witnesses appeared and tendered their evidence, and deputations representing all shades of Indian opinion submitted their views.

The task of the Joint Committee was a difficult one. It was confronted on almost all vital issues with conflicting and contradictory views, so that its eventual recommendations were in the nature of a compromise between those who wanted to go further and those who did not want to go as far. Even the Government of India's attitude towards some of the changes proposed by the Committee was unaccommodating. Looking back on that period, one cannot but admire the persistence and ability with which Montagu directed the passage of this Bill and its various amendments through Parliament. The Bill received the Royal Assent in December 1919, and became known as the Government of India Act, 1919.

The Rules framed under the Act of 1919 were no less important than the Act itself. These rules were approved by Parliament and it was in their provisions that, to a very large extent, the policy of the Act found expression.

The Government of India Act of 1919 laid down for the first time in definite terms the British Government's policy towards India. It will be useful to dwell to some extent on the broad features of this Act.

The declaration of August 1917 was embodied in the Preamble. The only change was the substitution of 'British India' for 'India', since India included both British India and the Indian States, and Parliament could not legislate for the latter.

The scheme of the Act followed the recommendation of the authors of the Joint Report that the earlier steps to be taken towards the realization of the new policy should be in the domain of the provinces. The provinces to which the provisions of the Act specifically applied were Madras, Bombay, Bengal, the United Provinces, the Punjab, Bihar and Orissa, the Central Provinces and Assam; but the Act permitted of their extension to other parts of British India. Burma, for instance, was accorded a constitution substantially identical with that enjoyed by the major Indian provinces and the provisions of the Act were extended subsequently to the North-West Frontier Province and partially to Coorg.

Hitherto there had been no formal division of the functions of the central and provincial governments. The administration of many subjects had been delegated to, or in practice rested with, the provincial governments. Under the Act, the spheres of the central and provincial governments were demarcated by a division of subjects into 'central' and 'provincial'. Generally speaking, 'central subjects' included all subjects directly administered by the Government of India or in which extra-provincial interests were dominant; whilst 'provincial subjects' included subjects in which the interests of the provinces essentially predominated.

The provincial subjects were divided into two categories, namely 'reserved' and 'transferred'. Each province was to be governed in relation to 'reserved' subjects by a Governor in Council, and in relation to 'transferred' subjects by a Governor acting with ministers, a system commonly known as dyarchy. In the selection of subjects to be transferred to ministers, the guiding principle followed was to include in the 'transferred' list those departments which offered the most opportunity for local knowledge and social service and those in which mistakes that might occur would not be irremediable. Broadly speaking, 'reserved' subjects comprised all subjects which were not transferred to ministers and embraced such subjects as land revenue, finance, and law and order.

At the head of each province there was to be a Governor appointed by His Majesty, ordinarily for a term of five years. Every Governor on appointment received an Instrument of Instructions defining his duties and responsibilities.

The strength of the Governor's Executive Council in each of the provinces was fixed as follows, namely, four in Madras, Bombay and Bengal; three in Bihar and Orissa, and two in the remaining provinces. Half the number in each of the provinces except Bihar and Orissa were Indians; in Bihar and Orissa there was only one Indian member.

The Act of 1919 did not alter the relations between the Governor and his Executive Council, nor the previous practice in regard to the transaction of business. Ordinarily, a member was expected to dispose of questions coming before him on his own initiative. Important cases were to be taken in Council and decided by a majority vote; but the Governor had power to override the decision of the Council in any case in which the safety, tranquillity or interests of the province, or part thereof, were in his judgment essentially affected, and any order so issued was the order of the Governor in Council.

Appointments of ministers were to be made by the Governor. No limit was prescribed as to their number; it rested with the Governor to decide how many ministers were required for the proper administration of the transferred departments. There were three ministers each in Madras, Bombay and Bengal and two in each of the other provinces. They were to hold office at the pleasure of the Governor; but no minister could hold office for a longer period than six months unless he were, or became, an elected member of the Legislative Council. The minister's salary and the provision of supply for his departments were subject to the vote of the legislature.

The Act, while directing that the Governor should be guided by the advice of his ministers, authorized him, if he saw sufficient cause, to dissent from their opinion and to require that action be taken otherwise than in accordance with that advice. In deciding whether the circumstances were such as to justify his acting against the advice of his ministers, the Governor was guided by his Instrument of Instructions.

A minister had the option of resigning if his advice were not accepted by the Governor, and the Governor had the ordinary constitutional right of dismissing a minister whose policy he believed to be either seriously at fault, or out of accord with the views of the Legislative Council. A minister who resigned, or was dismissed by the Governor, might have behind him the opinion of the legislature and the Governor might conceivably find it impossible to appoint a successor who would work with him. In that event the Governor would dissolve the legislature. If the new legislature proved equally obdurate, the only course open to the Governor, assuming that he felt it impossible either to give way on the point at issue or to effect a compromise, was to assume control of the administration of the departments concerned. The temporary administration of a subject could continue only until a minister was appointed; but in the last resort and if it proved impossible for him to find ministers willing to accept office, the Governor could move the Governor-General in Council to revoke or suspend the transfer of all such subjects.

It was the essence of the dualized system of government set up by the Act that there should be a clear division of responsibility between the two halves of the Government. This principle of separate responsibility was clearly laid down and emphasized in the Act, which directed that the orders and other proceedings of the Government should be so authenticated as to distinguish those relating to transferred subjects from other orders and proceedings.

Under the arrangements previously in force, the resources of the provincial government were derived from a share in the proceeds of certain heads of revenue, which share was based primarily on the estimated needs of the province. This system necessarily involved a degree of control and interference by the Government of India which could not be maintained if the popular principle in Government was to be given fair play in the provinces. The separation of the resources of the central and provincial governments was therefore an essential part of the reforms scheme. Certain sources of revenue, principally the receipts from provincial subjects, were allocated to the provinces; but since this allocation, whilst adding largely to the revenues of the provinces, reduced correspondingly those of the central government, each province was required to make good the deficit thus resulting by paying an annual contribution to the Government of India. In each of the provinces of Madras, Bombay, Bengal, the United Provinces, and the Punjab, the contribution so calculated amounted to about 60 per cent of the new revenues, and in the Central Provinces and Assam, where the margin of revenue over expenditure was small, to about 40 per cent. No contribution was demanded from Bihar and Orissa, a province already burdened with heavy expenditure. These contributions did not correspond with any equitable standard, but were dictated by the exigencies of the previous financial system. Provision was accordingly made in the rules for the gradual establishment of a standard ratio that would conform as closely as practicable to the financial capacity of each province. A further measure of relief was afforded by the assignment to each province of a share in the growth of the revenue from taxation on incomes.

With regard to the control exercisable by the Secretary of State and Parliament, the Act of 1919 brought into existence new sources of power. To the extent to which control by the legislature was admitted, the control of Parliament had inevitably to be relaxed. The Secretary of State and the Government of India retained power to safeguard the administration of central subjects, to decide questions arising between two provinces, and to carry out the duties imposed upon them by the Act or the rules made thereunder. Except for these defined purposes, the Secretary of State and the Government of India exercised no control over the administration of transferred subjects. On the other hand, there was no statutory divestment of control in relation to the reserved subjects administered by the

Governor in Council, since the responsibility of the Governor in Council was to the Secretary of State and to Parliament and not to the provincial legislature.

Under the 1919 Act, indirect election was abolished and was replaced by direct election, and the proportion of elected members in each of the provincial councils was fixed at not less than 70 per cent. The qualifications of voters, except for University constituencies, were based mainly on property and residence within the constituency. The number of members in the councils ranged from 53 in Assam to 139 in Bengal.

In the matter of communal representation, the authors of the Joint Report had felt that separate electorates should be accorded only to Muhammadans and to the Sikhs in the Punjab. At the same time they had stressed their strong aversion to the policy of communal representation which, for more reasons than one, they regarded as 'a very serious hindrance to the self-governing principle.' In the final result, however, communal representation was accorded not only to Muhammadans (on the basis of the Lucknow Congress-League Pact) and to the Sikhs in the Punjab, but also generally to Europeans, Anglo-Indians and Indian Christians, while in Madras and Bombay a definite proportion of non-Muhammadan seats was reserved, respectively, for non-Brahmins and Mahrattas.

Landholders, universities and commercial and industrial interests were given special representation, and provision was also made for the representation by nomination of communities or classes which might otherwise have failed to secure any, or adequate, representation on the councils.

Broadly speaking, the legislative sphere of the provincial legislatures was conterminous with the list of provincial subjects. On central subjects legislation was primarily reserved for the Indian legislature and could only be undertaken in the provincial councils with the previous sanction of the Governor-General. The rules made under the Act specified certain laws that could not be repealed or altered without the previous sanction of the Governor-General. Provision was also made for certain categories of bills passed by the provincial councils to be reserved for the consideration of the Governor-General.

With the exception of certain specified items of expenditure which were excluded from the jurisdiction of the provincial councils, the proposals of the Government for the appropriation of the provincial revenues had to be submitted to the vote of the councils. No such proposals however could be made except on the recommendation of the Governor. The sole function of the council was to assent or to refuse its assent to a demand, or to reduce its amount wholly or by the omission of any of the items of which it was composed. Control over expenditure being the essence of responsible government, the Governor had no power to restore any demand rejected by the Legislative Council in respect of transferred subjects. On the other hand, the responsibility of the legislature was not admitted in respect of reserved subjects and the Governor could, in the last resort, have his own way in regard both to legislation and supply.

The Act of 1919 did not alter the general structure of the central executive. The Government of India continued to be a purely official government responsible to the Secretary of State and to Parliament. Nevertheless, the creation of an Indian legislature with a large elected majority inevitably affected the character of the administration.

With respect to the Governor-General's Executive Council, the previous limitation of the number of members to six was removed. The Act, however, retained the requirement that three of the members should be persons who had been for at least ten years in the service of the Crown in India. The result of these changes was that henceforward there were not less than three Indian members in the Governor-General's Executive Council.

The Act made radical changes in the legislative arrangements of the central government. The former Indian (or Imperial) Legislative Council was replaced by a bicameral legislature consisting of a Legislative Assembly and a Council of State. The Legislative Assembly was the lower chamber, containing 145 members, of whom 105 were elected and 40 nominated. The elected members were chosen by an electorate which bore roughly the same proportion to the electorate for the provincial councils as the provincial quota of seats in the Assembly bore to the general and communal elective seats in the provincial councils. As in the case of the provincial councils, the total proportion of Muslim seats was fixed in accordance with the Lucknow Pact. Separate representation was also accorded to Europeans, Sikhs, landholders and Indian commerce. Communities, classes and interests which had secured inadequate representation by election were to be represented, so far as was practicable, by means of 14 nominated seats reserved for non-officials.

The Council of State, or upper chamber, was intended to be a revising body capable of exercising in relation to the Legislative Assembly a restraining though not an overriding influence, and its composition was a corollary of its functions. The total number of members was 60, of whom 34 were elected and 26 nominated. The qualifications for voters were based on a comparatively high franchise. Muhammadan representation was practically in accordance with the Lucknow Pact; separate representation was also accorded to Sikhs and to European commerce. The nominated members included 20 officials and 6 non-officials.

The powers exercised by the Indian legislature in the matter of the budget corresponded broadly with those which had been conferred on the provincial councils. As in England, they were exercised only by the lower house. Estimates of annual revenue and expenditure were to be laid before both chambers, but the proposals of the Government for the appropriation of the revenues were to be submitted to the vote of the Legislative Assembly alone. As in the case of the provincial councils, certain expenditure was excluded from the jurisdiction of the Assembly. The Governor-General in Council was empowered, if he was satisfied that any demand that had been refused by the Assembly was essential to the discharge of his responsibilities, to act as if it had been assented to by that body.

In the matter of legislation, the two chambers exercised co-equal powers. A bill could be introduced in either chamber and the assent of both the chambers was normally required to its enactment. Provision was made in the rules for the adjustment of any differences that might arise between them.

The responsibility for legislation on central subjects rested with the Governor-General in Council, just as the responsibility for legislation on reserved subjects was with the Governor in Council; and the Governor-General was duly empowered to secure any legislation which he considered to be essential for the safety, tranquillity or interests of British India, or any part thereof. The Governor-General was also empowered in cases of emergency to issue Ordinances which would have the like force of law as an Act passed by the legislature.

Normally every Council of State continued for five years and every Legislative Assembly and provincial Legislative Council for three years.

As regards the Secretary of State's Council, certain changes were made in its constitution; the Indian element was strengthened; in order to ensure a continuous flow of Indian experience and to relieve Indian members from the necessity of spending so long a period as seven years in England, the period of service on the Council was reduced to five years.

Lastly, provision was included in the Act for the appointment, after ten years, of a Statutory Commission, whose duty would be to examine the working of the new constitution in all its details in the provinces; to advise whether the time had come for full responsible government, or whether, and to what extent, the powers of self-government already granted should be extended, modified or restricted. The Commission was also empowered to inquire into the working of the Government of India, to advise in respect of the Government of India no less than in respect of the provincial governments. As explained by the Under-Secretary of State for India in the House of Commons: 'The reason for the ten years' experiment apparently was that we should have three consecutive Parliaments on which to base our decision as to the future.'

The authors of the Montagu-Chelmsford report were not unaware of the shortcomings of the scheme which they had recommended — and which was subsequently embodied in the Act. In their own words:

Hybrid executives, limited responsibility, assemblies partly elected and partly nominated, divisions of functions, reservations general or particular, are devices that can have no permanent abiding place. They bear on their faces their transitional character; and they can be worked only if it is clearly recognised that that is their justification and their purpose. They cannot be so devised as to be logical. They must be charged with potentialities of friction. Hope of avoiding mischief lies in facing the fact that they are temporary expedients for training purposes, and in providing that the goal is not merely kept in sight but made attainable, not by agitation but by the operation of machinery inherent in the scheme itself.

But these hopes were not realized. The Act was assailed from the first from both sides. An influential body of British opinion remained unconvinced as to India's capacity even for partial responsible government; while a powerful section of Indian opinion, which was impatient to reach its goal of *swaraj*, regarded the Act as 'inadequate, disappointing and unsatisfactory.'

## III

The new reforms were inaugurated by the Duke of Connaught (uncle of King George V) who came out to India in the beginning of 1921. He read the following message from His Majesty:

For years — it may be for generations — patriotic and loyal Indians have dreamed of Swaraj for their Motherland. Today you have the beginning of Swaraj within my Empire and the widest scope and ample opportunities for progress to the liberty which my other Dominions enjoy.

This was the first time that the word 'Swaraj' had been used in an official pronouncement. But the reforms had failed to rouse the enthusiasm of the people. Various factors had supervened between 1917 and 1921 to draw away large and influential sections of Indian opinion.

The war, in the first place, had come to be regarded more and more as a struggle between liberty and despotism and for the right of peoples to rule their own destinies. The advocacy of self-determination by President Woodrow Wilson had buoyed up the hopes of Indian nationalists. But as the discussions in Parliament on the Government of India Bill proceeded there grew the feeling that what had been promised by Britain in her hour of peril was being sought to be whittled down when the emergency ceased to exist.

Early in 1919 the Government of India, ignoring all protests and advice, passed the Rowlatt Act[1] to deal with revolutionary crime. The Act provided the executive with such wide and sweeping powers as to rouse widespread agitation throughout the country. The climax was the tragedy of Jallianwala Bagh on 13 April at Amritsar, where hundreds of defenceless persons were killed and over a thousand injured. This tragedy, in particular, and the subsequent severities of the régime of martial law in the Punjab engendered a profound and intense anti-British feeling.

It was against this background that the Congress held its annual session in Amritsar in December 1919. A section of Congressmen, led by Surendranath Banerjea, Tej Bahadur Sapru and V. S. Srinivasa Sastri, dismayed by the growth of extremist opinion in the Congress, had left the organization and founded the National Liberal Federation. The Federation, meeting in Calcutta, welcomed the Government of India Act and offered its full co-operation in the working of it.

[1] This Act took its name from the Chairman of the committee appointed to examine the emergency provisions in the Defence of India Act dealing with anarchical crime, with a view to the continuance of those provisions after the war.

At the Congress session in Amritsar there was a cleavage of opinion on the policy to be adopted with regard to the new reforms. Tilak and his followers were anxious to work the Act for what it was worth. This view was shared by Madan Mohan Malaviya as well as by Gandhiji, who had by this time definitely associated himself with Congress politics and who was very soon to take over its leadership. Another section of opinion, led by C. R. Das, advocated the rejection of the scheme. It was Gandhiji who brought about a compromise; and the following resolution was ultimately passed:

This Congress trusts that so far as may be possible the people will so work the reforms as to secure an early establishment of full responsible government and this Congress offers its thanks to the Right Honourable E. S. Montagu for his labours in connection with the reforms.

This offer of co-operation was, however, short-lived. Two factors influenced the attitude of the Congress in general and of Gandhiji in particular. One was the publication of the draft Treaty of Sevres, which proposed the liquidation of the Turkish Empire. The Sultan of Turkey being the Caliph, or religious head of the Muslim world, this naturally roused the religious sentiments of the Indian Muslims, who started an agitation known as the 'Khilafat movement' with the object of bringing pressure to bear on the British Government for the restoration of the Sultan to something like his pre-war position. The other was the unfeeling attitude of the British Parliament and a section of the British public in respect of the Punjab atrocities.

Gandhiji now became definitely a non-cooperator. He advised the Hindus to make common cause with the Muslims in a united mass non-cooperation movement to restore the position of the Caliph, to right the Punjab wrongs and to win *swaraj*. His influence became stronger with the death of Tilak in July 1920. At a special session held in Calcutta in August 1920 a resolution supporting his policy of non-cooperation was passed by a large majority. The non-cooperation movement was directed at the boycott of the legislatures, educational institutions and law courts. The voters were asked to abstain from exercising their franchise.

The first elections to the provincial and central legislatures were held in November 1920. The Congress, as well as the Khilafat Committee, boycotted the elections. The Muslim League took up a neutral attitude. The Liberal Federation was the only all-India party which contested the elections. In Madras the non-Brahmins had organized a party called the 'Justice Party' which emerged from the elections with great success. In the Punjab Sir Fazli Hussain formed the 'Unionist Party' (consisting of Muslims, Sikhs and Hindus) which secured a great measure of success in that province. These bodies were more a congregation of individuals than parties in the real sense. Nevertheless, the Justice Party and the Unionist Party formed ministries respectively in Madras and the Punjab. In the other provinces notable liberal leaders like Surendranath Banerjea, Dr Sachhidananda Sinha and Sir C.Y. Chintamani took office as ministers.

Taking the ten legislative bodies collectively (two chambers of the Indian legislature and eight provincial councils) there were 774 seats to be filled and for these there were 1,957 candidates. There were contested elections for 535 seats and for these 1,718 candidates were forthcoming. For only about half a dozen of the 774 seats was there no candidate nominated in the first instance, but all of these were subsequently filled through by-elections. None the less, a substantial portion of the electorate did not exercise its franchise.

The Congress session held in Nagpur in December 1920 was noteworthy for two outstanding achievements, attributable largely to Gandhiji's influence. One was the reaffirmation of the non-cooperation resolution. The other was the change in the constitution of the Congress. The President was given an executive known as the Working Committee, with an All-India Congress Committee to direct and control its activities. Similar organizations were set up in all provinces (divided on a linguistic basis) as well as in the districts. The goal of the Congress was changed to the attainment of *swaraj* by peaceful and legitimate methods.

The fact that the Congress boycott of the elections was not a success does not imply that the non-cooperation movement did not have a considerable effect both on the Government and the country at large. The extent of the enthusiasm and unity created at the time among the masses, culminating in the boycott of the Prince of Wales in 1921, was never so strong, even in the subsequent years of India's struggle for freedom. Had the non-cooperation movement not been ended by Gandhiji at a time when it was causing the utmost anxiety to the Government, the latter might possibly have been induced to take some action to appease Indian sentiment. But in February 1922 Gandhiji called it off. This was because of the Chauri Chaura episode, when a mob set fire to the police station, with the result that a police inspector and 21 police constables were burned to death. In the same month Montagu had a difference with the Cabinet and was obliged to resign, and in March 1922 Gandhiji was arrested and sentenced to a long term of imprisonment on a charge of sedition.

The position at the end of 1922 was that non-cooperation had been suspended; that the boycott of the legislatures had not proved effective, and that the Congress was for the time being without any definite policy of action. But no political party can remain static. A section of Congressmen, led by C. R. Das and Pandit Motilal Nehru, started thinking in terms of council entry. A resolution advocating council entry was rejected by the Congress at its annual session in Gaya in December 1922. C. R. Das thereupon resigned his presidentship of the Congress and announced the formation within the Congress of a group known as the 'Swarajya Party'. The next few months emphasized the differences between the 'No-changers' and the Swarajists. In September 1923 a special session of the Congress was held in Delhi and a compromise resolution was passed which permitted those who had no religious or conscientious objections to enter the legislatures.

In October 1923 the Swarajya Party published its election mani-festo. It declared that the immediate objective of the party was the speedy attainment of Dominion Status, that is, the right to frame a constitution adopting such machinery and system as were most suited to the conditions of the country and the genius of the people. As a necessary preliminary, the Swarajya Party demanded that the people of India should have effective control of the existing machinery and system of government. If this demand were not conceded, they would resort to a policy of 'uniform, continuous and consistent obstruction with a view to make government through the Assembly and the councils impossible.' In no case would any member of the party accept office.

In the elections of 1923 the Swarajists practically wiped out the Liberals. They gained a clear majority in the Legislative Council of the Central Provinces and secured a substantial number of seats in Bombay and the United Provinces, as also in the Central Legislative Assembly. In the Bengal Council they found themselves, though not in a majority, in a position to prevent the formation of any ministry in that province.

The Hindu-Muslim unity which Gandhiji sought to build up on the Khilafat issue did not last long, though his espousal of the cause had contributed considerably to its strength. While few among the

Muslims understood what 'Khilafat' stood for, all understood the cry of 'Islam in danger'. On this ephemeral issue, the true basis of which was not clearly perceived, Gandhiji endeavoured to cement an alliance between Muslims and Hindus. The first shock was the Moplah (Muslim) outbreak in Malabar in 1921; the second the repudiation by Turkey of the Khilafat itself and her rejection of all extraneous mediation in the matter. The temporary alliance thus came to an abrupt end, resulting in the reversion of the two communities to their mutual animosities.

There followed other efforts on the part of the Congress leaders to bring about an understanding between the two communities. Early in December 1923 the Bengal Swarajya Party formulated a pact known as the 'Bengal Pact'. This provided *inter alia* for separate representation to Muslims in the Bengal Council on a population basis; for representation on local bodies in the proportion of 60:40 according as either community was in a majority; and for the grant of 55 per cent of Government appointments to Muslims. The Congress, at its annual session in Coconada, rejected the Bengal Pact. Instead, it referred another draft pact, known as the 'Indian National Pact', to a special committee. A third pact was drawn up by the Punjab Muslim League early in 1924. But none of these pacts, nor similar efforts to bring about a communal understanding, achieved any tangible result; indeed, the communal situation instead of getting better became worse.

Let us turn to the activities of the Swarajya Party within the legislatures. The Governors were obliged to take over the administration of 'transferred subjects' in Bengal and the Central Provinces because the Swarajists refused to co-operate in the formation of ministries there. In the Central Legislative Assembly a resolution was moved in February 1924 by Dewan Bahadur T. Rangachari, recommending that steps should be taken at a very early date 'for revising the Government of India Act so as to secure for India full self-governing Dominion Status within the empire and provincial autonomy in the provinces.' To this resolution Pandit Motilal Nehru, the leader of the Swarajya Party, moved an amendment calling for a representative Round Table Conference to recommend a scheme of constitution for the establishment of full responsible government in India. The amendment was carried by an overwhelming majority of elected members, the elected Muslim members voting with the Swarajya Party. In the course of the debate, Sir Malcolm Hailey, then Home

Member, declared that 'responsible government' mentioned in the Preamble of the Government of India Act of 1919 did not necessarily lead to 'full dominion self-government'. 'It may be,' he said, 'that full dominion self-government is the logical outcome of responsible government, nay, it may be the inevitable and historical development of responsible government, but it is a further and final step.' There was no call for this gratuitous pronouncement. It only created further suspicion of the bona fides of the British Government and let loose an agitation from now on for the definition of the goal of His Majesty's Government's policy in India as 'Dominion Status'.

The only outcome of the resolution of February 1924 was the appointment of the Reforms Enquiry Committee, popularly known as the Muddiman Committee. The terms of reference to the Committee were as follows:

(1) To inquire into the difficulties arising from, or defects inherent in, the working of the Government of India Act and the Rules thereunder in regard to the central government and the governments of Governors' provinces; and (2) to investigate the feasibility and desirability of securing remedies for such difficulties or defects, consistent with the structure, policy and purpose of the Act, by action taken under the Act and the Rules, or by such amendments of the Act as appear necessary to rectify any administrative imperfections.

The Committee consisted of Sir Alexander Muddiman (who had succeeded Sir Malcolm Hailey as Home Member) as Chairman and the following members, namely, Sir Muhammad Shafi, Member of the Governor-General's Executive Council; Maharajadhiraja Sir Bijay Chand Mahtab Bahadur of Burdwan; Sir Tej Bahadur Sapru; Sir Arthur Froom; Sir P. S. Sivaswami Iyer; Sir Henry Moncrieff-Smith, Secretary to the Government of India, Legislative Department; M. A. Jinnah and Dr R. P. Paranjpye.

Pandit Motilal Nehru was offered a seat on the Committee but he declined to accept it, contending that no inquiry within the limited scope and extent prescribed by the terms of reference could yield satisfactory results; that it would no doubt be possible for the Committee to discover difficulties and defects and suggest remedies with the limitations laid down, but it was obvious that such remedies could not meet the situation. No member of the Swarajya Party came forward to give evidence before the Committee. Those Indian witnesses who did appear before the Committee and who had experience of the system of dyarchy, condemned it as unworkable.

The Muddiman Committee signed two reports on 3 December 1924. The Minority Report was signed by Sir Tej Bahadur Sapru, Sir Sivaswami Iyer, Jinnah and Dr Paranjpye. The main difference between the Majority and Minority Reports was in the recommendation of the latter for the appointment of a Royal Commission with wider terms of reference and a larger scope of enquiry, or any other agency, in order to make recommendations for placing the constitution on a permanent basis, with provisions for automatic progress in the future. Only such a course would in their view secure stability in the Government and the willing co-operation of the people.

The Reports were published in March 1925. Lord Reading's Government rejected the recommendation for the appointment of a Royal Commission; in its view the time for such an appointment had not yet come. At the same time, Lord Reading was not averse to the proposal for summoning a Round Table Conference of Indian leaders, if the situation demanded such a course. The political situation in Bengal was causing grave concern because of the terrorist movement and the Government of India was anxious, if possible, to placate C.R.Das (whose position in the Congress at the time was comparable with that of Gandhiji) and to bring about some settlement with him. C.R.Das was willing to offer his co-operation under certain conditions, and in his speech at the Faridpur session of the Bengal Provincial Congress Committee, he extended the hand of friendship. The Government might then, in all probability, have summoned a Round Table Conference of Indian leaders; but unfortunately the great leader died on 16 June 1925 and with his death the Government reverted to its policy of 'do nothing'.

This attitude was affirmed by Lord Birkenhead, the Secretary of State, who, on 7 July 1925, stated in the House of Lords that His Majesty's Government would not be diverted from its high obligations by the tactics of restless impatience, that the door of acceleration was not open to menace, still less would it be stormed by violence.

Following a tirade on the refusal of the Congress to co-operate in the working of the reforms, Lord Birkenhead proceeded to say:

To talk of India as an entity is as absurd as to talk of Europe as an entity. Yet the very nationalist spirit which has created most of our difficulties in the last few years is based upon the aspirations and claims of a nationalist India. There never has been such a nation. Whether there ever will be such a nation the future alone can show.

And towards the close of a long speech, he threw out the challenge:

But if our critics in India are of opinion that their greater knowledge of Indian conditions qualifies them to succeed, where they tell us that we have failed, let them produce a constitution which carries behind it a fair measure of general agreement among the great people of India. Such a contribution to our problems would nowhere be resented. It would, on the contrary, be most carefully examined by the Government of India, by myself and I am sure by the Commission, whenever that body may be assembled.

This challenge was taken up by Pandit Motilal Nehru on behalf of the Swarajya Party in the Central Legislative Assembly in September 1925, when the Muddiman Committee Report came up for discussion. He moved an amendment which came to be known as the 'National Demand'. It carried the support of all parties, including the Liberals and the Muslims. We need not go into the details of the demand because, after all, nothing came of it.

Lord Irwin was appointed Viceroy in April 1926. About a year later, in March 1927, His Majesty's Government announced their decision to appoint a Statutory Commission in advance of the prescribed date. This came as a surprise. Apparently the Viceroy and His Majesty's Government hoped by this move to bring down the communal temperature and to effect a change in nationalist opinion. There was also the anxiety of the Conservative Government in England, which no doubt felt that, if it could not itself settle the Indian issue, it might at least take steps while still in office to set up a Commission of its own choice.

The country at the time was in a state of frustration. The Congress had no active programme, except *khadi*[1]. The Swarajists had lost that cohesion and discipline which they had under C. R. Das. Some of its prominent leaders had left the party and accepted office under Government, while others had broken away and formed separate parties. The Muslim League was a leaderless organization; one of its sessions at about this time had to be adjourned for lack of a quorum. The communal situation was causing considerable anxiety, and successive unity conferences had only produced more disunity. In these conditions the appointment of the Commission, as we shall see, proved a blessing, particularly to the Congress.

The personnel of the Commission and its terms of reference were announced in November 1927. It consisted of seven members drawn

[1] Hand-woven cloth from hand-spun yarn.

from the three political parties in the British Parliament, under the chairmanship of Sir John (later Viscount) Simon. The hope entertained by His Majesty's Government that the announcement of the Commission would appease nationalist opinion was not realized. There never was an issue on which Indian opinion was so completely united. The exclusion of Indians from the personnel of the Commission was considered an affront, not only because it implied for them a position of inferiority, but because it denied them the right to participate in the determination of the constitution of their own country. The sop held out later, that Committees of the central and provincial legislatures could submit opinions and proposals to the Commission, only served to stiffen the opposition.

At the annual session of the Congress in Madras in December 1927, a resolution was passed advocating the boycott of the Simon Commission 'at every stage and in every form'. The Liberal Federation also refused to co-operate with the Simon Commission. Other political organizations followed suit. In the Muslim League there was a split. Jinnah and a considerable section were for boycotting the Commission, while Sir Muhammad Shafi and his group were against such a step. There were thus two sessions of the Muslim League held in December 1927. That led by Jinnah held its session in Calcutta and decided on boycott; the other, under the presidentship of Sir Muhammad Shafi (who had the support of the Government), met in Lahore and decided to co-operate. Except for the Shafi group of Muslims and the Justice Party of Madras, practically all political parties in India had turned their backs on the Simon Commission.

The Madras session of the Congress authorized its Working Committee to convene an All-Parties' Conference with a view to drawing up a constitution for India acceptable to all parties. The Jinnah wing of the Muslim League authorized its executive to confer with the Working Committee of the Congress and other organizations and to take part in the proposed All-Parties' Conference. This Conference met in Delhi in February and March 1928 and in Bombay in May that of year. Dr M. A. Ansari, who presided, informed the delegates that no agreement had been reached on the subject of communal representation and that the report of the sub-committee which had been formed to consider the question of the separation of Sind from Bombay was not yet ready for submission to the Conference. After much discussion, the Conference decided to appoint an influential committee under the chairmanship of Pandit Motilal

Nehru to determine the principles of a constitution for India and to prepare a report thereon. This Committee in fact prepared an admirable report known as the 'Nehru Report', which was published in August 1928, but the discussions at the All-Parties' Conference, which subsequently met again in Lucknow, were inconclusive, and the report was not adopted.

Enthusiasm for the Nehru Report was in any case killed by the rallying tactics of the Simon Commission, to whom the Muslims, Sikhs and Depressed Classes, now in a bargaining spirit, felt it in their interests to turn. When the All-Parties' Conference met again in Calcutta in the last week of December 1928, Jinnah moved certain amendments to the proposals of the Nehru Report which were not accepted. His group refused to participate further in the Conference. A few days later a Muslim All-Parties' Conference held in Delhi, which was attended even by some nationalist Muslims, formulated a series of demands on behalf of the Muslims and made it clear that no constitution, by whomsoever proposed or devised, would be acceptable to the Muslims, unless it conformed with those demands. It was at about this time that Jinnah, after consulting several Muslim leaders, formulated his 'fourteen points' for the safeguarding of the rights and interests of Muslims in any future constitution. These points were as follows:

1. The form of the future constitution should be Federal, with the residuary power vested in the provinces.

2. A uniform measure of autonomy shall be granted to all provinces.

3. All legislatures in the country and other elected bodies shall be constituted on the definite principle of adequate and effective representation of minorities in every province without reducing the majority in any province to a minority or even equality.

4. In the central legislature Muslim representation shall not be less than one-third.

5. Representation of communal groups shall continue to be by separate electorates provided that it shall be open to any community at any time to abandon its separate electorate in favour of joint electorates.

6. Any territorial redistribution that might at any time be necessary shall not in any way affect the Muslim majority in the Punjab, Bengal and the N.W.F. Province.

7. Full religious liberty, that is liberty of belief, worship, and observance, propaganda, association and education, shall be guaranteed to all communities.

8. No Bill or Resolution or any part thereof shall be passed in any legislature or any other elected body if three-fourths of the members of any community in that particular body oppose it as being injurious to the interests of that community.

9. Sind should be separated from the Bombay Presidency.

10. Reforms should be introduced in the North-West Frontier Province and Baluchistan as in other provinces.

11. Provision should be made in the Constitution giving Muslims an adequate share along with the other Indians in all the services of the State and in local self-governing bodies having due regard to the requirements of efficiency.

12. The Constitution should embody adequate safeguards for the protection of Muslim culture, and for the protection and promotion of Muslim education, language, religion, personal laws, and Muslim charitable institutions and for their due share in grants-in-aid.

13. No Cabinet, either central or provincial, should be formed without there being at least one-third of Muslim ministers.

14. No change shall be made in the Constitution by the central legislature except with the concurrence of the States constituting the Indian Federation.

When the Nehru Report came before the annual session of the Congress in Calcutta in December 1928, it was assailed by the left wing on the ground that it suggested only Dominion Status and not complete independence, which had been declared as the Congress goal at its previous session in Madras. In April 1928, the 'Independence of India League' had been formed, with Jawaharlal Nehru and Subhas Chandra Bose as Secretaries and S. Srinivasa Iyengar as President. The Congress session in Calcutta saw an almost open split between those who stood for Dominion Status and those who advocated Independence. Ultimately it was resolved that, if the British Parliament accepted the Nehru Report before 31 December 1929, the Congress would adopt the report in its entirety. In the event of its non-acceptance by that date, the Congress would insist on independence and organize non-violent non-cooperation to achieve it. (To this resolution there was an amendment to the effect that the Congress would be content with nothing short of independence. The amendment, in spite of Gandhiji's opposition, was lost only by a very narrow margin).

In the course of its tour the Simon Commission met with a hostile reception everywhere. Its proceedings were rigidly boycotted. The Central Provinces Legislative Council refused to appoint a committee to work with the Commission. The Legislative Assembly also rejected the proposal to elect members to the Indian Central Committee. Nevertheless, a Committee was formed, comprising three members elected by the Council of State and five members nominated by the Viceroy from amongst members of the Legislative Assembly. Sir Hari Singh Gour, one of the members of the Indian Central Committee, had to admit later that 'politically-minded India had organized and marshalled an effective boycott both of the Statutory Commission and its Indian wing.'

In May 1929 a general election took place in Britain resulting in the fall of the Conservative Government. Its place was taken by a Labour Government headed by Ramsay MacDonald. The Labour Party was the largest single party, though not possessing an absolute majority in the House of Commons. Lord Peel, who had succeeded Lord Birkenhead as Secretary of State, was replaced by Wedgwood Benn. Towards the end of June, Lord Irwin, the Viceroy, left for England for consultations with His Majesty's Government.

By this time the Simon Commission had finished their labours in India and had returned to England to draft their report. On 16 October 1929, Sir John Simon wrote to the Prime Minister suggesting that after the publication of the report a conference should be arranged between the representatives of His Majesty's Government and the representatives of British India and the Indian States 'for the purpose of seeking the greatest possible measure of agreement for the final proposals which it would later be the duty of His Majesty's Government to submit to Parliament.' Ramsay MacDonald accepted the suggestion on behalf of His Majesty's Government.

On his return to India on 31 October 1929, Lord Irwin announced that:

In view of the doubts which have been expressed both in Great Britain and India regarding the interpretation to be placed on the intentions of the British Government in enacting the Statute of 1919, I am authorised on behalf of His Majesty's Government to state clearly that in their judgment it is implicit in the declaration of 1917 that the natural issue of India's constitutional progress as there contemplated is the attainment of Dominion Status.

He also announced that after the Simon Commission and the Indian Central Committee had submitted their reports and when His Majesty's Government had, in consultation with the Government of India, considered these matters in the light of the material avai-lable, they would invite representatives of British India and of the Indian States to meet them separately, or together, for the purpose of conference and discussion in regard to both British-Indian and all-Indian problems.

## II

# ALL-INDIA FEDERATION—A LOST IDEAL

LORD Irwin's declaration of October 1929 was received with great satisfaction by all political parties in India. The Congress leaders met in Delhi and, on 2 November, a joint statement was issued over the signatures of Gandhiji, Pandit Motilal Nehru, Jawaharlal Nehru, Sir Tej Bahadur Sapru, Mrs Annie Besant and others. Appreciation was expressed of the sincerity underlying the declaration and the obvious desire of the British Government to meet Indian opinion. The leaders hoped that they would be able to tender their co-operation to His Majesty's Government in their effort to evolve a scheme of Dominion constitution suitable to India's needs. They considered it vital for the success of the Round Table Conference, firstly, that a policy of general conciliation should be adopted so as to introduce a calmer atmosphere; secondly, that political prisoners should be granted a general amnesty; thirdly, that the representation of the progressive political organizations should be effectively secured and that the Indian National Congress, as the largest among them, should have predominant representation. The leaders desired that it should be made clear that the proposed Round Table Conference would meet not to discuss *when* Dominion Status should be established, but to frame a constitution for India on that basis. Such clarification of the position was necessary in order to remove any doubt in the minds of the people. They concluded: 'We hold it absolutely essential that the public should be made to feel that a new era has come from today and that the new Constitution is to be but the register of that fact.'

Clarification was soon forthcoming, though not in the form or manner expected by the Congress leaders. A section of the British press launched a virulent campaign against the Viceroy's announcement of Dominion Status which, it was contended, marked a drastic change of policy and served but to undermine the work of the Simon Commission. Both Stanley Baldwin and Lloyd George, on behalf of their respective parties, disowned the declaration. There was an acrimonious debate in Parliament, where the speeches of the members were provocative and unrestrained.

The Labour Government, placed as they were with no majority in Parliament, were disposed to take up a defensive attitude. The Secretary of State attempted to allay the storm of opposition by explaining that there was actually no change of policy. But it was the speech of the former Secretary of State, Lord Birkenhead, in the House of Lords, that carried weight. Lord Birkenhead went to the extent of calling upon the Simon Commission to treat the Viceroy's declaration 'as irrelevance — in the old classic phrase as impertinence.' 'What man in this House,' he asked, 'can say that he can see in a generation, in two generations, in a hundred years, any prospect that the people of India will be in a position to assume control of the Army, the Navy, the Civil Service, and to have a Governor-General who will be responsible to the Indian Government and not to any authority in this country?'

The debates in Parliament not only came as a rude shock to the people of India, but effectively strengthened the hands of the Congress left wing, whose demand for independence could no longer be stifled.

As mentioned earlier, the Congress in Calcutta had decided to change its goal to that of complete independence if the demand for Dominion Status were not accepted by the British Parliament within one year. That year was almost over. The Congress was shortly to meet in Lahore and it was apparent that the views of the left wing would prevail. Vithalbhai Patel, President of the Indian Legislative Assembly, felt that only an authoritative pronouncement by the Viceroy would enable Gandhiji and Pandit Motilal Nehru to turn the tide. He accordingly arranged a meeting to take place on 23 December 1929 between the Viceroy and the leaders of the main political parties. Gandhiji and Pandit Motilal Nehru represented the Congress, Sir Tej Bahadur Sapru the Liberals, and Jinnah the Muslim League. The discussion was limited to the functions of the proposed Round Table Conference in London. The Congress leaders expressed the view that, unless previous assurance were given by His Majesty's Government that the purpose of the Conference was to draft a scheme for Dominion Status which His Majesty's Government would undertake to support, there would be grave difficulty about Congress participation. Lord Irwin explained that the Conference was designed to elicit the greatest possible measure of agreement for the final proposals which it would be the duty of His Majesty's Government to submit to Parliament, and that it was impossible for him or for His Majesty's Government in any way to prejudice the action of the Conference or to restrict the liberty of Parliament. The discussions proved infructuous.

At the session held in Lahore in December 1929, the Congress changed its creed to one of complete independence and decided not to attend the Round Table Conference. It also decided to boycott the legislatures and called upon the Congress members to resign. Further, the All-India Congress Committee was authorized to launch a programme of civil disobedience, including non-payment of taxes, whenever it deemed fit. The Congress Working Committee appointed Gandhiji as the sole authority to decide the time and manner of the launching of the civil disobedience movement.

The resolution passed in Lahore was assailed by leaders of all the other parties. Mohamed Ali, an erstwhile supporter of Gandhiji and the Congress, went to the extent of appealing to the Muslims not to participate in the Congress movement.

On 2 March 1930, Gandhiji wrote a letter to the Viceroy intimating his intention of launching a programme of civil disobedience.

In common with many of my countrymen I had hugged the fond hope that the proposed Round Table Conference might furnish a solution. But when you said plainly you could not give any assurance that you or the British Cabinet would pledge yourself to support a scheme of full Dominion Status, the Round Table Conference could not possibly furnish a solution for which vocal India is consciously and the dumb millions are unconsciously thirsting. Needless to say, there never was any question of Parliament's verdict being anticipated. Instances are not wanting of the British Cabinet, in anticipation of the Parliamentary verdict, having itself pledged to a particular policy. The Delhi interview having miscarried, there was no option for Pandit Motilal Nehru and me but to take steps to carry out the solemn resolution of the Congress arrived at in Calcutta at its session in 1928. But the resolution of Independence should cause no alarm, if the word 'Dominion Status' mentioned in your announcement had been used in its accepted sense. For, has it not been admitted by responsible British statesmen that Dominion Status is virtual Independence? What, however, I fear is, that there never has been any intention of granting such Dominion Status to India in the immediate future.

Lord Irwin replied that he regretted to learn that Gandhiji contemplated a course of action which was clearly bound to involve violation of order and danger to the public peace. Gandhiji was indeed faced with a serious problem. He had received no satisfaction from the Viceroy; on the other hand, he was bound to take some positive action because of the very strong left-wing pressure from inside the Congress. Though the civil disobedience resolution was passed in December 1929, Gandhiji did not make up his mind finally till March 1930. When he had no other alternative, he started the civil disobedience movement with his usual courtesy of informing the Government of what he proposed to do. He picked upon the seemingly trivial course of breaking the Salt law, which made a strong appeal to the masses and, contrary to expectations, proved a remarkable success. A feature of the movement was the participation in it of a large number of women and students. The boycott of British goods, particularly of cloth, was especially effective. Thousands of persons were imprisoned. By the third week of May, Gandhiji and all the Congress leaders were arrested. But the movement continued.

The recommendations of the Simon Commission were published in May. The recommendations, briefly, were that dyarchy in the provinces should be abolished and that ministers should be made responsible to the provincial legislatures in all departments, including the department of law and order. The Governor, however, was to retain special powers for the safety and tranquillity of the province and for the protection of minorities. He would also have full powers of intervention in the event of a breakdown of the Constitution. The franchise was to be extended and the legislatures enlarged. At the Centre, the Legislative Assembly (to be known as the 'Federal Assembly') would be reconstituted on the basis of the representation of the provinces and other areas of British India in accordance with population. The Council of State would continue as the Upper House, but its members would be chosen not on the basis of direct election, but by indirect election by the provincial councils or, if such were set up, by the second chambers in the provinces. There was to be no change in the central executive. An all-India federation was deemed to be the ultimate aim, but was not considered immediately practicable. Meanwhile, a closer association of British India with the Indian States might be effected by means of a 'Council for Greater India', which would deliberate on matters of common concern. The Commission also recommended that Burma, which was not a natural part of British India, should be separated and provided with a constitution of its own.

Shortly before the Simon Commission's recommendations were published, the report of the Indian Central Committee appeared. As was to be expected, its views were diametrically opposed to those of the Commission. The Committee wanted a substantial advance both at the Centre and in the provinces. It declared: 'We are convinced that there is no safe half-way house between an immediate advance on the lines we have indicated in our report and an ultimate surrender by the British Government, after years of agitation and bitterness, to India's insistent demand.'

The recommendations of the Simon Commission were considered by the Government of India in consultation with provincial governments. The Government of India's views were embodied in its despatch of September 1930 to the Secretary of State. Its recommendations were no less disappointing to Indian opinion than those of the Simon Commission. In any case, whatever interest Indians might have had in either was killed by the announcement of the proposed Round Table Conference.

The personnel of the Round Table Conference was announced on 11 September 1930. All shades of opinion and interests in British India, other than the Congress, were represented. The Indian States had a strong delegation, which included some of the prominent rulers. The delegates arrived in London towards the end of October. The formal opening of the conference by the King did not take place until 12 November. The actual work of the Conference began on 17 November. The interval was utilized for informal discussions between British-Indian delegates and representatives of the States.

Contrary to general expectation, the first Round Table Conference achieved outstanding results, the most important being the unanimous agreement of all parties, including the rulers, on the issue of federation. Up to this time, an all-India federation had been regarded as only a remote possibility. But at the very outset of the Conference Sir Tej Bahadur Sapru boldly declared himself for a federal system of government for India and invited the rulers to support his suggestion. The Maharajah of Bikaner and the Nawab of Bhopal stated on behalf of the rulers that they were prepared to come into the proposed federation provided their internal sovereignty was guaranteed. Sir Muhammad Shafi for one wing of the Muslim League and Jinnah for the other, also welcomed the proposal.

Several factors contributed to this unanimity of opinion among the Indian delegates. The rulers had seen the trend of the civil disobedience campaign in British India. They had no illusions as to what would happen if this campaign were extended to their States. Furthermore, if they stood in the way of progress in British India, in the existing temper of the country, they would be inviting immediate trouble to themselves. As for the Muslim League, it had always been opposed to a strong Centre. It envisaged that participation of the rulers in a Federation would ensure a Centre which would be limited to the minimum number of subjects, the residuary powers being retained by the federating units. Nor could a Labour Government, with its professed sympathy with Indian aspirations, turn down the unanimous recommendations of an Indian opinion consisting of Hindus, Muslims and Princes at a time when the civil disobedience campaign was going on in full force in India.

At the conclusion of this session of the Round Table Conference, Ramsay MacDonald defined the policy of His Majesty's Government thus:

The view of His Majesty's Government is that responsibility for the government of India should be placed upon Legislatures, central and provincial, with such provisions as may be necessary to guarantee, during a period of transition, the observance of certain obligations and to meet other special circumstances, and also with such guarantees as are required by minorities to protect their political liberties and rights.

His Majesty's Government has taken note of the fact that the deliberations of the Conference have proceeded on the basis, accepted by all parties, that the central Government should be a federation of all India, embracing both the Indian States and British India in a bicameral legislature. With a Legislature constituted on a federal basis, His Majesty's Government will be prepared to recognise the principle of the responsibility of the Executive to the Legislature.

Under existing conditions the subjects of Defence and External Affairs will be reserved to the Governor-General, and arrangements will be made to place in his hands the powers necessary for the administration of those subjects. Moreover, as the Governor-General must, as a last resort, be able in an emergency to maintain the tranquillity of the State, and must similarly be responsible for the observance of the constitutional rights of minorities, he must be granted the necessary powers for these purposes.

The Governors' provinces will be constituted on a basis of full responsibility. Their ministries will be taken from the Legislature and will be jointly responsible to it. The range of provincial subjects will be so defined as to give them the greatest possible measure of self-government. The authority of the Federal Government will be limited to provisions required to secure its administration of federal subjects, and to discharge its responsibility for subjects defined in the constitution as of all-India concern.

The Prime Minister concluded by hoping that the achievements of the Conference might enable those in India who had refused to co-operate in this work to be brought into its subsequent deliberations. The Prime Minister's announcement of policy was later endorsed by a resolution passed by both Houses of Parliament.

Lord Irwin took up the Prime Minister's statement as a starting-point from which to create a new situation. No Viceroy had ever made such genuinely sincere attempts to find a solution of the Indian impasse. Within a week of the statement he released Gandhiji and the members of the Working Committee. 'My Government,' he said, 'will impose no conditions on these releases, for we feel that the best hope for the restoration of peaceful conditions lies in discussions being conducted by those concerned under terms of unconditional liberty.... I am content to trust those who will be affected by our decision to act in the same spirit as inspires it.'

Shortly afterwards, meetings were arranged between the Viceroy and Gandhiji. Sir Tej Bahadur Sapru, M. R. Jayakar and V. S. Srinivasa Sastri exercised their influence on the Congress to bring about a settlement, which was ultimately signed on 5 March 1931 and was known as the 'Gandhi-Irwin Pact'. The Government agreed to release all civil disobedience prisoners; the Congress, on its part, agreed to suspend civil disobedience and to participate in the next Round Table Conference. Under the Pact, Gandhiji accepted the Federation outlined by the Prime Minister, but stipulated that the safeguards and reservations should be 'in the interests of India,' a phrase which was later subject to various interpretations. The Pact was unanimously accepted by the Central Legislature.

At the session of the Congress held in Karachi in March 1931, the Gandhi-Irwin Pact was ratified and Gandhiji was appointed as the sole representative of the Congress to the second session of the Round Table Conference. It may be remarked that the Congress had originally demanded that it should have predominant representation at the Round Table Conference and Lord Irwin was prepared, in view of the position of the Congress, to concede to it sixteen delegates. It was anticipated that the Congress would send a very strong delegation of prominent leaders. Its decision to send Gandhiji as its sole representative therefore came as something of a surprise.

The Second Round Table Conference was held in less auspicious circumstances. The Labour Government had now been replaced by a National Coalition Government. Though Ramsay MacDonald continued as Prime Minister, the Government was predominantly Conservative. Wedgwood Benn had been replaced by Sir Samuel Hoare (later Viscount Templewood), as Secretary of State for India. In India, Lord Irwin was succeeded by Lord Willingdon who, it may be remarked, never throughout his viceroyalty disguised his antipathy towards the Congress.

This session of the Round Table Conference lacked the enthusiasm which had marked the first. The representatives of the Muslims and other minorities were clamorous for a settlement of their claims before any business could be done. Gandhiji directed his attention to finding a solution of this problem, but after protracted negotiations he had to admit 'with deep sorrow and deeper humiliation' utter failure to secure an agreed solution of the communal problem. The representatives of the Muslims, the Depressed Classes, the Indian Christians, the Anglo-Indians and the British interests then met and produced a joint statement of their claims which, they said, should stand or fall as a whole. The initiative thus passed from the Congress to His Majesty's Government, to whom the minorities henceforward looked for the protection of their rights. As for the rulers, the communal disharmony in British India gave them quite sufficient excuse to sit back and watch developments.

At the conclusion of the Conference, Ramsay MacDonald reaffirmed the Government's adherence to the principle of responsible federal government (subject to certain reservations and safeguards during a transition period) and provincial autonomy. Referring to the communal problem, he said that though it constituted a formidable obstacle, it should not be permitted to be a bar to progress. It was a problem especially for Indians to settle by mutual agreement, but if that should continue to be impossible the Government would be compelled to apply a provisional scheme of its own. He added:

This would mean that His Majesty's Government would have to settle for you, not only your problems of representation, but also to decide as wisely and justly as possible what checks and balances the Constitution is to contain to protect the minorities from unrestricted and tyrannical use of the democratic principle expressing itself solely through the majority power.

With the advent of a coalition Government in England the whole atmosphere and temper of the Round Table Conference had changed. The sole outcome of this second session was the widening of the cleavage between the Congress and the minorities, especially the Muslim League. With the minorities in opposition and a British Government antagonistic to Indian aspirations, Gandhiji was unable to achieve anything. He returned from England a disappointed man.

During Gandhiji's absence, the political situation in India had rapidly deteriorated, especially in Bengal, the United Provinces and the North-West Frontier Province. The Viceroy had issued a series of Ordinances. Jawaharlal Nehru had been arrested in connexion with the proposed launching of a no-rent campaign by agricultural tenants in the United Provinces. Ghaffar Khan and his colleagues in the North-West Frontier Province had also been arrested. Immediately on his return from England, Gandhiji sent the following telegram to Lord Willingdon:

I was unprepared on landing yesterday to find Frontier and United Provinces Ordinances, shootings in Frontier and arrests of my valued comrades in both, on the top the Bengal Ordinance awaiting me. I do not know whether I am to regard these as an indication that friendly relations between us are closed, or whether you expect me still to see you and receive guidance from you as to the course I am to pursue in advising the Congress. I would esteem a wire in reply.

In the correspondence which ensued, Gandhiji received no satisfaction. The Congress Working Committee demanded a public enquiry on the working of the Ordinances. The Committee also passed a resolution stating that the Prime Minister's declarations were unsatisfactory and wholly inadequate in terms of the Congress demand. In the event of a satisfactory response not coming from the Government, the Working Committee called upon the nation to resume civil disobedience. In consequence, Gandhiji, along with other Congress leaders, was arrested — and for the next two and a half years the Congress remained in the wilderness.

Even after their return to India, a representative body of the delegates to the Round Table Conference continued to meet in Simla in an endeavour to reach agreement on certain outstanding problems, such as the representation of minorities in the legislatures. The Muslim representatives insisted that the question of communal representation should be decided first. But the delegates were unable to come to any agreement and His Majesty's Government had therefore to intervene. The Prime Minister announced his Communal Award on 16 April 1932. The Award related to the provincial legislatures. It accorded separate electorates for Muslims, Europeans, Sikhs, Indian Christians and Anglo-Indians. Seats were reserved for Marathas in certain selected general constituencies in Bombay. The Depressed Classes were given seats which were to be filled by election from special constituencies in which they alone could vote, though they were entitled to vote also in the general constituencies. A number of seats, also communally divided, were allotted to women. Special seats were allotted to labour, commerce and industry, mining and planting, and landholders.

The Muslim representation under the Award was as follows:

| Province | Muslim percentage of population | Total number of seats | Number of seats reserved for Muslims |
|---|---|---|---|
| Madras ... | 7·9 | 215 | 29 |
| Bombay excluding Sind | 9·2 | 175 | 30 |
| Bengal ... | 54·7 | 250 | 119 |
| The United Provinces | 15·3 | 228 | 66 |
| The Punjab ... | 57·0 | 175 | 86 |
| The Central Provinces | 4·7 | 112 | 14 |
| Assam ... | 33·7 | 108 | 34 |
| Sind ... | 70·7 | 60 | 34 |
| N.W.F. Province ... | 91·8 | 50 | 36 |
| Bihar and Orissa ... | 10·8 | 175 | 42 |

The Sikhs, who formed 13·2 per cent of the population of the Punjab, were given 32 seats in a house of 175.

Gandhiji had declared more than once that if an attempt were made to rend the Depressed Classes from the main body of the Hindus by means of separate electorates, he would resist it with his life. When the Communal Award was announced, he wrote to the Prime Minister informing him that, if the Award were not changed so far as the Depressed Classes were concerned, he would undertake a fast unto death. On 20 September 1932, he started his fast. This roused certain prominent Hindu leaders to get into immediate negotiation with B. R. Ambedkar, the leader of the Depressed Classes, as the result of which an agreement was reached on 24 September known as the 'Poona Pact'. His Majesty's Government accepted the Pact and Gandhiji broke his fast. The Poona Pact was more generous to the Depressed Classes than was the Award of His Majesty's Government.

Under the Pact, seats were reserved for the Depressed Classes out of the general non-Muhammadan seats in the provincial legislatures as follows: Madras 30, Bombay with Sind 15, Punjab 8, Bihar and Orissa 18, Central Provinces 20, Assam 7, Bengal 30, and United Provinces 20 — a total of 148 seats, as against 81 seats given by the Communal Award. Election to these seats would be by joint electorates, subject to the following procedure. All the members of the Depressed Classes registered in the general electoral roll in a constituency would form an electoral college, which would elect a panel of four candidates belonging to the Depressed Classes for each of the reserved seats by the method of the single vote; the four members getting the highest number of votes in such primary election would be candidates for election to each such reserved seat by the general electorate. Representation of the Depressed Classes in the central Legislature would be on the same principle of joint electorates and reserved seats by the method of primary election. These arrangements were to be in force for a period of ten years.

The third and last session of the Round Table Conference held in November 1932 was attended by only forty-six delegates. None of the important rulers was present. It was evident that they had lost their first enthusiasm for federation. It was at this session that the Secretary of State announced that His Majesty's Government had decided to give the Muslims in the central Legislature $33\frac{1}{3}$ per cent of the British-Indian seats. It had also been decided to constitute Sind into a separate province. Sind would be a predominantly Muslim province. As a counterbalance, it was decided later to create a separate province of Orissa.

In March 1933, the decisions taken by the Government in the light of the three Round Table Conferences, were published in a White Paper setting out His Majesty's Government's proposals for an Indian constitution. It was made clear that it was His Majesty's Government's intention to refer these proposals to a Joint Select Committee, after which it would be the duty of His Majesty's Government to introduce a Bill embodying its final plans.

In April, a Joint Committee of both Houses of Parliament was appointed, with Lord Linlithgow as Chairman, 'to consider the future government of India' with special reference to the White Paper proposals.

The year 1934 saw radical changes in Congress politics. It was decided to suspend the civil disobedience movement started in 1932.

The Swarajya Party was reconstituted and the policy of council entry was adopted. At its annual session held in Bombay in October, the Congress rejected the White Paper proposals and declared that the only satisfactory alternative was a constitution drawn up by a Constituent Assembly elected as far as possible on the basis of adult suffrage. Incidentally, the Congress had not rejected the Communal Award of His Majesty's Government, but had merely criticized it as a negation of nationalism. A section of Congressmen, led by Pandit Madan Mohan Malaviya, broke away and started the 'Congress Nationalist Party' the immediate policy of which was to reject the Communal Award. Towards the end of 1934, elections were held to the central Legislative Assembly. The Congress and the Congress Nationalist Party together secured more than half the number of elected seats. The Muslim League as a party did not contest the elections; Jinnah himself was returned as an Independent.

On 12 December 1934, a Bill based on the Joint Select Committee's recommendations was introduced in the House of Commons. In both Houses of Parliament its passage was resisted by a section of the Conservatives. Winston Churchill was its most vehement opponent. He characterized the Bill as 'a gigantic quilt of jumbled crochet work, a monstrous monument of shame built by pigmies.' Nevertheless, the Bill was ultimately passed by both Houses of Parliament and received the Royal Assent on 4 August 1935.

The Government of India Act of 1935 contemplated a Federation of British-Indian provinces[1] and Indian States. The provinces consisted of Madras, Bombay, Bengal, the United Provinces, the Punjab, Bihar, the Central Provinces and Berar, Assam, the North-West Frontier Province, Orissa and Sind. In a Federation so established were to be included the Chief Commissioners' provinces, namely, Delhi, Ajmer-Merwara, Coorg, British Baluchistan, the Andaman and Nicobar Islands and Panth Piploda.

In the case of the provinces, accession to the Federation would be automatic, but in the case of the Indian States it would be voluntary. The ruler of an Indian State would accede to the Federation by executing an Instrument of Accession which would have to be accepted by His Majesty and the Federation would be brought into existence by the

---

[1] Burma was separated from India in pursuance of the recommendation of the Indian Statutory (Simon) Commission, whose proposal was accepted in principle by His Majesty's Government. A Burma Round Table Conference was held in London in 1932 and the Burma Act was passed in 1935. The separation actually took place in 1937.

issue of a Royal Proclamation. But no such proclamation would be issued until the rulers of States, representing not less than half the aggregate population of the States, and entitled to not less than half the seats allotted to the States in the Federal Upper Chamber, had signified their desire to accede to the Federation, and both Houses of Parliament had presented an address to His Majesty praying that such a proclamation be issued.

The federal portion of the Act contained special provisions for the administration of defence, ecclesiastical affairs, external affairs and tribal areas. These subjects would be administered by the Governor-General 'in his discretion' assisted by counsellors. Other federal subjects would be administered by the Governor-General assisted by ministers responsible to the Federal Assembly. The Act also provided the Governor-General with special powers for the prevention of grave menace to peace and tranquillity and for safeguarding the financial stability of the country; for protecting the rights of minorities, for obtaining necessary supply and legislation, and for the promulgation of Ordinances. This portion of the Act was not brought into operation because of the outbreak of war and the consequent suspension of federal negotiations with the rulers.

But the Act also provided that, pending the establishment of Federation, the central Government and Legislature as they had existed previously, would continue with such changes as might be required to meet new conditions. In fact, these transitional provisions, embodied in Part XIII of the 1935 Act, continued in force till the date of the transfer of power.

The Government of India thus remained purely an official government under the control of the Secretary of State, but there were two vital changes.

Firstly, the relations of the Crown with the Indian States were no longer the concern of the Government of India. They passed to the Crown Representative, a new functionary (though the same individual held the offices of both Governor-General and Crown Representative). The Crown Representative exercised his functions in relation to the Indian States through the agency of the Political Department, local Residents and Political Agents.

Secondly, the relations of the Government of India with the provinces were on a strictly federal basis. The provincial governments were made completely autonomous and they and the central Government acted in mutually excluded spheres of administration. There were two lists of subjects, namely 'federal' and 'provincial'. The central Government administered the federal subjects, while the provincial governments had full authority in the provincial field. There was also a third list of subjects, called the 'concurrent list', on which the central and provincial legislatures were both competent to legislate, but the administration of which was left to the provincial governments. The concurrent list included such subjects as civil and criminal law, factories, labour welfare, etc. The intention was that in such matters the central Legislature would lay down the main principles applicable to the whole of British India, while the provinces might make variations to suit local conditions.

Under the Act of 1935, each of the eleven provinces was administered by a Governor appointed by His Majesty, normally for five years. The Governor was assisted by a council of ministers responsible to the legislature. The administration of 'excluded areas' (inhabited in the main by primitive people) was excluded from the purview of ministers, but in all other matters the administration was carried on with their advice. In those cases in which the Governor had a special responsibility, for example, for the prevention of grave menace to peace or tranquillity, or for the safeguarding of the interests of minorities, he could overrule his ministers; otherwise, he was obliged to act on their advice. In the exercise of his overriding powers, the Governor was answerable to the Governor-General and through him to the Secretary of State for India and Parliament.

Each province had a Legislative Assembly. The provinces of Madras, Bombay, Bengal, the United Provinces, Bihar and Assam also had a Legislative Council or Upper Chamber. All members of the Assembly were elected. The franchise was very wide; the total voting strength of the provinces taken together was about thirty millions. The population of the British-Indian provinces under the census of 1931 was two hundred and fifty-six millions; 11·5 per cent of the population was thus enfranchised. Separate electorates were provided for certain communities. The normal life of the Assembly was five years. The Upper Chamber was a permanent body, a proportion of whose members would retire and be replaced by fresh members every third year. Legislation in the provincial field had to be passed by both chambers, but the voting of supplies was the exclusive function of the Legislative Assembly.

There was one difference between parliamentary government in England and in India. In England, if a ministry was defeated, the

King had to find an alternative ministry or dissolve Parliament. In India, having regard to past experience of the working of representative government, provision was made in the Act (Section 93) that, if at any time the Governor of a province was satisfied that a situation had arisen in which the government of the province could not be carried on in accordance with the provisions of the. Act, he could by proclamation take upon himself the administration of the province.

The Chief Commissioners' provinces were governed directly by the central Government. Except in Coorg, which had a legislative council, these Chief Commissioners' provinces had no legislature of their own.

Since the federal and provincial governments were equal and independent authorities operating in exclusive spheres, there was more than a likelihood that in the legislative sphere the province and the Centre might trespass on each other's respective domains. A Federal Court was constituted for the purpose of resolving any disputes that might arise in this connexion. The Federal Court of India consisted of a Chief Justice and two judges.

I have here attempted to give only the broad features of the 1935 Act. I may mention that the Act had more enemies than friends. Its federal provisions, in particular, were condemned by almost all parties, including the Congress and the Muslim League. In fact, the only parties who declared themselves in favour of working the Act, both in the provinces and the Centre, were the National Liberal Federation and the Hindu Mahasabha.

When the Congress met in Faizpur in December 1936, there was fairly general opposition to the federal portion of the Act and in particular to the proposed safeguards and the Governor-General's overriding powers. It wanted complete responsibility at the Centre. The Congress repeated its resolve 'not to submit to this constitution or to co-operate with it but to combat it both inside and outside the legislatures so as to end it.' But there was an influential section which felt that the provincial portion of the Act should be accepted and worked. The Congress finally resolved to contest the elections to the legislatures without committing itself to any definite policy. The question of 'acceptance of office' was left over till after the general elections.

The Muslim League denounced the safeguards in the Government of India Act as making responsible government nugatory, but it recommended that 'having regard to the conditions prevailing at present in the country, the provincial scheme of the constitution be utilized for what it is worth.' The League whole-heartedly supported the Communal Award.

Early in 1936, the Muslim League (which had been in a moribund condition ever since the split in 1927) showed fresh signs of life with the election of Jinnah as its President. It appointed a Central Parliamentary Board to direct the elections.

Elections to the provincial legislatures under the Act of 1935 were held early in 1937. The Congress obtained a clear majority in Madras, the United Provinces, Bihar, the Central Provinces and Orissa. In Bombay it won nearly half the seats and could count on the support of a few sympathizers. In Assam and the North-West Frontier Province it was the largest single party. Only in Bengal, the Punjab and Sind was it in a minority. In Bengal the Krishak Proja Party of Fazlul Huq won a large number of seats, while in the Punjab the majority of the seats were captured by the Unionist Party led by Sikander Hyat Khan. Out of a total of 485 Muslim seats, the Muslim League was able to capture only 108. The Congress contested 58 Muslim seats and won 26.

In March 1937, the All-India Congress Committee passed a resolution permitting acceptance of office if the leader of the Congress Party in each provincial legislature 'is satisfied and is able to state publicly that the Governor will not use his powers of interference or set aside the advice of ministers in regard to their constitutional activities.' The Governors concerned explained that they could not give any such promise, whereupon the Congress leaders declined to take office. Interim ministries were therefore set up in those provinces in which the Congress was in a majority. The Unionist Party took office in the Punjab, and coalition ministries were formed in Assam, Bengal, Sind and the North-West Frontier Province.

The Congress demand led to much controversy, which was finally resolved by a statement by Lord Linlithgow, the Governor-General, on 22 June 1937. He made it clear that the 'special responsibilities' of the Governor did not entitle him to intervene at random in the administration of the province. They had been restricted in scope to the narrowest limits possible, within which field the Governors were anxious 'not merely not to provoke conflicts with their ministers to whatever party their ministers may belong, but to leave nothing undone to avoid and to resolve such conflicts.' Lord Linlithgow concluded by appealing to Indians to take advantage of the Act and to work it for all it was worth.

The Congress considered this statement as meeting their demand. In July 1937 the Working Committee resolved that Congressmen should be permitted to accept office. Congress ministries were formed in Madras, Bombay, the Central Provinces, Bihar, Orissa and the United Provinces. Shortly after, the ministry in the North-West Frontier Province was defeated and was replaced by a Congress coalition ministry. In October 1938 a Congress coalition ministry was also formed in Assam. These eight ministries continued in office till October 1939.

When the Congress decided to accept office there was a proposal that it should form coalition ministries with the Muslim League. As far as Bihar, Orissa and the Central Provinces were concerned, the League had no member at all in the legislatures and therefore the question did not arise. In the other provinces efforts in this direction did not materialize. The Congress decided to have homogeneous ministries of its own and chose Muslim ministers from amongst those who were members of the Congress Party. This was the beginning of a serious rift between the Congress and the League and was a factor which induced neutral Muslim opinion to turn to the support of Jinnah.

After the elections of 1937, the Congress started a programme of Muslim mass contact. But this did not meet with any success; on the other hand, it widened the gulf between the Congress and the League. Jinnah took serious umbrage at what he described as an adroit effort on the part of the Congress to take advantage of the weakness of the League and the presence of splinter parties among the Muslims, and so to divide the community. From now on Jinnah followed a two-pronged policy to consolidate the position of the League. The first was to win mass support. This he did by persistent propaganda that the Congress was only a Hindu body, in support of which he instanced the *Bande Mataram* song, the tricolour flag, the *Vidya Mandir* scheme of education and the Hindi-Urdu controversy. These were issues calculated easily to excite the Muslim masses. Side by side, he made a determined effort to bring all Muslim political parties under the banner of the League. Quite a number of Muslims who had been elected on non-League tickets to the legislatures, started trickling into the League camp. By 1938 Jinnah had consolidated his position to a considerable extent. When efforts were made by Gandhiji, Jawaharlal

Nehru and Subhas Chandra Bose to come to a settlement with Jinnah, he insisted that the Muslim League should be recognized as the one and only body that represented the entire Muslim community and that the Congress should speak only on behalf of the Hindus. The Congress could not accept such a position; in the words of Rajendra Prasad, it 'would be denying its past, falsifying its history and betraying its future.'

The underlying concept of an all-India federation was to preserve the essential unity of the country. But it is sad to reflect that in the clash of politics, the struggle for power, the wrangle for ascendancy, and the scramble for gains on the part of the political organizations, politicians and the Princes, the scheme of federation, became a tragic casualty. The Congress condemned it for reasons mostly divorced from facts and realities but largely under the pressure of a strong left wing. Jinnah and the other leaders of the Muslim League, embittered by the controversy on the issue of coalition ministries, now began to play with the idea of a separate State, and turned against the conception of an all-India federation. The Indian Princes, regardful only of their own parochial interests, made extravagant claims impossible of acceptance. But the final death-blow was given to it by the outbreak of the second World War which did not give time to its sponsors to stage even a decent burial.

# III

## WAR AND THE DEADLOCK

AUGUST 1939 was a month of international tension and anxiety. The peace of Europe, indeed of the whole world, hung perilously on a thread. The future of India was no less in the balance. The Congress was not long in framing its policy. On 11 August its Working Committee passed a resolution declaring that it was opposed to any imperialist war and that it was determined to resist any attempt to impose a war on India. It condemned the sending of troops to Egypt and Singapore. It protested against the prolonging of the life of the central Legislative Assembly and called upon all Congress members of the central Assembly to refrain from attending its next session. 'The Committee,' the resolution concluded, 'further remind provincial governments to assist in no way the war preparations of the British Government and to keep in mind the policy laid down by the Congress to which they must adhere. If the carrying out of this policy leads to resignations or the removal of the Congress ministers, they must prepare for this contingency.'

Despite the unequivocal nature of the resolution passed by the Congress Working Committee, there were still some prominent Congressmen who were anxious not to break with Britain. They were prepared to co-operate in the war effort; but they feared that, if they did so, they would lose the initiative to the left wing. Some of them hinted privately that a break could be avoided if only His Majesty's Government would give a unilateral assurance that at the end of the war full Dominion Status would be conceded to India.

The Council of the Muslim League passed a resolution on 27 August deploring the treatment meted out to Muslims by the British Government and stressing that if the latter desired the support of the Muslims of the world, the demands of Muslim India would have to be met without delay. The Council considered that it was premature to determine their attitude in the event of a world war; if a state of emergency arose the question would be decided by the Working Committee of the League.

In the non-Congress provinces of Bengal and the Punjab, although the respective Prime Ministers, Fazlul Huq and Sikander Hyat Khan, had recently become members of the Muslim League, the ministries remained independent of the League. In fact, both Prime Ministers publicly announced that the manpower and resources of their respective provinces would be placed unhesitatingly at the disposal of Great Britain and her allies.

In the event of war, Lord Linlithgow was keen that the Government of India should be vested with special authority for the purpose of co-ordinating the activities of the central and provincial governments. His Majesty's Government rushed a Bill through Parliament to secure this objective. The Government of India already had power in case of an emergency 'to make laws for a province or any part thereof with respect to any of the matters enumerated in the provincial legislative list,' but executive authority in regard to these subjects still remained with the provincial governments. Under the Government of India (Amendments) Act of 1939 the central Government was empowered, not only to give directions to a province as to the manner in which its executive authority should be exercised, but to make laws conferring executive authority in respect of provincial subjects on the central Government and its officers. The Congress protested against this amending Act 'which strikes at the very basis of provincial autonomy and renders it a farce in case of war, which in effect creates a war dictatorship of the central Government in India, and which makes provincial governments the helpless agents of Imperialism.'

On 3 September, as the result of Germany's attack on Poland, Britain declared war on Germany. On the same day, in a message to the people of India, Lord Linlithgow announced that India was at war with Germany and appealed for their sympathy and support. He followed this up by getting into touch with political leaders as to how best their co-operation could be secured in the war effort. He saw Gandhiji, Jinnah and the Chancellor of the Chamber of Princes separately on 4 September. Jinnah remarked later, 'After the war. . . suddenly there came a change in the attitude towards me. I was treated on the same basis as Mr Gandhi. I was wonderstruck why all of a sudden I was promoted and given a place side by side with Mr Gandhi.'

Gandhiji told the Viceroy that his sympathies in the war were with England and France from the purely humanitarian standpoint, but that he could not commit the Congress in any manner whatsoever on this issue. In a statement issued on 5 September he explained that he had not gone to the Viceroy as an envoy of the Congress and that there was no question of negotiations or understandings with the Viceroy. He was not thinking of India's deliverance. 'It will come, but what will it be worth if England and France fall, or if they come out victorious over Germany ruined and humbled?' Jinnah told the Viceroy that he could not commit the League without consulting its Working Committee. The Chancellor of the Chamber of Princes on the other hand offered, on behalf of the rulers, unconditional co-operation to Britain in the war effort.

Shortly after, the central Legislature passed the Defence of India Bill; the Congress party abstained from attending the session. On 11 September the Viceroy addressed both Houses of the central Legislature and read a message from the King. He announced at the same time the postponement of federation, but stressed that it still remained the objective of His Majesty's Government. Postponement of federation it was thought, would ensure the whole-hearted co-operation of the Princes, and also secure the support of Jinnah and the Muslim League. Even the Congress, the left wing of which was opposed to federation, was not likely to take umbrage at this decision.

Jawaharlal Nehru, who at about this time had proceeded on a tour of China, hurried back in order to take part in the discussions of the Congress Working Committee. On his return he publicly stated that 'in a conflict between democracy and freedom on the one side and Fascism and aggression on the other our sympathies must inevitably lie on the side of democracy.... I should like India to play her full part and throw all her resources into the struggle for a new order.' The Congress Working Committee met in Wardha and was in continuous session from 8 to 14 September. (Jinnah was specially invited to participate in the discussions, but he was unable to attend). In the Congress there were three divergent views. At one end was Gandhiji, who desired that whatever co-operation was given should be given unconditionally. At the other end were the leftists, notably Subhas Chandra Bose, who openly declared that 'Britain's difficulty was India's opportunity.' In fact Bose had, five months earlier at the Tripuri session of the Congress, advocated that an ultimatum should be given to Britain and if the demands were not accepted, a general mass civil disobedience movement should be launched. Between these two extremes were those who, while anxious not to embarrass the Government, still wanted some explicit declaration in regard to India's future. The Working Committee ultimately passed a lengthy resolution expressing sympathy with the democracies and condemning German aggression, but declaring that India could not associate herself freely in a war said to be fought for democratic freedom so long as that very freedom was denied to her and such limited freedom as she possessed was taken away from her. The resolution stressed that the war measures had been taken without the consent and against the wishes of the Indian people. The Congress was prepared to co-operate in order to remove Fascism and imperialism, but first of all they invited the British Government to declare in unequivocal terms what their war aims were in regard to democracy and imperialism and the new order that was envisaged and how, in particular, those aims were going to apply to India. 'The real test of any declaration is its application in the present, for it is the present that will govern action today and also give shape to the future.' A sub-committee, consisting of Jawaharlal Nehru, Abul Kalam Azad and Vallabhbhai Patel, was appointed to deal with questions that might arise out of the international situation.

Commenting on the Working Committee's statement of 14 September, Gandhiji remarked that he was sorry to find himself alone in seeking that whatever support was to be given to the British should be given unconditionally. At the same time he agreed that recognition of India as an independent nation seemed to be the natural corollary of the British profession with regard to democracy.

The attitude of the Muslim League was expressed in a resolution passed by its Working Committee on 18 September. Much of the resolution was devoted to the plight of the Muslim minority under Hindu domination in Congress-governed provinces, total condemnation of the Federation scheme, and an appeal to the British Government for greater protection for Muslims against Congress oppression. The resolution expressed deep sympathy with the Allied cause, but warned the British Government that it could count on full Muslim support only on two conditions: Muslims must be given 'justice and fair play' in the Congress provinces and an assurance that no declaration regarding the question of constitutional advance for India would be made, nor any constitution framed, without the consent and approval of the Muslim League.

About this time Vallabhbhai Patel, chairman of the Congress Parliamentary Sub-Committee, wrote to the ministers in the Congress-governed provinces that the Working Committee's statement should be taken as a background for the time being and that ministers should do nothing inconsistent with it and in particular should not allow their responsibility as provincial governments to be overridden. Patel also suggested that a suitable opportunity should be taken to get a resolution passed by the local legislatures on the lines of the Working Committee's statement.

The stand taken by the Congress had wide support for three reasons. These were, firstly, the popular view that despite India's whole-hearted support in 1914 she had not been generously treated after the war ; secondly, that her support in the present war — a conflict for which she was in no way responsible — had been taken for granted; and thirdly, that if this was to be a war for freedom, Indians had every right legitimately and logically to ask for some assurance about their own future.

Lord Linlithgow felt that some concession should be held out which would give the Congress and the League an excuse for co-operating despite their declaration that they would do so only at a price. He proposed to make it clear to the leaders that it was out of the question, in wartime, to consider constitutional changes, or to enter into any commitment as to future constitutional development, but that he would be prepared to agree to the constitution of a Defence Liaison Committee drawn both from inside and outside the legislature and including representatives of the Princes. Such a committee would be summoned to periodical meetings and over these meetings the Viceroy himself would preside to give confidential information and to bring to notice any points of difficulty of a general character arising out of the prosecution of the war.

The Secretary of State was concerned more particularly with the need for making an early announcement that would satisfy the Congress, the sort of statement that would at least indicate that His Majesty's Government did not intend to take a rigid stand on the literal provisions of the federal portion of the Act. It was impossible in the midst of a war to consider constitutional changes and no one could foretell the situation in which His Majesty's Government or India would find themselves after it was over. It was evident that when the time came to resume consideration of plans for federation, it would be necessary to reconsider the appropriateness of the details of the plan embodied in the Act. With regard to the proposed Defence Liaison Committee, the Secretary of State presumed that its functions would be purely advisory and consultative; that being so, he suggested some closer and more definite association than would arise out of a committee summoned only from time to time.

The Viceroy, on further consideration, felt that he should avoid the appearance of presenting a completely blank negative to the demands put forward by the Congress and by the League. He was prepared to make a public announcement of His Majesty's Government's policy, but only after discussion with the representatives of the various parties.

Accordingly, on 26 September the Viceroy met Gandhiji. The interview lasted for over three hours and covered a very wide field. Gandhiji began by giving an account of the Congress Working Committee's discussions at Wardha. He stated that, had he been ten or fifteen years younger, he would probably have taken the responsibility for drafting the resolution, in which event it might have emerged in a very different form. But he thought that the burden was more than he could carry by himself at his age and he had felt bound to take Nehru with him, even though their views might not coincide. Gandhiji's main demand was for a declaration of policy. He wanted Britain to follow the example she herself had set in dealing with South Africa after the Boer War. If Britain left India free to frame her own constitution so long as the elements concerned could agree among themselves, such confidence and political sense would be generously rewarded. From the point of view of the Congress Working Committee, it would have something with which to satisfy its followers; therefore, the clearer and fuller the declaration the better.

The Viceroy stressed the lack of agreement between the various parties and the extreme seriousness and gravity of the communal issue. His own idea of a declaration would be to avoid any mention in it of differences between communities, or quoting those differences as reason for proceeding with caution in the matter of commitments after the war. It was just possible that His Majesty's Government might be able to go so far as to say that it would reconsider the position under the Act at the end of the war and that agreement between the communities would be a condition precedent for future constitutional advance.

Gandhiji thought that a declaration on the lines suggested by the Viceroy was likely to create many difficulties. He pressed for something full and satisfying which would stand for all time, something which would give real and substantial ground for hope to India with regard to the fulfilment of her aspirations. The declaration, he said, was the essential thing to which everything else fell to be related.

Turning to the Executive Council, the Viceroy stressed the extreme difficulty of combining a system of cabinet with a system of departmental government, or of substituting for the present Council a body of active politicians. With respect to the possible methods of associating public opinion with the conduct of the war, Gandhiji indicated that he was strongly averse to a consultative committee. If there was to be any body to represent public opinion he thought it should be a committee of the legislature.

The Viceroy was reluctant—and Gandhiji fully appreciated his reluctance—to call an all-parties conference, as such a conference was likely to end in a communal wrangle. At the conclusion of the meeting the Viceroy expressed a desire to meet some members of the Working Committee of the Congress. Gandhiji suggested the names of Rajendra Prasad and Jawaharlal Nehru.

On 2 October the Viceroy interviewed Rajendra Prasad and Jawaharlal Nehru. The two leaders demanded a declaration which must be 'full-blooded, positive and unambiguous', which must use the phrase 'absolute freedom' for India at the end of the war, and which should provide for India's unfettered liberty to frame her own constitution by means of a Constituent Assembly. Such a declaration should be accompanied by an immediate share of power at the Centre. Both leaders were opposed to the idea of an all-parties conference; they were of the view that the Congress would not attend such a conference.

At the conclusion of the meeting, the Viceroy pointed out that it was his desire to take counsel with other important parties, including the Princes, and he suggested that the meetings of the Working Committee and the All-India Congress Committee, which were scheduled to meet shortly, might be postponed. Rajendra Prasad wrote later that 'any long postponement may be misunderstood and may give rise to speculations. . . . It is not however our intention to hurry things considering the grave issues involved and we shall advise the All-India Congress Committee not to make any final decisions.'

On 3 October a joint protest from the Liberals (represented by Sir Chimanlal Setalvad), the Scheduled Castes (represented by B. R. Ambedkar), the Hindu Mahasabha (represented by V. D. Savarkar), and the Parsis (represented by Sir Cowasjee Jehangir), was received by the Viceroy. The Viceroy was warned 'not to be misled into the position enunciated by Mr Gandhi or to regard the Congress and the Muslim League as representing the whole or even the bulk of India.' To concede the Congress claim to be the only party in the land would, they stressed, be a death-blow to democracy.

After his talks with the Congress leaders the Viceroy had a series of interviews with the leaders of various other political parties, including Jinnah and other representatives of the Muslims. As was to be expected, there arose a cacophony of opinions. Sir Sikander Hyat Khan, the Punjab premier, was opposed to the expansion of the Executive Council but was strongly in favour of a Defence liaison group. Savarkar promised full support to the war effort but pressed for an undertaking by His Majesty's Government that full Dominion Status would be granted after the war. Ambedkar was clear that the parliamentary system on the British model had failed in India. He was strongly opposed to any self-government at the Centre, nor was he in favour of an expanded Executive Council. C. Rajagopalachari, the premier of Madras, felt that a declaration of an 'extensive character' was essential and that it must create the impression that His Majesty's Government was prepared to accept whatever constitution was agreed upon by the various parties. Rajagopalachari insisted that it was important to secure an expansion of the Executive Council by the inclusion of political leaders. He was opposed to any mention in the Viceroy's declaration of a consultative committee, on the ground that it would merely strengthen the hands of the left wing. He was also against an all-parties conference, which he thought would do no good, either to India or to Britain, if held in time of war.

On 10 October the All-India Congress Committee passed a resolution dealing with the situation arising out of the war. After repeating the Congress protest against bringing India into the war without the people's consent, it stated that the Congress did not wish to take any decision precipitately and without giving every opportunity for the British Government to clarify its war and peace aims with particular reference to India. It endorsed the Working Committee's statement of 14 September and repeated the request for a declaration of its war aims by the British Government. It condemned Fascism and Nazi aggression and asserted that peace and freedom depended on the extension of democracy and the application of the principle of self-determination to all colonial countries. 'In particular, India must be declared as an independent nation and present application must be given to this status to the largest extent possible.' There was substantial opposition from the left wing, but the resolution was carried.

Referring to the All-India Congress Committee's resolution of 10 October, Gandhiji said that its merit lay in not fixing any time limit for the declaration demanded from the British Government and appealed to those impatient Congressmen who would take steps in active opposition to the war to defer action until the Congress High Command so decided.

The statement of His Majesty's Government's policy which had been awaited with so much interest was issued by the Viceroy on 17 October. With regard to the objectives of His Majesty's Government in the war, the Viceroy pointed out that Britain's war aims had already been dealt with in the Prime Minister's statement, to which he invited attention. 'This statement, I think, clearly establishes the nature of the cause for which we are fighting, and justifies, if justification is needed, the extension by India of her moral support and her goodwill to the prosecution of that cause.' Regarding His Majesty's Government's attitude towards the constitutional future of India, he mentioned the success of provincial autonomy and the inevitable suspension during the war of the federal scheme. He quoted the statement of Sir Samuel Hoare in the House of Commons on 6 February 1935 confirming that the natural issue of India's progress was the attainment of Dominion Status. He pointed out that the Government of India Act of 1935 was based on the greatest measure of common agreement which it was possible to obtain at the time. He gave an undertaking, on the authority of His Majesty's Government, that at the end of the war they would be very willing to enter into consultation with representatives of the several communities, parties and interests in India, and with the Indian Princes, with a view to securing their aid and co-operation in the framing of such modifications in the plan embodied in the Government of India Act as might seem desirable. For the purpose of the closer association of India with the prosecution of the war, the Viceroy announced his intention of setting up a consultative group representative of all the major political.parties in British India and of the Indian Princes, over which he would himself preside. This consultative group would be summoned at his invitation and would have as its object the association of public opinion in India with the conduct of the war and with questions relating to war activities.

The Working Committee, at its meeting held in Wardha on 22 and 23 October, condemned the statement as an unequivocal reiteration of the same old imperialistic policy. It decided that it could not give any support to Great Britain, for that would amount to an endorsement of the imperialist policy which the Congress had always sought to end. As a first step, it called upon the Congress ministries to resign, but warned Congressmen against any hasty action in the shape of civil disobedience, political strikes and the like.

Jinnah, on the other hand, preferred to sit on the fence. The Working Committee of the Muslim League did not definitely reject the Viceroy's declaration, but asked for further discussion and clarification. Its resolution empowered its President (Jinnah), should he be satisfied on those points, 'to give an assurance of support and co-operation on behalf of the Musalmans of India to the British Government for the purpose of the prosecution of the war.'

On 26 October there was a debate in the House of Commons on the political situation in India. Wedgwood Benn suggested that the Viceroy's Executive Council should be expanded to include political leaders. Sir Samuel Hoare indicated the readiness of His Majesty's Government, if certain conditions were secured, to associate Indian opinion in a still closer and more responsible manner with the conduct of the war by a temporary expansion of the Viceroy's Executive Council. This offer failed to placate the Congress. It refused to stay its hand and adhered to its decision that the Congress ministries should resign by 31 October.

The Premier of Madras tendered the resignation of his ministry on 27 October; it was accepted on the 30th. In each of the Congress provinces (except Assam) the local Assembly passed a resolution on the lines of the Working Committee's resolution of 14 September and the ministry thereafter resigned. The Governors, unable to find alternative ministries, assumed control under Section 93 of the Government of India Act and appointed officials as their advisers. In Assam, the Congress coalition ministry resigned, but an alternative ministry was appointed with Sir Mahomed Saadullah as premier. The remaining provinces of Bengal, the Punjab and Sind continued as before.

The decision of the Congress to resign was widely regretted. Even within the Congress there were some who were opposed to this course. We shall see, as we proceed, how it only weakened the bargaining power of the Congress.

On 1 November, in pursuance of Sir Samuel Hoare's offer, Lord Linlithgow invited Gandhiji, Rajendra Prasad and Jinnah for a joint discussion. Here the Congress was confronted with a dilemma. It was, the Viceroy said, the lack of agreement between the major communities, such as could contribute to the harmonious working of the Centre, that had prevented him from going further than the suggestion for a consultative group. The resolutions of the Congress Working Committee and of the League Working Committee showed only too clearly the gulf that existed between the two. The idea therefore was that they should discuss among themselves in order to arrive at a basis of agreement in the provincial field and thereafter let the Viceroy have proposals for the expansion of the Governor-General's Executive Council. Lord Linlithgow added that, in any arrangement at the Centre, it should be practicable to include one or possibly more representatives of other important groups; that the arrangement would be an *ad hoc* one for the period of the war, quite distinct from the much wider question of constitutional reform at the end of the war; that the position of anyone appointed to the Executive Council as a member of a political party would be identical in privileges and in obligation with that of the existing members; and that the arrangement would be within the general scheme of the existing Act. Both Gandhiji and Rajendra Prasad made it clear that it was impossible for the Congress to consider any subsidiary proposal unless the main issue concerning the clarification of Britain's war aims was first resolved.

The Viceroy repeated his offer in writing to the leaders the next day. Jinnah had a meeting with Gandhiji and Rajendra Prasad, who informed him that they were not in a position to discuss anything unless the British Government clarified its war aims. On 3 November, Rajendra Prasad sent a long reply to the Viceroy emphasizing that the crisis was entirely political and was not related to the communal issue; that it was impossible for the Congress to consider any steps towards co-operation unless Britain's war aims were enunciated, and that the Viceroy should not have dragged in the communal issue in this connexion. The letter demanded once more the determination of a constitution for India through a Constituent Assembly without external interference.

Jinnah also wrote to the Viceroy to say that he had met the Congress leaders, who refused to discuss any questions until the British Government clarified its war aims.

On 5 November the Viceroy published the correspondence that had passed between him and the leaders, together with a statement in which he reviewed the negotiations with the party leaders since the outbreak of war. He deplored the entire lack of agreement between representatives of the parties on fundamental issues, but said that he would not accept this failure and, in due course, would try again, in consultation with party leaders and the Princes, to attain unity.

Thus ended the first phase of the negotiations. At the start Lord Linlithgow had recognized that he could not leave the Congress out of his reckoning. It was not only the largest and most important political party in the country; it was at the time responsible for the government of eight of the eleven provinces, and so had it within its power seriously to impair the Government's capacity to prosecute the war effort. When, however, the Congress resigned office, Lord Linlithgow's attitude automatically changed. There was no longer any necessity to woo the Congress so far as the war effort was concerned, since the administration of the Congress provinces had been taken over by the Governors. It was not likely that the Congress would embark on a campaign of civil disobedience in view of its earlier commitments against Nazism and Fascism; international opinion, moreover, would condemn any such action as designed to thwart the war effort. In any case, the Viceroy felt assured that the Government had ample resources, if the Congress did decide to launch a civil disobedience movement, to deal with such a situation.

From now on, Lord Linlithgow began to lean more on the support of the Muslim League and to discountenance any move on the part of the Congress to return to office except on his own terms. It is significant that he should have insisted on a mutual settlement by the Congress and the League of their differences in the provincial field as a *sine qua non* for the expansion of his Executive Council—though barely two months previously he had expressed to Gandhiji his reluctance to call an all-parties conference because it would degenerate into a communal wrangle!

With the Congress in the wilderness and Jinnah's hands considerably strengthened, waverers among the Muslims began trickling into the League. For all practical purposes Jinnah was given a veto on further constitutional progress and, adroit politician that he was, he made the very most of the situation. On 5 November he addressed Lord Linlithgow, asking for assurances on four points, namely (1) that as soon as circumstances permitted, or immediately after the war, the entire problem of India's future constitution (apart from the Government of India Act, 1935) would be examined and reconsidered *de novo*; (2) that no declaration would, either in principle or otherwise, be made or any constitution be enacted by His Majesty's Government or Parliament without the approval and consent of the two major communities of India; (3) that His Majesty's Government would try to meet all reasonable national demands of the Arabs in Palestine, and (4) that Indian troops would not be used outside India against any Muslim power or country.

On 23 December the Viceroy sent a conciliatory reply to Jinnah in which he stated that his declaration of 17 October did not exclude reconsideration of any part either of the Act of 1935, or of the policy and plans on which it was based. With regard to the second point, His Majesty's Government was alive to the importance of the position of the Muslim community in India and full weight would be given to their views. In framing its policy for Palestine His Majesty's Government had endeavoured to meet all reasonable Arab demands. As for the assurance that Indian troops would not be used outside India against any Muslim power or country, the Viceroy stated that the question was hypothetical, since His Majesty was not at war with any Muslim power and that while it was impossible to give a guarantee in terms so wide, every precaution had been taken by His Majesty's Government to ensure that Muslim feeling in India on this matter was fully respected.

Meanwhile the All-India Congress Committee had met in Allahabad on 23 November and passed a resolution declaring that neither the claims of the minorities nor those of the Princes were a genuine obstacle to conceding the Congress demand for national independence and that the British Government was taking shelter under irrelevant issues in order to maintain imperialist domination in India. The resolution put the Constituent Assembly in the forefront of the Congress programme as the only democratic method of determining the constitution of a free country and the only adequate instrument for solving the communal and other difficulties. The Assembly should be elected on the basis of adult suffrage.

In the first week of December Jinnah called on Muslims throughout India to observe 22 December as a day of thanksgiving to mark their deliverance from the 'tyranny, oppression and injustice' of the Congress régime in the provinces. In fact, as early as 1938, the Muslim League had appointed a small committee under the chairmanship of the Nawab of Pirpur to enquire into certain atrocities alleged to have been committed by the Congress governments on the Muslims. The Pirpur Committee brought out a report, the one-sided findings of which confirmed those allegations. Jinnah wanted the British Government to appoint a Royal Commission of judges under the chairmanship of a Law Lord of the Privy Council to hold an enquiry into the charges. The Congress had no objection to the holding of such an enquiry, but at the instance of the Viceroy the matter was dropped. The Governors (on whom lay the special responsibility for safeguarding the legitimate interests of the minorities) were satisfied that there was no basis for the allegations. The Governor of one of the provinces in which the atrocities were alleged to have been committed, writing in February 1939 to the provincial premier, stated that 'the League has made very unfair attacks on you and your colleagues; they have referred to the "atrocities" committed by the Congress governments, but no Muslim to whom I have talked on this point could give me any definite instances of "atrocities".' The Viceroy felt that, while specific instances might admit of being proved in particular provinces, it would be most difficult for Jinnah to prove any general anti-Muslim action on the part of the Congress governments, and a finding that there was nothing substantial in the allegations would be damaging to Jinnah himself! Apart from anything else, if such an enquiry were held, it would most severely exacerbate communal bitterness and this the Viceroy was most anxious to avoid.

'Deliverance Day', 22 December 1939, was observed by the followers of the Muslim League throughout India with varying degrees of enthusiasm. The outlook at the end of the year was indeed gloomy. There seemed to be little prospect of finding a way out of the impasse. The Congress insisted on a Constituent Assembly at the end of the war; the League was opposed to the idea. The breach between the two could not have been more complete.

The Viceroy even discouraged the efforts of certain well-wishers to bridge the gulf between the Congress and the Government. There was G. D. Birla, for instance, who laid stress on the fact that it was of vital importance to make some move, but the Viceroy was not disposed to take any action.

Incidentally, in December 1939, Sir Stafford Cripps stayed in India for a few days on his way to China and made a statement to the press in which he indicated that some kind of Constituent Assembly (not necessarily quite in the form advocated by the Congress) should be set up after the war. He claimed considerable support in England for the broad conception that when the next move was to be made India's constitution should, to the largest possible extent, be framed by Indians in India.

Early in 1940 the Viceroy visited Nagpur and Bombay and took the opportunity of interviewing some of the political leaders there. He delivered an important speech on 10 January at the Orient Club in Bombay. In this speech he emphasized the necessity, in the interests of Indian unity, of the inclusion of the Indian States in any constitutional scheme. He also stressed the claims not only of the Muslim minority, but also of the Scheduled Castes, adding that His Majesty's Government was determined to see justice done to them. The British Government's objective in India, he declared, had been clear as to full Dominion Status of the Statute of Westminster variety and its concern was to reduce to the minimum the interval between the existing state of things and the achievement of that objective. He appealed to the leaders of political parties in India to get together and reach some agreement and thus help to end the deadlock as early as possible.

Before leaving Bombay, the Viceroy met Jinnah. The latter mentioned the terms which he had offered the Congress in November 1939 for an interim settlement for the duration of the war. These terms were five in number — coalition ministries in the provinces; legislation affecting Muslims not to be enforced if two-thirds of their number in a provincial Lower House were opposed to it; the Congress flag not to be flown on public institutions; understanding as to the use of *Bande Mataram*; and the Congress to cease wrecking tactics against the Muslim League. Jinnah told the Viceroy that, during the discussions in November, he had tried to prevail upon the Congress leaders to accept the Viceroy's offer to expand his Executive Council subject to agreement in the provinces, but that the Congress leaders would not look at the proposal. Jinnah remained pessimistic as to the prospect of democratic institutions in the western sense working well in India; collective Cabinet responsibility, he felt, must be abandoned.

The Viceroy also saw Bhulabhai Desai, leader of the Congress Party in the Central Legislative Assembly. Desai told the Viceroy that he himself was content with Dominion Status; that the difference between Dominion Status and Independence seemed unreal. There was, he said, no desire on the part of the Congress High Command to precipitate a crisis. Many felt that they ought not to offer active opposition in wartime, but there was a good deal of pressure and a desire for a *quid pro quo*. The Congress High Command could probably hold the position till the annual session of the Congress in March. If there could be an understanding that the provincial ministries would get back into office and that the Governor-General's Executive Council would be expanded, the absence of a Constituent Assembly might be regarded as less vital. He did not think that a proclamation or declaration by His Majesty's Government concerning the Constituent Assembly was necessarily an essential preliminary to doing business, but admitted that he could not commit himself even privately and that the Viceroy would have to consult Gandhiji. He added that some of the Congress leaders were deeply committed to the idea of a Constituent Assembly and might find it difficult to resile from that position. The Viceroy acquainted Desai with Jinnah's demands and asked him what the Congress was likely to concede to Jinnah. Desai said that the Congress was prepared to include in any ministry a Muslim nominated by the majority of Muslim representatives in a provincial Assembly, subject however to acceptance by such nominee of the principle of collective responsibility and ordinary Congress discipline. While the Congress would be entitled to claim reciprocity in Bengal and the Punjab, he doubted if it would in practice necessarily do so, though the position might be different in Sind. He stressed the importance which the Congress attached to majority rule and to collective responsibility in the Cabinet.

Gandhiji on his part was anxiously searching for a basis on which to bring about a peaceful solution. He did not want to break with the Government. In spite of the opinion of some of his colleagues, he saw in the Viceroy's speech the germs of a settlement. In a letter to the Viceroy he said:

I have read and re-read your Bombay speech. I like it. I write this, however, to put before you my difficulties. Dominion Status in terms of the Statute of Westminster and Independence are taken to be equivalent terms. If so, should you not use the term that fits India's case? I have no doubt that you had very good reasons for the way you dealt with the question of minorities, but I have serious doubts about the implications of your reference to that question. I do not at all understand the reference to the 'Scheduled Castes'. If you think you would like to see me about these difficulties of mine, you have but to wire or to write.

The Viceroy was himself anxious to meet Gandhiji. But he decided first to see the Punjab and Bengal premiers, Sir Sikander Hyat Khan and Fazlul Huq.

He saw Sir Sikander Hyat Khan on 25 January 1940 and acquainted him with the talks he had had at Bombay with Jinnah and Bhulabhai Desai. Sir Sikander was against forcing Muslim League representatives into Congress cabinets, the effect of which would ultimately be to weaken the League. He was also strongly opposed to any proposal for doing away with collective responsibility; it would put the Governors in a quite hopeless position if they had also to take up and consider the views of individual and contending ministers. With regard to the communal settlement, Sir Sikander suggested that committees might be set up in the provinces to protect minorities, with statutory powers to call for papers and, if necessary, hear witnesses, and a right thereafter to approach the Governor direct. If after approaching the Governor they were still not satisfied, they should be given the right of appeal to the Federal Court.

The Viceroy saw Sir Sikander Hyat Khan and Fazlul Huq together on 3 February. In this joint interview both premiers were against any reversal of the principle of collective responsibility. They were willing to admit the Congress into their ministries on the principle of a coalition with joint policies for carrying out a common programme. Both stressed that if the Congress were to secure concessions at the Centre without some offsetting concessions to the minorities in the provinces, the minorities would suffer a permanent loss of manoeuvring ground. They were particularly anxious to impress on the Viceroy the seriousness with which the Muslim League would view any concession of importance to the Congress if unaccompanied by some satisfaction of their own demands.

Two days later the Viceroy met Gandhiji. The latter made it clear that he had come, not only without the agreement of his colleagues, but despite the efforts which some of them had made to dissuade him from coming. He had done so because he had felt that if the Viceroy, under instructions from the British Cabinet, was in a position truly to reflect current British opinion, there was a chance of a settlement honourable to everyone. The Working Committee had given him no blank cheque so far as the negotiations were concerned. He personally had no anxiety about the prospects of reaching a settlement or the reverse. If carnage had to come he would look on without flinching, though he himself was a man of non-violence. His supporters had been begging him to 'declare war', but he had refused to do so unless they gave him their hearts and their complete obedience to the principles of non-violence. The Viceroy stressed that it was necessary that Gandhiji should be in a position to speak for and commit the Congress. If any real advance was to be made it was quite essential that Gandhiji, while taking his colleagues with him, should himself direct and maintain control over the activities of the Congress.

On the general issue of the future Indian constitution, Gandhiji said that His Majesty's Government ought to allow India to decide for herself by means of a Constituent Assembly in which all interests were adequately represented.

As for the Princes, he would be content with a referendum to States' subjects and if they were to say that they wished to remain under autocratic rule he would accept such a position, though that was unlikely to be the popular choice. For his part, he would accept for the moment the independence of British India alone, leaving the States to Great Britain, which had created them. He did not regard the problem of the Indian States as an urgent one.

Regarding the Muslim minorities, Gandhiji said that in order to satisfy their apprehensions the Congress would go the whole length and would guarantee to protect their religion, culture, personal law, language and the like. If the Muslims had a complaint against any Congress government, they could take the ministers to a tribunal set up under arrangements to be mutually agreed.

As for the Scheduled Castes, Gandhiji wondered whether Great Britain could protect their interests as effectively as the Congress. Was it Britain, for example, that had succeeded in opening temples to the Harijans? The achievements and progress of the Scheduled Castes in the past few years amply warranted the conclusion that they were adequately cared for.

On the question of European interests, he would only say that when the British parted with power they should *not* ask for special protection for them. The Constitution itself would contain certain appropriate safeguards for property and a provision that there would be no confiscation without compensation. Gandhiji was emphatic that such safeguards should find no place in a settlement between Britain and India; that they must be part of a spontaneous response of the Indian Government to the need to protect the legitimate interests and rights of property.

Referring to the Viceroy's offer of Dominion Status of the Statute of Westminster variety, Gandhiji stated that it was for India to choose her status and not for His Majesty's Government to make a limited offer. Let the proposed Constituent Assembly settle the whole question of status.

The Viceroy remarked that it was clear that Gandhiji, speaking for the Congress, and he for His Majesty's Government, were still a considerable distance apart. In the first place, His Majesty's Government retained a fixed intention to enable India, including the States, to attain Dominion Status at the earliest possible date. Secondly, the offer in regard to the expansion of the Governor-General's Executive Council still held good, which offer should be regarded as an earnest and token of the determination of His Majesty's Government to proceed towards responsible government at the Centre. But any attempt to expand this part of the offer into a cabinet government, the advice of which would have to be accepted by the Viceroy, would be resisted. The Viceroy said that his intention was to place four seats at the disposal of political parties, two for the Congress, one for the Muslim League and one to be filled from outside these two bodies.

Referring to the Scheduled Castes, the Viceroy stressed that the Poona Pact would continue to be in force till it was modified or replaced by mutual agreement. If, therefore, in any new arrangement the terms of the Poona Pact were to be disregarded without the consent of the Scheduled Castes, that would be a matter which would at once attract the responsibility of His Majesty's Government.

The Viceroy then mentioned the arrangements he had in mind for consulting Indian opinion on the question of the revision of the Constitution. He suggested that use could be made of a broad-based and representative federal legislature for the purpose. Though he had announced the suspension of the federal negotiations, His Majesty's Government would be prepared to resume those negotiations even during the war. As soon as the requisite number of

States had acceded, His Majesty's Government would inaugurate the federation. The Viceroy himself felt that federation could most appropriately be used as a means by which the goal of self-government within the Empire could be reached at the earliest possible moment. He concluded by saying that this was the offer which he was empowered to put forward on behalf of His Majesty's Government and the limits within which he could conduct negotiations.

With regard to coalition ministries in the provinces, Gandhiji said that he did not think there was any hope in that direction with the Muslim League in its present mood. He regretted very much to say that it was a question of satisfying office-seekers and place-hunters, a process which could not settle such a major issue. The Viceroy confessed that he was himself not enamoured of coalitions. The justification for the proposal was that it would mitigate the acerbities of communal antagonism and possibly lead to real progress later on. Gandhiji said he followed the argument but did not think that at that stage anything was to be gained by coalitions.

Gandhiji concluded that there was not sufficient common ground to render further discussion profitable. The truth was that the whole business was something that had to grow. He was quite sure that in due time it would develop in a direction which would make the resumption of negotiations fruitful. Meanwhile he thought it better not to attempt to conceal from the public that the discussion, though most friendly, had shown quite definitely that for the present no negotiations could be expected to yield constructive results.

The following day Gandhiji issued a statement to the press in which he elaborated the points he had raised with the Viceroy. He concluded: 'We parted as friends. I have no disappointment in me that the negotiations failed. That failure I am going to use, as I am sure His Excellency the Viceroy is going to use, as a stepping-stone to success. If that success does not come in the near future, I can only say Heaven help India and Britain and the world. The present war must not be decided by a clash of arms, but it must be decided by the moral strength that each party can show. If Britain cannot recognize India's legitimate claims, what will it mean but Britain's moral bankruptcy?'

After his talk with Gandhiji, the Viceroy invited Jinnah to see him. Jinnah was far from dissatisfied with the outcome of the Viceroy's interview with Gandhiji. But Lord Linlithgow felt that this should not make Jinnah imagine that he held the key to future progress.

He told Jinnah that though his efforts had for the moment received a setback, it did not mean that His Majesty's Government or he himself would relax their endeavours in the slightest degree to restore the normal working of the Act. It was most unsatisfactory that ex-Congress provinces should be governed under conditions approximating to those of 1860. Neither public opinion in Great Britain, nor Parliament, could countenance or acquiesce in the maintenance of such a position, unless they were satisfied that constant and active efforts were being made to escape from it.

Jinnah laid particular stress on what he called the dreadful effect of this suspense in India. The Viceroy never appeared to break with Gandhiji, always leaving the impression that he was going to see him again before long and that negotiations would be resumed. That naturally produced in the minds of the Muslims the fear that Congress governments might return to office at any moment. His Majesty's Government ought to make it clear to the Congress without undue delay that it was not going to permit its return to office. If the Congress ministries returned to office under existing conditions, there would, said Jinnah, be civil war in India. The Viceroy remarked that for a man in Jinnah's position that was a very grave utterance; but even if he meant what he said, the Constitution was part of the law of the land and must be respected in its existing form unless and until the law was altered. In fact, no opportunity would be missed, subject always to the protection of the legitimate interests of minorities, to persuade Congress ministries where they could rely on a majority to return to office.

With respect to the future constitution of India, Jinnah was clear that it was out of the question to go straight to Dominion Status, or anything approaching it, in existing conditions. But the Viceroy suggested the need for some positive and constructive effort. He warned Jinnah that it would be a great mistake to think that responsible opinion in any circle in Great Britain would accept the view that to stand still, much less to go back, was the right solution of their difficulties.

Towards the close of the interview Jinnah referred to the efforts being made by the League to form a ministry in the North-West Frontier Province, where the Congress ministry had resigned. He wanted the support of the Governor, Sir George Cunningham, in these efforts. He was convinced that there could be no more salutary lesson for the Congress and no better advertisement of the real position in India, whether before the country or throughout the world, than that a non-Congress ministry should be set up in the North-West Frontier Province. The Viceroy said that he would welcome the restoration of the normal working of the Constitution in that province by the appointment of a government with a majority in the legislature which would satisfy the test when the Assembly met, and promised to communicate Jinnah's view to the Governor.

The Working Committee of the Muslim League, which met shortly after Jinnah's talks with the Viceroy, professed not to be wholly satisfied on some of the points in the correspondence which had passed between Jinnah and the Viceroy in November and December 1939. The Committee empowered Jinnah to make further representations. It resolved also that a delegation should visit England as soon as possible to put the case of Muslim India before the British public, Parliament and Government.

An article contributed to *Time and Tide* by Jinnah left no room for doubt that the League would strenuously resist resumption of purely party governments in the provinces and any arrangements on similar lines at the Centre. The article concluded that the reform must recognize 'that there are in India two nations who must both share the governance of their common motherland.'

On 12 February the Secretary of State, in an interview with the *Sunday Times*, made an appeal to the Congress leaders. He declared that the experience of the working of the Act of 1935 had made it clear that the problem of minorities must be taken in hand by Indians themselves. 'Long range bombardments by leading personalities from the platform and the press are little likely to lead anywhere. What is wanted is an escape from the tyranny of phrases and a descent from idealism, from the abstract to the concrete.'

On 28 February the Congress Working Committee met in Patna and decided that only one resolution should be put forward at the forthcoming Congress session at Ramgarh. The resolution began with a severe indictment of British rule in India. It reiterated the inability of the Congress to participate in a war undertaken for imperialist ends; it re-affirmed that 'nothing short of complete independence can be accepted by the people of India,' and it stressed again the demand for a Constituent Assembly. 'The withdrawal of Congress ministries,' it stated, 'must naturally be followed by civil disobedience to which the Congress will unhesitatingly resort as soon as the Congress organization is considered fit enough for the purpose

or in case circumstances so shape themselves as to precipitate a crisis.'
The resolution left to Gandhiji the responsibility for declaring civil
disobedience when he was satisfied that strict discipline was being
maintained and the 'independence pledge' was being carried out.

The resolution met with strong disapproval in non-Congress circles.
The President of the National Liberal Federation criticized it as showing 'complete disregard of the realities of the internal and international situation.' Jinnah described it as a 'beautiful essay completely
devoid of statesmanship.' The President of the Central National
Mohammedan Association commented that 'the resolution is suicide'
and that the Muslims could never support the demand for complete
independence as opposed to Dominion Status.

On 24 February Jinnah informed the Viceroy that the Working
Committee of the Muslim League, while appreciating the sentiments
expressed in the Viceroy's letter of 23 December 1939, were not
satisfied, because it had not met their request for a definite assurance
that no declaration would be made, nor any constitution enforced by
His Majesty's Government or enacted by Parliament, without the
approval and consent of the Musalmans of India. The Viceroy's
letter still left the position of the ninety million Musalmans only in
the region of consultation and counsel, and vested the final decision
in Great Britain to determine the fate and future of Muslim India.
With regard to Palestine, a solution should be found to the satisfaction
of the Arabs; and with regard to the use of Indian troops, the assurance asked for was that they should not be used against any Muslim
power or country outside India, not that they should not be used for
the defence of the country in case of attack or aggression. In order
to give whole-hearted co-operation and active support in the prosecution of the war, the Committee felt they must be assured that the
future of the Musalmans of India was not left in the region of uncertainty or doubtful possibility. They wanted a clear assurance
that no commitments would be made with regard to the future
constitution of India, or any interim settlement be reached with any
other party, without the approval and consent of the Muslim League.
Jinnah concluded by saying that he would be very glad to place the
views of the Working Committee before the Viceroy in fuller detail
whenever the Viceroy found it convenient.

Accordingly, on 13 March the Viceroy invited Jinnah for an
interview. Jinnah began by referring to the possibility of the war
extending into Asia and suggested that both from the Muslim point

of view and that of His Majesty's Government, there was every reason for co-operation between the two. The Muslim world realized now, in a way which they had not done for very many years past, that there was a strong Muslim element in India. In his judgment, Great Britain had never been in greater need of the friendship and confidence of the Muslims everywhere, and he was perfectly clear that Muslim leadership could not work with Great Britain, save on a basis of confidence and partnership. What he wished to impress upon the Viceroy was that, if His Majesty's Government wished Muslim India to give definite and effective help, it must not 'sell the pass behind the backs of the Muslims.'

Jinnah also wished to make it clear that if His Majesty's Government could not improve on its present solution for the problem of India's constitutional development, he and his friends would have no option but to fall back on some form of partition of the country; that as the result of their discussion they had decided first of all, that the Muslims were not a minority but rather a nation; and secondly, that democracy for all-India was impossible. They did not want His Majesty's Government to get itself into the position of deliberately and progressively withdrawing and handing over the control of the country to a Hindu Raj, and in the intermediate stage of being forced into the position of helping it to hold the Muslims down with British bayonets. That was an intolerable prospect.

The Viceroy told Jinnah that there seemed to him to be three main possibilities. The first was, that in course of time the operation of the constitution embodied in the Act of 1935 would result in the complete removal of Hindu-Muslim differences and of the causes of collision between the two communities. That was the ideal for which Parliament had been striving. The second was, on the assumption that Britain was ultimately going to withdraw, that there would be a conflict between the two communities. What the result of such a conflict would be was a matter of opinion, but there was no doubt that the outcome would be disastrous. Thirdly, there might be some tripartite arrangement by which the presence of His Majesty's Government, in a manner as little out of tune with Indian aspirations as possible, would be needed in India, longer even than some imagined. In such an arrangement Britain would have predominant responsibility for Defence.

Jinnah said that the third of these possibilities was an excellent one so far as he was concerned, but even here difficulties would arise. He was in favour of a Muslim area run by Muslims in collaboration with Great Britain. He was fully aware that this would mean poverty, that the lion's share of the wealth would go to others, but the Muslims would retain their self-respect and their culture and would be able to lead their lives in their own way. That might be out of tune with the British conception of the future, but it provided the only means of making Muslim existence happy within a particular area, in addition to the.feeling that Muslims would be able to safeguard, because of their military power, even those of their community who were domiciled in the Hindu area. Jinnah was at pains to impress upon the Viceroy that the attitude which he represented was the expression of deep and sincere feeling and that there was no serious division within the Muslim fold with regard to it.

Throughout the interview the Viceroy remained non-committal, but he could not dispel the conviction from his mind that the Muslim attitude was undoubtedly hardening.

On 19 March the Congress held an open session in Ramgarh and passed the resolution already referred to. Various left-wing amendments were rejected and this had the effect of consolidating Gandhiji's position. He was more clearly in the saddle than ever before. The left wing, though still a factor to be reckoned with, had obviously failed to shake Gandhiji's general control.

Simultaneously with the Congress session at Ramgarh, was held an Anti-Compromise Conference, over which Subhas Chandra Bose presided. In the course of his presidential remarks he said:

What has distressed and bewildered us during the last year and a half is the fact that while on the one hand strong resolutions are passed and statements issued by the members of the Working Committee, simultaneously, other remarks are made and statements issued by Mahatma Gandhi, or by the rightist leaders, which create a totally different impression on the average mind. The result of all this has been that the British Government have ceased to take the Congress seriously and have formed the impression that however much the Congressmen may talk, they will not ultimately show fight.

The Muslim League held its annual session in Lahore towards the end of March. In his presidential address Jinnah said, 'Islam and Hinduism are not religions in the strict sense of the word, but are in fact different and distinct social orders, and it is only a dream that the Hindus and the Muslims can ever evolve a common nationality.' He declared that democracy was unsuited to India; that 'the Muslims are a nation, according to any definition of a nation, and they must have their homelands, their territory and their State.' The following resolution, which came to be known as the 'Pakistan Resolution', was passed:

Resolved that it is the considered view of this session of the All-India Muslim League that no constitutional plan would be workable in this country or be acceptable to the Muslims unless it is designed on the following basic principles, namely, that geographically contiguous units are demarcated into regions which should be so constituted, with such territorial readjustments as may be necessary, that the areas in which the Muslims are numerically in a majority as in the north-western and eastern zones of India should be grouped to constitute 'Independent States', in which the constituent units shall be autonomous and sovereign.

Beyond some speculation over the threatened civil disobedience campaign, the proceedings of the Congress session at Ramgarh created no surprise; its outcome was a foregone conclusion after the Working Committee's meeting at Patna. The Muslim League session at Lahore, on the other hand, roused widespread concern. Its proceedings undoubtedly shocked many sections of public opinion, for although the idea of partition was not new, nobody hitherto had taken it very seriously. The Hindus were angered; other minorities were displeased, and the best the average Muslim could say was that Jinnah did not mean it and was using it only as a bargaining weapon. Among Muslims in the Congress provinces there was considerable dismay; they saw themselves abandoned to an angered Hindu community wielding all the economic power.

The League's Lahore resolution provoked representatives of the various Muslim nationalist groups like the Ahrars, Jamiat-ul-Ulema and the Shia Political Conference, to gather in Delhi in April. Allah Bakhsh, the premier of Sind, presided over this 'Azad Muslim Conference'. The Conference supported the Congress plan for the Constituent Assembly and condemned the demand for partition put forward by the Muslim League. It disputed the claim of the Muslim League to be the only representative organization of the Muslims. It announced the determination of Muslims to fight shoulder to shoulder with their other countrymen for the attainment of complete independence. This conference continued to meet from time to time, but it failed to make any impression on the increasing hold of the League on the Muslim masses.

The growing breach between the Congress and the Government, especially after the Ramgarh session, was deeply deplored by many friends of the Congress. G. D. Birla went to Wardha in the last week of March and had many talks with Gandhiji. Later, on 2 April, Birla saw the Viceroy. He stressed the need for averting a crisis and for bringing about an atmosphere of trust. But the Viceroy told him that he would be better occupied in promoting enquiries by his own friends within the Congress designed to find some way out of the existing impasse. The only result of Birla's continued efforts was that he himself lost all prestige with the Viceroy.

There was a feeling among some of the Congress leaders that in his interview with the Viceroy on 5 February, Gandhiji had failed to present the Congress point of view with sufficient clarity. Abul Kalam Azad wrote to Gandhiji early in April suggesting that if he had made it clear from the very beginning that Dominion Status of the Westminster variety would not be acceptable to him, the Viceroy would have comprehended the situation; that he had led Lord Linlithgow instead to obtain a firm assurance from the Home Government that the Dominion Status to be conferred on India would be of the Westminster variety; that Gandhiji's subsequent unequivocal refusal of this offer had weakened Lord Linlithgow's credit with the Home Government and given him a genuine grievance against Gandhiji's attitude. Others, too, informed Gandhiji that at the interview he did not try to put any plank on the gulf that seemed to exist and that he had done the Viceroy an injustice by abruptly ending the conversation.

This moved Gandhiji to ask the Viceroy to confirm in writing that there was no misunderstanding and that he had in fact made it clear in their interview that Dominion Status, even of the Statute of Westminster variety, would not be acceptable to the Congress. The Viceroy confirmed that there was no misunderstanding. The gap between them was recognized by both to be too great to be handled by prolonged conversations, and both felt that the straightforward and courageous course was to conclude those conversations rather than protract them.

After the passing of the Ramgarh resolution — with its threat of civil disobedience — the Viceroy definitely turned his back on the Congress. With the Congress in opposition Lord Linlithgow felt that he should not alienate Muslim opinion or rub Jinnah the wrong way. There being no possibility of accommodating the divergent claims of the Congress, the Muslim League, the Depressed Classes and the Princes, the Viceroy felt that he could now afford to adopt a policy of 'wait and see'.

A White Paper on 'India and the War' was issued on 10 April. It detailed the events leading to the resignation of the Congress ministries and the negotiations that had taken place subsequently, ending with the resolutions of the Congress, the Muslim League and the Chamber of Princes. It concluded that, in view of the impasse, the Government had no option but to seek the approval of Parliament for the continuance of the Section 93 proclamations in the seven provinces. On 18 April Parliament approved their continuance. In the course of his speech in the House of Lords, the Secretary of State said:

But that does not mean that the future constitution of India is to be a constitution dictated by the Government and Parliament of this country against the wishes of the Indian people. The undertaking given by His Majesty's Government to examine the constitutional field in consultation with representatives of all parties and interests in India connotes not dictation but negotiation. Admittedly a substantial measure of agreement amongst the communities in India is essential if the vision of a united India which has inspired the labours of so many Indians and Englishmen is to become a reality, for I cannot believe that any Government or Parliament in this country would attempt to impose by force upon, for example, 80 million Moslem subjects of His Majesty in India a form of constitution under which they would not live peacefully and contentedly.

This particular portion of the Secretary of State's speech was underlined by the Viceroy in a letter to Jinnah dated 19 April 1940, as adequately meeting his demand for an assurance that no declaration would be made and that no constitution would be enforced by His Majesty's Government, or enacted by Parliament, without the approval and consent of the Musalmans of India.

The deadlock was thus complete. But events were soon to take a dramatic turn.

# IV

# THE AUGUST OFFER AND AFTER

THE war in Europe, after the crushing of Poland, was in a state of quiescence until April 1940, when Hitler suddenly invaded and overran Norway and Denmark. Events thereafter took a quick and dramatic turn. Holland and Belgium surrendered, France collapsed, and the British expeditionary forces had to retreat from Dunkirk.

The sudden disaster brought about a change of Government in Britain. In May 1940 Winston Churchill replaced Neville Chamberlain as Prime Minister, and L. S. Amery succeeded the Marquess of Zetland as Secretary of State for India.

A month later, Parliament passed the India and Burma (Emergency Provisions) Act providing 'in the event of a complete breakdown of communications with the United Kingdom' for the transfer to the Governor-General of powers normally exercised by the Secretary of State.

In India there was a certain amount of panic, but chiefly among the propertied classes. The attitude of the political parties was generally one of sympathy for the cause of Britain and her allies. Congress leaders proclaimed that advantage should not be taken of Britain's position to press their demand for independence. 'I am of the opinion,' said Gandhiji, 'that we should wait till the heat of the battle in the heart of the allied countries subsides and the future is clearer than it is. We do not seek our independence out of Britain's ruin; that is not the way of non-violence.' Nehru expressed his antipathy towards Nazism and he, too, declared that England's difficulty was not India's opportunity.

As soon as the new Government in Great Britain had been formed, the Viceroy sought to get some guidance from it with regard to the policy he should follow in dealing with the Indian problem. He

advised His Majesty's Government that the Congress was not thinking in terms of a resumption of office (indeed it could not hope to
resume office without an agreement with the Muslims) but there was
definitely less prospect of its embarrassing the Government in the
prosecution of the war. Nor did he anticipate any trouble, at least
in the present circumstances, from the Muslim League. In other
words, it was possible that the Government would be able to get on
with the war on the existing basis.

The Secretary of State, on the other hand, was not disposed to
stand still. His own idea was that a small committee should be
formed to explore the whole constitutional problem, provincial and
central; to set out the pros and cons of the various alternative solutions, and to indicate its own or alternative solutions, both as to the
constitution itself and the body which would take its suggestions
into definite consideration after the war. Thus, the whole problem
could be discussed in private and in a practical spirit, without any
party being committed to the results of the discussion.

While recognizing the attractiveness of the Secretary of State's
scheme, the Viceroy felt that the time was not ripe or opportune to
give it a trial. The position in fact was that while the Congress was
firm in its demand for self-determination and for a constitution to be
framed on the basis of a broadly-elected constituent assembly, with
which His Majesty's Government would have nothing to do, the
Muslim League's attitude was in flat contradiction. In the Viceroy's
view, it remained as important as ever to give the fullest weight to
the Muslim position at a time when the Muslims alone were working
the constitution in the provinces and when their assistance and support were so essential to His Majesty's Government, both from the
military point of view (they were providing 60 per cent of the army)
and because of possible reactions in other countries. As for the
Princes, they were content to remain very much as they were. The
Viceroy stressed the necessity of choosing the right moment for
any move.

The Secretary of State still felt that His Majesty's Government
would be incurring a grave responsibility if it let slip an opportunity
that might not recur of resolving a deadlock which seemed practically
certain to continue until some initiative by the Viceroy provided the
possibility of a way out. He suggested a revised plan. The Viceroy
should make an appeal to the leaders of all political parties to meet
him in order to consider whether, in the perilous situation of the war,

they could not agree to discuss among themselves ways and means of reaching sufficient accommodation to enable ministries to resume office with common consent in the provinces, and to enable political leaders to join the Viceroy's Executive Council, with the general purpose of placing India in a position of active and conscious co-operation in the effort of the Allies to crush Hitlerism. It should be made plain that response to the appeal would be provisional and entirely without prejudice to any principles to which the several parties had already committed themselves. To meet possible demands for an indication of further intentions, the Secretary of State would be prepared, subject to the approval of the Cabinet, to make an announcement of policy setting out His Majesty's Government's aims and commitments in this regard. The problem of bringing the States into any such plan raised difficult issues. The Princes might themselves refuse to take advantage of the appeal; but any such refusal should not justify abandonment of the scheme for the rest of India. It was ultimately decided that the Viceroy should hold further meetings with Gandhiji, Jinnah, and other political leaders.

Meanwhile there were one or two important developments. On 15 June the Working Committee of the Muslim League met to endorse Jinnah's policy and to authorize him to proceed with his negotiations with the Viceroy. No other member of the Committee was to negotiate with the Congress leaders without Jinnah's permission, nor were Muslims to serve on war committees pending further instructions from him.

On 17 June France sued for peace. In an article on 'How to Combat Hitlerism', Gandhiji contended that if non-violent resistance had been offered Europe would have added several inches to its moral stature. 'I have written these lines,' he said, 'for the European powers. But they are meant for ourselves. If my argument has gone home, is it not time for us to declare our changeless faith in non-violence of the strong and say we do not seek to defend our liberty with the force of arms but we will defend it with the force of non-violence?'

The Working Committee of the Congress, which met in Wardha on 17 June, announced that it could not accept Gandhiji's extreme stand on non-violence. 'Mahatma Gandhi desires the Congress,' ran the resolution, 'to be true to the creed of non-violence and to declare its unwillingness that India should maintain armed forces to defend her freedom against external aggression or internal disorder. The Committee are unable to go the full length with

Gandhiji; but they recognize that he should be free to pursue his great ideal in his own way and, therefore, absolve him from the responsibility for the programme and activity which the Congress has to pursue, namely the parallel organization of self-defence and the maintenance of public security throughout the country by Congressmen on their own and in full co-operation with the sympathetic groups.' The Committee added that the national struggle for India's independence must continue on its non-violent course; the war committees sponsored by Government should not be supported, and no Congressmen should contribute to the war funds or enlist in civil guards under official control.

The Viceroy interviewed Jinnah on 27 June and Gandhiji two days later.

Jinnah's attitude was that he was perfectly ready to co-operate but could only do so from inside the Government. He was prepared to work on the basis of the offer of November 1939 to expand the Executive Council and he was confident that not only the Muslim League, but the Hindu Mahasabha, the Sikhs and the Scheduled Castes would be prepared to do likewise. He urged that if the offer were renewed and the Congress refused to take advantage of it, His Majesty's Government should go ahead without waiting for the Congress. Regarding the Section 93 provinces, Jinnah suggested that the Governors should accept non-official advisers chosen from parties represented at the Centre. These advisers would eventually destroy the ascendancy of the Congress, either by winning the support of the existing legislatures, or by preparing the provincial constituencies to support non-Congress candidates at the next election. Once the monopolistic position of the Congress was seriously assailed, those naturally opposed to it would recover their self-reliance. Jinnah insisted that any declaration which His Majesty's Government might make should not preclude, when it came to the full-dress consideration of India's future constitution, a fair and unprejudiced hearing of the Muslim League proposal for the creation of two Indias. Further it was essential, if the Muslim League was to support the Government, that the declaration should make it clear that, whatever the constitutional status conceded to her, India should remain in relations with Britain.

At his interview with Gandhiji, the Viceroy tentatively sketched the lines of a possible declaration purporting to give India a status similar to that of the self-governing dominions within one year after the termination of the war. Appropriate machinery would be set up, in accordance with the agreement of those concerned, for the working out of a new constitution, subject to an agreed understanding with regard to British commercial interests, defence, external affairs, the rights of minorities and treaty obligations to the Princes. Gandhiji was against any such declaration. Nor was he in favour of any exploratory processes such as might fill up the time pending the end of the war; he thought they would be likely to produce a very early clash of interests and retard rather than advance progress.

After his interview Jinnah sent the Viceroy a memorandum containing certain tentative proposals. No pronouncement should be made by His Majesty's Government which would in any way militate against, or prejudice, the 'two nations' position which had become the universal faith of Muslim India. A definite assurance should be given by His Majesty's Government that no interim or final scheme of constitution would be adopted by the British Government without the previous approval and consent of Muslim India. The Muslim leaders should be treated as equals and have an equal share in the authority and control of the governments, central and provincial. During the war, the following provisional steps should be taken: the Governor-General's Executive Council should be enlarged within the framework of the existing constitution; Muslims should have equal representation with Hindus if the Congress came in, otherwise they should have a majority; in Section 93 provinces non-official advisers should be appointed with Muslims in a majority; there should be a War Council of not less than 15 members, including representatives of the Princes, which would meet at regular intervals; here again Muslims should have equal representation with Hindus if the Congress came in, otherwise the Muslims should have a majority. Lastly, the Muslim representatives on the proposed War Council and Governor-General's Executive Council, and the Muslim non-official advisers of the Governors, should be chosen by the League.

The Viceroy felt that if the initiative was to be held firmly in his own hands, he must put a curb on Jinnah's ambitions. He sent Jinnah a reply in which he pointed out that it was not a case of striking a balance between the different interests, or of preserving the proportions between the important parties; that there were other parties, apart from the Congress and the Muslim League, which might fairly claim to be considered for inclusion in an expanded

Executive Council, and that there was a very definite limit of numbers to any possible expansion. The Viceroy accepted the importance, in the event of any expansion, of securing adequate representation of Muslim interests, but there was no question of responsibility falling in greater or less degree on any particular section; the responsibility would be that of the Governor-General in Council as a whole. He also made it clear that, in accordance with existing law and practice, it must remain with the Secretary of State, in consultation with the Governor-General, to decide upon such names as they might submit to the King for inclusion in the Executive Council and that such persons could not be the nominees of political parties, however important. With regard to the Section 93 provinces, the Viceroy said that the responsibility for government vested exclusively in the Governor; whether, and if so, at what stage and in what strength, non-official advisers from political parties should be appointed, were clearly matters for consideration in the light of the circumstances of each province. The Viceroy agreed that Jinnah's idea of a War Council was worth considering, but here again there were many parties affected other than the League and the Congress. In conclusion, he stated that it would be constitutionally impossible for the choice of Muslim representatives for appointment to an expanded Executive Council, or as non-official advisers, to rest with the Muslim League, but that any suggestions that Jinnah might put forward would receive full consideration.

The Viceroy also had discussions with Savarkar, President of the Hindu Mahasabha, and with the Jam Saheb of Nawanagar, Chancellor of the Chamber of Princes.

An emergency meeting of the Congress Working Committee was held in Delhi from 3 to 7 July. A resolution was passed renewing the demand for an immediate and unequivocal declaration of full independence for India, and to this resolution was appended the following:

As an immediate step to giving effect to it, a provisional national government should be constituted at the Centre which, although formed as a transitory measure, should be such as to command the confidence of all the elected elements in the central legislature and secure the closest cooperation of the responsible governments in the provinces. The Working Committee are of opinion that, unless the aforesaid declaration is made and the national Government accordingly formed at the Centre without delay, all the efforts at organising the material and moral resources of the country for its defence cannot in any sense be voluntary or as from a free country, and will, therefore, be ineffective. The Congress Working Committee declare that, if these measures are adopted, it will enable the Congress to throw its full weight into the efforts for the effective organisation of the defence of the country.

Interpretations offered by members of the Working Committee varied in tone. Rajagopalachari, who was said to be the author of the resolution, described it as a 'positive approach' to Britain, while Nehru stressed the demand for independence and declared that Indians would shoulder the burden of India's defence only for that end and not as 'recruiting sergeants for British imperialism.'

Later, at a meeting held in Poona towards the end of July, in spite of opposition from the left wing, the All-India Congress Committee ratified this resolution. The Congress was thus committed to a programme which retained the principle of non-violence in the struggle for freedom, but abandoned it in the sphere of national defence, while demanding an acknowledgment of the complete independence of India and, as a minimum step towards it, the establishment of a provisional national government at the Centre. In the course of his speech on the resolution, Nehru emphasized that there must be a strict and brief time-limit for the offer contained in the resolution, after the expiration of which the offer should lapse.

As a result of the Viceroy's interviews with the political leaders, the Secretary of State agreed that there would be an advantage in issuing a declaration setting out the aims and intentions of His Majesty's Government. The Secretary of State himself produced a rough draft which he sent to the Viceroy for the latter's comments and criticisms. But this draft underwent so much change and revision as to make the final form of the declaration, with its added implications and safeguards, of even more doubtful acceptability to the political parties concerned.

The announcement—which was made by the Viceroy on behalf of His Majesty's Government on 8 August—came to be known as the 'August Offer'. Its object was declared to be the early achievement of that unity of national purpose in India 'as would enable her to make the fullest possible contribution in the world struggle against tyranny and aggression.' It drew attention to the declaration of October 1939 in which His Majesty's Government had made it clear that Dominion Status was its objective for India. His Majesty's Government had been ready to expand the Governor-General's Council to include a certain number of representatives of political parties and to set up a consultative committee, provided that some measure of agreement between the major political parties in the provinces was forthcoming. That agreement had unfortunately not been reached. Nevertheless, His Majesty's Government felt that it could no longer postpone the expansion of the Governor-General's Council and the establishment of a body which would more closely associate Indian public opinion with the conduct of the war. Accordingly, the Governor-General would invite a certain number of representative Indians to join his Executive Council and would also establish a War Advisory Council, including representatives of Indian States and of other interests in the national life of India as a whole.

With regard to the position of minorities in any future constitutional scheme, His Majesty's Government had already made it clear that no part, either of the Act of 1935, or of the policy and plans on which it was based, would be excluded from re-examination. The Government could not contemplate the transfer of its responsibilities for the peace and welfare of India to any system of government the authority of which was denied by large and powerful elements in India's national life, nor could it be a party to the coercion of such elements into submission to such a system.

There had been a very strong insistence that the framing of a new constitution should primarily be the responsibility of the Indians themselves, a desire with which His Majesty's Government was in sympathy and to which it wished to see given the fullest practical expression, subject to the fulfilment of those commitments and obligations which Britain's long connexion with India had imposed upon her. Fundamental constitutional issues could not be resolved decisively at a time when the Commonwealth was engaged in a struggle for existence, but His Majesty's Government would most readily assent to the setting up after the war, with the least possible delay, of a body representative of the principal elements in India's national life, in order to devise the framework of the new constitution. Meanwhile, it would promote in any way possible, every sincere and practical step that might be taken by representative Indians themselves to reach a basis of friendly agreement as to the form which the post-war body should take and the methods by which it should arrive at its conclusions.

The announcement ended with an appeal for co-operation in making a notable Indian contribution to the victory of the world cause which was at stake, and the hope that new bonds of union and understanding would emerge to pave the way towards 'the attainment by India of that free and equal partnership in the British Commonwealth which remains the proclaimed and accepted goal of the Imperial Crown and of the British Parliament.'

The Viceroy had sent advance copies of the announcement to the presidents of the Congress, the Muslim League and the Hindu Mahasabha, to enable them, if necessary, to consult their respective Working Committees, and invited them for separate discussions before they sent any formal reply. The Viceroy was hopeful that the Congress, no less than other parties, would, within the terms of the announcement, be prepared to co-operate in a central Government and in the proposed War Advisory Council. But Abul Kalam Azad, on being informed that he was not free to discuss the particular terms of the announcement, sent a reply to the effect that he could find in these terms no meeting ground for the Congress; that, apart from other fundamental questions, there was no kind of suggestion for a national government and that, in the circumstances, he was unable to find any scope for further discussion.

Gandhiji wrote to the Viceroy: 'I have very carefully read your pronouncement and slept over it. It has made me sad. Its implications frighten me. I cannot help feeling that a profound mistake has been made.'

Jinnah met the Viceroy on 11 and 13 August. He asked for clarification on a number of points but did not commit himself.

Savarkar saw the Viceroy on 13 August and about a week later sent him a letter which stated that the expansion of the Executive Council was looked upon by the Hindu Mahasabha as a step in the right direction. As far as Dominion Status was concerned, Savarkar for one was satisfied and intended to issue a statement to that effect. With regard to the minorities, he thought it a pity that the Government should deliberately have chosen terms too strong, too vague and too alarming to the Hindus. Any attempt to cut at the root of the indivisibility of India as a political unit 'could not fail to evoke an undying opposition from Hindudom as a whole.' With regard to war measures, a good beginning had been made, though haltingly, but he hoped that everything would come right as the central War Committee sat from day to day, shaping and strengthening the war effort. Savarkar submitted a panel of names for inclusion in an expanded Executive Council as well as in the War Advisory Council.

The Sikhs, the Scheduled Castes and other organizations declared their willingness to accept the August Offer.

Amery's speech in the House of Commons on 14 August by no means improved the situation. He said, 'India cannot be unitary in the sense that we are in this island, but she can still be a unity. India's future house of freedom has room for many mansions.' After referring to the attitude of different parties in India, he spoke of the Congress demand for complete independence. 'It is a demand,' he said, 'which really raises the whole unresolved constitutional issue and prejudges it in the sense favoured by the Congress and rejected by the minorities.' Amery spoke of the discouraging attitude shown in Congress quarters and hoped that the leaders would be willing to take their part, but added that if that should unfortunately not prove to be the case, the Viceroy would of course go ahead with those who were prepared to work with him and with each other.

The Congress Working Committee met in Wardha from 18 to 22 August and placed on record that 'the rejection of the Congress proposals is proof of the British Government's determination to continue to hold India by the sword.' The Committee decided to call an emergency meeting of the All-India Congress Committee at Bombay on 15 September.

A day after the Working Committee meeting, Rajagopalachari came out with what he called a 'sporting offer' to promote an agreement with the Muslim League. 'If His Majesty's Government agree to a provisional national government being formed at once, I will undertake to persuade my colleagues to agree to the Muslim League being invited to nominate the Prime Minister and to let him form a government as he would consider best.'

Gandhiji was genuinely disturbed by the trend of events. He wrote to the Viceroy on 29 August to say that if things went on as they were and if the Congress remained supine, it would die a slow death. If he could not help the British Government, at any rate he did not wish to embarrass it, but this desire could not be carried to the extent of committing *harakiri*. Before he took any steps, however, he would like to lay bare his heart and mind to the Viceroy.

The Viceroy felt that he could hardly be expected to re-start negotiations after Azad's curt refusal of his invitation. Moreover, such a step might raise suspicions in the minds of other parties. He informed Gandhiji that His Majesty's Government's decided policy was made clear in the announcement of 8 August; if, however, there were any points of misunderstanding to be cleared up he would be glad to see Gandhiji and talk over the position. At the same time, he would have to make it clear to the public that the initiative had not come from the Viceroy.

In acknowledging the Viceroy's letter, Gandhiji said that he would renew his request for an appointment after the forthcoming meeting of the All-India Congress Committee. He explained that he was not unaware that the Viceroy's statement and the Secretary of State's speech represented the decided policy of His Majesty's Government. Had they met, he would have sought clearance of his own doubts as to the manner in which that policy was being enforced, and set out more fully his grounds for dissatisfaction, which daily events were deepening. He added:

I do not at all mind the Congress wandering in the wilderness. Nor should I at present engage in a fight with the Government over their policy if it were based on grounds which could be understood by the plain man. But I must not be a helpless witness to the extinction of a great organisation which I have held under curb on the ground of refusal to embarrass His Majesty's Government at the present critical juncture. I must not have it said that for a false morality I allowed the Congress to be crushed without a struggle. It is this thought that is gnawing at me.

When the All-India Congress Committee met in Bombay, Azad, in his preliminary address, declared: 'The offer Great Britain has made through the Viceroy is not worth looking at. These events made us decide again to request Mahatma Gandhi to assume the active leadership of the Congress. I am glad to inform you that he has agreed to do this, as now there is no difference whatsoever between him and the Working Committee.' While expressing sympathy with the British people, as well as the peoples of other countries involved in the war, and admiration for the bravery and endurance shown by the British nation in the face of danger and peril, the Committee insisted on the fullest freedom to pursue its own policy based on non-violence.

'The Congress,' said Gandhiji, 'claims for itself the freedom to protect civil liberty in this country, but must have the right to state freely what we feel about the war. . . . I claim the liberty of going through the streets of Bombay and saying that I shall have nothing to do with this war, because I do not believe in this war and in the fratricide that is now going on in Europe.'

Soon after, the Working Committee passed a resolution calling upon Congress organizations to refrain from all civil disobedience pending definite instructions from Gandhiji, who regarded its suspension as indispensable for his forthcoming interview with the Viceroy and as a test of discipline.

The Congress rejected the August Offer mainly on the ground that their demand for a national government had not been conceded. In giving advance copies of it to the party leaders the Viceroy had hoped that before they made up their minds there would be an opportunity for discussion, but Azad summarily rejected it. If the Congress leaders had only discussed the details of the reconstitution of the Executive Council, it is possible that the Viceroy would have gone more than half way to meet the Congress. In wartime there was no question of converting the Executive Council into a national government. Lord Linlithgow was firm on this issue and so was His Majesty's Government. Had the Congress joined the Viceroy's Executive Council at the time, and with Congress ministries coming back into power in the provinces, the political situation would have changed immensely to the advantage of the Congress. Once the Congress rejected the offer the Viceroy was in no mood to carry on any further parleys with it.

The Working Committee of the Muslim League, which met from 31 August to 2 September, considered that the Viceregal announcement and Amery's clarification constituted a considerable advance towards the viewpoint taken by the League and recorded its satisfaction that 'His Majesty's Government have, on the whole, practically met the demand of the Muslim League for a clear assurance that no future constitution, interim or final, will be adopted by the British Government without the Muslim League's approval and consent.' The resolution reiterated the League's faith in the Pakistan scheme and went on to interpret the Viceregal announcement as conceding the League's principle of Muslim partnership in any wartime constitutional scheme. The ban on League members from accepting membership of war committees was accordingly lifted. But the League's full co-operation in the war effort was stated to be conditional on the Viceroy clearing certain points with Jinnah.

On 24 September the Viceroy had a long discussion with Jinnah. Commenting on the method of appointment of new members to the Executive Council, the Viceroy explained that he would be prepared to accommodate the leaders of parties as regards their first choice, or by negotiation behind the scenes to secure satisfactory alternative choices. But if the matter were to be handled on that basis, the practical test should be that, until possible names had been considered, duly recommended, accepted and publicly announced, there should be no mention of any names by the Muslim League. Jinnah agreed, though he felt he could not guarantee that there would be no leakage or intelligent anticipation.

With regard to the composition of the expanded Council, Jinnah stated that he wished to make it clear in the first place that, should the Congress change its mind and decide to come in, he would at once demand equal representation in the Council with the Congress. Since the Congress was not for the moment coming in, the League would not press this demand. Jinnah added that the Viceroy should guarantee that the Congress would not be admitted into the Executive Council before the end of the war unless the Muslim League agreed.

The Viceroy replied that in any major alteration of the basis and character of the Council and before taking in the Congress or any other party, the Governor-General would presumably take counsel with his colleagues. But he declined to concede to the Muslim League a 'veto' on the entry of the Congress; nor could he agree to do any business, either immediately or in terms of future arrangements, on the fifty-fifty basis suggested by Jinnah.

With regard to the distribution of portfolios, Jinnah said that if the Muslim League were not to have defence, it should not go to any other Indian political party. The Viceroy thought that if there were to be any question of handing over defence to an Indian, the majority community would surely have a powerful case and would press vehemently for that portfolio. But the Act of 1935 gave the Governor-General a special position in relation to defence. It was an issue of vital importance, raising most substantial practical considerations, and its future position in the constitution was one of the most significant matters which the post-war constitution-making body would have to take into account. Apart from all other considerations, there was the great advantage in wartime of keeping the Commander-in-Chief on the Executive Council.

Jinnah repeated his fear of being let down by the Government in the event of the Congress coming in later on and asked whether it would be possible for His Majesty's Government to drop the whole question of expansion. But the Viceroy made it clear that the intention was to go ahead.

Jinnah made a final attempt to improve the Muslim League position in terms of seats (two were earmarked for the League) on the Executive Council. He pressed hard for a third Muslim, but the Viceroy regretted that he was unable to consider the proposition.

On 26 September, Jinnah wrote to the Viceroy expressing regret that the latter had declined to meet him on a vital point so far as the Muslim League was concerned. This was, to quote his own words, 'that in the event of any other party deciding later on to be associated with your Executive Council to assist in the prosecution of the war, it should be allowed to do so on terms that may be approved of and consented to by the Muslim League Party, as we were entering into, so to say, a "War Contract".'

The Working Committee of the Muslim League met in New Delhi on 28 September and passed a resolution (which was confirmed by the All-India Muslim League on the following day) stating that, notwithstanding its desire from the very beginning to help in the prosecution of the war and the defence of India, it was unable to accept the offer for four reasons, namely:

(1) The inclusion of only two representatives of the Muslim League in the proposed expansion of the Governor-General's Executive Council, of which neither the total strength nor the number of additional members has so far been definitely determined, does not give any real and substantial share in the authority of the government at the Centre; (2) No indication has been given as to what would be the position of the Muslim League representatives in the event of any other party deciding at a later stage to assist in the prosecution of the war, and the Government agreeing to associate it with the Executive Council, which may involve a substantial modification and reshuffling of the Executive; (3) So far, the Government do not propose to appoint non-official advisers in those provinces which are being administered by the Governors under Section 93 of the Government of India Act, 1935. The Committee feel that without the association of the Muslim League representatives in the administration of those provinces it will not be possible to secure real and effective co-operation of the Musalmans; (4) The proposed War Advisory Council is yet in embryo and no information is available as to its constitution, composition and functions, except that it will probably consist of about 20 members and that the question of setting it up will be considered after the expansion of the Executive Council is complete.

The Working Committee of the Hindu Mahasabha, meeting in Bombay in the third week of September, declared that it was prepared to accept the offer contained in the Viceroy's announcement only 'on honourable terms of equity and justice.' The terms were a clear and definite declaration from the Government that it had not approved or accepted the Muslim League's demand for the partition of India; and also an undertaking that, if the Muslims were going to receive two seats in the Executive Council and five seats in the War Council, the Mahasabha would be given six seats in the Executive Council and fifteen seats in the War Council.

Thus briefly, the Congress had rejected the Viceroy's offer because it did not meet its immediate demand for a national government at the Centre and its ultimate demand for complete independence; the Muslim League refused to accept it unless its demands for fifty-fifty and the right of veto over Congress entry into the Executive Council were met; the Hindu Mahasabha (though it was indeed anxious to come in) insisted on the satisfaction of demands which were as unacceptable to the Muslims as were those of the Muslims to the Mahasabha. The only parties that could be counted on were the Liberals, the Sikhs and the Scheduled Castes.

Immediately after the All-India Congress Committee session in Bombay, Gandhiji renewed his request for an interview with the Viceroy—which he sought 'both as the guide of the Congress and your friend which you have allowed me to call myself.'

Gandhiji saw the Viceroy on 27 September. Discussion for the most part centred on the former's insistence on the right to preach against participation in the war effort. Free speech, maintained Gandhiji, was the test of Britain's professed devotion to democracy, the object for which she claimed to be fighting the Germans. The Viceroy asked Gandhiji whether, for instance, he contemplated investing every Congressman with the right of inducing labour to cease work on munitions and war stores. Gandhiji replied that, in his view, any such appeal delivered directly to labour and at the point of production would amount to a breach of non-violence. The Viceroy then inquired whether Gandhiji would be satisfied with the liberty allowed to conscientious objectors in England where, while the conscientious objector was absolved from the duty of fighting and allowed even to profess his faith in public, he was not permitted to carry his opposition to the length of trying to persuade others, whether soldiers or munition workers to abandon their allegiance, or discontinue their efforts. Gandhiji replied that this was not enough for him. The collective conscience of England was belligerent. India was a subject country. It was essential that, in India, liberty of speech should cover not only the objection of the individual to personal participation in war, but the objection of the nationalist to India's part in the war. He would not preach, he said, to workers at the works, but would make declarations to that effect at large.

In the course of the correspondence which ensued, Lord Linlithgow informed Gandhiji that 'it would clearly not be possible, in the interests of India herself, more particularly at this most critical juncture in the war, to acquiesce in the interference with the war effort which would be involved in freedom of speech so wide as that for which you have asked.' Gandhiji replied: 'It is unfortunate that we have not been able to arrive at an agreement on the single issue of freedom of speech. But I shall hug the hope that it will be possible for the Government to work out their policy in the spirit of the Congress position.' He declared that the Congress still desired to refrain from embarrassing the British Government, but it was impossible for it to make a fetish of such a policy by denying its creed.

In a statement dealing with his interview with the Viceroy, Gandhiji declared that 'the immediate issue is the right of existence, that is, the right of self-expression, which, broadly put, means free speech. This the Congress wants not merely for itself but for all.' And Gandhiji chose this issue as the plank on which to launch his campaign of civil disobedience.

On 13 October the Congress Working Committee met in Wardha. Gandhiji there unfolded his plan of individual civil disobedience, which was approved. He selected one of his earliest associates, Vinoba Bhave, to inaugurate the movement. Vinoba Bhave began on 17 October to deliver anti-war speeches; four days later he was arrested and sentenced to three months' simple imprisonment. Jawaharlal Nehru was chosen to follow Vinoba Bhave. On 31 October he too was arrested; he was subsequently tried and sentenced to four years' rigorous imprisonment. Churchill, who was shocked at the severity of the sentence, had to be assured that Nehru would in fact receive specially considerate treatment.

In the light of the refusal both of the Congress and the Muslim League to co-operate in an expanded Executive Council and a War Advisory Council, there seemed no practical purpose in going ahead with the implementation of the August Offer—at least until a sufficient degree of support was forthcoming to ensure that the expanded Executive Council and the War Advisory Council were really representative. The Viceroy could see no prospect of getting any Muslim League leader who would be prepared to disregard the League's mandate. The introduction of non-League Muslims would be regarded as an affront to the League and instead of bringing support to the war effort might only create further difficulties. The Hindu Mahasabha had no real following; in any case, its inclusion would be bitterly resented by the Muslims. Lastly, there was the risk that members of the Congress and the League in the central Assembly might join in combined opposition against an expanded council in which they were not represented. As things stood, there was no hope of securing a council with anything remotely approaching a working majority in the central legislature.

With this background, Lord Linlithgow, when addressing both Houses of the central legislature on 20 November, announced that since the major political parties were not prepared to take advantage of the opportunity offered to them by the announcement of 8 August, His Majesty's Government had decided that the Viceroy would not be justified in proceeding for the time being with the enlargement of the Executive Council or the establishment of a War Advisory Council. His Majesty's Government did not however propose to withdraw the proposals and was prepared to give effect to them as soon as it was convinced that a sufficient degree of representative support was forthcoming.

Speaking in London the following day, the Secretary of State appealed to Indians to study afresh the constitutional problem of India. Certain passages in his speech were taken by the Hindu press to imply encouragement of the Pakistan scheme for the division of India. But in a later speech Amery laid stress on the intimate connexion between the political unity given to India by British rule and the development of individual freedom and national self-government. Once broken up into separate and independent entities, India would relapse into a welter of contending powers in which free institutions would be suppressed, and in which no one element would be able to defend itself against external attack. The Viceroy's offer had been rejected, not because it was inadequate, but because the spirit of *India First* was not strong enough to overcome the insistence on unpractical demands on one side, or undue suspicion on the other.

The individual civil disobedience campaign continued, with Congress leaders courting imprisonment, but the movement suffered from lack of enthusiasm among the rank and file of Congressmen and from apathy among the general public. This was largely due to the fact that the movement was restricted to individuals, that the issues were not clear to the general public, and that publicity was not possible because of the restrictions placed by the Defence of India Rules on anti-war propaganda.

During Christmas week, the Hindu Mahasabha and the National Liberal Federation held their annual sessions in Madura and Calcutta respectively. Both demanded a declaration as to the date by which Dominion Status would be achieved. The one fixed the term at one year and the other at two years after the end of the war. Both denounced the Pakistan scheme of the Muslim League. The Mahasabha proclaimed that if the British Government did not satisfy its demand for declarations both in regard to Dominion Status and against the Pakistan scheme, it would resort to 'direct action', a threat which alarmed nobody and which was never carried into effect.

Abul Kalam Azad, the Congress President, was arrested early in January 1941 and convicted for making an objectionable speech.

Subhas Chandra Bose, the left wing leader, who was standing his trial for certain speeches and articles and had been released from jail in December as a result of a hunger strike, disappeared from his house in Calcutta at the end of January. It was learnt later that he had escaped to Germany.

In the middle of February there appeared press reports of a scheme attributed to a sub-committee of the Muslim League which had been commissioned to study the various proposals for Pakistan. The scheme postulated the creation of two sovereign Muslim States, the first comprising the existing provinces of the Punjab (with Delhi province added to it), Sind, the North-West Frontier Province and Baluchistan; and the second comprising Assam and Bengal. It assumed at the same time due recognition of the integrity and unity of Hyderabad and the other States governed by Muslim rulers. But Jinnah issued a statement that the League sub-committee had not formulated any proposals as such; it had only published certain details which would be discussed in due course by the Working Committee. When the Working Committee of the League met on 22 February, it merely re-affirmed the basic principles laid down in the Lahore resolution of 1940 and refrained from going into details. The following is the text of the resolution, which was later confirmed by the Council of the All-India Muslim League:

The Working Committee view with disapproval the recent pronouncements of Mr. Amery, Secretary of State for India, which are likely to create grave apprehensions in the minds of the Musalmans as they give an impression, contrary to his previous pronouncements, that His Majesty's Government are still contemplating the possibility of a constitution based on the economic and political unity of India. The term 'Indian', the Working Committee would like to point out, covers three times a greater range of peoples than the term 'European' does. It is unfortunate that Mr. Amery, having regard to his responsibility as the Secretary of State for India, should have allowed himself to indulge in slogans such as 'India First'. Musalmans of India are proud to be Indians and firmly believe in India for Indians. It is in that spirit that the Lahore resolution was adopted, because the Musalmans are convinced that it is the only solution of India's constitutional problem which will ensure peace, harmony and satisfaction among all elements, interests and inhabitants of this vast subcontinent.

The Working Committee re-affirm adherence to the resolution passed at the Lahore session of the All-India Muslim League laying down the basic principles on which the future constitution of India must be framed before it can be acceptable to the Musalmans of India, viz., that 'geographically contiguous units are demarcated into regions which should be so constituted, with such territorial readjustments as may be necessary, that the areas in which the Muslims are numerically in a majority, as in the north-western and eastern zones of India, should be grouped to constitute "Independent States" in which the constituent units shall be autonomous and sovereign.'

Some of the moderate elements in the League were disturbed at the extent to which the Pakistan idea had now caught on with the Muslim masses. Sir Sikander Hyat Khan, Premier of the Punjab, found himself in a particularly embarrassing position. Although he was a member of the Muslim League, he was also the head of a cabinet representing the Unionist Party, which included not only Muslims, but also Hindus and Sikhs. He expressed his intention of resigning from the League and he hoped to take with him all the members of the Unionist Party. Such a step, however, would have been contrary to the policy of maintaining the League as a solid political body and Sir Sikander was dissuaded from his purpose. Nevertheless, he took the opportunity of explaining his position vis-a-vis Pakistan in the course of a debate in the Punjab Legislative Assembly in March 1941.

He admitted that he was, but only in a qualified sense, the author of the Lahore resolution, the original resolution which he drafted having been radically amended by the Working Committee. He went on to say:

I have explained that Muslims are opposed to an all-powerful Centre because they are afraid that a communal oligarchy in power might undermine or altogether nullify the autonomy and freedom of the provinces. That is the suspicion that haunts them. It may not be well-founded but there it is; and we must face facts. How can we remove their doubts and misgivings? How best can we meet their objection? Here is my recipe for what it is worth: I say, give complete autonomy and freedom to the units and let them be demarcated into regions or zones on a territorial basis. Representatives of the units within each zone should represent their respective units, as also the region at the Centre. The Centre thus constituted will not be a domineering hostile Centre looking for opportunities to interfere with the work of provincial governments, but a sympathetic agency enjoying the confidence and support of the provinces, a body set up by the units to control and supervise the central administrative machinery and to see that the work entrusted to it by the provinces is carried on efficiently, amicably and justly. . . . It will not be a rigid Centre and it will consist of representatives of the units selected by the provincial legislatures or governments responsible to the people of the province. The Centre will be elastic in the sense that except for subjects entrusted to it by prior agreement, e.g. defence, maritime customs, currency and coinage and external affairs, only such other matters or powers will be delegated to the Centre as the units may by agreement decide to transfer, and for such period as may be specified in the instrument of delegation.

Sir Sikander concluded by stressing:

We do not ask for freedom, that there may be Muslim raj here and Hindu raj elsewhere. If that is what Pakistan means I will have nothing to do with it. . . . I have said so before and I repeat it once again here on the floor of this House. If you want real freedom for the Punjab, that is to say a Punjab in which every community will have its due share in the economic and administrative fields as partners in a common concern, then that Punjab will not be Pakistan, but just *Punjab*, land of the five rivers; Punjab is Punjab and will always remain Punjab whatever anybody may say. This then, briefly, is the political future which I visualise for my province and for my country under any new Constitution.

To my mind, his speech in the Punjab Assembly is of historic interest and I have included the full relevant text of it as an appendix[1] to this book.

[1] See Appendix I.

Up to this point Jinnah, though the cry of Pakistan had served his political ends admirably, had no definite idea of what he really wanted. For instance, in an interview with the Governor of Madras, he is reported to have said that his idea was that India should be divided into four regions, namely (1) Dravidistan (approximately the Madras Presidency); (2) Hindustan (Bombay and the Central Provinces); (3) Bengalistan (Bengal and Assam) and (4) the Punjab (with some exceptions), Sind and the North-West Frontier Province. These were to be self-governing Dominions, each completely separate with its own Governor-General and responsible to the British Parliament through the Secretary of State. They would be called Dominions, but they would not have the status of Dominions under the Statute of Westminster. The Governor-General would have control over foreign policy and defence. The Indian States would have the option to come into any of the Dominions they liked. Until they did so they would retain their previous position and there would be a Crown Representative for functions in respect of them.

Though Indian Muslims realized the efficacy of Pakistan as a political weapon, opinion amongst them was divided. There were some who believed that it could be used as a bargaining power against the Congress and the Hindu Mahasabha but who did not support the idea of separation from India; others believed that separation was the only practicable solution of the Hindu-Muslim problem. Gandhi-ji is reported to have said that Pakistan was 'an untruth'. By this he probably meant that it was a political manoeuvre only, and that the sentiment of a common Indian nationalism was no less strong in Muslims than was their faith in Islam. This might have been true at one time, but there were growing indications that an Islamic revival in militant form might yet be a real danger to the unity of India.

Certain prominent leaders of the Liberal Party once more attempted the thankless task of finding some way out of the political impasse. On the initiative of Sir Jagdish Prasad, an ex-member of the Governor-General's Executive Council, a Non-party Conference under the presidentship of Sir Tej Bahadur Sapru was held in Bombay in the middle of March 1941. This Conference was attended by leaders representative of practically all parties outside the Congress and the League. The Hindu Mahasabha was particularly well represented, those in attendance including Savarkar, B. S. Moonje and Shyama Prasad Mookerjee. But Muslim representation was negligible; it consisted of Sir Suleman Kasim Mitha, Fazl Ibrahim Rahimtoola and Sir Sultan Chinoy, none of whom was of much importance in the political world. A resolution adopted at the Conference stressed that, while India should not take advantage of Britain's difficulties in her heroic struggle, it was equally desirable that India's domestic problems should not be pressed to her disadvantage. The resolution emphasized the immediate need for 'reconstructing' the Governor-General's Executive Council so as to comprise non-official Indians drawn from important elements in the public life of the country: this would, of course, involve the transfer to Indians of all portfolios, including the vital ones of Finance and Defence.

Jinnah's reaction was that the claim put forward by the Non-party Conference, if accepted by the British Government, would mean the cancellation of the declaration of 8 August 1940 and would constitute the grossest breach of faith with Muslim India and other minorities. The underlying idea of the Conference seemed to be to get the British Government by hook or by crook to denounce and reject the Muslim League demand for the partition of India.

On 7 April, Sir Tej Bahadur Sapru had two lengthy interviews with the Viceroy, in the course of which he dwelt on the entirely non-communal outlook of the Bombay conference. The question as to how many Hindus or Muslims should form the reconstructed council would be a matter entirely for the Viceroy to decide. Responsibility would be to the Crown and not to the legislature. The executive at the Centre would be irremovable for the duration of the war. The Council might include non-official Europeans, or even European members of the Services who had retired, or businessmen. There would be no question as to who should hold which portfolio.

The Viceroy referred to the difficulty which the proposed council was likely to experience in the absence of any majority in the legislature. Sir Tej Bahadur countered by suggesting that difficulty with the legislature was only likely to arise over taxation, repressive legislation, or the status of Indians overseas and that the Congress would not make trouble for the new government. If the new government were defeated on, say, the Finance Bill or some other measure and that measure had to be put through by certification, it would be far more easily acquiesced in than would be the case of certification with the existing Executive Council. The Viceroy expressed his doubts. There followed an exchange of views on such points of detail as the discretionary powers of the Governor-General, the position of the Indian States, and the undertaking that the whole constitutional position would be reviewed after the war. Sir Tej Bahadur pressed for an announcement of a time-limit for the implementation of the new constitution after the war and the grant of Dominion Status. He also emphasized the difference between 'expanding' and 'reconstructing' the Executive Council and stressed the need for speed if the Government proposed to take any action.

In April 1941 Parliament approved the continuance in force for a further year, in the seven Congress provinces, of the proclamation under Section 93 of the Government of India Act. Amery took advantage of the occasion to refer to the Non-party Conference. He said: 'The resolution seems to me to have been directed to the wrong address.' The scheme, he added, would amount, not to a modification of the present form of government, but to its supersession by an entirely different type of government. 'That is certainly something going beyond what we think practicable in the midst of the ever-increasing strain and urgency of the war situation.' Amery concluded by saying that there was obviously no agreement between the two major communities such as would afford to the reconstructed Executive Council political support or even acquiescence in the legislature.

This evoked from Gandhiji a strong rejoinder:

Mr. Amery has insulted the Indian intelligence by reiterating *ad nauseam* that Indian political parties have but to agree among themselves and Britain will register the will of a united India. I have repeatedly shown that it has been the traditional policy of Britain to prevent parties from uniting. 'Divide and Rule' has been Britain's proud motto. It is the British statesmen who are responsible for the division in India's ranks and the divisions will continue so long as the British sword holds India under bondage.

About this time Jinnah made a move of some significance towards an alliance with the Princes. He told the Jam Saheb of Nawanagar, who was in Delhi for a meeting of the Chamber of Princes, that he hoped the Princes would not stab the Muslim League in the back. He (Jinnah) would readily consult the Jam Saheb as Chancellor about any constitutional proposals, on the understanding that the princely order would not cut across him. The Jam Saheb assured Jinnah that it was not the habit of the Princes to stab people in the back; that he had noted his suggestion, but thought that any undertaking of the kind ought properly to come from the Muslim League and not from Jinnah. Jinnah expressed his readiness to get it confirmed by the League, and actually sent a letter to the Jam Saheb, but there the matter rested.

By the middle of 1941, a serious change in the war situation had taken place. The Axis Forces had succeeded in rapidly overrunning Yugoslavia and Greece and in occupying islands in the Aegean Sea. Rashid Ali, the Regent of Iraq, was openly flirting with the Axis powers. Hitler's armies were marching through Russia. The Grand Mufti of Jerusalem had raised the banner of revolt in Palestine. The situation in North Africa was far from satisfactory. Rommel was approaching the Suez Canal.

The Viceroy decided that he could no longer afford to follow a policy of 'wait and see'. Since the Congress and the League were determined not to co-operate, he would invite the support of leaders from outside those parties. A *communiqué* was issued on 21 July announcing that, as a result of increased pressure of work in connexion with the war, it had been decided to enlarge the Executive Council of the Governor-General in order to permit the separation and redistribution of certain existing portfolios and the creation of the new portfolios of 'Information' and 'Civil Defence'. The number of the members of the Executive Council was raised from 7 to 12 and the Indian element from 3 to 8, the members being chosen from outside the League or the Congress fold.

Simultaneously it was announced that, in pursuance of the desire of His Majesty's Government to associate non-official opinion as fully as possible with the prosecution of the war, it had been decided to establish a National Defence Council, the strength of which would be about 30 members and would include representatives of Indian States and other elements in the national life of British India. The idea was that the National Defence Council would serve as a safety valve and as a method of improving liaison between the central Government on the one hand and the provinces and States on the other, but that it would have no executive authority.

In announcing these changes in the House of Commons, the Secretary of State claimed that the new members of the Executive Council were as representative of public opinion, and as responsible to it as was possible in face of the refusal of the Congress and the Muslim League to co-operate. The aim, he said, was to make full use of the vast and hitherto insufficiently tapped reservoir of Indian ability and patriotism; measures making a change in the spirit, if not the letter, of India's constitution were an earnest of the desire of His Majesty's

Government to transfer to Indian hands a steadily increasing share in India's destiny.

Gandhiji made a statement to the effect that the announcement did not affect the stand taken by the Congress, nor did it meet the Congress demands.

Jinnah squarely condemned the Viceroy's action, to which, he declared, Muslim India would not extend whole-hearted, willing, or genuine support.

The Hindu Mahasabha declared that the announcement was a step in the right direction, and suggested that a representative of the Sikhs should be included in the Executive Council.

On 24 August, a meeting of the Muslim League Working Committee was convened in Bombay to consider the conduct of those of its members who had accepted appointments to the Viceroy's Executive Council and the National Defence Council. Jinnah contended that the selection of such persons over the head of their leader was designed to divide the Muslim ranks and destroy the solidarity of the League. In accordance with the Working Committee's resolution, the three premiers who belonged to the League resigned from the National Defence Council. The Bengal premier, however, made it clear that he was taking this step against his better judgment and in order to preserve Muslim solidarity; at the same time, he resigned his membership of the Working Committee and Council of the League in protest against the President's 'arrogant and dictatorial conduct'. Sir Sultan Ahmed, the new Law Member of the Viceroy's Executive Council, and Begum Shah Nawaz, the only woman member appointed to the National Defence Council, refused to obey the command and held on to their respective appointments; they were, in consequence, expelled from the League.

Hitler's advance in Russia went on almost unchecked. In August 1941, Franklin D. Roosevelt, President of the United States of America, and Winston Churchill, the British Premier, had a meeting off the coast of Newfoundland on board the cruiser *Augusta*. The meeting gave birth to what came to be known as the 'Atlantic Charter', under which the two countries jointly subscribed to a common peace aim, affirming *inter alia* that 'they respect the right of all peoples to choose the form of government under which they will live and they wish to see sovereign rights and self-government restored to those who have been forcibly deprived of them.'

The Charter was greeted with great enthusiasm by the subject countries of the world, including India. But in the course of a speech in the House of Commons on 9 September, Churchill said:

The joint declaration does not qualify in any way the various statements of policy which have been made from time to time about the development of constitutional government in India, Burma and other parts of the British Empire. We are pledged by the Declaration of August 1940 to help India to obtain free and equal partnership in the British Commonwealth of races, subject, of course, to the fulfilment of the obligations arising from our long connection with India and our responsibilities to its many creeds, races and interests.

This caused considerable resentment in India, and in the Legislative Assembly a resolution recommending that the Atlantic Charter should be applied to India was discussed and passed without division. Ultimately, in the House of Commons, Amery said, in answer to a question, that the Government's previous declarations with regard to the goal of India's attainment to free and equal partnership in the British Commonwealth still held good, and that it continued to be His Majesty's Government's desire to see that goal attained with the least possible delay after the war under a constitution framed by agreement among Indians themselves.

By the middle of October the expansion of the Viceroy's Executive Council was completed. By then, many Congressmen who had participated in the individual civil disobedience campaign had been released on completing their sentences. An influential section was known to favour a change from Gandhiji's satyagraha programme. They suggested that the Congress should take back power in the provinces; that if the British Government refused to permit it to do so, it would provide a common platform for all believers in democracy both inside and outside the Congress; that the communal situation would not have become so bad if the Congress had not resigned office; and that, if the Congress took back power, less and less would be heard of Pakistan.

Gandhiji, however, refused to yield. In a long statement, issued at the end of October, he answered his Congress critics. It did not matter to him how few the satyagrahis might be; if they were only ten or two, they would represent the whole of the Congress. 'Does not one ambassador represent his people? To give up civil disobedience would be folly.'

The Council of the Muslim League met on 26 October and endorsed the decisions made by the Working Committee in August.

The expansion of the Executive Council and the establishment of the National Defence Council were condemned as 'designed to create a rift in the Muslim ranks.' Jinnah, after making a statement in the Indian Legislative Assembly, announced that his party would boycott the proceedings and led his followers out.

Meanwhile, there were important ministerial changes in Orissa and Bengal. Throughout October and November, efforts had been made to form a non-Congress ministry in Orissa. A few Congress members of the Assembly, headed by Godavaris Misra, declared their readiness to form a coalition with non-Congress groups. The Maharajah of Parlakimedi, one of the biggest zamindars of the province, took up the idea. Ultimately on 23 November, the proclamation under Section 93 was revoked in Orissa and a ministry was sworn in, with the Maharajah as premier and Misra and Moulvi Abdus Sobhan Khan as ministers.

In Bengal, ever since his resignation from the Working Committee of the Muslim League, Fazlul Huq's relations with his Muslim colleagues in the cabinet, particularly with Sir Nazimuddin and H. S. Suhrawardy, had been extremely strained. The premier's non-League supporters, the Forward Bloc and others, had formed a coalition. Opposed to them were the League members of the legislature, who had formed a purely Muslim League Party with Nazimuddin as its leader. In December 1941, Fazlul Huq's ministry was obliged to resign; but after some days of political manoeuvring, he returned as the head of a cabinet of nine members—five Muslims and four Hindus.

On 3 December, as a concession to public opinion, the Government of India announced that all civil disobedience prisoners whose offences had been formal or symbolic in character would be set free, including Nehru and Azad. In a press interview Gandhiji said that the releases 'cannot evoke a single responsive or appreciative chord in me.' He felt that the civil disobedience campaign should continue. In a later statement he said: 'The jail delivery that is going on apace of satyagrahis must be taken as a challenge to convene a meeting of the All-India Congress Committee which, the Government of India have been evidently induced to expect, will reverse the Bombay decision whose working is reflected in my conduct of the satyagraha campaign.' Gandhiji accordingly advised Azad to convene meetings of the Working Committee and of the All-India Congress Committee at an early date.

On 7 December, Japan struck at Pearl Harbour and the war in the Pacific began. The next day the Japanese forces occupied Shanghai and Siam and made a landing in British Malaya. Twenty-four hours later the Japanese Navy sank the two British battleships, *H.M.S. Repulse* and *H.M.S. The Prince of Wales,* thus crippling the naval strength in the Pacific. This was followed by a spectacular advance against what the Japanese propagandists called the A.B.C.D. Powers —America, Britain, China and the Dutch.

It was against this background that the Working Committee of the Congress met in Bardoli on 23 December. For a week the members discussed the new situation and ultimately passed the following resolution:

While there has been no change in the British policy towards India, the Working Committee must nevertheless take into full consideration the new world situation that has arisen by the development of the war into a world conflict and its approach to India. The sympathies of the Congress must inevitably lie with the peoples who are the subject of aggression and who are fighting for their freedom, but only a free and independent India can be in a position to undertake the defence of the country on a national basis and be of help in the furtherance of the larger causes that are emerging from the storm of war.

The whole background in India is one of hostility and of distrust of the British Government and not even the most far-reaching promises can alter this background, nor can a subject India offer voluntary or willing help to an arrogant imperialism which is indistinguishable from Fascist authoritarianism. The Committee is, therefore, of opinion that the resolution of the A.I.C.C. passed in Bombay on September 16, 1940 holds today and defines the Congress policy still.

Gandhiji did not fail to notice that while the Bombay resolution postulated that in no circumstances was violence to be met by violence, the Bardoli resolution envisaged situations which, if brought about, would find the Congress taking up the armed defence of the country by the side of the British. In a letter to Azad, he said that he had interpreted the Bombay resolution as meaning that the Congress was to refuse participation in the present or all future wars, on the ground, principally, of non-violence; he, however, discovered that most of the members differed from his interpretation and held that opposition need not be on the ground of non-violence. The resolution contemplated association with Britain in the war effort as a price for the guaranteed independence of India. 'If such was my view,' he said, 'and I believed in the use of violence for gaining independence, and yet refused participation in the war effort as the price of that independence, I would consider myself guilty of unpatriotic conduct. It is my certain belief that only non-violence can save India and the world from self-extinction. Such being the case, I must continue my mission, whether I am alone or am assisted by an organization of individuals. You will, therefore, please relieve me of the responsibility laid upon me by the Bombay resolution.'

Gandhiji's letter was considered by the Congress Working Committee. By a supplementary resolution he was once again relieved of the responsibility of leading the Congress. He was free to carry on his ideals; the Committee hoped that Congressmen would tender him full assistance in the prosecution of his mission.

The Muslim League Working Committee met at about the same time and declared that it was as ready and willing as before to shoulder the defence of the country, singly or in co-operation with other parties, on the basis that a real share and responsibility was given in the government at the Centre and the provinces.

The year 1942 opened with an appeal to the British Government by a group of prominent Indians for a bold stroke of far-sighted statesmanship, so as to transform the entire spirit and outlook of the administration in India. The signatories, headed by Sir Tej Bahadur Sapru and including M. R. Jayakar, V. S. Srinivasa Sastri, Sir S. Radhakrishnan, Muhammad Yunus, Sir Jagdish Prasad, Sir P. S. Sivaswami Iyer and others, appealed to the British Prime Minister 'in all sincerity but with the greatest emphasis to act, while there is still time for such action, so that India may line up with the other anti-Axis powers on a footing of absolute equality with them in the common struggle for the freedom of humanity.'

Meanwhile, the war was approaching the very threshold of India.

# V

# THE CRIPPS MISSION

WITH the westward advance of Japan into Asia, the atmosphere in India deteriorated in a disturbing manner. Exaggerated fears had driven thousands of people from Calcutta and other cities and fantastic rumours were in the air. The weakness of the Far Eastern defences, especially in Malaya, had shaken public confidence and the arrival of refugees from Burma and other places, with their tales of woe and suffering, had shocked the complacence built by generations of security.

Singapore fell on 15 February 1942; Rangoon was taken on 8 March, and in the words of Churchill, 'the shadow of a heavy and far-reaching military defeat' lay over India.

The seriousness of the war situation was brought closer home by the visit of Marshal Chiang Kai-shek and his wife, to India in February 1942. The Marshal had come to confer with the Government of India and in particular the Commander-in-Chief, on matters of common concern to China and India. He was able to meet several prominent leaders, including Gandhiji and Jinnah, and to renew his acquaintance with Nehru, who had visited China in the autumn of 1939. At the end of his visit, Marshal Chiang Kai-shek made an appeal to the people of India for help in the war, adding the hope that Britain would as speedily as possible give 'real political power' to the Indian people.

The exigencies of the war created a demand in Britain and the United States of America for a new declaration of policy towards India. Churchill himself formulated a scheme, which it was his intention to broadcast in the form of an appeal to the Indian people. The broad outlines of his draft appeal were as follows:

In India's grave danger all must unite to save her and must lay aside controversies.

No far-reaching changes in the executive government can be contemplated at this time.

India's best and most representative men from every community, party and province, as well as the Princes, should come forward to serve India and to lay the foundations for a new future based on India's complete freedom to control her own destiny within, it is hoped and believed, the fellowship of the British Commonwealth.

To this end, the Government would set up an Indian Council of Defence, to be elected by some form of proportional representation by existing members of provincial lower houses. Representatives of the Indian States in due proportion would be added to these British-Indian representatives. This Council would during the war be charged with helping the war effort in regard to munitions production, recruitment, organising A.R.P. and steadying public morale.

It would nominate for inclusion in the Viceroy's Executive Council a representative of the people of India who would attend meetings of the British War Cabinet and the Pacific War Council. Similarly, it would nominate a representative, or representatives, to the Peace Conference.

After the war, it would work out a new constitution for India. Its main conclusions on the constitution would be (in their nature and procedure for reaching them) an expression of the desire of the people of India as a whole. His Majesty's Government would accept a constitution so arrived at and would negotiate with the Council in regard to the fulfilment of British obligations.

In commending the scheme to the Viceroy, the Secretary of State pointed out how it left the executive and legislative position untouched. It proposed a popularly-elected Defence Council with representation on the War Cabinet in London, the Pacific Council and the Peace Conference, while it purported to fulfil His Majesty's Government's pledge of bringing Indian parties together on the constitutional issue by offering to accept this Council as the future constituent body. Such a plan provided an instrument for the eventual solution of the constitutional problem on lines which the Congress could not denounce as undemocratic and which His Majesty's Government could put before the Muslims and the Princes as being in keeping with its Declaration of August 1940. The Secretary of State hoped that the scheme would be generally acceptable at a time when danger to India herself was so obvious. The Viceroy would be able to go on with his Executive Council, possibly expanded, and with a larger and perhaps better consultative body which, while perhaps more openly critical than the existing National Defence Council, might also be more effective in promoting the war effort throughout the provinces. Even if the scheme were condemned by the main political parties, its rejection could throw no discredit on His Majesty's Government; it was more likely to show its goodwill and expose the unreasonableness of the Indian parties.

But the Viceroy felt that it was not possible for him to agree to the scheme. His chief objection to it was that his Executive Council would either be subservient to, or in dangerous conflict with, the new body it proposed to set up; also that it would precipitate the whole constitutional and communal controversy into the conduct of the war and the day-to-day government. The proposed plan would, he was convinced, infect the army with communal fever of the most catastrophic kind.

The Viceroy put forward a rough sketch of an alternative form of declaration on the following lines:

(a) That His Majesty's Government make no insistence on provisions in the post-war constitution of India for safeguarding British interests as such. These would be the subject of negotiation after the war.

(b) That His Majesty's Government regard their obligations as separate from British interests, and construe those obligations as requiring them to see that full power is transferred to a government under which different races, communities and interests in India have the prospect of living without fear.

(c) The Viceroy will renew his attempts to bring together the leaders of parties in order that both his Executive Council and the governments in the provinces might, within the framework of the existing constitution, enjoy the overwhelming support of the people of India. The position of official members would be one of those questions which the Viceroy would be prepared to discuss round the table as a practical problem of administration with his potential colleagues in a national government. The position of the Commander-in-Chief must remain unimpaired but a non-official member might be associated much more closely with the problems of co-ordination of Defence.

(d) The control of the India Office will be exercised with a progressively lighter hand.

(e) India's representatives in the War Cabinet and the Pacific War Council shall be instructed from India; British-Indian representatives at the Peace Conference shall be nominated and be directly responsible to a government in India.

(f) That His Majesty's Government stand by their pledges to afford to a body representative of the interests and communities of India the fullest opportunity to devise the framework of a constitution after the war.

That His Majesty's Government undertake to accept in advance any constitution so framed representing the will and desire of India as a whole.

Lord Linlithgow's personal view was that the practical help in winning the war likely to be gained by a successful declaration was limited. He was not sanguine that his sketch declaration would either win over or split the Congress, while it would run the risk of upsetting the Muslims, the Europeans and the Services. He would have preferred to postpone a declaration until the military situation had become clearer. He had considered the possibility of making a firm declaration about post-war constitutional progress without, for the moment, going beyond that expansion of his Executive Council which had already been under discussion with the Secretary of State. But if the new offer proved acceptable and leading politicians were prepared to co-operate, they would have to be taken in. Lord Linlithgow felt that any transfer of power would have to be effective and that the risks would have to be taken with open eyes; that such transfer should be based on the existing organs and machinery of government, Parliament retaining eventual control to ensure that His Majesty's Government would be in a position after the war to discharge its obligations as defined, and that during the interim period the Viceroy should be supported in resisting any developments that might impede the war effort. Co-operation between British India and the States was essential and it was equally essential to ensure that His Majesty's Government did not break its pledges to the Princes, Muslims and other minorities.

With regard to the problem of reconstructing his Executive Council, Lord Linlithgow was emphatic in his view that the discontinuance of official membership should not be promised as part of any declaration, having regard to the enormous burden which would be thrown upon any one man who held the office of Governor-General and Crown Representative, with the addition of an active cabinet of politicians with no practical conception of the difference between policy and administration.

Due weight was given to Lord Linlithgow's views and the proposed broadcast was deferred. Subsequently, Churchill set up a special India Committee of the Cabinet under the chairmanship of Attlee, with the Secretary of State, Viscount Simon, Sir John Anderson, Sir Stafford Cripps and Sir James Grigg as members. This Committee decided to abandon the original scheme and proposed a new form of declaration, the principal features of which were:

(a) Explicit acknowledgment that the future Indian Dominion can secede if it so wishes; (b) setting up of the most suitable future constitution-making body immediately after the war if Indians had not previously come to an agreement on the subject themselves; (c) option to any province not wishing to accede to the new constitution to stand out;[1] (d) the whole field of British obligations, as well as such continued military assistance as India might need, to be dealt with by a separate treaty to be concluded with the constitution-making body and to come into force simultaneously with the new constitution; (e) the negotiation of revised treaty arrangements with Indian States.

Lord Linlithgow's preliminary reaction was that the revised draft scheme had certain commendable features. It had the advantage of leaving intact the pledges in the Declaration of August 1940 without the necessity of repeating them in the same or different terms; it contained clear promises without any specific commitments, such as the replacement during the war of an Executive Council of selected and representative individuals by one of a purely political complexion. But he had himself fought shy of advertising local option. This was almost certain to produce protests from the Bengal and Punjab Hindus, from the Sikhs, and probably also from the Bengal Muslims. He was nevertheless prepared to take the risk for the sake of a precise and brief declaration which did not tie his hands in advance regarding the immediate future of the Executive Council. Lord Linlithgow thought that the Indian States should also have a free choice to adhere or not to adhere to the Union.

Following an exchange of telegrams on certain controversial details, the Viceroy received from the Secretary of State the text of a draft declaration 'as finally revised' by the India Committee of the Cabinet. The Viceroy had in the meantime taken the opportunity of consulting the Commander-in-Chief and of obtaining the views of provincial Governors. In the light of their reactions, he felt bound to re-define his position. It had been stressed that the 'local option' proposal, while it adequately met the case of Muslims in the provinces in which they were in the majority, was no substitute for existing pledges in the eyes of Muslims elsewhere (e.g. in the United Provinces, where communal feeling was bitter), or of the other minorities, such as the Sikhs, Scheduled Castes and backward communities, who also regarded the undertakings given in August 1940 as a

---

[1] This was intended to placate the Muslim League. It was based on the provision in the Government of India Act, 1935, governing the accession of Indian States.

charter of their rights. Local option would be interpreted as the acceptance of Pakistan and the effect would be particularly bad on the Punjab. The prospect of a predominantly Muslim and independent Punjab would seriously upset the Sikhs. In fine, local option would threaten the internal security of the Punjab, would affect the Services and would grievously damage the capacity to wage war. Lord Linlithgow therefore felt it necessary to warn His Majesty's Government against the consequences of a precise declaration of local option in the terms proposed. He suggested an alternative draft declaration which followed generally the lines of the India Committee's draft but which omitted 'local option' and instead placed the responsibility on the constitution-making body to produce a constitution acceptable to the various parties and interests. While leaving to Indians the prime responsibility for setting up a constitution-framing body, it provided that if Indian leaders themselves invited His Majesty's Government, either to frame a new constitutional structure, or to refer this task to some other appropriate authority, His Majesty's Government would be prepared to do so.

Meanwhile, the Viceroy proposed to try and bring about a political truce so as to enable him to reconstruct his Executive Council and give India a strong government for the prosecution of the war. The draft contained a reference to the possible return of parliamentary government in the Section 93 provinces. It also dealt with the *de facto* international status of India during the war and at the Peace Conference.

The Viceroy was informed that the India Committee had given very careful consideration to his views and had amended its draft declaration in certain important respects. But those amendments only gave rise to further controversy. The discussions were in fact abruptly concluded by the communication, on 10 March, of the War Cabinet's decision that in view of the difficulties and objections raised, it was not proposed to proceed with any public declaration. Instead, the Prime Minister would make an announcement to the effect that the War Cabinet had its plan for solving the deadlock; that it was not, for the time being at any rate, publishing anything, but that it was sending Sir Stafford Cripps out to India to endeavour to secure, by negotiations with the Indian political leaders, a sufficient body of agreement upon its policy.

The decision of the War Cabinet, taken in the stress of the war situation, carried certain initial handicaps which were bound to affect the progress of the forthcoming negotiations. In the first place, no definite agreement had been reached between the Viceroy and the War Cabinet on the details of the policy to be pursued. Nor was there, apparently, any understanding between the War Cabinet and Sir Stafford Cripps as to the extent to which he might go in the way of concession to possible demands. Furthermore, though it was Sir Stafford Cripps who was to negotiate a settlement, it would surely be the Viceroy who would have to implement the terms of such a settlement and there was no understanding or agreement on important details of policy between these two authorities. An atmosphere charged with so much uncertainty held but scant prospect of success for the Cripps venture.

On the other hand, the choice of Sir Stafford Cripps was a very special one. He had recently been appointed Lord Privy Seal; he was a member of the War Cabinet and leader of the House of Commons and he was reported to be a personal friend of Nehru. Because of the particularly high esteem in which he was held both in Britain and in India, his arrival was looked forward to with a certain amount of hope and expectation, at least in Congress circles, which included a section which was prepared to welcome a new declaration of policy.

The Muslim League was definitely not pressing for a new policy; its line was to support the August 1940 offer, provided Muslims were given the share they claimed in the central Government. Jinnah doubtless believed that the chance of securing a promise of Pakistan was remote. The rival demand for the independence of India as a unit held more appeal for world opinion and had two generations of popular agitation behind it, whereas the League's demand for Pakistan had been before the public for no more than a couple of years. The League, on the other hand, feared that sharing power with the Congress would reinforce those centralizing and unifying tendencies, inevitable in war, which would stifle in advance its ambition for a separate Muslim State.

By contrast, the Muslim premiers of Bengal and Sind (who relied upon Congress and Hindu support) feared that the play of long-term forces might squeeze them between the upper and nether millstones of the Congress and the Hindu Mahasabha on the one hand, and the Muslim League on the other.

Other minorities were on the look-out for a declaration of policy which would suit them, and threatened a hostile stand against one

that did not. The Sikhs denounced in advance a policy that left them
out of the central Government or accepted Pakistan, while the Depressed Classes were against a policy which, by exaggerating Muslim
representation or otherwise, deprived them of a share in power or
failed to safeguard their long-term future.

It was the Moderate party, comprising members of the Sapru
group, the non-Brahmins of Madras and others, who demanded the
least terms for the long-term future and made the clearest offer of co-
operation. They knew that in the long run they must go to the wall,
but their hope lay in seizing the opportunities of present power. Assuming the unwillingness of the Congress majority to form part of a
war government save on terms which His Majesty's Government
would not be prepared to grant, a division of power between Muslims
and the Moderate Hindu group seemed an obvious solution. But
Jinnah had already insisted that if the Congress did not come in, he
would share power only with those who stood for something in the
country, such as Sikh and Scheduled Caste leaders, not with individuals like the members of the Sapru group.

Churchill's announcement of the decision to send Sir Stafford
Cripps out to India was made in the House of Commons on 11
March. 'The crisis in the affairs of India arising out of the Japanese
advance,' he said, 'has made us wish to rally all the forces of Indian
life to guard their land from the menace of the invader.' In order to
clothe with precision the policy announced in August 1940 and to
convince all classes, races and creeds of Britain's sincere resolve, the
War Cabinet, he said, had agreed unitedly upon conclusions for
present and future action which, if accepted by India as a whole,
would avoid the alternative dangers, either that the resistance of a
powerful minority might impose an indefinite veto upon the wishes
of the majority, or that a majority decision might be taken which
would be resisted to a point destructive of internal harmony and
fatal to the setting up of a new constitution. In order to ensure that
the scheme would win a reasonable and practical measure of acceptance and thus promote concentration of all thoughts and energies
upon the defence of the country, Sir Stafford Cripps was being sent
to India to satisfy himself by personal consultation that the conclusions would achieve their purpose.

Sir Stafford Cripps arrived in Delhi on 22 March, armed with the
British Government's draft declaration, on the basis of which he was
to conduct negotiations with the leaders of Indian political parties

and communities. The first two or three days were spent in preliminary talks with the Viceroy, members of his Executive Council and other official advisers. Thereafter, Sir Stafford Cripps proceeded to interview the leaders of the various political groups and communities. Apart from Gandhiji, who attended in his personal capacity, the political leaders included Azad and Nehru, together with other members of the Congress Working Committee; Jinnah as representative of the Muslim League; Sir Sikander Hyat Khan, Fazlul Huq and other Muslims; Savarkar and other members of the Hindu Mahasabha; Ambedkar and M. C. Rajah (Depressed Classes); Sapru and Jayakar (Liberals); representatives of the Sikhs, Indian Christians, Anglo-Indians and Europeans; and representatives also of the Indian States, notably the Jam Saheb of Nawanagar (Chancellor of the Chamber of Princes), the Maharajahs of Bikaner and Patiala and the Chief Minister of Hyderabad.

On 29 March Sir Stafford Cripps addressed a large gathering of press representatives, with whom he held a series of frank discussions. 'The Constituent Assembly,' he said, explaining the implications of the Cabinet's draft, 'can start with a declaration of Independence.' It was completely free to decide whether the new Union of India should remain within the Empire or not. It was free to do anything —even to declaring that it did not want a Governor-General.

With reference to the position of the Indian States, he explained that they could not be forced to participate in the Constituent Assembly, or be compelled to choose their representatives in any particular manner. 'We have not the same control over the Indian States as we have over British India.'

The British Government, he said, could not transfer to the Government of India during the interim war period the responsibility for, and the control and direction of, the defence of India. 'The defence of India will not be in Indian hands, even if all the parties want it.... It would be dishonest to say that an Indian Defence Member would be responsible for the defence of India.'

Regarding the working of the new Executive Council under the proposed interim scheme, Sir Stafford Cripps said that it would have to be within the present constitution, but that a good deal could be done by changing the conventions or adopting new ones. One of the things he is reported to have said was that the Council could function as a Cabinet—a point which later became the subject of particular controversy.

Finally, Sir Stafford made it clear that 'the scheme goes through as a whole or is rejected as a whole.'

It was at this Conference that the draft declaration was released to the press. The object of His Majesty's Government was stated to be 'the creation of a new Indian Union which shall constitute a Dominion associated with the United Kingdom and other Dominions by a common allegiance to the Crown but equal to them in every respect and in no way subordinate in any aspect of its domestic or external affairs.' The terms of the declaration were as follows :

(a) Immediately upon cessation of hostilities steps shall be taken to set up in India, in the manner described hereafter, an elected body charged with the task of framing a new constitution for India.

(b) Provision shall be made, as set out below, for the participation of Indian States in the constitution-making body.

(c) His Majesty's Government undertake to accept and implement forthwith the constitution so framed subject only to :

(*i*) The right of any province of British India that is not prepared to accept the new constitution to retain its present constitutional position, provision being made for its subsequent accession, if it so decides. With such non-acceding provinces, should they so desire, His Majesty's Government will be prepared to agree upon a new constitution giving them the same full status as the Indian Union and arrived at by a procedure analogous to that here laid down.

(*ii*) The signing of a treaty which shall be negotiated between His Majesty's Government and the constitution-making body. This treaty will cover all necessary matters arising out of the complete transfer of responsibility from British to Indian hands ; it will make provision, in accordance with the undertakings given by His Majesty's Government, for the protection of racial and religious minorities, but will not impose any restriction on the power of the Indian Union to decide in future its relationship to other member States of the British Commonwealth. Whether or not an Indian State elects to adhere to the constitution, it will be necessary to negotiate a revision of its treaty arrangements so far as this may be required in the new situation.

(d) The constitution-making body shall be composed as follows, unless the leaders of Indian opinion in the principal communities agree upon some other form before the end of hostilities:

Immediately upon the result being known of the provincial elections which will be necessary at the end of hostilities, the entire membership of the Lower Houses of provincial legislatures shall, as a single electoral college, proceed to the election of the constitution-making body by the system of proportional representation. This new body shall be in number about one-tenth of the number of the electoral college. Indian States shall be invited to appoint representatives in the same proportion to their total population as in the case of representatives of British India as a whole and with the same powers as British-Indian members.

(e) During the critical period which now faces India and until the new constitution can be framed His Majesty's Government must inevitably bear the responsibility for, and retain the control and direction of, the defence of India as part of their world war effort; but the task of organising to the full the military, moral and material resources of India must be the responsibility of the Government of India with the co-operation of the peoples of India. His Majesty's Government desire, and invite, the immediate and effective participation of the leaders of the principal sections of the Indian people in the counsels of their country, of the Commonwealth and of the United Nations. Thus they will be enabled to give their active and constructive help to the discharge of a task which is vital and essential for the future freedom of India.

Sir Stafford Cripps, in a broadcast on 30 March, made an appeal to the Indian people to accept these proposals. 'It is with the greatest hope,' he said, 'that I look to the events of the next few days which may, if wisely handled, seal for ever your freedom and our friendship.' He concluded with the exhortation:

Let us enter upon this primary task of the defence of India in the now sure knowledge that when we emerge from the fire and the travail of war it will be to build a free India upon foundations wrought by the Indian peoples themselves, and to forge a long, lasting and free friendship between our two peoples. Regrets and recriminations as to the past can have no place beside the confident and sure hopes of the future, when a Free India will take her rightful place as a co-worker with the other free nations in that world reconstruction which alone can make the toil and the suffering of the war worth while. Let the dead past bury its dead, and let us march together side by side through the night of high endeavour and courage to the already waking dawn of a new world of liberty for all the peoples.

The interim proposals contained in part (e) of the declaration were, except in regard to defence, vague and nebulous. The long-term proposals contained certain features which were unpalatable to the Congress, such as 'provincial option' and the inclusion in the constitution-making body of States' representatives who would not be the choice of the States' people; but it was contended that such provisions were essential in order to make the scheme as a whole tolerable to other parties and interests in India, and to fulfil certain solemn pledges of His Majesty's Government. In any case, the immediate object of the Cripps mission was to secure full Indian

co-operation in the war effort and Sir Stafford Cripps was hopeful
that this co-operation would be forthcoming, even if the main political
parties rejected the constitutional part of the proposals.

Gandhiji, whose policy was one of 'total pacifism', described the
declaration as a 'post-dated cheque' and decided to take no part in
the discussions.

The Hindu Mahasabha rejected the long-term plan on the ground
that the option given to provinces to stay out of the Union would
destroy the unity of the country.

The Sikhs also protested. 'We shall,' they said, 'resist by all possible
means separation of the Punjab from the All-India Union.'

The Depressed Classes denounced the scheme for its failure to
provide the necessary safeguards for them. 'We are all of us absolutely convinced that the proposals are calculated to do the greatest harm
to the Depressed Classes and are sure to place them under an un-
mitigated system of Hindu rule.'

Other political parties also set forth their views. None of them,
including the Muslim League, was prepared to accept the proposals
as they stood.

It was clear from the start that the Mission would have to rec-
kon mainly with the Congress and the Muslim League. As actually
happened, the negotiations were held almost exclusively with the
Congress, represented by Azad and Nehru, while the Muslim League
stood by and awaited developments.

It was a foregone conclusion that the Congress would not accept
the long-term proposals, involving as they did the virtual partition
of the country. In fact, the Congress Working Committee had, on
2 April, adopted a resolution rejecting the Cripps offer. Azad
brought a copy of the resolution to Sir Stafford Cripps, but they
agreed not to publish it and to proceed instead with their negotiations
on the interim proposals. Despite, therefore, its opposition to the
main scheme, the Congress had apparently made up its mind to put
aside questions relating to the future in order to concentrate on the
immediate issues. Thus, the discussions centred round the interim
proposals in clause (e) of the declaration, with special emphasis on
the position of defence.

Sir Stafford Cripps had written to Azad on 1 April suggesting that
he would ask the Commander-in-Chief to meet him and Nehru in
order to explain to them the technical difficulties of the situation
connected with the defence proposals and so that they, too, might

make any suggestions as to the division of responsibilities in this sphere of government. The Indian leaders saw the Commander-in-Chief on 4 April. It was clear enough that there was to be an Indian Defence member, in addition to the Commander-in-Chief who would continue to be the Supreme Commander of the Armed Forces in India; but the point on which the leaders were anxious to secure an assurance was that an Indian Defence member would have reasonable status and be able to function effectively. On this point, Sir Stafford Cripps, after consulting His Majesty's Government, wrote on 7 April to both Azad and Jinnah as follows:

I am therefore authorised to propose to you as a way out of the present difficulties that (a) the Commander-in-Chief should retain a seat on the Viceroy's Executive Council as War Member and should retain his full control over all the war activities of the armed forces in India subject to the control of His Majesty's Government and the War Cabinet, upon which body a representative Indian should sit with equal powers in all matters relating to the defence of India. Membership of the Pacific Council would likewise be offered to a representative Indian. (b) An Indian representative member would be added to the Viceroy's Executive who would take over those sections of the Department of Defence which can organisationally be separated immediately from the Commander-in-Chief's War Department and which are specified under head (I) of the annexure. In addition, this member would take over the Defence Co-ordination Department which is at present directly under the Viceroy and certain other important functions of the Government of India which are directly related to defence and which do not fall under any of the other existing departments, and which are specified under head (II) of the annexure.

### ANNEXURE

(I) Matters now dealt with in the Defence Department which would be transferred to a Defence Co-ordination Department: (a) Public relations; (b) Demobilisation and post-war reconstruction; (c) Petroleum officer, whose functions are to calculate the requirements of, and make provision for, all petroleum products required for the Army, Navy, and Air Force, and for the civil departments, including storage and distribution; (d) Indian representation on the Eastern Group Supply Council; (e) Amenities for, and welfare of, troops and their dependants including Indian soldiers' boards; (f) All canteen organisations; (g) Certain non-technical educational institutions, e.g. Lawrence schools, K.G.R.I.M. schools, and the Prince of Wales' Royal Indian Military College; (h) Stationery, printing and forms for the Army; (i) Reception, accommodation, and social arrangements for all foreign missions, representatives and offices.

(II) In addition the Defence Co-ordination Department would take over many major questions bearing directly on defence but difficult to locate in any particular existing departments; examples are denial policy, evacuation from threatened areas, signals co-ordination, economic warfare.

The proposal was rejected by the Congress, which regarded the subjects listed for transfer as being of such ephemeral importance as to make the position of the Indian Defence member almost ludicrous.

At about this time, Colonel Louis Johnson, President Roosevelt's personal envoy, arrived in Delhi as head of the American Technical Mission. With Sir Stafford Cripps' permission he took an active part in the negotiations on the defence formula. A new formula, sometimes referred to as the 'Johnson formula', was presented to the Congress. It read as follows:

In amplification of clause (e) of the draft Declaration His Majesty's Government make the following proposition upon the subject-matter of the Defence of India:

(a) The Defence Department shall be placed in the charge of a representative Indian member with the exception of functions to be exercised by the Commander-in-Chief as War Member of the Executive Council.

(b) A War Department will be constituted which will take over such functions of the Defence Department as are not retained by the Defence Member. A list of all the retained functions has been agreed, to which will be added further important responsibilities including matters now dealt with by the Defence Co-ordination Department and other vital matters related to the defence of India.

This formula was considered by the Congress Working Committee, which amended it to read:

(a) The Defence Department shall be placed in the charge of a representative Indian member, but certain functions relating to the conduct of the war will be exercised, for the duration of war, by the Commander-in-Chief, who will be in control of the war activities of the armed forces in India, and who will be an extraordinary member of the national Cabinet for that purpose.

(b) A War Department will be constituted under the Commander-in-Chief. This Department will take over such functions as are to be exercised by the Commander-in-Chief. A list of such functions has been prepared and is attached.

(c) The Defence Member shall be in charge of all other matters relating to Defence including those now dealt with by the Defence Co-ordination Department.

The Working Committee's revised formula was very much on the lines of the 'Johnson formula', but it differed materially from the earlier approach to the problem by His Majesty's Government. Instead of reserving defence as the responsibility of His Majesty's Government and asking the Indian Defence Member to accept certain relatively unimportant subjects, the Working Committee's proposal was to consider the national Government responsible for the whole field of administration, including defence, but to reserve to the Commander-in-Chief, for the duration of the war, certain functions essential for the discharge of his responsibilities and the carrying out of military operations.

In forwarding the revised draft to Sir Stafford Cripps, Azad remarked:

The approach made in the draft you gave me this morning seems to us a more healthy one. With some alterations that we suggest, it might be the basis of further discussions. But it must be remembered that a very great deal depends on the allocation of subjects between the Defence Department and the War Department, and until this is done, it is not possible to give a final opinion.

There were further *pourparlers* between Johnson and the Congress on the one hand, and Sir Stafford Cripps, the Viceroy and the Commander-in-Chief on the other. Suffice it to say that on the afternoon of 8 April Sir Stafford Cripps finalized his formula as follows:

(a) The Defence Department shall be placed in the charge of a representative Indian member, but certain functions relating to the conduct of the war will be exercised by the Commander-in-Chief, who will be in control of the armed forces in India, and who will be the member of the Executive Council in charge of the War Department.

(b) This Department will take over such governmental functions as are to be exercised by the Commander-in-Chief as War Member. A list of such functions has been prepared and is attached.

(c) The Defence Member shall be in charge of all other matters relating to defence in the Defence Department and those now dealt with by the Defence Co-ordination Department in addition to other important matters closely related to defence.

(d) In the event of any new functions failing to be discharged in relation to defence or any dispute arising as to the allocation of any old functions it shall be decided by His Majesty's Government.

The War Department, for which the Commander-in-Chief will be Member, will be responsible for the governmental relations of General Headquarters, Naval Headquarters and Air Headquarters which include:

(*i*) Examining and sanctioning all proposals emanating from G.H.Q., N.H.Q. and A.H.Q.

(*ii*) Representing the policy of Government on all questions connected with the war which originate in or concern G.H.Q., N.H.Q. or A.H.Q.

(*iii*) Acting as the channel of communication between the Government of India and His Majesty's Government on all such questions.

(*iv*) Acting as liaison between these headquarters and the other departments of Government, and provincial governments.

Sir Stafford Cripps discussed the revised formula with the Viceroy. The latter did not agree generally with Sir Stafford Cripps' approach to the problem, nor was he in favour of the proposed allocation of subjects between the Commander-in-Chief and the Indian Defence Member. Nevertheless, Sir Stafford Cripps telegraphed the revised formula to His Majesty's Government as the basis on which negotiations were proceeding and with a strong recommendation for its acceptance. He urged that without it there was no prospect of success, but on this basis there was considerable chance of securing the agreement of the Congress. Simultaneously, the Viceroy communicated his own views to His Majesty's Government, who decided that it could not agree, especially during the period of war, to lessening in any material respect the powers of the Commander-in-Chief. Sir Stafford Cripps felt that he was unable to proceed further, and the negotiations came to an abrupt end.

Referring to the previous day's interview which he and Nehru had had with Sir Stafford Cripps, Azad wrote in his letter of 10 April as follows:

When we asked you for illustrative lists of subjects for the two departments you referred us to the old list for the Defence Department which you had previously sent us and which we had been unable to accept. You added that certain residuary subjects might be added to this but, in effect, there was not likely to be any such subject as the allocation was complete. Thus, you said that substantially there was no change between the old list and any new one that might be prepared. If this were so, and we were to go back ultimately to the place we started from, then what was the purpose of our searching for a new formula? A new set of words meaning the same thing made no difference.

Even if there had been any adjustment possible on this issue — and there was not — the negotiations would in any case have broken down on the question of a national government. When Sir Stafford Cripps had first come out, he had used phrases at his meetings with the Press which had been taken as promising a wholly Indian National Cabinet and in conversation with political leaders he had said that the relations of the Indian Government to the Viceroy were similar to those of the British Cabinet to the King. It is true that he subsequently pointed out that no major amendment of the constitution was possible, but it was assumed that by such a convention within the constitution, a national government distinct from the Viceroy would be set up. On 9 April, when Azad and Nehru approached him on the subject, Sir Stafford Cripps made it clear that there would be no essential change between the Viceroy's Executive Council and the new government and that such questions as conventions for the working of the government were matters for discussion with the Viceroy after a settlement had been made. It was in these circumstances that Azad decided to place before Sir Stafford Cripps a detailed statement of the position and attitude of the Congress towards the British Government's proposals. This he did in a long letter dated 10 April, which concluded with the words, 'While we cannot accept the proposals you have made, we want to inform you that we are yet prepared to assume responsibility, provided a truly National Government is formed. We are prepared to put aside for the present all questions about the future, though, as we have indicated, we hold definite views about it. But in the present, the National Government must be a cabinet government with full power and must not merely be a continuation of the Viceroy's Executive Council.'

Sir Stafford Cripps replied on the same day to the effect that a cabinet government would require constitutional changes which were impossible in wartime, and that such a cabinet (nominated presumably by the major political organizations) would be responsible to no one but itself, could not be removed and would, in fact, constitute 'an absolute dictatorship of the majority.' This suggestion would be rejected by all minorities in India, since it would subject all of them to a permanent and autocratic majority in the cabinet. Nor would it be consistent with the pledges already given by His Majesty's Government to protect the rights of those minorities. Sir Stafford Cripps accepted Azad's letter as being a clear rejection by the Congress Working Committee of His Majesty's Government's draft declaration, and the negotiations were thus abruptly terminated.

On 11 April, Azad sent another letter to Sir Stafford Cripps stressing the essential need, in the Congress view, of a truly national government. The Congress President declared:

We are not interested in the Congress as such gaining power, but we are interested in the Indian people as a whole having freedom and power. How the Cabinet should be formed and should function was a question which might have been considered after the main question was decided; that is, the extent of power which the British Government would give up to the Indian people....

You will remember that in my very first talk with you, I pointed out that the communal or like questions did not arise at this stage. As soon as the British Government made up its mind to transfer real power and responsibility, the other questions could be tackled successfully by those concerned. You gave me the impression that you agreed with this approach.

On the same day the Congress Working Committee published its previously-adopted resolution containing its reactions to the British Cabinet's proposals. The following extracts represent the main features of the resolution:

The Committee, while recognising that self-determination for the people of India is accepted in principle in that uncertain future, regret that this is fettered and circumscribed and certain provisions have been introduced which gravely imperil the development of a free and united nation and the establishment of a democratic State. . . . The complete ignoring of the ninety millions of people of the Indian States and their treatment as commodities at the disposal of their rulers is a negation of both democracy and self-determination. . . . The acceptance beforehand of the novel principle of non-accession for a province is also a severe blow to the conception of Indian unity and an apple of discord likely to generate growing trouble in the provinces, and which may well lead to further difficulties in the way of the Indian States merging themselves in the Indian Union. . . . Nevertheless the Committee cannot think in terms of compelling the people in any territorial unit to remain in an Indian Union against their declared and established will. . . . Any proposal concerning the future of India must demand attention and scrutiny, but in today's grave crisis, it is the present that counts, and even proposals for the future are important in so far as they affect the present. The Committee have necessarily attached the greatest importance to this aspect of the question and on this ultimately depends what advice they should give to those who look to them for guidance. For this the present British War Cabinet's proposals are vague and altogether incomplete, and it would appear that no vital changes in the present structure are contemplated. It has been made clear that the defence of India will in any event remain under British control. At any time defence is a vital subject; during wartime it is all-important and covers almost every sphere of life and administration. To take away defence from the sphere of responsibility at this stage is to reduce that responsibility to a farce and nullity, and to make it perfectly clear that India is not going to be free in any way and her government is not going to function as a free and independent government during the pendency of the war. The Committee would repeat that an essential and fundamental prerequisite for the assumption of responsibility by the Indian people in the present is their realisation as a fact that they are free and are in charge of maintaining and defending their freedom. ... The Committee therefore are unable to accept the proposals put forward on behalf of the British War Cabinet.

As soon as it was known that the Congress would not accept the proposals, Jinnah published the resolution of the Muslim League Working Committee rejecting the scheme—mainly on the ground that the post-war provisions permitting the partition of India were so framed as not to give real protection to the Muslims. The following are extracts from the League Working Committee's resolution of 11 April:

In the draft declaration a constitution-making body has been proposed with the primary object of creating one Indian Union. So far as the Muslim League is concerned, it has finally decided that the only solution of India's constitutional problem is the partition of India into independent zones; and it will therefore be unfair to the Muslims to compel them to enter such a constitution-making body whose main object is the creation of a new Indian Union. ... The right of non-accession has been given to the existing provinces which have been formed from time to time for administrative convenience and on no logical basis. ... With regard to the interim arrangement there is no definite proposal except the bare statement that His Majesty's Government desire and invite the effective and immediate participation of the leaders of the principal sections of the Indian people in the counsels of their country, of the Commonwealth, and the United Nations. The Committee are therefore unable to express their opinion until a complete picture is available. Another reason why the Committee are unable to express their opinion on the interim arrangements for participation in the counsels of the country is that Sir Stafford Cripps has made it clear the scheme goes through as a whole or is rejected as a whole, and that it would not be possible to retain only the part relating to immediate arrangements at the Centre and discard the rest of the draft scheme; and as the Committee has come to the conclusion that the proposals for the future are unacceptable it will serve no useful purpose to deal further with the question of the immediate arrangements.

It was Jinnah's complaint that 'the talks had been carried on with the Congress leaders over the heads of the Muslims, and other parties had been utterly ignored.'

At a press conference on 11 April, Sir Stafford Cripps was reported to have said that the negotiations had been prolonged in the case of the Congress only; that there had been many meetings and a number of formulae and suggestions especially upon the question of a defence minister; that the Congress had made it clear that they were not prepared to accept the scheme or to enter a national government; that, as a result, he had most regretfully to advise His Majesty's Government that there was not such a measure of acceptance of their proposals as to justify their making a declaration in the form of the draft; that the draft was therefore withdrawn.

Broadcasting that night from the Delhi station of All-India Radio, Sir Stafford Cripps said:

The Congress has, since the outbreak of the war, repeatedly demanded two essentials as the basis for its support of the Allied effort in the war. First, a declaration of Indian independence and, second, a Constituent Assembly to frame a new and free constitution for India. Both these demands find their place in the draft declaration. It was in the light of the demands and criticisms of the Indian leaders that the War Cabinet drafted their declaration, with the object of convincing the Indian peoples and world public opinion of the sincerity of their desire to offer freedom to India at the earliest practicable moment.

Sir Stafford Cripps deplored that in all the spate of criticism, those vital parts of the declaration with which all agreed had never been mentioned. With regard to the interim proposals, he said:

The immediate difficulties have been as regards the present. First, there was the difficulty as to defence. Upon that the attitude of the British Government was very simple. For many decades the defence of India has been in the charge of His Majesty's Government. That charge has been carried out for over twenty years by a Commander-in-Chief who was also Defence Member of the Viceroy's Executive Council. This has led to an organisation which places the control of the armed forces under a Defence Secretariat headed by the Commander-in-Chief. The Army in India — containing British and Indian units — the Navy and the Air Force all come under this supreme command.

The demand has been made that the defence of India should be placed in Indian hands. No one suggests that the Commander-in-Chief, as the head of the armed forces, should be under the Indian Government but, they say, his functions as Defence Member should be transferred to an Indian. This may sound simple but would mean a long and difficult reorganisation of the whole Defence Secretariat — an unscrambling of eggs scrambled many years ago — which would cause delay and confusion at the very moment when the enemy is at the gate and the maximum of speed and efficiency is essential in defence. The duty of the British Government to defend India and our duty to our American Allies who are giving such valuable help, makes such a course impossible. . . .

In their final letter addressed to me, the Congress Working Committee have stated that the temporary form of government envisaged during the war, is not such as to enable them to join the Government. They have two suggestions to remedy the situation. First, an immediate change of the constitution, a point raised at the last moment and one that everyone else has admitted to be wholly impracticable while the war is proceeding; and second, that they are prepared to enter a true national government with a cabinet of Indian leaders untrammelled by any control by the Viceroy or the British Government. Realise what this means—the government of India for an indefinite period by a set of persons nominated by the Indian parties, responsible to no legislature or electorate, incapable of being changed and the majority of whom would be in a position to dominate large minorities. It is easy to understand that the great minorities in India would never accept such a system. Nor could His Majesty's Government, who have given pledges to those minorities, consent to their being placed unprotected, while the existing constitution lasts, under a simple and possibly inimical majority rule. It would be a breach of all the pledges that we have given.

'We have tried,' he added, 'by the offer that I brought, to help India along her road to victory and to freedom. But, for the moment, past distrust has proved too strong to allow of present agreement.'

On the following day, April 12, Sir Stafford Cripps left for England. The abrupt end of the negotiations and his sudden departure were the subject of much speculation and conjecture. Even in Congress circles there was a sense of disappointment and surprise that Sir Stafford Cripps should have left so suddenly, without making any further attempt to reach a settlement. Some of them felt that Sir Stafford Cripps had deceived them in the interests of British propaganda in America; that he had made a great show of what he was offering on behalf of His Majesty's Government, but that as soon as it became a question of definite agreement on practical details his attitude had hardened and, at the critical moment of the negotiations when anyone who wanted a settlement would have played his last card for a compromise, he had nothing to offer but, on the contrary, rejected some of the things he had said previously. Others believed that agreement had been reached in principle but that it had been blocked by pressure from the authorities in England.

A simple explanation is the one I have given earlier in this chapter,

namely that there was no proper understanding between the Viceroy
and Sir Stafford Cripps, nor between Sir Stafford Cripps and the
British Cabinet. Sir Stafford had been over-confident of 'selling' at
least the interim proposals to the Congress, but in their discussions
both had reckoned without the Viceroy and His Majesty's Government. Four years later, in the course of his speech in the House of
Commons on 12 December 1946, Churchill made it abundantly
clear that His Majesty's Government had not been willing to support Sir Stafford Cripps to the extent to which he himself was prepared to go.

Commenting on 'That Ill-fated Proposal', Gandhiji wrote on
13 April as follows:

It is a thousand pities that the British Government should have sent a
proposal for dissolving the political deadlock, which, on the face of it, was
too ridiculous to find acceptance anywhere. And it was a misfortune that
the bearer should have been Sir Stafford Cripps, acclaimed as a radical
among the radicals and a friend of India. I have no doubt about his goodwill. He believed that no one could have brought anything better for
India. But he should have known that at least the Congress would not
look at Dominion Status even though it carried the right of secession the
very moment it was taken. He knew too that the proposal contemplated
the splitting up of India into three parts, each having different ideas of
governance. It contemplated Pakistan, and yet not the Pakistan of the
Muslim League's conception. And last of all, it gave no real control over
defence to responsible ministers.

Gandhiji proceeded to draw the following significant conclusions.
He said:

But it is no use brooding over the past or British mistakes. It is more
profitable to look within. The British will take care of themselves, if we
will take care of ourselves. Our mistakes or rather our defects are many.
Why blame the British for our own limitations? Attainment of independence is an impossibility, till we have solved the communal tangle. We
may not blind ourselves to the naked fact. How to tackle the problem is
another question. We will never tackle it, so long as either or both parties
think that independence will or can come without any solution of the
tangle. . . . Whether those who believe in the two-nation theory and communal partition of India can live as friends co-operating with one another
I do not know. If the vast majority of Muslims regard themselves as a
separate nation having nothing in common with the Hindus and others,
no power on earth can compel them to think otherwise. And if they want
to partition India on that basis, they must have the partition, unless the

Hindus want to fight against such a division. So far as I can see, such a preparation is silently going on on behalf of both parties. That way lies suicide. Each party will probably want British or foreign aid. In that case, good-bye to independence.

In the House of Commons on 28 April, the Secretary of State (Amery) stated:

Such a national government (as the Congress demanded) would have been responsible in the last resort neither to Parliament here under the existing constitution, nor to an agreed and fairly balanced constitution in India, but only to its own majority — a majority presumably of Congress or, at any rate, of Hindus. That demand, whether made by Sir Tej Bahadur Sapru and his colleagues, or by the Congress, was the one thing which the Muslims and other minorities were determined at all costs to reject. They were and are convinced that such a government would, in fact, prejudge the whole future situation to their detriment. There was, therefore, never any question in our view of conceding that demand because it was, in fact, if not in intention, a demand which precluded all agreed co-operation in India.

Sir Stafford Cripps said:

Government have not in any sense closed the door regarding India. . . . They are only too anxious that the matter should be settled at any time when a settlement looks likely or possible. They cannot put forward any proposals because the proposals they have put forward they believe are the best they can put forward.

Commenting on what precisely was meant by the withdrawal of the draft declaration, the Secretary of State explained:

What we have certainly not withdrawn is our main object and purpose, namely, that India should, as soon as possible, obtain full freedom under constitutional arrangements of her own devising and suited to her own peculiar conditions. On the other hand, the particular method suggested for arriving at a constitutional settlement, more particularly the present provincial basis, both for setting up a constitution-making assembly and for non-accession, is not meeting with sufficient support for us to press it further. It may be that alternative methods might arise which might form a better basis for the definition of boundaries and might give representation for smaller elements such as the Sikhs, whose natural aspirations we appreciate. It is for Indians themselves to improve on our suggestions if they can.

As regards the interim situation, the particular proposals made by Sir Stafford Cripps in order to secure the whole-hearted co-operation of the Congress as well as the other political parties have, of course, lapsed. The

Viceroy will, no doubt, be willing to consider practical suggestions within the framework of suggestion (e) of the draft declaration put forward by responsible party leaders, more particularly if put forward jointly and based on a broad measure of agreement.

Amery added that the main object of the draft declaration was to set at rest India's suspicions as to the British Government's intentions. 'Our ideal,' he concluded, 'remains a United All-India.'

The result of the Cripps negotiations, instead of bridging the gulf between the Government and the political parties in India, only served to widen it. The manner in which the negotiations had broken down tended to strengthen the doubts and suspicions in the minds of political leaders that there was no genuine desire on the part of His Majesty's Government to part with power.

# VI

## THE STALEMATE CONTINUES

THERE was profound disappointment in India at the failure of
the Cripps Mission, and perhaps no one felt more thwarted than
Rajagopalachari. Ever since the outbreak of the war, he had
been indefatigable in his efforts to bring about an understanding
between the Government and the Congress. After the failure of the
Cripps Mission, he was convinced that progress was impossible without agreement between the Congress and the League. The gulf
between them was very wide indeed, and the Congress High Command was reluctant to make any overtures to Jinnah. Nevertheless,
on 23 April 1942 Rajagopalachari managed to get two resolutions
passed by the Congress members in the Madras legislature. The
first recommended to the All-India Congress Committee (which was
about to meet in Allahabad) that Congressmen should acknowledge
the Muslim League's claim for separation, should the same be persisted in when the time came for framing the constitution of India,
and that negotiations should immediately be started with the Muslim
League for the 'purpose of arriving at an agreement and securing the
installation of a national government to meet the present emergency.'
The resolution urged that ' to sacrifice the chances of the formation
of a national government for the doubtful advantage of maintaining
a controversy over the unity of India is the most unwise policy' and
that it had become necessary to choose the lesser evil. The second
proposed the restoration of responsible government in Madras.

The passing of the resolution conceding the Muslim League's claim
for separation created a stir in the country. The Muslim League
was naturally jubilant at its ideal of Pakistan having been brought
down at last from the clouds of speculation to the level of practical
politics; but amongst Congress leaders there was a feeling of
general resentment against Rajagopalachari. The All-India Congress

Committee, meeting in Allahabad on 29 April, rejected his resolution by an overwhelming majority and adopted a counter-resolution 'that any proposal to disintegrate India by giving liberty to any component State or territorial unit to secede from the Indian Union or Federation will be detrimental to the best interests of the people of the different States and provinces and the country as a whole and the Congress, therefore, cannot agree to any such proposal.'

The core of the main resolution, which was carried almost unanimously at the All-India Congress Committee meeting in Allahabad, was that India's participation in the war was a purely British act and that not only the interests of India, but Britain's safety and world peace and freedom, demanded that Britain must abandon her hold on India. The Committee repudiated the idea that freedom could come to India through the interference of, or invasion by, any foreign nation, whatever the professions of that nation might be. In the event of an invasion taking place it must be resisted. The Committee called upon the people of India to offer complete non-violent non-cooperation to the invading forces and not to render them any assistance.

Undaunted by his failure at the All-India Congress Committee, Rajagopalachari undertook a campaign in Madras, in the course of which he pleaded for the forging of a national front, for the establishment of a national government and for the mobilization of the country for defence. Nehru and other Congress leaders took serious objection to Rajagopalachari's campaign, as being detrimental to the interests of the country. 'It appears to me,' said Nehru, 'that he is breaking to pieces the weapon which the Congress have fashioned after twenty-two years of innumerable sacrifices.' Rajagopalachari announced his intention of resigning his membership of the Congress and also his seat in the Madras Assembly in order to be absolutely free to continue his campaign to convert the Congress. At a meeting of the Congress members of the Madras legislature on 15 July, he formally resigned. Only seven of his colleagues followed him. The meeting rescinded the previous resolution conceding the League's claim for separation, and confirmed the resolutions of the All-India Congress Committee.

Gandhiji now began a series of articles in the *Harijan* in which he urged the British to 'Quit India'. Week by week Gandhiji harped on this theme. He wrote: 'If the British left India to her fate as they had to leave Singapore, non-violent India would not lose anything. Probably the Japanese would leave India alone.' Gandhiji referred to the conditions in which the people of India were living as a state of 'ordered anarchy'; if this ordered anarchy was to be replaced by complete lawlessness in India as a result of the withdrawal of the British, he was prepared to take that risk and could only hope that the people would evolve real popular order out of chaos.

The Congress Working Committee met in Wardha on 6 July. The discussions lasted about nine days. Finally two resolutions were passed. The first dilated on various hardships caused by the preparations for the defence of the country, such as the acquisition of land for military purposes, the requisitioning of boats and vehicles in threatened coastal areas, and the scarcity of salt resulting from war conditions. It advised the people to refuse compliance with military requirements in certain circumstances. The other resolution demanded that British rule in India must end immediately. Neither settlement of the communal tangle, nor effective resistance to foreign aggression, was possible while British authority lasted. On the withdrawal of British rule, responsible men and women of the country would come together to form a provisional government representative of all important sections of the people of India. Those representatives would confer with the representatives of Britain 'for the adjustment of future relations and the co-operation of the two countries as allies in the common task of meeting aggression.' In the alternative, the Congress would be reluctantly compelled to utilize all its accumulated non-violent strength in a widespread struggle, under the leadership of Gandhiji. Further, it was resolved that, since these issues were of most vital and far-reaching importance, they should be referred to the All-India Congress Committee for final decision.

The publication of the resolutions was greeted with a chorus of dissent and alarm. Jinnah made a statement in which he said:

The latest decision of the Congress Working Committee on July 14, 1942, resolving to launch a mass movement if the British do not withdraw from India is the culminating point in the policy and programme of Mr. Gandhi and his Hindu Congress of blackmailing the British and coercing them to concede a system of government and transfer power to that government which would establish a Hindu Raj immediately under the aegis of the British bayonet, thereby throwing the Muslims and other minorities and interests at the mercy of the Congress Raj.

Savarkar and other Mahasabha leaders called on their followers to give no active support to the Congress policy. Liberal leaders, headed by Sapru and Sastri, appealed for the abandonment of civil disobedience as it would be 'prejudicial to the best interests of the country in respect of defence and other matters.'

The reaction of His Majesty's Government was stiff and uncompromising. Amery in the House of Commons, as well as Sir Stafford Cripps in a broadcast to America, made it clear that the Government would not flinch from taking every possible step to meet the Congress challenge. The demand of the Congress for British withdrawal would, if conceded, completely disrupt the governmental machinery in one of the most vital theatres of the war at a time when every energy was needed for the struggle against the common enemy. It was therefore the earnest hope of the British Government that the people of India would not countenance a movement fraught with disastrous consequences for the Allied cause, but that they would, on the contrary, throw their all into the struggle against the Axis. Both Amery and Cripps re-affirmed that the British Government would stand firmly by the broad intentions embodied in the Cripps proposals.

Even the *Daily Herald* of London, the official mouthpiece of the British Labour Party, which had always been friendly to Indian aspirations, was constrained to point out to the Congress the unwisdom of its policy:

If you persist in demands which are at this moment impossible to grant, you will cripple your cause and humble the influence of us who are your proud and faithful advocates. You will do worse, you will convey to the world the impression that India's leaders are incapable of distinguishing between the ideal of the United Nations and the petty standards of nationalism; that you rate political strategy higher than the prospect of liberty, equality and fraternity with the progressive peoples of the earth.

Before we proceed to the All-India Congress Committee meeting, there are one or two events to be noted, the first being the removal of the ban on the Communist Party of India, which had been imposed eight years previously. The ban was lifted because, after the invasion of Russia by the Germans, the Communists in India had ranged themselves behind the Government in support of the war effort. Another was the expansion of the Viceroy's Executive Council which had taken place because of the growing complexity of wartime administration. The Defence Department was divided into 'War' under the Commander-in-Chief, and 'Defence' under an Indian Member. The division of subjects followed generally the lines which had been drawn during the Cripps negotiations. Matters relating to War Transport were separated from the Communications Department and placed in charge of a member of the European business community. The new council numbered fourteen besides the Commander-in-Chief; eleven were Indians, including a Sikh and a member of the Depressed Classes. Together with these changes had come the appointments of Sir A. Ramaswami Mudaliar and the Jam Saheb of Nawanagar as representatives of India in the War Cabinet and the Pacific War Council.

The All-India Congress Committee met in Bombay on 7 August. It approved and endorsed the Working Committee's resolution demanding the immediate end of British rule. If this demand were not conceded, it gave sanction for the starting of 'a mass struggle on non-violent lines on the widest possible scale' under Gandhiji's leadership. In the course of his speech, Gandhiji said that he would ask for an interview with the Viceroy. The Congress President proposed to address appeals to President Roosevelt, Marshal Chiang Kai-shek and Maisky, Russian Ambassador in Britain. But the Government struck quickly. In the early morning of 9 August, Gandhiji and the members of the Working Committee were arrested; before long, all important leaders of the Congress throughout the country had been taken into custody, and at the same time Congress committees were declared unlawful associations. Serious disorders followed the arrest of the Congress leaders. The Government however was ready and took firm steps to quell the disturbances.

With the Congress out of the way, the Muslim League and the Hindu Mahasabha became more vocal. In a resolution passed at Bombay on 20 August the Working Committee of the League condemned the Congress civil disobedience movement as an instrument for forcing the British Government and Muslims to surrender to Congress dictation, and directed Muslims to refrain from participating in it. At the same time it demanded from the British Government an immediate declaration guaranteeing to the Muslims the right of self-determination and a pledge 'that they will abide by the verdict of a plebiscite of Musalmans and give effect to the Pakistan scheme.'

The Working Committee of the Hindu Mahasabha met at the end of August and formulated demands which did not differ markedly from those of the Congress, except that they were more militant in tone and more openly antagonistic to the Muslim League. It set up a committee headed by Shyama Prasad Mookerjee 'to make a final effort for an Indo-British settlement on honourable terms,' but this had no result. There were various talks between Mookerjee and Jinnah which were equally fruitless.

There were still a few leaders, on the Congress as well as on the Muslim League side, who were anxious to bridge the gulf between the two parties. For instance, there was Sir Sikander Hyat Khan, who had drawn up a tentative formula for the solution of the communal problem. His scheme provided that, in the absence of a 75 per cent majority of members of the Punjab Legislative Assembly in favour of either accession or non-accession to the Indian Federation, the Muslim community should be given an opportunity of deciding on non-accession by means of a referendum; if they so decided, the non-Muslim portions of the Punjab should, by a similar referendum, be accorded the right to cut themselves adrift from the province. If it actually came to the point where non-Muslims decided to break adrift, it would mean (assuming the unit concerned to be a district) that the Ambala division and a large part of the Jullundur division, and also the Amritsar district, would cease to belong to the Punjab. If a smaller unit such as the *tehsil* were to be taken, at least a very large part of the areas mentioned, and possibly certain others, would disappear from the province. In either case a disastrous dismemberment of the Punjab would be involved. The underlying idea of Sir Sikander's scheme was to bring home to all reasonably-minded men that if it should ever eventuate, Pakistan would smash the Punjab as it existed. He was, however, dissuaded by the Viceroy from publishing or proceeding with his scheme.

After detaching himself from the Congress, Rajagopalachari was ploughing a lonely furrow, with little hope of raising a political crop. Early in November he had talks with Jinnah. He seems to have found him in a co-operative mood, in which he was almost inclined to be constructive about the future—so that the impression left on Rajagopalachari was that there was only a very small gap to be bridged. On 12 November he saw the Viceroy, acquainted him with the change in Jinnah's attitude and sought his permission to see and consult Gandhiji. The Viceroy, however, refused to give him this permission. In fact, the very next day an official *communiqué* was issued in which it was explained that special facilities could not be accorded for discussions with persons under restraint for revolutionary activities, whose expressed and published aims were wholly inconsistent with the maintenance of peace and order in India and the prosecution of the war.

Soon after this, Rajagopalachari made an offer to go to England if he were given facilities to do so. The Secretary of State saw no advantage to be gained from such a visit. He said in Parliament that, while the Government welcomed Rajagopalachari's endeavours to promote an agreed settlement of the Indian problem, it was clear that any such agreement must come about in India between the Indian parties.

If the Congress repudiated Rajagopalachari, Jinnah was no less distrustful of his moves. The Scheduled Caste leaders were also critical. Ambedkar said: 'Mr Rajagopalachari seems to feel like an orphan in the storm keenly feeling for the kith and kin whom he deserted in search of green pastures. Nobody can accept his proposals.'

The Muslim League now began to press its claims with increased vehemence. At a meeting of its Council, the League passed a resolution which said that as the Muslims of India were a nation and not a minority, they were entitled to autonomous homelands in the areas in the north-west and north-east where they were in a majority. The Muslims themselves should determine their fate by means of a plebiscite after the war. The League was ready to participate in a 'provisional government', provided its post-war claims were not prejudiced thereby; any provisional government so set up was likely to have a decisive voice in the negotiations immediately after the war and therefore the League must have 'parity' in any such government to ensure that its claims were not prejudiced. The Congress movement was condemned as an instrument for coercing both the British and the Muslims to surrender to the Congress demands.

Up to this time the Viceroy had given no indication of his attitude or line of policy towards the Muslim League's demand for Pakistan. The only reference which he had made to it was in a letter to Sir Tej Bahadur Sapru in which he had said that the matter should remain an open question for discussion after the war. There were, however, allegations that the Viceroy had been encouraging Jinnah in his demand. It was obvious that Lord Linlithgow could not afford to appear as a partisan in this issue, and at the Annual Meeting of the Associated Chambers of Commerce in Calcutta on 17 December he strove to dispel the impression. In the course of his speech he made a point of stressing the geographical unity of India, adding that a divided India could not carry the weight that it ought to carry, nor could it make its way in the world with a confident expectation

of success. This statement, however negative in character, was sufficient to rouse strong resentment in League circles.

Towards the end of December an unfortunate event took place —
the death of Sir Sikander Hyat Khan, the premier of the Punjab.
In any scheme of partition the Punjab was the deciding factor, and
Sir Sikander Hyat Khan had been consistently opposed to its division.
He was the only moderating influence in the League who could have
stayed Jinnah's hands. Hereafter there was no one to thwart Jinnah's
wishes.

The year 1942 ended with the writing by Gandhiji of a personal
letter to Lord Linlithgow, in which he hinted that he would have to
'crucify the flesh by fasting,' unless the Viceroy could convince him
of his errors. On 13 January 1943, Lord Linlithgow replied, 'If I am
right in reading your letter to mean that in the light of what has
happened you wish to retrace your steps and dissociate yourself from
the policy of last summer, you have only to let me know and I will
at once consider the matter further.' At the same time he asked
Gandhiji for any positive suggestion he might wish to put forward.

Replying, Gandhiji placed the whole blame for the events that
had taken place since 9 August at the door of the Government of
India. He put two alternatives to the Viceroy: '(1) If you want me
to act singly, convince me that I was wrong and I will make amends;
(2) If you want me to make a proposal on behalf of the Congress you
should put me among the Working Committee members.' The
Viceroy was not prepared to accept either of these suggestions;
instead, he insisted on having from Gandhiji not only an admission
of guilt but appropriate assurances with regard to the future.

Gandhiji replied that it was the Government that had 'goaded
the people to the point of madness.' At the close of his letter, he
stated: 'If then I cannot get soothing balm for my pain, I must resort to the law prescribed for the satyagrahi, namely, a fast according to capacity.' He gave notice that the fast would begin on 9 February and that it would continue for 21 days.

An announcement was issued that the Government of India proposed to release Gandhiji for the duration of his fast. The latter's
reaction to this was that if he were released there would be no fast in
the terms of his correspondence. The Government of India once
more announced that it was ready to set him at liberty for the duration of the fast, but that, if he was not prepared to take advantage of
that fact and decided to fast while under detention, he did so on his

own responsibility and at his own risk. The fast actually started on 10 February. An urgent appeal for his intervention was sent by certain prominent Indian leaders to Churchill, whose reply was as follows:

The Government of India decided last August that Mr. Gandhi and other leaders of the Congress must be detained for reasons which have been fully explained and are well understood. The reasons for that decision have not ceased to exist. . . . There can be no justification for discriminating. between Mr. Gandhi and other Congress leaders. The responsibility therefore rests entirely with Mr. Gandhi himself.

Three members of the Viceroy's Executive Council tendered their resignations and dissociated themselves from the Government's policy, whereafter an All-Parties' Conference (representative of every political organization except the Congress and the Muslim League) met in Delhi, with Sir Tej Bahadur Sapru in the Chair. The Conference passed long and detailed resolutions, which they forwarded to the Viceroy, recommending that, in the interests of the future of India and for the sake of international goodwill, Gandhiji should be released immediately and unconditionally.

The Government, however, stood firm. A few days after the beginning of the fast, it even issued a pamphlet fastening the responsibility for the disturbances which followed the sanctioning of a mass movement by the All-India Congress Committee on 8 August 1942 upon Gandhiji and the Congress High Command. At one stage of the fast Gandhiji's condition was reported to be critical, but after the eleventh day he began to pull round. Rajagopalachari and others were allowed to see him. The fast ended on 3 March.

The leaders of the All-Parties' Conference met again in Bombay during the second week of March. They asked permission for representatives to visit Gandhiji in order to explore avenues for reconciliation. It was proposed that a deputation, headed by Rajagopalachari, should meet the Viceroy for this purpose. The Viceroy did not receive the deputation, but his reply, together with the full text of the memorandum that had been submitted to him, were published in a Government *communiqué*. The Viceroy's reply pointed out that nothing positive had emerged as a result of the talks between Gandhiji and his friends during his fast and that there was no reason· to believe that he was any more ready to repudiate the policy as the result of which the Congress leaders were under detention. So long as Gandhiji's attitude and that of the Congress remained unchanged, special facilities for contact with him or other Congress leaders could not be given. On the suggestion that only if the deputation were permitted to consult Gandhiji could a genuine national government be formed, the Viceroy pointed out that the essential preliminary to such a government was that measure of agreement between parties, communities and interests which he had been so anxious to foster, but to which the excessive claims and the totalitarian ambitions of the Congress and its leaders had been so consistent an obstacle. The Viceroy's decision was applauded by the Muslim League, the official journal of which expressed the hope that 'the purposeless interference of political busybodies' would now cease. Other sections were vehemently critical. Rajagopalachari characterized the Viceroy's reply as 'revealing the Versailles spirit wishing to humiliate the Congress and others and influenced by passion and prejudice.'

The annual session of the Muslim League was held in Delhi at the end of April. The main resolution regretted the Government's failure to guarantee Muslim self-determination, warned the Government that the imposition of any kind of federal constitution would be forcibly resisted, and exhorted Muslims to face the effort and sacrifice required to reach the cherished goal of Pakistan. The session was dominated by Jinnah, who was elected President for the eighth time.

In 1939, when the war broke out, Jinnah could claim only a nominal hold on the Punjab. But by this time all the other provinces which he claimed for Pakistan, namely Assam, Sind, Bengal and the North-West Frontier Province, had come under the control of League ministries. It will be interesting to recount how this came about.

In ASSAM, as has been mentioned, the resignation of the Congress ministry shortly after the outbreak of the war, had been followed by a coalition ministry under Sir Mahomed Saadullah. But in December 1941, Rohini Kumar Choudhury, Education Minister in Assam, resigned his office and formed a new party. This brought about the downfall of the Saadullah ministry, and the administration was taken over by the Governor. Rohini Kumar Choudhury felt that he could form a ministry, but it would have to depend on the votes of the Congress for its stability. The refusal of two successive Governors—Sir Robert Reid and Sir Andrew Clow—to accept a ministry which depended for its support on a party which refused to co-operate in the war effort, destroyed Choudhury's hopes.

Sir Mahomed Saadullah was encouraged to explore the possibilities of forming a new ministry. Negotiations with the European members of the Assembly, whose support was necessary, created some delay. Ultimately, in August 1942, the Governor revoked the Section 93 proclamation and Sir Mahomed Saadullah took office with a majority. The internment of about half the number of Congress members of the Assembly by the end of that year, made his position secure for the time being.

In SIND the ministerial change had a special feature of its own. On 19 September Allah Bakhsh, the premier, wrote a letter to the Viceroy renouncing his titles of Khan Bahadur and O.B.E, which he stated he could not but regard as 'tokens of British Imperialism'. On 26 September he released this letter to the press. The Governor lost no time in declaring that the renunciation by Allah Bakhsh of his titles was inconsistent with his retention of his office, since such renunciation was out of harmony with the oath of allegiance which he had taken to His Majesty. The proper thing for Allah Bakhsh to do, therefore, was to resign; if he refused to do so, the Governor would have no alternative but to dismiss him. On 10 October, Sir Hugh Dow had a talk with Allah Bakhsh, who refused to resign. A *communiqué* was thereupon issued to the effect that the Governor had discussed his renunciation of his honours with Allah Bakhsh and, in the light of that discussion, had no option but to inform him that he no longer possessed the Governor's confidence and that therefore he could not continue to hold office. Allah Bakhsh commanded a majority in the legislature and whether the Governor could go to the length of dismissing him because he had renounced his titles was a moot point.[1] In any case, both the Governor-General and the Secretary of State acquiesced in the decision of the Governor. The fact remains that by his action Allah Bakhsh had played into the hands of the Muslim League. Sir Ghulam Hussain Hidayatullah, an experienced and opportunist politician who was at the time serving under Allah Bakhsh, immediately took office with the support of the Muslim League. His ministry comprised two members of the League, one independent Muslim and two Hindus. There was picketing in front of the houses of the Hindu ministers and this gave Ghulam Hussain Hidayatullah an excuse to announce that, in view of the hostile attitude of the Congress and in the interests of his own community, he had decided to join the Muslim League. Allah Bakhsh's party was still in a majority when he ceased to be the premier, but

[1] At a later stage, certain provincial ministers belonging to the Muslim League relinquished their titles, but they continued in office.

Sind politics were so opportunist that by the time the legislature met again Hidayatullah had no difficulty in getting a majority of the members behind him. He was even successful in getting the Assembly to pass a resolution claiming that the Muslims of India were a separate nation entitled to an independent status of their own, uncontrolled by a central government dominated by Hindus.

With regard to BENGAL, it was after Fazlul Huq's resignation of his premiership at the end of March 1943 that the province came to be administered by a predominantly Muslim League ministry. Fazlul Huq had been the premier of Bengal since the establishment of provincial autonomy in 1937. He had belonged originally to the Krishak Proja Party, which represented the interests of the agrarian tenantry. Subsequently he joined the Muslim League. Towards the close of 1941, as a result of differences with the League, he resigned and formed a new coalition ministry. Later on he was expelled from the Muslim League. Thereafter, members of the League in the Bengal Legislature joined together in opposition to Fazlul Huq's ministry. But it was the action of the Governor (Sir John Herbert) that actually brought about the downfall of Fazlul Huq's ministry — sooner than was expected. The Governor sent for Fazlul Huq on 28 March and required him to sign a letter of resignation which, according to the latter, had already been drafted. This letter — an interesting document in its way — was in the following terms:

Dear Sir John,

   Understanding that there is a probability of the formation of a Ministry representative of the parties in the event of my resignation, I hereby tender resignation of my office as Chief Minister in the sincere hope that this will prove to be in the best interests of the people of Bengal.

In less than two hours the Governor communicated his acceptance of the resignation. It would appear that the Governor had acted under the influence of the European group who were at that time openly aligned with the Muslim League against Fazlul Huq. The action was a hasty one, taken without consultation with the Governor-General. A serious difficulty was that the budget for 1943-44 had not been passed, although the financial year was about to begin. When Fazlul Huq, in the course of a debate in the Bengal Assembly on 29 March, admitted that he had resigned and that the Governor had accepted his resignation, the Speaker, maintaining that the ministry had ceased to exist, adjourned the House for a fortnight. Nothing could therefore be done to get the budget passed before the

end of the financial year, and the Governor took over the administration of the province. The Governor's rule continued until 24 April,
when Sir Nazimuddin formed a ministry which was mainly composed
of members of the Muslim League. Many of Fazlul Huq's erstwhile
supporters transferred their allegiance and nothing more was heard
about the formation of a 'ministry representative of the parties'. If
there was any one Muslim leader in Bengal who, despite his unpre-
dictable temperament, could have held a reasonable section of the
Muslims and Hindus of the province together, it was Fazlul Huq.
His temporary exit from the scene of Bengal politics at a crucial
juncture, and the death of Sir Sikander Hyat Khan, left the Muslim
League free to forge ahead with its plans for partition.

In the NORTH-WEST FRONTIER PROVINCE a Muslim League
ministry did not materialize until May 1943. Sir Feroz Khan Noon,
then a member of the Viceroy's Executive Council, had discussed
this question with the Governor (Sir George Cunningham) in
October 1942. Sir Feroz Khan urged that a Muslim ministry in the
North-West Frontier Province would show the world that the Muslim
League was predominant in North India, in spite of all that the
Congress could do or say. But the Muslim League had an insecure
majority in the Assembly and the time was not ripe for action—though
the position was to change some months later. Aurangzeb Khan,
the local Muslim League leader, obtained a promise of support from
20 Muslim members. There were 50 seats in all in the Assembly, of
which 22 belonged to the Congress Party; but ten of the Congress
members were in prison, while seven seats were vacant. Aurangzeb
Khan formed a cabinet of five ministers, as against four in the previous
cabinet, and by so doing was able to obtain an additional following.

Lord Linlithgow laid down his viceroyalty on 20 October 1943.
His $7\frac{1}{2}$ years' régime—longer than that of any other Viceroy—was
conspicuous by its lack of positive achievement. When he left India,
famine stalked portions of the countryside. There was economic
distress due to the rising cost of living and the shortage of essential
commodities. On the political side, Sir Tej Bahadur Sapru expressed
the general feeling thus: 'Today, I say, after seven years of Lord
Linlithgow's administration the country is much more divided than
it was when he came here.'

Lord Linlithgow had come to India full of zeal for the federal plan
which he hoped to inaugurate during his time. His efforts were
partly frustrated by the Princes, who had put forward various

demands which were difficult to meet; by the Congress which wanted no whittling down of responsibility at the Centre; by the Muslim League, which was opposed to a unified Centre and last, but not least, by a Political Department whose half-hearted efforts could not, or would not, rise to the occasion.

With the outbreak of war, Lord Linlithgow decided to shelve the question of federation. Thereafter he concentrated his whole attention on the winning of the war. In the beginning he tried to enlist the support of the Congress, and of Gandhiji in particular, in the war effort. But his purpose was to carry on the government with a minimum of change and this resulted in purely negative policies, so that such initial enthusiasm as some of the leaders evinced in the cause of the democracies soon evaporated. Once the Congress ministries resigned their offices, and particularly after the passing of the Ramgarh resolution in the spring of 1940, Lord Linlithgow resolutely turned his back on the Congress.

With the Congress in opposition, Lord Linlithgow had to look to Jinnah and the League, whose co-operation and support he could not afford also to lose. This led, as a natural consequence, to the building up of the Muslim League.

For this state of affairs the Congress must take its due share of blame. Had it not resigned from its position of vantage in the provinces the course of Indian history might have been very different. By resigning, it showed a lamentable lack of foresight and political wisdom. There was little chance of its being put out of office; the British Government would surely have hesitated to incur the odium of dismissing ministries which had the overwhelming support of the people. Nor could it have resisted a unanimous demand for a change at the Centre, a demand which would have been all the more irresistible after the entry of Japan into the war. In any case, it is clear that, but for the resignation of the Congress, Jinnah and the Muslim League would never have attained the position they did.

The fact is that Lord Linlithgow, by playing one party against the other, succeeded in retaining the initiative in his own hands. He was convinced that for the successful prosecution of the war no diminution of his own authority should be allowed, and in this policy he had ample support from Churchill and his Cabinet.

The selection of Field-Marshal Viscount Wavell to succeed Lord Linlithgow was as much a surprise to Lord Wavell himself as to the political parties and their leaders, some of whom regarded it as ominous that a soldier should have been appointed as Viceroy—particularly one who had been the Commander-in-Chief in the Government which suppressed the disturbances following the 'Quit India' resolution and the arrest of the Congress leaders. However, such speculation was dispelled by Lord Wavell himself when, soon after his appointment, he addressed a press conference in London. 'There is certainly no intention,' he said, 'to set up anything in the shape of military rule or to withdraw or weaken in any way the pledges and offers already made to India by His Majesty's Government.' Amery, too, in announcing the appointment in the House of Commons said that it did not imply any change in the settled policy to which His Majesty's Government were pledged with regard to the development of Indian self-government.

When Lord Wavell took over as Viceroy the war was not by any means over, but the turning point had been reached and victory was in sight. It was clear that once peace was established, it would be difficult to deny or delay the transfer of substantial power to Indian hands. Lord Wavell was mindful of the problem and began almost at once to set about preparing the conditions in which political power could be transferred.

The prospects were none too bright. The legacy left by his predecessor in office was difficult and onerous. To achieve any communal settlement between the political parties seemed practically impossible. At the session of the All-India Muslim League held in Karachi in December 1943, Jinnah invented a new slogan: 'Divide and Quit'. The League resolved to establish a 'Committee of Action' to organize Muslims all over India to resist the imposition of a unitary constitution and to prepare for the coming struggle for the achievement of Pakistan. On the other hand, the All-India Hindu Mahasabha, meeting in Amritsar, demanded the preservation of the integrity of India, the introduction of federation with a strong Centre, and the refusal to any province, community, or section, of the right to secede. The Muslim League maintained its hostility to the Congress policy, whereas the Mahasabha demanded the immediate release of the Congress leaders and other prisoners. The National Liberal Federation, meeting in Bombay, also desired the release of the Congress leaders in the hope that they would defer to popular opinion and abandon the policy which had led to the 'Quit India' movement.

Lord Wavell's first important political speech was his address to the joint session of the central legislature on 17 February 1944. 'The winning of the war is our first task,' he said, 'but it must not exclude preparation for the future.' To plan India's political future in any detail was a difficult problem. He could state what he knew to be the desire of the British people and of His Majesty's Government, which was to see India a prosperous and united country enjoying complete and unqualified self-government as a willing partner of the British Commonwealth. He went on to say that the Cripps Offer of March 1942 was still open to those who had a genuine desire to further the prosecution of the war and the welfare of India. But the demand for the release of the Congress leaders who were in detention was an utterly barren one, until there was some sign on their part of willingness to co-operate in the great tasks ahead. Of these tasks, one of the greatest was the preliminary examination of the constitutional problems of India by an authoritative body of Indians. The Government would be ready to give such a body every assistance it might desire in carrying out its task, and Indians were free to devise, if they could, a method which would produce agreement in the country more readily than the Cripps proposals. On the main problem of Indian unity, Lord Wavell declared, 'You cannot alter geography....India is a natural unit.' It was for Indians to decide how the two great communities and certain other important minorities, as well as the Indian States, should live within that unit and make the best use of its wealth and opportunities. Of the Congress, Lord Wavell said: 'I recognize how much ability and high-mindedness it contains, but I deplore its present policy and methods as barren and unpractical. I should like to have the co-operation of this element in solving the present and future problems of India. If its leaders feel that they cannot consent to take part in the present Government of India, they may still be able to assist in considering future problems.' But those responsible for the declaration of 8 August 1942 (the 'Quit India' resolution) could not be released till the policy of non-cooperation and obstruction had been withdrawn, 'not in sackcloth and ashes—that helps no one—but in recognition of a mistaken and unprofitable policy.'

The Viceroy's emphasis on Indian unity was, needless to say, resented by the Muslim League. 'This drawing in of geography,' its official daily said, 'without reference to history and psychology is a poor compliment to Lord Wavell's gift of statesmanship.' Jinnah himself accused Lord Wavell of 'fishing in Congress waters.'

The nationalist press and the Liberals condemned the Viceroy's refusal to release the Congress leaders. Sir Tej Bahadur Sapru considered the speech most disappointing; it was not calculated to inspire hope, to remove differences or to encourage the people.

In the central Legislative Assembly a number of Congress members (who had been boycotting it since the war began) made their appearance, and with them the Muslim League made common cause. The Government were defeated in a series of important divisions. In particular, the Finance Bill was thrown out. In his closing speech for the Opposition, Bhulabhai Desai (leader of the Congress Party) pleaded that he was not opposed to defending his country, but that he would not undertake the 'responsibility' of voting the taxes without the 'privilege' of directing their expenditure.

The death of Kasturba Gandhi on 22 February 1944 caused widespread sorrow. The fact that she was sharing her husband's detention added poignancy. Shortly before her death, Gandhiji had written a letter to the new Viceroy in which he insisted that the Congress and he were wholly innocent of the charges brought against them. 'Promises for the future,' he said, 'are valueless in the face of the world struggle in which the fortune of all nations and therefore of the whole of humanity is involved. Present performance is the peremptory need of the moment if the war is to end in world peace.... Therefore a real war effort must mean satisfaction of India's demand. "Quit India" only gives vivid expression to that demand, and has not the sinister and poisonous meaning attributed to it without warrant by the Government of India.'

To this the Viceroy sent a reply in which he expressed his sympathy with Gandhiji in his bereavement. He also enclosed a copy of his address to the central legislature as indicating his views on the political situation.

A considerable portion of Gandhiji's reply was devoted to a criticism of the speech. Lord Wavell had been making a succession of flying visits to famine-afflicted areas in the country. Gandhiji suggested that he should interrupt his usual flights all over India and descend upon Ahmednagar and the Aga Khan Palace (where Gandhiji and certain others were detained) 'in order to probe the hearts of your captives.'

Lord Wavell replied that he viewed the policy of the Congress as hindering and not forwarding India's progress to self-government and development. He believed that the greatest contribution the Congress could make towards India's welfare was to abandon the

policy of non-cooperation and to join wholeheartedly with the other
Indian parties and with the British in helping India forward in her
economic and political progress—not by any dramatic or spectacular
stroke, but by hard steady work towards the goal ahead.

Gandhiji retorted that co-operation required equality between
the parties and mutual trust, but equality was absent and Government distrust of the Congress could be seen at every turn. The result
was that suspicion of Government was universal. He asked whether
it was not high time that the Viceroy co-operated with the people
of India through their elected representatives, instead of expecting
co-operation from them. India, as Gandhiji visualized it, was one
vast prison containing four hundred million souls, and the Viceroy
was their sole custodian.

About this time there occurred an incident of some importance
politically. In any scheme of Pakistan, the Punjab was of crucial importance and Jinnah had long been anxious to consolidate his hold
over that province which, as has been mentioned already, was ruled
by the Unionist Party. The majority of the members of the Unionist
Party were Muslims, but all the important landholders in the
province were its supporters. In 1937, Sir Sikander Hyat Khan had
entered into a pact with Jinnah by which he agreed to persuade
every Muslim in the Legislative Assembly to join the Muslim League.
In return, Jinnah had agreed that the Unionist Party should continue
to function as such and that the League would not interfere in its
provincial policies. (Incidentally, Jinnah denied the existence of
such a pact, but that was years later, in 1944). After Sir Sikander's
death in 1942, Khizr Hyat Khan became the leader of the Unionist
Party and the premier of the Punjab. Jinnah thought that he could
coerce Khizr Hyat Khan into acceptance of his dictates. He went
to Lahore in April and insisted that the ministry's 'Unionist Party'
label should be changed to that of 'Muslim League Coalition'. The
premier consulted his non-Muslim colleagues in the ministry and
offered several alternative formulae as a compromise; he even
suggested that a Muslim High Court judge should arbitrate, but
Jinnah was adamant. Now, Khizr Hyat Khan had admitted into
his ministry Captain Shaukat Hyat Khan, son of the late premier.
Captain Shaukat's role was a dubious one. He was credited with
the intention of resigning and crossing the floor of the House
with a number of his supporters if the premier did not comply
with Jinnah's demand. But there was also a charge against this

minister that in the exercise of his powers he had committed a very serious case of injustice, in consequence of which he was dismissed by the Governor. The dismissal was taken by Jinnah as an affront to himself and the League, and soon after the Jinnah-Khizr talks broke down. The Committee of Action of the Muslim League called upon Khizr Hyat Khan for a statement of his case with a view to taking disciplinary action against him, but he ignored the challenge. Ultimately the premier was expelled from the League, but most of his supporters remained true to him and the Muslim members of his ministry severed their connexion with the League.

Meanwhile, the Liberal leaders continued their efforts to resolve the impasse. At a Non-party Conference at Lucknow, Sir Tej Bahadur Sapru referred to the frustration caused by the 'immobility of the Government' which would neither make proposals nor encourage proposals from others. The Conference passed a number of resolutions recommending the restoration of ministerial government in the Section 93 provinces; the reconstruction of the Governor-General's Executive Council as a truly national government with a prime minister; the release of the Congress leaders, and elections to the central and provincial legislatures. The Conference authorized its president (Sir Tej Bahadur Sapru) to prepare a memorandum for submission to the Viceroy.

Sir Tej Bahadur submitted a memorandum to the Viceroy in the course of which he pointed out that the Governors in Section 93 provinces had become autocrats, the like of which had never been seen before. Out of 18 advisers, only three were Indians. The Governor acting 'in his discretion' was not subject to the control of the Governor-General in Council, but only to the control of the Governor-General and the Secretary of State, so that he was free from all Indian influence, whether provincial or central. The memorandum pointed out that resentment against the continuance of Governor's rule under Section 93 was deep and strong, but it rarely came to the surface because of the drastic powers with which the officials were invested under the Defence of India Rules. The memorandum concluded with the suggestion that an attempt should be made in those provinces to establish coalition ministries, or ministries representing all the important elements in the legislature.

Lord Wavell replied that the suspension of the constitution was due to the refusal of the majority party to remain in office for reasons which had nothing to do with the provincial administration, and that if ministries were to be formed in some or all of these Section 93 provinces, the first move should come from the party or parties which were prepared to take office and establish a stable government. The Viceroy was anxious to see the political life of India restored to normal and progress made on the path of self-government, but he did not see how His Majesty's Government, or the Governor-General, could produce a 'national government' at the Centre and ministries in the provinces without some marked spirit of co-operation from outside. In his view, drastic constitutional changes should not be made in wartime; and a national government would have to be established within the framework of the existing constitution, a limitation which was apparently unacceptable to the Indian leaders. A national government should be a business rather than a political government, devoting its energies to the great administrative problems during the war and to preparations for post-war development; while some body should be formed to study the political problem with a view to arriving at a scheme for political settlement and the means of a change-over after the war.

Replying to the Viceroy, Sir Tej Bahadur made no secret of his deep regret at the decision of the Congress to withdraw from office. But the practical question was whether, for an error of judgment committed five years ago, the whole of the electorate should continue to be deprived of their constitutional rights. He suggested that it was open to a Governor in a Section 93 province to have executive councillors or advisers in place of ministers, and yet allow the legislatures to function. He could not speak for the Congress; nevertheless, he felt very strongly that, though it might possibly decline to assume the responsibility of office, it would probably not stand in the way of other parties forming ministries, and that it would place no unnecessary obstruction in the way so long as those who held office reflected public opinion in their actions and discharged their duties fairly and wisely. With regard to the national government at the Centre, Sir Tej Bahadur felt that changes even within the framework of the existing constitution could be brought about without imperilling the safety of the country, or without interfering with the effective prosecution of the war, by suitable conventions and by securing in fact and in practice as full a measure of freedom for the Government of India from outside control as might be possible. He fully realized the importance of a body being formed to study political problems for a permanent settlement and to provide the means of a change-over after the war, but he thought that such a body formed by a government which had not the support or backing of political parties had little chance of producing a favourable impression on the minds of the people at large.

In the existing political situation, the Viceroy was not in favour of setting up provincial executive councils the position of which, vis-à-vis hostile legislatures, was bound to be difficult. Both supply and legislation might have to be certified. Non-official advisers, too, would be in a difficult position. It was best to recognize Section 93 for what it was and not to attempt to dress it up as a democratic form of government. He agreed with Sir Tej Bahadur that a national government at the Centre would need the whole-hearted support of the political parties, and that such support was not forthcoming.

In the middle of April 1944, Gandhiji had an attack of malaria from which he did not make a quick recovery. There were grounds for fear of a sudden collapse, so that he was released unconditionally on 6 May on medical grounds.

On 17 June, Gandhiji wrote to the Viceroy expressing a desire to interview members of the Congress Working Committee in order to discuss a fresh approach and, as a preliminary, suggested that when he had recovered from his illness he should meet the Viceroy.

The Viceroy refused permission to Gandhiji to see the members of the Working Committee, nor did he feel that a meeting between themselves at that stage would serve any useful purpose. If, however, after his convalescence, and on further reflection, Gandhiji had a definite and constructive policy to propose for the furtherance of India's welfare, the Viceroy would be glad to consider it.

On 20 June, the Government published the correspondence which had passed between Lord Linlithgow, Lord Wavell and the Government of India on the one hand, and Gandhiji on the other, during the latter's detention.

On 11 July, the *Times of India* published what was said to be an interview given by Gandhiji to Stewart Gelder, a correspondent of the *News Chronicle*, London. At a press conference the next day, Gandhiji handed over the notes which he had prepared after his discussion with the British journalist. He said that he had not authorized the publication of the interview, or even its substance. He had told Gelder that his first business was to go to Delhi and, if he could, see the Viceroy and give him an idea of the way Gandhiji's mind was working.

The substance of the interview was that Gandhiji could do nothing without consulting the Congress Working Committee. If he met the Viceroy he would tell him that it was his purpose to help and not hinder the Allied war effort. He had no intention of offering civil disobedience. History could never be repeated; he could not take the country back to 1942. The world had moved on during the last two years and the whole situation had to be reviewed *de novo*. Today he would be satisfied with a national Government in full control of civil administration and would advise the Congress to participate in such a government if formed. It would be composed of persons chosen by the elected members of the central Assembly. The military would be allowed all the facilities they might require, but the control would be that of the national Government. Ordinance rule would give place to normal administration. The Viceroy would be there, but he would be like the King of England, guided by responsible ministers. Popular government would be automatically restored in all the provinces. So far as military operations were concerned, the Viceroy and the Commander-in-Chief would have complete control, subject to advice and criticism from the national Government. Thus the portfolio of defence would be in the hands of the national Government, which would be genuinely interested in the defence of the country and might render great assistance in the shaping of policies. The Allied forces would be allowed to carry on their operations on Indian soil, but the expense of the operations would not be borne by India.

On 15 July, Gandhiji wrote to Lord Wavell. He said that the Viceroy must have seen the authentic version of his interview with Gelder. He regretted its premature publication, as it was meant primarily to be shown to the Viceroy. But he thought that the publication would be a blessing in disguise if it enabled the Viceroy to grant at least one of his two requests — either that he (Gandhiji) should be permitted to see the members of the Working Committee, or that he should be granted an interview with the Viceroy.

The Viceroy replied that he could not usefully comment on the Gelder interview, but that if Gandhiji would submit a definite and constructive policy, he would be glad to consider it.

On 27 July, Gandhiji wrote to Lord Wavell to the effect that he was prepared to advise the Working Committee to renounce mass civil disobedience and to give full co-operation in the war effort, if a declaration of immediate Indian independence were made and a national government responsible to the central Assembly were formed, subject to the proviso that during the pendency of the war, military operations should continue as at present, but without any financial burden upon India.

Only a day later, on 28 July, there was a debate on India in the House of Commons. In the course of his speech, the Secretary of State said that Gandhiji's interviews and statements were not free from obscurities and reservations on particular points, but that they were all bound up with, and dependent upon, one central demand which did not leave any room for ambiguity. That was the demand for immediate recognition of India's independence under a provisional government in which the only powers reserved to the Viceroy would be those which dealt with the control of active military operations. All the reserve powers which were indispensable to ensuring that the various functions of administration were co-ordinated with the war effort, as also those indispensable to the safeguarding of the constitutional position for minority elements, were to d sappear. That was just the demand upon which the negotiations with the Congress had broken down two years ago. There was the further stipulation that India was to bear no part of the cost of her own defence. So long as these were the bases for his proposals, they obviously did not form even the starting-point for a profitable discussion, either with Lord Wavell or with the interned Congress leaders. They were in no sense a response to the Viceroy's invitation to Gandhiji to produce constructive proposals. The Secretary of State concluded that they could only continue to hope that the time would come when they would have before them proposals which would conform to conditions not arbitrarily imposed, but which were indispensable both because India was at war and because no agreed future constitution was yet in sight.

The Viceroy replied to Gandhiji on 15 August. He repeated that Gandhiji's proposals were very similar to those which had been made by the Congress President to Sir Stafford Cripps in April 1942 and rejected at that time for reasons given by His Majesty's Government. The British offer to India of unqualified freedom after the war had been made conditional upon the framing of a constitution agreed by the main elements of India's national life, and the negotiation of a treaty with Britain. The object of these conditions was to safeguard the racial and religious minorities, the Depressed Classes, and treaty obligations to the Indian States. If the Government were to be made responsible to the central Assembly, it would be necessary to alter the constitution and this was impossible during the period of the war. Until the war was over, responsibility for defence and military operations could not be separated from the other responsibilities of Government; and until the new constitution was in operation the British Government and the Governor-General must retain their responsibility over the entire field. With regard to India's share in the cost of the war, the existing financial arrangements could only be reopened at the instance of either the British Government or the Indian Government. The Hindus, the Muslims and the important minorities, were welcome to co-operate in a transitional government under the constitution, as it stood, but for such a government to succeed there must first be agreement in principle between those elements as to the method by which the future constitution should be framed.

Commenting on the Viceroy's reply, Gandhiji said that it was 'as clear as crystal that the British Government did not propose to give up the power they possess over the four hundred millions unless the latter develop strength enough to wrest it from them.'

The door having been closed by the Viceroy, some of the Congress leaders turned again to Jinnah. Rajagopalachari was convinced that there was no escape from some form of partition of the country if there were to be any progress in the constitutional field. Earlier, in 1943, he had drawn up a formula to serve as a basis for a settlement between the Congress and the League. He had shown it to Gandhiji and obtained his approval when he had been allowed to see him during his fast in February of that year. Now, in April 1944, he communicated the formula to Jinnah and had discussions and correspondence with him. The terms of the formula, which Rajagopalachari published on 10 July, were that the Muslim League should endorse the demand for independence and co-operate with the Congress in the formation of a provisional interim government for the transitional period; after the termination of the war, a commission should be appointed to demarcate those contiguous districts in north-west and north-east India wherein the Muslims were in an absolute majority, and in those areas there should be a plebiscite of all the inhabitants to decide the issue of separation from Hindustan; if the majority decided in favour of forming a separate sovereign State, such decision should be given effect to. It would be open to all the parties to advocate their points of view before the plebiscite was held. In the event of separation, a mutual agreement should be entered into for defence, commerce, communications and other essential purposes. Any transfer of population would be on an absolutely voluntary basis. These terms should be binding only in case of transfer by Britain of full power and responsibility for the governance of India. Jinnah agreed to place this formula before the League, but refused to take personal responsibility for accepting or rejecting it.

On 17 July, Gandhiji wrote to Jinnah suggesting that the two of them should meet. 'Do not regard me as an enemy of Islam or of Indian Muslims. I have always been a servant and friend to you and to mankind. Do not disappoint me.' Jinnah replied that he would be glad to receive Gandhiji at his house in Bombay on his return from Kashmir, probably in the middle of August.

The Working Committee of the Muslim League, which met in Lahore on 30 July, gave Jinnah full authority to negotiate with Gandhiji. But Jinnah's speech was not exactly helpful. While he did not conceal his pleasure that Gandhiji, at any rate in his personal capacity, had accepted the principle of partition, he dismissed the Rajagopalachari formula as offering 'a shadow and a husk, a maimed, mutilated and moth-eaten Pakistan.'

Gandhiji's willingness to discuss the partition of the country with Jinnah provoked bitter criticism, particularly from the Hindus in the Punjab and Bengal, who were aggrieved at the prospect of becoming a helpless minority in an Islamic State. The Sikhs were nervous about a settlement being reached over their heads. The Hindu Mahasabha was very bitter; Savarkar asserted that 'the Indian provinces were not the private properties of Gandhiji and Rajaji so that they could make a gift of them to anyone they liked.'

The offer to discuss the partition of India with Jinnah was, to say the least of it, inopportune. The League ministries in Bengal, Sind and the North-West Frontier Province were in none too stable a position. Moreover, the refusal of Khizr Hyat Khan, the premier of the Punjab, to change the 'Unionist Ministry' in the Punjab into a 'Muslim League Coalition Ministry', had not enhanced Jinnah's prestige. In these circumstances Gandhiji's move was calculated only to strengthen Jinnah's hands and further the cause of the Muslim League. This was a view which was shared by some prominent Congressmen.

On 6 August, *Dawn*, the official mouthpiece of the Muslim League, carried a leading article which stated that the first question was the acceptance of the principle of the carving out of portions of India for the creation of separate sovereign States. That alone would take them to the next stage of the marking of the frontiers of the State with due regard to its safety and solvency. It was not going to be a mere pencil scrawl on the map according to the density of population, because if the principle of creating sovereign States were conceded, it was also to be understood that the unit in the comity of nations must be self-supporting and that necessary adjustments would have to be made by negotiation and consent. The demand that Musalmans should precisely define the geographical lay-out of Pakistan, so that Hindus could sit on the fence and throw stones, did not appear to be a token of co-operation and sincerity, because the very basis of division, if conceded, would throw upon both parties the onus of sitting together and finding a solution that would enable the divided States to be economically self-supporting and nationally solvent in the larger sense of a term which embraced all aspects of sovereignty.

On 10 August, Rajagopalachari was compelled to state that if the conditions for an independent State were lacking in the Muslim majority areas, it would be good ground for advising the people at the time of the plebiscite to vote against separation, or for the total withdrawal of the demand. He said that it should not become a reason for asking for an expansion of territory involving the coercion of people outside Muslim majority areas, or for making other and fresh demands. In conclusion, he said that areas found to be lacking in self-sufficiency must be content to remain units within a larger State, for they could not aspire to independent sovereign status.

The Gandhi-Jinnah meeting took place on 9 September 1944. The talks continued under a veil of secrecy till the 27th, when the correspondence which had accompanied the talks was released and the failure to reach agreement was announced.

On 24 September, Gandhiji had made a concrete offer to Jinnah, stating that he was willing to recommend to the Congress and the country the acceptance of the claim for separation contained in the League's Lahore resolution of 1940, under certain terms and conditions. He had proceeded on the assumption that India was not to be regarded as two or more nations, but as one family consisting of many members, including those Muslims living in Baluchistan, Sind, the North-West Frontier Province, parts of the Punjab, Bengal and Assam, who desired to live in separation from the rest of India. These areas should be demarcated by a commission approved by the

Congress and the League and the wishes of the inhabitants should be ascertained through a plebiscite. If the vote were in favour of separation, it should be agreed that these areas should form a separate State as soon as possible after India was free. There should be a treaty of separation which should provide for the efficient and satisfactory administration of foreign affairs, defence, internal communications, customs, commerce and the like, which must necessarily continue to be matters of common interest between the contracting parties. The treaty should also contain terms for the safeguarding of the rights of minorities in the two States. Immediately on the acceptance of that agreement by the Congress and the League, the two would decide upon a common course of action for the attainment of India's independence. The League would however be free to remain out of any direct action to which the Congress might resort and in which it might not be willing to participate.

Jinnah replied the next day to the effect that Gandhiji had already rejected the fundamental principles of the Lahore resolution, since he did not accept that the Musalmans of India were a nation, nor that they had an inherent right of self-determination; that they alone were entitled to exercise their right of self-determination, and that Pakistan was composed of two zones, North-West and North-East, comprising six provinces namely Sind, Baluchistan, the North-West Frontier Province, the Punjab, Bengal and Assam, subject to territorial adjustments that might be agreed upon as indicated in the Lahore resolution. He added that the All-India Congress Committee's resolution passed at Allahabad in May 1942 and the one passed at Bombay on 8 August 1942 were a complete bar to any settlement on the basis of the division of India into Pakistan and Hindustan. He was emphatic that if the terms offered by Gandhiji were accepted, the existing boundaries of the Punjab, Bengal and Assam would be mutilated beyond redemption, leaving the Muslims with no more than the husk. Jinnah was against Gandhiji's proposal that even in those areas the right of self-determination should be exercised, not only by Muslims, but by all the inhabitants of those areas. Gandhiji's proposal was also that, if the vote were in favour of separation, Muslims should be allowed to form a separate State as soon as possible after India was free; whereas the Muslim League proposal was that the two parties should come to a complete settlement immediately and by their united front and efforts do everything in their power to secure the freedom and independence of the peoples of India on the basis of Pakistan and

Hindustan. Gandhiji had suggested that there should be a treaty of separation to provide for the efficient and satisfactory administration of foreign affairs, defence, communications, customs, commerce and the like, as matters of common interest; but Jinnah was clear that all these matters, which were the life-blood of any State, could not be delegated to any common central authority or government.

In the words of Gandhiji, the talks and the correspondence seemed 'to run in parallel lines and never touch one another.' On 27 September, Jinnah announced that it had not been possible to reach an agreement, but added: 'We trust that this is not the final end of our efforts.' Gandhiji commented that failure to reach agreement was no cau e for disappointment. 'The breakdown is only so called. It is an adjournment *sine die*.' The only practical result of these talks was to reveal, for the first time, the concrete features of the demand which the Muslim League had been pressing without so far defining —and further to enhance Jinnah's position and prestige amongst the Muslims generally.

# VII

## A NEW APPROACH

THE breakdown of the Gandhi-Jinnah talks convinced Lord Wavell that unless His Majesty's Government itself intervened there was no likelihood of arriving at any solution of the Indian problem. Meanwhile, in consultation with his advisers, he had formulated certain tentative conclusions which he decided to put before a conference of Governors. The Conference was held in August 1944. Lord Wavell told the Governors that His Majesty's Government was preoccupied with its vast undertakings elsewhere and, so long as the war con inued, had little time to devote to India's political problems. On the other hand, the position was that Germany was likely to be beaten by the end of the year and that the war with Japan would end about six months later. The political question would then inevitably have to be taken up and the promises made to India redeemed. Elections would have to be held at the Centre and in the provinces. The Defence of India Rules would lapse. There would be general demobilization, dispersal of labour from war industries, and the winding up of war establishments, involving large-scale unemployment and discontent. Economic problems would continue to be as difficult as ever. He thought that it would be wise to provide Indians with an outlet for their administrative and political energy and that, if Indian leaders could be induced to enter the central Government and if it were possible to get popular ministries back into office in the Section 93 provinces, that would be the outlet; but unfortunately the prospects were not favourable. He enquired whether, on the long-term view, the Governors were agreed that Government should sit back and await events, or that they should make a positive move. All the Governors were emphatic that, failing agreement between the Indian parties, a positive move was essential and that, in view of the rapidly approaching defeat of Germany, it should be made as soon as possible.

Fortified by the Governors' unanimous agreement, Lord Wavell proceeded to finalize his plan. The Viceroy would assemble a small conference of the principal leaders, including, besides Gandhiji and Jinnah, one representative each of the Congress and the Muslim League, of the Sikhs, Depressed Classes, non-Congress Hindus, non-League Muslims and Labour. The Viceroy would discuss with them the question of the composition of the transitional government. His own idea was that there should be an equal number of Hindus and Muslims, with one representative of the Depressed Classes and one Sikh, in addition to the Commander-in-Chief and the Governor-General. This transitional government would work within the existing constitution. Its task would be to prosecute the war against Japan with the utmost energy and to carry on the government of British India until the new constitution and treaty came into force; to appoint British-Indian representatives to the Peace Conference and other international conferences; to consider the composition of the Constituent Assembly, or other body, which would draft the constitution and negotiate the treaty with His Majesty's Government; and to secure the approval of the leaders of Indian opinion in the principal communities to the composition proposed.

The conference would also consider the best means of re-establishing popular governments in the Section 93 provinces, preferably with coalition ministries. If the conference agreed to the formation of a transitional government at the Centre and was able to propose acceptable members for it, the names would be submitted by the Viceroy to the Secretary of State for His Majesty's approval. The members would then take office. Provincial governments would be formed in Section 93 provinces simultaneously, or as soon as possible thereafter. If it were found necessary or desirable to hold elections for the central and provincial legislatures, they would be held after the new governments had taken office. When the new transitional government was well settled, the Viceroy would encourage it to prepare and communicate to His Majesty's Government proposals for the establishment of the constitution and treaty-making body. At that stage, the Princes would have to be brought into the negotiations. If the conference failed, there would be no alternative but to carry on the government with the existing Executive Council.

In communicating his plan to the Secretary of State the Viceroy admitted that there were obvious difficulties and risks, but stressed that the risks of following a policy of no action were much greater.

The Secretary of State, whilst sympathizing with the objective underlying the Viceroy's proposals, saw in them certain inherent practical difficulties. He was sure that, unless there were prior agreement between the political parties with regard to the constitutional future, there was bound to be such acute tension within the Council as would hamper the war effort and the day-to-day administration of the country. The Secretary of State also foresaw difficulties in regard to the composition of the interim Government. An important point was whether Jinnah should be allowed to nominate all the Muslim members to the Executive Council. If he were allowed to do so, important sections of Muslims in the Punjab and elsewhere would go unrepresented. Further, in attempting to conciliate the Congress and the Muslim League, there was the risk that those classes in India that had supported His Majesty's Government loyally in the past and whose co-operation was still essential, would be thrown overboard.

At the same time, Amery appreciated the arguments against allowing the situation to drift. He therefore suggested an alternative plan which he thought would, while evading some of the objections to the Viceroy's plan, show that the British Government was not content to sit still. His suggestion was that the existing Executive Council should be left untouched for the duration of the war. The Viceroy might announce his intention, in the face of the obviously unbridgeable gulf between the two main organized parties, to set up a conference of the other less unbalanced and irreconcilable elements in Indian polity, for the purpose of discussing the basis of a future constitution for India and framing proposals to that end. The nucleus of the conference might be the National Defence Council, which already included representatives of the Princes. This body could be reinforced by the premiers of non-Section 93 provinces, elder statesmen, representatives of the Depressed Classes and Labour, and representatives of the Fighting Services, including those of the Indian States. Even so, though it would not be unduly larger for general discussion, a small committee might be selected from within it to concentrate on planning. The selection of a chairman would be a critical point of the scheme, but should not present insuperable difficulty. There was much to be said for by-passing the Congress and the League; if that proved impossible, they might be invited to participate, but only on a relatively small scale. If they declined to participate, the conference would go to work without them. Secretariat and expert assistance might be provided by the Reforms Department; and advisers, especially those experienced in the working of federal constitutions, might be invited from the Dominions and foreign countries. Proposals emanating from the conference would no doubt be subject to eventual ratification by an elected body, the composition of which would have to be suggested by the conference. The Congress and the League would be represented on the elected body and this would provide an answer to criticism of their exclusion from, or non-participation in, the work of the conference. The Secretary of State thought that this plan would avoid the serious administrative difficulties inherent in the Viceroy's proposals during the critical war period; it would be an earnest of His Majesty's Government's determination to fulfil its promises; it would focus Indian political discussion on a constructive task, and it would evade the difficulty (which was a feature of both the Viceroy's proposed preliminary conference and transitional government) of having the Congress and the Muslim League confronting each other and dominating the discussions with their irreconcilable differences. It would also give full opportunity for the expression of the views of those who had stood by the British Government in recent years.

In Lord Wavell's view, the Secretary of State's alternative plan was quite impracticable. The Congress and the Muslim League could not be by-passed. They held the keys to the situation; they controlled the press, and they would undoubtedly sweep the polls in any elections that might be held. Preliminary agreement about the future constitution was not being insisted upon because such agreement was manifestly impossible. On the other hand, by working together, politicians might achieve a greater sense of realism, as had to a large extent happened after the Congress took office in 1937.

It was now that Amery, with characteristic boldness of vision, put forward an arresting thesis of his own. He said that he was coming increasingly to the view that India's main grievance and source of bitterness was not the existing Government of India, but Downing Street and the House of Commons. It was the suspicion, however unjust, that India's views were being overruled from Whitehall, that India's interests were being made subservient to British interests, and that her policy was being governed by the prejudice or party manoeuvres of British politicians. More than that, the situation was one which tended—at least subconsciously—to accentuate the irresponsibility of Indian politicians. At the back of their minds they were always thinking that by stating their case in its extreme form they might get something more out of the British Government when the latter had to come to a decision, and they could not bring themselves to believe that the British Government really meant to accept an Indian settlement and implement it. To that extent, he believed that there was something in Gandhiji's argument that the presence of the British in India impeded a settlement. The conclusion he drew from this was that instead of making Indian agreement an essential prerequisite to full self-government vis-à-vis Whitehall, the British Government should go the other way about and concede independence in the fullest sense as a prerequisite to an internal settlement in India. It was obvious that the British could not leave India to chaos and therefore the independence to be conceded would have to be to the Government of India as it existed at the time. Amery's idea was that the British Government should declare that they recognized India as enjoying the full freedom of status enjoyed by the Dominions under the Statute of Westminster, namely, full equality with Great Britain, and that Parliament in England should have no power to legislate for Indian affairs except at the request of an Indian Government. Though Amery was not unaware that his proposal might be considered 'wildly fantastic', he felt that it was not inconceivable that a situation might arise in which it would be possible for a Government in Britain to astound India and the world by the boldness of its action!

Here was a conception that was destined in the very near future to take practical and definite shape. That Amery was not able to translate his ideas into practice was largely due to environment and the circumstances of the time.

In fact, the key to the door of progress was controlled by Churchill, for at that critical time the rest of the British Cabinet largely subordinated their views to his policy and judgment. Lord Wavell felt that his own views would have a better chance of acceptance by the Cabinet if he wrote directly to Churchill. I had the privilege of seeing that remarkable document. It contained a bold and forthright expression of his views on the political situation as it existed at the time and pressed very strongly for a change of spirit, a change which would convince the average educated Indian that the British Government was sincere in its intentions and was friendly towards India. I recall, in particular, the way in which Lord Wavell opened and concluded his observations. He prefaced his letter by stating that during the five years or more during which he had had the privilege of serving under

Churchill, the latter must often have found him a difficult and troublesome subordinate. He himself had not always found Churchill an easy master, but he had never failed to serve him loyally and with unqualified admiration for his courage and strategy, and he had always told him the truth as he saw it without fear of consequences. Lord Wavell concluded his letter by saying that, as Churchill knew, he had no axe to grind; that he had not sought, nor had he desired his appointment as Viceroy, but since he had been placed in a position of such immense responsibility he was bound to place his views before him without partiality, favour or affection.

Simultaneously with the despatch of his letter to Churchill, Lord Wavell suggested to the Secretary of State certain practical measures which would be calculated to convince Indians of a change of spirit on the part of the British Government. These were a declaration by the British Prime Minister himself that His Majesty's Government definitely intended to give India self-government as early as possible; an assurance that the British Government did not intend to repudiate its debt to India, although the time and manner of repayment would require discussion; a gift or transfer of shipping to India against sterling balances to help tide over the transportation problem; a promise of modern ships to the Indian Navy at the end of the war; higher status for the Indian High Commissioner in London and the transfer to him of some of the business done in the India Office; conferment on the Indian representative in the United States of the status of Minister, and the transfer of Indian affairs from the India Office to the Dominions Office.

The Secretary of State hoped that the Viceroy's appeal to Churchill would have its effect. A change of spirit was essential, for both future and day-to-day relations between India and Great Britain, and nothing could carry so much conviction as a statement by the Prime Minister himself. The Secretary of State was inclined to support the specific proposals made by the Viceroy, though he felt that practical effect could not be given to some of them, at any rate until after the war. He reiterated that he himself would go a long way towards the recognition of India's self-governing status without waiting for a solution of her internal constitutional problems.

In the meantime there was a new move in the political field. Ever since the breakdown of the Gandhi-Jinnah talks a few of the Hindu and Muslim extremists had been carrying on a bitter controversy over the Pakistan issue and the use of the words 'civil war' was becoming far too frequent in public speeches. Sir Tej Bahadur Sapru, alarmed at the way in which the communal situation was deteriorating, wrote to Gandhiji suggesting the holding of an All-Parties Conference; but Sir Tej Bahadur himself was doubtful whether his proposal would lead to any satisfactory result and, after some discussion with Gandhiji, the suggestion was dropped. Another proposal was that Gandhiji should call a National Convention, but he was not agreeable to doing so. Subsequently, Sir Tej Bahadur suggested to Gandhiji that the Standing Committee of the Non-party Conference should set up a committee and prescribe for it certain duties. The object of this committee would not be to bring about a settlement in the sense that 'the document would be executed, signed, sealed and delivered,' but to understand the point of view of each party and to act as a sort of conciliation board by establishing contacts with the leaders of all parties, and then to recommend such solution as they thought fit. It would be open to the parties to accept it wholly or partially, or to reject it. Gandhiji accepted the suggestion, but said that the members of the committee should not belong to the Congress, the League, the Mahasabha, or any of the recognized parties, and that they should be persons who had not definitely committed themselves to any particular view since the breakdown of the Gandhi-Jinnah talks.

The Standing Committee of the Non-party Conference met on 19 November 1944, and decided to set up a committee 'to examine the whole communal and minorities question from a constitutional and political point of view, put itself in touch with the different parties and their leaders, including the minorities interested in the question, and present a solution within two months to the Standing Committee of the Non-party Conference.' Sir Tej Bahadur Sapru was authorized to appoint the members of the Committee.

Sir Tej Bahadur held a press conference the same day at which he explained that the proposed Committee would consist of people who were not actively associated with any of the recognized political parties and who had not publicly expressed opinions on the communal controversy. The Committee's object would be to lift the discussion of the communal and political problem from the partisan to the scientific and judicial level. He hoped that two ex-High Court judges, and possibly one or two Englishmen, would serve on the Committee, which would do all it could to ascertain the views of the various political parties. He said that if any party declined to co-operate, there would be no recriminations, though the fact would be recorded. Sir Tej Bahadur added that he had Gandhiji's support and he hoped that the Government would adopt a reasonable attitude to any approach by the Committee for information or statistics.

The Viceroy was apprehensive lest Sir Tej Bahadur Sapru's scheme should affect the consideration of his own proposals by the British Cabinet. Whilst recognizing the inappropriateness of making any move that might possibly be interpreted as an attempt to sabotage a genuine effort by Indian leaders to produce a settlement, he also felt that if the Government ceased to give consideration to the main principles of the problem every time the Indian leaders stirred the muddy waters, there would be no end to the business. His Majesty's Government should be prepared to move quickly when a good opportunity offered, but it could not be prepared unless it was clear about its general objective. The Viceroy accordingly urged on the Secretary of State that his proposals should be considered by the Cabinet, even though action might have to be delayed pending the result of the Sapru Committee's discussions.

The Cabinet felt that the Viceroy's proposal to summon a conference of political leaders was a matter that called for personal discussion and that the best time for the Viceroy to go to London would be after the outcome of the Sapru Committee's inquiries had become known.

The Viceroy insisted however that he should put his point of view to the Cabinet as early as possible and suggested that he should leave for England by the end of January 1945; but the Secretary of State advised that it would be convenient if he could come a little later, possibly in March.

On 3 December, Sir Tej Bahadur Sapru announced the names of the members of his 'Conciliation Committee'. He said that it was his intention to write to leaders of the various parties and organizations requesting them to agree to personal interviews. The Committee would be free to devise its own procedure. It was proposed to publish all important papers along with the report of the Committee. The field of work of the Committee was obviously limited. It was not attempting to frame a detailed constitution. Its purpose was to investigate whether there was a possibility of reconciling conflicting views and of suggesting a basis on which a constitutional structure might be built, and for this the Committee would welcome and be grateful for help from every quarter.

Shortly after this, Sir Tej Bahadur wrote to Jinnah asking whether he would meet him and one or two other members of the Committee with a view to clarifying certain points. Jinnah replied that he could not recognize the Committee of the Non-party Conference, or its Standing Committee, and that he was therefore unable to comply with the request. He added that he did not mean any discourtesy to Sir Tej Bahadur personally; that if the latter had desired to meet him otherwise than on behalf of the Non-party Conference he would have been glad to see him. Then there was Ambedkar, who was inclined at first to co-operate, but who later withdrew because he disliked the composition of the Committee. Despite these rebuffs, the Sapru Committee went ahead with its inquiries.

In his annual address to the Associated Chambers of Commerce in Calcutta in December 1944 the Viceroy said:

If I may be permitted to assume for the moment the role of medical adviser to political India, my advice would be something like this: I do not believe that your condition calls for a serious operation, I should certainly try all other possible remedies first. But I do not think that the 'Quit India' mixture or those Satyagraha pills have done you much good. I should suggest your leaving off medicines altogether, and you may find that you are not as ill as you think. Perhaps some fresh air and work in the fields would do you good. In other words, I do not believe that there are now real differences in principle between India and Britain, or that the communal problem, difficult though it is, is insoluble. But also I do not believe that we can solve our problems by mutual recriminations and by harping on past grievances and mistakes. Our best hope lies in working together without trying to lay down detailed conditions or to decide everything before we begin work. To return to the medical metaphor for a moment, I think the first requirement for a return to health is a faith cure, a belief in the good intentions of the British people and in their genuine desire for a settlement and for the welfare and self-government of the Indian people. I can certainly assure you that I should not be here if I did not believe in those.

He paid a tribute to the Government of India describing it as 'a preponderantly Indian Government which in spite of all the criticism and abuse heaped on it is doing an essential job of work for India and is doing it on the whole extremely well.' This did not mean that some other national government, based on the support of the main political parties, might not be more serviceable to India's needs. According to the Viceroy's conceptions a national government should be one formed to meet a national crisis in which 'none are for a party but all are for the State.' If it were possible to form such a national government during the war, it would quite clearly and quite definitely have to function under the existing constitution, and its primary task would have to be the sincere and whole-hearted support of the war effort. The Viceroy added that in the last decade His Majesty's Government had made two attempts to 'solve the deadlock' — the Act of 1935, and the draft declaration propounded by Sir Stafford Cripps. Both attempts had failed and after the second failure the British Government had said that they could do no more and that India herself must make a constructive suggestion. No such suggestion had yet emerged and the recent discussions between Gandhiji and Jinnah showed how intractable the communal problem still was. His Majesty's Government was naturally chary of a further advance until it felt that the spirit of compromise and co-operation was real, but its desire for a solution remained perfectly genuine.

The year 1945 began on an optimistic note, with rumours of a Congress-League alliance. Since 1944, when the Congress members had begun once more to attend the central legislature, Bhulabhai Desai had been working in close co-operation with Liaqat Ali Khan, the *de facto* leader of the Muslim League Party in the legislature, and there had been a certain amount of speculation with regard to a pact said to have been reached between them.

Bhulabhai Desai saw Sir Evan Jenkins, then Private Secretary to the Viceroy, on 13 January. This was followed by an interview with the Viceroy on 20 January. Bhulabhai Desai's plan was as follows:

Desai and Jinnah should be invited to form an interim Government at the Centre;

They would then consult the groups in the Indian legislature and submit names to the Governor-General for inclusion in the Executive Council. The selection would not be confined to members of the legislature;

Communal proportions within the Council would be settled by agreement. Bhulabhai Desai would be accommodating about this (he said that, speaking for himself, if the Muslim League insisted, he would agree to equality between them and the Congress, with a 20 per cent reservation for the rest);

The interim Government would work within the present constitution, but all the members of the Executive Council, except the Governor-General and the Commander-in-Chief, would be Indians;

As regards the long-term solution, there would be no commitments. The long-term solution might be easier when the interim Government had been in office for a year or so;

In the provinces, the existing ministries would not be interfered with, though there might be adjustments based on party agreements with which His Majesty's Government would not be concerned. Section 93 administrations would be replaced by coalition ministries including both Congress and League elements;

There would be no general elections either at the Centre or in the provinces;

*Détenus* would not be released before the formation of the interim central Government.

Desai claimed that these proposals had the support of Gandhiji, that they were based on informal talks with Liaqat Ali Khan, and that if the British Government really wanted a central Government with political backing they could get it now. He was confident that Jinnah was aware and had approved of what had passed between him and Liaqat Ali Khan.

The Viceroy suggested to the Secretary of State that Bhulabhai Desai's plan afforded an excellent opportunity of making progress in the political sphere. It not only accorded with his own proposals, but it had the advantage of being put forward by an Indian. The British Cabinet, however, raised a number of points of varying importance. It wanted to know what guarantee there was that Desai's interim Government would support the war effort; whether the intention was to deprive the Governor-General of the right to select his colleagues; how far the new members of the Council would be subject to control by their party caucuses; how far the Congress would support Desai; where the British Government stood on the 'Quit India' resolution; how minorities and non-Congress Hindus and non-League Muslims would be provided for; and so on. It was clear that the Viceroy could not answer these questions without seeing Desai and Jinnah. In authorizing him to do so, the Secretary of State emphasized that he was not to commit himself (or His Majesty's Government) in any way as to the acceptability or otherwise of the proposals; that he was merely to clear up, as far as possible, the points mentioned above, and transmit to His Majesty's Government any serious suggestion agreed to between Desai and Jinnah.

Meanwhile, Jinnah made a public statement disclaiming any knowledge of the Desai-Liaqat Ali pact. Desai was undeterred by Jinnah's disclaimer and continued to canvass support for his plan. Desai happened to meet me at about this time. He told me that no serious notice need be taken of Jinnah's disclaimer, which had been expressed in very guarded language; that he himself had acted with the knowledge of Gandhiji and that, if the Government accepted his plan, Jinnah would certainly participate, even though he might express dissatisfaction in public. I remember his quoting a Gujarati proverb to the effect that one might grumble about the food, but one would eat it all the same.

It was learnt that Jinnah was not likely to come to Delhi before March. Lord Wavell therefore asked Sir John Colville, the Governor of Bombay, to see Jinnah on his behalf and find out if he thought the Desai proposals worth pursuing and if so, whether he would come to Delhi as soon as possible for discussions with himself and Desai. Sir John Colville saw Jinnah, who stated that he knew nothing about the talks between Desai and Liaqat Ali Khan and that the proposals had been made without any authority from the League. He said he would be going to Delhi early in March and that he would be glad to discuss the matter with the Viceroy on his arrival. Unfortunately, when Jinnah reached Delhi, he fell ill and was unable to meet the Viceroy.

Lord Wavell now urged on the Secretary of State that his visit to England should no longer be put off. Bhulabhai Desai's proposals were after all only an incidental development of the general plan that he himself had put forward; indeed, he was more concerned to know the mind of His Majesty's Government than that of Jinnah or Desai. But the Sapru Committee's report was expected in May, and the Secretary of State suggested that it would be better, for this and other reasons, if the Viceroy postponed his visit till June. Lord Wavell, however, protested strenuously against any postponement and it was finally agreed that he should fly to England at the end of the third week of March. Sir Evan Jenkins and myself accompanied Lord Wavell to England. It was wartime and the news of the Viceroy's departure was not made public until he had reached London.

But let us complete the story of the Desai-Liaqat Ali pact. There can hardly be any doubt that Desai had in fact reached an understanding with Liaqat Ali Khan on the formation of a national government at the Centre and that the latter resiled from it when he found that Jinnah was not going to be helpful. Gandhiji himself admitted later that the Desai-Liaqat pact had received his blessing. Desai's formula was an attempt to break the political deadlock on the lines of an *ad hoc* practical compromise. Its merit was that it was not unduly ambitious; that it did not try to attack the main points of difference between the parties, and that it was well-timed, because of the progressive disposition of the Viceroy and his desire to achieve some kind of settlement. But Desai was later to be repudiated by Jinnah, as well as by the leaders of the Congress, and the ultimate result of his labours was his own political extinction!

Nor did the proposals of the Sapru Committee meet with any success. Its recommendations were published shortly after Lord Wavell's departure for London. The main features were that a national government should replace the present Executive Council at the Centre; that in the provinces the Congress ministries should resume office but with an admixture of non-Congress parties; that in the constitution-making body, representation of Hindus (excluding Scheduled Castes) and Muslims should be equal; that similar parity in the central Assembly should be conditional on Muslims agreeing to joint electorates with reservation of seats instead of separate electorates; that no decision of the constitution-making body should be valid unless it was supported by three-fourths of the members present and voting, and that His Majesty's Government, while accepting the decisions so made, should supplement them by its own awards where the requisite majority was not obtained. The Committee firmly rejected the Pakistan idea (though two of its members were willing— if no other basis for an agreed settlement were forthcoming—to consider a division of the country, subject to a definite agreement in respect of common matters of defence and economic development).

In spite of the eminent and talented personalities of which it was composed, the Committee failed in its efforts to advance the position. For one thing, the Committee was handicapped by the absence of any top-ranking Muslim. Its rejection of the Pakistan idea and the recommendation of joint electorates made the Muslim League's attitude all the more hostile. There was disapproval, even from non-Congress Hindus, who were unable to acquiesce in the proposal for parity between Muslims and Hindus other than the Scheduled Castes.

There is yet another matter to be noted—the position of the provincial ministries at that time. We have already mentioned how in May 1943 a Muslim League ministry was set up in the NORTH-WEST FRONTIER PROVINCE. Lord Wavell's policy of the gradual release of Congressmen resulted in an increase of Congress members in the provincial Assembly. On 12 March 1945, the Muslim League ministry in the North-West Frontier Province was defeated by twenty-four votes to eighteen, and Dr Khan Sahib, leader of the Congress Party, was invited by the Governor to form a new ministry. The Governor asked for an assurance of whole-hearted co-operation in the prosecution of the war. Dr Khan Sahib gave the necessary assurance and once more a Congress ministry was formed in the North-West Frontier Province.

Similarly, the position of the Muslim League ministry in ASSAM became more precarious as Congress members of the local legislature were released from detention. Sir Mahomed Saadullah, the premier, was obliged to open negotiations with Gopinath Bardolai, the leader of the Congress Party. Bardolai had already got permission from Gandhiji, either to form a ministry, or to join a coalition. Bardolai did not ask for any seats in the proposed new ministry, but he laid down certain conditions, which included the replacement of the non-Muslim ministers, the release of all political prisoners and the ending of all restrictions on political activity. In March 1945, Sir Mahomed Saadullah signed an agreement in pursuance of which a new cabinet was formed in Assam.

The ever-changing loyalties of the SIND politicians, guided solely by personal considerations, made a stable ministry in that province well-nigh impossible. In February 1945, the League ministry, headed by Sir Ghulam Hussain Hidayatullah, was defeated on a budget demand. The defeat was caused by the defection of several Muslim League members. The premier thereupon proposed to reconstruct his ministry on a coalition basis, that is, with Hindus and independent Muslims. One of the ministerships was offered to Khan Bahadur Moula Bakhsh, brother of the late Allah Bakhsh and leader of a small group of independent Muslims. Moula Bakhsh was duly sworn in as minister, but Jinnah insisted that he could not be included in the ministry unless he joined the Muslim League. Moula Bakhsh's refusal to bow to Jinnah's behest created another ministerial crisis. Sir Ghulam Hussain Hidayatullah eventually formed a new ministry, which was sworn in on 14 March 1945.

In BENGAL, because of stresses and personal ambitions among the League members, the position of Khwaja Sir Nazimuddin, the Muslim League premier, had become weak and insecure. Kiran Shankar Roy, leader of the Congress Party in the Bengal legislature, approached Nazimuddin with a view to the formation of a League-Congress coalition ministry. The proposal held obvious advantages, but meanwhile, on 28 March, owing to the defection of a number of members of his party, Nazimuddin's ministry was defeated and the whole of the budget demand under the head of agriculture was

rejected. The Speaker adjourned the House *sine die,* and the administration was taken over by the Governor under Section 93.

Reverting to the Viceroy's mission, Lord Wavell reached London on the evening of 23 March and began his discussions with
the Secretary of State and the India Committee immediately thereafter. The British Cabinet was preoccupied with so many other vital
matters that it was not possible to hold regular continuous meetings
to discuss the Indian problem. The Viceroy's plan of a conference
was generally accepted, but the discussions were prolonged over
certain important details—for instance, whether the conference
should be confined to a selected few, or be bigger and more representative; whether in the matter of representation of the Congress,
members of the party still under detention should be released unconditionally, or on parole; the question of Muslim representation in
the proposed new Executive Council, and the transfer of the subject
of external affairs to an Indian member. Sir Stafford Cripps, who
took a keen interest in the proceedings and who gave the Viceroy considerable support in getting his proposals accepted, was himself in
favour of a bigger and more representative conference. The general
plan was that the leaders, not only of the two main parties (Congress
and Muslim League), but of other parties as well, should be invited,
subject to some definite criteria being followed to prevent invitations
being issued on an arbitrary basis, and that those invited would not
be consulted separately by the Viceroy, but would sit together in
conference. Though Gandhiji and some of the members of the Congress Working Committee had been released, there were others who
were still under detention, and it was largely owing to the insistence
of Lord Wavell that it was agreed that they should be released unconditionally. Amongst other important decisions, besides the transfer of the subject of external affairs to an Indian member, were the
appointment of a British High Commissioner in India and parity of
representation for Muslims in the Executive Council. Meanwhile a
draft statement was prepared, which was discussed and re-discussed
and underwent many revisions before it was finally accepted.

While the discussions were still in progress, came the surrender of
Germany on 7 May. The fact that the end of the war with Japan
must follow in the very near future underlined the urgency of settling
the Indian problem as soon as possible.

On 4 June Lord Wavell arrived back in Delhi.

# VIII

## THE SIMLA CONFERENCE

ON the eve of Lord Wavell's departure, Amery made an announcement in the House of Commons to the effect that the Viceroy had been empowered to make proposals on the composition of an interim Government in India. This naturally raised a good deal of eager expectation, particularly as (owing to the ban on Congress activities and the detention of its leaders) the political life of the country at the time was practically at a standstill. The suspense was relieved on 14 June when Lord Wavell broadcast[1] his proposals — designed, as he said, 'to ease the present political situation and to advance India towards her goal of full self-government.' It was his intention, he announced, to hold a political conference in Simla on 25 June, to which would be invited twenty-one leaders, including premiers of provincial governments; persons who last held the office of premier in the provinces administered by Governors; the leader of the Congress Party and the Deputy Leader of the Muslim League in the central Assembly; the leaders of the Congress and the League in the Council of State; the leaders of the Nationalist Party and the European Group in the central Legislative Assembly; Gandhiji and Jinnah, as the recognized leaders of the two main political parties, and a representative each of the Sikhs and the Scheduled Castes. The purpose of the Conference would be to take counsel with the Viceroy with a view to the formation of a new Executive Council which would be more representative of organized political opinion. It was intended that the new Council would represent the main communities and would include 'equal proportions of Caste Hindus and Muslims.' Except for the Viceroy and for the Commander-in-Chief, who would hold charge of the war portfolio, it would be an entirely Indian Council. The subject of external affairs, which had hitherto

[1] See Appendix II.

been administered by the Viceroy, would be 'in charge of an Indian Member of Council, so far as the interests of British India are concerned.' The new Council would work under the existing constitution; there could be no question of the Governor-General agreeing not to exercise his constitutional power of overriding his Council in certain circumstances, but this power would not of course be exercised unreasonably. It was also proposed to appoint a British High Commissioner in India, as in the Dominions, to represent Great Britain's commercial and other interests in India. Lord Wavell made it clear that the formation of this interim Government would in no way prejudice the final constitutional settlement; also that the proposals were confined to British India and did not in any way affect the relations of the Indian Princes with the Crown Representative. The main tasks of the new Executive Council would be first, to prosecute the war against Japan; secondly, to carry on the government of British India (with its manifold tasks of post-war development) until a new permanent constitution could be agreed upon and come into force; and thirdly, to consider (when the members of the Government thought it possible) the means by which such agreement could be achieved. The third task, Lord Wavell said, was most important; neither he himself, nor His Majesty's Government, had lost sight of the need for a long-term solution, and the present proposals were intended to make such a solution easier. He considered that the proposals were not merely a step, but a stride forward and a stride in the right direction.

If the Conference were successful, Lord Wavell hoped that ministries would again be formed in the provinces which were being administered by the Governors and that such ministries would be on a coalition basis. It would be part of the functions of the Conference to discuss the appropriate time for fresh elections to the central and provincial legislatures. Orders had already been issued for the release from detention of the remaining members of the Congress Working Committee, and it would be for the new central Government and provincial governments to decide with regard to those others who were still in detention in consequence of the 1942 disturbances.

In conclusion, Lord Wavell appealed for the creation of an atmosphere of goodwill and mutual confidence. India's military reputation stood high and sympathy for India's aspirations had never been greater or more widespread. These were great assets, but there were also many pitfalls and dangers. There was something on all sides to forgive and forget. He himself believed in the future of India and would do his best to further her greatness.

A simultaneous statement[1] was made in Parliament by the Secretary of State. Explaining the proposals in the House of Commons, Amery said that the Cripps Offer of 1942 stood in its entirety. That offer contained two main principles—first, that no limit was set to India's freedom to determine her own destiny, whether within the Commonwealth or outside it, and secondly that this destiny could only be achieved by a constitution or constitutions framed and agreed to by Indians. No progress had been made towards the solution of the internal deadlock, but the wholehearted co-operation of every section was necessary for the tackling of the immediate problems. This could not be achieved without some real advance in the political field, but such an advance would have to be within the existing constitution, so as not to prejudge the future solution. For the same reason, there could be no question of making the executive responsible to the legislature. It was equally impossible to abrogate the Governor-General's overriding power over a majority decision of his Council. That was a power in reserve, not an instrument in everyday use; but so long as there was no Indian constitution under which controversial issues could ultimately be resolved, it was a necessary protection for the minorities, whether against immediate injury or against decisions which might prejudice the constitutional future. In any case, its main purpose was to safeguard Indian interests, and this applied no less to the Viceroy's obligation to protect the interests of the Indian States. The appointment of a British High Commissioner in India had been suggested in order to emphasize this aspect of the Viceroy's position, as well as for reasons of practical convenience. Amery said that the present members of the Executive Council had rendered great service, but they were not sustained as a body by that measure of co-operation, goodwill and understanding which was desirable for carrying out the task of reconstruction. Nothing could serve this cause better than the agreement of the political leaders to join the Executive Council. Amery added that the proposals owed everything to the initiative of Lord Wavell, to his deep sympathy with India's aspirations and to his firm belief in India's future greatness.

A reference to the new proposals was also made in the King's speech proroguing Parliament on 15 June. The King expressed the earnest hope that the invitation extended to the Indian political

[1] See Appendix III.

leaders would be accepted, so that the immediate tasks might be undertaken with the full co-operation of all sections of Indian public opinion.

The attitude of the press and the public towards the proposals was generally favourable. There was evident a disposition to await the outcome of the proposed conference and not to prejudice its chances of success by unfavourable criticism or comment. In particular, there was general acknowledgment of Lord Wavell's sincerity and of his earnest desire to end the political deadlock.

Immediately after the broadcast, the Viceroy sent invitations to all the political leaders, including Gandhiji and Jinnah. Abul Kalam Azad was not included among those who were originally invited, because it was thought that Gandhiji would agree to represent the Congress, and apparently also because of the risk (by including Azad) of offending Jinnah. But Gandhiji's reaction on receipt of the invitation was to point out that he represented no institution and that the function of representing the Congress belonged to the Congress President, or whomsoever the latter nominated. Accordingly an invitation was sent to Azad, who informed the Viceroy that the invitation would be placed before the Working Committee on 21 June and that a reply would be sent thereafter.

With regard to Gandhiji himself, the Viceroy stated that, whatever the technical position, he would value his help and hoped that he would be able to attend. If, replied Gandhiji, the Viceroy thought his help was desirable (purely in a personal capacity and without being a member of the Conference), he would make it a point to be at the Viceroy's service before and even during the Conference, assuming of course that the Working Committee also wished it. The Viceroy, who had invited Gandhiji for a preliminary talk on 24 June, said that he was looking forward to seeing him on that day and hoped that means would be found for him to take part in the proceedings of the Conference.

Other preliminary objections raised by Gandhiji in his correspondence with the Viceroy related to India's goal of independence and the question of parity of representation between Caste Hindus and Muslims. The broadcast, Gandhiji remarked, seemed 'rigorously to exclude the use of the word independence. Accordingly it seems to me to demand revision to bring it in line with modern Indian thought.' In reply, the Viceroy invited attention to the Secretary of State's speech wherein he had stated that there was no limit set to India's freedom to decide her own destiny, whether as a free partner in the Commonwealth, or even outside it. The Viceroy said that it was not practicable to modify the terms of the broadcast, which was a simple statement of the proposals approved by His Majesty's Government. This point was not referred to by Gandhiji in his subsequent correspondence with the Viceroy, but in a press interview on 18 June, when asked if he was satisfied with the clarification offered by the Viceroy and the Secretary of State concerning the question of independence, he replied that it was a question for the Working Committee to answer and that, though he had his own opinion, he did not wish to anticipate or influence the Working Committee.

With regard to parity of representation between Caste Hindus and Muslims, Gandhiji informed the Viceroy that the term 'Caste Hindus' rang untrue and offensive; that the Congress could not represent them, since it sought to represent without distinction all Indians who had desired and worked for independence, and that even the Hindu Mahasabha, which claimed to represent Hindus, would disclaim representing 'Caste Hindus'. In reply, the Viceroy informed Gandhiji that the term 'Caste Hindus' was not used with any offensive intention; it merely meant that there should be equality between Muslims and Hindus other than members of the Scheduled Castes. Subject to this, the exact composition of the Council would have to be decided after discussion at the Conference. Gandhiji insisted that unless a change was made to meet the objection taken on the question of parity between Caste Hindus and Muslims, religious division would become officially stereotyped on the eve of independence. Personally he would never subscribe to this; nor, if he knew its mind, would the Congress. In spite of having an overwhelmingly Hindu membership the Congress had always striven to be purely political. He added, 'I am quite capable of advising Congress to nominate all non-Hindus and most decidedly non-Caste Hindus. You will unconsciously but equally surely defeat the purpose of the Conference if parity between Hindus and Muslims is unalterable. Parity between the Congress and the League is understandable. I am eager to help you and the British people but not at the cost of fundamental and universal principles.' The Viceroy pointed out that he could not change his broadcast, nor did he think it desirable to discuss its details before the Conference met. None of the persons or parties was expected or required to accept or reject the proposals now. The only immediate question was whether the proposals were worth discussing at the Conference and it was to that question that an answer would be most helpful. To this Gandhiji replied that the fact that members were free to accept or reject the proposals cleared the ground for those who had been invited to attend, but if parity between Muslims and Caste Hindus was incapable of being altered by the British Government, his advice to the Congress would be not to participate in the formation of the Executive Council. 'Congress has never identified itself with Caste or non-Caste Hindus and never can, even to gain independence, which will be one-sided, untrue and suicidal. Congress to justify its existence for winning the independence of India must remain for ever free to choose the best men and women from all classes and I hope always will. That it has for the sake of conciliating the minorities chosen men to represent them, though they have been less than best, redounds to its credit, but that can never be pleaded to justify or perpetuate distinctions based on caste or creed. The Hindu Mahasabha is the body claiming to represent solely Hindu interests.'

Gandhiji made his position clear in one or two press statements. In a statement issued on 15 June, he expressed his approval of the Desai-Liaqat Ali pact and said that the proposed conference could do much useful work if it were put in its proper political setting and were at the very outset rendered immune from any fissiparous tendency. 'Undoubtedly,' he said, 'all invitees might appear as Indians conjointly bent on achieving India's natural goal, and not as persons representing several sections of the Indian society. That is how I have viewed the Bhulabhai-Liaqat Ali understanding which I suppose has laid the foundation for the forthcoming Viceregal Conference. Sri Bhulabhai Desai's proposal has no such colouring as the Viceregal broadcast would seem to have.' Again, on 18 June, Gandhiji said that, if the omission of the Hindu Mahasabha was a method of putting the Congress in its place and treating it as a sectional or Hindu body, the Congress would avoid the whole affair. But there was, he conceded, another construction, namely, that the British Government wanted to avoid the Conference being based on religious distinction and had therefore invited political representatives only. Against this favourable assumption had undoubtedly to be put the parity between Muslims and Caste Hindus. But, said Gandhiji, he had publicly announced that he believed this mistake, however grave, to be one of ignorance, and that if his assumption were correct it would be rectified. Gandhiji added that, thinking along the same lines, he accounted for the omission of the Muslim Majlis and similar bodies.

The members of the Congress Working Committee were released on 15 June. About a week later, the Working Committee met in Bombay. (This, incidentally, was after a lapse of nearly three years). The Committee decided that the Congress should participate in the Conference as an organization and permitted those whom the Viceroy had invited to attend.

On 15 June, *Dawn*, the official organ of the Muslim League, came out with a statement on the proposed reconstruction of the Executive Council, protesting that 'with regard to the Muslim moiety, the Musalmans will tolerate no infiltration of non-League stooges to humour any party.'

On the same day, Jinnah telegraphed that he would require some clarification of the broadcast, which he hoped would be available when he met the Viceroy (as previously arranged) on the 24th; that this would enable him to consult his Working Committee and decide upon their course of action, and that the date of the Conference should be postponed for the purpose by a fortnight. He reciprocated the Viceroy's appeal for co-operation and goodwill and assured him that the Muslim League would make its contribution to any just and reasonable interim provisional settlement. The Viceroy told Jinnah in reply that his intention was to deal at the Conference itself with any points requiring clarification; that he deprecated any discussions on the subject before the Conference met; that he preferred to adhere to the date, namely 25 June, for the opening of the Conference and hoped Jinnah would attend. The Viceroy also suggested that Jinnah might arrange for his Working Committee to meet at Simla. Jinnah sent a reply in which he said that he had noted the Viceroy's intention to deal at the Conference itself with points requiring clarification. He added that till he had a complete picture of the Viceroy's proposals, the Working Committee would not be able to deal with them. He suggested that the fixing of the meeting of the Working Committee on or before 25 June was fraught with difficulties. The Viceroy replied as follows:

May I take it (a) that you and others invited who are members of the Muslim League will attend the Conference on the 25th but (b) that you will wish to consult your Working Committee when the proposals have been made clear to you at the Conference. I suggest that long adjournment of the Conference might be most inconvenient to others attending and that your Committee might meet in Simla before the end of June.

Jinnah's response to this was that, after discussing with the Viceroy on the 24th, he would be better able to inform him, firstly whether the members of the League would attend the Conference on 25 June, and secondly whether the Working Committee should be called at the end of June as suggested by the Viceroy. Jinnah added that the press had reported that the Viceroy contemplated revising his broadcast plan without consulting the League; if that were true, it would lead to more difficulties and would serve further to retard the chances of success of the Viceroy's task.

The Hindu Mahasabha was aggrieved at not having been invited to the Conference. In any case, it was opposed to the proposal of parity between Caste Hindus and Muslims in the Executive Council and strongly worded resolutions were passed against the proposals. The Mahasabha even staged some public demonstrations of protest and declared a *hartal* on 8 July.

On 24 June, the Viceroy had separate interviews with Azad, Gandhiji and Jinnah.

Azad (who was accompanied by Govind Ballabh Pant, former Congress premier of the United Provinces), appeared to accept the general principles of the Viceroy's proposals. He agreed that it was essential for success that all parties should co-operate with the Viceroy and with one another in the prosecution of the war against Japan; that the new members of the Council should be first-class men, capable of really getting down to India's problems, and that they must be genuine political leaders who had the confidence of their parties and of India as a whole and who could take independent decisions. But he contended that the Working Committee had received inadequate notice of the Conference; that all Congress prisoners, especially those who were members of the All-India Congress Committee, should have been released, and that the Conference would have to adjourn to permit the Congress delegates to consult further with the Working Committee. The Congress, he said, was more interested in the end than in the means, and wanted to be clear that the proposals were intended to facilitate and not to obstruct a final settlement. He also raised the question of the Viceroy's overriding powers. The Viceroy explained that this was part of the chain of responsibility through him to the Secretary of State for India and to Parliament, and that the power must remain. Azad then referred to the defence portfolio. While the Congress had no objection to the Commander-in-Chief retaining this portfolio and would use its influence to support the war effort, it hoped that the Indian Army would be brought closer to the people and become a real national army. Further, the Congress regarded it as fundamental that the countries liberated from Japan should not be kept in subjection. Finally he dealt with the parity issue. The Congress, he said, would not fight on the principle of parity between Hindus other than Scheduled Castes and Muslims, but it would fight on the method of selection. The Congress must have a say in the representation of communities other than the Hindu community, and would not agree to Muslim names being put forward by only one communal organization.

Gandhiji gave his blessing generally to the proposals. But, like Azad, he pointed out that all political prisoners, and not merely the members of the Working Committee, should have been released. He maintained his objection to the term 'Caste Hindus' and said he would have preferred to call them 'Non-Scheduled Hindus'. He questioned the Viceroy about coalitions in provinces; in his view, the minorities should be represented in the provinces only by members of their body belonging to the Congress. The Viceroy told him that the essential thing was that the minorities should be represented by someone they trusted and that it was this psychological factor that was important. Gandhiji then referred to the position of the Secretary of State's Services, claiming that they should everywhere be responsible to the governments under which they worked and not to the Secretary of State. The Viceroy said that the Indian Civil Service could be trusted to carry out the instructions of the Executive. Gandhiji then inquired about the method of selecting the members of the new Council. The Viceroy told him that he would probably ask for panels of names. Gandhiji dealt with the parity issue on the same lines as Azad. Finally, he said that he did not regard himself as representing the Congress or any other body and would much prefer not to attend the Conference, but if the Viceroy wished, he would stay on in Simla for the period of the Conference.

Jinnah took the line that under the proposals the Muslims would always be in a minority, for the smaller minorities would vote with the Hindus. He suggested that if the majority of the Muslims were opposed to any measure, it should not go by vote. This arrangement, the Viceroy pointed out, would be quite undemocratic. Jinnah then claimed that the Muslim League had the right to nominate the Muslim members, and referred to the League's success in recent by-elections as justifying its claim to represent the whole of the Muslims of India. He was opposed to the representation of Punjab Unionists or Congress Muslims. He made it clear that the Muslims would expect a fair share of the key portfolios. He hinted at the possibility of adjourning the Conference so as to enable him to consult his Working Committee.

The way was now cleared for the holding of the Conference. The main problems that were likely to confront it were the question of parity between Muslims and Hindus other than Scheduled Castes in the new Executive Council, and the demand of the League to nominate the entire Muslim quota. Another factor of some importance was the apprehension of the Punjab Unionists that a Congress-League coalition at the Centre and in the Section 93 provinces would lead to political instability in the Punjab.

The Conference assembled in the Viceregal Lodge, Simla, at 11 a.m. on 25 June. There were twenty-one invitees.[1] By a coincidence, the Conference itself was made up, apart from the European, Scheduled Caste and Sikh representatives, of an equal number of Hindus and Muslims. In his introductory remarks, the Viceroy welcomed the delegates as men who by character and ability had risen to leadership in their provinces and parties. He asked for their help in a spirit of broad co-operation towards the good of India as a whole. What was proposed was not a constitutional settlement or a final solution of India's problems, nor did the plan in any way prejudge or prejudice the final issue. But if it succeeded, he was sure that it would pave the way towards a settlement. 'The statesmanship, wisdom and goodwill of all of us,' said the Viceroy, 'is here on trial, not merely in the eyes of India but before the whole world.' It was necessary to rise above the level of old prejudices and enmities and

---

[1] The members of the Conference were as follows: (1) Abul Kalam Azad, President of the Congress; (2) P. N. Banerjee, leader of the Nationalist Party in the Indian Legislative Assembly; (3) Bhulabhai Desai, leader of the Congress Party in the Indian Legislative Assembly; (4) Sir Ghulam Hussain Hidayatullah, Premier of Sind; (5) Hossain Imam, leader of the Muslim League Party in the Council of State; (6) M. A. Jinnah, President of the Muslim League; (7) Liaqat Ali Khan, Deputy Leader of the Muslim League Party in the Indian Legislative Assembly; (8) Khizr Hyat Khan, Premier of the Punjab; (9) B. G. Kher, ex-Premier of Bombay; (10) G. S. Motilal, leader of the Congress Party in the Council of State; (11) Khwaja Sir Nazimuddin, ex-Premier of Bengal; (12) Govind Ballabh Pant, ex-Premier of the United Provinces; (13) The Maharaja of Parlakimedi, ex-Premier of Orissa; (14) C. Rajagopalachari, ex-Premier of Madras; (15) Sir Henry Richardson, leader of the European Group in the Indian Legislative Assembly; (16) Sir Mahomed Saadullah, Premier of Assam; (17) Dr Khan Sahib, Premier of the North-West Frontier Province; (18) Ravi Shankar Shukla, ex-Premier of the Central Provinces; (19) Master Tara Singh (Sikhs); (20) Sri Krishna Sinha, ex-Premier of Bihar; (21) N. Sivaraj (Scheduled Castes).

Gandhiji did not attend, but stayed on in Simla for the period of the Conference.

of party and sectional advantage and to think of the good of the four hundred million people of India. He went on to say that until there was an agreed change in the constitution, he was responsible to His Majesty's Government for the good government and tranquillity of India, and that they would have to accept his leadership. He asked them to believe in him as a sincere friend of India and as one who would endeavour to guide the discussions of the Conference in what he believed to be the best interests of the country. He commended to them as a guide the words engraved on the column crowned by the Star of India in front of the Viceroy's House in New Delhi—'In Thought Faith, in Word Wisdom, in Deed Courage, in Life Service, so may India be great.'

The Viceroy announced that Sir Evan Jenkins and I would function as Secretaries to the Conference. He impressed on the members the importance of keeping the proceedings confidential. The sittings would not be open to the press, but at the end of each day a statement, drafted by the Secretaries, would be issued to it with the approval of the Conference.

Lord Wavell then referred to the copies of the Secretary of State's statement and his own broadcast, which had been put together in a convenient form for purposes of easy comparison and supplied to all the members. He proposed to go through the compilation page by page, so as to leave no doubt as to the scope and intention of the proposals. It was not the purpose at that stage to discuss the merits or demerits of the proposals, but only to ascertain whether their meaning was quite clear. Members would have an opportunity later on to discuss their general principles.

By way of introduction to the discussion the Viceroy stated that the proposals were not intended in any way as a substitute for the final goal of Indian self-government, but as a step towards it. They were put forward in the hope that working together on common problems might make the approach to a final settlement easier. He stressed the importance of the parties sending their very best men to the new Executive Council and of everybody sinking party differences so as to establish a real national government 'where none are for a party and all are for the State.' The same sincere determination to co-operate in a common programme was needed in the provinces. Both at the Centre and in the provinces the interests of the minorities— Indian Christians, Anglo-Indians and others—would have to be considered and dealt with sympathetically and generously.

The Conference thereafter proceeded to discuss the texts of the Secretary of State's statement and the Viceroy's broadcast. The points raised and the explanations given are dealt with below.

With reference to the expression 'Caste Hindus'[1], the Viceroy said that no offence was intended; that the expression simply meant Hindus not belonging to the Scheduled Castes.

With regard to the phrase, 'so far as the interests of British India are concerned', this only meant that relations with Indian States were a matter for the Crown Representative and that the Governor-General-in-Council had nothing to do with them.

The Viceroy observed that if the Conference were successful, the members of the new Executive Council would not be able to take office immediately, because the Ninth Schedule to the Government of India Act, 1935, required that three members of the Executive Council must be persons who had been in the service of the Crown for at least ten years and the Act would therefore have to be amended. Owing to the dissolution of Parliament, the amendment would have to wait till August. The Viceroy was considering whether there was any other means of doing something before then. Kher asked whether it would not be possible to amend the relevant provision by an Order in Council. The Viceroy replied that that was not possible.

Regarding the proposal to have a British High Commissioner in India, the Viceroy explained that, as things stood, if His Majesty's Government wished to safeguard British interests which impinged on Indian problems, it could only be done through the Governor-General. The proposal meant that British interests would be dealt with by the High Commissioner, instead of by the Governor-General or the departments of the Government of India. This was a step on the road to Dominion Status or Independence.

With regard to external affairs, if the Conference were successful, an Indian Member would be in charge of this portfolio instead of the Governor-General. Hossain Imam (leader of the Muslim League Party in the Council of State) raised the question whether the Commonwealth Relations Department would be amalgamated with the Department of External Affairs. The Viceroy said that this was a matter which could be discussed later. He was inclined to think that the Foreign Office and the Commonwealth Relations Department should both be in the external affairs portfolio; this he understood

---

[1] See paragraph 3 of the Viceroy's broadcast (Appendix II).

was the practice in the Dominions. Dr Khan Sahib said that he wanted to raise the point as to the treatment of tribal and frontier matters being part of the defence of India. The Viceroy explained that for the moment he was considering the whole question and it might be that tribal areas would have to be included in external affairs.

On the question of the power of the Governor-General to override his Executive Council in the interests of the safety, tranquillity and interests of British India, the Viceroy said that this was part of the chain of responsibility to Parliament.

He emphasized that the interim Government would not commit anyone for the future. If, however, the new Executive Council decided to put forward a long-term solution, it would be open to them to do so.

The Viceroy explained the three main tasks of the new Executive Council. Their first and most pressing task would be the effective prosecution of the war against Japan. With regard to agreement about the future constitution, he thought that after some experience of the working of government, the new Executive Council might constitute a body to study the various constitutions of the world, e.g. the U.S.A. and Canada, and to suggest whether any of their provisions would suit Indian conditions. The Viceroy made it clear that for the present the proposals did not affect the Indian States, but if the new Executive Council decided to take up the question of a long-term solution, it would be necessary to consider the question of associating the Indian States in the framing of a new constitution.

Govind Ballabh Pant raised the question of persons imprisoned before the disturbances of August 1942. Dr Khan Sahib pointed out that Section 401 of the Criminal Procedure Code permitted provincial governments to suspend, remit or commute sentences and that provincial governments would therefore ultimately decide the question.

The Viceroy explained that in provinces where there were ministries the question of fresh elections would be one for the provincial governments to decide.

After this the morning session of the Conference terminated.

The Conference reassembled at 2.30 p.m. and discussions on general principles followed.

Azad began by asserting that while he was aware that the present proposals were purely for an interim settlement, the Congress could not possibly be a party to anything, however temporary, that prejudiced its national character, tended to impair the growth of nationalism, or reduced the Congress directly or indirectly to the level of a

communal body. He attached considerable importance to the declaration that the provisional plan was only a preliminary step towards
facilitating and expediting the attainment of independence for
India. The Congress Working Committee wished to co-operate in
any reasonable way towards resolving the deadlock, but its decisions
would require to be confirmed by the All-India Congress Committee.
Information on the following points was necessary, namely (1) the
scope and functions of the proposed External Affairs Department;
(2) the giving of a national character to the Indian Army and the
removing of barriers isolating it from the national Government and
the people; (3) the policy with regard to the liberated countries in
South-East Asia after the war; and (4) the relations between the
national Government and the Indian States and States' people.

Jinnah said that he could not understand the relevance of some of
Azad's observations and suggested that the Viceroy should elucidate
those issues before he attempted to make his own observations. The
Viceroy proceeded to do so.

Dealing first with the External Affairs Department, the Viceroy
explained that the subjects under its control comprised foreign
affairs proper, e.g. relations with foreign countries such as the United
States, China, Afghanistan, Persia and Iraq; relations with the tribes
on the north-west and on the north-east of India; the administration of British Baluchistan, and the affairs of certain frontier States.
Foreign Affairs and Tribal Relations were administered by the
Governor-General in Council; British Baluchistan was the responsibility of the Governor-General in his discretion. The Frontier States
were in relations with the Crown Representative and were dealt
with in the External Affairs Department only as a matter of convenience. But at the same time, on all matters of policy affecting these
States, the External Affairs Department consulted the Political
Department before taking decisions. It was quite clear that foreign
affairs proper would be transferred to the new Indian Member.
The other subjects were under expert examination and he could not
say how they would finally be allotted.

The Viceroy said he was not quite clear what Azad had in mind
with regard to the Indian Army. No government could permit its
army to take part in politics. The Indian Army had done splendidly
during the war and had enhanced its own and India's reputation.
He believed it to be a contented army and he thought the delegates
did not realize what rapid progress had been made with indianization

during the war. He would certainly oppose any suggestion that the Indian Army should be brought into politics. On the other hand, he wished it to be a truly national army, efficient and contented.

The Viceroy explained that the future of the occupied territories in South-East Asia was a matter in which several governments were interested. The Government of India would be entitled to express any views it pleased, but it could not expect to have the last word.

Azad had referred to relations with the Indian States, which though part of India, were not under the jurisdiction of the Governor-General in Council. The Viceroy explained that the Government of India was in close relations with the Indian States, e.g. on commercial and economic matters, but unless a federal constitution, embracing both British-Indian provinces and States, were introduced, there could be no question of a central Government exercising control over the States.

On the question of the Congress goal of independence, the Viceroy referred to the Secretary of State's speech of 14 June, which made it quite clear that His Majesty's Government's offer was based on two main principles, namely (1) that no limit was set to India's freedom to decide her own destiny, whether as a free partner within the Commonwealth, or even without it; and (2) that this could only be achieved under a constitution or constitutions framed by Indians, to which the main elements were consenting parties.

In conclusion, the Viceroy assured Azad that there was nothing in the proposals to brand the Congress as a communal body.

At this stage Jinnah interjected with the remark that the Congress represented only Hindus. Dr Khan Sahib, the Congress premier of the North-West Frontier Province, objected vehemently to this statement. The Viceroy observed that the Congress evidently represented its members, and Jinnah said that he accepted this.

P. N. Banerjee (Nationalist leader, central Assembly) deplored the omission from the Conference of the Hindu Mahasabha, the non-Congress and non-League Muslim organizations (the Krishak Proja Party of Bengal, Momins, etc.) and the Indian Christians. He also said that Pandit Madan Mohan Malaviya should have been invited. He stressed that complete independence was the goal, and deprecated a communal approach to the problem. He said that parity between Hindus, other than the Scheduled Castes, and Muslims had been generally condemned throughout India and that the feeling on this subject was serious. He urged the immediate release of political prisoners.

Sir Henry Richardson (European Group leader, central Assembly) said that his party supported the proposals and if it could help in any way, it would be only too glad to do so.

Khizr Hyat Khan (Premier, Punjab) said that the proposals, though put forward as a short-term plan, must clearly affect the future to some extent. The reservation of defence might not be effective if the Army were to be subjected to financial control by an Indian member. He could not say how the proposals would affect the long-term solution until he knew the composition of the new Executive Council.

The Maharajah of Parlakimedi (ex-Premier, Orissa) welcomed the Conference, but said that the interests of persons who had supported the war effort should not be neglected.

Master Tara Singh (Sikhs) said that he approved the proposals in general, but that everything would depend on the spirit in which they were worked; that by coming together the parties might in the end drift further apart. The Sikhs did not identify themselves with the Congress, though in so far as the Congress favoured India's freedom they were in sympathy with it. He thought the future of the Indian Army needed careful consideration. It had its own history and traditions, and new ideas about it might injure people who had served the country well.

Sivaraj (Scheduled Castes) said that his community did not intend to be obstructive. If it asked for safeguards, it was doing so only for its own protection and certainly did not wish to stand in the way of progress. So far as he was able to judge, the proposals were for an interim arrangement and he did not understand how any general principles could apply to them.

Sir Mahommed Saadullah (Premier of Assam) criticized Banerjee's speech, asserting that the Conference was sufficiently representative and that he was against the inclusion of the Mahasabha.

Jinnah spoke at some length. He said that he understood His Majesty's Government's proposals to represent a stop-gap arrangement. They in no way affected the Congress stand for independence, or the Muslim League stand for Pakistan. The future constitution of India could only be framed by agreement, and the British Government had made it clear that it was not going to impose it on the country. The Muslim League could not in any circumstances agree to a constitution on any basis other than that of Pakistan; its attitude was fundamentally opposed to the Congress demand for a united India and a

common central Government. Jinnah then read out the resolution of
the Muslim League Working Committee of 20 August 1942, which
declared that 'the Muslim League has been, and is, ready and willing
to consider any proposals and negotiate with any party on a footing
of equality for the setting up of a provisional Government of India in
order to mobilize the resources of the country for the purpose of the
defence of India and the successful prosecution of the war,' provided
that the demand for Pakistan was conceded unequivocally. He recognized that the task of framing a constitution on the basis of Pakistan was a complex one and would take time. For that reason, unlike
the Congress, which wanted independence here and now, the Muslim
League did not demand that Pakistan should be conceded immediately. He did not himself doubt the sincerity behind His Majesty's
Government's offer and agreed that they should not examine it in a
spirit of carping criticism. He said that it would do no good to start
questioning each other's representative character and, so far as the
League was concerned, it was prepared to help in every way possible
without jeopardizing its own interests. He conceded that the Congress represented about 90 per cent of the Hindus, but claimed that
the Muslim League represented 90 per cent or more of the Muslims.
Of course, there were Muslim, Sikh and Scheduled Caste people in
the Congress, but they were not many. It would not be helpful to
suggest that the Congress had a hold over all communities. Jinnah
did not commit himself to any definite conclusion, but appeared to
support the proposals subject to a decision acceptable to him on the
question of communal parity.

The Viceroy answered the points taken by Banerjee and Sivaraj.
To the former he said that he had made the Conference as representative as he could without making it unwieldy. To the latter, he pointed out that the principles he had in mind were a sincere desire to
co-operate; the willingness to put forward first-class men to take office;
the determination to prosecute the war against Japan, and so on.

The Conference adjourned till the next day. Meanwhile, the Viceroy had a statement prepared in consultation with his advisers. This
statement split up the proposals for discussion into their component
elements under two heads, namely, (a) those primarily for agreement
between the parties and the Viceroy; and (b) those primarily for
settlement between the parties themselves.

When the Conference met again on 26 June, the Viceroy gave each
of the invitees a copy of the statement, which raised the following issues:

A. *Subject to agreement under B*, is the Conference prepared to agree to an Executive Council:

(*i*) publicly committed to the three tasks set out in the Viceroy's broadcast;

(*ii*) consisting of men of influence and ability recommended by the Conference, and prepared to take decisions and the responsibility for them;

(*iii*) with all portfolios (including external affairs) held by Indian Members, except the war portfolio which would be held by the Commander-in-Chief;

(*iv*) having within it an equal number of Muslims and Hindus other than Scheduled Castes; and

(*v*) working in all respects under the present constitution, including the constitutional provisions for control by the Secretary of State and the Governor-General.

B. *Subject to agreement under A*, is further agreement possible on:

(*i*) the strength and composition of the Executive Council by parties and communities; and

(*ii*) the method by which panels of names will be submitted to the Viceroy to enable him to make his recommendations for appointment to the new Executive Council.

The Viceroy suggested that the Conference should take Part A of the statement item by item and that the members should then proceed to make whatever observations they had to offer on them. On the first item regarding the three tasks of the new Council, G. S. Motilal (leader of the Congress Party in the Council of State) raised the question of the bearing of the proposals on the Cripps plan. This gave the Viceroy the opportunity of explaining that if the Council were reconstructed, it would continue until it broke down, or until a new constitution agreed by all the parties was framed; also that the Cripps proposals regarding a constitution-making body still stood if the parties thought that those proposals would afford the best way of finding a long-term solution.

As regards item (ii), Lord Wavell said that the men selected for the Executive Council must be men of influence and ability and such as were prepared to take decisions and the responsibility for them without reference to outside authorities. Govind Ballabh Pant suggested that what the Viceroy had said was an elementary principle governing all cabinets.

Items (i), (ii) and (iii) were accepted by the Conference. The discussions in fact proceeded smoothly until item (iv) relating to communal parity was reached. Banerjee said that as a nationalist he took strong exception to parity between Muslims and Caste Hindus, first because communalism was an antiquated idea and secondly, because Hindus could not be divided into two sections — Caste and non-Caste. The Executive Council should be selected on the basis of ability and capacity. It might consist wholly of Muslims, or of Scheduled Caste men, if they had the confidence of the people, but parity between Hindus and Muslims was illogical and absurd. It brought a community of 250 millions down to the level of a community of 90 millions. He pleaded only for fairness and justice. The newspapers had in recent weeks shown the strength of public feeling on this question. Also, he thought that the Scheduled Castes had not been fairly treated — they were in danger of being squeezed out. The Viceroy said that he and many others would agree that communalism was deplorable, but in India it was, at the time, a fact from which there was no escape. He was sure that if, later on, the Conference recommended names, fairness and justice would be borne in mind.

Banerjee went on to say that a good many people thought that the parity stipulation arose from the British desire to continue a system of 'divide and rule'. He did not take this view himself, but it was quite generally held.

Sivaraj confirmed the objection of the Scheduled Castes to the grant to Muslims of parity with Caste Hindus, without regard to the rights of other minorities. He referred to the 1940 discussions between Jinnah and Lord Linlithgow in which (according to Sivaraj) any weightage arranged at the expense of the Hindus was to be shared between the minorities. He thought that parity in the Executive Council might lead to Muslim claims for parity in the Services and in the Indian Army. He disagreed with Banerjee as to the position of the Scheduled Castes. It was right that they should be considered separately from the main Hindu community.

Jinnah said that Sivaraj had misinterpreted the suggestion made in 1940. At that time there was no definite mention of the Scheduled Castes, or of any minority other than the Muslims. His proposals to Lord Linlithgow concerned the entry of the Congress and the Muslim League into the Executive Council with one, or possibly two, members from the other minorities. The League had suggested parity with the Congress, but if the Congress stood out, it claimed a majority in the Executive Council — because it was clear that the main responsibility for the administration would then rest on the League. There had never been any question of a distribution of weightage over all the minorities.

Azad said that the Congress view was that the members of the Council should be appointed on a political and not on a communal basis. The Congress did not object to the parity proposal, but had strong views about the door through which the members would enter.

Pant expressed his dislike of communal parity. A national government formed on a communal basis was really a contradiction in terms. The Congress did not worry much about the number of places in the Council assigned to one community or another, but was concerned with the parties to which the members belonged.

The other delegates more or less agreed in principle to the parity proposal. Rajagopalachari said that he thought of the Hindus and Muslims as two electoral bodies rather than as two communities. Dr Khan Sahib expressed the view that only a revolution would cure the communal problem.

Banerjee asked the Viceroy to explain the genesis and basis of the parity proposal. The Viceroy replied that the proposal had been made on grounds of expediency and that Banerjee would have an opportunity of having his dissent recorded when the recommendations of the Conference took final shape.

On item (v), Banerjee suggested that a convention should be established from the outset by which the Viceroy would not overrule his Executive Council. Lord Wavell said this was not possible, but that the Viceroy's powers would not be used unreasonably. Sivaraj asked whether the Viceroy's veto would be sufficient to protect the position of the minorities, including the Depressed Classes; if not, the law should be amended. Lord Wavell read out the passage from Amery's speech in Parliament in which he had said that, so long as there was no Indian constitution under which controversial issues could ultimately be resolved, the Viceroy's overriding power was a necessary protection for the minorities, whether against immediate injury, or against decisions which might prejudice the constitutional future. This, he said, should reassure the minorities. Pant hoped that, as in the existing Council, the Viceroy would have no occasion to use his veto in the reconstructed Council, and Lord Wavell said that no one would be happier than himself if that were to be so. B. G. Kher said that he would prefer to rely upon their resources rather than on the Viceroy; what was required was goodwill and amity, and if the

Executive Council worked as a team it would not ordinarily be possible for the Viceroy to overrule them.

The Viceroy then passed on to Part B of the statement. He said that there were three possible methods of dealing with it. First, there might be a private discussion among the delegates, including, if necessary, discussions between the leaders and himself; secondly, the Conference might decide to appoint a committee to report to the Conference; thirdly, the first two methods might be combined. In any case, there would have to be a later discussion in a full meeting of the Conference. He would like to have the views of the Conference on these suggestions and its advice as to whether it would be suitable to have a general discussion on the strength of the Executive Council before the other matters were taken up. At the suggestion of Rajagopalachari, supported by Jinnah and Azad, it was decided to adjourn the Conference to enable the parties to consult among themselves.

The next meeting, on the 27th, lasted for about an hour. It was agreed that the meeting should be adjourned in order to enable Pant and Jinnah to continue the informal conversations which they had begun the previous day.

The Viceroy said it might help if he stated his own position. He wished to make it clear that he had three obligations to the British Government; first, however the composition of the new Executive Council might be arrived at, he must maintain equality of numbers as between Muslims and Hindus other than Scheduled Castes; secondly, he must make a positive act of selection and could not accept any names merely because they bore particular party labels; and thirdly, he must satisfy himself that the persons selected would work together harmoniously and without friction and would be capable of discharging the first two of the three tasks enumerated in his broadcast, and of approaching the third task in a spirit of conciliation. This meant that the new Council as a whole must command the confidence of the country. The Viceroy said that the result of the meeting between Pant and Jinnah would be reported to him and that, if necessary, he himself would be very ready to help. He gave an assurance that delegates from parties other than the Congress would have an opportunity of submitting names in due course. The Conference was adjourned till 29 June.

On the evening of the 27th, Jinnah saw the Viceroy and after a long discussion made it clear that while he could not agree to the appointment to the Executive Council of Muslims who did not belong to the League, he would be prepared to place before his Working Committee any formula which the Viceroy thought suitable.

When the Conference met for the fourth time on 29 June, it was evident that the Congress and the Muslim League had failed to agree. It was reported that Pant and Jinnah had met, that their discussions had been inconclusive, and that they could not see a way out. Accordingly, Lord Wavell felt that he must intervene. He informed the Conference that since no progress had been made and it was not certain that a further adjournment would be useful, it should be assumed that the discussions between the major parties had broken down. He had hoped that there would at least be some preliminary agreement between them, into which lesser interests could subsequently be fitted. It was possible that the present difficulties arose from concentration on party and communal quotas, or, in other words, from an attempt to find an arithmetical formula to which everyone was prepared to agree. He now proposed a different approach — more personal, if less logical — that might commend itself to the Conference. If all the interests represented at the Conference would send him by a specified date, lists of the persons whom they would like to be included in the Executive Council, he would consider them, possibly add some names of his own, and try to produce on paper a list of persons who would be acceptable to all concerned. He did not suggest that the various interests should confine themselves exclusively to the names of persons belonging to their own parties, but he would like a distinction made between people who were regarded as party members and others. If the Conference accepted this suggestion, he would ask that the lists should contain more names than the number of seats in the Council likely to be available to any one interest. He presumed that Jinnah and Azad would send him lists from the Muslim League and the Congress respectively. He would like not less than eight and not more than twelve names from each of the parties. Sivaraj (Scheduled Castes) might send him four, and the remaining delegates, namely Banerjee, the Maharaja of Parlakimedi, Khizr Hyat Khan and Master Tara Singh, might send three names each. He made it clear that these numbers referred to party members only and that any outside names submitted would be in addition. After scrutinizing the lists, and if necessary taking into consideration any additional names of his own, he would attempt to form on paper an Executive Council of the kind he and His Majesty's Government had in mind, and he would then put his proposals to the Conference.

Azad said that the difficulties concerned not only the composition but the strength of the Executive Council. The Congress could not give up their claim to include members of all communities in their list, and particularly the Scheduled Castes and Christians. Before sending his list he would want to consult his Working Committee. In reply to an inquiry from Jinnah, Azad affirmed that Muslim names would also be included in the Congress list.

Khizr Hyat Khan and the Maharaja of Parlakimedi suggested that the lists to be sent by the party leaders should be kept secret and that the party leaders should be consulted before the final list was placed before the Conference. The Viceroy explained that the lists sent to him would be kept secret and that before he put final proposals before the Conference he would consult the party leaders. Master Tara Singh suggested that if the final proposals were not accepted, there should be general elections, after which the Viceroy might try again.

Sivaraj objected to the Congress claim to nominate representatives of the Scheduled Castes. He said that they represented a separate element in the national life of India and had been recognized as such. He felt very strongly that the representation of Scheduled Castes in the Executive Council should be as favourable as that allowed to the Muslims. He would not press for parity but would insist that the number of Scheduled Caste members should bear the same ratio to their population as the Muslim members bore to theirs. He wished to consult the Working Committee of his Federation before he committed himself even to the sending in of a list.

Jinnah said that he was still without a complete picture of the Viceroy's proposal. According to his reading, the members of the Conference were attending in their personal capacity to advise the Viceroy in the selection of persons for the new Executive Council. He regarded certain matters as being of vital importance and when he knew exactly what was proposed he would take the League's decision. He himself sincerely desired to help and was fully appreciative of the Viceroy's intervention, but he was not prepared to commit himself immediately to sending in a list. He would like to consult his Working Committee first.

The Viceroy pointed out that he could not impose a settlement on any party or individual. But he had a responsibility, and his suggestion had been put forward in order to prevent a breakdown. Most of the delegates had promised to send in their lists within a week. He had no intention of requiring any delegate to put forward names in addition to the numbers asked for from his own party. He had only said that it might help him if the lists were also to include some outside names. In response to a request from Jinnah, the Viceroy promised to send him a written statement of the procedure suggested. He concluded by saying that he would inform the members as soon as possible of the date on which the Conference would meet again. (It was later decided to adjourn the Conference till 14 July).

By this time it was known throughout the country that the Conference was facing a crisis and that the question at issue was the manner in which the Muslim members of the Executive Council should be selected. The contentions of the Congress and the Muslim League became the subject of numerous statements by politicians and publicists all over India. It happened that at this time the fortunes of the Muslim League in the provinces were at a low ebb. Of the provinces which at one time had been controlled by predominantly League ministries, in the Punjab the Muslim members of the Unionist Party had definitely broken away from the League; in the North-West Frontier Province the Congress Party under Dr Khan Sahib had taken control; in Bengal, Nazimuddin had been defeated in the Assembly and the province was being administered by the Governor; while in Sind and Assam the Muslim League ministries were in power on Congress sufferance. These facts were publicly emphasized in numerous statements, many of them made by Muslims who did not profess allegiance to the League. Nevertheless, the spokesmen of the League continued to press the claim that it was the League, and the League alone, that represented the Muslims.

Both the Congress and the Muslim League convened meetings of their respective Working Committees. The Congress Committee met on 3 July, and by the 6th had selected a panel of names which they submitted to the Viceroy. The Muslim League Working Committee met on 6 July. On the next day Jinnah wrote to the Viceroy making three suggestions — first, that the Muslim League should not be asked to submit a panel, but that its representatives should be chosen on the basis of personal discussion between the Viceroy and himself; secondly, that all the Muslim members of the Council should be chosen from the League; and thirdly, that some effective safeguard, other than the Viceroy's veto, should be provided to protect Muslim interests from majority decisions of the Council. On the 8th the Viceroy received Jinnah and had prolonged discussions with him on these points. On the 9th the Viceroy sent him a written reply in which he made it clear that he could not give any guarantee to the Muslim League that the Muslim members would be selected exclusively from the League's list, any more than he could give a similar guarantee to the other parties. He pleaded for the League's co-operation in the important tasks on which decisions would have to be taken in the next two or three years and added that it would be his principal duty to see fair play between all parties, not only in the composition of the proposed Council but in its working. Jinnah replied on the same day stating that since the required assurances were not forthcoming, his Committee could not furnish any list.

Lists of names had meanwhile been received from the other delegates concerned and the Viceroy made his provisional selections, using his own judgment with regard to Muslim League representatives. He ascertained that his selections would be acceptable to His Majesty's Government if they were accepted by the different parties. He saw Jinnah on the afternoon of 11 July and told him that he was prepared to include four members of the Muslim League, but that the fifth place would have to go to a Punjabi Muslim who did not belong to the League. He gave Jinnah the names of the Muslims included in his selections and said that, if Jinnah wished to substitute other League members for the four he had chosen, he would consider his suggestions. He would indeed be glad if Jinnah himself would agree to serve. He made it clear that with his selections there would be parity not only between Hindus and Muslims, but between the Congress and the League. The Viceroy finally added that he had not yet consulted the Congress, who might possibly not accept the arrangement he proposed.

Jinnah said at once that it was impossible for the Muslim League to co-operate unless (a) all five Muslim members of the Council were taken from the League, and (b) the Governor-General's power of veto were reinforced by a special safeguard for the Muslims within the Council, e.g. a provision that no decision objected to by the Muslims should be taken except by a clear two-thirds majority, or something of the kind.

The Viceroy said that he could not accept either of these conditions. Jinnah replied that if that were so, the Muslim League could not co-operate. He said that his Working Committee appreciated the sincerity of the Viceroy's intentions and realized that members of the League, by taking office, could have done much for the Muslims of India. On the other hand, the Working Committee could not abandon certain fundamental principles. The Viceroy thereupon informed

Jinnah that this meant the failure of his efforts, and that he would make a statement to that effect to the Conference on 14 July.

Soon after his talk with Jinnah, Lord Wavell sent for Sir Francis Mudie (the Home Member), Sir Evan Jenkins and myself and informed us that he had been in communication with the Secretary of State and that it had been decided that the proposals should not be proceeded with. I personally was terribly disappointed, for I had been pressing consistently on the Viceroy that Jinnah's claim that the Muslim League represented the will of all the Muslims of India was quite untenable; that we could not let down the Unionist Party which alone, contrary to the League's claims, could speak for the Punjab; that in the interests of the Punjab we should not compromise with the League, but should go ahead with our plans. My argument was that if we conceded Jinnah's claims, we should logically be conceding his demand for Pakistan. Even on that basis, the Muslim League should not be entitled to a greater standing than that which was due to a future State of Pakistan,—which could not possibly claim to represent the millions of non-Muslims in the non-Pakistan areas of India. But the decision not to proceed with the proposals, we were told, was final and there was nothing more to be said.

On 11 July, the Viceroy saw Gandhiji and informed him that, in view of the unwillingness of the Muslim League to co-operate, except on its own terms, the Conference had failed. Gandhiji expressed no surprise but remarked that, as the Congress and the League, Hindus and Muslims, were irreconcilable, it would be necessary at some time for the British to decide between them. The Viceroy replied that an imposed settlement could hardly result in peace or self-government in India.

On 12 July the Viceroy explained the position to Khizr Hyat Khan, as well as to Azad and Pant, who showed some bitterness at the attitude of the Muslim League.

At the fifth and last session of the Conference on 14 July, the Viceroy made a statement in which he accepted full responsibility for the failure of the discussions. He said:

On the 29th June I undertook, with the approval of the Conference, to endeavour to produce a solution not based on any formula agreed in advance. I asked the parties to let me have lists of names, and said I would do what I could to produce a solution acceptable to the leaders and to the Conference.

I received lists from all parties represented here except from the

European Group (who decided not to send a list) and the Muslim League. I was, however, determined that the Conference should not fail until I had made every possible effort to bring it to a successful ending. I therefore made my provisional selections including certain Muslim League names, and I have every reason to believe that if these selections had been acceptable here, they would have been acceptable to His Majesty's Government.

My selections would, I think, have given a balanced and efficient Executive Council, whose composition would have been reasonably fair to all the parties. I did not find it possible, however, to accept the claims of any party in full. When I explained my solution to Mr. Jinnah he told me that it was not acceptable to the Muslim League, and he was so decided that I felt it would be useless to continue the discussions. In the circumstances I did not show my selections as a whole to Mr. Jinnah and there was no object in showing them to the other leaders.

The Conference has therefore failed. Nobody can regret this more than I do myself. I wish to make it clear that the responsibility for the failure is mine. The main idea underlying the Conference was mine. If it had succeeded, its success would have been attributed to me, and I cannot place the blame for its failure upon any of the parties. I ask the party leaders to accept this view, and to do all they can to ensure that there are no recriminations. It is of the utmost importance that this effort to secure agreement between the parties and communities should not result in a worsening of communal feeling. I ask you all to exercise the greatest possible restraint.

I have now to consider the next steps. I must remind you that, whatever happens, the first two of the three tasks mentioned in my broadcast — the prosecution of the war against Japan, and the carrying on of the administration and preparation for post-war development — must be performed by the Government of India for the time being in office. It will be my duty to see that these tasks are performed with the greatest energy that I can impose, and I cannot permit any hindrance to them.

I propose to take a little time to consider in what way I can best help India after the failure of the Conference. You can all help best by refraining from recriminations. The war against Japan must be carried on, and law and order must be maintained; and until I see my way more clearly than I do now, it may be difficult, perhaps impossible, to suggest any new move. No Government can carry on under the daily prospect of change or dissolution. I have to secure the stability and day-to-day efficiency of my Government, and it would be impossible to enter upon continuous or even frequent political discussions of this kind. Whatever decisions His Majesty's Government may take in the near future must therefore, in all probability, hold good for some little time.

I thank you all for the help you have given me, and for the restraint, patience and understanding which you have shown. Do not any of you be discouraged by this setback. We shall overcome our difficulties in the end. The future greatness of India is not in doubt.

Azad said that although the Viceroy had generously taken the blame for the failure of the Conference on his own shoulders, it really rested on those of others and it was important to recognize the true facts. The Viceroy had called the Conference, the delegates had accepted his invitation, and the Conference had assembled. Thereafter the Viceroy had been asked to clarify certain points in the proposals of His Majesty's Government, and he had done so. The Conference had then considered the strength and composition of the Executive Council, and was adjourned to enable the parties to arrive at an agreement on these matters. The difficulties of any agreement were well known. The Muslim League claimed the right to nominate all Muslim members of the Executive Council. This was a position which the Congress could not accept. By accepting it, the Congress would have reduced itself to a sectarian and Hindu organization, and thrown away the work of half a century. This was the Congress view and, as a Muslim, he agreed with it wholeheartedly. As a Muslim he was convinced that the Congress must carry the Muslims of India with it. The Congress had therefore rejected the Muslim League's claim, and private conversations had proved fruitless. The Viceroy was then compelled to intervene, and from the account he had just given of the further proceedings it was evident that he also had failed to convince the Muslim League. The Viceroy was right in rejecting its claim as he had apparently done. There was no doubt where the responsibility lay. In the circumstances it was now for the Viceroy to decide what to do. The communal problem had become so acute that, in the opinion of the Congress, it could only be solved by some final and just decision. The British Government could not divest itself of responsibility in this matter. There must be a decision based on justice and fair play, and such a decision, once taken, must be firmly enforced. A policy of expediency could produce no satisfactory results. By all means let the Viceroy consider the problem at leisure, but firmness would be needed and hesitation was only another name for weakness.

Azad concluded that he had reviewed and re-examined the line he had taken in the Conference, and was convinced that he had been right. The spirit which had animated him and his colleagues in the

Conference would continue to animate them outside it. He and his colleagues would not forget that the Viceroy had made a sincere attempt to solve the Indian problem. The difficulties had been insuperable, but the Viceroy had done his best and the Congress delegates were grateful.

The Viceroy thanked Azad and said he appreciated the efforts made by the Congress to help him. Azad had touched on the heart of a great problem about which he felt he could not say more at present. The Conference had to admit failure for the time being. Azad had referred to the weakness of a policy based on expediency. He would like to remind Azad that the British, with their long experience of politics and government, had found that many difficult problems could be solved only by compromise and on a basis of expediency.

Rajagopalachari said that postponement of a final solution until a great measure of agreement was reached was an understandable policy; but he could see no reason why an interim solution should be postponed. The negative attitude of any particular group or individual should not be allowed to stand in the way. He thought that the Viceroy might get away from communal principles and attempt a short-term solution on a territorial or administrative basis. The Congress had shown itself willing to co-operate even in a defective arrangement. He did not know the arrangement put forward by the Viceroy and rejected by Jinnah, but it was clear that the Conference had failed. He hoped the Viceroy would bear in mind the possibility of a settlement on a territorial or administrative basis.

Jinnah said he fully appreciated the efforts that the Viceroy had made and knew that he had done his best. He thought it unnecessary to apportion the blame for the failure of the Conference. The points at issue had been discussed at very great length and it was fruitless to go over them again. He fully endorsed what the Viceroy had said about communal bitterness and recriminations. It was essential that the parties should refrain from action that was likely to embitter party and communal relations. But when it was said, as it had been by the two previous speaker, that the Muslim League was responsible for the failure, he must remind the Conference of the fundamentals. The League and the Congress had an entirely different angle of vision. If the proposed Executive Council had come into being, every matter before it would have been looked at by the League and the Congress from entirely different points of view. The idea of Pakistan and the idea of a united India were incompatible. He recognized that pending a long-term solution the Viceroy had to carry on the government of the country whether the parties and communities agreed or not. He appealed to the Conference and to the Viceroy to put themselves in the shoes of the Muslim League. The League had repeatedly offered co-operation in the war effort and had raised no difficulties or obstacles. But the League was determined to have Pakistan. It would consider any proposal for an interim provisional government subject to two conditions: first, a declaration by His Majesty's Government giving Muslims the right of self-determination; and secondly the grant to Muslims of an equality with all other communities in the interim arrangement. The first of these conditions found no place in the present proposals. There had been an oblique reference to it in the Secretary of State's statement in Parliament and in the Viceroy's broadcast. This was not good enough, for an interim arrangement might well become permanent. As for the second condition, the proposals reduced Muslim representation to one-third. He himself had always felt great sympathy for the other minorities, but it was evident that since such minorities were not in a position to organize independent States of their own, they must take the Congress side. In the proposed new Council the Congress would thus have secured a permanent majority. The Viceroy's veto was an inadequate safeguard and the Muslim League would be content with nothing less than some form of veto exercisable on particular subjects by the League members, e.g. a provision that if a decision were challenged by a League member, it could be carried only if a specified majority were in favour of it. Again, as the composition of the proposed Council was admittedly communal, the Muslim League must insist that the Muslim members must be selected entirely by the League. He was told that this was not the national spirit, but the League did not accept the national spirit of the Congress. The League was the representative organization of all the Muslims of India. If it was expected to take administrative responsibility, it must be permitted to select its own men. The Congress had claimed two Muslims and the Punjab one Muslim. The League would apparently be left with two.[1] Moreover, the League objected strongly to the panel system suggested by the Viceroy. The Viceroy had reserved the right to select the members himself and to include non-League men among the Muslims. The Conference had really failed on this issue. It might be said that it was

[1] This was not in accordance with the offer made to him by Lord Wavell on 11 July — an offer of which no one else was aware.

a small point, but in fact it fundamentally affected the character and status of he League. Rajagopalachari had given some advice to the Viceroy. His own advice would be that the difference in the angle of vision between the Congress and the League would persist in any interim arrangement that might be devised. The League's fear was that the Congress would make use of any interim arrangement to consolida e its position and gradually to strangle Pakistan.

Banerjee deplored the fact that one party had been able to obstruct progress and suggested that the Viceroy should go ahead without the Muslim League; in any case, responsible government should be established in Section 93 provinces and all political prisoners should be released.

Khizr Hyat Khan admitted having asked for a seat for his own province. There were different schools of thought among the Muslims and he did not think any party should have a political monopoly.

Master Tara Singh suggested that the differences between the Congress and the Muslim League should be put to arbitration; he was quite prepared to agree to Pakistan if Jinnah on his part would agree to a separate State for the Sikhs. Pakistan was a far greater danger to the Sikhs than to the other communities.

Sivaraj said that the British were wrong in recognizing only two major parties. The sixty million members of the Scheduled Castes were a major element in the population and should be treated as such in any further attempt at a settlement.

The Viceroy thanked the delegates once more and said that he would take note of the observations made. The Conference then ended.

On the conclusion of the Conference the leaders of the main parties held a press conference at which they explained their respective viewpoints.

Azad said that the blame for failure rested mainly on the Muslim League, but he could not altogether absolve the British Government. If it had been really serious about settling the issue it would have foreseen the communal difficulties and been prepared to meet them. It ought not to have given the right of veto to any particular group to hold up the progress of the country. Azad contested the Muslim League claim to be the sole representative organization of the Muslims and pointed to the position in the provinces, in only two of which, namely Sind and Assam, the Muslim League ran the Government and even there it had to depend upon Congress support.

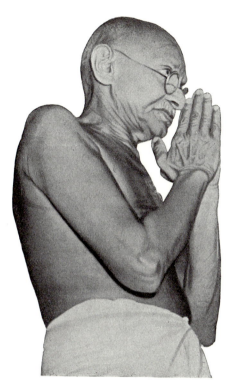

GANDHIJI

'Who has been our beacon light,
our guide and philosopher,
during the last thirty years'

*Rajendra Prasad's tribute in the*
*Constituent Assembly, 15 August 1947*

*Photograph by the courtesy of N. Parameswaran*

# 1. THE SIMLA CONFERENCE

Lord Wavell shaking hands with Ravi Shankar Shukla. Others in the picture are (L to R) Govind Ballabh Pant, Master Tara Singh, Jinnah, Maharajah of Parlakimedi, Hossain Imam, Srikrishna Sinha and Ghulam Hussain Hidayatullah

Lord Wavell speaking to G. S. Motila (L to R) The Author, Sir Evan Jenkin Lord Wavell, Lady Wavell, G. S. Motila P. N. Banerjea, N. Sivaraj, Master Tar Singh, Jinnah and Hossain Imar

Lord Wavell greeting Abul Kalam Azad, President of the Congress

2. THE SIMLA CONFERENCE

Author, Military Secretary to the Viceroy, Abul
Kalam Azad, Sir Evan Jenkins and Dr Khan Sahib

Lord Wavell receives Members of the Cabinet Mission at Palam Aerodrome in Delhi. (L to R) A. V. Alexander, Lord Pethick-Lawrence, Lord Wavell and Sir Stafford Cripps

The Cabinet Mission at work

abhı Sitaramayya, Vallabhbhai Patel, Shanker-
Deo, Lord Pethick-Lawrence and P. C. Ghosh

Cabinet Mission in discussion with Abul Kalam Azad.
(L to R) Lord Pethick-Lawrence, Abul Kalam Azad,
Asaf Ali, A. V. Alexander and Sir Stafford Cripps

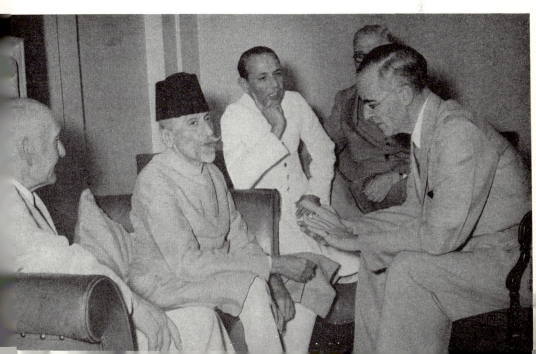

Members after being sworn in on 2 September 1946. (L to R)
Sarat Chandra Bose, Jagjivan Ram, Rajendra Prasad,
Vallabhbhai Patel, Asaf Ali, Nehru and Syed Ali Zaheer

5. THE INTERIM GOVERNM

Members after Muslim League nominees were sworn in on 26 October 19
(L to R) *Front Row*: Baldev Singh, John Matthai, C. Rajagopalachari, Neh
Liaqat Ali Khan, Vallabhbhai Patel, I. I. Chundrigar, Asaf Ali and C. H. Bhab.
*Back Row*: Jagjivan Ram, Ghazanfar Ali Khan, Rajendra Prasad and Abdur Rab Nish

Congress Members and Congress Premiers of Provinces :
(L to R) *Seated :* Srikrishna Sinha, Dr. Khan Sahib,
Harekrushna Mahtab, Ravi Shankar Shukla, Sir
Muzzafarali Qazilbash, T. Prakasam, B. G. Kher,
Govind Ballabh Pant and Gopinath Bardolai.
*Standing:* Sir Shafaat Ahmad Khan, John Matthai,
Baldev Singh, K. B. Sahai, Rajendra Prasad,
Nehru, Vallabhbhai Patel, Rajagopalachari, Asaf
Ali, Syed Ali Zaheer and C. H. Bhabha.

...nbers visiting Bengal in connexion with the Calcutta and Noakhali disturbances.
(L to R) Abdur Rab Nishtar, Liaqat Ali Khan, Nehru and Vallabhbhai Patel.

Departure for London : Lord Wavell and
Liaqat Ali Khan at the Palam airfield

7. CONSULTATIONS
   IN LONDON

The Secretary of State receiving Indian leaders in London:
(L to R) Jinnah, Baldev Singh, Lord Pethick-Lawrence and Nehru

8. CONSULTATIONS IN LONDON

Nehru and Jinnah with Sir Samuel Rungana-
dhan, Indian High Commissioner in London

9(a). GOVERNORS' CONFERENCE IN DELHI, APRIL 1947.

Lord and Lady Mountbatten with provincial Governors and their wives. *Middle Row:* Sir Olaf Caroe, Sir Andrew Clow, Sir Hugh Dow, Sir Francis Wylie, Sir John Colville, Lt.-Gen. Sir Archibald Nye, Sir Evan Jenkins, Sir Frederick Bourne, Sir Francis Mudie, Sir Chandulal Trivedi and Sir Akbar Hydari

9(b). THE VICEROY'S MEETING WITH LEADERS, 2 JUNE 1947.

*Round the table:* Lord Mountbatten, Jinnah, Liaqat Ali Khan, Abdur Rab Nishtar, Baldev Singh, J. B. Kripalani, Vallabhbhai Patel and Nehru, *Behind:* Sir Eric Miéville and Lord Ismay.

10 (a). PRESS CONFERENCE, 4 JUNE 1947

On Lord Mountbatten's right Vallabhbhai Patel. *Bottom Row:*
Author, Sir Eric Miéville, Lord Ismay, Sir George Abell and Ian Scott

10 (b). INAUGURATION OF THE PAKISTAN CONSTITUENT ASSEMBLY, 14 AUGUST 1947

Lord Mountbatten addressing the assembly, Jinnah seated on his left.

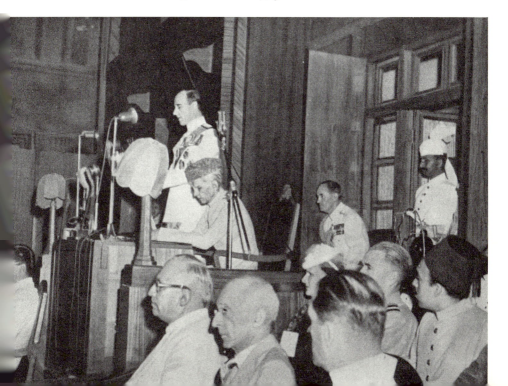

11. INDIA'S FIRST PRIME MINISTER
Lord Mountbatten swearing in Nehru on 15 August 1947

Jinnah said that the stand taken by the Muslim League ever since 1940 had been that it would be willing to participate in an interim Government at the Centre provided two conditions were assured. The first of these was that separate States would be established in Muslim majority areas after the war, or so soon as it might be possible; the second was that Muslims, being not a minority but a nation, should be accorded equality of numbers in the Executive. Lord Wavell's proposals had conceded neither of these conditions. It had suited the Congress to agree to proposals which did not prejudice its ultimate objective of a united India; as for the Muslim League, its representation would be about one-third in the proposed Council; the other minorities such as the Depressed Classes, the Sikhs and the Indian Christians shared the general viewpoint of the Congress and were likely to align themselves with that party; the result was that there would be no safety for Muslim interests. In these circumstances, to have accepted the arrangement suggested to them by the Viceroy would have been, Jinnah said, an abject surrender of all they stood for, and the death knell of the Muslim League. 'On a final examination and analysis of the Wavell plan,' said Jinnah, 'we found that it was a snare.' He added:

There was the combination consisting of Gandhi and the Hindu Congress, who stand for India's Hindu national independence as one India, and the latest exponent of geographical unity, Lord Wavell, and Glancy[1]-Khizr, who are bent upon creating disruption among the Muslims in the Punjab, and we were sought to be pushed into this arrangement, which, if we had agreed to, as proposed by Lord Wavell, we should have signed our death warrant.

Nehru said that the Muslim League represented mediaeval conceptions and fear complexes and that India would one day have to settle the problem of communalism if she wished to progress as a modern democratic State. He explained that the old conception of Nation States was now outmoded and that the real modern problems lay in the economic sphere.

The Simla Conference had met in an atmosphere of optimism. The initial doubts raised by the party leaders had given rise to concern, but once the Congress and the League leaders agreed to attend the Conference, there had been high hopes of an eventual agreement. Even after it was known that Jinnah had refused to submit his list, hope persisted that the Viceroy would find a way out. This sentiment

[1] Governor of the Punjab.

was not confined to any particular school of thought or opinion. For instance, just before the Viceroy communicated his final decision to the members, Hossain Imam, who attended the Conference in his capacity as leader of the Muslim League Party in the Council of State stopped me on my way to the Cecil Hotel and confided to me his feeling of distress over the imminent breakdown. He urged me even at that late hour to see Liaqat Ali Khan in order to find a way out of the impasse. He gave me the impression that the members of the Working Committee of the Muslim League were far from unanimous in rejecting the Viceroy's offer. Hossain Imam suggested that the Viceroy was not aware that a member of his own Executive Council was advising Jinnah to stand firm.

On arrival at the Cecil Hotel I telephoned to Liaqat Ali Khan, who readily agreed to meet me. I discussed the general situation with him that evening, stressing some of the dangers that would overtake the country if an agreement were not reached. He gave me the impression that the crucial issue with the League was the insufficiency of the Viceroy's veto to protect Muslim interests. His point was that no decision objected to by the Muslim members should be taken by the Executive Council except by a clear two-thirds majority. I assured him that, with goodwill on both sides, a formula on this point acceptable to all the parties could be devised, and that we could still save the situation. Liaqat Ali told me that he would consult Jinnah and let me know his reaction the next day. I never heard from him. His attitude during our discussion did not strike me as being in any way other than helpful. One can only draw one's own conclusions as to the reasons which deterred him from pursuing my suggestion.

The Conference at Simla had been conceived as a gathering of politically eminent persons who would sit together and collectively advise the Viceroy about the formation of a new central Government. Very soon, however, it became transformed into the familiar pattern of futile discussions between the Congress and the Muslim League, and between party leaders and the Viceroy. The formal sessions of the Conference served as the forum for party leaders to set out their points of view whilst other members functioned as the audience or chorus. Rajagopalachari made pointed reference to this in a statement soon after the Conference ended. He added that if it had been known that the sole purpose of the Conference was to get Jinnah to agree, failing which it would have to disperse, the Congress would have told Lord Wavell at the very start that it would be a waste of energy.

Lord Wavell was blamed for not following up his initiative by imposing an award of his own. But it must be said in his justification that the war with Japan was still to be won; that His Majesty's Government would not have supported the formation of an Executive Council which did not include the Muslim League — those 90 million Muslims who, according to Churchill, had eschewed any such non-cooperative tactics as had been adopted by the Congress and had consistently refrained from doing anything that would tend to thwart the war effort. Moreover, Amery's consistent view was that unless there were general agreement on the long-term plan the Congress and the League would not come together and, even if they did, would not work honestly together. The primary need was winning the war with Japan, and since one of the two important parties had refused to cooperate, the Viceroy was left with no alternative but to carry on as best he could with his existing Executive Council.

On the other hand, the abandonment of the plan undoubtedly strengthened the position of Jinnah and the League at a time when their fortunes were none too good. It weakened the position of those Muslims who had been opposing the League, particularly the Unionist Party in the Punjab, and since it was clear that Jinnah alone could deliver the goods, the wavering and middle-of-the-road Muslim politicians tended to gravitate to the Muslim League.

The Simla Conference afforded a last opportunity to the forces of nationalism to fight a rear-guard action to preserve the integrity of the country, and when the battle was lost the waves of communalism quickly engulfed it. Only the Hobson's Choice of partition was left.

# IX

## THE GENERAL ELECTIONS

VERY soon after the breakdown of the Simla Conference there came a sweeping change in the political outlook. This was caused by two important events. The first was the general election in Britain; the second the surrender of Japan.

The general election in Britain resulted in a resounding victory for the Labour Party, the first time that the Party had been able to secure a clear majority in the House of Commons. Churchill's caretaker Government gave place to a Labour Government, with Clement Attlee as Prime Minister and Lord Pethick-Lawrence as Secretary of State for India. Nationalist opinion in India acclaimed the Labour Party's success with jubilation. In a cable to Attlee, the Congress President said: 'Hearty congratulations to the people of Great Britain on the results of the election which demonstrate their abandonment of the old ideas and acceptance of a new world.' There was less enthusiasm among members of the Muslim League; but on the whole, the new British Government was welcomed by India with friendliness and goodwill.

The expected surrender of Japan was accelerated by the first atom bomb, which was dropped on Hiroshima on 6 August 1945, and on the 15th of that month victory over Japan was celebrated all over the country.

The end of the war brought to the fore the urgency of finding a permanent and lasting solution of India's constitutional problem. In a press statement issued immediately after the Simla Conference, Sir Stafford Cripps attributed its breakdown not so much to the composition of the interim Government as to the influence that any temporary arrangement was likely to have upon the more permanent decisions which would have to be made for the full and free self-government of India. Sir Stafford Cripps felt that, since emphasis had shifted once more from transitional arrangements to a permanent settlement, it was obviously desirable not to waste time by trying to arrive at a temporary arrangement, but rather to expedite the means of arriving at a permanent settlement in which the question of Pakistan must form a major issue. Sir Stafford urged that new elections should be held in India and that, with the representatives so elected, a constituent assembly should be formed to work out a new free self-governing constitution for British India, or such part of it as was ready to consent to such a constitution.

Sir Stafford's suggestion certainly fitted in with the view of the Muslim League, the Working Committee of which had already adopted a resolution calling for fresh elections to the provincial and central legislatures. The demand was reiterated by Jinnah in a speech on 6 August, in the course of which he charged Gandhiji and the Congress with having adopted spiteful and malicious devices to defeat the Muslim League at the Simla Conference. He said that the League had offered co-operation in an Interim Government only because of the war and that it was useless to talk of interim arrangements now; the need was to go ahead with plans for a permanent constitutional settlement. This, he said, should be on the basis of Pakistan; on that issue the Muslim League would never surrender. He added that his immediate purpose was to fight the elections so that, once and for all, everyone might be convinced of the League's representative character.

The Congress was also in favour of a general election, but contended that the elections would not be fair unless civil liberties were to be restored first and the Congress was enabled to function fully again. Other organizations joined in the demand for a general election.

The Viceroy himself was of the view that a general election should be held without delay. The last elections to the central Assembly had been in 1934 and to the provincial legislatures in 1936. Elections had subsequently been postponed, under the special powers of the Governor-General in the case of the central legislature, and by parliamentary legislation in the case of the provincial legislatures. There seemed to be no justification for putting off the elections any longer. During the first week of August the Viceroy held consultations with the provincial Governors, who agreed that the elections should be held as early as possible.

His Majesty's Government preferred to approach the whole problem in a more comprehensive way, but agreed with the Viceroy as far as the elections were concerned and requested him to expedite all the requisite preparatory measures to enable the elections to the central and provincial legislatures to be held during the cold weather.

On 21 August 1945 two announcements were made by the Viceroy: first, that elections to the central and provincial Assemblies would be held in the cold weather, and secondly, that the Viceroy would very shortly be paying a visit to England for consultation with His Majesty's Government. These announcements had a settling effect upon the political atmosphere. On 24 August Lord Wavell left for London, accompanied by Sir Evan Jenkins and myself.

Lord Wavell had long discussions with the Secretary of State and the India Committee of the Cabinet, in particular on such problems as the manner in which popular representatives could be associated with the administration; how ministries were to be restored in the provinces, and the procedure by which ultimate decisions in the matter of the future constitution should be taken. With regard to the procedure for reaching a final constitutional settlement, the British Government was inclined to rely on the suggestions contained in the Cripps proposals for 'provincial option'. Whether this particular feature of the proposals were to be retained or not, the provincial Assemblies would have to provide the starting point for the creation of a body to frame the future constitution. How would the provincial Assemblies elect their representatives for framing the constitution? An interesting suggestion put forward by one of the British ministers was that a convention of all the provincial Assembly members should be called to elect their representatives from the common gathering. It was claimed that the experience of sitting together and transacting business, even if it were only of a routine character, would have a valuable moral effect and would instil the feeling of belonging together. It was pointed out that in Trade Union assemblies in Great Britain procedure of this kind was common and was not known to lead to any undue confusion or trouble.

In the end, it was decided that these details could best be settled after ascertaining the views of the Indian leaders at the conclusion of the elections.

Lord Wavell returned to India on 16 September. On the 19th, he made the following announcement on behalf of His Majesty's Government:

As stated in the gracious speech from the Throne at the opening of Parliament, His Majesty's Government are determined to do their utmost to promote in conjunction with the leaders of Indian opinion the early realisation of full self-government in India. During my visit to London they have discussed with me the steps to be taken.

An announcement has already been made that elections to the central and provincial legislatures, so long postponed owing to the war, are to be held during the coming cold weather. Thereafter His Majesty's Government earnestly hope that ministerial responsibility will be accepted by political leaders in all provinces.

It is the intention of His Majesty's Government to convene as soon as possible a constitution-making body, and as a preliminary step they have authorised me to undertake, immediately after the elections, discussions with the representatives of the Legislative Assemblies in the provinces, to ascertain whether the proposals contained in the 1942 declaration are acceptable or whether some alternative or modified scheme is preferable. Discussions will also be undertaken with the representatives of the Indian States with a view to ascertaining in what way they can best take their part in the constitution-making body.

His Majesty's Government are proceeding to the consideration of the content of the treaty which will require to be concluded between Great Britain and India.

During these preparatory stages, the Government of India must be carried on, and urgent economic and social problems must be dealt with. Furthermore, India has to play her full part in working out the new World Order. His Majesty's Government have therefore further authorised me, as soon as the results of the provincial elections are published, to take steps to bring into being an Executive Council which will have the support of the main Indian parties.

Simultaneously, in a personal message, Lord Wavell underlined the importance of the announcement. It meant, he said, that His Majesty's Government was determined to go ahead. The fact that, in spite of having a great number of most important and urgent problems on its hands, it had taken time, almost in its first days of office, to give attention to the Indian problem, was an indication of its earnest resolve. The task of making and implementing a new constitution for India was a complex and difficult one which would require goodwill, co-operation and patience on the part of all concerned. Elections were necessary in order to know the will of the Indian electorate. After the elections, discussions would be held with the Indian leaders and with the representatives of the Indian States to determine the form which the constitution-making body should take. This procedure appeared to be the best way to give India the opportunity of deciding her destiny. His Majesty's Government and the Viceroy were well aware of the difficulties, but were determined to overcome them.

In a message broadcast on the same day, Prime Minister Attlee said that, although the Cripps proposals had not been accepted by the Indian parties, the British Government were acting in the spirit of those proposals. He gave an assurance that the British Government would not try to introduce into the proposed treaty any matter which was incompatible with the interests of India, and he appealed to Indians to make a united effort to evolve a constitution which would be accepted as fair by all parties and interests in India.

The reactions of the two main parties were not favourable. Jinnah and Liaqat Ali Khan reiterated on behalf of the Muslim League that no solution would be acceptable except on the basis of Pakistan. So far as the Congress was concerned, the two months of inaction that had elapsed after the failure of the Simla Conference served only to intensify its impatience. The All-India Congress Committee, meeting in Bombay on 21 September, passed a resolution which characterized Lord Wavell's proposals as 'vague and inadequate and unsatisfactory.' It pointed out the omission of any reference to independence, nothing short of which would satisfy the Congress and the country; criticized the proposal to make no immediate change at the Centre; set out a list of grievances, including a demand for the release of political prisoners; but wound up by directing the Working Committee to take steps to contest the elections in order to demonstrate the will of the people, especially on the issue of the immediate transfer of power.

The Government of India and the provincial governments now started preparations for holding the elections. The Viceroy had announced that there would be no major alterations in the franchise, as that would delay the elections considerably; but he promised to revise the electoral rolls as carefully and as thoroughly as possible. It was decided that elections to the central legislature should be held first; then elections to the provincial legislatures where ministries were functioning, and lastly, elections to the legislatures in provinces where ministries were not functioning. The Congress had demanded that in the last-named provinces ministries should be formed before the dissolution of the legislatures. But this was not accepted by the Government as the provincial Governors were opposed to it, as was also the Muslim League.

The Muslim League had already announced that it would fight the elections on the issue of Pakistan and the title of the League to represent all the Muslims. Jinnah and other League spokesmen declared that their demand was that the provinces of the Punjab, Sind, the North-West Frontier Province, Baluchistan, Bengal and Assam in their entirety should be formed into a separate sovereign State to be known as Pakistan. Muslims with any political ambitions had already begun to realize that their interests could lie only with Jinnah and the League. Many of them flocked to Jinnah's standard and he welcomed them like lost sheep. Among the notable persons who changed their allegiance was Abdul Qaiyum Khan of the North-West Frontier Province, who had not only been an ardent Congressman, but the Deputy Leader of the Congress Party in the central Assembly!

Nationalist Muslims found themselves in a particularly difficult position. They felt that, unless the Congress could reassure the Muslims, it would not be possible to win their support in the coming elections. Towards the end of August 1945, Abul Kalam Azad approached Gandhiji with a plan for a communal settlement. It was useless, he said, to enter into the causes of the communal problem or to apportion blame for it. Muslim fears could only be removed by devising a scheme under which they would feel secure. Any attempt to form a unitary government at the Centre would fail. Partition was against the interests of the Muslims themselves. As an Indian Muslim, he regarded partition as a defeatist policy and could not accept it. He suggested to the Congress that the future constitution of India must be federal with fully autonomous units; that the central subjects must only be of an all-India nature and agreed upon by the constituent units, and that the units must be given the right of secession. There must be joint electorates both at the Centre and in the provinces, with reservation of seats and such differential franchise as might be needed to make electorates reflect the strength of population of the communities. There must be parity of Hindus and Muslims in the central legislature and the central executive till such time as communal suspicion disappeared and parties were formed on economic and political lines. There should also be a convention by which the head of the Indian federation would, in the initial period, be Hindu and Muslim by turn. Hindu friends were exhorted to leave entirely to the Muslims the question of their status in the future constitution of India. If Muslims were satisfied that the decision was not being imposed on them by a non-Muslim agency, they would drop the idea of partition and realize that their interests would be best served by a federated and united India. Azad concluded by saying that once

Indians had acquired power, economic, political and class interests would oust purely communal interests.

What consideration the Congress Working Committee gave to this proposal is not known; but at its meeting in September 1945 it passed a resolution reiterating the Congress policy of independence, with particular emphasis on unity, adding a rider in regard to the right of secession in the following terms:

Nevertheless, the Committee declares also that it cannot think in terms of compelling the people in any territorial unit to remain in an Indian Union against their declared and established will. While recognising this principle, every effort should be made to create conditions which would help the different units in developing a common and co-operative national life. Acceptance of the principle inevitably involves that no changes should be made which result in fresh problems being created and compulsion being exercised on other substantial groups within that area. Each territorial unit should have the fullest possible autonomy within the union, consistently with a strong National State.

The resolution was not put before the All-India Congress Committee, but the question of the right of secession came up indirectly. Very strong speeches were made against the proposal. The Congress leaders declared that they would make no more approaches to the League, but would contact the Muslim masses direct and would try to reassure them by appropriate means through the election manifesto.

The Congress itself faced considerable organizational difficulties in preparing for the elections. Years in the wilderness had impaired the party machine; some of its leaders were still in prison and party funds and property had in many cases been sequestrated. These difficulties only added to the feeling of resentment against the Government. Some Congressmen glorified the activities which had brought them into conflict with the Government in 1942, and there were threats of another struggle after the elections if nothing satisfactory emerged.

Another problem gained considerable prominence about this time. This concerned certain Indian military personnel who had fallen into Japanese hands during the war and who had constituted themselves into an 'Indian National Army' under the leadership of Subhas Chandra Bose. At the conclusion of the war, over 20,000 of its members had been rounded up and repatriated to India. The Army authorities had evidence that certain officers among them had been guilty, not only of waging war against the King, but of 'gross brutality in the methods employed to induce their fellow-prisoners to join them.' It was proposed that they should be put on public trial in Delhi and an Ordinance was promulgated setting up a Military Tribunal for the purpose. The first batch of the accused included a Hindu, a Muslim and a Sikh. The place of trial was the Red Fort. The Congress took up the case of the accused and set up a panel of defence under Bhulabhai Desai, which included Sir Tej Bahadur Sapru and Nehru. The glamour of Subhas Chandra Bose's name and the fact that the Congress had taken up the cause of the accused evoked popular enthusiasm throughout the land. Demonstrations were held in different places, like Madura, Bombay, Calcutta, Lucknow and Lahore. In the disturbances that ensued, the police had in some places to open fire. When the Muslim League decided to associate itself with the defence of the I.N.A. accused, the agitation became countrywide. The Government had to bow to the storm; for though the accused were convicted, their sentences were in almost every case ultimately remitted.

The holding of the I.N.A. trials in Delhi was indeed a blunder. The Army authorities showed characteristic disregard of the political tension prevailing in the country at the time. If the purpose was to demonstrate the British Government's determination that no disloyalty in the armed forces would be tolerated, that purpose was certainly not accomplished. On the other hand, these trials provided excellent material for propaganda against the Government, which the parties used to full advantage.

The speeches made by some of the Congress leaders threatening another struggle, and the disturbances arising out of the trial of the I.N.A. prisoners, created so dangerous and tense a situation that the British Government felt bound to re-state their policy. On 4 December, the Secretary of State made a statement in the House of Lords in which he said that the full significance of the proposals contained in the Viceroy's announcement of 19 September had not been properly appreciated; that the holding of discussions for the setting up of a constitution-making body after the elections was not intended to delay matters; but that, on the other hand, His Majesty's Government regarded the setting up of a constitution-making body by which Indians would decide their own future as a matter of great urgency.

His Majesty's Government considered that it would be an advantage if members of the British Parliament could meet leading political

Indian personalities to learn their views at first hand, as also to convey in person the general desire of the people of England that India should speedily attain her full and rightful position as an independent partner State in the British Commonwealth. His Majesty's Government therefore proposed to send out to India as soon as possible a Parliamentary delegation, drawn from all the parties, under the auspices of the Empire Parliamentary Association.

The Secretary of State emphasized that during the transition towards complete self-government India would be passing through difficult times. No greater disservice could be done to a future Indian government and to the cause of democracy than to permit the foundations of the State to be weakened and the loyalty of its servants to those who were in authority to be undermined, before the new government came into being. His Majesty's Government would not therefore countenance any attempt to break down the loyalty of the administrative services or of the Indian armed forces. It would give full support to the Government of India in securing 'that their servants are protected in the performance of their duty and that the future constitution of India shall not be called into being by force or threat of force.'

There was wide appreciation of His Majesty's Government's anxiety to settle the Indian constitutional problem as urgently as possible. The warning against threats of force was not relished, though it was not entirely displeasing to the Congress High Command, who were themselves already concerned over the manner in which the country was heading towards violence. The proposed visit of the Parliamentary delegation did not evoke any interest, because it was thought to be only a device to fill the gap while the elections were in progress.

In a press statement Jinnah said that the British Government was groping in the dark; that the constitution-making body should be called into being only after the question of Pakistan had been settled, and that there should be two separate constitution-making bodies for the two parts into which India should be divided.

The Congress Working Committee met in Calcutta on 7 December and at the end of its session passed a comprehensive resolution, drafted by Gandhiji, re-affirming its faith in non-violence and stressing that such non-violence does not include burning of public property, cutting of telegraph wires, derailing trains and intimidation.

On the whole, Indian politics tended to settle into smoother channels.

In his address to the Associated Chambers of Commerce on 10 December, the Viceroy said that India's problem was not a simple one. It could not and would not be solved by repeating a password or formula. 'Quit India' would not act as the magic 'sesame' which opened Ali Baba's cave. It could not, and would not, be solved by violence. Disorder and violence were the very things that might check the pace of India's progress. There were various parties to the settlement, who must somehow or other reach a measure of agreement amongst themselves — the Congress, the minorities (of whom the Musalmans were the most numerous and the most important), the rulers of Indian States and the British Government. The objective of all was the same — the freedom and welfare of India. Lord Wavell appealed for goodwill on the part of all leaders. He said: 'We are going through a very difficult and testing time, and it will need coolness and wisdom if we are to avoid calamity. In so far as I can help by personal contact, I am always prepared to do so.' He then referred to a matter on which, as a soldier, he held strong views. This was the I.N.A. trials. He said:

A great deal of political heat and feeling has been engendered by the way in which the I.N.A. trials have been represented to the public. I will say nothing of the trials themselves or of the men under trial, it would be quite improper for me to do so. But I do propose to say something for the men who were prisoners of war but did not join the I.N.A., who, under pressure and punishment, under hardships and want, stood firm to their ideals of a soldier's duty, a soldier's faith. They represent some 70 per cent of the total men of the Indian Army who became prisoners of war in Malaya and Hong Kong. Whatever your political views, if you cannot acclaim the man who prefers his honour to his ease, who remains steadfast in adversity to his pledged faith, then you have a poor notion of the character which is required to build up a nation. I say to you that amongst all the exploits of the last five or six years for which the world rightly extols the Indian soldier, the endurance of those men in captivity and hardship stands as high as any. As a proof of what they endured as the price of their loyalty to their ideals of a soldier's duty, I will tell you this: the 45,000 Indian prisoners of war who stood firm are estimated to have lost about 11,000, or one quarter of their numbers, from disease, starvation and murder; the 20,000 who went over to our enemy's side lost only 1,500, or $7\frac{1}{2}$ per cent.

Meanwhile the elections to the central Legislative Assembly had been held and the complete results became available towards the end of December 1945. The Congress won an overwhelming success in the General constituencies, the Hindu Mahasabha and other opposing candidates preferring in most cases to withdraw rather than risk defeat. The Muslim League won every Muslim seat, the Nationalist Muslims forfeiting their deposits in many instances. The Congress secured 91·3 per cent of the votes cast in non-Muhammadan constituencies and the Muslim League 86·6 per cent of the total votes cast in Muhammadan constituencies. The final figures were, Congress 57; Muslim League 30; Independents 5; Akali Sikhs 2; and Europeans 8, making a total of 102 elected seats. In the previous Assembly the figures at the time of dissolution were, Congress 36; Muslim League 25; Independents 21; Nationalist Party 10, and Europeans 8. The results of the elections clearly emphasized that the Congress and the Muslim League were the only parties that counted in the country.

Both parties were jubilant over their victories. The Central Election Board of the Congress, in a bulletin issued on 6 January 1946 declared that the Congress stood vindicated; it was the biggest, strongest and most representative organization in the country.

The Muslim League celebrated 11 January as its day of victory, and Jinnah's message for the occasion congratulated the League on winning all the Muslim seats in the central Assembly.

The new year began with a broadcast message by the Secretary of State. Lord Pethick-Lawrence said that it was because 1946 would be a crucial year in India's age-long history that he felt he should like to speak to the people personally. He wanted Indians to realize that the British Government and the whole British people earnestly desired to see India rise quickly to the full and free status of an equal partner in the British Commonwealth. There was no longer any need for denunciations or organized pressure to secure recognition of India's due position in the world. 'The problem now,' said the Secretary of State, 'is a practical one. It is to work out a rational and acceptable plan of action. It must be a plan under which authority can be transferred to Indian control under forms of government which will willingly be accepted by the broad mass of India's people — so that the new India will not be torn and rent by internal strife and dissensions.' He pleaded for the active help of leading Indians in every community and of every way of thought, and concluded that it was only through moderation and compromise that great political problems could be solved. 'If we all bend our minds and wills to this high endeavour we can do something in 1946 for the greatness of India, for the future peace and prosperity of Asia and the world.'

The Parliamentary Delegation arrived in India on 5 January. It consisted of ten members — eight from the House of Commons and two from the House of Lords. The Delegation was led by Professor Robert Richards, a member of the Labour Party and at one time (in 1924) Under-Secretary of State for India. On the eve of the Delegation's visit the Secretary of State wrote to the presidents of the Congress and the Muslim League stating that the basic purpose of the Delegation was to make personal contacts. The delegates were coming as individuals; they were not empowered in any way to act on behalf of the British Government; but their impressions would of course be passed on by them to ministers and others in Parliament. He expressed the hope that co-operation would be extended to the Delegation.

The Parliamentary Delegation was in the country for about a month. It met almost all the important political leaders and its members were received everywhere with cordiality and friendliness.

In his talks with the members of the Delegation, Jinnah made it clear that he would take no part in an interim Government without a prior declaration accepting the principle of Pakistan and 'parity' with all other parties. He insisted on two constitution-making bodies. The drawing of the frontier between Pakistan and Hindustan would be a matter for negotiation between the two bodies. He did not envisage predominantly non-Muslim areas, like the Ambala Division of the Punjab, remaining in Pakistan, but insisted that Pakistan must be a living State economically and culturally. Any attempt to impose a unified constitution, or to accept a majority decision by a single constitution-making body, would be resisted, if necessary by force. He emphasized that Pakistan would remain within the Empire with a British Governor-General. Relations with Hindustan would be purely diplomatic; there would be no common currency, transport system, army, etc.

Nehru in his talks with the Delegation conceded that the British Government might have to declare for Pakistan, but that there would have to be a plebiscite in border districts to confirm it. He did not accept the election results to the central Assembly as being sufficient; the Muslims did not know what they were voting for.

Miss Muriel Nichol, one of the members of the Delegation, said after her meeting with Nehru: 'Without rancour or bitterness, and in a clear yet firm way, Pandit Nehru stated the Congress case for India's freedom. In meeting him I was not disappointed. He was tolerant in his views and as broad in his outlook as I had expected him to be. Tonight, I feel, I have really met a great man.'

In a farewell talk to press representatives Mr Richards, the leader of the Delegation, said:

The fact that we were here at the time of the general elections has enabled us to gauge something of the feeling in India on the one great question about which every party is united. There are deep divisions among you, but those divisions disappear in the unity with which you, in my opinion, very rightly demand a measure of self-government at this time. There are several views on that particular question, but I do say that we are all conscious of the fact that India has at last attained political manhood; and it will be the privilege of the Government in England, I hope, to extend and further that confidence which India has in herself and in her ability to take her place among the free nations of the world.

On 28 January, the Viceroy addressed the newly-elected central legislature in a seven-minute speech in which he emphasized the determination of His Majesty's Government to establish a new Executive Council formed from political leaders, and to bring about a constitution-making body or convention as soon as possible.

The Viceroy's speech was reassuring. Vallabhbhai Patel said, 'The ship has reached the shore. . . . The freedom of India is near at hand.' Jinnah, however, declared that the Muslim League was not prepared to consider anything short of immediate recognition of the Pakistan demand and that the League would not be prepared to co-operate in any interim arrangements until this principle had been made clear beyond all doubt and until it had been decided that there would be two constitution-making bodies, one for the Pakistan areas and the other for the rest of India. Subsequently, in an interview with the press, he added that if the British carried out their intention of calling a single constitution-making body, the only result would be a Muslim revolt throughout India.

Before we deal further with the elections, we must mention a serious and important incident which took place about this time. It was the revolt of certain R.I.N. personnel, which was followed by grave civil turmoil in Bombay. It started on 18 February, when ratings of the Signal School in Bombay went on a hunger-strike in protest against what their Central Strike Committee described as 'untold hardships regarding pay and food and the most outrageous racial discrimination,' and in particular against their Commander's derogatory references to their national character. They were joined later by ratings from other naval establishments. These persons got completely out of hand. They took possession of some of the ships, mounted the guns and prepared to open fire on the military guards. A very ugly situation developed. Admiral Godfrey, Flag Officer-Commanding, Royal Indian Navy, broadcast to the ratings calling upon them to surrender. At the same time efforts were made to secure guns and planes and to rush reinforcements to the scene. There were even some who tried to fish in the troubled waters. It was due largely to the efforts of Vallabhbhai Patel that, on 23 February, the ratings surrendered. In the meantime, contrary to the advice of Congress and Muslim League leaders, strikes and *hartals* were organized in Bombay and unruly crowds went about looting and setting fire to banks, shops, post offices, police posts and grain shops. The police had to open fire several times and the military had to be called in to assist before order could be restored. Over 200 persons were killed as a result of these disturbances, which had their repercussions in other centres such as Karachi, Madras and Calcutta.

The Army and the Air Force were not altogether unaffected. There was trouble in several places, though not of a serious character. On the whole, the provincial and subordinate services, including the police, remained loyal, and only the conduct of a section of the police in one province caused a certain amount of anxiety to the provincial government. These incidents were ominous portents for the future.

Elections to the provincial legislatures had meanwhile been going on apace. As has been mentioned earlier, elections were held first in the provinces of Assam, Sind, the North-West Frontier Province and the Punjab. In Assam, the Congress won all the General territorial seats and the League almost all the Muslim seats. The Congress Party, having captured fifty-eight out of 108 seats, was commissioned to form the Government and Gopinath Bardolai became the premier. The ministry consisted of five Hindus, one Indian Christian and one Nationalist Muslim. Two seats were offered to the Muslim League on condition that it would agree to work the Congress parliamentary programme, but the League rejected the offer because of the inclusion of a non-League Muslim in the ministry.

A piquant situation arose in Sind. The Muslim League captured twenty-seven seats, and one independent Muslim joined the party after the elections. The Nationalist Muslims won three seats, and a splinter group under G.M. Syed, which had broken away from the League just before the elections, captured four. The Congress secured twenty-one and, of the remaining seats, three went to Europeans and one to an independent Labour candidate. After the elections, the Syed group formed a coalition with the Congress and the Nationalist Muslims, which resulted in the position of two parties with twenty-eight members each. Subsequently the Labour member joined the coalition, which thus gained a majority. But the offer to form a ministry was made by the Governor to Sir Ghulam Hussain Hidayatullah, leader of the Muslim League Party. This was regarded as an act of partisanship and was greatly resented by Congress and nationalist opinion. Sir Ghulam Hussain Hidayatullah offered two Hindu seats to the Congress Party, but the latter insisted that the offer should be addressed to Syed, the head of the coalition. As it was an article of faith with the Muslim League not to have dealings with non-League Muslims, the matter was not proceeded with.

In the NORTH-WEST FRONTIER PROVINCE, the Congress won thirty seats (of which nineteen were Muslim), as against seventeen captured by the Muslim League. Other Muslims got two seats and the Akali Sikhs one. The Congress formed a ministry with Dr Khan Sahib as premier.

The results of the elections in the PUNJAB were considered to provide the key to the Muslim problem. Out of a total of eighty-six Muslim seats, the Muslim League had been able to win seventy-five. The Congress had won fifty-one seats, the Panthic Akali Sikhs twenty-two and the Unionists twenty, while the remaining seven had been won by independent candidates. As a result of changes in party loyalties that took place soon after the results came out, the final position became, Muslim League seventy-nine; Congress fifty-one; Panthic Akali Sikhs twenty-two; Unionists and Independents ten each. By-elections were pending in three constituencies. The Muslim League, as the largest single party, was entitled to the first offer to form a ministry; but as it could not claim an absolute majority in the Assembly it would have had to ally itself with some other party. The Congress and the Akali Sikhs formed a working alliance and, in their negotiations with the Muslim League, insisted upon three conditions: first, that the Congress should have the freedom to nominate as ministers persons belonging to any community, and not Hindus alone as the Muslim League insisted; secondly, that the Congress-cum-Akali Party should be allowed to nominate half the strength of the ministry; and thirdly, that extra-provincial questions, such as Pakistan, should not be brought before the provincial Assembly. These conditions proved unacceptable to the Muslim League, nor was the League able to reach any separate agreement with the Akali Sikhs, who insisted that assurances should be given with regard to the creation of a Sikh State in the event of the Muslim League pressing its claim for the establishment of Pakistan. Eventually a coalition party was formed which consisted of the Congress, the Unionists and the Akali Sikhs, under the leadership of Khizr Hyat Khan, who was invited by the Governor to form a ministry.

Of the provinces under Governor's rule, the first election results were announced in the case of BIHAR. In an Assembly of 152 members, the Congress won ninety-eight seats, including one Muslim seat; the Muslim League won thirty-four out of forty, the remaining five seats going to the Momins, who were pro-Congress; the other seats were won by independent candidates.

In the UNITED PROVINCES Assembly with a total of 228 seats, the Congress captured 152 seats, while the Muslim League won fifty-four of the sixty-six Muslim seats.

In BOMBAY, out of a total of 175 seats the Congress won 126, while the thirty Muslim seats all went to the Muslim League.

In MADRAS, the Congress won 165 seats out of a total of 215. The Muslim League won all the twenty-nine Muslim seats.

The last of the election results to come in were from the CENTRAL PROVINCES and ORISSA. In the former, which had 112 seats in the Legislative Assembly, the Congress won ninety-two seats and the Muslim League thirteen of the fourteen Muslim seats. In Orissa, where the Assembly was composed of sixty members, the Congress secured forty-seven seats and the Muslim League all the four Muslim seats.

In these six provinces, Congress ministries were formed and in each case the leader of the local Congress party negotiated with his opposite number in the Muslim League with a view to forming a coalition, but with no result.

In the BENGAL Assembly of 250 members, the Muslim League won 113 out of the total of 119 Muslim seats, and the Congress obtained eighty-seven. H. S. Suhrawardy, leader of the Muslim League, was invited to form a ministry. He held negotiations with the local Congress leaders with a view to forming a coalition ministry, but this proved fruitless and a ministry was formed by the Muslim League Party with the support of independent elements.

Though the League had thus won the majority of Muslim seats, it was able to form ministries only in two of the five provinces claimed for Pakistan, namely Bengal and Sind. Even there it had to secure the support of other parties and in particular that of the European group.

Lord Wavell had meanwhile been in consultation with the Secretary of State with regard to future action. His reading of the political situation was as follows. The Congress commanded the support of practically all Caste Hindus, and of certain other elements. It had the support of nearly the whole of the Press; it had the best organized — in fact the only well-organized — political machine; and it commanded almost unlimited financial support. Almost all educated Hindus, and especially the student class, were its enthusiastic followers. Indian business magnates, although strongly pro-Congress, were anxious for a solution without conflict and disorder. Most of the big landowners feared the Congress, and would have liked to support the Government, but few of them could be relied upon to give active aid.

The Viceroy realized that, generally speaking, there was no organized opposition to the Congress amongst Hindus in British India (except possibly in the Punjab) and nothing to put in its place if the British Government suppressed it. The Scheduled Castes were divided and many of them supported the Congress. The only real opposition to it came from the minorities, of which the Muslim League was of course the principal party, but it represented entirely sectional and not all-India interests. The League, though strongly anti-Congress, was not pro-Government or pro-British, and it would support the Government only to the extent of remaining neutral in a conflict between it and the Congress. Pakistan would remain inflexibly the League policy so long as Jinnah controlled it, even though many of his supporters might realize its disadvantages.

The Viceroy was confident that in a conflict with the Congress, he could count generally on the support of the officials, the Police and the Army. At the same time, it would be unwise to try the Indian Army too highly in the suppression of their own people, and as time went on the loyalty of even the Indian officials, the Indian Army and the Police might become problematical. A large number of British officials would probably take the first opportunity to retire, so that the British Government in India would be placed in a quite untenable position unless it found a very early solution, and this it should do at any cost. The chief problem was to find some kind of bridge between Hindu and Muslim.

With these considerations in mind Lord Wavell drew up a programme of action, the immediate objectives of which were: (a) to secure a reasonably efficient Executive Council, with representatives of the principal parties on a proportional basis, which would carry on the Government of India during the interim period; (b) to form a constitution-making body which would produce a workable and acceptable constitution; and (c) to bring about governments in the provinces on a coalition basis as far as possible. His plan was to take up each of these objectives in its turn and to proceed stage by stage.

Lord Wavell was not unaware of the possibility of Congress insistence on the abolition, or weakening, of the Governor-General's power of veto. He was, however, clear that no compromise was possible on this issue.

Turning to the Muslim League, the Viceroy's idea was that if Jinnah refused to participate in the interim Government he would tell him that the Government would be compelled to go ahead without the League. On the troublesome question of Pakistan, the Viceroy had no doubt in his mind that the Muslim League's demand for self-determination in genuinely Muslim areas would have to be conceded. At the same time there could be no question of compelling large non-Muslim populations to remain in Pakistan against their will. The effect of this would be that at least two divisions of the Punjab and almost the whole of West Bengal, including Calcutta, would have to be allowed to join the Indian Union. The attractiveness of Pakistan to the Muslims would thus largely disappear and only 'the husk', in Jinnah's own words, would remain. It was possible that such a plan might induce the League to remain in an all-India federation.

The Secretary of State and the British Cabinet found much to agree with in the Viceroy's analysis of the situation, but they felt grave doubts regarding his assumption that the stages of negotiation could be kept in watertight compartments. They felt that once discussion with the leaders began, even if only in regard to the Executive Council as proposed by the Viceroy, they would be bound to extend to the whole field.

In the view of His Majesty's Government, the situation demanded a different approach. It proposed sending a mission of Cabinet ministers (probably three in number, of whom the Secretary of State would be one) to conduct, in association with the Viceroy, negotiations with Indian leaders. This would allow a much greater latitude of local decision than would otherwise be possible and would overcome inherent difficulties in telegraphic communication.

The Viceroy welcomed the proposal, but he pointed out that the mission would have to stay in India till a satisfactory decision had been reached. It would create the worst possible impression if a high-grade mission were to leave without having achieved results.

On 19 February Lord Pethick-Lawrence in the House of Lords and Prime Minister Attlee in the House of Commons made a simultaneous announcement that in view of the paramount importance, not only to India and to the British Commonwealth, but to the peace of the world, of a successful outcome of discussions with leaders of Indian opinion, His Majesty's Government had decided to send out to India a special mission consisting of three Cabinet ministers to seek, in association with the Viceroy, an agreement with those leaders on the principles and procedure relating to the constitutional issue. The members of the Mission would be Lord Pethick-Lawrence, Secretary of State for India, Sir Stafford Cripps, President of the Board of Trade, and A. V. Alexander, First Lord of the Admiralty.

The announcement was well received throughout India. Azad said that it was a wise decision which would be appreciated by the country. Gandhiji appealed to the country not to suspect the bona fides of the Cabinet Mission.

Jinnah, on the other hand, reiterated the demands he had already put forward and said that he hoped to make the Cabinet Mission realize the true situation and to satisfy them that the division of India into Pakistan and Hindustan was the only solution of India's constitutional problem.

There was a debate in the House of Commons on 15 March on the Cabinet Mission's visit to India. Intervening in the debate, Attlee said that the tide of nationalism was running very fast in India and that it was time for clear and definite action. The Cabinet Mission was going to India in a positive mood. The temperature of 1946 was not the temperature of 1920, 1930, or even 1942. His colleagues were going to India with the intention of using their utmost endeavours to help her to attain freedom as speedily and as fully as possible. What form of Government was to replace the present régime was for India to decide, though he hoped that India would elect to remain within the British Commonwealth. In conclusion he said, 'We are mindful of the rights of the minorities and the minorities should be able to live free from fear. On the other hand, we cannot allow a minority to place their veto on the advance of the majority.'

This evoked criticism from Jinnah, who protested that the Muslims were not a 'minority' but a 'nation', and that it was futile to expect co-operation from the Muslim League if the machinery to be set up for the framing of the new constitution was to be a single constitution-making body or assembly.

Nehru, on the other hand, detected a pleasant change in the tone and approach of Attlee's speech.

Azad said that on the whole the speech had helped 'to create the desirable atmosphere which we want to maintain during the stay of the Cabinet Delegation in India. It has thrown light on certain basic problems and I believe its spirit will generally be appreciated in the country.'

Other political parties also welcomed the visit of the Cabinet Mission and offered their co-operation.

The decision of His Majesty's Government to send three Cabinet Ministers to confer with Indian political leaders was an unprecedented step. But the situation in India was equally unprecedented; a complete deadlock had been reached which, if peace and progress were to be maintained, had to be broken. There were genuine expectations that the Cabinet Mission, in consultation with the Indian leaders, would find some satisfactory solution. Past distrust gave place to new hope and belief that India was at last on the road to Freedom and Independence.

# X

## THE CABINET MISSION

### I

THE Mission of Cabinet ministers arrived in New Delhi on 24 March 1946. Their welcome had already been assured. The reference in the British Prime Minister's speech to India's independence had been particularly well received. The passage relating to the minority not being allowed to place a veto on the advance of the majority had aroused misgivings in the minds of the members of the Muslim League, but at a press conference on the day following the Mission's arrival, Lord Pethick-Lawrence found an opportunity to reassure them. He observed that 'while the Congress are representative of larger numbers, it would not be right to regard the Muslim League as merely a minority political party—they are in fact majority representatives of the great Muslim community.' The Secretary of State explained that 'the discussions now to begin are preliminary to the setting up of machinery whereby the forms of government under which India can realize her full independent status can be determined by Indians. The objective is to set up an acceptable machinery quickly and to make the necessary interim arrangements.' The Secretary of State also announced that 'the Viceroy, while continuing to carry the full load of his normal responsibilities, will join with us as our colleague in the discussions with Indian leaders.'

Thus, unlike the procedure adopted at the time of the visit of Cripps in 1942, the Viceroy was to be not merely a consultant, but an effective partner in the efforts of the Cabinet Mission to find a solution of the Indian problem.

Sir Stafford Cripps, on behalf of the Mission, repudiated the suggestion that they had come with a ready-made solution. 'We really have no scheme,' he said, 'either on paper or in our heads, so its non-disclosure means nothing except that it is not there, and I hope that will be quite clear to everyone.'

The Cabinet Mission spent their first week in Delhi conferring with the Viceroy on their future programme, and acquainting themselves with the Indian situation generally by discussions with the provincial Governors and members of the Viceroy's Executive Council. The next fortnight was given to interviews with party leaders and out-standing personages, the premiers of provinces, leaders of the oppo-sition in the central and provincial legislatures, representatives of minorities and special interests, Princes and their ministers, and so on. In all these interviews and discussions there loomed the one outstand-ing issue, underlining the difference of approach between the Congress and the Muslim League — a United India *versus* Pakistan. Indeed, the desire for a united India was not confined to the Congress; it was shared by almost everyone outside the Muslim League.

It is not necessary to embark on a detailed survey of the numerous interviews and meetings held by the Cabinet Mission; nor is it pro-posed to deal with the negotiations with the representatives of the Indian States (since this has already been covered in my book dealing with the integration of the Indian States ); but this chapter would not be complete without some mention being made of the attitude and views which were expressed by the leaders of the more important political parties in India.

The Congress case was presented on 3 April by Abul Kalam Azad. It proceeded on the basis of independence and on the assumption that the future constitution would be determined by a constitution-making body. It was obvious from the Congress point of view that in the intervening period there should be an interim government at the Centre which would be responsible for all subsequent stages, includ-ing the setting up of the constitution-making body. With regard to the composition of the central Government, elections having taken place everywhere, the wishes of the provincial governments should be ascertained. In an interim government, of say fifteen members, there might be eleven provincial representatives, and four places might go to representatives of the minorities. This did not necessarily mean that there should be one member from each province; members would be chosen by the provincial governments, but they need not come from within the province nor need they be members of the legislatures.

Regarding the future constitution, what the Congress had in mind was a federal government with a limited number of compulsory federal subjects such as defence, communications and foreign affairs, and autonomous provinces in which would vest the residuary powers. There should be a list of optional subjects, so that it would be open to any province to decide for itself the extent to which it would be federated over and above the subjects in the compulsory list. The Congress plan was that on the completion of the work of the constitution-making body, a province should have three choices: (1) to stand out of the constitution, (2) to enter the constitution by federating for the compulsory subjects only and (3) to federate for the compulsory as well as for the optional subjects.

Sir Stafford Cripps asked whether Azad would be prepared to consider a separate optional list for the Muslim majority provinces, but Azad said that the idea was inconsistent with a single federal structure. The Secretary of State said he would like to put the matter differently. Assuming, for the sake of argument, that the Punjab, the North-West Frontier Province and Sind stood out of the optional list but had a number of matters in common, he did not see how they could be prevented from coming together under the Congress proposal, even if it meant federation within a federation. Azad said that this was a matter which would have to be examined further, though he thought he could concede the point provided that the compulsory link between the different parts of India was not in any way interfered with.

Arguing against the Muslim League demand, Azad stated that autonomy with regard to optional subjects could be granted, but that the Congress could never agree to the partition of India. The kind of Pakistan about which Muslims spoke — many of them did so without understanding what it meant — would do them no good.

The Secretary of State asked Azad if he realized that his proposal for the selection of members of the Executive Council by the provinces would give eight seats to the Congress and only two or three to the Muslim League. Sir Stafford Cripps inquired if Azad agreed to equality, or near equality, of Hindu and Muslim members. Azad said that under his proposal Muslims would not get more than two or three seats on the Executive Council, but arrangements could be made to give them more; he personally doubted whether the Congress would agree to 'parity'.

With regard to the machinery for deciding the character of the new constitution, Azad said that the Congress had originally considered that the constitution-making body should be elected on the widest possible franchise, but he now thought a short cut was urgently required. There was no reason why the provincial legislatures should not be taken as federal colleges to choose the constitution-making body. There should be one federal college voting together and not in provincial compartments. Azad agreed that it was not possible to compel the Indian States to come in, but the proposition could be made attractive to them. It was fundamental however that the people's representatives should not be left out. They could be chosen by *prajamandals*[1] or through the All-India States People's Conference.

Gandhiji was interviewed immediately after the meeting. The Secretary of State said that the Mission would like to have Gandhiji's advice as to what he would like to see happen, especially in relation to the position of the Muslim League. Gandhiji began by pointing out that he had come in his personal capacity and that the Secretary of State's question was one that should be put to the authorized representatives of the Congress. The Cabinet delegation, he said, would have a much greater measure of difficulty to contend with than any other mission to India. If they meant business, he would advise them to take such action as would produce a hearty friendship. This could not be done without the release of the political prisoners now in custody. For the same reasons the Salt Tax should be removed. Salt should be free for the poor man.

Gandhiji said that he had spent eighteen days in discussions with Jinnah. He claimed to be a sincere friend of the Muslims, but he had never been able to appreciate the Pakistan demanded by Jinnah. The substance of Pakistan, as Gandhiji understood it, was independence of culture and the satisfaction of legitimate ambitions. Rajagopalachari's formula had given concrete form to a proposal to meet this demand. If that were put into shape, it should serve as the basis for negotiation; and unless he himself were to be reasoned into it he could not go further because, beyond that, Pakistan was an 'untruth'.

In Gandhiji's view the two-nation theory was most dangerous. The Muslim population, but for a microscopic minority, was a population of converts. They were all descendants of Indian-born people. Gandhiji was opposed to the two-nation theory, or to two constitution-making bodies. After having exhausted all friendly resources, if the Mission felt that a stage must arrive when they must say that there should only be one constitution-making body, they must take the risk and go ahead. In any case, there must be a considerable interim period. What was to happen in that period? Gandhiji

[1] States people's associations.

suggested that Jinnah should be asked to form the first Government with a personnel chosen from the elected members of the legislature. The Viceroy would appoint them formally, but in fact Jinnah would choose them. If he refused, then the offer to form a Government should be made to the Congress. Gandhiji said in conclusion that he did not underrate the difficulties of the situation which the Mission had to face. Indeed, if he were not an irrepressible optimist, he would despair of any solution.

Jinnah was interviewed by the Mission on 4 April. He was invited to give his reasons for thinking it better for the future of India that there should be a separate Pakistan. Jinnah replied that throughout her history, from the days of Chandragupta, there had never been any Government of India in the sense of a single government. After the British had come they had gradually established their rule in a large part of India, but even then the country had only been partly united. The Indian States had been separate and sovereign. It was said that India was one, but this was not so. 'India was really many and was held by the British as one.'

Hindu-Muslim tension had begun to develop at the first transfer of a small amount of power in about 1906 and to meet it the British Government had given separate electorates. A similar situation had arisen at the time of the Montagu-Chelmsford Reforms. In the discussions of 1930-35 no agreement could be reached on the communal question and the British Government had been obliged to give an award. In deference to the wishes of the Muslims, Sind had been separated from Bombay and the North-West Frontier Province was made a Governor's province. All these decisions had been taken by Great Britain.

The British Government was now saying that it would give complete independence to India inside or outside the Empire. To whom, asked Jinnah, was the government of this sub-continent, with its fundamental differences, to be transferred?

The differences in India were far greater than those between European countries and were of a vital and fundamental character. Even Ireland provided no parallel. The Muslims had a different conception of life from the Hindus. They admired different qualities in their heroes; they had a different culture based on Arabic and Persian instead of Sanskrit origins. Their social customs were entirely different. Hindu society and philosophy were the most exclusive in the world. Muslims and Hindus had been living side by side in India for a thousand years, but if one went into any Indian city one would see separate Hindu and Muslim quarters. It was not possible to make a nation unless there were essential uniting factors.

How would His Majesty's Government put 100 millions of Muslims together with 250 millions whose whole way of life was so different? No government could survive unless there was a dominant element which could provide a 'steel frame'. This frame had hitherto been provided by the British, who had always retained the key posts in the Civil Service, the Police and the Army. It was necessary to have a 'steel frame' for an independent India, but Jinnah could see none. He had therefore come to the conclusion, after years of experience, that there was no other solution but the division of India. There were in India two totally different and deeply rooted civilizations side by side and the only solution was to have two 'steel frames', one in Hindustan and one in Pakistan. He agreed that it would be convenient to have common railways, customs and so forth, but the question was, by what government would those services be controlled? He certainly contemplated treaties and agreements governing such matters, which could be settled once the fundamentals of Pakistan were agreed.

Explaining the Cabinet Delegation's position, the Secretary of State said that up to a point he accepted the view that India had been united by British control and by the British Army, Navy and Air Force; but he would not go so far as to say that it was solely so united. He thought that Hindus and Muslims had not only acquiesced in, but had co-operated in supporting that unity. The Cabinet Mission had come to decide the ways and means by which the domination of the British authority in India was to come to an end. Therefore they had to decide into whose keeping the repository of force was to be given. What they wanted to know was whether there was any agreement as to the repository to which this power should be transferred. The Congress wanted a 'united India'; the rulers were prepared to join an all-India federation; but Jinnah insisted on two Indias with nothing more than treaties and agreements between them. If the British Government had to withdraw its forces and its government from India, it was entitled to know the situation in India. Would it find itself faced with a major head-on collision between the two main communities? If there were no other answer it would have to consider what it should do, but the British would certainly not stay to pull the chestnuts out of the fire. Moreover, the Cabinet Mission had come as the representatives of one of the world's great Powers. They had to look at the position in India as part of the world situation in the interests of the preservation of peace. They were entitled to ask whether India would be able to stand up for herself in the world. She would not be able to stand up at all at sea; and as a land power only to some extent. Therefore, the British Government presumed that it would be invited to assist in India's defence. The British Government would have to consider the conditions on which it would be prepared to do this and it might expect some return, for example, India's help in the defence of adjacent territories such as Malaya, Burma and Ceylon. But there must also be a solution of India's affairs with effective provision for her defence against external aggression, and the British Government was entitled to know whether the new set-up in India would be of a kind with which it could in practice co-operate.

The case of the Sikh community was presented by Master Tara Singh, Giani Kartar Singh and Harnam Singh, as well as by Baldev Singh. The first three were interviewed together, though each had his own individual views to put forward. The Mission wished particularly to know whether, if it were given the choice, the Sikh community would prefer the transfer of power to a single body, or to more than one body; if power were to be transferred to two bodies, which of them would the Sikh community wish to join; and if such a thing were practicable and could be arranged, would the Sikhs wish to have a separate autonomous State of their own?

Master Tara Singh said that he stood for a united India and for some sort of coalition government of all communities. The Hindus and Muslims were not united and would remain antagonistic for some time; in that situation the Sikhs in a united India would have a degree of bargaining power. If India were divided the Sikhs would come under the majority of one community or the other; in that case, they would prefer a separate independent Sikh State with the right to federate either with Hindustan or Pakistan.

Giani Kartar Singh said that the Sikhs would feel unsafe in either a united India or in Pakistan. They should have a province of their own where they would be in a dominant, or almost dominant, position. In reply to Sir Stafford Cripps, who asked what would be the area of the proposed Sikh State, Giani Kartar Singh suggested that it should be the whole of the Jullundur and Lahore divisions, together with the Hissar, Karnal, Ambala and Simla districts of the Ambala division and the Montgomery and Lyallpur districts.

Harnam Singh was opposed to the partition of India. Such a step, he said, would be against the wishes of the Sikh community. A divided India would be a prey to foreign invasion and there could be no safeguard except in an independent Sikh State. He advocated an increased representation of Sikhs in the proposed constitution-making body and pleaded for a separate one for Sikhs if there were to be more than one constitution-making body.

Baldev Singh, who was a minister in the Punjab Government at the time, was interviewed separately. He gave a brief description of the manner in which the position of the Sikh community had deteriorated since 1914 and how impossible it would be for it to exist unless it were given special protection. Sir Stafford Cripps asked specifically how 'Khalistan' could be formed, to which Baldev Singh replied that it would be the Punjab, excluding the Multan and Rawalpindi divisions, with an approximate boundary along the Chenab river. An area comprising the Ambala division, the Jullundur division and the Lahore division was the smallest that could be contemplated. But the Sikhs strongly favoured a united India; they considered the division of India unwise because the small States on the frontier would be at the mercy of great powers and so be a source of danger to India. In Baldev Singh's view the best solution was a united India, with safeguards for minorities in the form of weighted communal proportions in the legislatures. Questioned as to the nature of the safeguards which he would regard as adequate, Baldev Singh said that in some of the British-Indian provinces, e.g. Bombay, weightage was given to Muslims as against the Hindus. If, in the Punjab legislature, the Muslims were content to have forty-five per cent of the seats instead of fifty-one per cent, and the balance were to be divided between the Hindus and the Sikhs, then Sikh interests could be protected.

Ambedkar was interviewed on behalf of the Scheduled Castes Federation. In reply to an enquiry as to the method of representation of Scheduled Castes in the constituent assembly, he said that he did not want a constituent assembly at all. It would be dominated by the Caste Hindus, and the Scheduled Castes would be no more than a small minority which would always be outvoted. All the assurances of protection which His Majesty's Government had given to the minorities would go by the board. His own proposal was that the tasks envisaged for the constituent assembly should be divided into two classes, namely (a) constitutional questions properly so called, e.g. the relations between the legislature and the executive and their respective composition and functions, and (b) communal questions. Matters under (a) should be referred to a commission presided over by an eminent constitutional lawyer from Great Britain or the U.S.A. The other members should be two Indian experts and one representative each of the Hindu and Muslim communities. The terms of reference should be the Government of India Act of 1935 and the commission should be required to recommend what changes should be made in the Act as it stood. Matters under (b) should be referred to a conference of the leaders of the different communities. If the conference failed to arrive at an agreed solution, His Majesty's Government should make an award.

Ambedkar claimed that, before they left, the British must ensure that the new constitution guaranteed to the Scheduled Castes the elementary human rights of life, liberty and the pursuit of happiness, and that it restored their separate electorates and gave them the other safeguards which they demanded. The Secretary of State suggested that Indian politics had been dominated by two issues, the question of winning independence from British rule and the Hindu-Muslim problem. Once these were out of the way, party divisions would probably be on economic issues. Surely the Scheduled Castes would have a better chance of securing their rights by allying themselves with the left wing than by relying on the British, who were about to hand over power. Ambedkar reiterated that so long as there were joint electorates, Scheduled Caste voters would be so few that Hindu candidates could safely ignore their wishes. Caste Hindus would never support Scheduled Caste candidates. Separate electorates were fundamental; without them the Scheduled Castes would never have their own representatives.

Jagjivan Ram, Radhanath Das and Prithvi Singh Azad attended together as representatives of the All-India Depressed Classes' League. They said that the League was opposed to any proposal which would impair the integrity of the country; that, in its view, the division of India into Pakistan and Hindustan would not provide a solution to the minority problem but would produce fresh problems; that it was also opposed to the setting up of more than one constituent assembly. The new constitution should contain provisions for the safeguarding of the language, culture etc. of the minorities and the rights and interests of the Scheduled Castes. With regard to the interim Government, the Depressed Classes' League was opposed to weightage being given to any community by depriving another community of its legitimate share; but if it were decided to give weightage, the Scheduled Castes should also be given weightage. The interim Government should be responsible to the legislature; and defence, finance and foreign affairs should be handed over to the Cabinet, whose members should be elected by the various provincial legislatures. Special provision should be made for the representation of the minority communities, and Scheduled Caste members of the provincial assemblies should form an electoral college to select persons for inclusion in the central Government.

Jagjivan Ram said that the difference between the Scheduled Castes Federation (led by Ambedkar) and the Depressed Classes' League was that, whereas the Federation held that the Scheduled Castes were not Hindus but a religious minority of their own, the League held that the Scheduled Caste masses considered themselves Hindus and that they had sacrificed much for the cause of Hinduism. The Depressed Classes' League pressed for special representation in the legislature and in the Services in order to enable the Scheduled Castes to raise themselves to the level of the rest of the country.

Shyama Prasad Mookerjee and L. B. Bhopatkar represented the Hindu Mahasabha. They handed in a memorandum which urged that His Majesty's Government should immediately declare India free and independent; that the integrity and indivisibility of the country should be maintained at any cost and that partition would be economically unsound, disastrous, politically unwise and suicidal. The Mahasabha would not agree to any suggestion that Hindus and Muslims should be represented in the central Government on the basis of equality.

Mookerjee stressed that the Mahasabha could not compromise on the Pakistan issue. His own idea, which he had put to Jinnah some years ago, was that representatives of the two communities should meet and that each should explain in what respects it wanted protection from the other. The Mahasabha would be willing to concede the fullest measure of autonomy to the provinces and would give minorities the maximum protection in respect of their languages, religions and customs.

Sir Tej Bahadur Sapru and M. R. Jayakar, the Liberal leaders, were also interviewed, separately. Sir Tej Bahadur Sapru stressed the necessity for the immediate formation of an interim Government. He had, he said, always recognized that the Muslims should be given a satisfactory measure of power, but he saw grave risks in partition. A strong Centre was vital for India; the fullest autonomy should be given to the Muslim provinces; but defence, foreign affairs and such matters as War Transport should have to remain under central control. Consistently with this, any principle of safeguards could be provided for the Muslims and made enforceable in the courts of law.

Sir Tej Bahadur advised the Mission not to attempt to by-pass the Muslim League. They should make the most liberal offer possible to the Muslims — short of the division of India. He believed that there were thousands of Muslims who were not convinced of the case for Pakistan; all that the elections had shown was that the Congress and the Muslim League were the two biggest parties in India.

He suggested that, in order to save Jinnah's face, the provincial boundaries could be revised to give solid Muslim majorities in certain provinces. There should be an equality of Muslims and Caste Hindus in the central Government. He stated that he would object most strongly to two constitution-making bodies, but that if there were one body sitting in two parts, that would be altogether different and it might be possible to get the Congress to agree to the idea.

Jayakar suggested that there were two things which the Mission had to do — first, to set up an interim Government commanding the confidence of the main political parties, and secondly, to establish the machinery for subsequent action. In his view the whole idea of Pakistan was based on slogans, in none of which was there much substance. He considered that a confederation of States was as bad as Pakistan. He commended the views and conclusions of the Sapru Committee with regard to the Centre. He believed that the powers reserved to the Centre should be as few as possible, though they should include foreign affairs, courts, customs, emergency powers, etc. In these matters and especially in defence, the Centre should be very strong. He also shared the view that the Muslims should be given parity with the Caste Hindus in the Cabinet and that they should also receive weightage in the legislatures and in the Constituent Assembly.

On or about 10 April and while these interviews were still in progress, Jinnah called together in Delhi a convention of over four hundred members of the various legislatures recently elected on the Muslim League ticket. A lengthy resolution was passed which demanded a sovereign and independent State of Pakistan, comprising the six provinces of Bengal and Assam in the north-east, and the Punjab, the North-West Frontier Province, Sind and Baluchistan in the north-west of India; the setting up of two separate constitution-making bodies by the peoples of Pakistan and Hindustan for the purpose of framing their respective constitutions, and the provision of safeguards for the minorities. The acceptance of the Muslim League demand for Pakistan, and its implementation without delay, were declared to be the sine qua non for Muslim League co-operation and participation in the formation of an interim Government at the Centre. Any attempt to impose a constitution or to force on them an interim Government contrary to their demand would leave the Muslims no alternative but to resist such imposition by all the means possible for their survival and national existence.

There followed a large number of statements by Congress and other party leaders contesting Jinnah's point of view.

The members of the Cabinet Mission had themselves already been studying various alternative schemes with a view to finding a common formula on which to bring the leaders of the Congress and the Muslim League together. The outstanding issue was Pakistan. If a sovereign State were to be established in the north-west and north-east of India, it would not be fair to include in it, against the will of those concerned, large blocs of territory inhabited predominantly by non-Muslims. The problem was to devise some constitutional arrangement which would secure the essence of the Muslim League demand and at the same time be acceptable to the Congress. That was no easy task. The Mission had before them the idea, for instance, of an Indian Union confined to defence and foreign affairs, having under it two federations of Pakistan and Hindustan; but they felt that in approaching the two parties there was some danger of selling different articles under the same name. Jinnah was apparently resolved not to budge from his position. His way of arriving at his goal was to dissolve the existing central structure and to rebuild it on the basis of Pakistan; once the Pakistan State came into being he would be prepared to construct a Centre on some sort of agency basis through a treaty. The Congress, on the other hand, would start with the existing Centre and subtract the optional subjects. There was a wide difference between these two conceptions. The first involved, for example, the undoing of the Indian Army and re-creating it as two armies; the second meant that the main army would remain under the central Government, though Hindustan and Pakistan might have smaller forces of their own.

The Mission felt that they should see both Jinnah and Azad again with a view to exploring, in discussion with each of them, the possibilities of a compromise. Jinnah was interviewed on 16 April, Azad on the following day.

At the interview on 16 April the Secretary of State told Jinnah that the Mission recognized the importance of the claims which he had put forward on behalf of his community, but that it was essential to reach an agreement between the parties, and if this could be done on the main issue other matters would fall into place. If there were no agreement the prospects for the people of India, for Great Britain and for the world, would be gravely affected. The Mission were therefore approaching Jinnah on the one hand, and the Congress on the other, with a view to closing the gap between the two parties.

After having considered with the greatest care the case which Jinnah had put forward, the Mission had come to the conclusion that the full and complete demand for Pakistan in the form presented by Jinnah had little chance of acceptance. He could not, in their view, reasonably hope to receive both the whole of the territory (much of it inhabited by non-Muslims) which he claimed, and the full measure of sovereignty which he said was essential. If the full territories were insisted upon and if there were to be a reasonable prospect of agreement, some element of sovereignty must be relinquished. On the other hand, if full sovereignty was desired, the claim to the non-Muslim territories could not be conceded. The Mission believed that progress might be possible in one of two ways. First, agreement might be reached on a separate State of Pakistan consisting of say, Sind, the North-West Frontier Province, Baluchistan and the Muslim majority districts of Bengal, the Punjab and Assam. The inclusion of Calcutta in the Pakistan territory could not be justified on any principle of self-determination, and its being treated as a free port seemed to be a doubtful proposition. On this basis it would clearly be necessary to contract a defensive alliance with Hindustan and enter into special treaty relations with it. Under this scheme the Indian States would be at liberty to join Hindustan or Pakistan, or to remain outside. No doubt there would be points in this scheme which would not appeal to Jinnah; but the Mission did not think that they, for their part, could press the Congress to go further than this to meet his point of view. The Secretary of State emphasized that this proposal was not a scheme which the Cabinet Mission put forward as one which they considered the best, or even as desirable, but as a possibly hopeful line along which agreement might be achieved.

Alternatively, the Congress and the Muslim League might sit down together and try to evolve an agreed scheme for an Indian Union. If the League accepted the principle of a Union Centre for the essential subjects, say defence, foreign affairs and communications, it might then be possible to include in one federation the whole of the province of Sind, Baluchistan, the North-West Frontier Province, the Punjab and Bengal, *plus* perhaps the Sylhet district of Assam. In such a Union the two parties might have equal representation. Whether the Indian States would come into the Union as a separate federation would be a matter for negotiation. There might be a provision that any party to it could secede after a certain period, say fifteen years. A set-up of this kind would secure a very strong Muslim federation and might possibly be acceptable to the Congress.

Jinnah asked how Pakistan would come in under the proposed all-India Union. The Secretary of State said that briefly there were two propositions—a small Pakistan with sovereign rights and a treaty relation, and a larger Pakistan which would function together with Hindustan on terms of equality within an all-India Union for the essential purposes of defence and foreign affairs. Under the second alternative, said Sir Stafford Cripps, there would be two federations linked by a Union Centre. The Indian States would come in either at the Union or at the federation level and there would be equal representation of Hindustan and Pakistan at the Union level. The communal balance would be retained at the Centre by some means even if the Indian States came in.

Jinnah asked how the Union executive would be formed. Sir Stafford Cripps said that the federations would choose the members of the Union executive. Jinnah asked how, if there was equal representation, decisions were to be reached. Sir Stafford Cripps replied that there would be no Union Parliament; the responsibility would go back to the two federations if agreement could not be reached, and differences could only be decided by inter-governmental agreement. Jinnah doubted whether such an arrangement would work in practice. Decisions would have to be taken every day on many important questions, especially in regard to defence. From what had been said, he had not been able to get anything which would enable him to say that the Union idea was worth considering.

The Secretary of State emphasized that the essence of the Union scheme was the equality of the two component parts, which made it entirely different from a Centre in which the Hindus had a majority. Of course, the Secretary of State did not know whether the Congress would agree to this principle of equality, but it was the essence of the proposal. Jinnah said that no amount of equality provided on paper would work. Equality could not exist between the majority and a minority within the same governmental system. He did not think that the domination of the Muslims by the Hindus could be prevented in any scheme in which they were kept together. It was only when the Muslims were the majority in Pakistan and the Hindus in Hindustan that there could be sufficient united force running through the State from the top to the bottom to provide a 'steel frame' which could hold it together.

The Secretary of State said that Jinnah seemed to be turning to the other alternative and he asked his views on that. Jinnah said that once the principle of Pakistan was conceded, the question of the territory of Pakistan could be discussed. His claim was for six provinces, but he was willing to discuss the area. The first question was whether the principle of Pakistan was accepted. Jinnah contended that his claim for six provinces was a reasonable demand, but he could not possibly agree that Calcutta should go out merely for the sake of five or six lakhs of Hindus (largely Depressed Classes who would prefer Pakistan) most of whom were imported labour. The Secretary of State said that the Mission's immediate object was to find a basis of agreement; they did not think that agreement could be reached on the basis that Calcutta should be included in Pakistan. Jinnah stressed that he could not in any event accept the exclusion of Calcutta.

The Secretary of State said that he wished to emphasize that the Mission did not consider that either of these two alternatives would be readily acceptable to the Congress. Jinnah replied that the Congress was in a very strong position; even if the whole of his claims were granted, the Congress got three-quarters of India. At worst, it would lose Calcutta, some part of Western Bengal (Burdwan) and the Ambala Division. The Secretary of State said that the Congress would lose much more than this. It would lose the unity of India, which alone would make India a strong entity in the outside world. Further, if Pakistan were conceded, the difficulty of getting the Indian States into a united India would be greatly increased. Jinnah still adhered to his view that the Congress stood to lose nothing and declared that the 'unity of India' was a myth.

The Secretary of State pointed out that if Jinnah did obtain, otherwise than by agreement, more than the Muslim-majority districts, he would find himself in a very vulnerable position later. He would have a large internal element of Hindu population, as well as external opposition from a hostile Hindustan. Pakistan would be in two parts, divided by a power which would be hostile to both of them. That seemed to the Secretary of State to be an exceedingly difficult and dangerous position to be in. But Jinnah said that he thought that this was an exaggerated statement of the position; all the non-Muslims could not be counted as Hindus.

He went on to say that if the Congress pressed the British Government to make an award, it was very likely that, in order to appease them, the latter would give some part of the six provinces of Pakistan to Hindustan. The Secretary of State interposed to say that the consequences of no agreement were much worse than that. A settlement without agreement would lead to chaos, and the whole future prospect for the Indian people would be blighted. Jinnah retorted that these arguments should be put before the Congress. If he made a concession, he would have lost it before the negotiations began. It was the Congress that should make a proposal.

The Secretary of State said that Jinnah was not being asked to commit himself to anything, but merely to say whether he would prefer the matter to be considered on the basis of sovereignty and a small area, or on the basis of a Union and a larger area. Jinnah replied that he could not accept the Union principle; on the other hand, he claimed the six provinces, and if the Congress thought it was too much they should say what they considered he ought to have. Subsequently, Jinnah said that he understood from the Mission that there was a chance of a settlement on the basis of the first alternative. If the Congress would say that on that basis they wanted certain defined areas taken from Pakistan, he was willing to discuss whether what they proposed was reasonable, fair and workable. He would try his very best to reach agreement with the Congress; but if what they proposed struck at the heart of Pakistan, or if the principle of Pakistan was not accepted, it was no use pursuing the matter.

The Secretary of State suggested that Jinnah should think the matter over and see whether he could not revise his attitude with regard to the second alternative. Meanwhile, had he any opinion to express on whether the two alternatives should be put to the Congress on the following day? Jinnah merely said that the more the Congress was encouraged to lop off parts of the Pakistan which he claimed, or to reduce its sovereignty, the less possibility would there be of an agreed settlement.

At the interview with Azad on the 17th, the Secretary of State said that the Mission considered that the Pakistan question was the main issue and they hoped very much that it would be possible for agreement on this subject to be reached between the Congress and the Muslim League. The Mission had seen Jinnah and put some general suggestions to him. They were awaiting his response and till then would prefer not to say anything, except that they felt sure that in any discussions on these subjects they could count on the Congress showing a spirit of compromise.

The Secretary of State was particularly anxious to know Azad's views on the structure of the federal Centre. Azad said that, as he had already explained, there would be two lists of central subjects, compulsory and optional; he agreed that the compulsory list should include foreign affairs and defence and that, broadly speaking, the optional list would cover all the remaining central subjects under the existing constitution. The Secretary of State said that he would like to envisage the position clearly under this proposal. If some provinces decided not to opt for the second list a Centre would come into being which would have different relations with two sets of provinces, some federated for a wider range of subjects than others. This seemed to involve the sub-division of the Centre into two parts dealing with (a) the provinces that had opted for the full range of subjects and (b) the provinces that were federated for the compulsory subjects only. If there were anything in the nature of Pakistan the provinces within it could not be prevented from agreeing on their own to pool some of their subjects in the optional field; this would work out in practice as separate centres for Pakistan and Hindustan, with a super-Centre above them dealing with the compulsory subjects. Azad said that this was a matter which he must discuss with the Working Committee. There were many other matters which needed to be discussed, such as the future relationship between Britain and India. The Mission suggested that Azad might like to send them a list of those matters so that they could consider them before they met him again.

Neither of these interviews produced anything like promising results. Nor did further personal contacts made by members of the Mission individually prove fruitful. Jinnah was entirely immovable in his demand for Pakistan. He remained firmly opposed to a common legislature or executive, even on the basis of equal representation. Meanwhile, Gandhiji and Nehru informed Sir Stafford Cripps that the proposal for an all-India Union on a three-tier basis would not be acceptable to the Congress.

The Cabinet Mission proceeded to Kashmir for a short respite. While there, they decided that they must adopt a new line of approach. The gist of their plan was that an interim Government should be formed forthwith. The interim Government would be responsible for setting up an all-India commission from the elected members of the provincial and central Assemblies, whose duty it would be to determine (a) the provisions to be made in any constitution or constitutions for the protection of the minorities, and (b) whether there should be one or two sovereign States in British India. If within thirty days there was no agreement on (b), the question would be put to the vote; and if the dissentient minority amounted to more than a certain prescribed percentage, the question would be decided by a method equivalent to a plebiscite. The Muslim representatives in each of the provincial Assemblies of Sind, the North-West Frontier Province, the Punjab and Bengal (with the addition of the district of Sylhet in Assam) would meet separately and vote as to whether they desired the particular province to be excluded from the rest of India. In the event of seventy-five per cent of such representatives deciding in favour of exclusion, that province would be excluded. Baluchistan would also be excluded if it were decided to exclude the contiguous provinces. It would be open to the non-Muslim representatives of any non-Muslim majority district, or districts contiguous to the main part of India, to meet and to vote as to whether they desired their districts to remain within the rest of India and so to be divided out from the excluded province. As soon as these decisions had been arrived at, there would be set up one or two constituent assemblies, as the case might be, to determine the new constitution or constitutions for India. The Mission appreciated that the North-West Frontier Province would probably vote against separation, but that, if the neighbouring provinces decided for it, the North-West Frontier Province would also have to be separated.

The proposed scheme was certainly an ingenious one. It was put before Jinnah by Sir Stafford Cripps on 24 April, after the Mission's return from Kashmir. Jinnah rejected the plan; so also did the Congress leaders when it was put to them. But Sir Stafford Cripps did not relax his efforts; he prepared a revised confederation plan. This however, had certain inherent defects. Finally, it was decided to fall back upon the original three-tier scheme, and Jinnah said that if he could be assured that the Congress was prepared to consider the three-tier scheme he would put it to the Muslim League Working Committee.

The difficulty was that this proposal had already been considered and rejected by the Congress. But when Sir Stafford Cripps saw Azad on the morning of the 26th, the latter himself raised the question of a three-tier constitution. He said that he thought he could get the Congress Working Committee to agree to a single federation which would be broken up into two parts, legislating for optional subjects. Sir Stafford Cripps asked if it would be possible for him to say to Jinnah that the Congress was prepared to negotiate on the basis of two federations having two separate legislatures, with a Union executive and legislature above them for compulsory subjects. Azad said that he hoped to get the Working Committee to agree to meet the Mission and representatives of the Muslim League to discuss the possibility of a settlement.

Sir Stafford Cripps thereupon saw Jinnah once more and explained to him the position which had been reached with the Congress in regard to the possibility of a joint meeting of Congress and League representatives and the Cabinet Mission. Jinnah was in a difficult mood; but in the end he agreed to put the proposal for a joint meeting to his Working Committee, provided the Mission sent him a letter specifically making that proposal.

It was in these circumstances that, on the evening of 27 April, letters couched in practically identical terms were sent by the Secretary of State to the presidents of the Congress and the League. It was stated that the Mission had decided to make one further attempt to obtain agreement between the two parties, but they appreciated that it would be useless to ask the parties to meet unless they were able to place before them a basis of negotiation likely to lead to agreement. Accordingly, each of the parties was invited to send four negotiators to meet the Mission, with a view to discussing the possibility of agreement upon a scheme based on the following fundamental principles.

The future constitution of British India would comprise: (a) a Union government dealing with foreign affairs, defence and communications, and (b) two groups of provinces, the one predominantly Hindu and the other predominantly Muslim, dealing with all other subjects which the provinces in the respective groups desired should be dealt with in common. The provincial governments would deal with all other subjects and would have all the residuary sovereign rights. The Indian States would take their appropriate place in the structure on terms to be negotiated with them.

The Congress reply was to the effect that, while the Secretary of State's letter referred to certain 'fundamental principles' (and these required amplification and elucidation), there was no mention of the basic issue of India's independence and the consequent withdrawal of British troops from India, and that it was only on this basis that the Congress could discuss the future of India or any interim arrangement. There were other points of disagreement, but as the Secretary of State himself pointed out, all these matters could be discussed at the meeting. The Congress agreed to send the following representatives to the proposed conference, namely, Azad, Nehru, Vallabhbhai Patel and Abdul Ghaffar Khan.

The President of the Muslim League also mentioned that there were several important matters, both of principle and detail, in the Secretary of State's letter, which called for elucidation and clarification. The following persons, however, were nominated to participate on behalf of the League in the proposed tripartite discussion, namely Jinnah, Mahommed Ismail Khan, Liaqat Ali Khan and Abdur Rab Nishtar.

The Conference took place in Simla between the 5th and 12th of May, but despite the valiant efforts of the Mission, the disagreement between the two parties — as we shall see later — proved too wide to be reconciled.

# XI

## THE CABINET MISSION

### II

WHEN the Cabinet Mission decided to invite representatives of the Congress and the Muslim League to confer
with them in Simla, it was not with any hope of securing
an immediate settlement of their differences, but rather in the belief
that, by bringing the two parties together, they would narrow the gap
and be able eventually to effect some satisfactory compromise.

The Conference was held in Simla. It opened on 5 May 1946 with
a short address by Lord Pethick-Lawrence, followed by preliminary
statements by the parties. The Conference then proceeded to deal
with items of an agenda[1] which had been drawn up by the Mission.
After two days of discussion the gulf between the two parties was still
as wide as ever.

On 6 May, the President of the Congress wrote to the Secretary of
State saying that he was somewhat mystified and disturbed at the
vagueness of the talks and some of the assumptions underlying them.
The letter reiterated the Congress stand in regard to independence
and its demand for the withdrawal of British troops from India.
Regarding the provisional interim Government, the Congress desired
that it should function, as far as possible, as a Government of free
India and that it should undertake to make all arrangements for the

---

**[1] AGENDA**

1. Groups of Provinces:
   - (a) Composition.
   - (b) Method of deciding group subjects.
   - (c) Character of group organisation.
2. Union.
   - (a) Union subjects.
   - (b) Character of Union constitution.
   - (c) Finance.

3. Constitution-making machinery.
   - (a) Composition.
   - (b) Functions
     - (i) in respect of the Union;
     - (ii) in respect of groups;
     - (iii) in respect of provinces.

transitional period. The Congress was entirely opposed to any executive or legislative machinery for groups of provinces or units of the Federation. That would result in creating three layers of executive and legislative bodies — an arrangement that would be cumbrous, static, disjointed and that must lead to continuous friction. Nor was such an arrangement, so far as the Congress was aware, to be found in any country. The Congress was also against parity as between groups in the executive or legislature. 'We are emphatically of opinion,' the letter went on to say, 'that it is not open to the conference to entertain any suggestions for a division of India. If this is to come, it should come through the Constituent Assembly, free from any influence of the present governing power.'

On 8 May, the Secretary of State sent the presidents of the Congress and the Muslim League a list[1] of 'suggested points for agreement between the representatives of the Congress and the Muslim League.'

In a long letter to the Secretary of State Jinnah protested that these points were a fundamental departure from the original formula proposed by the Secretary of State; that there were many objectionable features in the new suggestions, and that no useful purpose would be served by a discussion of them.

The Secretary of State sent him a reply in which he attempted to clear up some of the misapprehensions expressed in his letter and

---

[1] SUGGESTED POINTS FOR AGREEMENT BETWEEN THE REPRESENTATIVES OF THE CONGRESS AND THE MUSLIM LEAGUE

1. There shall be an all-India Union Government and Legislature dealing with foreign affairs, defence, communications, fundamental rights and having the necessary powers to obtain for itself the finances it requires for these subjects.

2. All the remaining powers shall vest in the provinces.

3. Groups of provinces may be formed and such groups may determine the provincial subjects which they desire to take in common.

4. The groups may set up their own executives and legislatures.

5. The Legislature of the Union shall be composed of equal proportions from the Muslim-majority provinces and from the Hindu-majority provinces whether or not these or any of them have formed themselves into groups, together with representatives of the States.

6. The Government of the Union shall be constituted in the same proportion as the Legislature.

7. The constitutions of the Union and the groups (if any) shall contain a provision whereby any province can by a majority vote of its Legislative Assembly call for a reconsideration of the terms of the constitution after an initial period of 10 years and at 10 yearly intervals thereafter.

For the purpose of such reconsideration a body shall be constituted on the same basis as the original Constituent Assembly and with the same provisions as to voting and shall have power to amend the constitution in any way decided upon.

8. The constitution-making machinery to arrive at a constitution on the above basis shall be as follows:

hoped that it would be possible for him to attend the conference on the 9th afternoon.

The Congress President also wrote to the Secretary of State pointing out that some of the suggestions were entirely opposed to the views of the Congress. The letter stressed the Congress objections to the compulsory grouping of provinces and parity. The only reasonable course, in the view of the Congress, was to have a constituent assembly with perfect freedom to draw up its constitution with certain reservations to protect the rights of minorities. Thus, the Congress might agree that any major communal issue should be settled by consent of the parties concerned, or where such consent was not obtainable, by arbitration. The letter proceeded to point out several obvious omissions and defects, from the Congress point of view, in the Secretary of State's memorandum, and stressed that the Federal Union should have the power to raise revenues in its own right; that currency and customs should in any case be included in the Union subjects; that provision should be made in the Union list for other subjects such as Planning, and that the Union should have power to take remedial action in case of a breakdown of the Constitution and in grave emergencies.

'If,' the letter concluded, 'an agreement honourable to both the parties and favourable to the growth of a free and united India cannot be achieved, we would suggest that an interim provisional Government responsible to the elected members of the central Assembly be formed at once and the matters in dispute concerning the Constituent

A. Representatives shall be elected from each provincial Assembly in proportion to the strengths of the various parties in that Assembly on the basis of 1/10th of their numbers.

B. Representatives shall be invited from the States on the basis of their population in proportion to the representation from British India.

C. The Constituent Assembly so formed shall meet at the earliest date possible in New Delhi.

D. After its preliminary meeting at which the general order of business will be settled, it will divide into three sections, one section representing the Hindu-majority provinces, one section representing the Muslim-majority provinces and one representing the States.

E. The first two sections will then meet separately to decide the provincial constitutions for their group and, if they wish, a group constitution.

F. When these have been settled it will be open to any province to decide to opt out of its original group and into the other group or to remain outside any group.

G. Thereafter the three bodies will meet together to settle the constitution for the Union on the lines agreed in paragraphs 1—7 above.

H. No major point in the Union constitution which affects the communal issue shall be deemed to be passed by the Assembly unless a majority of both the two major communities vote in its favour.

9. The Viceroy shall forthwith call together the above constitution-making machinery which shall be governed by the provisions stated in paragraph 8 above.

Assembly between the Congress and the League be referred to an independent tribunal.'

Nevertheless, the 'suggested points for agreement' were taken up for discussion when the Conference met on 9 May. Nehru made the suggestion that one or more representatives of each side should sit together, with an umpire, to discuss the points still at issue and that, in the event of disagreement, the umpire's decision should be accepted as final. Jinnah said that he would like to discuss this proposal with Nehru. There was a short interval, after which it was agreed to adjourn the Conference till the 11th afternoon to enable Nehru and Jinnah to continue their discussions.

Incidentally, on 9 May the members of the Viceroy's Executive Council, including the Commander-in-Chief, placed their respective portfolios at the disposal of the Viceroy in order to facilitate the formation of a new interim Government.

The next meeting of the Conference, on the 11th afternoon, was not a success. It transpired that Jinnah had refused to accept the decision of an umpire. After some discussion, it was agreed to adjourn the Conference till the next evening. In the meantime, each of the parties was asked to furnish a statement setting out its attitude on the points that were still outstanding.

The Muslim League submitted a memorandum setting out its minimum demands, 'by way of an offer', in the following terms:

(1) The six Muslim provinces (the Punjab, North-West Frontier Province, Baluchistan, Sind, Bengal and Assam) shall be grouped together as one group and will deal with all other subjects and matters except foreign affairs, defence and communications necessary for defence, which may be dealt with by the constitution-making bodies of the two groups of provinces — Muslim provinces (hereinafter named Pakistan Group) and Hindu provinces — sitting together.

(2) There shall be a separate constitution-making body for the six Muslim provinces named above, which will frame constitutions for the group and the provinces in the group, and will determine the list of subjects that shall be Provincial and Central (of the Pakistan Federation) with residuary sovereign powers vesting in the provinces.

(3) The method of election of the representatives to the constitution-making body will be such as would secure proper representation to the various communities in proportion to their population in each province of the Pakistan Group.

(4) After the constitutions of the Pakistan Federal Government and the provinces are finally framed by the constitution-making body, it will be

open to any province of the group to decide to opt out of its group, provided the wishes of the people of that province are ascertained by a referendum to opt out or not.

(5) It must be open to discussion in the joint constitution-making body as to whether the Union will have a legislature or not. The method of providing the Union with finance should also be left for decision of the joint meeting of the two constitution-making bodies, but in no event shall it be by means of taxation.

(6) There should be parity of representation between the two groups of provinces in the Union executive and the legislature, if any.

(7) No major point in the Union Constitution which affects the communal issue shall, be deemed to be passed in the joint constitution-making body, unless the majority of the members of the constitution-making body of the Hindu provinces and the majority of the members of the constitution-making body of the Pakistan group, present and voting, are separately in its favour.

(8) No decision, legislative, executive or administrative, shall be taken by the Union in regard to any matter of a controversial nature, except by a majority of three-fourths.

(9) In group and provincial constitutions, fundamental rights and safeguards concerning religion, culture and other matters affecting the different communities will be provided for.

(10) The constitution of the Union shall contain a provision whereby any province can, by a majority vote of its Legislative Assembly, call for reconsideration of the terms of the constitution, and will have the liberty to secede from the Union at any time after an initial period of ten years.

These, it was stated, were the principles of the League's offer for a peaceful and amicable settlement and this offer stood in its entirety and all matters mentioned therein were interdependent.

The following were the points suggested on behalf of the Congress as a basis for agreement:

1. The Constituent Assembly to be formed as follows:

(*i*) Representatives shall be elected by each provincial Assembly by proportional representation (single transferable vote). The number so elected should be one-fifth of the number of members of the Assembly and they may be members of the Assembly or others;

(*ii*) Representatives from the States on the basis of their population in proportion to the representation from British India. How these representatives are to be chosen is to be considered later.

2. The Constituent Assembly shall draw up a constitution for the Federal Union. This shall consist of an All-India Federal Government and

Legislature dealing with foreign affairs, defence, communications, fundamental rights, currency, customs and planning, as well as such other subjects as, on closer scrutiny, may be found to be intimately allied to them. The Federal Union will have necessary powers to obtain for itself the finances it requires for these subjects and the power to raise revenues in its own right. The Union must also have power to take remedial action in cases of breakdown of the constitution and in grave public emergencies.

3. All the remaining powers shall vest in the provinces or units.

4. Groups of provinces may be formed and such groups may determine the provincial subjects which they desire to take in common.

5. After the Constituent Assembly has decided the constitution for the All-India Federal Union as laid down in paragraph 2 above, the representatives of the provinces may form groups to decide the provincial constitutions for their group and, if they wish, a group constitution.

6. No major point in the All-India Federal Constitution which affects the communal issue shall be deemed to be passed by the Constituent Assembly unless a majority of the members of the community or communities concerned present in the Assembly and voting are separately in its favour. Provided that in case there is no agreement on any such issue, it will be referred to arbitration. In case of doubt as to whether any point is a major communal issue, the Speaker will decide, or, if so desired, it may be referred to the Federal Court.

7. In the event of a dispute arising in the process of constitution-making, the specific issue shall be referred to arbitration.

8. The constitution should provide machinery for its revision at any time subject to such checks as may be desired. If so desired, it may be specifically stated that the whole constitution may be reconsidered after ten years.

The Congress also submitted the following note to show in what respects its own proposals differed from those embodied in the Muslim League's memorandum:

(1) We suggest that the proper procedure is for one constitution-making body or Constituent Assembly to meet for the whole of India and later for groups to be formed, if so desired, by the provinces concerned. The matter should be left to the provinces and if they wish to function as a group they are at liberty to do so and to frame their constitution for the purpose.

In any event Assam has obviously no place in the group mentioned, and the North-West Frontier Province, as the elections show, is not in favour of this proposal.

(2) We have agreed to residuary powers, apart from the central subjects, vesting in the provinces. They can make such use of them as they like and, as has been stated above, function as a group. What the ultimate nature of such a group may be cannot be determined at this stage and should be left to the representatives of the provinces concerned.

(3) We have suggested that the most suitable method of election would be by single transferable vote. This would give proper representation to the various communities in proportion to their present representation in the legislatures. If the population proportion is taken, we have no particular objection, but this would lead to difficulties in all the provinces where there is weightage in favour of certain communities. The principle approved of would necessarily apply to all the provinces.

(4) There is no necessity for opting out of a province from its group as the previous consent of the provinces is necessary for joining the group.

(5) We consider it essential that the Federal Union should have a Legislature. We also consider it essential that the Union should have power to raise its own revenue.

(6 & 7) We are entirely opposed to parity of representation as between groups of provinces in the Union executive or legislature. We think that the provision to the effect that no major communal issue in the Union constitution shall be deemed to be passed by the Constituent Assembly unless a majority of the members of the community or communities concerned present and voting in the Constituent Assembly are separately in its favour, is a sufficient and ample safeguard for all minorities. We have suggested something wider, and including all communities, than has been proposed elsewhere. This may give rise to some difficulties in regard to small communities, but all such difficulties can be got over by reference to arbitration. We are prepared to consider the method of giving effect to this principle so as to make it more feasible.

(8) This proposal is so sweeping in its nature that no government or legislature can function at all. Once we have safeguarded major communal issues other matters, whether controversial or not, require no safeguard. This will simply mean safeguarding vested interests of all kinds and preventing progress, or indeed any movement in any direction. We, therefore, entirely disapprove of it.

(9) We are entirely agreeable to the inclusion of fundamental rights and safeguards concerning religion, culture and like matters in the constitution. We suggest that the proper place for this is the All-India Federal Union constitution. There should be uniformity in regard to these fundamental rights all over India.

(10) The constitution of the Union will inevitably contain provisions for its revision. It may also contain a provision for its full reconsideration at the end of ten years. The matter will be open then for a complete reconsideration. Though it is implied, we would avoid reference to secession, as we do not wish to encourage this idea.

The gap between the two parties, as evidenced by the views set out in their respective memoranda, was indeed so wide that there seemed no possible hope of reaching any settlement. This does not mean that both parties had not gone some way to modify their original views; but whatever efforts they had made were not sufficient to bridge the gap. The price which Jinnah demanded for entering into a common Union Centre was the right of the Muslims to frame their own group and provincial constitutions for the 'six Muslim provinces' through a separate constitution-making body — in other words, the virtual recognition of Pakistan. This the Congress was not prepared to concede.

The Conference met again, as scheduled, on the evening of 12 May, but after a short session it was agreed that no useful purpose would be served by further discussion and the Conference was brought to a conclusion. This fact was announced in an official *communiqué*, which was followed by another explaining that, though the Conference had failed to evolve an agreed plan, the Mission's work was very far from ended and that it was their intention to issue a statement in the course of the next few days expressing their views as to the next steps to be taken.

The promised statement[1] was published on 16 May. It recalled that the British Prime Minister had charged the Cabinet Delegation with the mission of helping India to attain her freedom as speedily and fully as possible. The Delegation and the Viceroy had accordingly done their utmost to assist the Indian parties to reach agreement on the fundamental issue of the unity or the division of India. After prolonged discussions they had succeeded in bringing the Congress and Muslim League together in a conference at Simla. Both pasties had been prepared to make considerable concessions, but had been unable to reach a final agreement. The Mission had therefore decided to put forward what they considered to be the best possible arrangements whereby Indians might decide for themselves the future constitution of India, and meanwhile an interim Government might be set up at once to carry on the administration.

The Mission had examined closely and impartially the possibility of a partition of India. They felt that if there were to be internal peace in India, it must be secured by measures that would assure to the Musalmans a control in all matters vital to their culture, religion and economic and other interests. They had considered the proposal for a separate sovereign State of Pakistan consisting of the six provinces claimed by the Muslim League; they had also considered the alternative of a smaller sovereign Pakistan consisting of the Muslim-majority areas only. The first of these alternatives they were unable to

[1] See Appendix IV.

recommend, because it would not solve the communal minority problem and because they could see no justification for including large areas, in which the population was predominantly non-Muslim, in such a separate State. The second was regarded by the Muslim League as quite impracticable, because it involved the exclusion of the whole of the Ambala and Jullundur divisions in the Punjab, the whole of Assam, except the Sylhet District, and a large part of Western Bengal, including Calcutta. The Delegation themselves were convinced that any solution which involved a radical partition of the Punjab and Bengal would be contrary to the wishes and interests of a very large proportion of the inhabitants of those provinces; moreover, any division of the Punjab would of necessity divide the Sikhs. There were other weighty administrative, economic and military considerations against the creation of a separate sovereign Pakistan. The Delegation were therefore unable to advise the British Government to transfer power in India to two entirely separate sovereign States. This decision did not, however, blind them to the very real apprehensions of the Muslims that their culture and political and social life might become submerged in a purely unitary India in which the Hindus must be a dominating element.

With regard to the Indian States, paramountcy could neither be retained by the British Crown nor transferred to the new Government. In other words, all rights surrendered by the States to the paramount power would go back to them. The States' representatives had assured the Cabinet Mission that the States were ready and willing to co-operate in the new development of India. The precise form which their co-operation would take must be a matter for negotiation.

The Cabinet Mission recommended that the new constitution should take the following basic form.

(1) There should be a Union of India, embracing both British India and the States, which should deal with the following subjects: foreign affairs, defence, and communications; and should have the powers necessary to raise the finances required for the above subjects.

(2) The Union should have an executive and a legislature constituted from British-Indian and States' representatives. Any question raising a major communal issue in the legislature should require for its decision a majority of the representatives present and voting of each of the two major communities as well as a majority of all the members present and voting.

(3) All subjects other than the Union subjects and all residuary powers should vest in the provinces.

(4) The States will retain all subjects and powers other than those ceded to the Union.

(5) Provinces should be free to form groups with executives and legislatures, and each group could determine the provincial subjects to be taken in common.

(6) The constitutions of the Union and of the groups should contain a provision whereby any province could by a majority vote of its Legislative Assembly call for a reconsideration of the terms of the constitution after an initial period of ten years and at ten-yearly intervals thereafter.

The Mission stressed that it had become necessary for them to make these recommendations as to the broad basis of the future constitution, because, in the course of their negotiations, it had become clear to them that, not until this had been done, was there any hope of getting the two major communities to join in the setting up of the constitution-making machinery which they proposed should be brought into being forthwith.

Turning to the constitution-making body, the Mission felt that election based on adult franchise, although the most satisfactory, would lead to a wholly unacceptable delay. The alternative was to utilize the recently elected provincial Legislative Assemblies as the electing bodies. These Assemblies did not, however, fairly reflect the relative size of the population of the different provinces, or of the different elements within each province. In order to overcome this difficulty, the Mission proposed that the fairest and most practicable plan would be:

(a) to allot to each province a total number of seats proportional to its population, roughly in the ratio of one to a million, as the nearest substitute for representation by adult suffrage.

(b) to divide this provincial allocation of seats between the main communities in each province in proportion to their population.

(c) to provide that the representatives allocated to each community in a province shall be elected by members of that community in its Legislative Assembly.

For this purpose they proposed to recognize only three main communities, General, Muslim and Sikh. The 'General' community would include all persons other than Muslims or Sikhs. Special arrangements were proposed for the smaller minorities, who, on the population basis, would have little or no representation. They would be represented on the Advisory Committee which would be set up to advise the Constituent Assembly on all matters affecting the rights of the minorities.

The representatives of the provincial legislatures so elected would meet together at New Delhi as one body, together with representatives of the Indian States, as soon as possible. After a preliminary meeting for the election of a chairman and for other business, the representatives would separate into three sections, as follows:

Section A — Madras, Bombay, United Provinces, Bihar, Central Provinces and Orissa.

Section B — Punjab, North-West Frontier Province and Sind.

Section C — Bengal and Assam.

These three sections of the Constituent Assembly would decide the provincial constitutions for the provinces within their group; also whether any group constitution should be set up — and if so, with what provincial subjects it should deal. Provinces would have the power to opt out of the groups by a decision of their new legislature when the new Union constitution had come into force. After the group constitution had been settled the three sections of the Constituent Assembly would reassemble, together with representatives of the Indian States, for the purpose of settling the Union constitution.

In the Union Constituent Assembly, any resolutions varying the recommendations made by the Cabinet Mission as to the basic form of the constitution, or the raising of any major communal issue, would require a majority of the representatives, present and voting, of each of the two major communities.

It would be necessary to negotiate a treaty between the Union Constituent Assembly and the United Kingdom to provide for certain matters arising out of the transfer of power.

The Mission stated that the Viceroy would forthwith request the provincial legislatures to proceed with the election of their representatives.

While the constitution-making was in process, the administration of India would have to be carried on. For this purpose, it was stated that the Viceroy hoped to set up immediately an interim Government having the support of the major political parties, in which all the portfolios, including that of the War Member, would be held by Indian leaders having the full confidence of the people. The British Government, recognizing the significance of the changes in the Government of India, would give the fullest measure of co-operation in the accomplishment of its tasks of administration to the Government so formed and in bringing about as rapid and smooth a transition as possible.

The Mission concluded by saying that, in the absence of an agreement, they were laying before the Indian people proposals which they hoped would enable them to attain their independence in the shortest time and with the least risk of internal disturbance and conflict. The alternative to their acceptance would be a grave danger of violence, chaos and even civil war. They therefore hoped that these proposals would be accepted and operated in the spirit of accommodation and goodwill in which they were offered. They concluded with the words: 'We hope that the new independent India may choose to be a member of the British Commonwealth. We hope in any event that you will remain in close and friendly association with our people. But these are matters for your own free choice. Whatever that choice may be we look forward with you to your ever increasing prosperity among the great nations of the world, and to a future even more glorious than your past.'

The publication of the Cabinet Mission's Statement was followed by broadcasts[1] by the Secretary of State and the Viceroy. Sir Stafford Cripps also addressed a press conference[2] at which he explained the background and implications of the Statement which, he stressed, was 'not merely the Mission's statement, but the Statement of His Majesty's Government,' and expressed the hope that the Indian people would accept it in the spirit of co-operation in which it had been drawn up. This was followed by another press conference[3] at which the Secretary of State answered numerous questions on the various aspects of the Cabinet Mission plan.

In his broadcast the Secretary of State outlined the various steps that would have to be taken and the machinery that would have to be set up for the framing of a constitution for India, such as the summoning of representatives to New Delhi; their division into sections or groups to decide initially upon provincial or group matters; the formation of a special committee to formulate fundamental and minority rights for inclusion in the constitution; the position of the Indian States, and the establishment of an interim Government. Emphasizing what he described as the fundamental issue, the Secretary of State said:

The future of India and how that future is inaugurated are matters of vital importance not only to India herself but to the whole world. If a great new sovereign State can come into being in a spirit of goodwill,

---

[1] See Appendixes V and VI.　　　　　　　[2] See Appendix VII.

[3] See Appendix VIII.

both within and without India, that of itself will be an outstanding contribution to world stability.

The Viceroy claimed in his broadcast that the proposals in the Statement offered a reasonable basis on which to found India's future constitution. They preserved the essential unity of India and in particular removed the danger of the disruption of the Indian Army. They offered the Muslims the right to direct their own essential interests, their religion, education, culture, and economic and other concerns in their own way and to their own best advantage. To another great community, the Sikhs, they preserved the unity of their homeland — the Punjab — in which they played, and could still play, so important and influential a part. They provided, in the special committee which formed a feature of the constitution-making machinery, the best chance for the smaller minorities to make their needs known and to secure protection for their interests. They sought to arrange a means for the Indian States, great and small, to enter by negotiation into the polity of a united India. They offered to India the prospect of peace — a peace from party strife, the peace so needed for all the constructive work there was to do. And they gave the people of India the opportunity of complete independence as soon as the Constituent Assembly had completed its labours.

Referring to the particular and immediate task of forming an interim Government, the Viceroy said that, except for the Governor-General, it would be a purely Indian government and would include (if he could get the persons he wanted) recognized leaders of the main Indian parties 'whose influence, ability and desire to serve India are unquestioned.'

The reactions of the Press to the Cabinet Mission's proposals were generally favourable. It was recognized that, in the absence of agreement between the two main parties, mediation by the British Government was inevitable. It was also recognized that the Mission had made a sincere effort to secure to both parties the essentials of the position which they wished to safeguard. There was therefore reason to hope that the scheme would be generally acceptable and that this would remove the preliminary obstacles to the formulation of a constitution for India.

Gandhiji was among the first to come out with his views. The Cabinet Mission's Statement, he said, was not an award. The Mission had tried, but failed, to bring the parties together and so they recommended to the country what in their opinion was worthy of acceptance by it. It was open to the Constituent Assembly to vary the proposals, to reject or improve upon them; otherwise, the Constituent Assembly could not be a sovereign body. Thus the Mission had suggested certain subjects for the Union Centre; the Constituent Assembly could, if they chose, add to them or reduce them. Similarly, it was open to the Constituent Assembly to abolish the distinction of Muslims and non-Muslims which the Mission had felt forced to recognize. As regards grouping, no province could be compelled to belong to a group against its will. Subject to these interpretations, Gandhiji said the Mission had brought something of which they had every reason to be proud. 'Whatsoever the wrong done to India by British rule, if the Statement was genuine, as he believed it was, it was in discharge of an obligation they had declared the British owed to India.'

The first indication of the views of either of the main parties was given by Jinnah on 22 May, when he made a long statement in which he described the Cabinet Mission's Statement as 'cryptic with several lacunas.' He regretted that the Mission should have negatived the League's demand for the establishment of a complete sovereign State of Pakistan which, he said, was the only solution of the constitutional problem of India and which alone could secure stable government and lead to the happiness and welfare, not only of the two major communities, but of all the peoples of the Indian sub-continent. Though he criticized points in the Cabinet Mission's plan, he refrained from making any suggestion that the proposals as a whole should be rejected. He preferred to leave the decision as to the acceptability or otherwise of the Statement to the unprejudiced judgment of the Muslim League Working Committee and Council.

On 24 May, after much deliberation, the Congress Working Committee adopted a resolution raising various points in regard to the Statement — particularly in the light of the Congress objectives, which they defined as follows, namely independence for India; a strong though limited central authority; full autonomy for the provinces; the establishment of a democratic structure in the Centre and in the units; the guarantee of the fundamental rights of each individual so that he might have full and equal opportunities of growth, and, further, that each community should have the opportunity to live the life of its choice within the larger framework. The Committee regretted to find a divergence between those objectives and the proposals made on behalf of the British Government.

Among the important points raised by the Committee was that

relating to the grouping of provinces. The Committee found the provision for initial grouping inconsistent with the freedom promised to the provinces in this respect. 'In order to retain the recommendatory character of the Statement, and in order to make the clauses consistent with each other, the Committee read paragraph 15 to mean that, in the first instance, the respective provinces shall make their choice whether or not to belong to the section in which they are placed.'

Another matter to which the Congress Working Committee took exception was the inclusion of Europeans in the electorate for the Constituent Assembly for the group comprising Bengal and Assam. The fact was that, in spite of their very small numbers (which would not entitle them to any representation in the Constituent Assembly on the basis of one member for one million of population), the Europeans enjoyed under the existing constitution a weighted representation in the Bengal and Assam Assemblies. Under the operation of proportional representation, this was likely to give them six seats in the Constituent Assembly for the north-eastern group. For obvious reasons, the Congress was anxious that the Europeans should not be in a position to hold the balance in this group.

It was pointed out that in Baluchistan it would be improper for any nominated individual to speak for the whole of a province which he did not represent; while in Coorg, only the elected members from the General constituencies should participate in the election.

The Congress also raised the question of the representation of the peoples of the States in the Constituent Assembly, and the question of the status and powers of the interim Government. Above all, the Congress stressed that the interim and long-term proposals should be regarded as part of the same picture. They preferred to defer their decision on the Cabinet Mission's proposals till the complete picture was available.

Immediately after this, on 25 May, the Cabinet Mission and the Viceroy issued the following statement:

The Delegation have considered the statement of the President of the Muslim League dated 22nd May and the resolution dated 24th May of the Working Committee of the Congress.

2. The position is that since the Indian leaders, after prolonged discussion, failed to arrive at an agreement, the Delegation put forward their recommendations as the nearest approach to reconciling the views of the two main parties. The scheme stands as a whole and can only succeed if it is accepted and worked in a spirit of co-operation.

3. The Delegation wish also to refer briefly to a few points that have been raised in the statement and resolution.

4. The authority and the functions of the Constituent Assembly, and the procedure which it is intended to follow are clear from the Cabinet Delegation's statement. Once the Constituent Assembly is formed and working on this basis, there is no intention of interfering with its discretion or questioning its decisions. When the Constituent Assembly has completed its labours, His Majesty's Government will recommend to Parliament such action as may be necessary for the cession of sovereignty to the Indian people, subject only to two matters which are mentioned in the Statement and which we believe are not controversial, namely, adequate provision for the protection of the minorities (paragraph 20 of the Statement) and willingness to conclude a treaty with His Majesty's Government to cover matters arising out of the transfer of power (paragraph 22 of the Statement).

5. It is a consequence of the system of election that a few Europeans can be elected to the Constituent Assembly. Whether the right so given will be exercised is a matter for them to decide.

6. The representative of Baluchistan will be elected in a joint meeting of the Shahi Jirga and the non-official members of the Quetta Municipality.

7. In Coorg the whole Legislative Council will have the right to vote, but the official members will receive instructions not to take part in the election.

8. The interpretation put by the Congress resolution on paragraph 15 of the Statement to the effect that the provinces can in the first instance make the choice whether or not to belong to the section in which they are placed does not accord with the Delegation's intentions. The reasons for the grouping of the provinces are well known and this is an essential feature of the scheme and can only be modified by agreement between the parties. The right to opt out of the groups after the constitution-making has been completed will be exercised by the people themselves, since at the first election under the new provincial constitution this question of opting out will obviously be a major issue and all those entitled to vote under the new franchise will be able to take their share in a truly democratic decision.

9. The question of how the States' representatives should be appointed to the Constituent Assembly is clearly one which must be discussed with the States. It is not a matter for decision by the Delegation.

10. It is agreed that the interim Government will have a new basis. That basis is that all portfolios, including that of the War Member, will be held by Indians; and that the members will be selected in consultation with the Indian political parties. These are very significant changes in the Government of India, and a long step towards independence. His Majesty's Government will recognise the effect of these changes, will attach the fullest weight to them, and will give to the Indian Government the

greatest possible freedom in the exercise of the day-to-day administration of India.

11. As the Congress statement recognises, the present constitution must continue during the interim period; and the interim Government cannot therefore be made legally responsible to the central legislature. There is, however, nothing to prevent the members of the Government, individually or by common consent, from resigning, if they fail to pass an important measure through the legislature, or if a vote of non-confidence is passed against them.

12. There is of course no intention of retaining British troops in India against the wish of an independent India under the new constitution; but during the interim period, which it is hoped will be short, the British Parliament has, under the present constitution, the ultimate responsibility for the security of India and it is necessary therefore that British troops should remain.

The Sikhs were considerably disturbed by the Cabinet Mission's proposals which, they felt, would leave them without sufficient safeguards against a Muslim majority in the Punjab and in the north-west group. The Akali leader, Master Tara Singh, said that under the proposed constitutional set-up the Sikhs were doomed. At a representative conference of Sikhs held at Amritsar on 10 June, the Cabinet Mission's proposals were rejected. Master Tara Singh and some other Sikh leaders declared their determination to fight the Mission's plan. They even appointed a committee of action under an ex-officer of the 'Indian National Army'.

The Working Committee of the All-India Scheduled Castes Federation were also dissatisfied with the plan.

The Congress disagreed with the Mission's proposals in regard to the compulsory grouping of provinces and the voting rights of Europeans, but at this stage it was more concerned with the arrangements proposed for the interim Government. On 25 May, Azad wrote to the Viceroy suggesting that in informal conversations the Viceroy had stated that it was his intention to function as a constitutional head of the Government and that in practice the interim Government would have the same powers as a Dominion cabinet. Azad sought written confirmation of this from the Viceroy. He added that a convention might be established to recognize the responsibility of the interim Government to the central Legislative Assembly.

The Viceroy replied that he had never stated that the interim Government would have the same powers as a Dominion cabinet. The whole constitutional position was entirely different. What he had said was that he was sure that His Majesty's Government would treat the new interim Government with the same close consultation and consideration as a Dominion government. Nevertheless, he gave the following assurance to Azad:

His Majesty's Government have already said that they will give to the Indian Government the greatest possible freedom in the exercise of the day-to-day administration of the country; and I need hardly assure you that it is my intention faithfully to carry out this undertaking.

I am quite clear that the spirit in which the Government is worked will be of much greater importance than any formal document or guarantees. I have no doubt that, if you are prepared to trust me, we shall be able to co-operate in a manner which will give India a sense of freedom from external control and will prepare for complete freedom as soon as the new constitution is made.

The considerations that weighed with the Viceroy in giving this assurance were based on the impression he had gathered from Azad that, once the main question regarding the status and powers of the interim Government had been settled to the satisfaction of the Congress, there would be no difficulty about the composition of the cabinet. Subsequent events proved this to be an over-simplication of the problem.

Turning to the Muslim League — on 6 June the Council of the All-India Muslim League passed a resolution accepting the Cabinet Mission's proposals, subject however to a host of reservations. The Council protested against the references made and the conclusions recorded in the Statement with regard to the Muslim demand for the establishment of a full sovereign State of Pakistan, and reiterated that a separate sovereign Pakistan was still the unalterable objective of the Muslims in India. Having regard, however, to the grave issues involved, and prompted by its earnest desire for a peaceful solution, and inasmuch as the basis and the foundation of Pakistan were inherent in the Mission's plan by virtue of the six Muslim provinces in Sections B and C, the League accepted the Mission's scheme and was willing to join the constitution-making body, keeping in view the opportunity and the right of secession of provinces or groups from the Union which had been 'provided in the Mission's plan by implication.' It also reserved the right to revise its policy and attitude at any time during the deliberations of that body, or of the Constituent Assembly, or thereafter if the course of events so required. The Council authorized Jinnah to negotiate with the Viceroy in regard to arrangements for the proposed interim Government at the Centre and to take such decisions and action as he deemed fit and proper.

On 8 June Jinnah wrote to the Viceroy stating that during the discussions the Viceroy had assured him that there would be twelve portfolios, namely, five League, five Congress, one Sikh and one Indian Christian or Anglo-Indian; and that the most important portfolios would be equally divided between the League and the Congress. This weighed with the Council of the All-India Muslim League in accepting the Cabinet Mission plan of 16 May. Any departure from this assurance, directly or indirectly, would lead to very serious consequences and would not secure the co-operation of the League. The Viceroy denied that he had given any assurance on this point, though he did indicate that the 5 : 5 : 2 ratio was what he had had in mind and he hoped that agreement would be reached on that basis.

The Viceroy subsequently invited Nehru and Jinnah for a joint consultation. Jinnah replied that until the Congress had given its decision on the long-term plan of 16 May, no purpose would be served by any discussion on the nature and composition of the interim Government. The joint consultation did not therefore take place.

On 12 June the Viceroy saw Nehru. The Congress President was ill at the time. The Viceroy confronted Nehru with entirely new proposals, which went all the way to meet the demands of the Muslim League in regard to the constitution of the interim Government. Nehru suggested, however, that there should be fifteen members in the interim Government including five Congress (all Hindus), four Muslim League, one non-League Muslim, one non-Congress Hindu, one Congress Scheduled Caste, one Indian Christian, one Sikh and one Congress woman. Lord Wavell expressed his inability to negotiate on this basis, which he felt would be entirely unacceptable to Jinnah.

The next day Azad wrote to the Viceroy stating that Nehru had reported the gist of their conversation to the Congress Working Committee. He pointed out that the Committee had repeatedly averred that they were opposed to parity in any shape or form. In the composition of the cabinet now suggested by the Viceroy there was parity between Hindus, including the Scheduled Castes, and the Muslim League. The position was in fact worse than it had been at Simla in June 1945 when the parity proposed was between Caste Hindus and Muslims, leaving additional seats for Scheduled Caste Hindus. The Muslim seats had not then been reserved for the Muslim League only, but could include non-League Muslims. The present proposal placed the Hindus in a very unfair position and at the same time eliminated the non-League Muslims. The Congress Working Committee were not prepared to accept such a proposal.

With regard to the convention requiring that major communal issues should be decided by separate group voting, Azad said that this convention, along with parity, would make the working of the Government almost impossible and deadlock a certainty.

The Congress President added that the Working Committee were strongly of the opinion that, for the more efficient administration of the country and in order to give adequate representation to the smaller minorities, the interim Government should consist of fifteen members.

In view of the strong attitude taken up by the Congress, the Viceroy gave up his formula of 5 : 5 : 2. He now suggested an Executive Council of thirteen members, six Congress (including a member of the Scheduled Castes), five Muslim League and two representatives of the minorities. He met Jinnah and put the new proposal before him. Jinnah said that if the Congress would agree to that formula he would place it before his Working Committee for consideration. But the formula was turned down by the Congress.

A complete deadlock was thus reached. The Cabinet Mission and the Viceroy finally decided to issue a statement setting out their own proposals for the composition of an interim Government. In forwarding advance copies to Azad and Jinnah the Viceroy said:

As the Statement shows, the Cabinet ministers and I are fully aware of the difficulties that have prevented an agreement on the composition of the interim Government. We are unwilling to abandon our hope of a working partnership between the two major parties and representatives of the minorities. We have therefore done our best to arrive at a practicable arrangement taking into consideration the various conflicting claims, and the need for obtaining a Government of capable and representative administrators. We hope that the parties will now take their share in the administration of the country on the basis set out in our new Statement. We are sure we can rely on you and your Working Committee to look to the wider issues and to the urgent needs of the country as a whole, and to consider this proposal in a spirit of accommodation.

The Statement, which was issued on 16 June, announced that it was proposed to set up an Executive Council of fourteen persons (all of whom were mentioned by name), six belonging to the Congress, including a representative of the Scheduled Castes, five to the Muslim

League, one Sikh, one Indian Christian and one Parsi. The list included the names of Nehru and Jinnah. The Statement stressed that the proposed distribution of seats should not be treated as a precedent for the solution of any other communal question; that it was an expedient put forward to solve the present difficulty only and to obtain the best available coalition government. It was made clear that if any one of those invited were unable for personal reasons to accept, the Viceroy after consultation would invite some other person in his place; also that if the two major parties, or either of them, proved unwilling to join, the Viceroy would proceed with the formation of an interim Government which would be as representative as possible of those willing to accept the Statement of 16 May.

The Sikhs rejected the interim proposals as they had rejected the long-term plan and refused to agree to any Sikh representative joining the Executive Council.

On 19 June, Jinnah wrote to the Viceroy asking for clarification of the following points in the Statement of 16 June, namely, whether the proposals for the setting up of an interim Government were final, or whether they were still open to any further change; whether the total number of fourteen members would remain unchanged during the interim period; if any of the persons invited as representatives of the minorities were unable to accept the invitation to join, would the vacancy or vacancies be filled up by the Viceroy, and would the leader of the Muslim League be consulted and his consent obtained; whether the proportion of members of the Government, community-wise, would be maintained and the representation given to the minorities be adhered to without any modification; and whether, in view of the substitution of fourteen members for the original twelve and the change made in the original formula, there would be a provision that the Executive Council should not take a decision on any major communal issue if the majority of the Muslim members were opposed to it.

The Viceroy replied that until he had received acceptances from those invited to take office in the interim Government, the names in the Statement could not be regarded as final, but no change of principle would be made without the consent of the two major parties; that no change in the number of fourteen members would be made without the agreement of the two parties; that if any vacancy occurred among representatives of the minorities the Viceroy would naturally consult the two main parties before filling it; that the proportion of members community-wise would not be changed without the agreement of the two parties, and that no decision on a major communal issue[1] could be taken in the interim Government if the majority of either of the parties were opposed to it.

Jinnah was not slow to take advantage of these commitments, which had been made by the Viceroy without sufficient and timely consideration. The contents of his letter to the Viceroy leaked out to the Press and when the Congress Working Committee saw it they asked the Viceroy for the full correspondence. Accordingly, the gist of the correspondence was communicated to Azad. The Viceroy wrote to Jinnah on 22 June saying that he understood from reports in the Press that there was a strong feeling in Congress circles that a Muslim of their choice should be included among the representatives of the Congress in the interim Government. The Viceroy said that it would not be possible for him or the Cabinet Mission to accept such a request.

The Viceroy's assurances to Jinnah, coupled with his insistence that the Congress should not nominate a Muslim, went far towards influencing the decision of the Congress Working Committee which met at Delhi on 25 June. The Committee passed a resolution rejecting the proposals for an interim Government. 'In the formation of a provisional or interim Government,' it said, 'Congressmen can never give up the national character of the Congress or accept an artificial and unjust parity, or agree to the veto of a communal group.' Dealing with the Statement of 16 May, the resolution re-emphasized that the proposals fell short of the Congress objective of immediate independence. The limitation of the central authority as contained in the proposals, as well as the system of grouping of provinces, weakened the whole structure and was unfair to some provinces such as the North-West Frontier Province and Assam, and to some of the minorities, notably the Sikhs. The Committee decided however that the Congress should join the proposed constituent assembly 'with a view to framing the constitution of a free, united and democratic India.' The Committee concluded that it was essential that a representative and responsible provisional national government should be formed at the earliest possible date.

In communicating this resolution to the Viceroy on 25 June, the

---

[1] Both the Cabinet Mission and the Viceroy had assumed in their discussions with Azad that the latter had accepted as a self-evident proposition that, in a coalition Government, it would not be possible to force through communal issues in the face of the opposition of either of the main parties. Subsequently Azad denied acceptance of this principle in relation to the interim Government.

Congress President reiterated the Congress objections to the Statement of 16 June, namely the non-inclusion of any nationalist Muslim;
parity, and the power of veto given to the Muslim League in the provisional Government. With regard to the Statement of 16 May, Azad
asserted that he and his party accepted the proposals and were prepared to work them with a view to achieving their objective, but that
they adhered to their own interpretation of some of the provisions of
the Statement, such as that relating to the grouping of provinces.

Immediately after the Congress decision, the Cabinet Mission
saw Jinnah and informed him that the scheme of 16 June had fallen
through; that the Congress had, however, accepted the Statement of
16 May; and that, since both the Congress and the League had now
accepted that Statement, it was proposed to set up a coalition Government, including both parties, as soon as possible. In view, however,
of the long negotiations which had already taken place, and since
everyone had other work to do, the Mission felt it better to have a
short interval before proceeding with further negotiations. This was
confirmed by a letter, which was issued on the same day, but which
Jinnah said did not reach his hands till late that night!

Meanwhile, Jinnah had gone straight from his interview with the
Mission to his Working Committee, which passed a resolution by
which it agreed to join the interim Government on the basis of the
Statement of 16 June.

Thus a new situation had developed. Paragraph 8 of the Statement of 16 June stated that 'in the event of the two major parties or
either of them proving unwilling to join in the setting up of a coalition Government on the above lines, it is the intention of the Viceroy
to proceed with the formation of an interim Government which will
be as representative as possible of those willing to accept the Statement of May 16th.' Jinnah interpreted this to mean that if the
Congress rejected the interim Government proposals, but the League
accepted them, the Viceroy would at once be obliged to form a government consisting of representatives of the Muslim League and any other
parties which had accepted the Statement of 16 May. In a letter to
Jinnah, the Viceroy repeated what the Mission and he had already
told him as to the course which the Mission proposed to adopt. But
Jinnah held to his own interpretation and insisted that the Mission
had gone back on their word by postponing the formation of the interim Government; that the long-term plan and the formation of the
interim Government formed one whole, and that it was undesirable to

proceed with one part, i.e. the elections to the Constituent Assembly, and to postpone the other. The Viceroy denied that they had gone back on their word, and added that there was no intention of postponing the elections to the Constituent Assembly, arrangements for which had already been put into operation.

The negotiations for an interim Government had failed. Meanwhile the existing Executive Council had lost some of its members by resignation, so that it became necessary to make transitional arrangements at the Centre pending further negotiations with the parties. Accordingly, the Viceroy decided to set up a caretaker Government composed of officials, who would function until such time as his efforts with the political leaders could be renewed.

The Cabinet Mission left India on 29 June, after a stay of more than three months. It had been a strenuous period of difficult and sustained negotiations conducted in the sweltering heat of an Indian summer, from which the Cabinet ministers could have derived no mental consolation or physical relief. But they had not allowed their efforts to flag. There was Sir Stafford Cripps on the one hand, with his indefatigable energy and flashes of intellectual genius, and Lord Pethick-Lawrence on the other, with his essentially practical outlook and undoubted sympathy for Indian aspirations — a combination which might surely have been expected to produce the results for which everyone had hoped. In fact, the Mission did not succeed in all that they had set out to do. The Congress and the Muslim League had indeed accepted the long-term plan, but their acceptances had been conditioned by their own interpretations of almost all the controversial issues. However, there were two positive achievements. First, the problem of the future of India had been brought down from the clouds of nebulous theories to the plane of hard realities; secondly, there had been the welcome realization that the Labour Party in England meant to keep their pledge to withdraw from India as soon as possible. Hereafter it was not to be so much a struggle to wrest power from the British, as a dispute as to how that power, once inherited, should be shared by the parties concerned.

Meanwhile, both parties were going ahead with their preparations for the elections to the Constituent Assembly.

# XII

## THE INTERIM GOVERNMENT

### I

THE Congress Working Committee's resolution accepting the Cabinet Mission plan was submitted for ratification to the All-India Congress Committee, which met in Bombay on 6 July 1946. Strong opposition was expressed by the leaders of the Socialist Party, but the influence of Gandhiji and of the Working Committee prevailed. The resolution was ratified.

At this session, Nehru took over the Congress presidentship, to which he had been elected a couple of months before, from Azad. In the course of his speech winding up the proceedings of the Committee, Nehru said that as far as he could see, it was not a question of the Congress accepting any plan, long or short. It was merely a question of their agreeing to enter the Constituent Assembly, and nothing more than that. They would remain in that Assembly so long as they thought it was for India's good and they would come out when they thought it was injuring their cause. 'We are not bound by a single thing except that we have decided for the moment to go to the Constituent Assembly.'

Speaking at a press conference Nehru admitted that, in agreeing to go into the Constituent Assembly, the Congress had inevitably agreed to a certain process of going into it, i.e. the election of candidates; 'but what we do there we are entirely and absolutely free to determine.' Referring to the two provisos laid down by the Mission, namely proper arrangements for minorities and a treaty between India and England, he stressed that he would have no treaty with the British Government if they sought to impose anything upon India; as for the minorities, it was a domestic problem and 'we shall no doubt succeed in solving it. We accept no outsider's interference in it, certainly not the British Government's interference, and therefore these two limiting factors to the sovereignty of the Constituent Assembly are not accepted by us.'

With regard to the question of grouping, Nehru said:

The big probability is, from any approach to the question, there will be no grouping. Obviously, section A will decide against grouping. Speaking in betting language, there is a four to one chance of the North-West Frontier Province deciding against grouping. Then group B collapses. It is highly likely that Bengal and Assam will decide against grouping, although I would not like to say what the initial decision may be since it is evenly balanced. But I can say with every assurance and conviction that there is going to be finally no grouping there, because Assam will not tolerate it under any circumstances whatever. Thus you see this grouping business, approached from any point of view, does not get us on at all.

Dealing with the powers of the proposed Union Centre, Nehru said that defence and communications would embrace a large number of industries necessary for their support. Foreign affairs must inevitably include foreign trade policy. It was equally inevitable that the Union must raise its finances by taxation, rather than by any system of contribution or doles from the provinces. Further, the Centre must obviously control currency and credit; and there must be an over-all authority to settle inter-provincial disputes and to deal with administrative or economic breakdowns.

Nehru's statements on the Cabinet Mission plan were at once taken up by Jinnah. He characterized them as 'a complete repudiation of the basic form upon which the long-term scheme rests and all its fundamentals and terms and obligations and rights of parties accepting the scheme.' Jinnah suggested that His Majesty's Government should make it a point at the forthcoming debate in the British Parliament, 'to make it clear beyond doubt and remove the impression that the Congress has accepted the long-term scheme.'

In an editorial, *Dawn* (the League's official daily) posed the question whether the British Government was going to delude itself and mislead the world with the illusion that the Congress had accepted the long-term plan, or whether it was going to make it clear that, should any party proceed inside the Constituent Assembly on any other basis than that prescribed in the Statement of 16 May, the plan would be deemed to have failed and the Constituent Assembly would be dissolved?

On 18 July, Lord Pethick-Lawrence, the Secretary of State, said in the House of Lords:

Before I leave this matter of the Constituent Assembly, I should perhaps say a few words regarding some recent reports from India as to the intentions of the parties in joining the Constituent Assembly. We saw both parties shortly before we left India and they said to us quite categorically that it was their intention to go into the Assembly with the object of making it work. Of course, they are at perfect liberty to advance their own views of what should or should not be the basis of a future constitution. That is the purpose of the Constituent Assembly, to hammer out agreement from diverse opinions and plans. Likewise, they can put forward their views as to how the Constituent Assembly should conduct its business. But having agreed to the statement of May 16 and the Constituent Assembly elected in accordance with that statement, they cannot, of course, go outside the terms of what has been agreed. To do so would not be fair to other parties who come in and it is on the basis of that agreed procedure that His Majesty's Government have said they will accept the decisions of the Constituent Assembly.

The same day, in the course of his speech in the House of Commons, Sir Stafford Cripps said:

There were two main points which the Congress were stressing as to the Statement of May 16th. The first was as to whether provinces were compelled to come into the sections of the Constituent Assembly in the first instance, or whether they could stay out if they wished. We made it quite clear that it was an essential feature of the scheme that the provinces should go into sections, though if groups were formed they could afterwards opt out of those groups.

A fear was expressed that somehow or other the new provincial constitutions might be so manoeuvred as to make it impossible for the province afterwards to opt out. I do not know myself how such a thing would be possible, but if anything of that kind were to be attempted it would be a clear breach of the basic understanding of the scheme.

The essence of the constitution-making scheme is that the sections A, B and C mentioned in paragraph 19 should have the opportunity of meeting together and deliberating upon the desirability of forming a 'Group' and upon the nature and extent of the subjects to be dealt with by the group. If when the pattern of the group definitely emerges any province wishes to withdraw from the group, then it is at liberty to do so after the first election under the new constitution when, with no doubt a wider electorate than at present, that matter can be made a straight election issue.

The statements failed to reassure the League. At the meeting of the Council of the All-India Muslim League in Bombay on 27 July, Jinnah accused the Cabinet Mission of bad faith and of having 'played into the hands of the Congress.' He condemned the Congress for its 'pettifogging and higgling attitude.' He said that the League had gone to the limit of concession, but the Congress had shown no appreciation of the sacrifices it had made; the League therefore had no alternative but to adhere once more to the national goal of Pakistan. Other members of the Council followed Jinnah's lead; even those who wished to counsel moderation considered it wise to express themselves cautiously in the face of the general feeling.

A resolution drafted by the Working Committee was then placed before the Council. It was passed without dissent. The resolution stated that, in accepting the long-term plan of the Cabinet Mission, the League had been influenced by the assurance given to its President that there would be five members each belonging to the Congress and the League in the interim Government, together with two members representing the minorities. The Cabinet Mission had gone back on this assurance; and when the League accepted the arrangements proposed in the Statement of 16 June and the Congress rejected them, they refused to let the League form the Government, thus committing a breach of faith. The resolution held that the Congress had not in fact accepted the Mission's long-term plan, as was evidenced by their resolutions about grouping, and that therefore, even according to the interpretation which the Mission put upon the disputed passage in their Statement of 16 June, the Congress was not eligible to participate in the formation of the interim Government. The resolution pointed to the terms of the Congress resolution and the statements of Azad and Nehru in support of the contention that the Congress, relying upon its majority, intended to upset the clear intentions of the scheme in regard to the grouping of provinces and to make the Constituent Assembly function as a sovereign body, that is, unfettered by any basic limitations of function or procedure. On this point, the Secretary of State and Sir Stafford Cripps had merely been content to say, in the recent debate in Parliament, that for any party to go beyond what had been agreed to would not be fair to the other party. Therefore the Muslim League Council had felt that their interests would not be safe in the Constituent Assembly and had decided that the acceptance of the scheme contained in the Cabinet Mission's Statement of 16 May should be revoked.

Another resolution authorized the Working Committee to draw up a plan of 'direct action' and called upon all members of the League to renounce any titles which they had received from the Government.

Immediately after the resolution had been passed, Jinnah declared: 'What we have done today is the most historic act in our history. Never have we in the whole history of the League done anything except by constitutional methods and by constitutionalism. But now we are obliged and forced into this position. This day we bid goodbye to constitutional methods.' He recalled that throughout the fateful negotiations with the Cabinet Mission the other two parties, the British and the Congress, each held a pistol in their hand, the one of authority and arms and the other of mass struggle and non-cooperation. 'Today,' he said, 'we have also forged a pistol and are in a position to use it.'

The Working Committee of the League followed up the Council's resolution by calling upon Muslims throughout India to observe 16 August as 'Direct Action Day'. On that day, meetings would be held all over the country to explain the resolution passed by the Council of the All-India Muslim League.

Jinnah's speech, as well as the resolution passed at the Muslim League session, were based on a number of assumptions which were open to question. For one thing (as has been pointed out earlier) Jinnah had never been given an assurance that the ratio of 5:5:2 would be adhered to in the composition of the interim Government. He had also been informed, before the Muslim League Working Committee decided to accept the Statement of 16 June relating to interim arrangements, that with the acceptance of the long-term plan by the Congress, the Viceroy was bound, in the light of paragraph 8 of the Statement of 16 June, to make a renewed attempt to form a government representative of both the major parties, since both had accepted the Statement of 16 May.

The decision of the Muslim League was widely regretted. Congress leaders now began to explain that their objection had not been to the principle of grouping, but to grouping being forced upon a province by the weight of the majority of a bigger province placed in the same section; and that the use of the expression 'sovereign' in relation to the Constituent Assembly implied not that the Assembly would be unfettered by any conditions and would be free to make its decisions by a majority vote, but that it would not be subject to control from any external authority.

It may be recalled that the Congress had questioned the right of Europeans of the Bengal and Assam Legislative Assemblies to vote in the election of representatives to the Constituent Assembly. As a sequel, the European party in the Bengal Legislative Assembly decided to abstain from voting in the election of candidates to the Constituent Assembly. A similar decision was taken by the European members of the Assam Legislature.

By the end of July 1946, elections were completed for the 296 seats assigned in the Constituent Assembly to the British-Indian provinces. The Sikh seats were not filled for reasons which will be explained later. The Congress won all the general seats except nine. The Muslim League won seventy-three seats, that is, all but five of the seats allotted to Muslims. The method of filling the ninety-three seats allotted to the Indian States was a matter for negotiation between the parties concerned.

Whilst the elections were in progress, the Viceroy had been in correspondence with the Secretary of State on the subject of the formation of an interim Government to replace the caretaker Government at the Centre. As agreed, the Viceroy wrote to the presidents of the Congress and the Muslim League (on 22 July) as follows:

I declared my intention of replacing the present caretaker Government of officials by an interim coalition Government as soon as possible ; and am now putting to you as President of the Congress/Muslim League the proposals set out below.

I think you will probably agree with me that our negotiations both this summer and last year were hampered by the attendant publicity. I am therefore seeking your co-operation in conducting at any rate the preliminary stages of the negotiations on a strictly personal and secret basis between myself and the two Presidents. I very much hope that you will prevent this correspondence being known to or discussed in the Press until we have seen whether we can find some basis of agreement. I realise of course that you will have at some stage to secure the approval of your Working Committee; but I believe it will be best to try and reach some basis of agreement between ourselves as a first step. I propose the following for your consideration :—

(a) the interim Government will consist of 14 members;

(b) Six members (to include one Scheduled Caste representative) will be nominated by the Congress;

Five members will be nominated by the Muslim League;

Three representatives of minorities will be nominated by the Viceroy. One of these places will be kept for a Sikh. It will not be open to either the Congress or the Muslim League to object to the names submitted by the other party, provided they are accepted by the Viceroy;

(c) Distribution of portfolios will be decided after the parties have agreed to enter the Government and have submitted their names. The Congress and the Muslim League will each have an equitable share of the most important portfolios;

(b) The assurances about the status of the interim Government which I gave in my letter dated 30th May to Maulana Azad will stand.

I would welcome a convention, if freely offered by the Congress, that major communal issues can only be decided by the assent of both the major parties, but I have never thought that it was essential to make this a formal condition since in fact a coalition Government could work on no other basis.

I sincerely trust that your party will agree to co-operate in the administration of India on the above basis, while the work of constitution-making proceeds. I am confident that this will be of the greatest possible benefit to India. I suggest that we should not spend further time in negotiation; but should try out at once a Government on the basis proposed above. If it does not work, and you find the conditions unsatisfactory, it will be open to you to withdraw, but I am confident that you will not.

Would you be good enough to let me know very soon whether the Congress/Muslim League will enter in the interim Government on this basis? I have written in similar terms to Mr. Jinnah/Pandit Nehru and enclose a copy of my letter to him.

Nehru replied on 23 July. He agreed with the Viceroy on the need for secrecy; but it was not possible for him even as Congress President to function by himself in such matters without any reference to his colleagues. The situation, he stressed, had changed in many ways and it was not possible to pick up the old threads again where they had been left off.

Nehru said that the assurances which the Viceroy had given to Azad in his letter of 30 May with regard to the status of the interim Government were very far from satisfying the Congress, which had all along attached the greatest importance to what it called the 'independence of action' of the interim Government. This meant that the Government should have perfect freedom and that the Governor-General should function only as a constitutional head. Nor would it be proper for the Governor-General to select representatives of the minorities.

Nehru concluded that, in view of what he had stated above, he was wholly unable to co-operate in the formation of a Government on lines suggested by the Viceroy. So far as he knew the mind of the Congress, it would want the political independence issue settled before it could enter any Government.

The Viceroy was inclined to regard Nehru's letter as being in the nature of a challenge. He felt that the Congress had taken up this attitude because it believed that the Labour Government would not only not take action against it, but would be compelled to acquiesce in any demands it might make. He proposed to the Secretary of State that he should see Nehru and have a personal talk with him.

The Secretary of State agreed that the Viceroy should see Nehru, but suggested that if no progress towards agreement resulted from the conversation and if the situation showed signs of moving towards a crisis, it might be desirable to ask both the Congress and the Muslim League to send representatives to London to discuss the position; in that event, the Viceroy would also have to go to London to participate in the conversations as a continuation of the Cabinet Mission's work.

Meanwhile there came the resolution of the Council of the All-India Muslim League rejecting the Cabinet Mission plan. At his meeting with Nehru, the Viceroy suggested that this resolution was partly a reaction to the language used by him and other Congress leaders since the meeting of the All-India Congress Committee in Bombay. It would be most unfortunate, said the Viceroy, if the League did not join the Constituent Assembly. Here was a chance for the Congress to show real statesmanship by giving the Muslim League assurances which would bring its representatives into the Constituent Assembly. Nehru said he did not see what assurances could be given. The Viceroy pointed out that the League's principal grievance was the feeling that the proposals with regard to grouping would not be given a fair chance.

The Viceroy went on to say that they were pledged to go ahead with the Constituent Assembly so far as circumstances permitted, but he did not see how, without the Muslims, they could get much further than a constitution for group A provinces. Nehru said that the intention of the Congress had been to form a Committee of all parties at the first meeting of the Constituent Assembly, to discuss the implications of the central subjects, not to extend them, in order to give the groups a basis on which to work.

The Viceroy said that he was anxious to form an interim Government as soon as possible, but that it was impossible to go beyond the assurances given in his letter to Azad regarding the status and powers of the interim Government. He expressed a desire to see Nehru again as soon as possible after the meeting of the Congress Working Committee which was to take place in Wardha on 8 August.

The situation was causing the Government no little anxiety. Communal tension had already increased in the towns as a result of the Muslim League's call for 'direct action'; moreover, there was widespread labour unrest in the country. Lord Wavell felt that a representative central Government was most urgently needed. Since that was not practicable in the immediate circumstances he was anxious, even though he was against the idea of a Government dominated by one party, to get the Congress in while keeping places for the Muslim League and the Sikhs. In that event the Congress might recognize the necessity for direct negotiations with Jinnah and might ask the Viceroy to postpone the Constituent Assembly until some arrangement had been reached.

The Secretary of State foresaw grave risks in the loss of initiative on the part of Government. He felt that it was impossible to allow Jinnah's non-cooperation to hold up the formation of an interim Government and that the Viceroy should therefore meet Jinnah as soon as possible and press him to allow members of the Muslim League to enter it. Should Jinnah be willing, the Viceroy might represent to Nehru that even though the League had not accepted the Statement of 16 May it was of overwhelming importance to have it in the interim Government.

The Viceroy was not in favour of this course, which would put up Jinnah's stock and increase his intransigence. Moreover, he could scarcely disregard the commitment to form a Government as representative as possible of those who had accepted the Statement of 16 May.

Meanwhile, on 31 July, Jinnah sent his reply to the Viceroy's letter of 22 July in regard to the interim Government. As he expressed it, the Viceroy's basis for the formation of an interim Government gave the go-by to all the important terms that were favourable to the Muslim League. It straightway broke the principle of parity. The Scheduled Castes had been let down, inasmuch as one of them was proposed to be nominated by the Congress and not by their own spokesmen. It would next be open to the Congress to nominate a 'Quisling Muslim'. Moreover, the distribution of portfolios would be 'equitable' and not 'equal' as had originally been proposed. As to the assurance about safeguards, he said that the Viceroy did not seem to attach much importance to it. This was a very clear and substantial departure that was most detrimental to the Muslim League and was obviously intended to appease the Congress. Jinnah concluded that in his opinion there was no chance of his Working Committee accepting the Viceroy's proposal.

The Secretary of State finally agreed that it would not be desirable to see Jinnah immediately and that an offer should be made to Nehru to form an interim Government. It was left to the Viceroy to decide whether the Muslim League places should be kept vacant or not. If the Congress declined to come in, the situation would have to be considered further.

Unless the Congress asked the Viceroy to postpone it, the Constituent Assembly should be summoned, as already arranged, in the first week of September. The Secretary of State hoped that by that time the Congress might be prepared to give Jinnah such assurances as to its procedure as would enable the Muslim League representatives to attend. The Secretary of State fully shared the Viceroy's dislike of an interim Government dominated by one party, but in view of the grave political situation in the country he agreed on the necessity for forming an interim Government with popular support.

On 6 August the Viceroy wrote to Nehru that, with the concurrence of His Majesty's Government, he had decided to invite him to make proposals for the formation of an interim Government on the basis of the assurances contained in his letter of 30 May to Azad. It would be for Nehru to consider whether he should first discuss the proposals with Jinnah. If he could reach an agreement with the latter, the Viceroy would naturally be delighted, since, as Nehru would probably agree, a coalition Government could best effectively direct the destinies of India at this critical time. The Viceroy had hoped to get the Constituent Assembly started in the first week of September, but the situation arising out of the Muslim League resolutions had to be considered. He concluded by saying that he had no objection to Nehru showing his letter of 22 July, as well as the present one, to the Congress Working Committee.

Two days later Lord Wavell replied to Jinnah's letter of 31 July. He stated that he was sorry things had gone the way they had, but it would not be profitable to enter into a detailed discussion of the points raised by him in his letter. He would only remind Jinnah that the basis of representation suggested was the same as the one which the Muslim League Working Committee had accepted at the end of June, namely 6:5:3. He said that in view of the League resolutions of 29 July, he had decided to invite the Congress to make proposals for an interim Government and he was sure that if they made a reasonable offer of a coalition, he could rely on Jinnah for a ready response.

The decision to go ahead without the Muslim League had been taken not without considerable misgiving. The attitude of the Muslims generally was causing the Government serious anxiety. It was apprehended that if Jinnah made a call for 'direct action', there would be a ready and immediate response. If the ministries went out in Bengal and Sind and there was a Muslim mass movement, the Government might lose control of East Bengal and of much of the countryside in Sind, and serious communal rioting might occur in the more populous towns of the Punjab and the United Provinces. The police were at least seventy per cent Muslim in Sind and the Punjab, and fifty per cent in the United Provinces; so it was impossible to count on them. The same was true of the Muslim police in East Bengal. In the North-West Frontier Province, the Congress ministry provided a safety-valve and immediate trouble was unlikely. What stood out clearly was that, especially in the Muslim provinces, any attempt to go ahead with constitution-making without Muslim participation would have very serious results.

The Congress Working Committee, meeting in Wardha on 8 August, decided to accept the invitation extended to Nehru to form an interim Government and authorized him to negotiate with the Viceroy.

The Working Committee also took stock of the fears expressed by the Sikhs in regard to their position in the Punjab. We have already seen how the Sikhs had reacted to the Cabinet Mission's proposals. The Congress High Command called upon the Congress Sikhs to file their nominations for elections to the Constituent Assembly. This they did, whereupon the Akalis (a communal organization of the Sikhs) nominated their own candidates. The ultimate result was that all the Sikh nominations were withdrawn and no Sikh was elected to the Constituent Assembly.

In the first week of July, Baldev Singh wrote to Prime Minister Attlee seeking his personal intervention for the remedying of the wrong that had been done to the Sikh community by the Cabinet Mission. It was fairly clear, Baldev Singh said, that the overriding factor which had weighed with the Mission in formulating their views had been to give every consideration possible to the Muslim League. The League, on the other hand, had made it plain that it accepted the proposals with the object of opting out the so-called Muslim areas and establishing an independent and sovereign Muslim State. Baldev Singh emphasized that the Mission had admitted the injustice of including predominantly non-Muslim areas (mainly Sikh) within a sovereign Pakistan State. The Mission had recognized the weight of Sikh fears against a Muslim majority domination. It was true that they had rejected the demand of a sovereign Muslim State; nevertheless, by imposing the group system, they had involved the Sikhs in what must in the end amount to a perpetual Muslim communal rule; and they had made no provision whatever for the Sikh areas to opt out of this domination, or for the protection of Sikh cultural, social, or even religious rights, on the basis assured to Hindus and Muslims. The Sikh community felt that this was palpably unjust. A very salutary provision had been made for the resolving of major communal issues in the Constituent Assembly as between Hindus and Muslims; but the Sikhs, who were one of the three main communities of India, had been ignored. Baldev Singh urged that this provision should in fairness be extended to the Sikh community as well.

In his reply Attlee said that he had given close consideration to the matter and was quite clear that the Statement of 16 May could not be altered in the way the Sikhs desired. At the same time, the Viceroy was very ready to discuss the position with the President of the Congress, and he would have been prepared to do likewise with the President of the Muslim League had not the League decided to withdraw their acceptance of the Statement of 16 May. It was unfortunate that the Sikh community should have decided meanwhile not to elect their representatives to the Constituent Assembly. It was obviously more difficult to raise with any other party the position of the Sikhs in the Constituent Assembly when, through their own decision, they remained outside it. He hoped that in any event the Sikh community would decide to co-operate in the process of constitution-making. It would surely be a mistake if the Sikh community refused to use the opportunity which had been offered to them simply because they assumed in advance that the mere weight of voting power would be used to injure their vital interests and to deny their natural aspirations. He assumed that the Constituent Assembly would face its problems in quite a different spirit.

The Congress Working Committee, noting all these factors, passed a resolution assuring the Sikhs that the Congress would give them all possible support in removing their legitimate grievances and in securing adequate safeguards for the protection of their just interests in the Punjab.

The Panthic Board met on 14 August and, while reiterating that the Cabinet Mission proposals were unjust to the Sikhs, decided, in response to the Congress appeal, to accept the Statement of 16 May. The Board also advised the Sikh M.L.A.s to elect their representatives to the Constituent Assembly. There being no provision in the Cabinet Mission plan for by-elections to the Constituent Assembly, these elections did not take place till much later.

By another resolution the Congress Working Committee sought to enlist the co-operation of the Muslim League. The resolution ran as follows:

The Working Committee of the Congress regret to note that the Council of the All-India Muslim League, reversing their previous decision, have decided not to participate in the Constituent Assembly. ... The Committee further note that criticisms have been advanced on behalf of the Muslim League to the effect that the Congress acceptance of the proposals contained in the Statement of May 16 was conditional. The Committee wish to make it clear that, while they did not approve of all the proposals contained in this statement, they accepted the scheme in its entirety. They interpreted it so as to resolve the inconsistencies contained in it and fill the omissions in accordance with the principles laid down in the Statement. They hold that provincial autonomy is a basic provision and each province has the right to decide whether to form or join a group or not. Questions of interpretation will be decided by the procedure laid down in the Statement itself, and the Congress will advise its representatives in the Constituent Assembly to function accordingly.

The Committee have emphasised the sovereign character of the Constituent Assembly, that is, its right to function and to draw up a constitution for India without the interference of any external power or authority, but the Assembly will naturally function within the internal limitations which are inherent in its task, and will further seek the largest co-operation in drawing up a constitution of free India, allowing the greatest measure of freedom and protection for all just claims and interests. ... The Committee hope that the Muslim League and all others concerned in the wider interests of the nation, as well as of their own, will join in this great task.

This resolution did not satisfy Jinnah. In a statement issued soon after, he expressed the view that, but for its phraseology, the resolution was only a repetition of what had been the Congress stand from the beginning. For instance, it repudiated grouping and emphasized once more the sovereign character of the Constituent Assembly, which meant that it would not be bound by anything laid down in the Statement of 16 May and would be free to decide every question by a majority. Jinnah concluded that 'the situation remains as it was and we are where we were.'

After the meeting of the Congress Working Committee, Nehru wrote to the Viceroy to say that he had consulted the Working Committee and that he was prepared to undertake the responsibility of forming a provisional national Government. Both the Working Committee and he had a Government in mind which would consist of good representatives of the main elements in India. The Congress would have welcomed the formation of a coalition Government with the Muslim League; but in view of the resolution adopted by the League and the recent statements made on its behalf, it was not possible to expect that it would agree to co-operate at this stage and any premature attempt to induce it to do so might produce a contrary result. He suggested that the best course was for the Viceroy to make a public announcement to the effect that he had invited the President of the Congress to form the provisional Government and that the latter had accepted the invitation. It would then be possible for the Congress to approach the Muslim League and invite its co-operation. He added that the Congress would welcome the League's co-operation but that, in the event of refusal, the Congress was prepared to go ahead without it.

A *communiqué* was issued accordingly by the Viceroy. On the following day, 13 August, Nehru wrote to Jinnah regarding the Viceroy's invitation to him and his acceptance of it. He felt that his first step should be to approach Jinnah and seek his co-operation in the formation of a coalition Government, and he suggested a personal discussion.

On 15 August Jinnah replied stating that he knew nothing of what had transpired between the Viceroy and Nehru, nor had he any idea of what agreement had been reached between them. If the Viceroy had commissioned Nehru to form an Executive Council and had already agreed to accept and act upon his advice, it was not possible for Jinnah to accept such a position. However, if Nehru cared to meet him on behalf of the Congress to settle the Hindu-Muslim question and resolve the serious deadlock, he would be glad to see him.

In his reply, Nehru made it clear that there was no arrangement between the Viceroy and himself, except what was contained in the

Viceroy's brief offer and the Congress acceptance. He regretted Jinnah's decision, but suggested that perhaps on fuller consideration he might be agreeable to reconsider it. The latter finally agreed to meet Nehru. They had a long and amicable discussion which did not however lead to any result.

Nehru later reported to the Viceroy that he had offered Jinnah five seats in an interim Government of fourteen, and that he had made it clear to him that any names proposed by the Muslim League would be accepted by the Congress. Jinnah had asked how the minorities would be nominated, and Nehru had replied that, as he had been asked to make proposals, he would naturally suggest the names of minority representatives for the consideration of the Viceroy. Jinnah complained that under the proposed arrangement it would be open to the Congress to nominate a non-League Muslim. Nehru told him that he did not see how the League could object, if it came out of the Congress quota.

The Muslim League's decision to observe 16 August as 'Direct Action Day' was followed by the taking out of processions and the holding of meetings in almost every big town. The Bengal and Sind ministries declared the 16th a public holiday. The Muslim press was flooding the country with propaganda calculated to encourage communal bitterness and defiance of law and authority. The premier of Bengal, Suhrawardy, went to the extent of saying that if the Congress were put into power, the result would be 'the declaration of complete independence by Bengal and the setting up of a parallel Government.' He added, 'We will see that no revenue is received by such central Government from Bengal and consider ourselves as a separate State having no connexion with the Centre.'

The sequel to all this was the unprecedented holocaust in Calcutta, where for four or five days beginning from 16 August, riot, murder, arson and pillage were rampant, involving very heavy damage to life and property. According to a rough official estimate at the time, nearly 5,000 lives were lost, over 15,000 persons were injured and about one hundred thousand were rendered homeless. (A Commission set up under the chairmanship of Sir Patrick Spens, the Chief Justice of the Federal Court, to inquire into the communal rioting in Calcutta, was later wound up — in consequence of the partition of the country).

To revert to the interim Government negotiations, on 17 August Nehru explained to the Viceroy that his idea was to include in the

Government six Congress nominees and three minority representatives and to fill the five Muslim seats with non-League Muslims. The Viceroy suggested the possibility of leaving the Muslim seats open for a time, but Nehru demurred on the ground that it would give the Government an appearance of instability. The rest of the discussion was devoted to a preliminary consideration of names and portfolios.

On the following day Nehru met the Viceroy again. The greater part of that interview was devoted to a discussion of the possibilities of a further approach to Jinnah. The Viceroy suggested that, in view of the happenings in Calcutta, Jinnah might now be inclined to co-operate, and that it was a matter of grave responsibility that every possible effort should be made to secure his co-operation. Nehru thought that the events in Calcutta had made it even more difficult to approach Jinnah. However, he agreed to consult the other members of the Working Committee in Delhi.

The Viceroy was personally averse to the acceptance of Nehru's proposal to fill the five Muslim seats with non-League Muslims. He felt that it would not be possible for him to recommend to His Majesty's Government more than one non-League Muslim. One seat might go to an Anglo-Indian, but the remainder should be left vacant rather than be filled by 'stooge' Muslims.

On 19 August, Nehru wrote to the Viceroy that he had consulted his colleagues, whose reaction was identical with his. He contended that he had accepted the Viceroy's invitation to make proposals for the formation of an interim Government on the understanding that the responsibility would be his and that of the Congress. Proceeding on that basis, he had approached Jinnah for the co-operation of the Muslim League, but without success. He had then decided to go ahead without the League. He had tried to get as good and representative a team as possible and had already approached various individuals on that basis. The Viceroy's new proposals had changed the whole approach to the problem and put an end to the responsibility, which, at his suggestion, the Congress had undertaken. If the Congress were now to be asked to revert to the previous stage, it would be placed in an embarrassing and unenviable position, and the difficulties inherent in the situation, especially in view of the recent happenings in Calcutta, were likely to be considerably increased.

On the same day Jinnah issued a statement to the press, the tone and temper of which convinced the Viceroy that it would be useless to make any approach to Jinnah.

Azad, who throughout the negotiations had striven to build up an attitude of co-operation and conciliation towards the League, was particularly concerned over the tragic events in Calcutta and their possible repercussions throughout the country. At an interview with the Viceroy, he severely criticized the Bengal ministry (Premier Suhrawardy in particular) and alleged that, although the Government of Bengal had apprehended trouble, they had not taken sufficient precautions; that they had been much too late in enforcing Section 144 and a total curfew, and in calling out the troops. The declaration of a public holiday on 16 August had made the hooligans of Calcutta's underworld believe that they had the licence of the Government to behave as they liked. He was now apprehensive of what might happen in the United Provinces and Bihar, where the Muslims were in a minority.

Azad also referred to the proposed interim Government. He said that at one time he had considered leaving the Muslim seats vacant, but he now held the view that to leave them vacant would create a feeling that the Government was not complete or stable. He asked if it was not possible for the Viceroy to make an indirect approach to Jinnah and to give him such reassurance as might persuade him to come in. The Viceroy promised to consider the matter, but added that the attitude of the League made the position very difficult.

The Viceroy then referred to Jinnah's account of his conversation with Nehru. The latter was alleged to have told Jinnah that in the proposed interim Government the Viceroy's veto would not be exercised and that the Government would be responsible to the legislature. The Viceroy reminded Azad of their previous discussions on these points. He reiterated that he had no intention of giving up his powers, though he hoped that he would not have to exercise them. The interim Government could not constitutionally be responsible to the legislature. If Nehru had made the remarks attributed to him by Jinnah, they would naturally have increased Jinnah's reluctance to come into the Government. Azad said that he did not know exactly what Nehru had said, but that the Congress would be prepared to reassure Jinnah on both these points.

The Viceroy then said that the real stumbling block was the question of a Nationalist Muslim and that he did not quite see how this obstacle was to be got over. Azad maintained that the Congress could not give up the nomination of a Nationalist Muslim.

There were further discussions between the Viceroy and Nehru in regard to the strength and personnel of the interim Government. Nehru wanted to increase the strength to fifteen by the inclusion of an Anglo-Indian, but the Viceroy was averse to any increase which would make it more difficult for the Muslim League to join. It was ultimately decided to keep the strength at fourteen. The names of six Congressmen, a Sikh, an Indian Christian and a Parsi, as well as three out of five Muslims, were agreed upon.

On 22 August, Nehru wrote a letter to the Viceroy stating that the Congress had been anxious to form a coalition with the Muslim League and that they would continue to work to that end; but he wanted to make it clear that the Congress idea of a coalition did not mean a submission to the demands or the peculiar ways which the League had adopted. A coalition could only come into existence on the clear understanding that the League could nominate its five representatives and not interfere in any way with the choice of the Congress representatives, including a Nationalist Muslim. The country needed a strong, virile, active and stable Government, which knew its mind and had the courage to go ahead. To give an impression to the country and the people that the new Government was merely a casual and temporary one which was awaiting the favour of the Muslim League would be to undermine the prestige and authority of the Government. That way would not even lead to the coalition for which they hoped. The only proper approach was to make it clear that, while the new Government would always welcome co-operation, it proposed to carry on firmly even if this were denied. He did not believe that co-operation would come out of the appeasement of wrong-doing, hence his dislike of approaches, direct or indirect, which had an appearance of that type of appeasement and were always likely to be misunderstood.

On 24 August a press *communiqué* was issued stating that the King had accepted the resignations of the existing members of the Governor-General's Executive Council and that His Majesty had been pleased to appoint in their places the following: Pandit Jawaharlal Nehru, Sardar Vallabhbhai Patel, Dr Rajendra Prasad, M. Asaf Ali, C. Rajagopalachari, Sarat Chandra Bose, Dr John Matthai, Sardar Baldev Singh, Sir Shafaat Ahmad Khan, Jagjivan Ram, Syed Ali Zaheer and Cooverji Hormusji Bhabha. Two more Muslim members would be appointed later. The interim Government would take office on 2 September.

On 24 August there was also a broadcast by the Viceroy, who

referred to the formation of the interim Government as a very momentous step forward taken on India's road to freedom. What the Viceroy had set out to secure was a Government of Indians as representative as possible of political opinion in the country; but although five seats out of fourteen had been offered to the Muslim League, though assurances were given that the scheme of constitution-making would be worked in accordance with the procedure which had been laid down, and though the interim Government was to operate under the existing constitution, it had not been possible to secure a coalition. No one could be more sure than the Viceroy that it was a coalition Government representing both the main parties that was needed in the interests of all the parties and communities in India; and this was a view that was shared by the Congress President and his colleagues, whose efforts, like those of the Viceroy, would still be directed to persuading the League to join the Government.

Under the offer which had been made and which was still open to the Muslim League, they could propose five names in a Government of fourteen, of which six would be nominees of the Congress and three would be representatives of the minorities. Provided that those names were acceptable to the Viceroy and approved by His Majesty, they would be included in the Government which would at once be reconstituted. The Muslim League need have no fear of being out-voted on any essential issue; a coalition Government could exist and function only on the condition that the two main parties were satisfied. The Viceroy would see that the most important portfolios were equitably shared. He sincerely hoped that the League would reconsider its policy and decide to participate in the Government.

Meanwhile, said the Viceroy, the administration of India had to go on and there were large issues to be decided. He was glad that the representatives of a very large body of political opinion in the country would be his colleagues in carrying on the Government and he welcomed them to his Council. He was also glad that the Sikhs had decided to participate in the Constituent Assembly and in the interim Government.

The Viceroy stressed what he had already made clear, namely that he would fully implement His Majesty's Government's policy of giving the new Government the maximum freedom in the day-to-day administration of the country. As a sop to the provinces ruled by Muslim League ministries, the Viceroy declared that the new Government had neither the power nor any desire to trespass on the field of provincial administration.

With reference to 'the recent terrible occurrences in Calcutta,' the Viceroy appealed not only to sober citizens but to the young and to the discontented to recognize that no conceivable good to themselves, or to their community, or to India, could come either from violent words or from violent deeds. It was essential that law and order should be maintained in all the provinces ; that the protection of the ordinary peaceable citizen should be assured with a firm but impartial hand, and that no community should be oppressed. Incidentally, he paid his tribute of admiration to the troops who had been called out as a last resort to restore order in Calcutta for their behaviour in a duty which was the most exacting and unpleasant on which troops could be employed.

'The War Member in the new Government,' he said, 'will be an Indian, and this is a change which both the Commander-in-Chief and I warmly welcome.'

He appealed to the press to use its very great influence on the side of moderation and compromise, bearing in mind that the interim Government could be reconstituted at any time if the League decided to come in.

Referring to the Constituent Assembly, he said it was desirable that its work should begin as early as possible. He assured the Muslim League that the procedure laid down in the Statement of 16 May regarding the framing of provincial and group constitutions would be faithfully adhered to ; that there could be no question of any change in the fundamental principles proposed for the Constituent Assembly in paragraph 15 of the Statement, or of a decision on the main communal issue, without a majority of both major communities; and that the Congress was ready to agree that any dispute on interpretation might be referred to the Federal Court. He sincerely hoped that the Muslim League would reconsider its decision not to take part in a plan which promised to give them so wide a field in which to protect the interests of, and to decide the future of, the Muslims of India.

In conclusion, the Viceroy stressed that never were tolerance and soberness in thought and action more necessary ; never were the wild speaking and rash deeds of a few fraught with greater danger for so many millions. He therefore appealed to all Indians in any authority and with any influence, to show by their good sense and restraint that they were worthy of their country and that their country was worthy of the freedom it was to receive.

But even this appeal failed to convince Jinnah, who said that the Viceroy had struck a severe blow to the Muslim League and Muslim India. He reiterated his demand for the division of India. With regard to the Constituent Assembly he said :

Then he (the Viceroy) proceeds to say that there can be no question of any change in the fundamental principles proposed for the Constituent Assembly in paragraph 15 of the Statement of May 16 and he echoes that the Congress are ready to agree that any dispute on interpretation may be referred to the Federal Court. But how can we expect an agreement on the terms and fundamentals of the Statement of May 16 when one party puts one interpretation contrary to the authoritative statement of the Mission dated May 25, and the other party puts a different interpretation which is more in accord with the Statement of May 25.

But he complacently goes on to say that any dispute on interpretation may be referred to the Federal Court. To begin with, there is no provision for such a dispute being referred to the Federal Court, and secondly, on the very threshold the parties fundamentally differ in their interpretation regarding the basic terms. Are we going to commence the proceedings of the Constituent Assembly with litigation and law suits in the Federal Court? Is this the spirit in which the future constitution can be framed affecting 400 million people of this sub-continent?

'If,' he concluded, 'the Viceroy's appeal is really sincere and if he is in earnest, he should translate it into concrete proposals by his deeds and actions.'

# XIII

## THE INTERIM GOVERNMENT

## II

SOON after making the announcement on the formation of an interim Government the Viceroy flew to Calcutta to acquaint himself at first hand with the tragic happenings there. What he saw and learnt convinced him that if some sort of agreement between the two major communities was not brought about soon, the Calcutta happenings would be repeated with varying degrees of recklessness all over India.

Lord Wavell was particularly struck by a point of view put forward by Khwaja Nazimuddin, who was himself a prominent Muslim League leader. The latter suggested that if the Congress would make an unequivocal statement that provinces could not opt out of groups except as laid down in the Statement of 16 May, or if the Viceroy or His Majesty's Government would state plainly that they would not permit the Congress to put any other interpretation on grouping than that meant by the Mission, the League would reconsider coming into the Constituent Assembly. With regard to the interim Government, it was just possible (the six Congress names having already been announced) that if the League were allowed to fill the Muslim quota of five seats, Jinnah might come in and this would get over the 'Nationalist Muslim' difficulty.

These factors were responsible for the definite change that became so evident in the Viceroy's attitude and policy after his return from Calcutta. He felt that he must see Gandhiji and Nehru immediately. He met them on 27 August, and after giving a description of conditions in Calcutta, he stressed that the only way to avoid similar trouble all over India was to set up coalition Governments both in Bengal and at the Centre. While recognizing the difficulty of reopening negotiations with the Muslim League, he felt sure that this was what the country expected. The crux of the matter lay in the Congress interpretation of grouping in the Constituent Assembly. He thought that the only chance of a peaceful transfer of power in India was that the Congress should make a categorical statement that it accepted the position that the provinces must remain in their sections, as intended by the Mission, until after the first elections under the new Constitution. He made it clear that he would not undertake the responsibility of summoning the Constituent Assembly until this point was settled. He handed over to Gandhiji and Nehru the draft of a formula which he thought might satisfy the Muslim League. It ran thus:

The Congress are prepared in the interests of communal harmony to accept the intention of the Statement of May 16th that provinces cannot exercise any option affecting their membership of the sections or of the groups if formed, until the decision contemplated in paragraph 19 (viii) of the Statement of 16th May is taken by the new Legislature after the new constitutional arrangements have come into operation and the first general elections have been held.

Gandhiji said that he thought this was a matter for the interim Government, but the Viceroy contended that it was a matter for the Congress which had challenged the interpretation of the Mission. Gandhiji went into legalistic arguments about the interpretation of the Mission's statement, but the Viceroy asserted that he was a plain man and not a lawyer; he knew perfectly well what the Mission meant, and compulsory grouping was the whole crux of the plan.

The discussions, which went on for some time and now and then became rather heated, proved inconclusive. In the end, Gandhiji and Nehru agreed to take away the formula.

Immediately after the interview Gandhiji wrote a letter to the Viceroy in which he said that he took it that it was their purpose to devise methods to prevent a repetition of the recent terrible events in Calcutta, and that the question was how best to do it. The Viceroy's language at their interview, said Gandhiji, had been minatory. He had threatened not to convene the Constituent Assembly if the formula suggested by him was not acted upon by the Congress; if such was really the case, then he should not have made the announcement inviting Nehru to form an interim Government. But having made it, he should recall the action and form another ministry enjoying his full confidence. If British arms were to be kept in India for the preservation of internal peace and order, the interim Government would be reduced to a farce. The Congress could not afford to impose its will on warring elements in India through the use of British arms. Nor could it be expected to adopt what it considered a wrong course because of the brutal exhibition recently witnessed in Bengal. Such submission would itself lead to an encouragement and repetition of such tragedies. The vindictive spirit on either side would go deeper, while waiting for an opportunity to exhibit itself more fiercely when occasion occurred. And all this would chiefly be due to the continued presence in India of a foreign power strong in and proud of its arms. Gandhiji affirmed that he said this neither as a Hindu nor as a Muslim. He wrote only as an Indian. So far as he was aware, the Congress claimed to know both the Hindu and Muslim mind more than the Viceroy or any Britisher. Unless, therefore, the Viceroy could wholly trust the Congress Government which he had announced, he should reconsider his decision.

The Viceroy felt on the other hand that if Congress intentions were as Gandhiji's letter suggested, the result of its being in power could only be a state of virtual civil war in many parts of India. He wrote to Nehru asking him to place his formula before the Congress Working Committee. In doing so, he realized that if the Working Committee rejected his proposal, the Congress might refuse to come into the interim Government. In that case he would carry on with the caretaker Government, and perhaps His Majesty's Government would consider inviting Nehru, Jinnah and himself to London for consultation.

Nehru replied to the Viceroy on 28 August, stating that he had placed the formula before the Working Committee, who were considerably surprised at the sudden change in the Viceroy's approach to the question. The Congress position with regard to the Constituent Assembly and grouping had been made clear in the Working Committee's resolution of 10 August. This resolution, so far as Nehru knew, had not been misunderstood by anyone, not even by the Viceroy in his broadcast of 24 August. In their public statements and in their private talks with the Viceroy, he and the Congress leaders had made it clear that any dispute as to the interpretation of the clauses relating to grouping might be referred to the Federal Court and that they would abide by its decision. What the Viceroy now suggested was at variance with what the Congress leaders had themselves said, as well as with his own broadcast. It meant that there would be no reference of this particular matter to the Federal

Court and that the Congress should accept the interpretation put upon it by the Cabinet Mission and the Viceroy, as distinguished from the legal interpretation which might be put upon it by the Federal Court. This approach was new. The Congress was extremely anxious to do everything in its power to promote communal harmony, but the way suggested by the Viceroy seemed to it to lead to a contrary result. To change the declared policy of the Congress, which was generally acknowledged to be fair, because of intimidation, was surely not the way of peace, but an encouragement of further intimidation and violence. The Congress was therefore unable to accept the Viceroy's proposal.

Nehru proceeded to say that the Viceroy's reference to the non-summoning of the Constituent Assembly unless the course suggested by him was adopted by the Congress had produced a feeling of resentment in the Working Committee. If this was the Viceroy's view and he was going to act upon it, then the whole structure built up during recent months would fall to the ground. The Congress was clearly of the view that it was now both a legal and a moral obligation to go on with the Constituent Assembly. The Assembly had already been elected and though it had not met, it already existed and must start functioning at an early date. It could not be held up because some people did not choose to join it and disturbances took place in the country. The Congress agreed that it was desirable for all concerned to join the Assembly and that it should make every effort to win the co-operation of others, but if some people refused to join, then the Constituent Assembly must proceed without them.

The Viceroy however adhered to his view. He told Nehru that the problem was not a legal but a practical one. Even if the Congress view in regard to sections and grouping were to be referred to the Federal Court and be accepted by it, the Congress would gain nothing. The Muslim League would inevitably refuse to take part, and the process of constitution-making would be held up while communal stresses in the country would get progressively worse. The Viceroy was sure that it would be unwise to call the Constituent Assembly till there was a firmly agreed view on the question of grouping.

Nehru admitted the practical aspects of the problem, but stressed in his reply that those aspects included other considerations; that any change made at the present stage would raise great resentment among the minorities, particularly the Sikhs; it would also produce a feeling of uncertainty and lack of finality. He reminded the Viceroy that the matter had been considered in all its aspects by the All-India Congress Committee, which had issued its directions to the Working Committee in the resolution it had passed, and that as a subordinate body the Working Committee, could not go against the spirit and letter of the resolution. If the point at issue were referred to the Federal Court, he did not know what the decision would be. For its part the Congress had agreed to abide by it even if the decision went against it. It was premature to say what the Muslim League would do then. That would depend, not only on the decision itself, but on many other factors. With regard to the Constituent Assembly, he felt sure that an indefinite postponement of it would not only be wrong in principle, but would have harmful practical results, even from the point of view of gaining the co-operation of the Muslim League.

His Majesty's Government fully appreciated how grave was the danger of widespread and violent communal trouble unless the Congress came to terms with the League, and agreed with the Viceroy that a determined effort should be made to get them to do so. At the same time, His Majesty's Government felt that the Viceroy should not take any steps which were likely to result in a breach with the Congress. Though the public statements of some of the Congress leaders had been equivocal, the Congress could always take the stand that from the outset it had never altered its position on the question of grouping. It was necessary to play for time in order that the effect of responsibility might make its impression on the members of the new Government. Meanwhile, His Majesty's Government was anxious that the interim Government, the formation of which had already been publicly announced, should take office at once. If the Congress could be persuaded to agree to a postponement of the summoning of the Constituent Assembly until October, that would provide a period of time for further discussion. The Viceroy might be able to find a *modus vivendi* in India, but if not, His Majesty's Government was willing to consider the proposal that Nehru, Jinnah and the Viceroy should be invited to England for discussions.

The interim Government was sworn in on 2 September. On the eve of the Government's assumption of office one of its members, Sir Shafaat Ahmad Khan, was the victim of a murderous assault and there were communal clashes in Bombay and Ahmedabad.

Gandhiji expressed the general feeling of apprehension in the country when he said, 'We are not yet in the midst of civil war but we are nearing it.'

On 7 September Nehru broadcast from All-India Radio. He said that the interim Government was part of a larger scheme, which included the Constituent Assembly. The Assembly would soon be meeting to give shape to the constitution of a free and independent India. There had been much heated argument about sections and groupings in the Constituent Assembly, but the Congress was perfectly prepared to accept, indeed had accepted, the position of sitting in sections which would consider the question of formation of groups. On behalf of his colleagues and himself he wished to make it clear that they did not look upon the Constituent Assembly as an arena for conflict, or for the forcible imposition of one point of view over another. That would not be the way to build up a contented and united India. What they sought were agreed and integrated solutions with the largest measure of goodwill. They would go to the Constituent Assembly with the fixed determination to have a common basis of agreement on all controversial issues. He invited those who differed from him and his colleagues to enter the Constituent Assembly as equals and partners with them, with no binding commitments. It might well be that when they had met and faced common tasks their present difficulties would fade away.

Jinnah gave an interview to a representative of the London *Daily Mail*, on 8 September. Referring to Nehru's broadcast 'which is applauded by the Congress newspapers as an assurance to the Muslim League on the vexed provincial grouping', he said that those were very vague words. 'He has made no definite proposals to me; you cannot butter parsnips with words; I have been stabbed and kind words will not stop the bleeding.' He said he would never go to London to plead his case, but if the British Government were to invite him to London to start a new series of conferences on an equal footing with other negotiators he would accept.

In Benga , the position of Suhrawardy, the Premier, was anything but comfortable. Public resentment against his ministry was very strong. Suhrawardy felt that only a coalition Government in Bengal could restore public confidence; but Jinnah, to whom he put the proposal, definitely ruled it out.

At this stage there arose between the Viceroy and the Secretary of State a conflict of views as to the method of dealing with the deadlock. Theirs was a common purpose, but they differed in their approach to the problem. While the Secretary of State was inclined to give the new Congress Government some time so that the responsibilities of office might guide it to adjust its attitude towards the demands of the Muslim League, the Viceroy was for taking immediate steps to clinch the issue. In the Viceroy's view it was essential that the Statement of 16 May should be adhered to; he would rather lose the co-operation of the Congress at the Centre and in the provinces than go ahead with constitution-making on a one-party basis, which the Cabinet Mission had never intended.

This rigid attitude of the Viceroy was based on one important consideration. While in Simla, the Cabinet Mission had given an assurance to the Muslim League — an assurance that had not however been made known to the Congress at the time — that decisions in the sections would be by a majority vote of the representatives of the provinces within the section; also that the constitutions for the provinces would definitely be framed by the sections. The Viceroy felt that His Majesty's Government was in honour bound to respect this assurance. But there were great practical difficulties in the way of implementing an assurance which had been given at the time without full consideration. If, as a result, the League came in and the Congress withdrew, the position would certainly not be bettered.

The Viceroy had discussions with Nehru, as well as with Rajagopalachari, but no satisfactory results emerged. At about this time Suhrawardy said in Delhi that if Jinnah felt that there was a spirit of co-operation on the Congress side, he would take less than his present demands. The Viceroy felt that now was the time to send for Jinnah in order to reach a settlement. The Secretary of State agreed to the course. Nehru, when consulted, said that he could not object to the Viceroy sending for Jinnah.

The Viceroy saw Jinnah on 16 September. He began by saying that he was very sorry that events had taken the turn they had since their last meeting. There had been much misunderstanding, and some hard things had been said, but it was necessary now to look forward and not back. Agreement about the Constituent Assembly and a representative coalition Government was essential to the progress of India and to avoid disaster. He said that he had invited Jinnah to come to him in order to ascertain his difficulties and to see whether an agreement could not be reached. It was clear that the Congress was prepared to implement the basic principle of the

Statement of 16 May, i.e. the meeting of provinces in sections, and this should surely get over one of his chief difficulties.

Jinnah replied that past happenings would have no effect on his present decision. The soul of the scheme of 16 May had been mutilated. The only good thing in it was the provision for sections and grouping; and the only guarantee for the successful working of the scheme was that it should be implemented with honour and goodwill. That the League had always intended to do, but the Congress obviously had not, and therefore it became impossible for the League to continue its acceptance.

He thought that the Viceroy had committed a great mistake in forming the present one-party Government, and dilated on the intensity of Muslim feeling among all classes and in every part of India. The Viceroy said that he appreciated the point, but surely it would be better for the League to enter the Constituent Assembly and see how it worked. Jinnah said that there were many points to be decided before he entered the Constituent Assembly, but he did not specify them. The Viceroy pointed out that the real guarantee was that no majority could ride roughshod over an influential minority; if they tried to do so, it simply would not work. The Hindus would be in a majority in the Union Assembly, but it would be quite useless for them to force through provisions which would be unacceptable to the Muslims, because the latter would certainly refuse to accept them and would walk out. Similarly, in groups B and C, the Muslims would be the majority, but they would have to satisfy the minorities or they would not get a workable constitution. While agreeing with this, Jinnah said that in sections B and C, the Muslims would have a bare majority, whereas in the Union Assembly and in section A the Hindu majority would be overwhelming. The Viceroy replied that the principle of the majority satisfying the minority still held good.

Jinnah asked what the Viceroy proposed with regard to the interim Government, to which the latter replied that the proportion would be the same as had already been accepted by him, viz. 6:5:3. While he was still striving to get the Congress to give up its claim to the inclusion of a Nationalist Muslim in the Cabinet, he did not encourage Jinnah to expect any concession from the Congress. In fact, the Viceroy told him that if the negotiations broke down on that issue alone, Jinnah would be in a very weak position in world opinion generally.

Jinnah said that there was no hope of his supporters agreeing to a solution on the lines suggested. The Viceroy said that it would be most unfortunate if they did not agree, as the consequences would be most serious. He suggested that Jinnah should think the matter over and come and see him again.

Jinnah's next interview with the Viceroy was on 25 September. The main topic discussed was the interim Government. Jinnah pressed for acceptance of a convention that major communal issues in the interim Government would only be decided by a vote of both communities. He explained the fears of the Muslim League of being outvoted, since some of the minority representatives might vote with the Congress. The Viceroy explained that if a matter involving a major communal issue came before the Cabinet, the party leader concerned would see it from the papers circulated. It would then be open to him to approach the leader of the opposite party. If the two party leaders failed to agree, the issue would be brought before the Viceroy, whose duty it would be to reconcile their differences and prevent the issue being brought before the Cabinet. The convention that Jinnah had in mind would not be really effective, and would throw on the Viceroy the onus of deciding what was a major communal issue, which would be just as responsible a task as the exercise of his veto. In the ultimate analysis, if the decision given was not acceptable to either party, they could resign from the Government. Jinnah agreed that a convention would not be wholly effective; but said that he wanted it in order to satisfy his supporters.

Jinnah did not seem to take much interest in the matter of portfolios, but he showed some anxiety in regard to the position of the Vice-President. He suggested that the vice-presidentship of the Cabinet should be held in rotation. The Viceroy told him that this would be rather a clumsy arrangement, and that it would be better to agree on a distribution between the parties of other important offices, such as the Vice-Chairmanship of the Co-ordination Committee of the Cabinet.

Jinnah observed that while the question of the interim Government could be settled by his Working Committee, the question of the Muslim League coming into the Constituent Assembly would have to go to the whole Council, since it was the Council that had decided to resile from their original agreement. He said that it would be necessary to create a favourable atmosphere and that he could not be rushed on this issue. There were two essential matters on which a decision would have to be reached before he could agree to recommend to his Council that they should come into the Constituent Assembly. The first was that the procedure for meeting in sections must be made quite clear; the second was that there must be some agreement on how certain matters were to be settled, e.g. when the group and provincial constitutions impinged on the Union subjects, or vice-versa. Again, who was to decide on the interpretation of the Statement of 16 May, particularly with regard to paragraph 15? He seemed to agree that these matters should be referred to the Federal Court. He added that there would have to be a good deal of discussion on the procedure of the Constituent Assembly before it met. If three hundred or so members met without a measure of agreement between the principal parties, no reasonable results would be achieved.

The Viceroy promised to see Nehru as early as possible and to discuss with him the points that had been raised. He asked Jinnah whether he would agree to meeting Nehru. It would be much better if the participation of the Muslim League in the Government appeared to arise from agreement between the two leaders. Jinnah expressed his readiness to meet Nehru if he could be certain of a favourable agreement on the points he had raised, but he did not wish it to appear that he had gone to the Congress to ask for favours.

The next day the Viceroy discussed the issues with Nehru. He told him he was confident that a settlement could be secured on the participation of the Muslim League, both in the interim Government and in the Constituent Assembly, if the matter were handled with wisdom and statesmanship. He gave an account of his interview with Jinnah and said that he thought he could persuade Jinnah to approach Nehru for direct negotiations, provided the latter could give him an assurance that the Congress would be prepared to be generous; in particular, that if the principle of complete freedom of nomination by the parties was accepted, the Congress would not insist on nominating a Nationalist Muslim. The Viceroy emphasized that a coalition Government was the need of the country. It was not his idea to create a 'King's Party' in the Cabinet. He desired it to work as a team and hoped to interfere as little as possible.

Nehru said in reply that at the recent All-India Congress Committee meeting a resolution had been proposed that the Congress should on no account give way on the issue of a Nationalist Muslim. The resolution had been withdrawn on the assurance that the Congress would not give way on this issue. The Viceroy maintained that the principle need not be sacrificed, but it would be wrong to throw away an opportunity of a coalition on a comparatively minor issue.

The Viceroy also had an interview with Gandhiji. He outlined the result of his discussions with Jinnah and followed the general line of argument he had taken with Nehru. Gandhiji entirely agreed that the Muslim League should come in, but that the issue of a Nationalist Muslim was a difficult one. If it were merely a question of a Congress 'right', they could make concessions on it; but if it was a 'duty', the matter was on a different footing. He suggested that the proper way of settling the matter would be by a meeting between Jinnah and Nehru.

Gandhiji wished to know what His Majesty's Government would do if the worst happened and the Muslim League did not come in. His personal view was that, in that event, it would be no use for the Constituent Assembly to meet, and it would be quite honourable for His Majesty's Government to say that its scheme could not be maintained. The Viceroy agreed that it was a possible line of argument, but asked for Gandhiji's solution of the problem if the worst did happen. Gandhiji replied that though the Constituent Assembly should be dropped, the interim Government should go on, the vacant Muslim seats being filled by other prominent non-League Muslims. The Viceroy was not prepared to accept Gandhiji's solution; he was not going to allow the present negotiations to fail, but if that should happen, His Majesty's Government would be obliged to reconsider the whole position.

The Viceroy continued his efforts to bring about a settlement with Nehru and Jinnah. He informed Jinnah on 2 October that he had failed to secure any concession from the Congress over the Nationalist Muslim issue. He emphasized at the same time that it was in the obvious interest of the Muslim League to come into the Government at once and unconditionally. On the distribution of portfolios and other issues the Viceroy would see that the League got fair treatment. Jinnah did not enter into any argument on the Nationalist Muslim issue, but said that if he was to have any chance of satisfying his Working Committee he must show them some success on other points, e.g. a safeguard on major communal issues, the vice-presidentship, and the question of minorities. Finally, he agreed to summon his Working Committee as soon as possible and undertook to send the Viceroy a note setting out the points on which he required elucidation.

The following are the nine points on which Jinnah sought elucidation:

(1) The total number of the members of the Executive Council to be fourteen.

(2) Six nominees of the Congress will include one Scheduled Caste representative, but it must not be taken that the Muslim League has agreed to, or approves of, the selection of the Scheduled Caste representative, the ultimate responsibility in that behalf being with the Governor-General and Viceroy.

(3) The Congress should not include in the remaining five members of their quota a Muslim of their choice.

(4) Safeguard: there should be a convention that on major communal issues, if the majority of Hindu or Muslim members of the Executive Council are opposed, then no decision should be taken.

(5) Alternative or rotational Vice-Presidents should be appointed in fairness to both the major communities as it was adopted in the U.N.O. Conferences.

(6) The Muslim League was not consulted in the selection of the three minority representatives, *i.e.* Sikh, Indian Christian and Parsi, and it should not be taken that the Muslim League approved of the selection that had been made. But in future, in the event of there being a vacancy owing to death, resignation or otherwise, representatives of these minorities should be chosen in consultation with the two major parties — the Muslim League and the Congress.

(7) Portfolios: the most important portfolios should be equally distributed between the two major parties — the Muslim League and the Congress.

(8) The above arrangement should not be changed or modified unless both the major parties — the Muslim League and the Congress — agree.

(9) The question of the settlement of the long-term plan should stand over until a better and more conducive atmosphere is created and an agreement has been reached on the points stated above and after the interim Government has been reformed and finally set up.

After consultation with Nehru on 4 October, the Viceroy replied as follows:

(1) This is agreed.

(2) I note what you say and accept that the responsibility is mine.

(3) I am unable to agree to this. Each party must be equally free to nominate its own representatives.

(4) In a coalition Government it is impossible to decide major matters of policy when one of the main parties to the coalition is strongly against a course of action proposed. My present colleagues and I are agreed that it would be fatal to allow major communal issues to be decided by vote in

the Cabinet. The efficiency and prestige of the interim Government will depend on ensuring that differences are resolved in advance of Cabinet meetings by friendly discussions. A coalition Government either works by a process of mutual adjustment or does not work at all.

(5) The arrangement of alternative or rotational Vice-Presidents would present practical difficulty, and I do not consider it feasible. I will however arrange to nominate a Muslim League member to preside over the Cabinet in the event of the Governor-General and the Vice-President being absent.

I will also nominate a Muslim League member as Vice-Chairman of the Co-ordination Committee of the Cabinet, which is a most important post. I am Chairman of this Committee, and in the past have presided almost invariably, but I shall probably do so only on special occasions in future.

(6) I accept that both major parties would be consulted before filling a vacancy in any of these three seats.

(7) In the present conditions all the portfolios in the Cabinet are of great importance and it is a matter of opinion which are the most important. The minority representatives cannot be excluded from a share of the major portfolios and it would also be suitable to continue Jagjivan Ram in the Labour portfolio. But subject to this, there can be equal distribution of the most important portfolios between the Congress and the Muslim League. Details would be a matter for negotiation.

(8) I agree.

(9) Since the basis for participation in the Cabinet is, of course, acceptance of the Statement of 16 May, I assume that the League Council will meet at a very early date to reconsider its Bombay resolution.

When informed that discussions were taking place between the Congress and League leaders, the Nawab of Bhopal (at the instance, it is said, of Gandhiji) took a hand in attempting to bring about a rapprochement between the two parties. A meeting was in fact arranged between Jinnah and Gandhiji, as a result of which a formula was evolved. The agreed formula, according to Jinnah, was as follows:

The Congress does not challenge and accepts that the Muslim League now is the authoritative representative organisation of an overwhelming majority of the Muslims of India. As such and in accordance with democratic principles they alone have today an unquestionable right to represent the Muslims of India. But the Congress cannot agree that any restriction or limitation should be put upon the Congress to choose such representatives as they think proper from amongst the members of the Congress as their representatives.

When this formula was communicated to Nehru, he expressed some dissatisfaction with its wording. The Congress, he said, was willing to accept the Muslim League 'as the authoritative representative

organization of an overwhelming majority of the Muslims of India'
and that 'as such they have today an unquestionable right to represent the Muslims of India', *provided that*, for identical reasons the
League recognizes the Congress as the authoritative organization
representing all non-Muslims and such Muslims as have thrown in
their lot with the Congress.

Nehru stressed that the Congress could not agree to any restrictions
or limitations to be put upon it in choosing such representatives as
it thought proper from amongst the members of the Congress. No
formula, he concluded, was therefore necessary; each organization
must stand on its own merits.

On Jinnah's insistence that the formula agreed between him and
Gandhiji should be accepted by the Congress, Nehru pointed out
that there was an important omission; that in the formula drafted by
Gandhiji there was also the following paragraph:

It is understood that all the ministers of the interim Government will
work as a team for the good of the whole of India and will never invoke the
intervention of the Governor-General in any case.

Jinnah maintained that this addition was not part of the formula.
Nothing came out of this episode.

Further discussion concerned Jinnah's 'nine points', on which the
Viceroy had already sent his reply. Nehru refused to accept the
League's claim that it must be consulted on future appointments
(to the interim Government) of representatives of minorities. The
Congress, he said, could not allow its position vis-à-vis the Scheduled
Castes or other minorities to be challenged by the League. Nor could
the Congress agree to the demand that the office of Vice-President
should be held in turn by members of both parties. Instead, an offer
was made that the vice-chairmanship of the Cabinet Co-ordination
Committee would be given to a member of the Muslim League; or,
in the alternative, a League member of the Cabinet would be the
leader of the House in the central Assembly. With regard to the procedure for settling such differences of opinion as might arise over a
major communal issue, the Congress view was that matters coming
before the Cabinet should not be referred to a Court; that agreement
should always be reached, and that if this were not possible the matter
should be referred to arbitration. The net result of the discussions was
to accentuate the bitterness between the two parties and to cause
further confusion in the public mind.

On 4 October Nehru wrote to the Viceroy stating that the Cabinet must necessarily function together. If any procedure were adopted which would encourage separate groups to function separately, it would seriously militate against the whole conception of Cabinet Government which he and his colleagues were seeking to evolve and which they had in a large measure already succeeded in evolving during the past month. The Viceroy assured Nehru that he himself was most anxious that the Cabinet should work as a team and hoped they would be able to achieve this.

When the Viceroy saw Jinnah, the latter sprang a surprise by asking whether, since the Congress had the right to nominate a Muslim in its quota, he could nominate a representative of Scheduled Castes or other minority in his quota. The Viceroy admitted that he could do so, but pointed out that such a nomination would not help towards a harmonious working of the Cabinet. He confirmed this in writing on 12 October.

On 13 October Jinnah wrote to the Viceroy as follows:

The Working Committee of the All-India Muslim League have considered the whole matter fully and I am now authorised to state that they do not approve of the basis and scheme of setting up the interim Government, which has been decided by you, presumably with the authority of His Majesty's Government.

Therefore, the Committee do not, and cannot agree with your decision already taken, nor with the arrangements you have already made.

We consider and maintain that the imposition of this decision is contrary to the Declaration of August 8, 1940, but since, according to your decision we have a right to nominate five members of the Executive Council on behalf of the Muslim League, my Committee have, for various reasons, come to the conclusion that in the interests of Musulmans and other communities it will be fatal to leave the entire field of administration of the central Government in the hands of the Congress. Besides, you may be forced to have in your interim Government Muslims who do not command the respect and confidence of Muslim India, which would lead to very serious consequences; and, lastly, for other very weighty grounds and reasons which are obvious and need not be mentioned, we have decided to nominate five on behalf of the Muslim League in terms of your broadcast dated August 24, 1946, and your two letters to me dated 4 October 1946 and 12 October 1946, respectively, embodying clarifications and assurances.

Jinnah's letter was followed by an interview with the Viceroy at which Liaqat Ali Khan was present. The question was again raised of the nomination of a non-Muslim Scheduled Caste member in the Muslim League quota. Jinnah said that he appreciated the Viceroy's anxiety that the two parties should work together as a team in as much harmony as possible, but that he and his colleagues had their own interests to consider. The Viceroy agreed that they were of course the final judges of their party interests, but it appeared to him that their interests, as well as those of India as a whole, would be best served in the long run by not making this challenge to the Congress.

The Viceroy then spoke to Jinnah on the long-term issue and stressed that the presence of the Muslim League in the interim Government would be conditional on their reconsideration of their Bombay resolution and acceptance of the Statement of 16 May. Jinnah said that he realized this, but that it would be necessary to secure certain guarantees from the Congress and that the Council of the Muslim League must be called together to withdraw their Bombay resolution. The Viceroy said that this should be done as soon as possible.

The next day the Viceroy informed Nehru of what had transpired between him and the Muslim League leaders. He showed him Jinnah's letter of acceptance. He also told him that it was the intention of the Muslim League to include a non-Muslim. Nehru asked about the long-term issue; was it to be assumed that Jinnah had accepted this? The Viceroy said that he had explained to Jinnah that his entry into the interim Government must be considered as conditional on his acceptance of the long-term plan and that Jinnah had replied that he was prepared to call a meeting of his Council to reverse its Bombay decision as soon as he was satisfied that the Statement of 16 May would be observed.

On 14 October Jinnah sent the names of five nominees on behalf of the Muslim League. They were: Liaqat Ali Khan, I.I. Chundrigar, Abdur Rab Nishtar, Ghazanfar Ali Khan and Jogendra Nath Mandal. Mandal belonged to the Scheduled Castes and was a minister in the Muslim League ministry of Bengal.

In order to make places for these five nominees (there were already two vacancies), the Congress decided that Sarat Chandra Bose, Sir Shafaat Ahmad Khan and Syed Ali Zaheer should retire from the interim Government.

On 15 October a press *communiqué* was issued that the Muslim League had decided to join the interim Government; that in order to make it possible to re-form the Cabinet three members had resigned; and that His Majesty the King had been pleased to appoint the five nominees of the Muslim League to be members of the interim Government. The distribution of portfolios would be settled later.

Nehru said in a letter to the Viceroy on the same day that he did not wish to raise any objections to the names proposed by the Muslim League, but that he owed it to the Viceroy to tell him how deeply he regretted the choice which the Muslim League had made. The choice itself indicated a desire to have conflict rather than to work in co-operation. This was especially evident in the choice of a member of the Scheduled Castes.

The Muslim League's decision to enter the interim Government was received with relief, although it was regretted that no agreement had been reached between the two parties and that the League had accepted from the Viceroy precisely what it had refused from the Congress. Gandhiji, while praying for the best, declared that the League's entry into the Cabinet had not been straight. He could not sense any generosity in the nomination of a Harijan in their quota of five seats, especially when he knew what was happening in East Bengal. He was, therefore, forced to wonder whether they had come into the Cabinet 'also to fight'.

# XIV

## THE CONSTITUENT ASSEMBLY

THE Muslim League had decided to enter the interim Government with but one purpose — and that was not to allow the Congress to consolidate its position to the detriment of the League's interests. Indeed, Jinnah had made this abundantly clear to the Viceroy. There could therefore be no question of the League and the Congress representatives working together as one team. Nehru's apprehensions in this behalf had fallen on deaf ears. Nor had any condition been imposed on Jinnah to withdraw his campaign of 'direct action'.

In fact, the Viceroy had been determined to bring the Muslim League into the interim Government. It was his hope, and that of His Majesty's Government, that once the League came in, the two parties, by working together, would arrive at some measure of understanding in regard to the future. But it was a case of hoping against hope. For one thing, even after its entry into the Government the League continued its campaign of 'direct action' — which included, besides such measures as non-payment of taxes and the defiance of law and order, the economic boycott of Hindus and the organization of Muslim National Guards. This led the Hindus in Bengal and other provinces to increase the activities of the Hindu volunteer bodies.

In about the second week of October 1946, there was a large-scale outbreak of lawlessness and hooliganism in the Noakhali and Tipperah districts of East Bengal. Large forces of armed police and military had to be employed to control the situation. The number of deaths was not great, but the loss of property was considerable. Referring to these disturbances, a prominent politician, who himself hailed from East Bengal, reported that whereas the lawlessness had been given the colour of pure goondaism, in fact it was not so; it was an organized attack engineered by the Muslim League and carried out with the connivance of the administrative officials. The attacks, he said, were made by people armed with guns and other deadly weapons; roads had been dug up and other means of communication cut off to prevent ingress and egress; canals had been blocked and strategic points were being guarded by armed insurgents.

Two of the Muslim League's nominees to the interim Government were openly indulging in belligerent speeches. One even went as far as to declare that the events in East Bengal were but part of the all-India battle for Pakistan. This impelled Nehru to write to the Viceroy insisting that he should obtain an assurance of co-operation and team-work from the Muslim League before admitting its representatives into the interim Government. The speeches of these two Muslim League members, he said, pointed clearly to a course of action which was in direct opposition to the co-operative and harmonious working of the interim Government. He also wanted it clearly confirmed that the Muslim League had accepted the Statement of 16 May.

The Viceroy had already seen and tackled Jinnah on the issue of rescinding the League Council's resolution rejecting the Cabinet Mission plan. The latter said that he could summon the Council at fifteen days' notice, but that he must first be satisfied as to certain matters. Asked what these matters were, he referred to the statements of Gandhiji and other Congress leaders which, according to him, indicated that the Congress had not really accepted the Statement of 16 May. On this point, Nehru, to whom the Viceroy passed on the gist of his conversation with Jinnah, declared that the Congress had made its position clear on many occasions in formal resolutions of the Working Committee, and that it was not prepared to discuss the matter any further.

The Viceroy informed Nehru that he had made it clear to Jinnah that the Muslim League's entry into the interim Government was conditional on its acceptance of the Cabinet Mission's statement of 16 May and that Jinnah should call his Council at an early date to ratify the acceptance; and that Jinnah had assured him that the Muslim League was coming into the interim Government and the Constituent Assembly with the intention of co-operating.

Nehru was not satisfied. He reminded the Viceroy that in the case of the Sikhs he had called for a definite resolution of their acceptance of the Statement of 16 May, and that a previous vague resolution on the subject passed by the Sikh Panthic Board had not been considered sufficient. He wanted to know quite clearly what the Muslim League's view was on the subject.

The fact was that the Viceroy was unable to make any headway with Jinnah regarding the acceptance by the League Council of the Statement of 16 May. In his reply to Nehru, the Viceroy merely repeated his conviction that 'the deplorable state of tension which exists between the two main communities in India can only be relieved by the two parties working together in co-operation in the central Government.' 'It has,' he added, 'always been my object to achieve this; and I do devoutly trust that this new interim Government, in spite of the inauspicious conditions in which it is being formed, will result in a feeling of co-operation that will bring peace and progress to India. The sooner we can start on this great task the better.'

In the matter of the distribution of portfolios, the Viceroy's view was that one of the three portfolios of External Affairs, Home, or Defence should be made available to the Muslim League. Nehru was strongly opposed to any change, not because these portfolios were more important than the others, but, as he put it, because of 'past and present happenings and apprehensions for the future.' To hand over Defence or Home to representatives of the Muslim League would, he stressed, give rise to serious misgivings; the handing over of External Affairs, especially after certain recent events on the North-West Frontier, would be an equally false step. The Viceroy was particularly keen on the transfer of the Home portfolio, but the Congress was adamant. Ultimately, it was decided to allot to the Muslim League representatives the five portfolios of Finance, Commerce, Communications, Health and Law. They took office on 26 October 1946 and the interim Government was reconstituted as follows:

Jawaharlal Nehru (Vice-President of the Executive Council— External Affairs and Commonwealth Relations); Vallabhbhai Patel (Home, Information and Broadcasting); Baldev Singh (Defence); John Matthai (Industries and Supplies); C. Rajagopalachari (Education); C. H. Bhabha (Works, Mines and Power); Rajendra Prasad (Food and Agriculture); Asaf Ali (Railways); Jagjivan Ram (Labour); Liaqat Ali Khan (Finance); I. I. Chundrigar (Commerce); Abdur Rab Nishtar (Communications); Ghazanfar Ali Khan (Health); and Jogendra Nath Mandal (Law).

Now that the Muslim League had entered the interim Government, the Viceroy proceeded to urge upon Jinnah the necessity for its representatives to join the Constituent Assembly. Jinnah, however, adopted an evasive attitude. Meanwhile, the League's representatives in the interim Government refused to accept Nehru's leadership, or the convention of collective responsibility. The interim Government, as Liaqat Ali Khan described it, 'consisted of a Congress bloc and a Muslim bloc, each functioning under separate leadership.'

The East Bengal happenings resulted in reprisals by the Hindus in places as widely separated as Chapra, Ahmednagar and Ahmedabad. The repercussions in Bihar towards the end of October and early November were particularly dreadful. The wave which swept the central parts of Bihar, however, quickly subsided. The provincial Government's efforts to control the situation were materially assisted by the Viceroy's visits to Bihar; by Gandhiji's resolve to fast to death if the disturbances did not stop within twenty-four hours; by Nehru's aerial tour and stern warnings to the rioters; and by the personal influence exerted in the province by Rajendra Prasad.

On 17 November, shortly after the Bihar disturbances, Jinnah wrote to the Viceroy arguing, in answer to the demand that he should summon his Council, that the Congress had not from the very beginning accepted the Statement of 16 May. He referred in this connexion to a letter which Nehru had written two months back to the Congress premier of Assam. The Congress position, Nehru had declared, was clear — that provincial autonomy must be maintained and a province must decide both as to grouping and its own constitution.

Jinnah also referred to one of Gandhiji's pronouncements, made on 23 October, in which he had said:

The Constituent Assembly is based on the State paper. That paper has put in cold storage the idea of Pakistan. It has recommended the device of 'grouping' which the Congress interprets in one way, the League in another and the Cabinet Mission in a third way. No law-giver can give an authoritative interpretation of his own law. If, then, there is a dispute as to its interpretation, a duly constituted court of law must decide it.

In these circumstances, said Jinnah, it would be futile for him to summon his Council. He went on to refer to the 'ruthless massacres of Muslims' in various parts of Bihar, and concluded by urging the Viceroy to announce immediately the postponement of the Constituent Assembly *sine die* and to concentrate every ounce of energy on restoring peace and order.

The position was that a provisional date, namely 9 December, had been fixed for the first meeting of the Constituent Assembly, and Nehru and his colleagues were pressing for the issue of invitations. The question was whether, in view of the fact that the Muslim League had not yet rescinded its Bombay resolution, these invitations should be issued. It was clear that the League had no immediate intention of calling its Council, and the Viceroy felt that if the Constituent Assembly were to meet with only Congress representatives, there would be grave and widespread disorder in the country. The main obstacle, he thought, in the way of Muslim League participation was the fact that there had never been an unequivocal declaration by His Majesty's Government as to the meaning of that part of the Statement of 16 May which referred to the manner of working the sections. A clear statement, if made immediately, would restore the confidence of the Muslim League and help the Viceroy to persuade it to attend the meeting of the Constituent Assembly on 9 December.

The Secretary of State suggested that the Viceroy might make it clear in his letter summoning the Constituent Assembly that it was His Majesty's Government's intention that sections should be free to settle their own procedure for determining matters allocated for decision by them, and that, in default of agreement between the representatives of the major communities, the decisions should be taken by majority vote. At the same time, the Secretary of State was doubtful if such a statement would bring in the Muslim League. What Jinnah was probably seeking was not an assurance as to the Cabinet Mission's intentions, but an assurance that those intentions would be enforced by His Majesty's Government. The latter assurance His Majesty's Government could not give, since it was not possible for it to control what happened in the Constituent Assembly.

Meanwhile, the Viceroy had seen Jinnah again. The latter, in reverting to the subject of the Bihar disturbances, made special mention of the refugee problem and raised the question of an exchange of population[1]. In particular, Jinnah stressed that to call the Constituent Assembly would be the greatest possible mistake and would lead to terrible disaster, particularly in the Muslim provinces. The Viceroy said that he did not see how he could postpone the meeting. He suggested that the right policy for the Muslim League was to come into

[1] The Muslim League members of the interim Government, in the course of discussions with the Viceroy, also brought up the subject of rehabilitation in Bihar and handed him a note containing the following requests:

(a) that the relief organization to be established in Bihar should be under the Governor and not the Government; (b) that the head of the relief organization should be British or Muslim, not Hindu; (c) that it should keep in touch with the Muslim League Committee in Bihar under Nazimuddin and Feroze Khan Noon; (d) that the troops should not be withdrawn for a long time to come.

The Viceroy said he would make a note of these points but that, as regards the troops, it was impossible that they should remain indefinitely in the province.

the Constituent Assembly and negotiate with the Congress; it could always walk out if it did not get satisfaction. The Muslim League had the guarantee that provinces would meet in sections. On the question of procedure the intentions of His Majesty's Government were quite clear, but it was of course impossible for it to force a method of procedure on the Constituent Assembly; all it could do was to refuse to recognize a constitution which had not been arrived at in accordance with its essential requirements. Everything ultimately rested on agreement between the parties concerned. The Congress could not make a constitution for the whole of India without the Muslim League; nor could the League force a constitution on Assam, or any other province in sections B and C, against the consent of the Congress. The alternative to agreement was civil war, which was likely to be disastrous for the Muslims and would break up the Indian Army. Nor could the British remain on indefinitely in India until the parties reached agreement.

Jinnah retorted by accusing the British Government of putting the Muslims gradually under Hindu rule. A settlement between the two communities, he said, was quite impossible. If the British were going, they had better go at once, or else they should draw up their own plan for a constitution and make an award. He thought that the British should give the Muslims their own bit of country, however small it might be, and they would live there, if necessary on one meal a day!

That same afternoon, the Viceroy interviewed Nehru. He told him what Jinnah had said about the Constituent Assembly, but added that he felt the issue could not be put off indefinitely and that, if Nehru so recommended, he would issue the invitations at once. Nehru advised that the invitations should be issued. The first session of the Assembly would, he thought, last for about ten days and would concern itself with formal matters of procedure, the appointment of committees and so on. The Assembly would then break up until April, the intervening period being employed in discussions by the sections. The Viceroy said he would issue the invitations, but hoped that before 9 December there would be informal discussions between the Congress and the League which might result in the League coming into the Constituent Assembly.

After his talks with Jinnah and Nehru, the Viceroy felt that a statement by His Majesty's Government, or by himself, would not be of any use, especially as Jinnah apparently wanted an understanding with the Congress first. The situation was worsening. He warned the Secretary of State that they were very near what would amount almost to open civil war between the communities, and that the calling of the Constituent Assembly might possibly precipitate the outbreak. Nevertheless, he did not think that it was possible to delay the Constituent Assembly further without changing their whole policy, and he felt that they must take the risk.

On 20 November the Viceroy issued invitations for the meeting of the Constituent Assembly. Jinnah characterized it as 'one more blunder of a very grave and serious character.' The Viceroy, he said, was blind to the seriousness of the situation and the realities facing him and was playing into the hands of the Congress and appeasing them in complete disregard of the Muslim League and other organizations and elements in the national life of the country. He called upon the representatives of the Muslim League not to participate in the Constituent Assembly and emphasized that the Bombay resolution of the Muslim League Council still stood.

In the light of Jinnah's unequivocal declaration, the Viceroy sent for Liaqat Ali Khan and told him that he could not agree to the representatives of the League remaining in the interim Government unless the League accepted the long-term plan. Liaqat Ali Khan replied that the League members were ready to resign whenever the Viceroy required them to do so, but they would not accept the long-term plan unless His Majesty's Government declared that the provinces would meet in sections; that the representatives in the sections would decide, by a majority if necessary, whether there would be groups; that the sections, again by a majority if necessary, would frame the provincial constitutions and the group constitutions, if any; and further, that His Majesty's Government must undertake not to implement the results unless this procedure was observed. If His Majesty's Government was unable to give such a guarantee, it was useless for the League even to come in and negotiate. He added that if His Majesty's Government was afraid of the Congress and had not the courage or honesty to maintain the Cabinet Mission plan, then the Muslims had been thrown to the wolves and must accept the position and do the best they could by themselves, for it was useless to expect mercy from the Congress. The Viceroy argued that the Constituent Assembly would contain a majority of reasonable men and that the Muslims would be able to secure good terms by negotiation. But in spite of all the Viceroy's pleadings and arguments, Liaqat Ali Khan refused to be convinced.

The Viceroy was impelled to fall back with even more insistence on the proposal that His Majesty's Government should give an assurance that the sections would reach decisions by a majority vote. He could not guarantee the reaction of the Congress and had to admit the possibility of Congress resignations at the Centre and in the provinces, followed perhaps by widespread violence. But if His Majesty's Government decided to adopt the line of surrender to the Congress point of view, the result would be something approaching civil war, which would lead to the eventual break-up of the Indian Army and chaos throughout India, since the Muslim League had been driven to the point of desperation and would use the religious issue to stir up trouble.

A point had been reached when the next step might make all the difference between ordered progress and complete anarchy for the country. A unilateral assurance by His Majesty's Government in the terms proposed was not likely to solve the problem. In the first place, one might well ask why the Muslim League had not insisted upon such an assurance before deciding to enter the interim Government. Moreover, to be of any effect, an assurance by His Majesty's Government should have the agreement of the Congress. On this issue the Congress had adopted a middle course; they agreed to enter into sections, but refused to commit themselves regarding the method of voting inside the sections. In the published papers, including the Statement of 25 May, all that His Majesty's Government had laid down was that the parties should enter into sections, and that the sections would draft provincial constitutions and group constitutions if it were decided to form groups. The Congress might very well insist that it had made it clear that it would enter into sections, and that it was not part of His Majesty's Government's plan to impose a further condition — that the procedure to be followed in sections should be by majority vote.

There was another consideration. The purpose of the Constituent Assembly, in the words of the Secretary of State, was 'to hammer out agreement from diverse opinions and plans — and likewise they can put forward their views as to how the Constituent Assembly should conduct its business.' If His Majesty's Government were to make a pronouncement on one point of procedure, it might be forced also to make pronouncements on others.

In the ultimate analysis, if a stable constitution was to be evolved, it would have to carry with it the agreement of the two major parties.

Nehru was reflecting genuine Congress feeling when he said that it was not the Congress intention to use its majority to make the Constituent Assembly an arena of conflict. His Majesty's Government's intervention at this stage would only have the effect of making the minorities look to it for support, rather than to settle their differences by discussion and adjustment in the Constituent Assembly itself.

The position briefly was that the communal veto made it possible for the Muslim League to ensure that the Union Centre was not too strong. The League could achieve the substance of Pakistan if it could but utilize its majority in sections B and C to secure strong group constitutions and provincial constitutions of its own choice; this it could do even against provincial opinion. Indeed, His Majesty's Government was back where it had started; the issue was Pakistan *versus* a United India, and it was on this issue that the battle still raged.

In any case, the Secretary of State felt that one more effort should be made to bring about a settlement between the two main parties and that the best method of achieving this would be to invite two representatives each of the Congress and the League to London to discuss with His Majesty's Government how best the meeting of the Constituent Assembly on 9 December could be made effective and profitable.

In agreeing that representatives of the Congress and the League should be invited to London, the Viceroy suggested that a representative of the Sikhs should also be invited.

In the meantime, at the annual session of the Congress which met in Meerut in the third week of November, Congress leaders demanded that the League should either accept the Cabinet Mission plan and come into the Constituent Assembly, or quit the interim Government. Addressing the Subjects Committee of the Congress, Nehru charged the Viceroy with failure to carry on the Government in the spirit in which he had started. 'He is gradually removing the wheels of the car and this is leading to a critical situation.' He declared that, ever since its entry into the interim Government, the League had pursued its aim to enlist British support. In fact it had been endeavouring to establish itself as the 'King's Party' in the Government. The British Government, meanwhile, had been exploiting the position for its own purposes. Nehru added that there was a mental alliance between the League and the senior British officials. The atmosphere, he said, had become so strained that the Congress members had twice threatened to resign. 'Our patience is fast reaching the limit. If these things continue, a struggle on a large-scale is inevitable.' Referring to the Constituent Assembly he said that the League members were welcome to join it, but stressed that whether they came in or stayed out, the work would go on. Vallabhbhai Patel declared that 'the Leaguers are trying to wage a war of nerves against the Congress. But we are not going to run away so easily from the interim Government. It is only when we are convinced that His Majesty's Government have gone back on their pledge and betrayed us that we shall get out.'

The Congress adopted a resolution declaring that it stood for an independent sovereign Republic of India, wherein all power and authority would be derived from the people. It declared that *swaraj* could not be real for the masses, unless it made possible a society in which democracy extended from the political to the social and economic spheres, in which there would be no opportunity for the privileged classes to exploit the bulk of the people. By another resolution, the Congress warned the people against the danger of retaliation in communal quarrels.

Liaqat Ali Khan protested that the League bloc had never once invoked the Viceroy's special powers, nor asked for his or the British Government's intervention in any matter. Jinnah said that he had never for one single moment conveyed to the Viceroy anything, by way of assurance or otherwise, except that the long-term settlement could only be considered and decided by the Council of the Muslim League. The interim Government, he said, was no more than the Viceroy's Executive Council under the Act of 1919. To call it a 'cabinet' was a complete misconception. 'You cannot turn a donkey into an elephant by calling it an elephant.' The Constitution gave no special position of pre-eminence to the Vice-President beyond that of presiding at meetings of the Council when the Viceroy was absent.

Nehru retorted that whatever might be the League's intention, its policy of stressing the legal position and preventing the Government from functioning as a cabinet must inevitably make it into a kind of 'King's Party' and increase the power and influence of the Viceroy. Liaqat Ali Khan did not want, he said, to enlarge the freedom of the interim Government, but to restrict it, as he was thus completely in line with the desire of the representatives of the British Government.

On 26 November the Viceroy saw Nehru, Liaqat Ali Khan and Baldev Singh and conveyed to them His Majesty's Government's invitation to London. Liaqat Ali Khan welcomed the suggestion, but wished to consult Jinnah, who was in Karachi; Nehru refused the invitation, and Baldev Singh saw no point in his going unless both parties accepted. Later on that same day, after consultation with his colleagues, Nehru wrote to the Viceroy stating that they attached great importance to the holding of the Constituent Assembly on 9 December and that the invitation to London appeared to reopen the whole problem which had been settled to a large extent by the Cabinet Mission's statement and by the formation of the interim Government. Any impression in the public mind that these decisions were being reopened would be fatal. He and his colleagues were convinced that the departure of the Congress representatives for London would be interpreted to mean that, at the instance of the League, the Cabinet Mission's plan was going to be abandoned or substantially varied and that they were parties to it. It would mean giving in to the League's intransigence and threats of violence, and this would have disastrous consequences. In these circumstances they could not accept the invitation to London, but would welcome consultations with the representatives of the British Government in India, whenever necessary.

Prime Minister Attlee thereupon sent a personal message to Nehru requesting him to visit London, since it was not possible for him or his colleagues to come to India. The object of their talks would be to try and ensure a successful meeting of the Constituent Assembly on 9 December. There was no intention of abandoning either the decision to summon the Constituent Assembly or the plan put forward by the Cabinet Delegation. It was the desire to see that this was implemented in full, and not any desire to abandon or alter it, that had prompted him to ask Nehru and his colleagues to come to London. All three members of the Cabinet Delegation individually and collectively had asked him to urge upon Nehru the supreme importance of this opportunity of their meeting and discussing the situation before any further untoward events took place in India.

In deference to the Prime Minister's wishes, Nehru agreed to go to London, but stressed that he would have to return by 9 December in time for the meeting of the Constituent Assembly. Vallabhbhai Patel, who was to have accompanied Nehru as the other representative of the Congress, was unwilling to go.

It had been already arranged that Jinnah and Liaqat Ali Khan would represent the Muslim League in London. But the League now insisted on knowing what had passed between the British Prime Minister and Nehru; and on being furnished with copies of the correspondence, Jinnah telegraphed from Karachi that it would not be possible for them to attend. Once more Prime Minister Attlee had to intervene and, as the result of a personal message from him, Jinnah agreed to go.

Nehru, Baldev Singh, Jinnah and Liaqat Ali Khan, together with the Viceroy, arrived in London on 2 December. The discussions which followed failed to bring about an agreement. On 6 December the British Government issued a statement announcing that no settlement had been achieved, but that this was only to be expected since the Indian representatives had to consult their colleagues before any final decision could be reached. The statement went on to say that the main difficulty had been about paragraph 19 (v) and paragraph 19 (viii) of the Cabinet Mission plan of 16 May.[1]

With regard to these paragraphs, the Statement continued as follows:

The Cabinet Mission have throughout maintained the view that the decisions of the sections should, in the absence of agreement to the contrary, be taken by a simple majority vote of the representatives in the sections. This view has been accepted by the Muslim League, but the Congress have put forward a different view. They have asserted that the true meaning of the Statement read as a whole is that the provinces have a right to decide both as to grouping and as to their own constitutions.

His Majesty's Government have had legal advice, which confirms that the Statement of May 16 means what the Cabinet Mission have always stated was their intention. This part of the Statement as so interpreted must therefore be considered as an essential part of the scheme of May 16 for enabling the Indian people to formulate a constitution which His Majesty's Government would be prepared to submit to Parliament. It should therefore be accepted by all parties in the Constituent Assembly.

It is however clear that other questions of interpretation of the Statement of May 16 may arise, and His Majesty's Government hope that if the Council of the Muslim League are able to agree to participate in the Constituent Assembly they will also agree, as have the Congress, that the Federal Court should be asked to decide matters of interpretation that may be referred to them by either side, and will accept such decision, so that the procedure both in the Union Constituent Assembly and in the sections may accord with the Cabinet Mission's plan.

On the matter immediately in dispute, His Majesty's Government urge the Congress to accept the view of the Cabinet Mission, in order that the way may be open for the Muslim League to reconsider their attitude.

If, in spite of this reaffirmation of the intention of the Cabinet Mission, the Constituent Assembly desires that this fundamental point should be

[1] See Appendix IV.

referred for the decision of the Federal Court, such reference should be made at a very early date. It will then be reasonable that the meetings of the sections of the Constituent Assembly should be postponed until the decision of the Federal Court is known.

There has never been any prospect of success for the Constituent Assembly except on this basis of an agreed procedure. Should a constitution come to be framed by a Constituent Assembly in which a large section of the Indian population had not been represented, His Majesty's Government could not of course contemplate — as the Congress have stated they would not contemplate — forcing such a constitution upon any unwilling parts of the country.

Before its issue, the statement was read to the Indian leaders. Jinnah asked what the position would be if the decision of the Federal Court on the matter immediately in dispute was contrary to the British Government's interpretation. The Secretary of State told him, in the presence of Nehru, that they would, in that case, have to consider the position afresh.

Nehru took the line that the statement amounted to a variation and extension of the Statement of 16 May and that he and his colleagues would have to consider the whole situation. Baldev Singh said that the Sikh position was worsened by the statement and that the Sikhs might withdraw from the Constituent Assembly if the Federal Court ruled that the British Government's interpretation was right.

Immediately after the London discussions, Nehru and Baldev Singh returned to India. But Jinnah and Liaqat Ali Khan stayed on for some time longer in England, where Jinnah made a number of speeches reiterating his demand for Pakistan, the alternative to which, he declared, was civil war.

The Constituent Assembly met on 9 December. The absence of the Muslim League representatives was widely regretted, but there were no serious demonstrations anywhere against the meeting of the Assembly, in spite of the Muslim League's demand for its postponement.

Sachhidanand Sinha as the oldest member took the Chair until the Assembly elected its President. Later, Rajendra Prasad was unanimously elected as President. The most important and politically significant resolution, known as the 'Objectives Resolution', was moved by Nehru. It envisaged the Indian Union as 'an independent Sovereign Republic' comprising autonomous units with residuary powers, wherein the ideals of social, political and economic democracy would be guaranteed to all sections of the people and adequate safeguards would be provided for minorities and backward communities and areas. Nehru described the resolution as 'a declaration, a pledge and an undertaking before the world, a contract with millions of Indians and therefore in the nature of an oath which we mean to keep.' His repeated statement that the House must rise above group or party politics was interpreted as a hint that, though the Assembly could not surrender on any fundamental matters, any reasonable grievance of the Muslim League would be satisfied. M. R. Jayakar moved an amendment suggesting that the discussion be postponed to a later date so as to enable representatives not only of the League, but of the Indian States, to participate in the Constituent Assembly. His suggestion, which was backed outside the House by Sir Sultan Ahmed (Constitutional Adviser to the Chamber of Princes) and the Dewans of Hyderabad, Travancore, Mysore and Bikaner, was ultimately accepted, in the hope, expressed by the President, that members of the League might attend by the time the resolution next came before the House. The Assembly was adjourned till 20 January.

On 22 December the Congress Working Committee issued a lengthy statement clarifying its attitude towards the British Government's statement of 6 December. The Committee criticized this statement and subsequent statements in Parliament as additions to, and variations of, the Cabinet Mission's statement of 16 May, on which the whole scheme of the Constituent Assembly had been based. The Committee added, however, that while the Congress had always been willing to agree to a reference to the Federal Court, any reference at a time when none of the other parties were prepared to join in it or to accept it, and one of them did not even accept the basis of the scheme, became totally uncalled for and was unbecoming and unsuited to the dignity of either the Congress or the Federal Court.

Referring to the question of grouping, the Working Committee reiterated its opinion that the British Government's interpretation in regard to the method of voting in the sections was not in conformity with provincial autonomy, which was one of the fundamental bases of the Cabinet Mission's scheme. The Committee emphasized that it was anxious to avoid anything which might come in the way of the successful working of the Constituent Assembly and was prepared to do everything in its power to seek and obtain the largest measure of co-operation, provided that no fundamental principle was violated. In view of the importance and urgency of the issues facing the country and the far-reaching consequences which must follow any decisions, the Working Committee decided to convene an emergency meeting of the All-India Congress Committee early in January to consider the latest developments and to give such directions as it might deem fit.

At the meeting of the All-India Congress Committee in Delhi on 5 January 1947, Nehru moved the following resolution:

The A.-I.C.C. having considered the events that have taken place in the country since the Meerut session of the Congress in November last, the statement issued by the British Government on December 6, 1946, and the statement of the Working Committee of December 22, 1946, advises Congressmen as follows:—

The A.-I.C.C. endorses the statement of the Working Committee of December 22, 1946, and expresses its agreement with the view contained therein.

While the Congress has always been agreeable to making a reference to the Federal Court on the question of the interpretation in dispute, such a reference has become purposeless and undesirable owing to the recent announcements made on behalf of the British Government. A reference could only be made on an agreed basis, the parties concerned agreeing to abide by the decision given.

The A.-I.C.C. is firmly of the opinion that the constitution for a free and independent India should be framed by the people of India on the basis of as wide an agreement as possible. There must be no interference whatsoever by any external authority and no compulsion of any province or part of a province by another province. The A.-I.C.C. realises and appreciates the difficulties placed in the way of some provinces, notably Assam, Baluchistan, Sind and the N.-W.F.P. and the Sikhs in the Punjab, by the British Cabinet scheme of 16 May 1946 and more especially by the interpretation put upon it by the British Government in their statement of December 6, 1946. The Congress cannot be a party to any such compulsion or imposition against the will of the people concerned, a principle which the British Government have themselves recognised.

The A.-I.C.C. is anxious that the Constituent Assembly should proceed with the work of framing a constitution for free India with the goodwill of all the parties concerned and, with a view to removing the difficulties that have arisen owing to varying interpretations, agree to advise action in accordance with the interpretation of the British Government in regard to the procedure to be followed in the sections.

It must be clearly understood, however, that this must not involve any compulsion of a province and that the rights of the Sikhs in the Punjab should not be jeopardised. In the event of any attempt at such compulsion, a province or part of a province has the right to take such action as may be deemed necessary in order to give effect to the wishes of the people concerned.

The future course of action will depend upon the developments that take place and the A.-I.C.C. therefore directs the Working Committee to advise upon it, whenever circumstances so require, keeping in view the basic principle of provincial autonomy.

Nehru emphasized the importance of proceeding through the channel of the Constituent Assembly, which had already come into existence and could not be dissolved without its own consent. It could be a very useful instrument if a conflict arose with the British Government, whereas, if they rejected the interpretation of the British Government, the latter might amend the Statement of 16 May.

Most of the speakers opposed the resolution. Among them were the leaders of the Congress Socialist Party, the representatives from Assam and even some right-wing Congressmen. One of the Assam members, a minister in that province, indicated that the attitude of Assam would depend upon the response of the Muslim League; if the League adopted a conciliatory attitude and reassured the minorities in the sections, Assam would sit in its section; otherwise the Assam members of the Constituent Assembly would abide by the mandate given to them by the Assam Legislative Assembly and refuse to participate in the work of the section. The debate occupied two days, after which the resolution was passed by a majority.

The Sikhs now began to press for procedural safeguards in section B, similar to those conceded to the Muslims in the Union Constituent Assembly, and started to elaborate a scheme for the partition of the Punjab. There were signs of a Hindu movement for the creation of a separate province of West Bengal, while the utterances of the Congress leaders of Assam showed that they were finding it difficult to decide upon their future course of action.

Public interest now centred upon the reactions of the Muslim League. Jinnah announced that the Working Committee of the League would be summoned, but the date subsequently fixed for its meeting, namely 29 January, caused dismay — since it was apparent that the Muslim League had no intention of participating in the Constituent Assembly, which was due to meet on the 20th. The views expressed by various League leaders and pro-League journals indicated dissatisfaction with the Congress resolution. On 25 January Liaqat Ali Khan issued a statement in which he held that the Congress veto given to provinces and parts of a province had completely negatived the principle of decision by a majority of votes in the sections; he asked the Congress, if this were not so, to give categorical answers to certain questions, some of which were concerned with the procedure in the sections and one with the reference of disputed points of interpretation to the Federal Court. No direct answers were returned to these questions, but Azad explained that the Congress objection was against any attempt to frame a provincial constitution by majority vote in the sections in such a way as would make it difficult for the province to exercise its eventual freedom to remain in the group or to opt out of it. Subject to this caveat, the Congress had accepted in full the British Government's statement of 6 December. Azad concluded that the League could now have no excuse for remaining away from the Constituent Assembly.

The Working Committee of the Muslim League met in Karachi and passed a resolution emphasizing that the League's view of the interpretation of the Statement of 16 May had been upheld by His Majesty's Government. Referring to the reservation in the Congress resolution on grouping, it proceeded to say: 'These qualifying clauses, in the considered opinion of the Working Committee of the All-India Muslim League, confer the right of veto within the section on "a province", and what is more absurd, on "a part of a province", as well as on the Sikhs in the Punjab, and therefore they completely nullify the so-called "acceptance" by the Congress of the December 6th Statement.' The Congress had not accepted the British Government's suggestion of reference to the Federal Court of disputed points; and the plain meaning of the British Government's declaration against coercing unwilling parts of the country had been distorted. The Constituent Assembly, it pointed out, in spite of its lack of Muslim representation, had taken vital decisions about the future constitution. It had gone beyond the functions prescribed by the Cabinet Mission Statement and had even tried to fetter the discretion of the sections; it was merely 'a rump' and a body totally different from that which had been contemplated by the Cabinet Delegation. Since the Congress, the Sikhs and the Scheduled Castes had not accepted the Statement, the Muslim League Working Committee called upon the British Government to declare that the plan of 16 May had failed and demanded that the Constituent Assembly, the elections to and the summoning of which had been *ab initio* illegal, should be dissolved forthwith. In these circumstances, the Working Committee declined to call the Council of the League to reconsider its decision of July 1946.

The Constituent Assembly met on 20 January. During its session of six days, Nehru's resolution on 'Objectives' was passed. Some important committees were also appointed. A number of places were left vacant on these committees to be filled by nomination by the President, the intention being to reserve them for the Muslim League. Controversial measures, such as a proposal for the redistribution of provinces on a linguistic basis, were dropped.

On 1 February, in an interview with Nehru, the Viceroy told him how much he regretted the Muslim League decision, which seemed to leave no loophole. A final break between the Congress and the League would have serious effects on the country. There could be no question of His Majesty's Government dissolving the Constituent Assembly or reversing its policy, but obviously a Constituent Assembly without the League and possibly without the States could not make an acceptable constitution for India as a whole. The Viceroy added that the Congress was in a position to demand the resignation of the Muslim League members from the interim Government, but whether it would be possible to carry on the administration of the country more effectively with the League in active opposition than with it in the Government, was a matter for careful consideration. The crisis had come at an awkward time, with the Budget session of the Assembly just about to begin.

Nehru said that the work of the Constituent Assembly would go on, but obviously they could not force a constitution on a reluctant province. He thought that they would probably draw up a model provincial constitution and then send it round to the provinces for discussion by the provincial Assemblies. They would also discuss matters with the States Negotiating Committee and see how far the States were prepared to co-operate with the Constituent Assembly. The meetings of the various committees had been postponed till the end of February in the hope that the Muslim League and the States would join. As to the interim Government, Nehru agreed that the matter required careful consideration. It was not merely that the League had refused to join the Constituent Assembly, but that, until the Bombay resolution was withdrawn, it was committed to a policy of direct action, i.e. of active opposition to the Government of which it formed a part.

On 5 February the Viceroy received a demand from the Congress and minority members for the resignation of the League representatives from the interim Government. The signatories pointed out that the resolution of the Muslim League was not merely for non-participation in the Constituent Assembly, but for a total rejection of the Cabinet Mission scheme and for a programme of direct action. It seemed impossible to them that this policy and programme could proceed side by side with membership of the interim Government. The two were incompatible. If the Cabinet Mission scheme was to be worked out, as they thought it should be, then those who rejected it could not continue as members of the interim Government; there was no other alternative.

The next day the Viceroy saw Liaqat Ali Khan and informed him of the Congress demand for the resignation of the Muslim League members from the Cabinet. This was obviously no surprise to Liaqat Ali Khan. He contended that the Congress had not in fact accepted the Mission's plan. If His Majesty's Government really considered that the Congress had accepted the Plan, the Muslim League would reconsider its position. But then it would be the responsibility of His Majesty's Government to see that the Congress 'did keep on the rails laid down by the Mission for the Constituent Assembly.'

The very next day, Liaqat Ali Khan wrote a long letter to the Viceroy reiterating the terms of the Karachi resolution of the Muslim League Working Committee. He particularly emphasized that if the basis of participation in the interim Government was acceptance of the Statement of 16 May, neither the Congress, which had not accepted it, nor the Sikhs, who had definitely rejected it, had any greater right to have their representatives or nominees in the Government than had the Muslim League. In the circumstances it was extremely presumptuous on the part of the nine members of the Executive Council to demand that their Muslim League colleagues should resign.

The Viceroy was in sympathy with the Muslim League's contention and was himself of the view that the Congress had not in fact accepted the Cabinet Mission plan. His personal inclination was to call upon the Congress to accept the plan without any reservations. On the other hand, the Congress had taken the stand that there should be 'no compulsion of a province' and that 'the rights of the Sikhs must not be jeopardised,' and there seemed to be no question of any compromise. My advice to the Viceroy at the time was that, in attempting to placate the League, he should not take any step that might cause the withdrawal of the Congress from the interim Government, as that would lead to a much more serious political situation.

Nevertheless, the Viceroy put his proposal to the Secretary of State, namely that His Majesty's Government should issue a statement calling upon the Congress to confirm that the relevant passages in its resolution dealing with sections and grouping, which had given rise to Muslim League doubts, were not intended to limit or qualify the Congress acceptance of the Cabinet Mission plan. If this were done, there was at least a slender chance of getting the League into the Constituent Assembly.

The Secretary of State was not satisfied that the issue of a statement by His Majesty's Government would in any way improve the situation. He was more concerned to know whether the Congress members were likely to resign from the interim Government if the Muslim League members were retained.

It was at this stage (on 13 February) that Nehru addressed a letter to the Viceroy reiterating his demand for the resignation of the members of the Muslim League from the interim Government. He stated that the present situation could not continue for long and that it was urgently necessary to come to a decision and give effect to it. The Congress and the minority members had made their position clear and could add nothing to it. The Muslim League had also made its position clear by its Karachi resolution. On the basis of these facts a decision had to be taken. Nehru asked the Viceroy to let him know what His Majesty's Government proposed to do in the matter. Delay in taking any decision, or in a decision which they thought was not proper or in conformity with the facts of the situation, would necessarily lead the Congress and minority members to reconsider their position in the interim Government.

Two days later Vallabhbhai Patel made it clear in a press interview that the Congress would withdraw from the interim Government if the representatives of the Muslim League were allowed to remain in it. The League must either get out of the interim Government, or change its Karachi decision.

The position that confronted His Majesty's Government was grave enough in all conscience. To ask for the resignation of the League representatives from the interim Government would have serious repercussions in India and in the Muslim countries of the world. To allow the Congress to resign would lead to even more disastrous consequences. His Majesty's Government had already committed itself to hand over power to Indian hands. The Cabinet Mission plan had been devised with the purpose of effecting a peaceful transfer of power with the agreement of the main political parties in India. His Majesty's Government had now exhausted all its resources to bring about such an agreement. The general situation in the country was alarming. The central Government was a house divided against itself. In further communal disorders, it was doubtful if the loyalty of the Army and the Services could be relied upon. His Majesty's Government therefore took a bold and momentous decision, namely to fix a definite date for its withdrawal from India. The Labour Government decided on this course in the hope that, besides establishing its bona fides, a time limit would serve as a challenge to bring home to the Indian parties the imperative need for coming to a mutua understanding.

On 20 February Prime Minister Attlee made a statement[1] in Parliament announcing His Majesty's Government's definite intention to take the necessary steps to effect the peaceful transfer of power into responsible Indian hands by a date not later than June 1948. It wished to hand over its responsibility to authorities established by a constitution approved by all parties in India in accordance with the Cabinet Mission plan, but unfortunately there was at present no clear prospect that such a constitution and such authorities would emerge. If then, it should appear that an agreed constitution would not have been worked out by June 1948, it would have to consider to whom it should transfer the powers of the central Government, 'whether as a whole to some form of central Government for British India, or in some areas to the existing provincial Governments, or in such other way as may seem most reasonable and in the best interests of the Indian people.'

Simultaneously with this statement it was announced that Lord Wavell would be succeeded as Viceroy in March by Admiral the Viscount Mountbatten, who would be entrusted with the task of 'transferring to Indian hands responsibility for the government of British India in a manner that will best ensure the future happiness and prosperity of India.' Lord Wavell's appointment, it was explained, had been a wartime one, and the opening of this 'new and final phase in India' was the appropriate time to terminate this war appointment. Attlee paid a tribute to Lord Wavell for the devotion and high sen e of duty with which he had discharged the high office during a very difficult period and announced that His Majesty had been pleased to approve the conferment on him of an Earldom.

[1] See Appendix IX.

The Viceroy saw Nehru on 21 February and pressed upon him the necessity of getting the Muslim League into the Constituent Assembly. The Viceroy adverted to the passages in the All-India Congress Committee's resolution of 6 January which seemed to need some explanation if the Muslim League was to be persuaded to join the Constituent Assembly. In the course of the discussion which ensued, Nehru argued that His Majesty's Government had recognized that they could not contemplate forcing an unwelcome constitution upon unwilling parts of the country; it was only logical that large minorities inside a province, such as the Hindus in Bengal and the Hindus and Sikhs in the Punjab, could also not be compelled into an unacceptable constitution. There was some argument on the interpretation of the words 'parts of the country' in the last paragraph of the Statement of 6 December. Nehru argued that 'parts of the country' could mean 'parts of a province'. The Viceroy said that was certainly not the intention of His Majesty's Government. If the resolution of the All-India Congress Committee merely meant to emphasize the obvious truth that any constitution (provincial, group or central) could only be framed with the consent of the great majority of the people, the Congress should say so; but if it implied that a part of a province could secede during the process of constitution-making, it was entirely inconsistent with the acceptance of the Cabinet Mission plan. The Viceroy urged that it was for the Congress to make its intention clear to the League.

The Viceroy saw Liaqat Ali Khan the same day. The latter pointed out that His Majesty's Government's Statement required careful consideration. He wanted to know if the Constituent Assembly was still going to function. As Finance Minister he could argue that, since it was not a fully representative Assembly as contemplated by the Mission's statement, there was no justification for spending public money on it. The Viceroy replied that the issue raised was arguable, but from a practical point of view neither the Finance Member, nor the Governor-General, nor His Majesty's Government could really stop the Constituent Assembly from continuing to function. The Viceroy repeated his advice that the Muslim League should come into the Constituent Assembly and argue out its case there. Liaqat Ali Khan saw no prospect of the two parties ever coming together. Finally, the Viceroy told him that the Statement of His Majesty's Government was a challenge to Indian statesmanship; that Hindus and Muslims had to live together in India on some terms; that they were now left to decide these for themselves without British support or interference, and the results would show whether they were capable of self-government or not.

Nehru publicly welcomed the British Government's decision as 'wise and courageous.' He said:

The clear and definite declaration that the final transference of power will take place by a date not later than June 1948 not only removes all misconception and suspicion, but also brings reality and a certain dynamic quality to the present situation in India. That decision will undoubtedly have far-reaching consequences and puts a burden and responsibility on all concerned. It is a challenge to all of us and we shall try to meet it bravely in the spirit of that challenge. I trust that we shall all endeavour to get out of the ruts and end the internal conflicts that have frustrated our efforts and delayed our advance and accept this burden and responsibility keeping only the independence and advancement of India in view.

Jinnah refused to comment on the Statement, but declared that the Muslim League would not yield an inch in its demand for Pakistan.

His Majesty's Government's decision to quit India was hailed by all progressive elements throughout the world as a bold and sincere step, although there were not a few, even in India, who considered it a leap in the dark.

The announcement was debated in the House of Lords. Viscount Templewood (who, as Secretary of State for India had piloted the Government of India Bill of 1935 through the House of Commons) moved that the British Government's decision to hand over India 'under conditions which appear to be in conflict with previous declarations of the Government on this subject and, without any provisions for the protection of minorities or discharge of their obligations, is likely to imperil the peace and prosperity of India.' He described the Statement as 'unconditional surrender, at the expense of many to whom we have given specific pledges for generations past, which would lead to a division of India under the worst possible circumstances.'

Lord Simon supported Viscount Templewood. 'I sadly fear,' he said, 'that the end of this business is not going to be the establishment of peace in India, but rather that it is going to degrade the British name.'

When it looked as though the division might go against the Government, it was the intervention of Lord Halifax that turned the scales. His was the most important and historic contribution to the whole debate. He said:

With such knowledge as I have, I am not prepared to say that whatever else may be right or wrong, this step must on all counts certainly be judged to be wrong ... for the truth is that for India today there is no solution that is not fraught with the gravest objection, with the gravest danger. And the conclusion that I reach — with all that can be said against it — is that I am not prepared to condemn what His Majesty's Government are doing unless I can honestly and confidently recommend a better solution... I should be sorry if the only message from the House to India at this moment was one of condemnation, based on what I must fully recognise are very natural feelings of failure, frustration and foreboding.

In winding up the debate Lord Pethick-Lawrence, the Secretary of State for India, pointed out that the only alternative to the present policy of the Labour Government was to start all over again the unhappy procedure of arrest and imprisonment without trial, so coming into conflict with what was a rapidly growing and determined body of people in India. Viscount Templewood finally withdrew his motion.

In the House of Commons the Government's motion was debated for two days. Speaking on behalf of the Government, Sir Stafford Cripps said that it was faced with only two alternatives. The first was that it could attempt to strengthen British control in India by the expansion and reinforcement of the Secretary of State's services, as well as by a considerable reinforcement of British troops. Both would have been required, so that the British would have been in a position to discharge for as long as might be necessary their administrative responsibility, while awaiting an agreement amongst the Indian communities. Such a policy entailed a definite decision that the British would remain in India for at least fifteen to twenty years. The second alternative was to make a further attempt to persuade the Indians to come together, while at the same time warning them that there was a limit to the time during which the British were prepared to remain in control while awaiting agreement among the communities. He explained:

The first alternative we had no hesitation in putting aside. It would be contrary to all we have said, and to the policy of this country, to prolong our stay in India for more than a decade against the wishes of the Indians — and there can be no shadow of doubt that it would be against their wishes. It would be politically impracticable, from both a national and an international point of view, and would arouse the most bitter animosity of all parties in India against us.

Even if we had been prepared to make available the extra troops that would be required to deal with opposition by the Indian people over that period of years, it is certain that the people of this country — short as we are of manpower, as we all know — would not have consented to the prolonged stationing of large bodies of British troops in India, for a purpose which was not consistent with our expressed desire that India should achieve self-government at as early a date as possible. Such a decision would, as I have said, have met with the hostility of all Indian communities, as indeed has been shown by the reaction to the statement the other day. We should, therefore, have had to rule India through the Governor-General and the Governors without any representative Indian Government. We therefore ruled out the first alternative, as both undesirable and impracticable.

In choosing the second alternative, he said, the British Government was quite definite in fixing the date of its withdrawal, but necessarily less so in naming its successors.

On the question of how the devolution of authority was to be carried out if a central Indian authority was not evolved, Sir Stafford Cripps said:

We shall be forced to choose the most appropriate government or governments to which to hand over power. It might be the then existing provincial governments or some form of combined government for parts of India. If it should eventuate that a large group of provinces, but not all, agree upon the form of the constitution, then it may be necessary to hand over separately in areas which have not been fully represented. We could not accept the forcing of unwilling provinces into a united Indian Government if they have not been represented in the making of the constitution.

The prominent speakers on the opposition side were Winston Churchill, R. A. Butler and Sir John Anderson. The last mentioned, when moving a detailed amendment to the Government motion on behalf of the Conservative Party, characterized the decision to withdraw by June 1948 as 'a gamble and an unjustifiable gamble'. The opposition criticism was based on three main considerations: firstly, that it was a departure from the agreed policy embodied in the Cripps Offer of 1942; secondly, that by fixing a time limit for withdrawal Britain had lost its bargaining power vis-a-vis India; and, thirdly, that the course adopted by the Government would lead to developments contrary to its expectations, that is to say, it would accentuate rather than minimize Indian differences.

Winston Churchill condemned the Constituent Assembly as having been elected on an 'inadequate and unrepresentative franchise'. The establishment of an interim Government from among the party leaders meant that India would be delivered over to politicians who had no claim to represent the mass of the people. 'In handing over the

Government of India to these so-called political classes we are handing over to men of straw of whom in a few years no trace will remain.' He advanced a suggestion that, instead of fixing a date, the aid and advice of the United Nations Organization should be sought. He concluded: 'Many have defended Britain against their foes, none can defend her against herself. But, at least, let us not add — by shameful flight, by a premature hurried scuttle — at least, let us not add to the pangs of sorrow so many of us feel, the taint and smear of shame.'

In winding up the debate, Prime Minister Attlee made one of the most forceful and convincing speeches of his career. Explaining why the decision had been taken to fix a date, he emphasized that 'the dangers of delay, the dangers of hanging on, were as great as the dangers of going forward.' He was sure that the whole House would wish Godspeed to the new Viceroy in his great mission. 'It is a mission, not as has been suggested, of betrayal on our part, it is a mission of fulfilment.' The censure motion was defeated by 337 votes to 185.

We have already seen how, after the general elections of 1945, the Muslim League had been able to set up ministries only in Bengal and Sind. In Sind the League had captured twenty-two seats out of forty-five and by selecting one of its members as Speaker, its strength had been reduced to twenty-one. The remaining twenty-three members of the Sind Assembly had combined to form a coalition opposition, but the one representing the labour constituency had been neutral, so that the coalition strength had dropped to twenty-two. The Speaker resigned his office and thus the League and coalition strength became even. Neither side was now prepared to sacrifice a vote by allowing one of its members to become Speaker. The Governor declared that in the circumstances the House could not function; he therefore dissolved the Assembly and called for fresh elections — which resulted in a League majority in the Assembly and a League ministry in the province.

In Bengal, where the Muslim League ministry had continued in office, the communal situation was causing considerable anxiety. The Working Committee of the Bengal Hindu Mahasabha went to the length of instituting an investigation into the feasibility of a separate Hindu province in West Bengal.

In Assam there was already a strong feeling that the province, being predominantly non-Muslim, should not have been grouped in section C. There followed a mass migration of Muslims from East Bengal who proceeded to take possession of Assam's reserved grazing lands. The Assam ministry took action against this movement, which had assumed the shape of a planned invasion and, as a consequence, the Assam Muslim League started preparations, with the assistance of the Bengal Muslim League, for a large-scale campaign against the ministry.

To understand the position in the Punjab, it is necessary to touch a little on the background. Ever since 1920, and up to the death of Sir Sikandar Hyat Khan in 1942, the general consensus of opinion among the Muslims in the Punjab was that a united Punjab under a Government representing Muslims, Hindus and Sikhs was the right solution. After the death of Sir Sikander Hyat Khan, the Muslim wing of the Unionist Party disintegrated and the Muslim League — with its demand for Pakistan — began to gain an increasing hold over the masses. The Muslim League was indeed determined to establish undiluted Muslim rule over the Punjab. It had fought the general election in 1946 on this issue, and had said nothing since to reassure the Hindus and the Sikhs. The failure of the League to form a ministry after the general election had been due more to its uncompromising communal outlook than to any other cause. So far as the Sikhs were concerned, the League leaders had refused to discuss their future, or to give them any assurances. The Sikhs felt that they could hardly throw in their lot with a party the avowed policy of which was to treat them as inferiors in a Muslim country. Nor were the Hindus, on whom the attitude of the League had made a bad impression, prepared to submit to undiluted Muslim rule.

It was inevitable that, having failed to form a ministry, the Muslim League should be sore. Thenceforth its leaders concentrated all their energies upon overthrowing the coalition ministry headed by Khizr Hyat Khan. Their grievances were based ostensibly on the issue of the suppression of civil liberties. Agitation proceeded on the familiar lines of defiance of orders prohibiting meetings and processions; crowds, including women and students, making demonstrations before Government House, the Secretariat, Legislative buildings, Magistrates' courts and jails; the shouting of League slogans; the hoisting of League flags on Government buildings in place of the Union Jack, and interference with railway traffic. By the third week of February the communal situation had become serious and notably so in Gujrat, Lahore, Amritsar and Jullundur. The Muslim League agitation created great apprehensions in the minds of the Sikhs and the Hindus. Khizr Hyat Khan was warned by his colleagues that if he did not suppress the League agitation with all the resources at his disposal, the Hindus would have to act on their own initiative. The Sikh leader, Master Tara Singh, declared that the League agitation had as its purpose the domination of the Punjab by the Muslims and he called on the Sikhs to prepare themselves to face the danger that threatened them. Both Hindus and Sikhs now began to feel that their safety lay in a separate province for themselves.

Sir Evan Jenkins, Governor of the Punjab, tried his best to bring about a settlement between the parties. He repeatedly stressed on the League leaders that the Punjab could only go forward as a powerful State if the Muslims took their proper place; that their numerical majority entitled them to leadership, but that the League should abandon their extreme communal attitude; that in order to retain their natural leadership they had to consider the non-Muslim minorities as partners and not as inferiors or subordinates, and that no one party could rule the Punjab. The advice fell on deaf ears; nothing came out of the Governor's attempts at reconciliation.

It was when the situation was causing the utmost concern that there came His Majesty's Government's announcement of 20 February 1947. Khizr Hyat Khan's position was extremely difficult. He could neither oblige the League, nor offend the Hindus and Sikhs. Ultimately he felt that he had no alternative but to resign, which he did on 2 March. The reasons given by him for his resignation were that His Majesty's Government's statement of 20 February made a coalition government, including the Muslim League, essential to the safety of the Punjab; that the League would not negotiate with the minorities unless faced with reality, and that the League would not be faced with reality so long as the Muslim Unionists acted as a buffer between them and the minorities. Khizr Hyat Khan's resignation came as a great surprise, even to his colleagues. The Muslim League was naturally jubilant.

Sir Evan Jenkins now warned the Viceroy that the Muslim League would not be able to form a ministry and that during the next sixteen months order could only be maintained in the Punjab, whether in a communal ministry or under Section 93, by the use of force. Nevertheless, he adopted the constitutional procedure of calling upon the Khan of Mamdot, leader of the provincial Muslim League, to form a ministry. As expected, both the Hindus and the Sikhs refused to co-operate and the Governor was obliged, on 5 March, to take over the administration under Section 93.

Communal rioting broke out again on a large scale. From street fighting in Lahore the trouble developed into a frenzy of stabbing and killing which spread to other towns such as Multan, Rawalpindi and Amritsar. Vigorous measures were taken by the Governor to check the communal fighting. In addition to his other worries, he was faced with a threatened strike from the subordinate Services for more pay. Needless to say, there was no question amidst the general communal situation of setting up any alternative ministry in the Punjab; therefore, right up to the transfer of power the province continued to be administered under Section 93.

The events in the Punjab had their reactions in the North-West Frontier Province, where the League organized demonstrations against the Congress ministry. The provincial Government was compelled to resort to large-scale arrests, the most important being that of the Pir of Manki Shariff, a prominent Muslim Leaguer. His arrest was strongly resented by his followers, who included a section of the tribal people.

Apart from the communal situation, the food position was disquieting. The rising prices and the reluctance of the cultivator to part with his grain provided the very conditions in which agitators thrive. The communists took full advantage of the position and exploited it for their own ends. Strikes were frequent and the economic situation was deteriorating.

It was in this atmosphere that the Congress Working Committee met on 5 March to consider the British Government's statement of 20 February. The Committee welcomed it, but required, as a corollary, that the interim Government should be recognized in the intervening period as a Dominion Government with full control over the Services and administration. The Committee reiterated its acceptance of the Cabinet Mission plan and the interpretation of it by the British Government; it welcomed the decision of a number of States to join the Constituent Assembly, and invited the elected Muslim League members to take their seats. The resolution declared that the Constituent Assembly was a voluntary body, so that the constitution framed by it would apply only to those areas which accepted it; similarly, no province or part of a province which desired to join the Indian Union could be prevented from doing so. It appealed to all parties and groups to discard violent and coercive methods, and to co-operate democratically and peacefully in the making of a constitution.

Another resolution declared that it had become incumbent on the people of India to prepare themselves jointly and co-operatively for the transfer of power so that it might be made peacefully and to the advantage of all. The Muslim League was invited to nominate representatives to meet representatives of the Congress, in order to discuss methods of ensuring a peaceful transfer of power. The resolution also stated that the Committee would keep in touch with the representatives of the Sikhs and other groups concerned, with a view to co-operating with them in the measures that had to be taken and in safeguarding their interests.

A third resolution narrated the recent events in the Punjab, and suggested that, in order to avoid compulsion of any section, the province should be divided into two parts so that the predominantly Muslim portion might be separated from the predominantly non-Muslim portion.

The Muslim League continued to be officially silent regarding the British Government's decision to transfer power by June 1948, nor was there any direct response to the invitation to discuss the situation with the Congress. The Muslim League press issued severe criticisms of the Congress proposal to divide the Punjab; nor was the solution entirely agreeable to certain pro-Congress sections. The Congress President explained in a press interview that the Congress had only suggested a division of the Punjab as a means of putting an end to violence, and that the same remedy would hold good for Bengal if the circumstances in that province were similar.

On 9 March 1947 Nehru wrote to Lord Wavell enclosing copies of the resolutions passed by the Congress Working Committee. Nehru said that it was the intention of the Congress to approach the Muslim League for a joint meeting to consider the situation. They wanted to do everything in their power to get the Muslim League representatives into the Constituent Assembly, so that all might function in terms of the Cabinet Mission's statement of 16 May. If, unfortunately, this were not possible, then the Congress would try to lay down a course of action which would avoid friction and conflict. It was with this object in view that they had sought a meeting with the League and had also suggested the division of the Punjab into two parts. This principle would, of course, apply to Bengal also. The proposal was not a pleasant one for the Congress to contemplate, but such a course was preferable to an attempt by either party to impose its will upon the other. Recent events in the Punjab demonstrated—if such demonstration were necessary—that it was not possible to coerce the non-Muslim minority in the province, just as it was not possible or desirable to coerce the others. The Congress felt that the suggested way out would be fair to all parties. If the League accepted the British Cabinet Mission's scheme of 16 May and co-operated in the Constituent Assembly, the question did not arise in this form. But even so, it was worth considering whether Bengal and the Punjab should not both be divided into smaller provinces. In the event of the Muslim League not accepting the Cabinet Mission's scheme and not coming into the Constituent Assembly, the division of Bengal and the Punjab would become inevitable.

The Viceroy told Nehru that he would forward the Congress resolutions to the Secretary of State. He himself was convinced that the best chance for the peaceful and orderly progress of India lay in the whole-hearted acceptance by both parties of the plan laid down by the Cabinet Mission. Until the results of the Congress approach to the League were known, it would, the Viceroy thought, be premature to consider the question of the partition of the Punjab and Bengal.

The Viceroy's hope of an amicable settlement between the Congress and the League was far from being fulfilled, for a new crisis was brewing. Liaqat Ali Khan, as Finance Member, had in his budget proposals suggested a twenty-five per cent tax on all business profits of more than one hundred thousand rupees. This was interpreted in Congress circles as an attempt to penalize the Hindu capitalists (who largely financed the Congress) and to bring about dissension between the right wing and the socialist group within the Congress Party.

By the time Lord Wavell left India, the general situation was so bleak that it looked as though the country was heading for certain disaster. With the Muslim League conducting a civil disobedience campaign against two provincial ministries, and its representatives in the central Government openly preaching 'direct action', Hindu-Muslim differences were further accentuated. Even some members of the Services, at least in the upper levels, had given up their traditional loyalty and impartiality and had begun openly to take sides in the political controversy. The precarious food position, the steadily deteriorating economic situation, and widespread labour unrest added to the threatening symptoms of a general collapse. It is particularly creditable to Nehru that he should, in the face of all this, have come to the defence of Lord Wavell. He could have enlarged on the differences that there had been between himself and the Viceroy. Instead, he emphasized the heavy burden that Lord Wavell had carried and paid special tribute to his sincerity and desire to serve India's interests.

# XV

## THE EVOLUTION OF A PLAN

LORD MOUNTBATTEN arrived in Delhi on 22 March 1947. He was the thirty-fourth and last of the British Governors-General of India. Even before he was sworn in, Lord Mountbatten wrote to Gandhiji and Jinnah inviting them to Delhi for discussion. Gandhiji at that time was touring in Bihar on his mission to restore communal peace.

On the morning of 23 March Lord Wavell left Delhi. Lord Mountbatten was sworn in the next day; he broke tradition by making a speech at the swearing-in ceremony. He said that his was not a normal Viceroyalty. His Majesty's Government were resolved to transfer power by June 1948, and since new constitutional arrangements must be made and many complicated questions of administration resolved, it meant that a solution had to be reached within the next few months. He believed that all the political leaders in India felt, as he did, the urgency of the task before them. He hoped soon to be in close consultation with them; he would give them all the help he could. In the meanwhile he appealed to everyone to do his best to avoid any word or action which might lead to further communal bitterness or add to the toll of innocent victims. He paid tribute to Lord Wavell, who had done much to take India along the path of self-government. He concluded: 'I am under no illusion about the difficulty of my task. I shall need the greatest goodwill of the greatest possible number, and I am asking India today for that goodwill.'

The first task that confronted the new Viceroy was to resolve the crisis within the interim Government over the budget proposals of Liaqat Ali Khan. Lord Mountbatten had a series of interviews with the members of the interim Government, particularly with Nehru and Liaqat Ali Khan who were in strong disagreement over the question of taxing business profits. Ultimately a compromise was reached whereby the percentage of tax was substantially reduced.

The second immediate problem was to bring about a truce between the two communities. This was vital for a peaceful transfer of power. The Viceroy had discussions with Gandhiji, as also with Jinnah. The two leaders signed a joint appeal for peace, in which they deeply deplored the recent acts of lawlessness and violence that had brought the utmost disgrace on the fair name of India and the greatest misery to innocent people. They denounced for all time the use of force for the achievement of political ends and called upon the communities of India, to whatever persuasion they might belong, not only to refrain from all acts of violence and disorder, but to avoid both in speech and writing any incitement to such acts. This appeal certainly enhanced the prestige of Lord Mountbatten; but it failed to produce the desired effect of lessening the communal tension.

Before his departure for India Lord Mountbatten had been given a directive by Prime Minister Attlee as to the broad lines of policy which he was to follow.

The objective of His Majesty's Government was to obtain a unitary Government for British India and the Indian States, if possible within the British Commonwealth, through the medium of a Constituent Assembly set up in accordance with the Cabinet Mission plan. Since, however, the basis of the Cabinet Mission plan was agreement between the two major parties, there could be no question of compulsion; and if Lord Mountbatten by 1 October 1947 found that there was no prospect of reaching a settlement on the basis of a unitary Government, he was to report the steps which he considered should be taken for the handing over of power on the due date.

With regard to the Indian States, Lord Mountbatten was directed to urge those rulers of Indian States where democratic progress had been slow to go forward more rapidly and to advise the rulers generally to reach fair and just arrangements with British India in regard to their future relationships.

Lord Mountbatten was further directed to bear in mind that the transfer of power must be in accordance with Indian defence requirements. He was to impress upon the Indian leaders the importance of avoiding a break in the continuity of the Indian Army and the need for continued collaboration with His Majesty's Government in the security of the Indian Ocean.

Lord Mountbatten had a remarkably careful yet quick and

business-like method of working. As soon as he finished an interview with a leader, and before proceeding to the next, he would dictate a résumé of the talk, a copy of which would be circulated to each member of his staff. He held staff conferences every day, sometimes twice and even thrice a day, to study and discuss how events were shaping.

The Governor-General's normal staff in India consisted of three Secretaries, namely, Secretary (Personal), better known as the Private Secretary, who was in charge of the personal correspondence of the Viceroy and also dealt with the work that came up to the Viceroy from the departments of the Government of India; Secretary (Public), who dealt with all correspondence between the Governor-General and the provincial Governors on matters in which the Governor-General exercised control over the provincial Governors; and Secretary (Reforms), who was the Constitutional Adviser to the Governor-General. These three Secretaries were directly under the Governor-General, that is, outside the Government of India Secretariat. In addition, Lord Mountbatten had brought his own staff with him from England, among whom were some notable persons. His 'Chief of Staff' was Lord Ismay, who had been Military Secretary to Lord Willingdon when the latter was Viceroy of India, and had been Churchill's Personal Military Adviser and Liaison Officer with the Combined Chiefs of Staff throughout the War; then there was Sir Eric Mieville, who had been Private Secretary to Lord Willingdon in India and later Assistant Private Secretary to King George VI. He had also brought with him Captain R. V. Brockman as 'Personal Secretary', Lieutenant Colonel V. F. Erskine Crum as 'Conference Secretary', and Alan Campbell-Johnson[1] as 'Press Attaché'.

In his very first interview with Lord Mountbatten, Gandhiji suggested that the Viceroy should dismiss the existing Cabinet and give Jinnah the option of forming a new one; that the selection of the members should be left entirely to Jinnah—they might be all Muslims, or all non-Muslims, or they might be representatives of all classes and creeds. If Jinnah accepted the offer, the Congress would guarantee to co-operate freely and sincerely, so long as all the measures that the Cabinet might bring forward were in the interests of the Indian people as a whole. The sole referee of what was, or was not, in the interests of India as a whole would be Lord Mountbatten in his personal capacity. Jinnah should, on his part, undertake on behalf of the League, or of any other parties represented in the Cabinet, that

[1] Author of 'Mission with Mountbatten'.

they would do their utmost to preserve peace throughout India. There should be no Muslim National Guards, or any other form of private army. Within the above limits, Jinnah would be perfectly at liberty, for example, to plan for Pakistan and even to put his plans into effect before the transfer of power, provided that he was successful in appealing to reason and did not use force. If Jinnah refused, the same offer should be made *mutatis mutandis* to the Congress.

It was Gandhiji's undoubted intention to bring about some sort of peace between the two communities, but there were inherent practical difficulties in his proposal. It failed in any case to win the support of his colleagues. Indeed, he wrote to the Viceroy to say that his plan was not acceptable to the Congress and that he was personally handing over all future negotiations to the Working Committee. But Lord Mountbatten requested him to stay on and exert his influence in favour of the acceptance of the Cabinet Mission plan.

Lord Mountbatten was required by his 'directive' to find an agreed solution for a united India on the basis of the Cabinet Mission plan and he set about most expeditiously and zealously on this path. But in the course of his talks with the party leaders, particularly with Jinnah and his colleagues, he became more and more convinced that there was no prospect of an agreed solution on that basis and that an alternative plan for the transfer of power had to be found and implemented without loss of time, in order to ease the growing political tension. Such an alternative plan would have to follow the policy laid down by His Majesty's Government in its statement of 20 February, that is, that if a constitution based on the Cabinet Mission plan was not likely to be worked out by a fully representative Constituent Assembly, by June 1948, 'His Majesty's Government will have to consider to whom the power of the central Government in British India should be handed over on the due date, whether as a whole to some form of central Government for British India, or in some areas to the existing provincial Governments, or in such other way as may seem most reasonable and in the best interests of the Indian people.' Accordingly, in consultation with his advisers, he drew up an outline of an alternative plan, the broad basis of which was the demission of authority to the provinces, or to such confederations of provinces as might decide to group themselves in the intervening period before the actual transfer of power. The plan provided that the members of the Legislative Assemblies of Bengal and the Punjab should meet separately in two parts, i.e. representatives of the predominantly Muslim areas, and representatives of the predominantly non-Muslim areas; and if both sections of each of these Assemblies voted for partition, then that province would be partitioned. Under the plan, in the event of the partition of Bengal, the predominantly Muslim district of Sylhet in Assam would have the option of joining the Muslim province. The plan also envisaged the holding of an election in the North-West Frontier Province to ascertain the wishes of the people of that province. Thus the responsibility for the division of the country was to be placed on the shoulders of the Indian people themselves.

The Viceroy put this plan before a conference of Governors on 15 and 16 April. He acquainted the Governors with the talks he had had with the party leaders and invited their opinion on the tentative plan. Sir Evan Jenkins had always held the view that partition of the Punjab would be disastrous. Crude population figures were not necessarily the only criterion. Within the districts the communities were not evenly distributed and the city and town populations often had a different communal composition from that of the adjoining countryside. In some districts the population of tehsils differed widely. In his view, partition would not solve the minorities problem, since the divided provinces would still have considerable and probably discontented minorities. Sir Frederick Burrows, the Governor of Bengal, was unwell and unable to attend the conference, but J. F. Tyson, I.C.S., represented him and conveyed his point of view. Sir Frederick Burrows was against the partition of Bengal. There were many Muslims in Bengal who were not, in his opinion, in favour of such a course. If Bengal were divided, there was no doubt that East Bengal would become a rural slum.

Consultation with the Governors certainly gave Lord Mountbatten a good idea of the colossal administrative difficulties involved in a transfer of power based on partition. But the problem that actually confronted him was, if it became inevitable to divide the country— and Lord Mountbatten was sure that no other solution would be acceptable to Jinnah—how was this to be brought about with the willing concurrence of the parties concerned? The greater the insistence by Jinnah on his province-wise Pakistan, the stronger was the Congress demand that he should not be allowed to carry unwilling minorities with him. Nehru, for instance, in a public speech on 20 April declared: 'The Muslim League can have Pakistan, if they wish to have it, but on the condition that they do not take away other parts of India which do not wish to join Pakistan.' But perhaps the more authoritative pronouncement was that made by Rajendra Prasad, President of the Constituent Assembly, when the Assembly met on 28 April:

While we have accepted the Cabinet Mission's Statement of May 16, 1946, which contemplated a Union of the different provinces and States within the country, it may be that the Union may not comprise all provinces. If that unfortunately comes to pass, we shall have to be content with a constitution for a part of it. In that case, we can and should insist that one principle will apply to all parts of the country and no constitution will be forced upon any unwilling part of it. This may mean not only the division of India, but a division of some provinces. For this we must be prepared and the Assembly may have to draw up a constitution based on such a division.

In Bengal, the demand for the creation of a separate province of West Bengal was gaining in popularity. It was endorsed by the provincial Congress and the Hindu Mahasabha and was reinforced by a campaign of protests against the misbehaviour of Punjabi Muslim policemen who had recently been recruited by the provincial Government. At this stage, Suhrawardy (the Premier) came out with a proposal for 'a sovereign, independent and undivided Bengal in a divided India.' Sarat Chandra Bose, the Congress left wing leader, supported the proposal, but it received little support from either the Muslim League or the Congress.

Jinnah issued a statement that the proposal for the partition of Bengal and the Punjab was 'a sinister move actuated by spite and bitterness.' He said that the principle underlying the Muslim demand for Pakistan was that Muslims should have a national home and a national State in their homelands comprising the six provinces of the Punjab, the North-West Frontier Province, Sind, Baluchistan, Bengal and Assam. If the Punjab and Bengal were partitioned, all the other provinces would have to be cut up in a similar way. Such a process would strike at the root of the administrative, economic and political life of the provinces which for nearly a century had been developed and built up on that basis and had grown and were functioning as autonomous provinces. He suggested that an exchange of population would sooner or later have to take place and that this could be effectively carried out by the respective Governments in Pakistan and Hindustan. He finally demanded the division of the Defence forces and stressed that the States of Pakistan and Hindustan should be made absolutely free, independent and sovereign.

Jinnah's statement drew the retort from Rajendra Prasad that the demand for the division of the Punjab and Bengal was in the terms of the Muslim League's Lahore resolution of 1940 and that it could not claim any areas which were not contiguous and in which the Muslims were not numerically in a majority. He said that if there was to be a division of India, then it should be as complete and thorough as possible, including the division of the Punjab and Bengal, so that there might not be any room for contention or conflict. If it required the division of the defence forces, that also should be brought about, and the sooner the better.

The Hindu and Sikh legislators of the Punjab and the non-Muslim members of the central Assembly and Constituent Assembly from that province met in New Delhi and passed a resolution that the only solution of the political problem of the Punjab lay in a just and equitable division of the province, and that the non-Muslim population must be assured of such territories and assets as they were entitled to according to their numbers and stake in the province. Safeguards were also demanded for the preservation of the integrity and homogeneity of the Sikh community.

At the same time, some of the extremists among the Sikhs started an agitation for a separate State of their own, to be called 'Khalistan', while in the North-West Frontier Province the idea was being mooted of a separate Pathan State. Taking their cue from Jinnah, the local bodies of the Muslim League in the United Provinces and Bombay began to demand the right of self-determination for Muslims in certain areas in those provinces.

The communal tension in the country was thus steadily going from bad to worse. Serious communal outbreaks and incidents of stabbing and arson were occurring in various districts of the Punjab. The unrest in that province led to disturbed conditions in the adjoining provinces, including Delhi. In the North-West Frontier Province the Muslim League agitation against the Congress ministry had taken a turn for the worse. Lord Mountbatten convened a conference which was attended by Nehru, the Governor (Sir Olaf Caroe) and Dr Khan Sahib, and, as a result, the provincial Government decided to release all political prisoners not charged with violence who had been arrested in connexion with the Muslim League agitation, and to withdraw the ban on public meetings. But, backed by Jinnah, the League leaders in detention refused to accept their freedom, or to suspend agitation, unless the Congress ministry resigned or a general election were ordered. There followed disturbances and attacks on trains resulting in many casualties among the Hindus. The frontier tribes were also affected. Towards the end of April Lord Mountbatten visited the province. This had a calming effect on the League demonstrators as well as on the tribes; but the League campaign of civil disobedience continued.

In the face of the progressively deteriorating situation in the country, Lord Mountbatten felt that if the procedure for the transfer of power was not finalized quickly, there was a possibility that at least in some parts of the country there would be no authority to whom power could be transferred. He revised his tentative plan in the light of his discussions with the Governors and party leaders and sent this revised plan to London with Lord Ismay and George Abell on 2 May. I should mention that by this time Lord Listowel had succeeded Lord Pethick-Lawrence as Secretary of State.

Lord Mountbatten urged that His Majesty's Government's approval should be communicated to him by 10 May. His purpose was to call a meeting of party leaders on 17 May in order to ascertain their reactions. In the afternoon of the same day he would also see the members of the States' Negotiating Committee and apprise them of the plan. If the party leaders did not accept the plan and were themselves unable to produce an agreed alternative solution, His Majesty's Government would demit power in accordance with its own plan.

Thus, within six weeks of his arrival and after constant and ceaseless effort, Lord Mountbatten had produced a plan which marked the first stage towards the transfer of power. In all his discussions with party leaders and others, despite the divergent views which he was forced to adjust and reconcile, there was nowhere any evidence of an attempt to question either his own impartiality or the bona fides of His Majesty's Government.

Pending receipt of His Majesty's Government's approval to the proposed plan, Lord Mountbatten decided to go up to Simla for a short respite. His secretarial staff was divided into three parts. One part had gone with Lord Ismay to London, a small group stayed in Delhi, and Sir Eric Miéville and I accompanied the Viceroy to Simla.

I had always been opposed to the plan which Lord Ismay and George Abell had taken to London. The theory that the provinces should become initially independent successor States was particularly abhorrent to me. But my protests and my views in the discussions with the Viceroy's advisers went in vain. The main consideration which influenced me was this, that if the transfer took place unilaterally without the willing consent of the party leaders and there was no strong central Government to which that power could be transferred, the whole country would inevitably drift into chaos and civil war.

It was at Simla that, for the first time, I had an opportunity of explaining my point of view to the Viceroy in person. As a matter of fact, it was while Lord Wavell was still conducting negotiations with the party leaders, but when agreement between the Congress and the Muslim League on the Cabinet Mission plan seemed — to me at least — to be impossible of achievement, that I had attempted to devise a fresh approach to the problem.

It was late in December 1946, or early in January 1947, that I had a lengthy discussion with Vallabhbhai Patel. A united India under the Cabinet Mission plan was, I suggested, an illusion; the three-tier constitutional set-up envisaged was unwieldy and difficult to work; I saw no future for the country under this plan. Besides, Jinnah showed no sign of resiling from his demand for a separate, independent sovereign State for the Muslims — a demand in which the League had the sympathy, if not the support, of a large section of British opinion and, what was even more important from our point of view, the sympathy of most of the British element in the Services. My personal view was that it was better that the country should be divided, rather than that it should gravitate towards civil war. If we agreed to partition, Jinnah obviously could not ask for those portions of the Punjab, Bengal and Assam which were predominantly non-Muslim. The crucial problem was the basis on which power could be transferred. In a divided India this could best be to two central governments on the basis — a point on which I laid particular stress — of Dominion Status. By consenting to accept Dominion Status, the Congress would be gaining three great advantages. Firstly, it would ensure a peaceful transfer of power. Secondly, such acceptance would be warmly welcomed by Britain, and the Congress would by this single act have gained its friendship and goodwill. The third concerned the future administration of the country. The civil services at the higher levels were manned largely by Britishers, and if India insisted on independence there was no question but that the British element had it in their power to create endless trouble at the time of the transfer of power. It might be possible to carry on the civil administration somehow; but certainly India could not, during the transitional period, do without some help on the defence side. The Indian Army was largely·officered by Britishers, almost entirely so in the higher ranks, while the Navy and Air Force had to be built up virtually from scratch. After all, the test of sovereignty was the power to amend one's constitution, which remained unaffected by the acceptance of Dominion Status. India could at any time, if she so desired, walk out of the Commonwealth. Moreover, the Princes, with their past associations with the British Crown, would be reassured and be more willing to negotiate.

I pointed out that if the transfer of power took place on the basis of Dominion Status, it would enable the Congress to have at one and the same time a strong central Government, able to withstand the centrifugal tendencies all too apparent at the moment, and to frame a truly democratic constitution unhampered by any communal considerations. Nobody could have been better aware of the situation in the country than Vallabhbhai Patel; he had already been in charge of the Home portfolio for some months. Like the great statesman that he was, he assured me that if power could be transferred at once on the basis of Dominion Status, he for one would use his influence to see that the Congress accepted it. In his presence I dictated the outline of a plan, which I later sent by special messenger to London to be handed over to the Secretary of State. (With Lord Wavell's concurrence, I had been conducting some correspondence with the India Office on the issue of the transfer of power on this basis). I could not very well convey to the Secretary of State that Patel had agreed, as that might have compromised his position, but I did say that I had reason to believe that the Congress would accept Dominion Status. It might well be that the Secretary of State was feeling that in view of the unequivocal demand of the Congress for complete independence there was no ground for assuming that the Congress would accept a transfer of power on the basis of Dominion Status. In any case, no action was taken on my proposals—which, incidentally, Lord Mountbatten mentioned having seen in London before coming out to India.

Nehru, accompanied by Krishna Menon, arrived in Simla on 8 May. They stayed as guests of the Viceroy at Viceregal Lodge. Lord Mountbatten suggested that I should discuss my plan with Nehru and find out his reactions, and I had discussions with him on that and the next day. I was not allowed to disclose to him the plan which Lord Ismay had taken to London, and so I did not say anything about it. As a result of my talks with Nehru, I gathered the impression that he was not averse to the proposed transfer of power on the basis of Dominion Status. I reported this to the Viceroy, who on 10 May called a conference which was attended by Nehru, Sir Eric Miéville and myself. At this conference Lord Mountbatten told Nehru that I had been working on a scheme for the early transfer of power on the basis of Dominion Status long before his arrival in India and he asked me to give Nehru an outline of the scheme. I repeated much of what I had already discussed with Nehru. The broad outlines were that the Muslim majority areas should be separated from India and that the transfer of power should be to two central Governments, India and Pakistan, on the basis of Dominion Status, each having its own Governor-General. Pending the drafting of a constitution by the respective Constituent Assemblies, the interim constitution for each of the two Dominions would be based on the Government of India Act of 1935, suitably adapted for the purpose. The existing Indian legislature would be dissolved and its place taken by the respective Constituent Assemblies, to which the central Government in each case would be responsible.

The Viceroy remarked that whereas it seemed to him that it would be a fairly easy matter, assuming His Majesty's Government agreed, to transfer power at a very early date on a Dominion Status basis to the Union of India, there would for some time to come be no authorities in Pakistan to whom power could be transferred. I assured him that this problem would not present any insuperable difficulty and that we could find a solution.

Nehru explained his own reaction to the scheme. He said that it was very desirable that there should be a transfer of power as soon as possible on a Dominion Status basis. He added that the basic reason for wanting an early transfer of power, apart from the desire of the Indians to control their own affairs, was that developments in India would not otherwise take place as they should. The present system of frequent reference to His Majesty's Government was producing the psychology of always looking elsewhere for decisions; of continual bidding by the different parties; of a lack of reality, and of an absence of self-reliance. However, the possibility of the division of India constituted the real difficulty.

On the same day the Viceroy received from London the plan which had been taken by Lord Ismay, as finalized and approved by the British Cabinet. This embodied certain important modifications which the Cabinet had made in the original plan. A press *communiqué* was now issued to the effect that the Viceroy had invited Nehru, Jinnah, Patel, Liaqat Ali Khan and Baldev Singh to meet him in Delhi on the morning of 17 May, when he would present to them the plan which His Majesty's Government had approved for the transfer of power to Indian hands. The Viceroy also invited the members of the States' Negotiating Committee to meet him on the same afternoon.

Events now took a dramatic turn. Lord Mountbatten was worried by the amendments which His Majesty's Government had made in the plan which he had sent to London. He felt that they considerably worsened the prospects of the acceptance of the plan by the party leaders. Furthermore, he saw great possibilities in my alternative plan, especially after Nehru's favourable reaction to it. At a meeting with his staff he declared, 'I have an absolute hunch that I must show the amended version of the plan to Nehru and obtain his reactions before I agree to the amendments.'

On the night of 10 May Lord Mountbatten showed Nehru the plan as he had received it from London. Nehru turned it down most vehemently and made it clear that the Congress would in no circumstances accept it.

When I saw Nehru on the morning of the 11th, I found that his usual charm and smile had deserted him and that he was obviously upset. I was not aware that Lord Mountbatten had actually shown him the plan but Nehru told me that he had seen it and that its whole approach was wrong. He said that up to the time of the Statement of 20 February the approach had been on the basis of a Union of India. But the draft plan was from the wrong end, that is to say, it encouraged units to cut adrift from the Union and the States to stand out. He did not like the provision as to Baluchistan, nor did he like the paragraph relating to the North-West Frontier Province. I told him that I myself did not like the plan, but that I was sure we could find a new approach. He was too agitated however to listen to me.

While I was still with Nehru an urgent summons came for me from Lord Mountbatten, and I went across immediately to see him. He told me that he had shown the draft plan to Nehru and he was not sorry that he had done so. The consequences would have been disastrous if he had followed up his programme for a conference of party leaders. In doing so he would have completely misled His Majesty's Government, which had been under the impression till then that Nehru would accept the plan. The problem was how best to retrieve the situation. I told the Viceroy what had taken place at my further meeting with Nehru and suggested that the most promising line of action was to proceed on the basis of my plan. The transfer of power to two central Governments on the basis of Dominion Status was a proposition that was likely to be accepted by the Congress as it would ensure an early demission of power. The only question was whether Jinnah would accept a truncated Pakistan. But Jinnah knew that Gandhiji was opposed to any division of the country and that the Congress could not possibly agree to let him have areas in which non-Muslims were in a majority. I reminded Lord Mountbatten that he himself had gained the impression that Jinnah was reconciled to the idea of the partition of the Punjab and Bengal; whereas the plan approved by His Majesty's Government would break up the country into several units, my plan would retain the essential unity of India while allowing those areas to secede which did not choose to remain part of it.

Meanwhile, Nehru had sent a note to the Viceroy embodying his reactions to His Majesty's Government's plan. He said that the picture presented by the proposals was an ominous one. 'Not only do they menace India but also they endanger the future relations between Britain and India. Instead of producing any sense of certainty, security and stability, they would encourage disruptive tendencies everywhere and chaos and weakness. They would particularly endanger important strategic areas.' In these proposals the whole approach had been changed completely. Starting with the rejection of an Indian Union as the successor to power, they invited the claims of large numbers of successor States who would be permitted to unite if they so wished into two or more States. Nehru had no doubt that a pronouncement by His Majesty's Government on the lines proposed would provoke wide and deep resentment all over India and that no responsible leader, outside the Muslim League, would be able to persuade the country either to accept or to acquiesce in the proposals. Hitherto all the British proposals and all discussions had been based on the idea of a united India. The Cabinet Mission had considered every aspect of a totally divided India and rejected it. Those considerations remained unchanged, and indeed the disorder and violence of recent months added further weight to them.

The present proposals, he said, involved a complete retraction by His Majesty's Government of its previous decisions and pledges, the virtual scrapping of the Constituent Assembly and the casting overboard of the Cabinet Mission plan. The inevitable consequences of the proposals would be to invite the Balkanization of India; to provoke certain civil conflict and add to violence and disorder; to cause a further breakdown of the central authority, which alone could prevent the growing chaos, and to demoralize the Army, the Police and the central Services. The proposal that each of the successor States should conclude independent treaties, presumably also with His Majesty's Government, was likely to create many 'Ulsters' in India, which would be looked upon as so many British bases on Indian soil and would create an almost unbridgeable gulf between National India and the British people.

The approach to the Princes was no doubt logical and consistent with the unfortunate position in respect of Paramountcy; but introduced at this stage it showed an obvious shift of emphasis and was a direct invitation, at least to the major States, to remain independent kingdoms, presumably as allies or feudatories of Britain. People's organizations everywhere demanded union, but the rulers would be encouraged to resist their demands and in the States themselves there might well be civil war.

Nehru emphasized that acquiescence on the part of the Congress in the splitting up of those areas which were predominantly League in their loyalty was in no wise an acquiescence in throwing overboard the all-India basis of future settlement. It was only a stretching of the Cabinet Mission plan to make opting out operable in keeping with its oft-repeated policy of non-coercion. The partition of provinces to which the Congress had agreed was not at all inconsistent with an all-India Union of both separated parts with the retention of separate identities.

Nehru then proceeded to go into certain details of the proposals. He described the so-called self-determination in the case of Baluchistan as 'preposterous'. It left the future of that province to a single individual who would be chosen by a group of sardars and nominated persons who obviously represented a vested semi-feudal element. Baluchistan had an importance as a strategic frontier of India and its future could not be dealt with in so partial and casual a manner.

There could be no objection to the surrender of a part of Assam to East Bengal if the people concerned so wished, but some such procedure should be equally applicable to parts of Sind.

With regard to the North-West Frontier Province, the proposals implied, in effect, a decision by His Majesty's Government that the province must reverse, or at least be given an opportunity to reverse, its present decision to remain in the Constituent Assembly. The sole reason for this appeared to be the violence and rapine which had been indulged in by adherents of the Muslim League or others in the province. The Congress had agreed that the North-West Frontier Province, like other areas, should be given the fullest opportunity to express its own desires for the future, but this must be done in common with other parts of India at the proper time and in the proper context. His Majesty's Government's proposals appeared to have been founded on the assumption that violence could render null and void previous and recent decisions arrived at by constitutional procedure.

With regard to treaties with frontier tribes, to give public assurance to the tribes that they could have treaties with whomsoever they liked was to invite them to profit by internal difficulties in India and to create a situation on the Indian frontier which would be a menace not only to India, but to neighbouring areas in Asia. Moreover, if the North-West Frontier Province remained with the Union, an alliance between the tribal areas and another State would create grave difficulties for the North-West Frontier Province and India as a whole.

If, said Nehru, it was indeed His Majesty's Government's sole purpose to ascertain the wishes of the people of India and to transfer power with the least possible dislocation, the purpose would not be advanced or achieved by these proposals. Before the people chose, they should have a proper picture of what they were choosing. Two or three vague proposals with no clear background would produce nothing but confusion, and the transfer of power, instead of being made without dislocation, would be obstructed by violence, by a mass of complications and by weakness of the central Government and its organs.

If, Nehru went on, there was to be any genuine assessment of opinion, the only practical way was for two constitutions, two appeals and two prospects to be placed before the people. This meant that the Constituent Assembly must proceed with the constitution-making on the basis of an all-India Union with full freedom for provinces and effective guarantees for all. In the same way, the League could prepare its own schemes and present its own proposals on an equal level, and the two constitutions could be presented to all the provinces of India on a plebiscite basis on such terms as might be agreed upon.

Until these decisions are made, the Government of India must remain as one. In view of the impending British withdrawal, the Coalition forming the central Government must be a Cabinet with joint responsibility based upon full Dominion autonomy. It may be made clear that the central Government will not take any steps to prejudice self-determination or subsequent partition and such other guarantees as are necessary may also be given so as to assure the League in regard to certain agreed matters.

Nehru had no doubt that the Congress would not accept the proposals contained in the plan and that it would not be prepared to acquiesce in the throwing overboard of the basic all-India Union, or accept the theory of provinces being initially independent successor States.

We now had a meeting with Nehru. After listening to a re-statement of his objections to the plan received from London, we proceeded to explain to him how our new plan would meet those objections. At the end of the meeting the Viceroy asked him whether the Congress would accept a plan based on our discussion. He replied that he would have to see the draft before he could commit himself.

In view of this new development, it was decided that the conference of party leaders which had been summoned to meet on 17 May should be postponed to 2 June, and a *communiqué* was issued to that effect.

After the meeting with Nehru I returned to my hotel. I had only two or three hours in which to prepare an alternative draft plan and I set to work on it at once. The Viceroy was anxious to show the draft to Nehru and to ascertain his reactions before he left Simla that evening, and I had barely got the draft into shape when Sir Eric Miéville came and took it away to the Viceroy.

That night I dined at Viceregal Lodge. I found that Lord Mountbatten had completely regained his buoyant spirits and good cheer. He told me that he had shown the draft to Nehru, who had said that the approach contained in it was on proper lines and that it would not be unacceptable to the Congress.

I was keeping Vallabhbhai Patel informed of the developments in Simla and he was delighted by the turn of events. He assured me that there would be no difficulty in the Congress accepting Dominion Status. In fact, he had already made a public statement on 9 May suggesting that power should be transferred to the Indian Government on the basis of Dominion Status, with the Viceroy standing out.

Lord Mountbatten returned to Delhi on 14 May. He had already apprised the Secretary of State of the developments in Simla and communicated to him an outline of the alternative plan. Immediately on his arrival in Delhi, he received an invitation from the Prime Minister to go to London. His Majesty's Government had been confronted with an entirely new situation, and without personal consultation with the Viceroy (who alone could give them a clear picture of the background) it was impossible for it to come to a firm decision.

The Viceroy felt that he should get the consent of the leaders of the three parties to the alternative plan before leaving for London, and he plunged into this task with his characteristic drive. He asked me to prepare a draft 'Heads of Agreement' to be shown to the leaders for their acceptance.

On 16 May I drew up a draft 'Heads of Agreement' the features of which were as follows:

(a) That the leaders agree to the procedure laid down for ascertaining the wishes of the people whether there should be a division of India or not;

(b) That in the event of the decision being taken that there should only be one central authority in India, power should be transferred to the existing Constituent Assembly on a Dominion Status basis;

(c) That in the event of a decision that there should be two sovereign States in India, the central Government of each State should take over power in responsibility to their respective Constituent Assemblies, again on a Dominion Status basis;

(d) That the transfer of power in either case should be on the basis of the Government of India Act of 1935, modified to conform to the Dominion Status position;

(e) That the Governor-General should be common to both the Dominions and that the present Governor-General should be reappointed;

(f) That a Commission should be appointed for the demarcation of boundaries in the event of a decision in favour of partition;

(g) That the Governors of the provinces should be appointed on the recommendation of the respective central Governments;

(h) In the event of two Dominions coming into being, the Armed Forces in India should be divided between them. The units would be allocated according to the territorial basis of recruitment and would be under the control of the respective Governments. In the case of mixed units, the separation and redistribution should be entrusted to a Committee consisting of Field Marshal Sir Claude Auchinleck and the Chiefs of the General Staff of the two Dominions, under the supervision of a Council consisting of the Governor-General and the two Defence Ministers. This Council would automatically cease to exist as soon as the process of division was completed.

After the Viceroy had approved the draft 'Heads of Agreement', I took it to Nehru, Patel and Baldev Singh and had discussions with them; Sir Eric Miéville did likewise with Jinnah and Liaqat Ali Khan.

Thereafter, the Viceroy had consultations with Nehru and Patel on behalf of the Congress; Jinnah and Liaqat Ali Khan on behalf of the League; and Baldev Singh on behalf of the Sikhs. In the light of these discussions the new plan was finalized. The Viceroy was anxious to obtain the acceptance of it by the leaders in writing if possible. Nehru readily complied on behalf of the Congress. In his letter he stated that the Congress accepted the plan generally, but that its acceptance was strictly subject to the other parties agreeing to it as a final settlement and to no further claims being put forward. This plan, as the Congress understood it, was a continuation of the Cabinet Mission plan, with suitable variations to fit in with the existing situation and in order to bring about an abiding settlement. In the event of the Muslim League failing to accept it, the Congress would urge strict adherence to the Cabinet Mission scheme under which the interim Government had been formed. In that interim Government there was no place for those who finally rejected the Cabinet Mission scheme. In the event of the partition of the country, the clause in paragraph 19 of the Cabinet Mission scheme dealing with the major communal matters would have no further significance. The Congress agreed that if during the interim period there were to be two States, the Governor-General should be common to both. Nehru said that the Congress would be happy if Lord Mountbatten would continue in this office and help them with his advice and experience.

Jinnah and Liaqat Ali Khan seemed willing to accept the general principles of the plan, but refused to state their acceptance in writing.

On 18 May the Viceroy left for London. I accompanied him. En route we stopped at Karachi, and Lord Mountbatten took the opportunity to discuss the new plan with Sir Francis Mudie, the Governor of Sind. Mudie was of the view that the Muslim League would accept the plan, but at the same time he emphasized the need for an early demission of power. We reached London the next day and Lord Mountbatten went straightway into discussion with the Prime Minister and with the India and Burma Committee of the Cabinet.

Throughout these discussions, Lord Mountbatten kept in constant touch, through Sir Eric Miéville who had stayed behind in Delhi, with Nehru and Jinnah, so that they were both kept fully informed throughout the evolution of the plan to its final stages.

The Cabinet ended by approving the new plan and by finalizing the statement[1] of His Majesty's Government. This statement began with a reference to the Cabinet Mission plan of 16 May 1946. It

[1] See Appendix X.

stated that His Majesty's Government had hoped that it would be possible for the major parties to co-operate in the working of the plan, but the hope had not been fulfilled. It had always been the desire of His Majesty's Government that power should be transferred in accordance with the wishes of the Indian people themselves. The task would have been facilitated if there had been agreement among the Indian political parties. In the absence of such agreement the task of devising a method by which the wishes of the Indian people could be ascertained had devolved on His Majesty's Government. His Majesty's Government wished to make it clear that it had no intention of attempting to frame any ultimate constitution for India. That was a matter for the Indians themselves. Nor was there anything in the plan to preclude negotiations between the communities for a united India.

It was not the intention of His Majesty's Government to interrupt the work of the existing Constituent Assembly. At the same time, it was clear that any constitution framed by it could not apply to those parts of the country which were unwilling to accept it. The problem was how to settle the best practical method of ascertaining the wishes of the people of such areas, whether their constitution should be framed by the existing Constituent Assembly, or by a new and separate Constituent Assembly consisting of the representatives of those areas which might decide not to participate in the existing one. When this had been done it would be possible to determine the authority or authorities to whom power should be transferred.

The Statement laid down that the provincial Legislative Assemblies of Bengal and the Punjab (excluding the European members) should meet in two parts, one representing the Muslim majority districts and the other the rest of the province. For the purpose of determining the population of the districts, the 1941 census figures should be taken as authoritative. The Muslim majority districts in those two provinces were as set out in the appendix to the Statement.

The members of the two parts of the Legislative Assembly sitting separately would be empowered to vote whether or not the province should be partitioned. If a simple majority of either part decided in favour of partition, division would take place and arrangements would be made accordingly.

Before the question of partition was decided, it was desirable for the representatives of each part to know in advance which Constituent Assembly the province as a whole would join in the event of the two parts deciding to remain united. Therefore, if any member of either part of the Legislative Assembly so demanded, a meeting should be held of all the members of the Legislative Assembly (other than Europeans) at which a decision would be taken on the issue.

In the event of partition being decided upon, each part of the Legislative Assembly would, on behalf of the areas represented by it, decide whether its constitution should be framed by the existing Constituent Assembly, or by a new and separate one.

The partition of Bengal and the Punjab according to Muslim majority districts and non-Muslim majority districts was a preliminary step of a purely temporary nature. As soon as a decision involving partition had been taken for either province, a Boundary Commission would be set up by the Governor-General, the membership and terms of reference of which would be settled in consultation with those concerned.

The Legislative Assembly of Sind (excluding the European members) would also at a special meeting take its own decision as to whether its constitution should be framed by the existing, or a new and separate Constituent Assembly.

With regard to the North-West Frontier Province, it would be necessary, in view of its special position, to give it an opportunity of reconsidering its position in the event of the whole or any part of the Punjab declaring against joining the existing Constituent Assembly. A referendum would be made to the electors of the present Legislative Assembly to choose between the existing Constituent Assembly and a new and separate one.

The Governor-General was examining how best British Baluchistan, in view of its geographical situation, could be given a similar opportunity of reconsidering its position.

Though Assam was predominantly a non-Muslim province, the district of Sylhet, which was contiguous to Bengal, was predominantly Muslim. If it should be decided to partition Bengal, a referendum would be held in Sylhet district to decide whether the district should continue to form part of the Assam province or should be amalgamated with the new province of East Bengal. Should the referendum result in favour of amalgamation with East Bengal, a Boundary Commission, with terms of reference similar to those for the Punjab and Bengal, would be set up to demarcate the Muslim majority areas of Sylhet district. In any case the rest of the Assam province would continue to participate in the proceedings of the existing Constituent Assembly.

If partition of Bengal and the Punjab should be decided upon, it would be necessary to hold fresh elections in order to choose representatives for the respective Constituent Assemblies on the scale of one for every million of the population, according to the principle contained in the Cabinet Mission plan. Similar elections would be held for Sylhet in the event of its being decided that this district should form part of East Bengal.

Negotiations would have to be initiated as soon as possible on the administrative consequences of any partition that might be decided upon.

Agreements with the tribes of the North-West Frontier of India would have to be negotiated by the appropriate successor authority.

After expressing full sympathy with the desire of the major political parties for the earliest possible transfer of power, the statement announced that His Majesty's Government was willing to hand over even earlier than June 1948. Accordingly, it proposed to introduce legislation during the current session of Parliament for the transfer of power in 1947 on a Dominion Status basis to one or two successor authorities, according to the decisions taken under the plan. That would be without prejudice to the right of the Constituent Assemblies to decide in due course whether the parts of India which they represented should remain within the British Commonwealth.

It was decided that Lord Mountbatten should present this plan to the Indian leaders on 2 June. Lord Mountbatten and party returned to India on 31 May 1947.

# XVI

## ACCEPTANCE OF THE PLAN

DURING Lord Mountbatten's absence in England a new complication had arisen. Jinnah demanded a 'corridor' to link West and East Pakistan. Nehru characterized the demand as fantastic and absurd and other Congress leaders strongly opposed it. Serious doubts arose as to whether Jinnah really desired any settlement at all. The Viceroy took up the matter with him on his return to India and prevailed upon him not to persist in this demand.

Another matter had been creating more than a ripple in the political situation. At his prayer meetings, Gandhiji had been pressing his views in favour of a United India and had gone so far as to declare that, if necessary, the Cabinet Mission plan should be imposed by force. But Sir John Colville, acting as Viceroy during Lord Mountbatten's absence, saw Gandhiji and was able to assure Lord Mountbatten that it was not Gandhiji's intention to sabotage the new plan.

Before Lord Mountbatten's departure for England, Nehru and Patel had asked him to invite J. B. Kripalani, the Congress President, to the proposed meeting of leaders. They pointed out that since both of them were in the interim Government, the presence of Kripalani would help in winning over the organizational side; moreover, his position as President of the Congress was analogous to that of Jinnah. Lord Mountbatten agreed to invite Kripalani, but decided that, in fairness, Jinnah should be given the right to bring with him one more League representative.

On 2 June, at the Viceroy's House, was held the historic conference attended by the seven leaders — Nehru, Patel and Kripalani on behalf of the Congress; Jinnah, Liaqat Ali Khan and Abdur Rab Nishtar on behalf of the League, and Baldev Singh representing the Sikhs.

The Viceroy opened the conference by explaining that he had asked the minimum number of party leaders to come to the meeting so that it could be held in a friendly atmosphere. During the last five years he had taken part in a number of momentous meetings at which the fate of the war had been decided; but he could remember no meeting at which the decisions taken could have such a profound influence on world history as those which were to be taken now. The way in which power was transferred would affect not only India, but the whole world.

He said that before he left for India in March, he had been given no indication of the necessity for speed in formulating proposals for the transfer of power. He had been led to believe in London that, if his recommendations were submitted so as to enable legislation to be introduced in Parliament by the beginning of 1948, that would be time enough. But from the moment of his arrival in India a terrific sense of urgency had been impressed upon him by everybody to whom he had spoken. They wanted the present state of political uncertainty to cease. He had come to realize that the sooner power was transferred the better it would be.

He explained how hard he had tried to obtain agreement on the Cabinet Mission plan. His Majesty's Government had set great store by that plan. He had, however, to report to His Majesty's Government that Jinnah and the Muslim League had been unable to withdraw their rejection of the plan, and maintained their view that it could not be made to work.

The Viceroy said that gradually, over the course of the last two and a half months, he had begun to see the degree of acceptance by the different parties of the various alternative plans. The position that had been reached was that the Congress would not agree to the principle of the partition of India, although they accepted the principle that Muslim majority areas should not be coerced; while Jinnah, who demanded the partition of India, would not agree to the principle of the partition of provinces. The Viceroy had made clear to His Majesty's Government the impossibility of a full acceptance of the demands of one side and not of the other.

He mentioned that during his recent visit to London there had been discussions both on the Cabinet Mission plan and the issue of partition. He had tried to put forward what he believed to be the points of view of both parties on these matters — not only to the Cabinet but to the members of the Opposition, including Churchill. He was happy to state that the members of the Opposition were broadly in agreement with the policy which His Majesty's Government intended to adopt. Government and Opposition were at one in their desire to help India.

The Viceroy went on to say that he was most distressed about the position of the Sikhs. He did not think that any single question had been discussed in London at such great length as this. He had repeatedly asked the Sikh leaders whether they desired the partition of the Punjab. The Sikhs were so spread out over the Punjab that any partition would necessarily divide their community: nevertheless they still declared themselves to be in favour of partition. For the purpose of 'notional partition' different formulae had been examined, but no solution had been found to safeguard the interests of the Sikhs. It had not been possible to adopt any principle other than division between Muslim majority and non-Muslim majority areas. The notional partition would be entirely provisional. The Boundary Commission, on which Sikh interests would of course be represented, would have to work out the best permanent solution.

Referring to the problem of Calcutta, the Viceroy said that this had also received careful consideration in London. The question had arisen as to whether a referendum should be held in Calcutta. It had been suggested that the vote of the Scheduled Castes might result in a decision in favour of Calcutta joining East Bengal. He had sought the Governor's advice on this point and was satisfied that there was no basis for the suggestion that the Scheduled Castes would prefer Muslim to Hindu rule. In any case, the definite decision of the Cabinet was that no exception to the general rule could be made in the case of Calcutta.

The Viceroy mentioned that under the new arrangement the India Office would be abolished.

He next referred to the 'new and very important feature' in paragraph 20 of the Statement under the heading 'Immediate Transfer of Power'. The leaders had always impressed upon him that after partition (if it was decided upon), the transfer of power should take place with the utmost speed. Accordingly, he had pressed on His Majesty's Government that the necessary legislation should be rushed through during the present parliamentary session. The Prime Minister had agreed and Churchill had given an assurance that the Opposition would facilitate the passage of the Bill.

The Viceroy pointed out that power would be demitted in the first instance on the basis of Dominion Status. Thereafter the new Indian Government, or Governments, would be completely free to withdraw from the Commonwealth whenever they so wished.

The Prime Minister had particularly impressed upon him the supreme need for secrecy concerning the statement until it was made in Parliament. The Viceroy therefore asked that every possible step should be taken to prevent a leakage before the following afternoon. This applied particularly to the new paragraph 20 regarding Dominion Status.

The Viceroy added that His Majesty's Government had expressed a wish to be associated in any defence agreement or treaty between the two new Dominions which were to be set up. It felt that the situation would be impossible if either of these Dominions, having British officers and equipment, were to allow other nations to come in and establish bases in their territories. The Viceroy conveyed His Majesty's Government's readiness to help both Dominions with British officers for administration, as well as for their defence forces.

The Viceroy pointed out that the plan had been formulated as a result of many talks with the Indian leaders. There had been some small drafting alterations in the statement since it had last been seen by them. These had been designed purely for clarification and were subject to their general agreement.

Copies of the statement of His Majesty's Government were then handed round. The Viceroy asked the leaders to take copies to their Working Committees, to discuss the statement with them that day and to let him know their reactions by midnight. He did not intend to ask either side to agree categorically to the terms of the statement, but requested assurances from both that they would do their best to have everything worked out peacefully.

Nehru stated that the Congress generally accepted the plan, though it could never give its complete approval to it. Jinnah said that it was perfectly true to say that neither side agreed with certain points in the plan, and he added that its formal acceptance by the Muslim League would have to come later. The decision could not be left to the leaders and the Working Committee alone. They would have to bring the people round and much explanation would be necessary.

The Viceroy said that he was willing to take the risk of accepting the word of the leaders, in whom he had complete confidence. At the same time, he would like to get the preliminary agreement of the Working Committees whose decisions, he repeated, should be communicated to him before midnight.

Jinnah said that he thought he would be successful in obtaining the support of the All-India Muslim League Council, but felt that it was better not to pre-determine the issue. He would go 'to his masters, the people,' with no intent of wrecking the plan, but with the sincere endeavour to persuade them to accept it.

Nehru pointed out that he and Patel had been committing themselves, step by step, to the present plan and had given their personal assurances. Owing to the peculiar nature of the case, the leaders themselves had to make decisions. He and his colleagues had been caught in the tempo of events. The urgency of the situation made it difficult for them to be vague. Nehru said that a letter would be sent to the Viceroy that evening giving an account of the Congress Working Committee's reaction to the statement.

Jinnah felt himself unable to report the views of the Muslim League Working Committee in writing. However, he would come and see the Viceroy and make a verbal report.

The Viceroy mentioned in conclusion that he intended to make a broadcast over All-India Radio the following evening. It would be recorded in London and relayed all over the world. He said that he would be most grateful if Nehru and Jinnah would broadcast immediately after him. They might give their personal assurances of support for the plan and say that they would use their best endeavours to ensure its peaceful acceptance by their respective parties. Both Nehru and Jinnah agreed. At the same time the Viceroy accepted Nehru's suggestion that Baldev Singh should also broadcast.

Soon after his interview with the leaders, the Viceroy saw Gandhiji. The latter, as we have seen, had been preaching at his prayer meetings against the very idea of partition. The Viceroy recounted to him the various steps which had led to the present position. He pointed out those features in the plan which conformed to Gandhiji's ideas, and explained the reasons for such features as were not in harmony with his views. In the end he was able to persuade Gandhiji that the plan was the best in the circumstances. It was Gandhiji's day of silence; but he wrote a friendly note, which reassured the Viceroy.

The Congress Working Committee met on 2 June and decided to accept the plan. Kripalani, the Congress President, wrote a long letter to the Viceroy, in the course of which he said:

I do not wish to enter into any detailed examination of the proposed statement of HMG. It has been produced after considerable consultation and I am desired to say by my Committee that we are prepared to accept it and to recommend to the All-India Congress Committee to do likewise. We do so in the earnest hope that this will mean a settlement. We feel that the situation in India, political and economic, as well as communal, demands more than ever a peaceful approach to all our problems. These problems cannot be solved by methods of violence, and there can be no submission to such methods.

While we are willing to accept the proposals made by HMG, my Committee desire to emphasize that they are doing so in order to achieve a final settlement. This is dependent on the acceptance of the proposals by the Muslim League and a clear understanding that no further claims will be put forward. There has been enough misunderstanding in the past and in order to avoid this in the future it is necessary to have explicit statements in writing in regard to these proposals.

Regarding the position of the Sikhs in the Punjab, Kripalani said that His Majesty's Government's plan would result in injury to them unless great care were taken and their peculiar position in the Punjab were fully appreciated.

Baldev Singh, on behalf of the Sikhs, accepted the principle of partition as laid down in the plan, but stressed that care should be taken to meet their demands when framing the terms of reference for the Boundary Commission.

The Viceroy saw Jinnah that night. Jinnah would not give anything in writing, but he assured the Viceroy that he would do all in his power to get the plan accepted. He said that his Working Committee were hopeful that the plan would be accepted by the All-India Muslim League Council, but that constitutionally it was not possible to reply on behalf of the Council. Lord Mountbatten, however, was not to be put off. He asked whether he would be justified in advising the Prime Minister to go ahead and make his announcement on 3 June — to which Jinnah replied in the affirmative. Jinnah explained that it would require at least a week to assemble the Council of the All-India Muslim League. Lord Mountbatten realized that a week's delay would be absolutely fatal at that stage. He therefore told Jinnah that he would inform the meeting of the leaders on the following day that he was satisfied with the assurances he had received from Jinnah; all he asked was that Jinnah should nod his head in assent when that statement was made. Jinnah agreed.

The Congress President's letter of acceptance raised two other points: one was the question as to what would happen in case one of the Dominions should decide to secede from the British Commonwealth, while the other decided to remain in it; the second was the choice of independence to be given in the referendum to the North-West Frontier Province. According to the Congress, should India decide to go out of the Commonwealth it would not be proper for Pakistan to continue as a Dominion. This virtually amounted to a demand that Pakistan should be expelled from the Commonwealth if India should decide to secede. At the instance of the Viceroy, I explained to Patel that His Majesty's Government could not possibly accept the point of view of the Congress; that if India decided to secede from the Commonwealth, this could not affect Pakistan's right, if she so wished, to continue as a Dominion, and that it would be putting His Majesty's Government in a very embarrassing position to have to deal with such an issue. With regard to the North-West Frontier Province, I told him that it was at Nehru's own request that the original proposal to allow every province the right to vote for Hindustan, Pakistan or independence had been dropped and that it was Lord Mountbatten's view that the issue of independence could not be re-introduced for only one province at this stage. Patel agreed on both points. Meanwhile Lord Mountbatten had explained the position to Nehru, who also agreed.

The next morning (3 June) the Viceroy's conference with the leaders was resumed. He acquainted them with the replies he had received from the three political parties. He said that he had received written assurances from the Congress and the Sikhs, and a verbal assurance from the Muslim League. The Viceroy turned towards Jinnah, who nodded his head in assent. The Viceroy went on to say that the plan represented as complete an agreement as it was possible to get and that, in his judgment, what was being done was in the best interests of the people of India.

Baldev Singh desired that instructions to the Boundary Commission should be included in His Majesty's Government's Statement, but the Viceroy persuaded him not to press the point.

During all these discussions, amidst the general glow of apparent friendliness, there arose occasional sparks of friction — such as Liaqat Ali Khan's attack on the speeches delivered by Gandhiji at his prayer meetings — which threatened to wreck the proceedings. It was indeed a remarkable feat that Lord Mountbatten should have succeeded by his tact and charm in keeping the discussions within bounds.

Immediately after his meeting with the party leaders the Viceroy communicated to the Secretary of State the assurances given him by Nehru, Jinnah and Baldev Singh in regard to the acceptance of the plan. Attlee announced the plan in the House of Commons on 3 June; hence it came to be known as 'the June 3rd Plan'.[1]

Speaking on behalf of the Opposition, Winston Churchill was particularly cautious. It appeared, he said, that the two conditions which had been foreseen at the time of the Cripps Mission, namely, agreement between the Indian parties, and a period of Dominion Status in which India or any part of it might freely decide whether to remain in the British Commonwealth or not, 'would seem to have been fulfilled by the proposal.' The Opposition, while preserving freedom on points of detail, would not oppose any Bill to confer Dominion Status on the various parts of India on the basis of His Majesty's Government's Statement. He concluded by saying: 'The Prime Minister said that credit was due to the Viceroy. There are matters about which it is extremely difficult to form decided opinions now, but if the hopes that are enshrined in this declaration should be borne out, great credit will indeed be due to the Viceroy, and not only to the Viceroy, but to the Prime Minister who advised the British Government to appoint him.'

In a broadcast which the Prime Minister made that night he said: 'As the Indian leaders have finally failed to agree on the Cabinet Mission's plan for a united India, partition becomes the inevitable alternative.' He explained that the twofold purpose of the plan was firstly, to make possible the maximum degree of co-operation and harmony between the political parties in order that the partition, if decided upon, might involve as little loss and suffering as possible; and secondly, to enable the British Government to hand over their responsibilities in an orderly and constitutional manner at the earliest opportunity. The plan, he added, provided for the handing over of power that year to one or two governments, each having Dominion Status.

On the evening of 3 June the Viceroy broadcast over All-India Radio. He gave a short account of his discussions with the leaders of the political parties. He said that it had always been his firm opinion that, with a reasonable measure of goodwill between the communities, a unified India would be by far the best solution; but it had been impossible to obtain agreement on the Cabinet Mission plan or on any other plan that would preserve the unity of India. The Muslim League had demanded the partition of India, and the Congress had used the same argument for demanding, in that event, the partition of certain

[1] See Appendix X.

provinces. The argument seemed unassailable, though he was as much opposed to the partition of provinces as he was to the partition of India. Hence it was left to the people of India themselves to decide the question of partition. It was necessary, in order to ascertain the will of the people of the Punjab, Bengal and part of Assam, to lay down boundaries between the Muslim majority and remaining areas, but he wished to make it clear that the ultimate boundaries would be settled by a Boundary Commission and would certainly not be identical with those which had been provisionally adopted.

Referring to the position of the Sikhs, the Viceroy said that they were so distributed that any partition of the Punjab would inevitably divide them. It was sad to think that the partition of the Punjab, which the Sikhs themselves desired, could not avoid splitting them to a greater or lesser degree. The exact degree of split would be left to the Boundary Commission, on which they would of course be represented.

The Viceroy went on to say that the whole plan might not be perfect, but, like all plans, its success would depend on the spirit of goodwill with which it was carried out. He had always felt that the transfer of power should take place at the earliest possible moment. The proposal which he had put forward, and which he was glad to say had been accepted, was that His Majesty's Government should transfer power immediately to one or two Governments of British India, each having Dominion Status. His Majesty's Government had already taken in hand the drafting of the necessary legislation, which it was proposed to introduce in Parliament during the current session. It was not the intention of His Majesty's Government to impose any restriction either on India as a whole, or on the two States if there were partition, to decide in the future their relationship to each other and to other member States of the British Commonwealth.

The Viceroy concluded: 'I have faith in the future of India and I am proud to be with you all at this momentous time. May your decisions be wisely guided and may they be carried out in the peaceful and friendly spirit of the Gandhi-Jinnah appeal.'

Immediately thereafter, His Majesty's Government's Statement was also broadcast and released to the Press.

There followed broadcasts by the Indian leaders. Nehru said that the announcement envisaged on the one hand the possibility of certain areas seceding from India and, on the other the promise of a big advance towards complete independence. It was with no joy in his heart

that he commended these proposals, though he had no doubt in his
mind that it was the right course. He emphasized that the united
India that they had laboured for was not one of compulsion and coercion, but a free and willing association of a free people. 'It may be
that in this way we shall reach that united India sooner than otherwise and that she will have a stronger and more secure foundation.'
He referred to the violence in the country as 'shameful, degrading
and revolting' and stressed that political ends were not to be achieved
by methods of violence. He expressed his deep appreciation of the
labours of the Viceroy ever since his arrival at a critical juncture in
India's history. He also paid tribute to Gandhiji, who had led the
nation unfalteringly for over a generation through darkness and
sorrow to the threshold of freedom.

Jinnah appealed to every community, particularly to Muslim India,
to maintain peace and order. The plan, he said, did not in some important respects meet the Muslim League point of view and it was for
the League to consider whether it should be accepted as a compromise
or a settlement. On that point he did not wish to prejudge the decision of the Council of the All-India Muslim League, but so far as he
had been able to gather, the reaction in League circles in Delhi had
been hopeful. He, too, paid tribute to the Viceroy, who had battled
against various forces very bravely. The impression that the Viceroy
had left on Jinnah's mind was that he was actuated by a high sense
of fairness and impartiality. It was up to everyone to make the Viceroy's task less difficult and to help him as much as possible to fulfil
his mission of the transfer of power in a peaceful and orderly manner.
He called upon the provincial Muslim League of the North-West
Frontier Province to withdraw the movement of civil disobedience.

Baldev Singh said that the plan steered a course which was obviously above the conflicting claims. It was not a compromise; he preferred to call it a settlement. 'It does not please everybody, not the
Sikh community anyway, but it is certainly something worth while.
Let us take it at that.'

Lord Mountbatten addressed a press conference on 4 June. Vallabhbhai Patel was in the chair. In his introductory speech Lord Mountbatten gave the background of how the June 3rd plan had been
evolved. He pointed out that at every stage and at every step he had
worked hand in hand with the leaders and that the plan had come
as no shock or surprise to them. All the leaders had wanted speed in
the actual transfer of power, but power could not be transferred to

one or two separate governments unless those governments had a constitution. One of the governments was not even in being, nor was it certain that it was coming into being. The other government would presumably take some time in framing its constitution. The Government of India Act of 1935, suitably modified, provided the obvious answer to this difficulty. He stressed that independence through Dominion Status was complete and that the different administrations were at liberty to opt out of the Commonwealth whenever they pleased. He meant it most sincerely when he said that power would be transferred completely by the end of the year.

The questions put to the Viceroy were numerous and varied. Many were of a trivial character, but to every one the Viceroy gave a crisp and apt reply. Among the points raised were three which were of special interest. The first was, what would happen if the Muslim League Council rejected the plan? The second was, whether the basic determining factor in drawing the boundaries of the provinces would be the communal majority of the population, or whether other considerations such as property, economic viability, etc., would also be included in the terms of reference? The third related to the referendum in the North-West Frontier Province.

The first, the Viceroy remarked, was a hypothetical question. As for the second, he pointed out that His Majesty's Government, least of all the present Labour Government, could hardly be expected to subscribe to a partition on the basis of landed property. With regard to the third question, the Viceroy explained that, compared to Bengal and the Punjab, the North-West Frontier Province Legislative Assembly had a heavier minority weightage viz., twelve seats out of fifty, although the minorities in that province only represented something like five per cent; that its referendum would be a perfectly straightforward one, and that he proposed to depute for the purpose such British officers of the Indian Army, selected by himself, as could be relied upon to be completely impartial. As to why the voters had not been given the alternative to opt for independence, the Viceroy said it was a question of politics; if they could get the Congress and the Muslim League to agree, he too, would of course agree.

But the most important of the questions centred on paragraph 20 of the Statement, which concerned the immediate devolution of power on the basis of Dominion Status. In this connexion the Viceroy explained that the British Commonwealth of Nations was a completely free association of peoples. Each State was completely independent, and, as far as he knew, they decided their own future. There was no power that he knew of to force them to stay in if they wanted to go out. People seemed to have some doubts about the term 'Dominion Status'. It was, he said, absolute independence in every possible way, with the sole exception that the member States were linked together voluntarily. In fact, they looked to one another for support, mutual trust and, in due course, affection.

Finally Lord Mountbatten made it clear that the transfer would be in 1947 and not in June 1948. He said, 'I think the transfer could be about the 15th of August.'

He appealed to the press to aim at one thing when putting out their news and their leading articles — peaceful, quick and speedy settlement, which all of them so sincerely desired.

Ian Stephens, who was editor of *The Statesman* at the time, writing six years after the event, described this press conference thus: 'For sheer intellectual range and vigour, for assured grasp of minutiae, yet brilliant marshalling of the main lines of a long, difficult argument, it was an extraordinary performance.'

The Viceroy also had a meeting with Gandhiji. Some time later, addressing his usual prayer meeting, Gandhiji said: 'The British Government is not responsible for partition. The Viceroy has no hand in it. In fact he is as opposed to division as Congress itself. But if both of us, Hindus and Muslims, cannot agree on anything else, then the Viceroy is left with no choice.' It was, he added, on the basis of the plan that agreement could be reached.

The announcement of the plan resulted in an immediate improvement in the general situation. The Muslim League mass movements in Assam and the North-West Frontier Province were abandoned, and it was only in parts of the Punjab and in Calcutta that there were sporadic disturbances.

The plan had its opponents as well. The Working Committee of the Hindu Mahasabha met in Delhi and passed a resolution which stressed: 'India is one and indivisible and there will never be peace unless and until the separated areas are brought back into the Indian Union and made integral parts thereof.' The Mahasabha even called for an all-India 'Anti-Pakistan Day'.

The extremists on the Muslim side were also dissatisfied; and the Khaksars, a group of militant Muslims (who demanded a Pakistan stretching from Karachi to Calcutta), staged demonstrations when the All-India Muslim League Council met in Delhi. Strangely enough, the Communists, who had been backing Jinnah's demand for Pakistan, now changed their tune. They said that partition and Dominion Status together would enable Britain to maintain her control over India, but they did not explain how this would be possible.

Progressive opinion throughout the world applauded the June 3rd plan as a courageous effort to resolve the Indian deadlock and praised the Labour Government for its courage in handing over power to Indian hands. Walter Lippmann, the famous American political commentator, wrote in *The Washington Post*:

Perhaps Britain's finest hour is not in the past. Certainly this performance is not the work of a decadent people. This on the contrary is the work of political genius requiring the ripest wisdom and the freshest vigour, and it is done with an elegance and a style that will compel and will receive an instinctive respect throughout the civilised world. Attlee and Mountbatten have done a service to all mankind by showing what statesmen can do not with force and money but with lucidity, resolution and sincerity.

The Council of the All-India Muslim League met in New Delhi on 10 June and passed a resolution noting with satisfaction that the Cabinet Mission plan had been abandoned. The only course open was the partition of India as proposed in His Majesty's Government's Statement of 3 June. The Council was of the opinion that, although it could not agree to the partition of Bengal and the Punjab, or give its consent to such partition, it had to consider His Majesty's Government's plan for the transfer of power as a whole. The resolution gave full authority to Jinnah to accept the fundamental principles of the plan as a compromise and empowered him to take all steps and decisions in that connexion.

The resolution provoked Nehru into writing a letter to the Viceroy in which he pointed out that, though the Cabinet Mission plan had been modified to a large extent, they were still functioning in many ways in accordance with the plan. Thus the Indian Constituent Assembly had been meeting and would continue to meet under that plan. It was therefore incorrect to say that the Cabinet Mission plan had been abandoned. By objecting to the partition of Bengal and the Punjab, the Council of the Muslim League had definitely rejected one of the basic provisions in the scheme. He went on to say that the Council had accepted the fundamental principles of the plan as a compromise, but it was not clear what they considered those fundamental principles to be. The point was whether the plan was accepted as a settlement or not. The report of the speeches that had been delivered led to the conclusion that it was looked upon as a step to be utilized for the enforcement of further claims. The Council had given full authority to Jinnah to take all steps and decisions which might be necessary in connexion with the plan, which meant that the Council itself had not accepted the plan as a settlement, but had given authority to Jinnah to do so if he chose. The least that could be done now was for Jinnah to accept the plan in its entirety as a settlement on behalf of the Muslim League. Unless this were done clearly in writing, there was every likelihood that difficulties would arise in the near future.

Between Nehru and Jinnah, the Viceroy was in a distinctly difficult position. In the light of past experience, the Congress was anxious to pin down the League, while Jinnah as usual was reluctant to commit himself to anything. In the end, Lord Mountbatten persuaded Nehru not to take the League Council's resolution at its face value.

Meanwhile, a joint conference of various Sikh organizations was held in Lahore. Though welcoming the division of the Punjab, the Conference placed on record its considered view that no partition of the province which did not preserve the solidarity and integrity of the Sikh community would be acceptable to the Sikhs.

The All-India Congress Committee met in Delhi on 14 June and passed a resolution accepting the June 3rd plan. This resolution included an eloquent exposition of the essential unity of India:

Geography and the mountains and the seas fashioned India as she is, and no human agency can change that shape or come in the way of her final destiny. Economic circumstances and the insistent demands of international affairs make the unity of India still more necessary. The picture of India we have learnt to cherish will remain in our minds and our hearts. The A.I.C.C. earnestly trusts that when the present passions have subsided, India's problems will be viewed in their proper perspective and the false doctrine of two nations in India will be discredited and discarded by all.

However much the secession of some parts of the country was to be regretted, the Committee accepted this possibility in the circumstances then prevailing. Congressmen in particular and the people in general were exhorted to forget petty differences and disputes and to stand by — vigilant, disciplined and prepared to serve the cause of India's freedom.

The resolution was moved by Govind Ballabh Pant, who said that acceptance of the June 3rd plan was the only way to achieve freedom and liberty for the country. It would assure an Indian Union with a strong Centre which could ensure progress. The Congress had worked hard and sacrificed everything for the sake of unity. The choice today was 'between accepting the June 3rd plan or committing suicide.' He argued that the present plan was better than the Cabinet Mission plan with its groupings and sections and its weak Centre.

In seconding the resolution, Azad disagreed with Pant that the June 3rd plan was better than the Cabinet Mission plan. He had all along held the view that the Statement of 16 May was the best solution of the problem; to that view he continued to adhere. But the choice before the Congress was not which plan to accept and which to reject, but whether the present state of indecision and drift should continue. Taking into consideration all the factors, the Working Committee had come to the decision that an immediate settlement was urgently required. Referring to the provinces which sought to cut themselves away from India, Azad said: 'The division is only of the map of the country and not in the hearts of the people, and I am sure it is going to be a short-lived partition.'

Opposition to the resolution came mostly from Nationalist Muslims, members of the Hindu minorities in the proposed Pakistan provinces, and from Purshottamdas Tandon. In an impassioned speech, Tandon said that the decision of the Working Committee was an admission of weakness and that it arose out of a sense of despair. Accepting the June 3rd plan would benefit neither the Hindus nor the Muslims. The Hindus in Pakistan would live in fear and the Muslims in India would do the same.

Intervening in the debate, Nehru asserted that there was no question of any surrender to the Muslim League. The Congress had all along been against coercing any unit to remain under the Indian Union. It was wrong to suggest that the Congress Working Committee had taken fright and therefore surrendered, though it was correct to say that they were very much disturbed at the prevailing madness.

Patel said that, looking at the Cabinet Mission's proposals in the light of his experience in the interim Government during the past nine months, he was not at all sorry that the Statement of 16 May had gone. Had they accepted it, the whole of India would have gone the Pakistan way. Today they had seventy-five to eighty per cent of India, which they could develop and make strong according to their genius. The League could develop the rest of the country.

The issue was clinched when Gandhiji supported the resolution. He said that he was not pleading on behalf of the Working Committee, but the All-India Congress Committee must weigh the pros and cons of its rejection. He said that his views on the plan were well known. The acceptance of the plan did not only involve the Congress Working Committee. There were two other parties to it, the British Government and the Muslim League. If at this stage the All-India Congress Committee rejected the Working Committee's decision, what would the world think of it? The consequences of rejection would be the finding of a new set of leaders, who would not only be capable of constituting the Congress Working Committee but of taking charge of the Government. They should not forget that peace in the country was very essential at this juncture. The Congress was opposed to Pakistan and he was one of those who had steadfastly opposed the division of India. Yet he had come before the All-India Congress Committee to urge the acceptance of the resolution on India's division. Sometimes certain decisions, however unpalatable they might be, had to be taken. The resolution was carried by 157 votes to twenty-nine, thirty-two members remaining neutral.

Acharya Kripalani, the Congress President, made a most forceful and memorable speech, in the course of which he answered the charge that the Working Committee had taken the decision out of fear. He said:

I must admit the truth of this charge, but not in the sense in which it is made. The fear is not for the lives lost, or of the widows' wail, or the orphans' cry, or of the many houses burned. The fear is that if we go on like this, retaliating and heaping indignities on each other, we shall progressively reduce ourselves to a stage of cannibalism and worse. In every fresh communal fight the most brutal and degraded acts of the previous fight become the norm.

Thus was the plan accepted by the three main political parties. But acceptance was one thing; its implementation was a different matter altogether. Here was a task which normally should have taken years to accomplish but which had to be compressed into the short space of a few weeks! It was a task before which anybody would have quailed, for it was one which seemed verily to tempt the Gods.

# XVII

## THE IMPLEMENTATION OF THE PLAN

THE June 3rd Plan having been accepted by the parties concerned, the next task of His Majesty's Government and the Viceroy was to concentrate on the problem of its early implementation. There was so much to be done within such a limited time. The verdicts of the provinces had to be ascertained; parliamentary legislation had to be hurried through; if partition were decided upon, the administrative services and armed forces had to be divided, assets and liabilities to be apportioned and the boundaries in the disputed areas to be settled — all these tasks had to be carried through more or less simultaneously. A strict chronology of events might help to stress the pressure and the acute sense of urgency with which the work was done, but such a narrative would be disjointed. It is not as though one problem was tackled first and another later. A broad survey, arranged so as to treat each of the problems separately, will make for a clearer understanding.

### Verdict of the Provinces

The June 3rd plan had laid down that the question whether or not India should be partitioned was a matter to be decided by the Indian people themselves. I have already explained the procedure prescribed in the plan for deciding this question. In Bengal the provincial Legislative Assembly met on 20 June and decided by 126 votes to ninety in favour of joining a new Constituent Assembly. The members from the non-Muslim majority areas of West Bengal then met and decided by fifty-eight votes to twenty-one that the province should be partitioned and that West Bengal should join the existing Indian Constituent Assembly; while the members from the Muslim majority areas of East Bengal met and decided by 106 votes to thirty-five that the province should not be partitioned and, by almost the same majority of votes, that East Bengal should join a new Constituent Assembly and that Sylhet should be amalgamated with that province.

The voting in Bengal passed off in a comparatively peaceful atmosphere, but in the Punjab there were demonstrations and communal disorders. The Punjab Legislative Assembly met, in fact, under a strong police guard. It decided by ninety-one votes to seventy-seven to join a new Constituent Assembly. The members from the Muslim majority areas of West Punjab then decided, by sixty-nine votes to twenty-seven, against the partition of the province; while the members from the non-Muslim majority areas of East Punjab decided, by fifty votes to twenty-two, that the province should be partitioned and that East Punjab should join the existing Indian Constituent Assembly.

The Sind Legislative Assembly met on 26 June and decided by thirty votes to twenty to join a new Constituent Assembly.

There was some difficulty in settling the procedure for ascertaining the wishes of the people of Baluchistan. Nehru had suggested the possibility of sending a commission to meet the tribal *jirgas* and of holding a referendum in Quetta town. But the Chief Commissioner, Sir Geoffrey Prior, advised that such a course was not feasible. The Viceroy finally decided that the Shahi *jirga* and the non-official members of the Quetta Municipality should be summoned in order to decide the future of the province. The members of these bodies met and unanimously decided to join a new Constituent Assembly. The seven Hindu and Parsi members of the Quetta Municipality did not attend the meeting.

With regard to Sylhet, neither the Congress nor the Muslim League was confident as to the outcome of the proposed reference to the Assembly voters from that district. Liaqat Ali Khan, for instance, pointed out that while the Muslims formed 60·7 per cent of the population, they formed only 54·27 of the total electoral roll; he suggested that the number of Muslim votes should therefore be multiplied by a factor which would equate the voting strength of the Muslims with their population strength. The Congress, on the other hand, claimed that the voters in the Labour and in the Commerce and Trade constituencies of the district should be allowed to participate in the referendum. Ultimately, the referendum was confined to voters in the General, Muhammadan and Indian Christian constituencies. It was held early in July. A majority of the voters — 239,619 to 184,041 — were in favour of separation and joining East Bengal.

In the North-West Frontier Province, though the Muslim League campaign of civil disobedience had been withdrawn, the situation was still tense. Sir Olaf Caroe had been replaced as Governor by General Rob Lockhart. The referendum in the province was entrusted to British officers of the Indian Army with experience of the frontier, under a Referendum Commissioner, Brigadier J. B. Booth. The June 3rd plan offered to the voters of the North-West Frontier Province Legislative Assembly the choice either to join a new Constituent Assembly or to continue with the existing one. Khan Abdul Ghaffar Khan, the Congress leader, objected to the people being asked to vote on a communal question; further, he urged that they should have the choice to vote for an independent Pathanistan. When the question was put to the Viceroy, he replied that he could not change the procedure without the consent of both the parties. While the Congress was willing to meet Ghaffar Khan's point of view, Jinnah was firmly opposed to it. The latter characterized the demand for an independent Pathanistan as 'insidious and spurious', but declared that in Pakistan the North-West Frontier Province would enjoy full autonomy. His demand not having been conceded, Ghaffar Khan appealed to his followers to boycott the referendum. Incidentally, the Government of Afghanistan had begun to take an interest in the Pathanistan demand, claiming that the territory west of the river Indus was populated by Afghans and that these people should be given a right to decide their future. Lord Listowel, the Secretary of State for India, in an address to foreign, American and Empire journalists, repudiated Afghanistan's interference. He said:

Afghanistan has no right to interfere, as they are trying to interfere, in the rights of the North-West Frontier Province. Pathans have been willing quite contentedly to remain in the North-West Frontier Province for a long time. It will give rise to all sorts of difficulties if we allow any movement to break up the North-West Frontier Province.

The referendum in the North-West Frontier Province was held from 6 to 17 July. Of the total electorate of 572,798, slightly over 50 per cent took part — 289,244 voting for, and 2,874 voting against joining a new Constituent Assembly.

Thus in effect East Bengal, West Punjab, Sind, Baluchistan and the North-West Frontier Province all voted for Pakistan.

Later, fresh elections were held in Sylhet, in West and East Bengal, and in West and East Punjab, for the election of representatives to the respective Constituent Assemblies. No fresh election was held in the North-West Frontier Province, in view of the fact that there was no change in the boundaries of that province; it already had its elected representatives[1] in the existing Constituent Assembly and those members had merely to be transferred to the new Constituent Assembly. For similar reasons no fresh election was held in either Baluchistan or Sind.

### INDIAN INDEPENDENCE BILL

No sooner had the partition of the country been decided upon than His Majesty's Government set about the task of preparing and finalizing, in consultation with the Viceroy and his advisers, the draft of the Indian Independence Bill. The Bill in its final form consisted of only twenty clauses and three schedules. But the size of the Bill is no index to the amount of labour that went to the making of it. I can say this with some assurance because here in India, I, as Reforms Commissioner, was in charge of the Bill. Nor can I forget the very able assistance rendered, both in connexion with the Bill and the adaptations to the Government of India Act, 1935, by Sir George Spence, K. V. K. Sundaram and S. V. R. Cook. I should like to pay a special tribute to Sir George Spence. In all my thirty-seven years' service in the Government of India, there was none among the many distinguished Law Secretaries who occupied so outstanding a position as did Sir George Spence in his time, respected and trusted as he was by British and Indian alike. He was already suffering from the strain of overwork when the Indian Independence Bill came under consideration; but he felt that he owed a duty to this country and, regardless of his health, stayed on till the work on the Bill and the adaptations to the 1935 Act was completed — a gesture which was highly appreciated by the Indian leaders. But for his unrivalled knowledge and the assistance of K. V. K. Sundaram and S. V. R. Cook, it would not have been possible to deal so satisfactorily with the Bill and the adaptations to the 1935 Act for India and Pakistan in the short time at our disposal.

Departing from parliamentary practice, Lord Mountbatten (with His Majesty's Government's approval) showed the draft Bill before its presentation to Parliament to the Indian party leaders, including Gandhiji, who attended the initial meeting convened in the Viceroy's

---

[1] Abul Kalam Azad was originally elected to the Constituent Assembly from the North-West Frontier Province. After partition he resigned and later was elected from Bihar.

House for the purpose of discussing its provisions. The Congress leaders and their advisers held their discussions next door to the room in which the Muslim League leaders and their advisers were holding theirs. The Congress comments were then shown to the League leaders, and vice versa. Thus, in the final revision of the Bill the comments of the Indian leaders were taken fully into account.

I have included in this book, as a matter of historical interest, the Indian Independence Act[1], as also a photostat[2] of the Congress memorandum on the draft Bill showing Nehru's corrections in his own hand and his signature at the end.

In its final stages the Bill kept the India Office as well as the Viceroy and his advisers practically sleepless for two nights. The Bill was introduced in the House of Commons by the Prime Minister on 4 July. On the same date the Secretary of State, Lord Listowel, addressed foreign and Empire journalists at the India Office. He said: 'This is a Bill unique in the history of legislation in this country. Never before has such a large portion of the world population achieved complete independence through legislation alone.' He went on to say that on 15 August India would achieve complete independence; that the people of India would start their new status on the same footing as other members of the Commonwealth and would also gain the advantages enjoyed by other members through their mutual cooperation; that there would be a new partnership between the East and the West which would bring healthy results for the whole world. Regarding the position of the India Office, Lord Listowel said that it would cease to be a separate office; that the Secretary of State would not function, and that the Secretary for Commonwealth Relations would look after the affairs of the new Dominions. Referring to the Congress choice of retaining the name of India for their Dominion, he said: 'The name "India" has certain practical advantages, as the name has been used in treaties and international documents. Retaining the name of India will make it easier for the Dominion to continue as a member of the United Nations Organization. There will be no difference in the status of the two Dominions, as Pakistan may also become a member of the United Nations Organization.'

In the course of the debate high tributes were paid to Attlee as well as to Lord Mountbatten. At one stage Lord Winterton, referring to Lord Mountbatten, said of him: 'No man since Wellington has been

---

[1] See Appendix XI.　　　　[2] See Appendix XII.

given such twin gifts of leadership in the military and constitutional fields.'

In the House of Lords there were two notable speeches. Lord Samuel, among other things, said:

It may be said of the British Raj as Shakespeare said of the Thane of Cawdor, 'Nothing in his life became him like the leaving of it....' This Bill is a moral to all future generations; it is a Treaty of Peace without a War.

Lord Halifax, including in his speech words of praise for Lord Mountbatten, said:

I think it has meant much for the long-term hopes which we may all cherish that the approach of His Majesty's Government to this tangled problem should have been inspired, as I think it has been, with courage and imagination, supported as it has been by the indomitable vigour and unrivalled resource of His Majesty's Government's representative in India today.

At the stage of the introduction of the Bill in Parliament, Lord Mountbatten had entrusted me with the task of explaining its provisions to a press conference. Vallabhbhai Patel, in his capacity as Minister for Information and Broadcasting, presided at this conference. In his introductory remarks, Patel stressed the fact that on 15 August 1947 India would be completely free, adding: 'And that is the greatest achievement of India and, one may say, it is one of the greatest acts done in history by any Power.'

At this press conference attention was for the most part directed to the future of the Indian States. I have already dealt with this aspect in my book on their integration. I made a point of explaining that clause 6 ( dealing with the powers of the new Dominion legislature) was the pivotal provision in the Bill and that, while my replies on other matters more or less represented my own personal views, so far as clause 6 was concerned they represented the authoritative views of the Viceroy and His Majesty's Government. Clause 6 established beyond doubt or dispute the sovereign character of the legislature of each of the new Dominions, giving to each the fullest measure of independence. Sub-clauses (2), (4) and (5) removed every possible element of subordination to, or dependence on, the Parliament of the United Kingdom. In particular, the power to amend or repeal 'this or any existing or future Act of Parliament' in so far as it affected the

Dominions, constituted a complete and unreserved transfer of sovereign power.

A question was posed whether clause 1 of the Bill prevented the subsequent recognition by the British Parliament of any more dominions than two in India, to which Patel replied by making it clear that the jurisdiction of the British Parliament over India ended with this Bill.

I may add that, in accordance with the June 3rd plan, the Bill provided that the Constituent Assembly of each of the two Dominions would be the legislature of the respective Dominions. Thus the existing central Legislative Assembly and Council of State were automatically dissolved.

The Bill also provided that, until the Constituent Assemblies of the respective Dominions made other provision, each of the Dominions would be governed in accordance with the Government of India Act, 1935, suitably modified and adapted.

The Indian Independence Bill was passed by the House of Commons on 15 July and by the House of Lords on the following day. There were no amendments. The Bill received the Royal Assent on 18 July. The Government of India Act, 1935, as modified and adapted, was brought into operation by the India (Provisional Constitution) Order, 1947, made by the Governor-General on 14 August 1947.

## THE CHOICE OF GOVERNORS-GENERAL

The question as to who should be the first Governor-General of Pakistan has an interesting history. In the 'heads of agreement' shown to the party leaders[1] there was a provision that the Governor-General should be common to both Dominions and that the present Governor-General should be re-appointed. There was no comment on this from either of the parties and it was assumed that it had been accepted. Accordingly, provision was made in the draft Indian Independence Bill that, unless and until a provision to the contrary was made by a law of the legislature of either of the Dominions, the same person might be Governor-General of both the Dominions. Nehru had already requested Lord Mountbatten to continue as Governor-General of India and it was assumed that Jinnah would make a similar offer. Jinnah himself had suggested that there should be a 'Super-Governor-General' over the Governors-General of the

---

[1] See Chapter XV, p. 366.

two Dominions. But it was hoped that if Lord Mountbatten continued as Governor-General of both the Dominions during the transition period, it would facilitate the division of assets and liabilities and that the partition of the defence forces could be smoothly accomplished. This was the only feasible solution we could think of that would meet Jinnah's suggestion of a Super-Governor-General. The proposal had been put to Jinnah more than once, but he would not commit himself. Finally, on 23 June, the Viceroy saw Jinnah and pressed him to give his earnest consideration to the question. Jinnah stated that whatever decision he took would not be on the ground of not wanting Lord Mountbatten, in whom he had implicit trust and confidence, but that the rule of his life was always to consider the interests of his people. He promised to convey his decision to the Viceroy within the next two or three days.

Jinnah did not, however, give a definite reply till the evening of 2 July, when he intimated to the Viceroy that he himself would like to be the Governor-General of Pakistan. On the morning of 5 July Liaqat Ali Khan confirmed this in writing and requested the Viceroy to recommend Jinnah's name for His Majesty's approval. The letter expressed the hope at the same time that Lord Mountbatten would stay on as Governor-General of the Dominion of India.

This unexpected development placed Lord Mountbatten in an awkward position. He had now to consider whether it would be proper for him to stay on as Governor-General only of the Dominion of India. He held consultations with Nehru and Patel, who repeated that it was their wish that he should continue as their Governor-General. They also desired that Sir John Colville and Sir Archibald Nye should continue as Governor of Bombay and Governor of Madras respectively.

There is no doubt that it would have been an ideal arrangement if Lord Mountbatten could have stayed on as Governor-General of both the Dominions. But even as Governor-General of India, he could still be of immense service to both Dominions. It was his personality, more than his official position, that had helped to bring about some measure of common action between the two parties and that had prevented a bad situation from getting worse. His staying on as Governor-General of India would act as a stabilizing influence. The task of the Partition Council would be made much easier, so also would the work of the Arbitral Tribunal. (In fact, it was due solely to Lord Mountbatten's perseverance that half-a-dozen issues, which had been referred to the Arbitral Tribunal, were withdrawn after agreement had been reached on all of them in the Partition Council). It was generally recognized that Lord Mountbatten's continued presence would not only ensure a smooth partition but would also help to bring about more friendly relations between India and Pakistan.

So far as India itself was concerned, Lord Mountbatten's presence would be of great help in solving the problem of the Indian States. It would also have a reassuring effect on serving British officers, particularly in the Armed Forces, where their retention for at least some time was indispensable.

It was however a personal question, and despite all the arguments Lord Mountbatten was not happy about staying on. He wanted at least to be sure of the reactions of His Majesty's Government and other party leaders in Britain, particularly of Winston Churchill. The Prime Minister was definite that Lord Mountbatten should accept the Governor-Generalship of India. The Opposition leaders, both Conservative and Liberal, shared the Prime Minister's view. Churchill sent a special message to Lord Mountbatten pointing out how useful a role he could play as Governor-General. Lord Mountbatten finally decided to accept the offer. He met Nehru and Patel and told them that he would stay on, but that he would remain only for the transition period. He explained that, in order to stress the non-partisan nature of his appointment, the Prime Minister proposed to say in his announcement that the appointment had also been approved by Jinnah and the Muslim League. The Congress leaders raised no objection. Accordingly, Attlee announced in the House of Commons that Jinnah had been appointed Governor-General of Pakistan and that Lord Mountbatten had accepted the invitation of the Congress leaders to remain on as the Governor-General of India, an appointment which also had the approval of Jinnah and the Muslim League.

### RECONSTITUTION OF THE INTERIM GOVERNMENT

A crisis had now developed within the Government which threatened to wreck the plan. For a long time past the Congress had been insisting that the Muslim League was not entitled to be represented in the Government, since it had not accepted the Cabinet Mission's long term plan. If the June 3rd plan was to go through, it was essential that both parties should continue to be represented in the central Government until the transfer of power. If, as a result of Congress pressure, the Muslim League members left the Government, or as a protest against their failure to do so the Congress members resigned, the plan would certainly be wrecked and no other solution would be available for the transfer of power. This problem caused Lord Mountbatten and his advisers more worry and trouble than did any other problem at this time. In fact, this was one of the considerations that prompted Lord Mountbatten to press for the transfer of power earlier than the stipulated period. Various methods of tackling this question were considered, but none of them was altogether free from objection. Ultimately it was decided to defer its consideration till after the Indian Independence Bill had been passed.

Subsequently, the device adopted was not to ask the Muslim League representatives to resign, but to withdraw all the portfolios and re-allocate them so that the Congress wing of the Cabinet would take charge of affairs pertaining to the Dominion of India, while the League representatives would take charge of the corresponding portfolios in so far as Pakistan was concerned. Matters of common concern to both Dominions would be dealt with jointly by both wings under the chairmanship of the Governor-General. The existing departments would be manned by the staff who had elected to remain in India and would be in charge of the ministers representing India. The personnel who had chosen to serve in Pakistan would be withdrawn from the existing departments, and would staff departments which would at once be organized in Delhi to take charge of matters concerning Pakistan. Thus, in effect, two separate provisional Governments were established, one for India and one for Pakistan, each to deal with its own business and to consult the other on matters of common concern. A *communiqué* announcing these arrangements was issued by the Viceroy on 19 July.

A similar procedure was adopted for partitioned Bengal and Punjab.

## THE MECHANICS OF PARTITION

Almost simultaneously with the acceptance of the June 3rd plan an examination was begun of the steps that would be necessary to effect the early partition of the country. Informal discussions were held on my initiative among a number of officers, and on the basis of the conclusions reached a note on procedure was prepared by W. H. J. Christie, i.c.s., Additional Private Secretary to the Viceroy. This dealt with such matters as the division of staff organizations and records, services and institutions, assets and liabilities of the Government of India; future economic relations; domicile, diplomatic relations, etc. It suggested in particular the setting up of a Partition Council and expert committees to deal with the various matters which would have to be tackled. This note, which had developed into a thirty-three page document entitled 'The Administrative Consequences of Partition', was produced by Lord Mountbatten before the party leaders at the end of the meeting at which they had accepted the June 3rd plan. The effect it made on those present was indicated by the complete silence which followed. For the first time the party leaders had been made to realize the magnitude of the task that confronted them. There were many meetings and much argument on the proposal for a Partition Council. Jinnah questioned the authority of the Government of India to make arrangements for the partition of the country —a responsibility which, in his view, was entirely that of His Majesty's Government. Lord Mountbatten eventually persuaded him to agree to the setting-up of a Partition Committee, which consisted of Vallabhbhai Patel, Rajendra Prasad, Liaqat Ali Khan and Abdur Rab Nishtar, with Lord Mountbatten as Chairman. Later, when the provinces decided on partition, this Committee was replaced by a Partition Council. The Congress continued to be represented in the Council by Patel and Rajendra Prasad, with Rajagopalachari as alternate member; while Jinnah and Liaqat Ali Khan, with Abdur Rab Nishtar as alternate member, represented the Muslim League. By an Order of the Governor-General under the Indian Independence Act, 1947, the Partition Council continued in existence even after 15 August. Its composition was then altered to include two members drawn from each of the Dominion Cabinets. India's representatives were Patel and Rajendra Prasad, while Pakistan was represented by such ministers as were able to attend the meetings in Delhi.

An Arbitral Tribunal was set up at about the same time as the Partition Council for the settlement of questions on which the two Governments might not be able to reach agreement. The Tribunal was composed of one representative each of India and Pakistan, with Sir Patrick Spens, ex-Chief Justice of India, as President.

The Partition Council worked through a Steering Committee of two senior officials, H. M. Patel, I.C.S., representing India and Chaudhuri Mahomed Ali representing Pakistan. The Steering Committee was assisted by ten expert committees of officials representing both

India and Pakistan. These expert committees covered the entire field of administration : organization, records and personnel; assets and liabilities; central revenues; contracts, currency and coinage; economic relations (trade and controls) ; domicile; foreign relations, and the armed forces.

The Steering Committee's duty was to ensure that concrete proposals were evolved and put up within a specified time to the Partition Council for decision, and thereafter to take steps to implement those decisions.

The expert committees, which began their investigations in the third week of June, were able to put up agreed recommendations on a large number of subjects, while the Steering Committee was successful in reaching agreement on most of the unsettled points. H.M. Patel, Chaudhuri Mahomed Ali and the officials serving on the expert committees performed a truly prodigious task, leaving only a few matters for settlement by the Arbitral Tribunal after 15 August. Even on these matters, and before the Arbitral Tribunal could take up their investigation, one more attempt (in which Lord Mountbatten played a big part) was made to reach mutual agreement. Representatives of Pakistan — Ghulam Mohamed and Sir Archibald Rowlands — met Vallabhbhai Patel, Rajendra Prasad and Rajagopalachari in Delhi. After a brief discussion, they remitted the issues to Chaudhuri Mahomed Ali and H. M. Patel, who were able to evolve formulae which were accepted by their respective principals; and all references to the Arbitral Tribunal were withdrawn.

### THE DIVISION OF THE ARMED FORCES

It was one of the inevitable consequences of partition that the Indian Armed Forces should be divided. In fact, both the Congress and the Muslim League insisted that they must have their own armed forces under their control before 15 August. The Indian Armed Forces, which had functioned for so long and with such distinction as closely knit units displaying the highest qualities of comradeship and common sacrifice, gave place to two sets of armed forces, both necessarily weakened. As Baldev Singh, the Defence Minister, remarked at the time:

Rarely in peace time has a fighting force suffered such great vicissitudes during so short a period as the Indian Army during the days of its partition. Following the decision to partition the country, the Army had to be divided and the reconstitution, which began immediately, meant the breaking up of battalions, regiments, installations, training institutions, etc.

When the matter first came up at a meeting between the Viceroy and the party leaders, the question was posed whether the division should be on a communal or on a territorial basis. Kripalani, the Congress President, pointed out that it was a question intimately connected with that of nationality. Jinnah supported this view, adding that it would be his purpose in Pakistan to observe no communal differences and that all those who lived there, regardless of creed, would be full-fledged citizens. At that stage it was agreed that the division should be on the basis of citizenship (which in its turn would be based on geographical considerations), subject to the stipulation that an opportunity should be given to those who happened to be resident in that part of India in which their community was a minority, to transfer their homes and citizenship to the other part. Subsequently however, the Partition Council decided that from 15 August the Indian Union and Pakistan would each have within its own territories forces under its own operational control, composed predominantly of non-Muslims and Muslims respectively.

The Partition Council's decision involved the splitting up of the three services of the armed forces and the establishment of separate headquarters in India and Pakistan so that they might be in a position to take over their respective commands on 15 August. The existing armed forces had to be sorted out, and meanwhile had to remain under a single administrative control. The task was undertaken by Field Marshal Sir Claude Auchinleck, Commander-in-Chief, who was re-designated, from 15 August, as Supreme Commander. He worked under the direction of the Joint Defence Council, of which Lord Mountbatten was Chairman, and the Defence Ministers of India and Pakistan, together with the Supreme Commander, were members. The original proposal was that the Joint Defence Council should include both Governors-General in its composition, but Jinnah suggested that if the Governor-General of India would be the independent Chairman he would agree to his own name being omitted.

The Joint Defence Council continued to function till 1 April 1948; but the Supreme Commander ceased to be a member of it from 1 December 1947, when his post was abolished. The Supreme Command was closed down under somewhat unhappy circumstances. At an earlier date Sir Claude Auchinleck had himself made the proposal that the Command should be wound up on 31 December 1947. But

Patel had begun to question Sir Claude Auchinleck's impartiality and, despite Lord Mountbatten's protests, insisted that the Supreme Command should end at once. Meanwhile, Sir Claude Auchinleck also had represented to the Joint Defence Council that it was not possible for him and his officers to discharge their tasks in the absence of 'the necessary spirit of goodwill and co-operation between the principal parties concerned.' The matter was referred to His Majesty's Government, which felt that it had no option but to close down the Supreme Command on 30 November.

The withdrawal of British troops from India, which had started on 17 August 1947, was completed on 28 February 1948, when the last contingent, the Somersetshire Light Infantry, left the shores of India.

### SERVICES AND COMPENSATION

Ever since May 1946, when it was clear that power would definitely be transferred to Indian hands, the question of compensation to members of the Secretary of State's services had been a live issue. Lord Mountbatten had, in fact, discussed this problem with His Majesty's Government before coming out to India as Viceroy and had later held discussions with the members of the interim Government.

On 30 April 1947, the Viceroy made an announcement setting out the decisions reached by His Majesty's Government on the position of the members of the Secretary of State's services, as well as officers and British warrant officers of the Indian Armed Forces. The Government of India was anxious, and His Majesty's Government shared its anxiety, that the administration should not be weakened by the loss of experienced officers. The Government of India therefore undertook to give those members of the Secretary of State's services who continued to serve under it and in the provinces their existing scales of pay, leave, pension rights, etc.

On the question of compensation, His Majesty's Government felt that there was a radical difference in the effect which the transfer of power would have upon the position of European and Indian officers respectively. The former would no longer be serving under the ultimate control of the Parliament of their own country and, as it could not be maintained that their position would be the same as in the past, they were undoubtedly entitled to compensation. Indian officers on the other hand would continue to serve their own country on the same terms as before and these would be guaranteed by the

Government of India, or by the provincial Governments, as the case might be. The same case for compensation did not therefore arise. There were however certain exceptions, namely those Indian officers who had not been invited to continue to serve after the transfer of power, or who could satisfy the Governor-General that their actions in the course of duty during their service prior to the transfer of power had damaged their prospects, or that the appointments offered to them were such as could not be regarded as satisfactory in the altered circumstances, or who could show to the satisfaction of the Governor-General that they had legitimate cause for anxiety about their future in the province and that no suitable transfer could be arranged. The same principles of compensation applied to European officers and other ranks of the Defence Services and the Indian Medical Service.

The Government of India accepted liability for the payment of retiring or proportionate pensions, while the British Government undertook to pay compensation to the European officers and those Indian officers in the special categories referred to for loss of their careers and prospects.

Most of the European officers on the civil side were reluctant to accept service in India and preferred to take compensation. In the defence forces, however, a large number agreed to continue in service.

## BOUNDARY COMMISSIONS

In accordance with the June 3rd plan, it was decided to set up two Boundary Commissions, one to deal with the partition of Bengal, as also the separation of Sylhet from Assam, and the other to deal with the partition of the Punjab. Each Boundary Commission would consist of a Chairman and four members, two nominated by the Congress and two by the Muslim League.

With the consent of both parties Sir Cyril (later Lord) Radcliffe was appointed the Chairman of both Commissions. The remaining members were all High Court judges. Thus, the members of the Bengal Commission were Justices C. C. Biswas, B. K. Mukherji, Abu Saleh Mahomed Akram and S. A. Rahman, while the members of the Punjab Commission were Justices Mehr Chand Mahajan, Teja Singh, Din Mahomed and Muhammad Munir.

These Commissions were required by their terms of reference to demarcate the boundaries of the two parts of the respective provinces on the basis of ascertaining the contiguous majority areas of Muslims and non-Muslims. The Bengal Commission was required in addition to demarcate the Muslim majority areas of Sylhet district and the contiguous non-Muslim majority areas of the adjoining districts of Assam. Their task was a difficult one. Besides having to plod through a maze of facts and figures, the members had to contend with a mass of evidence bristling with divergent opinions and contradictory suggestions.

In Bengal, there were only two groups of districts which were not a cause of anxiety to the Commission. These were the indisputably non-Muslim majority areas of Midnapore, Bankura, Hooghly, Howrah and Burdwan, and the Muslim-majority areas of Chittagong, Noakhali, Tippera, Dacca, Mymensingh, Pabna and Bogra. Except for these, all the other areas, including Calcutta, were subject to contention and rival claims. Similarly in the Punjab, there was much controversy and dispute over the three divisions of Lahore, Multan and Jullundur, as also a portion of the Ambala Division.

Nor were differences of opinion confined to those who tendered evidence before the Commissions; there were differences among the members themselves. Neither as regards Bengal nor the Punjab were the members able to reach any satisfactory agreement. It was finally agreed that the Chairman should give his own award. Sir Cyril Radcliffe was ready with his award only on 13 August. It was Lord Mountbatten's plan to hand over copies of the award to the leaders of the Congress and the Muslim League immediately after he had received them from Sir Cyril Radcliffe, but since he was going to Karachi on the 13th, he could not possibly summon the party leaders on that date. The earliest he was able to get the leaders together from Karachi as well as Delhi to receive the Radcliffe award was on 17 August, and copies were handed over on that day; in fact, before the meeting on the 17th, no one, not even Lord Mountbatten, had seen or read the award.

The Congress had claimed for West Bengal about fifty-nine per cent of the area and forty-six per cent of the population of the province. Under the Radcliffe award, only thirty-six per cent of the area and thirty-five per cent of the population were assigned to West Bengal. Of the total Muslim population of Bengal only sixteen per cent came under West Bengal, while as many as forty-two per cent of non-Muslims remained in East Bengal. The non-Muslims of Bengal complained that the area of West Bengal under the award, as compared with that in the notional division, had shrunk by about 4,000 square miles; they protested against the transfer to East Bengal of Khulna and the Chittagong Hill Tracts and deplored the absence of any link between Darjeeling and the rest of West Bengal. The Muslims, on the other hand, deplored the loss of Calcutta, Murshidabad, and part of Nadia district.

In the Punjab the Congress framed its demands on the basis of the protection of the cultural and religious life of the Sikhs, strategic considerations, economic security and a rational distribution of the irrigation system, river waters, canal colonies, etc. Thus it claimed for East Punjab all that portion of the province east of the river Chenab. The Sikhs supplemented the Congress claims by asking for a few more districts such as Montgomery and Lyallpur and certain sub-divisions of the Multan division. The Muslim League other hand demanded not only the three complete divisions of Rawalpindi, Multan and Lahore, but also a number of tehsils in the Jullundur and Ambala divisions. The Radcliffe award however allocated to East Punjab only thirteen districts, comprising the whole of the Jullundur and Ambala divisions, the Amritsar district of the Lahore division, and certain tehsils of the Gurdaspur and Lahore districts. East Punjab obtained control over three of the five rivers of the united Punjab, namely the Beas, Sutlej and the upper waters of the Ravi. About thirty-eight per cent of the area and forty-five per cent of the population were assigned to East Punjab. West Punjab, on the other hand, obtained under the award about sixty-two per cent of the area and fifty-five per cent of the population, together with a major percentage of the income of the old province. The non-Muslims of the Punjab, especially the Sikhs, bitterly resented the loss of Lahore and the canal colonies of Sheikhupura, Lyallpur and Montgomery, while the Muslims protested against the retention of the Mandi hydro-electric project by East Punjab and the severance of certain tehsils from the notional West Punjab.

As might have been anticipated, the Radcliffe award satisfied none of the parties. The Hindu press characterized it as self-contradictory, anomalous and arbitrary and as unjust to the Hindus of Bengal and the Punjab. The Muslim press declared that Pakistan had been cheated; that the award was a biased decision, an act of shameful partiality. Nonetheless, all were agreed that the award should be accepted for the time being and that adjustments might be sought later by negotiation.

# XVIII

## THE BIRTH OF TWO DOMINIONS

AMONG the varied and complex problems involved in the setting up of the two Dominions there was one issue in particular over which the Congress and the League could not see eye to eye. The Government of India had been a single international personality enjoying membership of fifty-one international bodies and being bound by numerous treaties, conventions and agreements. The establishment of two independent Dominions raised the question as to which Dominion would inherit the international obligations and privileges of pre-partition India, and which would constitute the successor State so far as membership of the United Nations Organization was concerned.

The Congress claimed that the Dominion of India would continue as the international personality of pre-partition India. The Muslim League, on the other hand, maintained that the existing Government of India would, on 15 August, disappear altogether as an entity and would be succeeded by two independent Dominions of equal international status, both of which would be eligible to the existing rights and obligations.

The advice which I tendered to the Viceroy, after consulting the Legislative Department, was that the remainder of India, after the northern and eastern portions had been separated,[1] would remain identifiable with pre-partition India, and that its identity as an internationally-recognised State would not be affected. It was our definite view that neither variation in the extent of a State's territory, nor change in its constitution, could affect the identity of the State. There were numerous instances where loss of territory was not considered to destroy the identity of a State. In the case of India herself the separation of the province of Burma in 1937 did not affect the

---

[1] The portions earmarked for separation represented about 29 per cent of the area and about 35 per cent of the population of British India.

identity of India as an international entity and as a member of the League of Nations, and other international obligations previously undertaken by India-cum-Burma had devolved on India. On the establishment of the two new Dominions, the major portion of the territory, with its Capital, would still be included in the Indian Dominion, and the same machinery of government would carry on the administration as before. As for changes in the constitution, it had been established beyond question that a change in the form of government did not in any way alter the international personality of a State; it was the States, not the governments of those States, which were members of the Family of Nations. In other words, the identity of a State was independent of its form of government.

An important exception was the case of international obligations which were of exclusive territorial application to an area comprised in the Dominion of Pakistan (e.g. treaties relating to the North-West Frontier). Such obligations ran with the land and were only capable of being discharged by the State within the borders of which the territory was situated. Such obligations, with the rights associated with them, would therefore devolve on the Dominion of Pakistan. There might also be treaties to which the entire British Empire was a party and which might have territorial application to India as a whole. The rights and obligations under such treaties would be inherited by both Dominions.

These questions were referred to the Secretary of State, who agreed with our view. In the course of the discussions of the Indian Independence Bill in the House of Commons, the Government spokesman clarified the position thus:

The question of the international status of the two new Dominions is not one which will be finally determined by the terms of this Bill. It is a matter for members of the U.N.O. and other foreign States as much as for H.M.G. in the U.K. Our own view is that the new Dominion of India continues the international personality of existing India and that she will succeed as a matter of International Law to membership of the U.N.O., which existing India enjoys as an original signatory of the San Francisco Charter. Similarly representatives of the Dominion will in our view be entitled to membership of existing international organizations and specialised agencies in which India has hitherto participated. Our hope is that on establishment of the new Dominion of Pakistan she will be accepted as a new member of the Family of Nations and that she will before long be able to make her proper contribution to international goodwill and collaboration. H.M.G. will do all in their power to bring this result about.

The Muslim League leaders however remained unconvinced and continued to claim for Pakistan the position of an original member of the United Nations Organization. The question was therefore referred to the U.N.O. for decision. Dr Ivan Kerno, Assistant Secretary-General for Legal Affairs of the United Nations Organization, who examined the question, made the following recommendations:

The situation is that of a part of an existing State breaking off to form a new State. On this analysis, there is no change in the international status of India; it continues as a State with all its treaty rights and obligations, and consequently with all the rights and obligations of membership in the United Nations. The territory which breaks off, Pakistan, will be a new State; it will not have the treaty rights and obligations of the old State, and it will not, of course, have membership in the United Nations.

In International Law, the situation is analogous to the separation of the Irish Free State from Great Britain, and of Belgium from the Netherlands. In these cases, the portion which separated was considered as a new State; the remaining portion continued as an existing State with all the rights and duties which it had before.

Apart from separation, the Independence Act has effected a basic constitutional change in India. The existing State of India has become a Dominion, and consequently has a new status in the British Commonwealth of Nations, independence in external affairs, and a new form of Government. This, however, does not affect the international personality of India, or its status in the United Nations.

Dr Kerno's conclusions were as follows:

The new Dominion of India continues as an original member State of the United Nations with all rights and obligations of membership.

Pakistan will be a new non-member State. In order to become a member of the United Nations, it would have to apply for admission pursuant to Article 4 of the Charter and its application would be handled under the pertinent rules of procedure of the General Assembly and the Security Council.

The representatives of India on the Economic and Social Council and the representative of India participating in the discussion of the Indonesian case in the Security Council should be requested to submit new credentials after August 15 issued by the Head of the Government, or the Foreign Minister of the new Dominion of India.

Accordingly, on 14 August 1947 Lord Mountbatten promulgated the Indian Independence (International Arrangements) Order, 1947, according to which membership of all international organizations, together with the rights and obligations attached to such membership, devolved solely upon the Dominion of India. Pakistan was left to apply for membership of such international organizations as she chose to join. The rights and duties under international agreements to which pre-partition India had been a party devolved upon both and would, if necessary, be apportioned between them, such rights and obligations as had exclusive territorial application devolving exclusively upon the Government of the territory to which they related. (I may add that Pakistan applied for separate membership of the United Nations Organization, which was granted three days after Pakistan came into existence).

It was also agreed that the existing diplomatic relations abroad should continue to function for India, leaving Pakistan to make its own arrangements in this respect.

Apart from the question of international obligations and privileges, there were a few ancillary questions, such as the relationship of the two Dominions with border tribes, domicile and nationality, passport restrictions and the position of Indian nationals abroad.

His Majesty's Government had entered into treaties and engagements with the border tribes on the North-West Frontier and in Baluchistan. Since India was geographically separated from, and Pakistan was contiguous to these areas, it devolved on Pakistan to negotiate fresh agreements with the border tribes.

With regard to the tribes located on the north-east frontier, there were no formal treaties and engagements; the Government of India's policy had been merely to extend gradually to those areas the benefits of settled administration. In view of the geographical position of the north-east frontier, the responsibility in relation to these border tribes remained with the Indian Dominion.

With regard to domicile and nationality, the position before partition had been that nationality in British India was governed by the British Nationality and Status of Aliens Act, 1914, and to some extent also by the Indian Naturalisation Act. All inhabitants of India enjoyed the status of British subjects, both in and outside India. Since the inhabitants of both Dominions would continue to be British subjects as citizens of two member nations of the British Commonwealth, no immediate change was called for.

The question was considered of instituting a passport system between the Dominions of India and Pakistan. It was decided that, at least for some time to come, no restrictions should be imposed on the movement of persons from one Dominion to the other.

It was also agreed that the two Dominions should, as far as possible, adopt 'a common policy in matters affecting Indians abroad so as to enable them *inter alia* to secure racial equality and civic rights.'

While these details were being arranged calmly and smoothly between the two Dominions, the communal situation in the Punjab, which had eased to some extent after the announcement of the June 3rd plan, began seriously to deteriorate. The immediate cause of the tension was the statement of the Muslim League—to which the Sikhs strongly reacted—that only the notional division of the Punjab as described in the June 3rd plan would be acceptable to them.

Lord Mountbatten lost no time in dealing with the situation. He summoned a meeting of the Partition Council, to which he invited Baldev Singh, the Defence Minister. After the meeting the following *communiqué* was issued:

At their meeting at 5 p.m. on Tuesday, July 22, 1947, the members of the Partition Council (which included Sardar Baldev Singh for this item) decided to issue the attached statement:

Those present were:

In the chair: His Excellency the Viceroy.

For the future Government of India: The Hon'ble Sardar Vallabhbhai Patel and the Hon'ble Dr. Rajendra Prasad.

For the future Government of Pakistan: Mr. Jinnah and the Hon'ble Mr. Liaqat Ali Khan.

On behalf of the Sikhs: The Hon'ble Sardar Baldev Singh.

Now that the decision to set up two independent Dominions from August 15 has been finally taken, the members of the Partition Council, on behalf of the future Governments, declare that they are determined to establish peaceful conditions in which the processes of partition may be completed and the many urgent tasks of administration and economic reconstruction taken in hand.

Both the Congress and the Muslim League have given assurances of fair and equitable treatment to the minorities after the transfer of power. The two future Governments re-affirm these assurances. It is their intention to safeguard the legitimate interests of all citizens irrespective of religion, caste or sex. In the exercise of their normal civic rights all citizens will be regarded as equal, and both the Governments will assure to all people within their territories the exercise of liberties such as freedom of speech, the right to form associations, the right to worship in their own way and the protection of their language and culture.

Both the Governments further undertake that there shall be no discrimination against those who before August 15 may have been political opponents.

The guarantee of protection which both Governments give to the citizens of their respective countries implies that in no circumstances will violence be tolerated in any form in either territory. The two Governments wish to emphasise that they are united in this determination.

To safeguard the peace in the Punjab during the period of change-over to the new conditions, both Governments have together agreed on the setting up of a special Military Command from August 1, covering the civil districts of Sialkot, Gujranwala, Sheikhupura, Lyallpur, Montgomery, Lahore, Amritsar, Gurdaspur, Hoshiarpur, Jullundur, Ferozepore and Ludhiana. With their concurrence Major-General Rees has been nominated as Military Commander for this purpose and Brigadier Digambar Singh (India) and Colonel Ayub Khan (Pakistan) have been attached to him in an advisory capacity. After August 15, Major-General Rees will control operationally the forces of both the new States in this area and will be responsible through the Supreme Commander and the Joint Defence Council to the two Governments. The two Governments will not hesitate to set up a similar organization in Bengal should they consider it necessary.

Both Governments have pledged themselves to accept the awards of the Boundary Commission, whatever these may be. The Boundary Commissions are already in session; if they are to discharge their duties satisfactorily, it is essential that they should not be hampered by public speeches or writings threatening boycott or direct action, or otherwise interfering with their work. Both Governments will take appropriate steps to secure this end; and, as soon as the awards are announced, both Governments will enforce them impartially and at once.

This statement was the first joint declaration of policy by the spokesmen of the two Governments on a matter of fundamental importance. It had a reassuring effect throughout the Punjab and Bengal for the time being, and was regarded as a charter of rights by the minorities in both the Dominions. The Boundary Force, set up on 1 August, consisted of about 50,000 officers and men, a high proportion of the officers being British. This was possibly the greatest military force ever assembled for the express purpose of maintaining civil peace and it gave to everyone a feeling of confidence.

As the day for the transfer of power drew nearer and as the sheets in Lord Mountbatten's specially devised tear-off calendar became fewer and fewer, the activity in the Government departments reached fever pitch. There was no department that was not in one way or another concerned with the partition arrangements, and energies were concentrated almost exclusively on this task. The Government of India had issued a general order that top priority should be given to the execution of the work connected with the setting up of the

Pakistan headquarters. Speedy action was taken to provide building materials, and also for the installation of telephones, at Karachi
and Dacca. The officers and staff who had opted for Pakistan were
relieved as soon as possible and facilities were given for their immediate transit to their new headquarters. The departments gave special
attention to the duplicating of files, to the division of office furniture
and equipment, etc., and to the despatch of such articles as refrigera-
tors, duplicators and calculating machines to Karachi. Although no
agreement had yet been reached on the question of the division of
cash balances, the Government of India transferred a sum of Rs 20
crores to enable the new State to start functioning with sufficient cash
in hand.

On 7 August Jinnah bade farewell to India and all his old associations and flew to Karachi. The first act of the Constituent Assembly
of Pakistan, which met on 11 August, was to elect him as its President.
In the course of his presidential address Jinnah said:

You are free; you are free to go to your temples, you are free to go to
your mosques or to any other place of worship in this State of Pakistan.
You may belong to any religion or caste or creed — that has nothing to do
with the fundamental principle that we are all citizens and equal citizens
of one State. Now, I think we should keep that in front of us as our ideal,
and you will find that in course of time, Hindus would cease to be Hindus,
and Muslims would cease to be Muslims, not in the religious sense, because
that is the personal faith of each individual, but in the political sense as
citizens of the State.

The Constituent Assembly passed a resolution conferring on Jinnah
the honorific of Qaid-e-Azam (great leader), a title by which he
had been called by Muslim Leaguers for some years. Liaqat Ali Khan
in moving the resolution, hailed Jinnah as 'the Ataturk or the Stalin
of our State.' The Constituent Assembly also decided that the Muslim League flag, with a white strip near the mast, should be the flag
of the Pakistan Dominion.

On 13 August Lord Mountbatten flew to Karachi and on the
following day addressed the Pakistan Constituent Assembly. He first
read His Majesty's message of greetings and warmest wishes to the
new Dominion. The message affirmed that all sections of opinion
within the British Commonwealth would assist Pakistan in the uphold-
ing of democratic principles, and gave assurances of His Majesty's
interest and support.

In his speech Lord Mountbatten said that he was speaking to them that day as their Viceroy. From the next day the Government of the new Dominion of Pakistan would rest in their hands, and he himself would be the constitutional head of their neighbour, the Dominion of India. The next day two new sovereign States would take their place in the Commonwealth, not young nations, but the heirs of old and proud civilizations. Referring to Pakistan he said:

The birth of Pakistan is an event in history. We, who are part of history, and are helping to make it, are not well-placed, even if we wished, to moralize on the event, to look back and survey the sequence of the past that led to it. History seems sometimes to move with the infinite slowness of a glacier and sometimes to rush forward in a torrent. Just now, in this part of the world our united efforts have melted the ice and moved some impediments in the stream, and we are carried onwards in the full flood. There is no time to look back. There is time only to look forward.

Lord Mountbatten then paid tribute to the leaders in general, and Jinnah in particular, for having helped to arrive at a peaceful solution for the transfer of power. He reminded his audience of the Gandhi-Jinnah appeal and quoted the assurances given to minorities by the Partition Council in their statement of 22 July. The honouring of those words would mean nothing less than a charter of liberty for a fifth of the human race. He concluded by referring back to the period when the East India Company had received its Charter nearly four centuries ago. The great Emperor Akbar was on the throne, his reign marked by a degree of political and religious tolerance such as had perhaps never been known before or since. 'Akbar's tradition has not always been consistently followed by the British or Indians, but I pray for the world's sake that we will hold fast, in the years to come, to the principles that this great ruler taught us.'

Lord Mountbatten flew back to Delhi on 14 August. I should like to mention here an episode connected with the inauguration ceremony at Karachi. Some days before Lord Mountbatten left for Karachi, information was conveyed to him that there was a conspiracy by some Sikh leaders to bomb Jinnah during the inauguration procession at Karachi. Lord Mountbatten passed on this information at once to the Muslim League leaders, who demanded that all the Sikh leaders should be arrested. In the absence of definite proof, which no one was able to adduce, Lord Mountbatten took the advice of the existing Governor and the Governors-designate of West and East Pakistan and decided that it would be of no avail to arrest the Sikh leaders. He insisted, however, that he himself should drive in the car with Jinnah in the procession, so that if there were any risk they would both share it. Ultimately this was done. Nothing happened.

Pakistan officially became a Dominion on 15 August 1947, when Jinnah was sworn in as Governor-General and the new Pakistan Cabinet headed by Liaqat Ali Khan was also sworn in.

Jinnah broadcast a message over the Pakistan Radio. He said that the birth of the independent sovereign State of Pakistan marked the fulfilment of the destiny of the Muslim nation which had made great sacrifices in the past few years in order to have its own homeland. He paid tribute to all the valiant fighters in this cause.

He went on to say that the creation of the new State gave the citizens of Pakistan an opportunity to demonstrate to the world how a nation containing many elements could live in peace and amity and work for the betterment of all its citizens, irrespective of caste or creed. Their object should be 'peace within and peace without.' He assured the minorities that so long as they fulfilled their duties and obligations as loyal citizens of Pakistan they had nothing to fear. 'We have no ambitions beyond the desire to live honourably and let others live honourably.'

Before we deal with the inauguration of the new Indian Dominion, let us pause for a moment to dwell on two other matters.

One of these was the meeting of the Constituent Assembly in Delhi. I have already explained how the first three sessions of the Constituent Assembly were boycotted by the Muslim League members. After the acceptance of partition, however, Jinnah and the League leaders agreed that Muslim League members from the non-Pakistan provinces should participate in the Constituent Assembly. Liaqat Ali Khan issued an appeal to such League members to attend the Constituent Assembly and play their part in the framing of the future constitution of the Union of India, with a view to securing the rights of Musalmans by means of adequate and effective safeguards in the constitution. When the Constituent Assembly began its fourth session on 14 July, the Muslim League members from the non-Pakistan provinces took their seats and declared themselves to be 'loyal and law-abiding citizens of India.'

It was now clear that the functions of this Constituent Assembly would be confined to the future Indian Dominion; that the Assembly was no longer bound by the provisions in the Cabinet Mission plan, and that it was free to have a federation of its own choice, with as strong a Centre as it desired. With the disappearance of the Cabinet Mission plan, sections, groups, double majority, residuary powers with provinces, opting out, revision after ten years, the Centre limited only to three or four subjects — had all gone by the board.

The other matter was the problem of the Indian States. Under the Cabinet Mission plan, paramountcy would only have lapsed after the Constitution had been set up and power transferred to the successor government; but under the June 3rd plan power was to be transferred on 15 August 1947 and paramountcy was to lapse on that day. Thus, there were hardly two months in which to solve this problem. I need not repeat[1] here the various discussions and negotiations that took place with the rulers and the States' ministers. It will suffice to say that by 15 August 1947 the rulers of all the States geographically contiguous to India, with the exception of Hyderabad, Junagadh and one or two States in Kathiawar with Muslim rulers, had signed the Instrument of Accession and the Standstill Agreement. The fundamental unity of the country having been ensured, India became one federation with the provinces and the States as integral parts.

On the night of 14 August the Constituent Assembly met and, in a moving speech, Nehru called upon the members to take a pledge of dedication to the service of India:

Long years ago we made a tryst with destiny, and now the time comes when we shall redeem our pledge, not wholly or in full measure, but very substantially. At the stroke of the midnight hour, when the world sleeps, India will awake to life and freedom. A moment comes, which comes but rarely in history, when we step out from the old to the new, when an age ends, and when the soul of a nation, long suppressed, finds utterance. It is fitting that at this solemn moment we take the pledge of dedication to the service of India and her people and to the still larger cause of humanity.

Nehru concluded by saying that they had all to labour and work hard to give reality to their dreams. Those dreams were for India, but they were also for the world; all the nations and peoples were too closely knit together today for any of them to imagine that they could live apart. Peace had been said to be indivisible; so was freedom, so was prosperity, and so also was disaster, in this One World that could no longer be split into isolated fragments. To the people of India Nehru made an appeal for co-operation in the great adventure of building 'the noble mansion of free India where all her children may dwell.' The Constituent Assembly endorsed the request of the Congress

---

[1] See my book, *The Story of the Integration of the Indian States.*

leaders that Lord Mountbatten should become the first Governor-
General. Soon after its meeting, Rajendra Prasad and Nehru went
over to Government House and conveyed to him the request of the
Constituent Assembly. Lord Mountbatten feelingly replied, 'I am
proud of the honour and I will do my best to carry out your advice in
a constitutional manner.'

On the morning of 15 August Lord Mountbatten in a colourful
ceremony was sworn in as Governor-General by the late Chief Justice
Kania, and the new cabinet, headed by Nehru, was sworn in by the
Governor-General.

Lord Mountbatten then drove in state to the Chamber of the Constituent Assembly. Rajendra Prasad read congratulatory messages
from all over the world felicitating the birth of the new Dominion.
Lord Mountbatten read out the King's message. 'Freedom-loving
people everywhere will wish,' the message said, 'to share in your cele-
brations, for with this transfer of power by consent comes the fulfilment of a great democratic ideal to which the British and Indian peoples alike are firmly dedicated. It is inspiring to think that all this
has been achieved by means of peaceful change.'

In his speech Lord Mountbatten touched briefly upon the negotiations which had led to the evolution and acceptance of the June 3rd
plan. He applauded the wisdom, tolerance and friendly help of the
leaders which had enabled the transfer of power to take place ten and
a half months earlier than had originally been intended. He also
commended the ministers and officials who had laboured day and
night to carry out the partition of a sub-continent of 400 million inhabitants and the transfer of power to two independent Governments
in less than two and a half months.

Referring to the Indian States, Lord Mountbatten acclaimed Patel
as a far-sighted statesman and stressed that by the implementation
of the policy of accession there had been established a unified political structure in the new Dominion of India.

He went on to say: 'From today I am your constitutional Governor-
General and I would ask you to regard me as one of yourselves devo-
ted wholly to the furtherance of India's interests.' He added that he
proposed to ask to be released in April 1948, so that India should be
at liberty to have one of her own people as her Governor-General.
He made a reference to the many problems confronting the country.
He paid tribute to Gandhiji, whom he described as the architect of
India's freedom through non-violence. In conclusion, he hailed Free

India's first Prime Minister, Jawaharlal Nehru, as a world-renowned leader of courage and vision. 'Under his able guidance, assisted by the colleagues whom he has selected, and with the loyal co-operation of the people, India will now attain a position of strength and influence and take her rightful place in the comity of nations.'

In reply, Rajendra Prasad gratefully acknowledged that 'while our achievement is in no small measure due to our own sufferings and sacrifices, it is also the result of world forces and events and, last though not least, it is the consummation and fulfilment of the historic tradition and democratic ideals of the British race.' After paying a special tribute to Lord Mountbatten, he concluded: 'The period of domination of Britain over India ends today, and our relationship with Britain is henceforward going to rest on a basis of equality, of mutual goodwill and mutual profit.'

On 15 August, too, Lord Mountbatten issued a broadcast to the United States of America, to celebrate the second anniversary of the Allied victory over Japan. Lord Mountbatten said:

Two years ago today I had just returned from the Potsdam Conference and was in the Prime Minister's room in 10, Downing Street, when the news of the Japanese surrender came through. Here, as I speak to you tonight in Delhi, we are celebrating an event no less momentous for the future of the world — India's Independence Day. In the Atlantic Charter, we — the British and Americans — dedicated ourselves to champion the self-determination of peoples and the independence of nations. Bitter experience has taught us that it is often easier to win a war than to achieve a war aim; so let us remember August 15th — V. J. Day — not only as the celebration of a victory, but also as the fulfilment of a pledge.

Needless to say, there was tumultuous joy on that day all over India. Nehru and the Congress leaders were acclaimed with demonstrative joy and affection. Driving in state in Delhi, Lord and Lady Mountbatten were greeted by the enthusiastic crowds with prolonged and resounding cheers. What a contrast — this acclamation to His Majesty's representative — with say, the boycott[1] of the Prince of Wales in 1921. For with independence had come a remarkable change in the attitude of the Indian people towards the British. The upsurge of goodwill was an augury for the future.

Thus ended a most important and memorable chapter in India's chequered history — the end of 182 years of British rule. Prince

---

[1] It is interesting to recall that, on that occasion, Lord Mountbatten was in the Prince of Wales's party as a member of his staff.

Bismarck is quoted as having said: 'Were the British Empire to disappear, its work in India would remain one if its lasting monuments.' From 1765, when the East India Company took over the collection of the revenues of Bengal, Bihar and Orissa, the British had gradually built up in India an administrative and political system hitherto unknown. They brought about the consolidation and unity of the country; they created an efficient administrative organization on an all-India basis; it was they who for the first time introduced the rule of law; and they left to India that most precious heritage of all, a democratic form of government. As long as there is an India, Britain's outstanding contributions to this country will continue to abide.

# XIX

## THE AFTERMATH OF PARTITION

WHILE Delhi and the rest of India were celebrating the advent of Independence, the fate of the minorities in areas directly affected by the partition of the country was hanging perilously in the balance. The Muslim League's 'Direct Action' campaign, followed by the Calcutta killing and disturbances in the Noakhali district of East Bengal and in Bihar, and further bloodshed and arson in the Punjab and the North-West Frontier Province, had already thrown the country into a dangerous state of communal frenzy. The joint appeal issued by Gandhiji and Jinnah at the instance of Lord Mountbatten, soon after the latter assumed the Viceroyalty, failed to bring about any marked change in the relations between the two communities. The announcement of the June 3rd plan and its acceptance by the political leaders did serve temporarily to stem the tide of communal hostilities, but when the Muslim League in the Punjab declared that it would resist any change in the notional division of the province, the Sikhs immediately launched a violent counter-agitation, and the situation once more began to deteriorate dangerously. We had anticipated that there might be communal trouble in the border districts directly affected by the partition, but we felt that the Boundary Force of mixed composition under Major-General Rees, an enormous and carefully picked body, would be able to cope with the situation. As for the rest, we had no reason to believe that the Governments concerned would not themselves be able to control any sporadic outbursts that might occur in their respective Dominions. We had the guarantee of the political leaders as set out in their joint statement of 22 July, as also the specific assurances in regard to the protection of minorities given by Jinnah in his address to the Constituent Assembly and in his broadcast to the people of Pakistan. It is true that the situation was full of fear and foreboding;

but we had not expected to be so quickly and so thoroughly dis-
illusioned.

In fact, not only before the transfer of power, but also immediately
thereafter, Gandhiji and the Congress leaders had appealed to the
Hindu and Sikh minorities in Pakistan areas not to run away but to
stay in their homes and to face the situation bravely. Master Tara
Singh had also advised the non-Muslims of West Punjab to stay on
in their homes. But soon after the announcement of the Radcliffe
Award on 17 August, a determined campaign to drive out the Hindus
and Sikhs was evident all over West Punjab and the North-West
Frontier Province. There were serious disturbances in the Lahore,
Sheikhupura, Sialkot and Gujranwala districts. A massacre on an
unprecedented scale took place in Sheikhupura in West Punjab. This
was followed by a violent anti-Muslim reaction in Amritsar. Thereafter communal frenzy gripped the people on both sides of the border, taking a heavy toll of lives and creating an exodus of population
between the two Dominions, the like of which has never before been
known in history. The Hindus and Sikhs in West Pakistan made
for the Indian border by the shortest possible routes — from Narowal
to Dera Baba Nanak, from Lahore to Amritsar, from Kasur to
Ferozepore, from Montgomery to Fazilka, from the Muslim State
of Bahawalpur to Bikaner, from Mirpur Khas to Jodhpur. This
they did by air, by train, by car, by bus — by almost every conceivable means of transport, as well as in foot convoys. What started as a
trickle very soon developed into a flood which, sweeping through East
Punjab, engulfed the city and province of Delhi and overflowed into
the western districts of the United Provinces.

The uprooted millions were in a terrible mental state. They had
been driven from their homes under conditions of indescribable hor-
ror and misery. Not many had the time to plan their evacuation; most
had to move out at the shortest possible notice. They had been subjected to terrible indignities. They had witnessed their near and dear
ones hacked to pieces before their eyes and their houses ransacked,
looted and set on fire by their own neighbours. They had no choice
but to seek safety in flight, filled with wrath at what they had seen, and
full of anguish for numberless missing kinsmen who were still stran-
ded in Pakistan and for their womenfolk who had been abducted.

All classes of people joined the stream of refugees. There were the
rich, who had been reduced overnight to poverty and penury; there
were petty tradesmen and office-workers for whom the future was

bleak and uncertain, and there were the Sikhs who had borne the main brunt of the communal fury.

The holocaust in Western Pakistan had its repercussions in East Punjab. The streams of fleeing refugees with their tales of woe and suffering made a profound impression on the people. In vain were appeals made to them to remember that retaliation was no remedy. The spirit of revenge was abroad, working up communal bitterness to a frenzied pitch, till all restraint was thrown to the winds and there ensued a wholesale attack on Muslims. The trouble spread to Patiala and the East Punjab States and to the western districts of the United Provinces, especially Meerut and Saharanpur, the States of Bharatpur and Alwar, and ultimately to Delhi. The Muslims in these areas now started a mass exodus to the Pakistan border.

While panic-stricken refugees poured into the city of Delhi, the Capital buzzed with rumours of a deep-laid, long-prepared Muslim conspiracy to overthrow the new Government of Free India and to seize the Capital. Such rumours may now seem, if not baseless, at least extremely improbable, but so credulous had the people then become that they were very widely believed. Had not Delhi, before the advent of the British, been the seat of Muslim empires for centuries? Had not the Capital been the cradle of Muslim culture? The Muslim League High Command functioned from Delhi and it was from Delhi that the campaign of 'Direct Action' had been organized and conducted through the length and breadth of the country. The militant National Guards had a well-knit organization in the city. The Khaksars (who had made their appearance in Delhi early in the year) also boasted of a number of adherents. It was the general belief that plans had been made before the announcement of the June 3rd plan to organize and equip the Muslim community for communal violence. The majority of the ammunition dealers in the city were Muslims and it was easy for them to help their co-religionists in obtaining a wide variety of weapons and ammunition. There were also Muslim blacksmiths and arms-repairers who were alleged to have given a hand in the fabrication of bombs, mortars and other ammunition.

The first recorded communal incident in Delhi took place in a predominantly Muslim locality. On 21 August there was an explosion in a house belonging to a Muslim science student. It is believed that he had been trying to prepare a bomb. A few days later the first stabbing was reported from the vicinity of the Diwan Hall and the Wavell Canteen, the two places where arrangements had been made for the reception of incoming refugees. On 25 August, an altercation ensued between a Hindu worker and a Muslim worker in the Birla Mills, which led to a free fight; but the police were able to control it and to restore order very quickly.

The local administration was very soon faced with a task far beyond its capacity. Many of those of its Muslim officers who were drawn from the Punjab had opted to serve Pakistan. Their withdrawal caused an almost crippling depletion of the officer cadre. More than fifty per cent of the civil and almost seventy-five per cent of the armed police force had been drawn from amongst the Muslims and all of them had their heart in, and were keen to opt for, Pakistan. They obviously could not be relied upon in an emergency; in fact, there were persistent rumours that they were planning to go over to the Muslim side together with their firearms. Nor were the non-Muslim sections of the force more reliable. Many of the Hindu policemen had been drawn from the Punjab and they had heard of what had happened to their friends and relations in the western part of the province. The gaps in the officer cadre had been hastily filled by optees from West Pakistan who had themselves witnessed or experienced the worst features of communal fury in West Punjab and the North-West Frontier Province. Few of them were in a fit mental state to take strong action against rioters. For some time only a handful of troops were present in the Capital and they could not be reinforced quickly, because many of the formations which had fallen to the share of India were still locked up in Pakistan. In an effort to preserve order with the help of the limited manpower at his disposal, the District Magistrate of Delhi imposed an extended curfew from the afternoon of 28 August to the early hours of 1 September. The Old City seemed peaceful and quiet during this period but, as was discovered later, forces bent on mischief were busy making offensive and defensive preparations on a considerable scale in areas which were either predominantly inhabited by Muslims, or into which non-Muslim refugees had penetrated. On the morning of 4 September, the explosion of a bomb in a Hindu locality in Karolbagh was the signal for a serious outbreak of rioting and there occurred numerous isolated cases of arson and of looting and stabbing in different parts of the city. Muslim and Hindu localities were so intermingled that each locality feared an attack from its neighbour. An atmosphere of nervousness and apprehension pervaded the entire Capital.

In the beginning, the use of firearms was exceptional. But on

7 September some Muslims shot and killed a few Hindus. Their action was probably only defensive, but it was provocative in the tense atmosphere that prevailed. Trouble broke out afresh on a large scale and firearms were freely used. Some of the houses in certain Muslim localities were converted into powerful bastions where firearms were collected and stored for use. One of these houses was later found to contain considerable subterranean stores of arms and ammunition and even wireless sets. Firearms and ammunition were actually dug up from graveyards. In a situation such as this, the small police force was completely helpless and troops had to be called upon to give assistance. These comprised a small body of Gurkhas, the Rajputana Rifles, and the 4th Battalion, the Madras Regiment. The last-mentioned were rushed to Delhi from Poona. They were disposed in the areas of Sadar Bazar, Subzimundi, Paharganj and Karolbagh. Even with the help of the troops it was not easy to restore order. If it had been only a question of protecting the few against the onslaughts of the many, perhaps the troops — even though small in number — might have proved equal to the task. But both sides seemed well provided with firearms, were equally well organized and determined and were employing guerilla tactics. The task of restoring law and order called for patience and perseverance, as well as a certain degree of ruthless determination. The troops, particularly the Madras Regiment (commanded by Lieutenant-Colonel Sherrif, a Muslim officer from Madras), performed many difficult and unpleasant tasks with remarkable courage and impartiality.

Organized rioting apart, sporadic and isolated incidents of looting, stabbing and arson were frequent in many parts of the city. Muslim shops situated in predominantly Hindu areas were the chief targets for loot and needy refugees were the chief beneficiaries. Stabbing was developed into an art. The tragedy was that for the most part it was women, children and the aged who were the victims. Stabbing did not take place only in the alleys. Groups of bloodthirsty ruffians would even rush into houses and drag people out of them to be stabbed. For days together, no effective protection could be given against treacherous, sneaking and silent killing by individuals impelled by an uncontrollable urge to settle the score; an eye for an eye, a tooth for a tooth.

The passion for revenge found expression in many ways, and arson was one of them. Delhi had six fire engines and all of them were kept more than busy; they had scores of small and big fires to attend to. On the night of 7 September one could see from housetops in New Delhi red clouds and smoke curling up from numberless points in the Old City.

Not all, however, had lost their balance; indeed, there were numerous instances of brave conduct in defence of the helpless, by both individuals and institutions. When a mob attacked a Muslim family, a Congressman intervened and dared them to kill him before laying their blood-stained hands on the Muslim family. Hundreds of Hindus took their Muslim neighbours into protective custody and escorted them to refugee camps, and many institutions mounted guards to protect their Muslim members.

Verily, only a thin line divides the man from the beast — and order from chaos. Even though not more than a small section of the population was directly involved in the riots, the uncertainty of the moment, the prevailing atmosphere of nervousness and apprehension, and the fear of one's own neighbour, all but paralysed the normal life of the Old City. While Muslims from the disturbed areas were fleeing to refugee camps in search of security, others — Muslims and non-Muslims alike — were unwilling or unable to leave their homes. Their families would not let them go because they did not know what might befall them on the road. The bread-winner hesitated to go out because he was afraid of what might happen to his family in his absence. And so for days together, shops remained unopened, offices ceased to function, health services were disrupted and communications were disorganized.

Conditions in New Delhi had never before deteriorated to so serious an extent. In Connaught Place a number of shops were looted and there were also cases of stabbing. There was sufficient apprehension and uncertainty to induce almost the entire Muslim population of New Delhi to move out to the shelter of refugee camps. Nor was there a sense of security among the Hindus. The concentration of Muslims, particularly the turbulent Meos from the neighbouring villages round about the Lodi Road area, was a potential source of trouble. The lurid glow of fires in the horizon, the all-night shooting and the screaming and shrieking of victims, were enough to unnerve anyone. Food and milk were scarce and the majority of the staff absented themselves from the central Government offices. Telephones worked fitfully and for two days the mail was not delivered at all. Even the airports were not spared by the rioters and air services were badly interrupted.

When the trouble spread to the areas surrounding Delhi, to the villages of the neighbouring States of Alwar and Bharatpur and the adjoining districts of the United Provinces and East Punjab, large numbers of people — mostly Muslims — trekked into Delhi and greatly added to the already complex problem of protecting the local Muslim population.

This account of the deterioration in Delhi is but a reflection of how the situation had developed in East Punjab, the western districts of the United Provinces and some of the Punjab and Rajasthan States. The new province of East Punjab had not yet had time to reorganize its administration; even its Capital had not been settled, when there came this unforeseen challenge to law and order, which resulted in a complete — though short-lived — breakdown of the administration. Under the pressure of refugees fleeing from terror it was with the greatest difficulty that some semblance of order could be maintained even in the western districts of the United Provinces.

The task that confronted the Government of India was threefold. Firstly, they had to retrieve the law and order position and to stop the communal frenzy; secondly, they had to bring about a sense of security among the Muslim minority and, if that was not possible, at least to afford those who wanted to go away to Pakistan safe transit across the frontier; and thirdly, they had a moral duty by their brethren across the borders, to ensure the peaceable transfer of Hindus and Sikhs to India and to provide for their resettlement.

It was particularly essential that Delhi should be saved from the impending chaos at whatever cost. Danger to the Capital meant a threat to the very existence of the nascent Dominion. It was clear that some extraordinary and forceful action was necessary to retrieve the position. I felt that it was only Lord Mountbatten's presence in the Capital that would save the situation. Because of criticisms on both sides, the Punjab Boundary Force had been dissolved, and the authority of the Joint Defence Council over it having come to an end, Lord Mountbatten felt that there was no necessity for his immediate presence in Delhi. He had therefore gone to Simla for ten days for a well-earned rest. He could scarcely have foreseen a situation that might develop so seriously as to affect his return to Delhi. I mentioned to Vallabhbhai Patel my idea of ringing up Lord Mountbatten to tell him how serious the situation was and to request him to return immediately. He readily fell in with my suggestion and assured me that the Prime Minister would also agree. On my telephonic request,

Lord Mountbatten returned at once to Delhi and on his arrival I met him and explained the situation. Immediately afterwards he had a discussion with Nehru and Patel. That very evening an Emergency Committee of fifteen was set up. It consisted of Cabinet Ministers, the Commander-in-Chief, representatives of the Supreme Command, the Chief Commissioner of Delhi, the Inspector-General of Police, the Director-General of Civil Aviation and representatives of the Medical Department and Railways. The Cabinet Ministers were Nehru, Vallabhbhai Patel, Baldev Singh (Defence), John Matthai (Railways) and K. C. Neogy (who was nominated as minister in charge of refugees). Others were co-opted as and when required. C. M. Trivedi, Governor of East Punjab, together with his Premier and Home Minister, also attended the meetings when called upon. The energetic and indefatigable Vernon Erskine Crum was appointed Secretary of the Committee.

Nehru and Patel insisted that Lord Mountbatten should be the Chairman. The Emergency Committee promptly plunged into an earnest examination of ways and means of dealing with the situation. Daily meetings were held in Government House, where urgent problems were discussed, decisions formed and officers entrusted with the task of ensuring that those decisions were implemented at once. The minutes of each meeting were circulated within two hours of the dispersal of the meeting, so that the officers concerned were able to take action on the same day and report to the Committee at its next meeting. A special feature was the institution of a Map Room, the purpose of which was to provide factual and up-to-date information to all concerned with regard to the place and number of disturbances and the location and movement of refugees. Every day, before the meeting, the members of the Committee were taken to the adjoining Map Room so that they could make themselves acquainted with the up-to-date position. The facilities provided in the Map Room were specially appreciated by members of the foreign embassies and by press correspondents.

On the morning of 9 September an *ad hoc* committee was set up to deal specifically with the crisis in the Capital. The idea at first was that this Committee should be composed of the Chief Commissioner of Delhi (who happened to be a Muslim), the Sub-area Commander and the Inspector-General of Police. H. M. Patel, I.C.S., who was then the Cabinet Secretary, came to my office and we discussed this between ourselves. We both felt that a Committee of the nature proposed would be inadequate to deal with the situation, which had already deteriorated to an alarming extent. In our view the situation was so serious that a Minister from the central Cabinet ought straightway to be deputed to head a Special Emergency Committee for Delhi. I mentioned this informally to Lord Mountbatten, who put the idea to Nehru and Vallabhbhai Patel. C. H. Bhabha, then Commerce Minister, was selected to undertake this onerous responsibility.

Bhabha convened a meeting at his house of a few senior officers, including the Chief Commissioner and the Deputy Commissioner and senior police officials of the Delhi administration, and a tentative plan for dealing with the crisis was placed before it for discussion.

The general sense of the meeting appeared to be against any change in the arrangements already proposed. But before any decision could be reached, news was received that in the vicinity of Ajmere Gate some Muslims armed with automatic weapons had run amuck and were shooting down Hindus at sight. The Deputy Commissioner and two police officers immediately left the meeting for the scene of the alleged shooting and a feeling of helplessness overwhelmed those who were left behind. The meeting dispersed. H. M. Patel and I went to Vallabhbhai Patel's residence and told him of the discussion. Just then some one brought in the news that a few Hindus had been killed by Meos in the Lodi Road area; and a minute later a man rushed in to say that a Muslim had been butchered not very far from Vallabhbhai Patel's residence. In a voice charged with the deepest anguish, he exclaimed: 'What is the point in waiting and discussing here: why don't you all get on with the business and do something, and do what you think is right?'

We returned to Bhabha's house. It was agreed that the first step was for the Central Emergency Committee to approve of the new special Committee for Delhi, and for this Committee to meet immediately afterwards in the Town Hall (situated in the heart of the Old City).

Next morning the Central Emergency Committee formally set up the special Committee, with Bhabha as Chairman and H. M. Patel as Vice-Chairman. It was left to Bhabha to call upon suitable non-officials to work on the Committee. Immediately after this decision was taken, Bhabha — accompanied by Shyama Prasad Mookherjee (then Industries and Supply Minister) and H. M. Patel — proceeded to the Town Hall in Old Delhi. The Chief Commissioner and other officers of the Delhi Administration and a few prominent non-official citizens of Delhi had already assembled there. Those present were in a far more chastened mood, for the situation had continued to worsen during the night. No plan was put forward for discussion. Bhabha merely said that it had been decided to appoint a special Emergency Committee for Delhi with himself as Chairman and H.M. Patel as Vice-Chairman, and that he had been given the authority to co-opt other members. He added that those present might regard themselves as members. There was no voice of dissent. Thus was born the Delhi Emergency Committee, upon which lay the duty of rescuing the Capital from chaos and bringing it back to normal life. The Committee was fortunate in having as its Secretaries two young and brilliant officers of the Indian Civil Service — L. K. Jha and K. B. Lall. The latter belonged to Delhi and not only enjoyed the friendship and confidence of persons professing diverse faiths, but had the advantage of contacts with political and social workers and professional men in many different walks of life. With their drive and initiative these officers soon welded together a mixed crowd of volunteers, officials and non-officials, men and women, Hindus, Muslims, Christians and Parsis into a wonderful team.

I have already referred to a tentative plan which had been prepared to deal with the Delhi situation. This owed its origin to H.M. Patel and K. B. Lall. It was extraordinarily simple. It recognized that the local administration had broken down. It envisaged that emergency arrangements had to be improvised while no new centralized administration could be built up because of the paucity of personnel and the breakdown of communications. The province was therefore to be divided into five zones, each of which was to be entrusted to an administrator to be drawn from amongst the senior officers of the Government of India. The administrators were to be allowed their respective quotas of men and material; and each zonal group was to be asked to rely on its own initiative and resources to do what appeared to be best in the circumstances, and only to keep the headquarters informed of the situation from time to time and of its regional requirements. To begin with, a skeleton headquarters organization would be located at the Town Hall with a mobile reserve at its disposal and with wireless facilities for the maintenance of contact with zonal administrators. The idea was to secure maximum decentralization and effective co-ordination with a view to making the best possible use of the limited man-power available at the time.

Old and New Delhi were divided into four zones, the rural area constituting a fifth. It was decided that the maximum co-ordination

possible between the magistracy and the police, as also other organs
of local administration, should be achieved at the zonal level. The
system yielded quick results. The zonal administrators were generally
successful in putting a stop to large-scale rioting. Of necessity, they
had to concentrate on danger spots. In the worse-affected zones,
since they could not induce the Muslims to stay on in their homes,
they did the next best thing: they arranged to escort them to refugee
camps. In the less-affected zones, they created a sense of security,
repelled attempts by refugees to infiltrate and made it possible for the
Muslims to stay on in their homes.

The Committee's headquarters at the Town Hall came to be known
as the ' Central Control Room ', whence flowed directives and instructions to zonal organizations and workers over the wide area of Old
and New Delhi and the surrounding villages, and into which flowed
an almost unending stream of demands and requirements for assistance of every conceivable kind from various sections of the public
and official and semi-official bodies. Every evening a meeting would
be held at which the day's occurrences, problems and difficulties
would be reviewed and suitable instructions issued. The following
morning Bhabha would inform the Central Emergency Committee
of the general situation in the Capital and receive instructions as to
any particular action it might wish the Delhi Committee to take.
Nehru and Vallabhbhai Patel made frequent visits to the Headquarters and also toured the affected areas, keeping themselves fully
in touch with the situation.

A notable factor, which contributed immeasurably to the restoration of law and order in Delhi, was the steadfastness and loyalty of
the majority of its citizens, who were more than ready to give their
help and co-operation. The Committee needed men and women
of determination and devotion to duty, who would readily undertake any task, however disagreeable, and who would shirk nothing,
even if physical risk were involved. And such men and women
were not wanting. Nothing was more inspiring and nothing cheered
one so much as the spontaneous way in which men and women of
all ages, classes and shades of opinion came forward to work at all
hours — if need be, round the clock — in a disciplined manner at
a task which they realized was one of great humanity. I, for one,
look back on this in order to draw fresh inspiration whenever I find
current events thoroughly depressing.

H. M. Patel's pivotal position as Cabinet Secretary proved a boon, for he was able to obtain authority from the Cabinet to requisition the services of any central Government officer he needed. This authority was freely used, though with discretion. A number of young officers were detailed for whole-time duty with the Committee, while quite a number of us volunteered to perform part-time service. Probationers of the Indian Administrative Service, then under training at the Administrative Training School, were also called upon to serve and did so with extraordinary enthusiasm.

The strength of the armed forces at the disposal of the Delhi Committee was very limited and reinforcements were expected to come in only later. A contingent of armed police was contributed by the Central Provinces, and the Governor-General made available the services of his Bodyguard (which had not yet been partitioned) and they rendered yeoman service, driving round in pairs of armoured cars — one car in each pair being manned by Punjabi Musalmans, and the other by Sikhs. All of them carried out their duties in an exemplary manner. For the rest, the Committee had to rely on the citizens of Delhi. Every possible source of trained and disciplined man-power was tapped — the Officers' Training Corps, the Territorials, Scout organizations, the Jamiat-ul-Ulema[1], Congress volunteers. Each of these separate organizations had its accredited representative in the Control Room, to whom each made a daily report and from whom it received daily orders regarding disposition of its resources in men and material.

Communications constituted what was perhaps the most important single basic problem. The public transport system was virtually at a standstill; only a few ventured to go out on cycles or on foot, and even the voluntary workers of the Control Room had to be picked up from their homes and transported back to them. The Defence Department helped with trucks and jeeps. Help was obtained from unofficial sources; cars and trucks were requisitioned even from refugees, and soon an impressive transport fleet was built up.

Sanitation was the next big problem; for sanitary arrangements, particularly in Old Delhi, had broken down completely. A week's accumulation of filth is enough to cause despair to any health authority, and loot and arson had multiplied the problem tenfold. The inhabitants of each locality were now called upon to organize volunteer squads to clean up the roads. Even after the sweepers had been persuaded to come back to work, a large number of volunteers from

_____
[1] An association of Muslim divines.

the Congress, the Jamiat-ul-Ulema, student unions and Boy Scouts, had to be drafted to assist them. Here too, the Army helped by placing at the disposal of the Control Room a hygiene squad which made it possible for the badly affected parts of the town to be thoroughly disinfected. It was only after a week of sustained effort that it could be said that the city had been saved from the danger of epidemic.

Food distribution arrangements had been thoroughly disrupted. Ration shops remained closed and authorized ration distributors were unwilling to stir out of their houses to replenish their stocks. Without further delay the Control Room organized a system for the delivery of rationed foodgrains to shopkeepers at their shops. Fortunately, there were enough stocks of foodgrains available; only salt and fuel were in short supply and these had to be brought in rapidly to replenish the reserve.

But the most urgent and difficult of all the problems was the care of refugees, both Muslim and non-Muslim. Those non-Muslims uprooted from Pakistan naturally expected to find at least food and shelter in the Capital of India. They cast longing eyes on houses occupied by Muslim residents of the city and they looked around for opportunities to strike new roots in the land to which they had been driven by communal fury. So long as their primary needs remained unsatisfied, they constituted a standing menace to law and order.

Then there were the Muslims living in mixed localities in Delhi and the surrounding rural areas, who had left their homes to seek safety in hastily improvised camps. Some took themselves for safety and shelter to the spacious mausoleum of Emperor Humayun, while others went to the Purana Qila, where the Pakistan High Commissioner had organized a small camp primarily for Government servants who had opted for Pakistan. Muslims of all classes congregated in these camps —Punjabi businessmen, doctors, lawyers, professors, Government officials, craftsmen, artisans and labourers. In the beginning the Pakistan High Commissioner tried to look after their requirements, but the job became too big for his limited staff, and even the efforts of the local administration, with its hands full of other and manifold responsibilities, proved inadequate. Many thousands of Meos from the neighbouring States of Bharatpur and Alwar and even some Afghan nationals and Kashmiri Muslims, who had been living in the disturbed areas, sought safety in these camps.

The Committee had to act here with special speed, for there were over a hundred thousand persons to be cared for and the numbers were increasing. Arrangements for food, filtered water, sanitary and medical facilities were quickly improvised. Three officers of the Indian Civil Service were detailed to work as Camp Commandants; the Indian Administrative Service Training School supplied them with a few deputies, and many non-officials joined in. Assistance was rendered to the official organization by a devoted band of women, including the wives of British and other European officials. Help came from various social organizations in Delhi, and Christian missions also contributed volunteers. Lady Mountbatten herself was indefatigable in organizing and carrying out works of relief and welfare. She was a frequent visitor to the camps; she not only gave help from her own household, but did not rest content until bit by bit the requirements of the camps had been satisfactorily met. After all these years, if anything stands out prominently in my mind, it is the services rendered by Lady Mountbatten, as also by Mrs Sucheta Kripalani, whose zealous work for the relief of the refugees was beyond praise. Lady Mountbatten formed, and became the Chairman of, the United Council for Relief and Welfare and her organizational ability was recognized by all who had the privilege of being associated with her.

Every foot of the covered accommodation in the precincts of Purana Qila and Humayun's Tomb was occupied. Scores of tents were pitched and every possible contrivance was used to improvise shelter. The Air Force lent command trailers for the use of the Camp Commandants. Although the semblance of an office had been set up on the first day, the Camp Commandants had no means of communication with the mass of humanity placed under their charge, until the Navy provided them with loud hailers. A loudspeaker system was also rigged up from civilian sources and powerful searchlights were erected with the help of the Army. The Military Engineering Service and the Central P.W.D. helped to lay on a water system and steps were taken to put in an emergency telephone connexion.

In the early stages, labour and equipment were simply not available. There were tents to be pitched, drains to be cleared, sanitation to be looked after, and volunteers were needed for the distribution of foodgrains and to maintain law and order. To set an example, the Camp Commandant and his officers themselves went round the Camps with shovels, filling up a drain here and digging a trench there. There was no job which was too mean or too specialized for the volunteers.

An efficient supply and services organization at the Control Room made it possible to cope with an unending stream of demands for supplies, all of the highest priority. The camps sent in their indents every day, and every evening the Camp Commandants discussed their problems and difficulties with the authorities at headquarters. A portion of the needed supplies came by way of donations, and stocks from shops and godowns were also freely requisitioned. In diverse ways the varied and enormous requirements of over a lakh of people were met within a week, and life in the camps became more organized and tolerable.

Even nature added to the suffering of the refugees. The September rains were exceptionally heavy that year. Few were able to keep dry under such improvised shelters as existed, while the influx of refugees into the camps continued. At one time it was thought that another refugee camp would have to be organized. But in the meantime the efforts to stamp out lawlessness in the city had been meeting with success. There was a distinct improvement in the law and order situation and sufficient confidence had been re-instilled in the minds of the Muslim inhabitants, at least in some areas, to make them stay on in their homes.

Within less than two weeks normal conditions had been restored in the city. The sense of insecurity among the Muslims perhaps took longer to disappear, though it would not be incorrect to say that by the first week of October a Muslim could move about the city without any danger to life or limb. So long as the camps in Purana Qila and Humayun's Tomb remained, the Control Room too had to remain, for there was no other organization which could have taken over the responsibility of running these two camps with their population of over 150,000. But gradually the camps emptied. Many of the Muslim refugees went to Pakistan; others returned to their homes in Delhi and the neighbouring areas.

The movement of refugees[1] from and to Pakistan was one of the most difficult problems which the Central Emergency Committee had to tackle. I do not propose to enter into the innumerable difficulties

[1] It has been estimated that up to the middle of 1948 about 5½ million non-Muslims were brought across the border from West Punjab and other provinces of Western Pakistan. About the same number of Muslims moved into Pakistan from East Punjab (including the East Punjab States), Delhi, the United Provinces, Ajmer-Merwara, Alwar, Bharatpur, Gwalior and Indore. During the same period about 1¼ million non-Muslims crossed the border from Eastern Pakistan into West Bengal. These figures do not of course take into account about 400,000 non-Muslims who later migrated to India from Sind. There is today hardly a Hindu or a Sikh to be found in Western Pakistan.

that confronted the Committee, or attempt to describe how they were tackled and solved. I will only say that the task was of truly Himalayan proportions and that it seemed to me, at the start, to be beyond our capacity and resources. The enormous nature of the task can be gauged by the fact that within a period of three months the Government had managed to evacuate nearly 4,500,000 refugees across the borders. Arrangements had to be made for the reception of the non-Muslim refugees from Pakistan in specially improvised refugee camps; for their food, shelter and other amenities, and for their eventual dispersal and resettlement in various States, a particular problem being the resettlement of refugees from the urban areas. And all these refugees had to be resettled within a reasonably quick time, otherwise they were likely to be a source of continuing trouble to the Government. Simultaneously, the Muslim refugees — those who were desirous of going to Pakistan — had to be assembled in camps and arrangements made for their safe transit across the border. Convoys, generally several thousand strong, were moved across from each side under military escort, each Government being responsible for the welfare and safety of all refugees while in their respective territories. Special trains were also requisitioned for the purpose. There were some deplorable incidents, at least in the initial stages, when trains and convoys were attacked. I recall a particular occasion when, at Amritsar, Sikhs refused to allow Muslim refugees from India to pass through the city on their way to the Pakistan border because of attacks which were being made on non-Muslim convoys and trains in Pakistan, accompanied by massacre and the abduction of women. If these refugees were not allowed to pass through the city, it would mean their having to make a detour round Amritsar, involving many days of delay. This was a problem that was causing considerable anxiety to General Thimayya. At the time he was in command of the military forces responsible for maintaining law and order in East Punjab, including the safe conduct of refugee convoys to and from Pakistan. Vallabhbhai Patel made up his mind to go to Amritsar and I accompanied him. There a conference was convened of all the Sikh leaders including the Maharajah of Patiala. To understand the attitude of this 'over-blamed people', one must appreciate the fact that the Sikhs had been driven out of their homes, contrary to all their hopes and expectations; that they had been deprived of their lands and property, their shrines and holy places; that their losses in men and property had been comparatively greater than those of any other community affected by the communal upheaval; that nearly forty per cent of the entire Sikh community had been reduced to penury and had become refugees, with the necessity of having to start life afresh. In their hour of tragedy and frustration Vallabhbhai Patel realized that the Sikhs could only be brought round by sympathetic understanding, and brotherly treatment. They were still well-fitted to play a very big part in the development and security of the country. He handled the situation at Amritsar with admirable tact and understanding and persuaded the Sikh leaders to allow the Muslim refugees to proceed through the city without molestation or hindrance. That same evening he addressed a public meeting. In the vast gathering I could distinguish none but Sikhs. He spoke to them for more than an hour. The crowd was at first very sullen, but in the end, by his forthright approach and sincerity, he was able to win them over.

In East Punjab the administration, as I have already said, had virtually broken down. C. M. Trivedi, the Governor, had decided to make his Government's headquarters—at least temporarily—at Jullundur. He set to work with a small nucleus staff, and the rest of the Government secretariat was located in various places in East Punjab, wherever accommodation was available. His first task was to protect the Muslims in East Punjab and to give them safety in the refugee camps till they could be repatriated to Pakistan. The other problem was to look after the refugees pouring in from West Punjab, most of whom naturally preferred to strike root in East Punjab and the Punjab States. The food position was far from satisfactory and, as a result of partition, the administrative personnel at his disposal was extremely inadequate. Trivedi and his Government were given all the help which the Government of India could give, but the magnitude of the task that confronted him will probably never be realized. That he was able to solve all his manifold problems so quickly and efficiently was indeed due to his great administrative capacity. In this task he had the confidence and support of his ministers, particularly that of the Premier, Gopichand Bhargava, and the Home Minister, Swaran Singh.

The main flood of the two-way exodus had spent itself by the close of December and thereafter the situation in the country was sufficiently under control to enable the central Government and the provincial Governments concerned to give their attention more fully to the problem of refugee rehabilitation. A ministry was specially created for the purpose at the Centre, while corresponding organizations were set up in East Punjab and elsewhere. The responsibilities of the Central Emergency Committee gradually devolved on these new organizations and in due course the Committee came to an end.

It is gratifying to note that while the north was in the throes of a communal holocaust, the rest of India remained comparatively peaceful. In Bengal, particularly in Calcutta, the situation might have become serious but for one man, and that man was Gandhiji. Though the Hindus and Muslims of the province had fraternized on 15 August, a couple of weeks later news of the atrocities in the north brought about a threatening recrudescence of communal trouble. Gandhiji immediately began a fast 'to end only if and when sanity returns to Calcutta.' The entire police force of north Calcutta undertook a 24 hour fast in sympathy, while continuing on duty. Within four days there was complete peace. After one of Gandhiji's prayer meetings on the Calcutta maidan, thousands of Hindus and Muslims mingled and embraced one another. No word of Government could have given so much confidence and assurance as this one man alone had inspired in the minorities on either side. Perhaps the best description of Gandhiji's part in maintaining communal peace in Bengal was made by Lord Mountbatten when, in a broadcast, he referred to Gandhiji as 'the one-man boundary force who kept the peace while a 50,000 strong force was swamped by riots.'

The communal holocaust, the two-way exodus of refugees, their protection and the rehabilitation of those who had come to India—all these provided the Government of India, at a time when the administrative machinery was already out of joint as a result of partition, with a task which was as stupendous as any nation ever had to face. If in its initial stages the situation had not been controlled with determination and vigour, the consequences would have brought down the Government itself. It is to the eternal credit of Lord Mountbatten that he agreed to take over the helm of responsibility at that critical stage, and it redounds to the statesmanship of Nehru and Patel that they unhesitatingly and confidently offered it to him.

There are critics who argue that if the transfer of power had taken place in June 1948, as originally planned, instead of in August 1947, the bloodshed that followed immediately after the partition could have been avoided. It is easy to be wise after the event. When in July 1947 the communal situation looked like getting out of hand, Lord Mountbatten took the precaution of getting assurances from the Congress, as well as from the Muslim League, that the minorities would be protected in their respective Dominions. These assurances were repeated by Nehru as well as by Jinnah on the day the respective Dominions were established. Had both the Dominions stood firmly by their pledges, would it have made any difference whether the transfer of power took place in August 1947 or in June 1948; and if it were not the purpose and policy of one or other of the Dominions to adhere to its pledge, could not the catastrophe that occurred immediately after August 1947 have happened equally in June 1948?

Then again, it has been said that if a planned exchange of population had been arranged before the transfer of power, the communal holocaust would have been avoided. But could there be any question of an exchange of population between two sides which had agreed and publicly announced that they would retain their respective minorities? Indeed, the Congress was definitely against any exchange of population. The Sikhs and Hindus would never have entertained the idea of leaving their homes in West Punjab. Nor, for obvious reasons, could the British Government have enforced it. The question of an exchange of population could only have been raised, if at all, after the two Dominions had come into being. But no sooner had the Dominions been established than communal frenzy broke out, resulting in the disastrous consequences already described.

The communal exodus from East Bengal in the early stages after partition was but a trickle. It assumed critical proportions much later, and then the Hindus from East Bengal also had to undergo severe hardships and privation. In fact, it was when the West Pakistan officials had established themselves in East Bengal that the exodus of Hindus began in earnest. It has always been my belief that the East Bengal Muslims, if left to themselves, would have been content to live with their Hindu brethren as one family, and that it was the policy of the West Pakistan officials that was responsible for the mass exodus of Hindus from East Bengal. The flood of refugees has already severely strained the resources of the West Bengal Government, while more and more continue to come across the border. If this influx is not stopped and mutual goodwill and understanding are not established, this issue is bound to overshadow any other that faces the Indian and Pakistan Governments.

# XX

## CONCLUSION

DESTINY seems to have linked the course of Indo-British relations with the month of August. It was in August 1765 that Emperor Shah Alam II formally granted the *Dewani* of Bengal, Bihar and Orissa to the East India Company. In August 1858 was passed the 'Act for the Better Government of India', when British India was placed under the direct government of the Crown. August 1917 will be remembered for its famous announcement, when the British Government for the first time declared the goal of their policy in India to be responsible government. It was in August 1947 that the British handed over power and left the country. The manner both of their coming and of their going was unique. They came to trade, but stayed to rule. They left of their own will; there was no war, there was no treaty — an act with no parallel in history.

The main factor responsible for the early transfer of power was the return of the Labour Party with an absolute majority in 1945. Almost the first thing they did on assuming office was to set about finding a solution of the Indian problem, a solution that would be acceptable to the two main political parties in the country, namely the Congress and the Muslim League. When they found that the parties were unable to come to any agreement, they themselves produced a plan. This was the Cabinet Mission plan, to which the Congress and the Muslim League at first reacted favourably, but on which subsequently they disagreed fundamentally on points of interpretation. The Labour Government then tried the expedient of bringing the leaders of the two parties inside an interim Government, in the hope that by working together they might come to an understanding on the long-term plan. But now the position became much worse; in coming into a common Government the leaders merely brought their outside differences inside the Cabinet. The Government of India was a house divided against itself, and the communal situation, instead of getting better, deteriorated to a state bordering on civil war. The Labour Government decided that the only way to redeem their pledge, while making the leaders face the grave realities of the situation, was to announce that the British would hand over power and would quit India by a definite date. The Labour Government's action was described in Parliament as a gamble and a betrayal. But let me quote the words of Sir Austen Chamberlain on another famous occasion:

Now and again in the affairs of men there comes a moment when courage is safer than prudence, when some great act of faith, touching the hearts and stirring the emotions of men, achieves a miracle that no art of statesmanship can compass.

The British Government's decision to quit India not only touched the hearts and stirred the emotions of Indians; it produced an immediate reassuring effect on the whole of South-East Asia and earned for Britain, as at no other time, universal respect and goodwill.

Though through the centuries many attempts had been made to bring India under one central Government, it was the proud claim of the British that it was they who for the first time created an Indian Empire, extending from Kashmir in the north to Cape Comorin in the south, and from Baluchistan in the west to Assam in the east. It is a sad reflection that the British who achieved that unity could not bequeath it to their successors. But sadder still is the thought that Jinnah, the hero of my generation, a great nationalist in his time and one who fought many a battle for the freedom of his country, should later have fought so successfully against its freedom, and should eventually, almost single-handed, have brought about its division.

I have indicated how Jinnah took over the Muslim League, which was then moribund, and in a few years made it the most powerful Muslim organization. When the Congress ministries resigned from the provinces and withdrew their support from the war effort, Lord Linlithgow inevitably leaned upon the Muslims. The League grew rapidly in the sunshine of favour. It consolidated its position and soon reached the stage of asserting that the Muslims were a nation and demanding separation from the rest of India of all the provinces in which they were a majority. It was at this stage that the British Government, in their declaration of 1942, gave the right to the provinces to accede or not to accede to the Union and even to form a separate Union or Unions. This was a radical departure from the policy hitherto adopted. In the discussions leading up to the passing of the Government of India Act of 1935, it had never been contemplated that the accession of the British-Indian provinces to the Federation should be optional.

This was really the death-blow to Indian unity, and subsequent assertions of their preference for a united India by British authorities carried no weight. It was definitely a victory for Jinnah. Hereafter he could afford to stand on this declaration. When it was made in 1942, the Pakistan resolution was only two years old, and the League position, even in the Muslim-majority areas, was none too strong. But in spite of that, His Majesty's Government conceded the substance of Jinnah's demand; and this attitude persisted in all the subsequent negotiations.

When, in 1942, Sir Stafford Cripps announced His Majesty's Government's policy, the opinion was widely expressed that the British were bent upon the division of the country; that they wanted to create a Middle Eastern sphere of influence, and in pursuance of that policy wished to bring about the creation of a separate Pakistan. This would accord with their traditional liking for Muslims, with their policy of protecting the Straits and the Suez Canal from Russian influence, and with their new but overwhelming interest in the oil of Iran, Iraq and Arabia.

On the other hand, by surrendering its position of vantage and resigning its ministries in eight provinces out of the eleven, the Congress left the field entirely to the Muslim League and to the Government. If it had not resigned, it could have insisted on and got an immediate change at the Centre, especially after Japan joined the war. His Majesty's Government would not have taken the drastic step of dismissing the Congress ministries from office. Moreover, the Congress opposition to the war effort and the League's *de facto* support for it convinced the British that the Hindus generally were their enemies and the Muslims their friends, and this consideration must have added force to the silent but effective official support for the policy of partition.

Gandhiji's original instinct was sound. He stood for unconditional co-operation in the war. He was not supported by his own party, and Government was unhelpful in meeting his immediate demands. Eventually, when he found no way out and Jinnah's demand grew insistent, Gandhiji conceded self-determination for Muslim-majority areas, insisting only that there should be a central authority for the administration of certain essential subjects common to both the States. But Jinnah rejected this proposal.

When the Cabinet Mission arrived in 1946 they were thus confronted with the League's demand for a province-wise Pakistan and the Congress refusal to concede any more than a truncated Pakistan consisting merely of Muslim-majority areas.

The Cabinet Mission attempted to preserve a united India. But it was no more than a facade of unity. If their plan had worked, it would have resulted in the Muslim League securing, in substance, a province-wise Pakistan. In any case, the three-tier constitution was so unwieldy and carried with it so much potentiality for friction that it could never have been worked. Moreover, the whole structure was vitiated by an inherent instability, in that any provincial Assembly could call for a reconsideration of the terms of the constitution 'after an initial period of ten years and at ten yearly intervals thereafter.'

When the Labour Government found that no agreement between the parties was possible, either in the working of the interim Government or of the Constituent Assembly, on the basis of the Cabinet Mission plan, it made the bold decision that the British would quit India by a specified date. The League by this time had raised communal consciousness to such a pitch that a united India by peaceful agreement was no longer possible. The Muslim masses were behind the League; in fact, they supported the League more solidly where they were in a minority than in the Muslim-majority provinces. Even the safeguards and protection demanded for their community by the Nationalist Muslims went so far that, if acceded to, they would have prevented for all time the growth of a united nation.

In India, the province which more than any other held the key to the problem of partition was the Punjab. Official opinion in the province was divided, but Sir Bertrand Glancy, who was the Governor of the province up to 1946, was a strong advocate of a united Punjab; and his successor, Sir Evan Jenkins, who was Governor at the time of the partition, was no less so. If anyone knew the Punjab, it was surely Sir Evan Jenkins. Moreover, not all the Muslim leaders were for partition. Khizr Hyat Khan, the premier of the Punjab and leader of the Unionist Party, put up a fight in the earlier stages, but succumbed to pressure later. It has been alleged that, while he had ample resources to fight the election in 1946, he failed to use them. It is possible that if he had been given sufficient official encouragement, he would have fought against the disintegration of the province.

But when, owing to his resignation, the Unionist Party was dissolved, the fate of the Punjab was sealed.

When Lord Mountbatten arrived on the scene, he soon realised that the Cabinet Mission plan was unacceptable to the parties, and some form of partition was inevitable. He prepared a plan, the basis of which was demission of power to the provinces, or to such confederations as the provinces might decide to form before the transfer of power. The responsibility for partition was left to the popular choice. When this plan was shown to Nehru he reacted strongly against it. Thereupon Lord Mountbatten fell back on the alternative plan of two Dominions, of which Pakistan would comprise the Muslim-majority areas only. The Congress agreed to this, and by accepting Dominion Status removed one of the great obstacles which had hitherto stood between them and the British. Thereafter the League was no longer able to derive advantage from the fact that it had agreed to remain within the Commonwealth while the Congress claimed complete independence. Thenceforth things moved smoothly, and in every step that Lord Mountbatten took he carried the support of the party leaders.

The Congress had accepted the division of the country on two considerations. In the first place, it was clear from the unyielding attitude of the Muslim League that a united India would either be delayed or could only be won at the cost of a civil war. Secondly, it was hoped that the establishment of a separate Muslim State would finally settle the communal problem which had for so long bedevilled Indian politics and thwarted all progressive aspirations, that India and Pakistan would thereafter live in peaceful relations with each other, and that all men of goodwill on either side would be free to concentrate on improving the economic conditions of the common people.

India's disillusionment came as a startling blow almost immediately after the partition. Those who had the welfare of both Dominions at heart, who were earnestly desirous that they should live as good neighbours, viewed the trend of events with grave concern. My personal feelings at this stage can best be recalled by the following excerpts from an article which I contributed to the *Statesman* of 21 October 1947:

Hardly had the two Dominions been ushered into separate existence when mass migrations of the minority populations from both sides began. . . .

At present less than half the total number of the people to be moved have crossed the frontier, but those concerned have so utterly lost confidence in their respective Governments that it is doubtful whether the process will come to an end until practically all the non-Muslims from Western Pakistan have crossed into India, and similarly practically all the Muslims in East Punjab have crossed into Pakistan.

The result will be that Western Pakistan will be left as a purely Muslim State, while India will still contain large numbers of Muslims.

The consequences of this require serious consideration. Throughout the centuries India has been subjected to repeated invasions from the North-West, and the popular mind is particularly sensitive to a Muslim Power (the biggest in the world) commanding the country's historically dangerous frontier. Add to this the bitterness of the present persecutions and migrations, which will take generations to wipe out, and we have a potentially dangerous situation.

Another factor contributing to the insecurity is Pakistan's expansionist policy in the matter of the States' accession. Pakistan was established as a State in which Muslims would be enabled to find scope for self-development; but the Dominion has sought to rope in States peopled predominantly by non-Muslims, even if situated far from the territories of Pakistan.

It was not without reason that the late President Roosevelt gave to *freedom from fear* pride of place among his Four Freedoms. A sense of security is the primary essential before progress. Public opinion in India will therefore insist upon adequate military precautions on the frontiers of India, and no responsible statesman will be able to ignore the demand. This will naturally lead to counter-preparations on the Pakistan side....

This is a danger which must be averted. Mahatma Gandhi has been insisting that freedom would lose its significance if the lot of the common man were not improved. Similarly, the agitation for Pakistan was based upon the need for the Muslims to build up their life in their own way. Neither object can be achieved if the two States' resources are frittered away in futile military preparations. It is imperative that a way be found for building up a basis of security for both.

In essential respects their interests are bound up with each other.... Why then should not both recognise this, and join up formally in mutual union for the three essential subjects of defence and foreign affairs (mutually dependent), and communications upon which defence depends? In this lies salvation.

Pakistan may be loath to surrender the sentimental satisfaction of a separate national State for the Muslims. But a union at the top for these three subjects would not affect the separate existence of the two States for other matters. Muslims would still have their separate homelands, with complete control in essential economic matters. They would remain free to develop Muslim traditions and political institutions on their own lines, unhampered by outside interference....

A week after this article was written the tribal invasion of Kashmir began. Thereafter, events gravely affecting the relations between the two countries followed one another in quick succession. The result was further bitterness and estrangement.

Pakistan today is an Islamic State. There is no minority problem in West Pakistan, while East Pakistan is being steadily drained of its Hindus. India on the other hand still has a population of about forty million Muslims, besides other minorities, to protect and care for. Gandhiji particularly emphasized that the minorities were a sacred trust in the hands of the majority. It was a cause most dear to his heart. He lived for it — indeed he eventually died for it! India will surely be true to his precepts. I have no doubt that, despite the heavy strain which the policy of Pakistan imposes on the Government of India, the latter will steadfastly maintain and fulfil its great ideal of a truly secular State.

That the future of the two countries depends upon mutual good relations is almost a truism. The partition of August 1947 was surely not intended to sunder for all time the ties that for a century and a half have bound India together as one administrative, political and economic unit. Geographically and economically at least, those ties persist in spite of the partition and the serious effect which its aftermath has had upon the economy of the Punjab and Bengal. The prosperity of the Punjab was due to the sweat and toil of irrigation engineers. There is no reason why East and West Punjab should not continue to enjoy the fruits of those labours by mutual give and take. Similarly, the economy of West Bengal is inextricably tied up with that of East Bengal, and vice versa. Neither side can afford to ignore the circumstances of geography and the economic interests which draw them together. Economically it is the common man who must suffer, but the suffering of the common man can surely be assuaged on both sides by the healing touch of good neighbourliness. It is never too late for men of goodwill to take stock of realities, for the leaders to sit down calmly and dispassionately, and together evolve some common machinery which would not merely minimize the rigours of partition but, by banishing all sense of fear and conflict, would bring about for both countries enduring peace and progress.

# APPENDIX I

*Demands For Grants*

GENERAL ADMINISTRATION

*Communal Harmony*

*Premier (Sir Sikander Hyat Khan)*:... My honourable friend then went on and asked what was the Prime Minister's view about Pakistan. He repeated that question several times and other members of the opposition who followed him also repeated it. My honourable friend, I take it, put that question to me in my personal capacity and not as a member of the Government. Obviously he is only anxious to ascertain my personal views on the subject; and in any case Government as such is not concerned with this controversy. I propose, therefore, to answer his question in my individual capacity and not as Premier. But before answering his question I should like to put him a question to make sure that he understands his own question (*laughter*). May I ask on which particular Pakistan scheme he wants my opinion? Does he even know how many schemes there are?

*Sardar Ajit Singh*: The one that you framed.

*Premier*: I did not frame any Pakistan scheme. My honourable friend should not be impatient. I will presently give him the genesis of the various schemes. He will then know what colossal ignorance prevails about these schemes and will be sorry for his interruption. Now, which Pakistan scheme has my friend in mind? There is in the first place the Pakistan scheme of Maulana Jamal-ud-Din Afghani. Has he studied it? Does he want my views on it?

*Sardar Lal Singh*: We want to know the views of the Premier about the one passed at Lahore.

*Premier*: No Pakistan scheme was passed at Lahore. But I will deal with the Lahore resolution also, to which he is apparently referring, in due course. As for Pakistan schemes, Maulana Jamal-ud-Din's is the earliest, but he does not want my views on that. Then there is the scheme which is attributed to the late Allama Iqbal of revered memory. He, however, never formulated any definite scheme, but his writings and poems have given some people ground to think that Allama Iqbal desired the establishment of some sort of Pakistan. But it is not difficult to explode this theory and to prove conclusively that his conception of Islamic solidarity and universal brotherhood is not in conflict with Indian patriotism and is in fact quite different from the ideology now sought to be attributed to him by some enthusiasts. I presume that my honourable friend opposite does not want my views on the non-existent scheme attributed to the great poet-philosopher of the East, Dr. Iqbal.

Then there is Chaudhri Rahmat Ali's scheme (*laughter*). Does he want my opinion about that? This is how Mr. Rahmat Ali produced his Pakistan. P for Punjab, A for Afghanistan including Pathanistan, i.e., the North-West Frontier Province, K for Kashmir, S for Sind and the last three letters 'tan' of Baluchistan. I am not sure if Iran is also included. This is Chaudhri Rahmat Ali's scheme. He put forward this scheme a few years ago, and it was widely circulated in this country and also published in the press. It was also given wide publicity at the time in a section of the British press. But there is another scheme also which my honourable friend has probably never heard of; it was published in one of the British journals — I think the *Round Table* — and was conceived by an Englishman. Does he want my opinion about that scheme? (*S. Ajit Singh*: No!) Then my honourable friend probably wants my opinion on some Pakistan scheme which does not exist outside his imagination.

I will now try to satisfy the curiosity of my hon'ble friend Sardar Lal Singh by dealing with the Lahore resolution, which is now popularly known as the Pakistan scheme. When that resolution was passed it was termed the Lahore resolution; the word Pakistan was not used at the League meeting and this term was not applied to the League resolution by anybody until the Hindu press had a brain-wave and dubbed it Pakistan. They have sown the wind and must now reap the whirlwind.

It has been said that I am the author of the Lahore resolution. I have no hesitation in admitting that I was responsible for drafting the original resolution. But let me make it clear that the resolution which I drafted was radically amended by the Working Committee, and there is a wide divergence in the resolution I drafted and the one that was finally passed. The main difference between the two resolutions is that the latter part of my resolution which related to the centre and co-ordination of the activities of the various units, was eliminated. It is, therefore, a travesty of fact to describe the League resolution as it was finally passed as my resolution. It must be taken as the official resolution of the Muslim League which was ratified by the Muslim League.

My hon'ble friends can call it Pakistan or by whatever name they like. They dubbed it Pakistan, and it is now popularly known as Pakistan. The ignorant masses have now adopted the slogan provided by the short-sighted bigotry of the Hindu and Sikh press. If I may venture a word of protest and advice, I consider it a fatal mistake on the part of the Hindus and Sikhs to raise this hare. They probably wanted to create an atmosphere among the Hindu and Sikh masses against the resolution. That was their object and I think they have succeeded to some extent, but they overlooked the fact that the word Pakistan might have an appeal — a strong appeal — for the Muslim masses. It is a catching phrase and it has caught popular imagination and has thus made confusion worse confounded. The unsophisticated masses are incapable of distinguishing between the various schemes, and I am almost certain that the average Muslim himself does not realise the implications of Pakistan or even know which particular scheme he is supporting. The result is that political adventurers have been provided with vast opportunities of exploiting the ignorant, each according to his own inclinations and convenience. Some preach Maulana Iqbal's version of Pakistan, others Maulana Jamal-ud-Din's; and I noticed that a leading Muslim daily of Lahore in its Pakistan number started with Maulana Jamal-ud-Din's scheme, and then drifted into a rambling discourse on the Lahore resolution of the League — a confused hotch-potch of ideas picked up from here and there.

A vast majority of educated Muslims, however, do not believe in any of these schemes. Take the President of the League himself. He is not a believer in any extra-territorial scheme. He stands by the Lahore resolution to which our Hindu friends have given the name of Pakistan. Mr. Jinnah naturally, like everybody else, sees the advantage in adopting a catch-phrase which appeals to the masses. If the Hindus and Sikhs can exploit it why not the Muslim League? The Muslims like it; so it is a convenient slogan to sway the Muslim masses. The Hindus and Sikhs started the cry of Pakistan and now the Muslims have taken it up. Both sides are now responsible for popularising the Pakistan bogey which did not exist until it was created by the opponents of the League and is now being utilised by both to exploit the masses. I personally think that it is largely due to this fact that the proposals, which should have been considered on their merits, are being opposed or supported merely on the basis of the word 'Pakistan'. As I have already said, it is a great mistake to give the Lahore resolution a name, which from the Hindu and Sikh points of view is provocative, and is undesirable even from the Muslim point of view, as it has already created a great deal of confusion among the Muslims.

*Dr. Shaikh Muhammad Alam:* There was also one scheme of Bhai Parmanand.

*Premier:* Yes, that is so. However, we need not worry about nomenclatures. It is the substance which matters. My honourable friends have asked me to state my position regarding the future destiny of India. I will do so with pleasure but in my individual capacity. My views are well known to my honourable friends in this House and they are known to the people outside, and also to the political leaders. Since my honourable friends opposite want me to reiterate them, I will repeat them for their benefit. This is what I visualise regarding the future status and constitution of my country. As I have repeatedly declared, it is my fixed conviction that the future destiny of India lies in accepting a position of freedom within the British Commonwealth. I have repeatedly said so, and my reasons are that at the present moment, when powerful nations are trying to make fresh alliances to save themselves from extinction it would be criminal folly on the part of India to cut adrift from the British Commonwealth, which is the main and perhaps the only safeguard against aggression so far as we are concerned. But for the British Navy which is defending the vital sea route to India, we would be at the mercy of that powerful enemy in the East who is looking for an opportunity to extend his domain westwards. Without the Singapore base and the invincible Navy, which is stationed there to protect us, Burma and India would have been attacked in the early stages of the war. Again, is it not the British Navy and the Imperial Forces, including our own, which are protecting us on our western frontier? We are not out of danger yet. We are still in danger, and I repeat that it is a real danger. Can any sane person believe that we can become an independent nation, or retain our independence when we secure it, by a mere declaration that we are independent? I make bold to say that there can be only one answer to that question — an emphatic 'No!' We are not in a position at present to defend ourselves or our country single-handed. We need protection and that protection we can get only from that powerful comity of nations known as the British Commonwealth. That is my view. Of course, if my honourable friends opposite feel that they can derive satisfaction from slogans, however unreal and fallacious they may be, or by shutting their eyes to obvious facts, they can please themselves. If they wish to live in a fool's paradise they can do so, but that will not bring them or India any nearer to the goal we have in view. We must look at the problem as practical men and face facts. Now let us put aside for the moment sentimental considerations and examine the position from a purely practical, or if you prefer, a mundane, materialistic point of view. Within the British Commonwealth the component units have certain privileges as also certain obligations. Hitherto India has been a dependent dominion; and while we have been fulfilling our obligations we have not so far been granted the privileges which are enjoyed by the other Dominions. We have been fighting along with the British and Imperial troops in every theatre of war. And what have we got in return? Nothing so far. We want freedom for our country, freedom in the sense that we shall have full control of our own affairs, as an equal and autonomous unit within the British Commonwealth.

We have hitherto been denied some of the coveted privileges which the other partners enjoy although we have unhesitatingly fulfilled our obligations. Now the time has come when we shall ask for the extension of those privileges to us on the same footing as the other free dominions. One of the privileges for which I will ask is that the other partners should extend to me unstinted support and assistance against aggression, just as I have given them unconditional and wholehearted support in the last war and during the present war. I want that assurance because we are not at present strong enough to ward off aggression without the help of our co-partners in the Commonwealth. I can legitimately ask for that assurance because as a member of the Commonwealth it is my privilege to requisition their help until I become strong enough to defend my country without their assistance. After the war we will ask the British Government and the British people to make India a full-fledged member of the British Commonwealth, and we would also stipulate that they must, as a matter of duty and honour, protect us from foreign aggression until we are strong enough to stand on our own feet. So apart from other considerations, from the point of view of the safety and integrity of India alone it would be criminal folly even to think of severing our connection with the British Commonwealth. That is my position with regard to the future status of India after the war.

As for the principles on which the new constitution should be based, there again my views are well known. I believe and, in spite of the various developments which have taken place since my scheme was originally published, I adhere to my belief that my proposals provide an equitable basis and perhaps the only basis for the solution of the constitutional problem. Under my scheme every unit will enjoy complete autonomy in its internal affairs. It is fortunate that the population of India is so distributed in the various units that in four out of the eleven British Indian Provinces Muslims are in the majority — though in two of these they have just a bare majority — while in the remaining seven provinces Hindus are in the majority. If any of my honourable friends considers that this natural distribution of the population is a misfortune, then I can only say that he is a short-sighted bigot. I repeat that it is our good fortune that Providence has so distributed the population that it provides the fullest opportunity and scope to the two major communities, within their respective territorial spheres, to exercise and enjoy rights of a majority, subject, of course, to the rights and privileges of the minorities. If we accept this principle, which to my mind is a rational principle, then all those difficulties which are of our own making, and which obstruct our constitutional progress, will disappear as if by a magic wand.

As I understand it, what the Muslims desire is that where they are in a majority they should not be thwarted by anybody in the exercise of their inherent rights as a majority when they are prepared to give constitutional guarantees to the minorities for the protection of their rights and interests in the Muslim-majority provinces. At the same time they are willing to concede — and they cannot reasonably deny to the Hindus what they claim for themselves as a just right — the same rights and privileges to the Hindus in the provinces in which they happen to be the majority community. Surely that is not an unfair proposition. Since the Hindus will benefit from this proposal in seven out of eleven provinces, why should they grudge the same facilities and privileges to the Muslim in the four Muslim-majority provinces? I am sure that if the problem is examined dispassionately, in the light of the observations I have made, nobody with any sense of justice and fairplay will deny that the solution I have suggested will secure for all concerned their due rights and share in the administrative, political and economic spheres without trenching on the legitimate rights of the majority, be it a Hindu or a Muslim majority.

Moreover, the Muslims fear that if the provinces are not free and autonomous, there will always be a danger of undue and unwarranted interference from the Centre, which will be dominated by Hindus. They argue that so far as the seven Hindu-majority provinces are concerned, they will be 'on velvet' the whole time because they will have a Hindu government in the provinces and Hindu majority at the centre. It is conceivable, they say, that a central government with a Hindu majority would use its authority and influence to strengthen the position of Hindu provinces in the political, economic, social and cultural fields at the expense of the Muslim-majority provinces on the one hand, while on the other they would try to undermine the authority and position of the latter by unnecessary interference and unjust restrictions and obstruction. These doubts and misgivings may be unfounded. The mutual mistrust, which holds the field, is unfortunate and tragic, but the fact remains that the suspicion and mistrust does exist and I do not see how it is to be removed except by some such device as I have suggested. In their present mood neither of the major parties seems capable of examining any scheme or proposal on its merits from howsoever unimpeachable a source it may emanate. The result is that we are sinking deeper and deeper into the political quagmire. It is time that we made an effort to end this stalemate. This is possible only if we make up our minds to face facts and to look at the problem from a realistic point of view like practical men, like men of honour. If we genuinely desire a solution we must make an approach with a broadminded and just outlook and not from a narrow selfish point of view. By all means let us safeguard our legitimate rights and interests, but that does not mean that we should try to thwart others when they evince a similar desire to protect their rights and interests. After all, if we want freedom for all, why should we try to thwart others? Why should we adopt tortuous and dubious methods to frustrate the reasonable claims and legitimate demands of the various communities or classes, and why should we by such dishonourable methods try to hoodwink the masses and to throw dust in their eyes? To put it mildly, such tactics are most dishonest and are most unjust and unfair to our province, our motherland (*applause*).

The facts are that in seven provinces Hindus are in a majority. In those provinces let Muslims accept that majority and co-operate with them. In four provinces the Muslims are in a majority. In these provinces Hindus and Sikhs should accept that position and co-operate as honourable partners. After all, we have to live together — as we have been living together for the last thousand years or more — and no one can convert a majority into a minority or vice versa by squabbling among ourselves. Let us accept the position as we find it and willingly come to an understanding without grudging the majority its rightful share, whether it be a Hindu majority or Muslim. That is a simple and straightforward method of composing our differences, and once we accept this principle as a basis for settlement it should be a simple matter to settle the details. At the moment the issues are confused because we do not approach the problem in an honest and straightforward manner. We look at it either through communal glasses or through sectional glasses; or else with the object of thwarting the other party by raising false issues and dishonest slogans, such as religion in danger, Khalsa raj, Hindu raj and Muslim raj. Such tactics, apart from misleading the ignorant masses and thus creating bitterness, take us further away from our goal. If we make up our minds to view the problem from a common angle and from the point of view of India as a whole, and at the same time concede to every unit the right to manage its own affairs with common and reciprocal safeguards for the minorities, I think all our difficulties and doubts will disappear and we will then be able to look forward to a bright future, for which every patriotic Indian is yearning.

You may well ask how do I propose to keep the units together, and what would happen if there is no central authority and all the provinces and States are free. I have explained that Muslims are opposed to an all-powerful centre because they are afraid that a communal oligarchy in power might undermine or altogether nullify the autonomy and freedom of the provinces. That is the suspicion that haunts them. It may not be well-founded, but there it is; and we must face facts. Now, how can we remove their doubts and misgivings? How best can we meet their objection? Here is my recipe for what it is worth; I say, give complete autonomy and freedom to the units, and let them be demarcated into regions or zones on a territorial basis. Representatives of the units within each zone should represent their respective units as also the region at the centre. The centre thus constituted will not be a domineering, hostile centre looking for opportunities to interfere with the work of provincial governments, but a sympathetic agency enjoying the confidence and support of the provinces — a body set up by the units to control and supervise the central administrative machinery and to see that the work entrusted to it by the provinces is carried on efficiently, amicably and justly. You can call it the central government or a co-ordination committee, or call it by any other name you like. But as I have said, if you face the facts squarely and examine the problem dispassionately, you cannot but come to the same conclusion as myself, that a centre agreed to by the various interests of their own free will would be a much stronger centre than one arbitrarily superimposed and composed of individuals elected independently of the provincial legislatures or governments. The latter type will not work smoothly or even justly for the simple reason that there will be a perpetual tug-of-war between the centre and the units. At any rate two-thirds of India, including Rajasthan will not find it easy to accept a centre which, for reasons mentioned by me, does not enjoy their confidence or willing co-operation. Would a centre set up with the consent of the units and enjoying their confidence be stronger and more powerful, or one that is imposed on them without their consent and which does not represent the provincial assemblies or governments? Of course, the former. I beg to submit that my proposals will not only secure freedom and autonomy to the provinces but will also consolidate the country on a basis of mutual confidence and goodwill, which will enormously add to the strength of India as a whole. Once the idea of domination and interference is abandoned the problem becomes quite simple. Then Muslims would not be justified in asking for a complete severance from the rest of India. I am sure they will not. If they still persist, then I think that they would be worthy of being sent to a lunatic asylum. All they can reasonably ask for is that there shall not be a domineering centre which may undermine their power and authority in the Muslim-majority provinces.

Some of my honourable friends over there, or on this side of the House, might consider that if power to administer important subjects is delegated to the centre, it may tempt them to bully the provinces. My answer is 'No!' It will not be a rigid  centre, and it will consist of representatives of the units selected by the provincial legislatures or governments responsible to the people of the province. The centre will be elastic in the sense that except for subjects entrusted to it by prior agreement, e.g. defence, maritime customs, currency and coinage and external affairs, only such other matters or powers will be delegated to the centre as the units may by agreement decide to transfer, and for such period as may be specified in the instrument of delegation. As regards actual administration of these subjects, they can be administered by committees on which every region must be represented, or in the alternative by a representative executive. Again, the decisions need not be on a bare majority basis. Once the basic issues are settled it should not be difficult to devise means whereby an adequate and effective voice is assured to the representatives of every region, and the danger of

any section being overwhelmed by a sheer communal majority is completely eliminated. You can lay down a two-thirds or even a three-fourths majority for any administrative act to be effective. I am merely giving you an
idea; it will be for the experts to devise a suitable scheme. My point is that
once there is agreement on the basic principles, it should not be difficult
to secure agreement in matters of detail. For instance, it should be possible
to lay down in the constitution that the central machinery will not be rigid
but capable of modification by agreement among the parties concerned.
Again, it might be advisable to make a provision which would enable a
region — provided a specified number of units demand it — to secede within
a prescribed period of say 10, 15 or 25 years. This may be necessary in
order to satisfy the units that, if in spite of the safeguards in the constitution, it is found that their rights are not adequately secure, they will have
an opportunity to reconsider their position. If the units or a region find
that they do not get a fair deal at the centre they should have the right to
transfer their constitutional relationship from the centre direct to the Crown
— but only after a fair and honest trial. There will then be justification for
doing so. Now, before that contingency has arisen, it is not reasonable to
ask for it. Indeed, the remedy suggested is worse than the disease, and instead of doing good it would do considerable harm to the units as also to
the interests of the country as a whole.

My point then is that we should try to devise an agency which would be
set up with the consent of the units and administer at the centre subjects of
common interest such as customs, currency, defence and foreign affairs.
Without some co-ordinating central agency it may be difficult to secure an
equitable distribution of financial burdens and resources. I give you an
illustration. Punjab is not a maritime province, but we pay our share of
customs duty on the goods and merchandise we import from abroad. How
are we going to realise our share of the income from this source? If we are
isolated, we cannot claim a share of receipts from maritime customs. Bombay, Karachi and Calcutta, as ports of maritime provinces, will levy and
retain the whole amount. Unless there is a central agency to collect and
distribute these dues or utilise them for some agreed common purpose, the
maritime provinces will gain at the expense of land-bound units, such as
the Punjab and the United Provinces.

Again I visualise several other difficulties in this connection. For instance, if all the numerous Indian States and provinces are isolated in water-
tight compartments, and Mr. Fazlul Huq decides to come to Lahore for
consultation with the Nawab Sahib of Mamdot in regard to certain matters relating to 'Bangsam' — I believe that is the name proposed for the
Bengal-cum-Assam combination by Chaudhri Rahmat Ali, the originator
of Neo-Pakistan — this is what would happen. He will start from Calcutta,
but as soon as he passes Asansol he will be stopped at the Bihar frontier and

asked to show his passport and get his luggage examined. The Bihar customs authorities will demand that. He will next arrive at the frontier of the United Provinces and the same process will be repeated. From there he will proceed to the borders of the Punjab, where he will be stopped again and his passport and kit will be examined. In short, he will experience the same inconvenience to which a traveller is subjected in the Balkans where after every few minutes you are stopped by the customs officials to get your luggage and passport checked (*interruptions*).

It may be argued that some system can be easily introduced, such as the European countries have amongst themselves, to arrange such matters. True, we can also make similar arrangements by treaties and covenants, but even so the customs and passport formalities and the difficulties I have enumerated will not be eliminated unless we have a common agency to deal with these subjects. You must have a central agency to control these subjects, which are of common interest to all the units, if you want to avoid unnecessary inconvenience and harassment. Similarly, with regard to customs charges, uniformity can be achieved only by setting up an agreed coordinating agency. Surely we do not want a state of affairs where each unit is free to levy at each frontier a customs duty which may vary — say from five to fifty rupees — on a particular article. This may lead to unhealthy competition and chaotic conditions. It is not inconceivable that landbound provinces might even find their trade and commerce completely paralysed.

Then, take defence — a very important and vital subject. I have dealt with customs and now I will deal with defence. A few short-sighted enthusiasts say that they will be able to look after the defence of their own bit of the country. They argue that once they are free to manage their own affairs, every unit will have an army of its own; and when they have secured their independence they will willingly undertake the responsibility of maintaining an adequate military force. In theory the proposition may appear plausible and even attractive to those reckless enthusiasts who seldom take the trouble of calculating the financial and other implications of any such undertaking. They fail to realize that a well-equipped army is an expensive affair. Assuming for a moment that the bigger units may be able to maintain some kind of troops as the Indian States do now, who will, for instance take the responsibility of defending the North-West Frontier of India? Surely you cannot expect the North-West Frontier Province to do so. It is the province which would be the first to be overrun by any invader who may come from that direction. No sane person will contend that the North-West Frontier Province can afford to provide and finance a force capable of keeping in check an army equipped with modern armaments. How can you possibly expect them to bear the burden? It is obvious, therefore, that some arrangements will have to be made either to subsidise them or set up a force on an all-India basis which will defend the country against aggressors from without — and also deal with internal aggression, if necessary — and will be paid for by the country as a whole.

How will you do it? Who will look after that force and see that it is maintained properly and efficiently, and effectively controlled? If we consider the matter dispassionately we cannot but come to the inevitable conclusion that it is essential to have some kind of central agency to deal with defence matters. We have not only to guard our north-west frontier but also our eastern frontiers in Bengal and Assam. Moreover, we have to defend our extensive coastal line running from Chittagong in the east down to Madras and Tuticorin, and from there up the Malabar coast and Bombay right up to the Persian border. Apart from large land forces we would need a powerful navy and an efficient and strong air force to protect us. And it all costs money — and for a country the size of India it would involve an expenditure of not crores but *arabs* and *kharabs*.

But let us for a moment leave aside these wider issues and examine the matter from the point of view of our own province. Punjab provides the bulk of the Indian Army — our proportion in the peace-time strength is about 52 per cent; our war-time contribution is even higher (*cheers*). Why? Because from time immemorial we have had to bear the brunt of attacks by invaders from the north-west and have long and glorious traditions as clean and stout fighters (*hear, hear*). We are the natural custodians of India and have proved our worth on the battlefields at home and abroad and have thus acquired the proud distinction and title of being known as 'the sword arm' of India (*cheers*). But that does not mean that we can on that account afford to cut adrift from the rest of India and still hope that we will be able to defend our province and our neighbours against organized aggression from outside. Apart from other considerations, we cannot afford to pay for the upkeep of even a small force, much less for a force more than half the size of the present Indian army. We want independence and freedom like everyone else, but we cannot become independent merely by declaring that we are free because we have our own army. Who will pay for that army? I am quite clear in my mind that we cannot afford it — even with the vast resources of my friend the Nawab of Mamdot, neither he nor all of us put together would be equal to the task of keeping up a modern army of any size (*laughter and hear, hear*). Can any province single-handed defend itself or bear the burden of its own defence? My answer is, no; and this is a consideration which cannot be brushed aside lightly, and would need careful examination when we sit together to settle the scope and functions of the central agency. Unless we have strong, efficient and up-to-date defence forces our independence will not be worth a day's life; let us make no mistake about it.

Next take currency. Here again, if the matter is left to the units to do as they like, we may have several hundred different currencies: there are eleven provinces and over six hundred Indian States. Just imagine what would happen if a person proceeds from Lahore to Calcutta. When he gets to Delhi he will have to change his money for Delhi money, and when he enters the United Provinces from Delhi he will have to provide himself with the currency of that province, and exchange it again on entering Bihar and then Bengal. So he will have to change his currency several times before he gets to Calcutta. But there again the matter can be easily settled if you have a uniform currency and a central agency to control it. Take again the case of a traveller from Lahore to Bombay; in addition to the British Indian provinces he will have to traverse several — more than a dozen — Indian States. In Rajputana alone there are numerous States — and my honourable friend Raja Ghazanfar Ali Khan will be able to tell you how many Indian States you have to cross on your way to Bombay as he knows that part of the country intimately. My own impression is that in Central India and Rajputana jurisdiction changes after every few miles. But this formidable problem would be automatically solved if we have a common currency controlled by an agreed central agency. Once we establish ourselves in water-tight compartments it would become exceedingly difficult, if not altogether impossible, to find an agreed solution of these difficulties. In the absence of uniform practice and procedure it might take several days instead of 36 hours to get to Bombay from Lahore, because at every provincial and State boundary customs formalities will have to be fulfilled and currency will have to be exchanged.

These matters are not so simple of adjustment as some of us might think. If you want freedom — real freedom — you will not get it by shouting slogans and catchwords. We will have to put our heads together and devise a plan which will ensure that the freedom which we ask for and obtain for ourselves must also be granted to our neighbours, our co-citizens. Every country and every unit must have the same measure of freedom as a matter of right. So far as we in the Punjab are concerned, let me assure you that we will not countenance or accept any proposal which does not secure freedom for all (*cheers*). We do not desire that Muslims should domineer here, just as we do not want the Hindus to domineer where Muslims are in a minority. Nor would we allow any body or section to thwart us because Muslims happen to be in a majority in this province. We do not ask for freedom, that there may be Muslim Raj here and Hindu Raj elsewhere. If that is what Pakistan means I will have nothing to do with it. If Pakistan means unalloyed Muslim Raj in the Punjab then I will have nothing to do with it (*hear, hear*). I have said so before and I repeat it once again here, on the floor of this House (*cheers*). If you want real freedom for the Punjab, that is to say a Punjab in which every community will have its due share in the economic and administrative fields as partners in a common concern, then that Punjab will not be Pakistan, but just *Punjab*, land of the five rivers; Punjab is Punjab and will always remain Punjab whatever anybody may say (*cheers*). This, then, briefly is the political future which I visualise for my province and for my country under any new constitution.

*Malik Barkat Ali*: The Lahore resolution says the same thing.

*Premier*: Exactly; then why misinterpret it and try to mislead the masses? As for the people who come to the province from outside, I have no quarrel with them; they have every right to come and express their views; but their function is only to advise us — as a matter of fact we should welcome friendly advice. But after they have given their advice they must leave it to us to decide the course and action which we consider suitable for our province. If I am asked, for instance, by the United Provinces Muslims to go there and advise them on any particular issue, I will be glad to do so. But I will go there merely as an adviser and it would be for them to refuse or accept my advice as they think best. Why should we in the Punjab worry if my advice is not accepted? Similarly, we in the Punjab are prepared to listen to the views of friends from outside but the final decision to accept or reject those views must rest with us. To put it briefly, we want for the Punjab the same right of self-determination which others want — self-determination which Mr. Gandhi wants, which Mr. Jinnah wants, which the Congress and the Muslim League want and which others demand. I ask for nothing more than what other parties or units in India ask for themselves, namely, the right of self-determination. So, how can they with any reason or justification deny me that right which they claim for themselves?

Supposing the Hindus of the seven provinces in which they are in a majority suggest that we must accept a particular type of constitution for the Punjab and India, and if we do not consider it to be suitable I will say to them: 'Thank you very much for your suggestions and advice, but I am sorry I cannot accept it because it does not suit the Punjab.' Similarly, if the Muslims from those very provinces try to press on us their point of view and we find that their proposals or suggestions are against the interests of the Punjab, we cannot but give them the same reply as to the Hindus. We should make it clear to them that matters pertaining to the proposed new constitution can only be settled by discussion and in consultation with our Hindu and Sikh friends. That seems to me to be the rational position, one which we can reasonably adopt and should adopt. Any other course would lead to further confusion and might eventually result in bloodshed; and if unfortunately it comes to that, the responsibility will be of those who exploit the unsophisticated masses by catchwords and slogans. I have given this warning before and I repeat it today in the hope that it will bring home to all concerned the danger of rousing the passion of the ignorant masses and disseminating bitterness by word of mouth. As I have said, these matters must be considered calmly and dispassionately and we should not be carried away by sentimental slogans. I have told you how I feel about it. It is possible that my viewpoint may not be acceptable to some of you; I may be wrong but I am open to conviction as every fair individual should be.

I may, however, add that my views and conclusions are based on considerations which should be close to the heart of every patriotic Indian. I have given a great deal of thought to this problem and I have put before you my considered views. The future destiny of our province and our country depends mainly on those who are in a position to lead the masses. If they give the correct lead and approach the problem fairly and squarely from a common angle and not from a communal angle, then and only then can we hope to achieve the ideal we have set before us. We must try to understand the other man's point of view just as we expect him to appreciate our point of view. Once we decide to deal with the problem in a spirit of mutual confidence and trust, its solution will not be difficult.

One word to my Sikh friends before I conclude. I have often heard them say: 'We are nationalists and therefore we will not allow any partition of India' — very laudable sentiments. I have no quarrel with their sentiments or their opposition to the partition of India. But I should like to point out to my Sikh friends that if they press for a powerful and superimposed centre at the expense of the provinces, they will be doing gross injustice to the Punjab and incalculable harm to their community. They should not forget that they constitute only one per cent of the population of India and even if they get a 100 per cent weightage they cannot expect to get more than 2 per cent representation at the centre. Now let me put to them this question. Would they prefer to be partners in a concern in which they would be entitled to only one per cent representation and can at best expect a 2 per cent share, or would they be better off where they get a 20 per cent share although they constitute only a little over 12 per cent of the population? Which is the better choice? If they are honest there can be only one answer to that question. In the Punjab, their home province, they will have the same status as Punjabis as their Muslim and Hindu brethren. Here they will have a 20 per cent share as equal partners in a purely Punjabi concern. At the centre they will occupy an insignificant position and their feeble voice will be lost in the multitude of voices from other units and communities. If they are the real nationalists they profess to be, then they will, I am sure, agree with me that the freedom to which we aspire and for which we should strive must be freedom for all and not for any particular community, party or unit. That is the kind of freedom I visualise for the Punjab — freedom for Muslims, Hindus and Sikhs, Christians and others as Punjabis; freedom for the Punjab as also for the other units, subject of course to agreed limitations which may be necessary to ensure the integrity of the units and the country as a whole; freedom which would be unassailable by anybody from within the country or from outside.

Let us, as an earnest of that larger, wider freedom, which we hope to secure, close our ranks in our own province. You know the well-known adage that an isolated stick can be easily snapped but they become unbreakable if they are tied together in a bundle (*cheers*). We are passing through critical times, and I appeal to all communities and parties to join together and unite in order to meet any aggression from outside or trouble from within. Let me warn my Sikh friends that if they are misled into adopting an attitude detrimental to the interests of the Punjab, they will be doing untold harm to their community and betraying their province. For instance, if they say that they would prefer one per cent share at the centre rather than have 20 per cent in their own province — and even my honourable friend Sardar Lal Singh should be able to distinguish between one per cent and 20 per cent although he is a Jat — (*An honourable member*: Sir Chhotu Ram is also a Jat). . . . Yes, but he is an exception to the rule and if you would only follow him like other Jats you also would not make any mistakes. Moreover, if the Sikhs adopt a dog-in-the-manger policy in the matter of apportionment of power between the centre and the units, they will confirm the suspicion that their non-agriculturist leaders in sympathy with their Hindu kith and kin are using them as a cat's-paw for the sake of others.

There is also the danger that the anxiety on the part of certain Sikh leaders to bring the Sikhs in line with the non-agriculturist Hindus, under the plausible pretext that if they join hands with the Hindus they will be able to domineer over Muslims through the centre, might in reality be an attempt to merge the Sikhs into the Hindu community. I am, however, sure that no genuine or honest Sikh will, or can, take up that attitude because apart from religious considerations any such consummation would deprive them of the political, economic and other privileges which they enjoy as an important minority. Once the distinction which distinguishes Sikhs from Hindus is removed or even blurred, they will no longer be entitled to claim or retain the concessions which they now enjoy in the matter of representation, services and in other spheres, for the simple reason that they will cease to be a separate entity.

I will not detain the House much longer. I have frankly put forward my point of view and I will request my friends on both sides of the House to give it their earnest thought and consideration. Let me once again appeal to you and to our co-citizens outside the House that we should examine this problem not from any petty communal or sectarian point of view but from the point of view of the Punjab as a whole. Whatever our differences, they are capable of composition. Let us strive together for a freedom which will ensure liberty and freedom for all and which will enable us to live together as brothers and become so united that no power could part us asunder. Let us live together as Punjabis and act as Punjabis and then in consultation and in agreement with the other units — both British provinces and Indian

States — devise an equitable and just scheme for the centre which will enable us to stand together against any common enemy from without and, at the same time, eliminate the possibility of any internal friction. I have indicated the lines on which it should be possible to achieve our common objective. Let us join hands in order to preserve and maintain peace and harmony within the province, and unite with the rest of India to face with courage and confidence the danger from without. And let us above all show to the rest of India that we in the Punjab stand united and will not brook any interference from whatever quarter it may be attempted. Then and then only will we be able to tell meddling busybodies from outside: 'Hands off the Punjab!' (*prolonged applause*).

# APPENDIX II

## BROADCAST SPEECH OF
## THE VICEROY, LORD WAVELL,
## 14 JUNE 1945

I have been authorised by His Majesty's Government to place before Indian political leaders proposals designed to ease the present political situation and to advance India towards her goal of full self-government. These proposals are at the present moment being explained to Parliament by the Secretary of State for India. My intention in this broadcast is to explain to you the proposals, the ideas underlying them, and the method by which I hope to put them into effect.

This is not an attempt to obtain or impose a constitutional settlement. His Majesty's Government had hoped that the leaders of the Indian parties would agree amongst themselves on a settlement of the communal issue, which is the main stumbling-block; but this hope has not been fulfilled.

In the meantime, India has great opportunities to be taken and great problems to be solved, which require a common effort by the leading men of all parties. I therefore propose, with the full support of His Majesty's Government, to invite Indian leaders both of central and provincial politics to take counsel with me with a view to the formation of a new Executive Council more representative of organised political opinion. The proposed new Council would represent the main communities and would include equal proportions of Caste Hindus and Moslems. It would work, if formed, under the existing constitution. But it would be an entirely Indian Council, except for the Viceroy and the Commander-in-Chief, who would retain his position as War Member. It is also proposed that the portfolio of External Affairs, which has hitherto been held by the Viceroy, should be placed in charge of an Indian Member of Council, so far as the interests of British India are concerned.

A further step proposed by His Majesty's Government is the appointment of a British High Commissioner in India, as in the Dominions, to represent Great Britain's commercial and other such interests in India.

Such a new Executive Council will, you realise, represent a definite advance on the road to self-government. It will be almost entirely Indian, and the Finance and Home Members will for the first time be Indians, while an Indian will also be charged with the management of India's Foreign Affairs. Moreover Members will now be selected by the Governor-General after consultation with political leaders; though their appointment will of course be subject to the approval of His Majesty the King-Emperor.

The Council will work within the framework of the present constitution; and there can be no question of the Governor-General agreeing not to exercise his constitutional power of control; but it will of course not be exercised unreasonably.

I should make it clear that the formation of this interim Government will in no way prejudice the final constitutional settlement.

The main tasks for this new Executive Council would be:

First, to prosecute the war against Japan with the utmost energy till Japan is utterly defeated.

Secondly, to carry on the Government of British India, with all the manifold tasks of post-war development in front of it, until a new permanent constitution can be agreed upon and come into force.

Thirdly, to consider, when the Members of the Government think it possible, the means by which such agreement can be achieved. The third task is most important. I want to make it quite clear that neither I nor His Majesty's Government have lost sight of the need for a long-term solution, and that the present proposals are intended to make a long-term solution easier.

I have considered the best means of forming such a Council; and have decided to invite the following to Viceregal Lodge to advise me:

Those now holding office as Premier in a provincial Government; or, for Provinces now under Section 93 Government, those who last held the office of Premier.

The Leader of the Congress Party and the Deputy Leader of the Muslim League in the Central Assembly; the leader of the Congress Party and the Muslim League in the Council of State; also the leaders of the Nationalist Party and the European Group in the Assembly.

Mr. Gandhi and Mr. Jinnah as the recognised leaders of the two main political parties.

Rao Bahadur N. Siva Raj to represent the Scheduled Classes.

Master Tara Singh to represent the Sikhs.

Invitations to these gentlemen are being handed to them today and it is proposed to assemble the Conference on 25 June at Simla, where we shall be cooler than at Delhi.

I trust that all those invited will attend the Conference and give me their help. On me and on them will lie a heavy responsibility in this fresh attempt to make progress towards a final settlement of India's future.

If the meeting is successful, I hope that we shall be able to agree on the formation of the new Executive Council at the Centre. I also hope that it will be possible for Ministries to re-assume office and again undertake the tasks of government in the provinces now administered under Section 93 of the Constitution Act and that these Ministries will be coalitions.

If the meeting should unfortunately fail, we must carry on as at present until the parties are ready to come together. The existing Executive Council, which has done such valuable work for India, will continue it if other arrangements cannot be agreed.

But I have every hope that the meeting will succeed, if the party leaders will approach the problem with the sincere intention of working with me and with each other. I can assure them that there is behind this proposal a most genuine desire on the part of all responsible leaders in the United Kingdom and of the British people as a whole to help India towards her goal. I believe that this is more than a step towards that goal, it is a considerable stride forward, and a stride on the right path.

I should make it clear that these proposals affect British India only and do not make any alteration in the relations of the Princes with the Crown Representative.

With the approval of His Majesty's Government, and after consultation with my Council, orders have been given for the immediate release of the members of the Working Committee of Congress who are still in detention. I propose to leave the final decision about the others still under detention as the result of the 1942 disturbances to the new central Government, if formed, and to the provincial Governments.

The appropriate time for fresh elections for the central and provincial legislatures will be discussed at the Conference.

Finally, I would ask you all to help in creating the atmosphere of goodwill and mutual confidence that is essential if we are to make progress. The destiny of this great country and of the many millions who live in it depends on the wisdom and good understanding of the leaders, both of action and of thought, British and Indian, at this critical moment of India's history.

India's military reputation never stood higher in the world than it does at present, thanks to the exploits of her sons drawn from all parts of the country. Her representatives at international conferences have won high regard for their statesmanlike attitude. Sympathy for India's aspirations and progress towards prosperity was never greater or more widespread. We have thus great assets if we can use them wisely. But it will not be easy, it will not be quick; there is very much to do, there are many pitfalls and dangers. There is on all sides something to forgive and forget.

I believe in the future of India, and, as far as in me lies, will further her greatness. I ask you all for your co-operation and goodwill.

# APPENDIX III

1. During the recent visit of Field-Marshal Viscount Wavell to this country His Majesty's Government reviewed with him a number of problems and discussed particularly the present political situation in India.

2. Members will be aware that since the offer by His Majesty's Government to India in March 1942 there has been no further progress towards the solution of the Indian constitutional problem.

3. As was then stated, the working out of India's new constitutional system is a task which can only be carried through by the Indian peoples themselves.

4. While His Majesty's Government are at all times most anxious to do their utmost to assist the Indians in the working out of a new constitutional settlement, it would be a contradiction in terms to speak of the imposition by this country of self-governing institutions upon an unwilling India. Such a thing is not possible, nor could we accept the responsibility for enforcing such institutions at the very time when we were, by its purpose, withdrawing from all control of British-Indian affairs.

5. The main constitutional position remains therefore as it was. The offer of March 1942 stands in its entirety without change or qualification. His Majesty's Government still hope that the political leaders in India may be able to come to an agreement as to the procedure whereby India's permanent future form of government can be determined.

6. His Majesty's Government are, however, most anxious to make any contribution that is practicable to the breaking of the political deadlock in India. While that deadlock lasts not only political but social and economic progress is being hampered.

7. The Indian administration, over-burdened with the great tasks laid upon it by the war against Japan and by the planning for the post-war period, is further strained by the political tension that exists.

8. All that is so urgently required to be done for agricultural and industrial development and for the peasants and workers of India cannot be

carried through unless the wholehearted co-operation of every community and section of the Indian people is forthcoming.

9. His Majesty's Government have therefore considered whether there is something which they could suggest in this interim period, under the existing constitution, pending the formulation by Indians of their future constitutional arrangements which would enable the main communities and parties to co-operate more closely together and with the British to the benefit of the people of India as a whole.

10. It is not the intention of His Majesty's Government to introduce any change contrary to the wishes of the major Indian communities. But they are willing to make possible some step forward during the interim period if the leaders of the principal Indian parties are prepared to agree to their suggestions and to co-operate in the successful conclusion of the war against Japan as well as in the reconstruction in India which must follow the final victory.

11. To this end they would be prepared to see an important change in the composition of the Viceroy's Executive. This is possible without making any change in the existing statute law, except for one amendment to the Ninth Schedule to the Act of 1935. That Schedule contains a provision that not less than three members of the Executive must have had at least 10 years' service under the Crown in India. If the proposals I am about to lay before the House meet with acceptance in India, that clause would have to be amended to dispense with that requirement.

12. It is proposed that the Executive Council should be reconstituted and that the Viceroy should in future make his selection for nomination to the Crown for appointment to his Executive from amongst leaders of Indian political life at the Centre and in the provinces, in proportions which would give a balanced representation of the main communities, including equal proportions of Moslems and Caste Hindus.

13. In order to pursue this object, the Viceroy will call into conference a number of leading Indian politicians, who are the heads of the most important parties, or who have had recent experience as Prime Ministers of provinces, together with a few others of special experience and authority. The Viceroy intends to put before this conference the proposal that the Executive Council should be reconstituted as above stated and to invite from the members of the conference a list of names. Out of these he would hope to be able to choose the future members whom he would recommend for appointment by His Majesty to the Viceroy's Council, although the responsibility for the recommendations must of course continue to rest with him, and his freedom of choice therefore remains unrestricted.

14. The members of his Council who are chosen as a result of this arrangement would of course accept the position on the basis that they

would wholeheartedly co-operate in supporting and carrying through the war against Japan to its victorious conclusion.

15. The members of the Executive would be Indians with the exception of the Viceroy and the Commander-in-Chief, who would retain his position as War Member. This is essential so long as the defence of India remains a British responsibility.

16. Nothing contained in any of these proposals will affect the relations of the Crown with the Indian States through the Viceroy as Crown Representative.

17. The Viceroy has been authorised by His Majesty's Government to place this proposal before the Indian leaders. His Majesty's Government trust that the leaders of the Indian communities will respond. For the success of such a plan must depend upon its acceptance in India and the degree to which responsible Indian politicians are prepared to co-operate with the object of making it a workable interim arrangement. In the absence of such general acceptance, existing arrangements must necessarily continue.

18. If such co-operation can be achieved at the Centre it will no doubt be reflected in the provinces, and so enable responsible Governments to be set up once again in those provinces where, owing to the withdrawal of the majority party from participation, it became necessary to put into force the powers of the Governors under Section 93 of the Act of 1935. It is to be hoped that in all the provinces these Governments would be based on the participation of the main parties, thus smoothing out communal differences and allowing Ministers to concentrate upon their very heavy administrative tasks.

19. There is one further change which, if these proposals are accepted, His Majesty's Government suggest should follow.

20. That is, that external affairs (other than those tribal and frontier matters which fall to be dealt with as part of the defence of India) should be placed in the charge of an Indian Member of the Viceroy's Executive so far as British India is concerned, and that fully accredited representatives shall be appointed for the representation of India abroad.

21. By their acceptance of and co-operation in this scheme, the Indian leaders will not only be able to make their immediate contribution to the direction of Indian affairs, but it is also to be hoped that their experience of co-operation in government will expedite agreement between them as to the method of working out the new constitutional arrangements.

22. His Majesty's Government consider, after the most careful study of the question, that the plan now suggested gives the utmost progress practicable within the present constitution. None of the changes suggested will in any way prejudice or prejudge the essential form of the future permanent constitution or constitutions for India.

23. His Majesty's Government feel certain that, given goodwill and a genuine desire to co-operate on all sides, both British and Indian, these proposals can mark a genuine step forward in the collaboration of the British and Indian peoples towards Indian self-government and can assert the rightful position, and strengthen the influence, of India in the counsels of the nations.

# APPENDIX IV

## STATEMENT OF
## THE CABINET MISSION AND THE VICEROY,
## 16 MAY 1946

1. On March 15th last, just before the despatch of the Cabinet Delegation to India, Mr. Attlee, the British Prime Minister, used these words:

'My colleagues are going to India with the intention of using their utmost endeavours to help her to attain her freedom as speedily and fully as possible. What form of government is to replace the present régime is for India to decide; but our desire is to help her to set up forthwith the machinery for making that decision. . . . I hope that India and her people may elect to remain within the British Commonwealth. I am certain that they will find great advantages in doing so. . . . But if she does so elect, it must be by her own free will. The British Commonwealth and Empire is not bound together by chains of external compulsion. It is a free association of free peoples. If, on the other hand, she elects for independence, in our view she has a right to do so. It will be for us to help to make the transition as smooth and easy as possible.'

2. Charged in these historic words we — the Cabinet Ministers and the Viceroy — have done our utmost to assist the two main political parties to reach agreement upon the fundamental issue of the unity or division of India. After prolonged discussions in New Delhi we succeeded in bringing the Congress and the Muslim League together in conference at Simla. There was a full exchange of views and both parties were prepared to make considerable concessions in order to try and reach a settlement but it ultimately proved impossible to close the remainder of the gap between the parties and so no agreement could be concluded. Since no agreement has been reached we feel that it is our duty to put forward what we consider are the best arrangements possible to ensure a speedy setting up of the new constitution. This statement is made with the full approval of His Majesty's Government in the United Kingdom.

3. We have accordingly decided that immediate arrangements should be made whereby Indians may decide the future constitution of India and an interim Government may be set up at once to carry on the administration

of British India until such time as a new constitution can be brought into being. We have endeavoured to be just to the smaller as well as to the larger sections of the people; and to recommend a solution which will lead to a practicable way of governing the India of the future, and will give a sound basis for defence and a good opportunity for progress in the social, political and economic field.

4. It is not intended in this statement to review the voluminous evidence that has been submitted to the Mission; but it is right that we should state that it has shown an almost universal desire, outside the supporters of the Muslim League, for the unity of India.

5. This consideration did not, however, deter us from examining closely and impartially the possibility of a partition of India; since we were greatly impressed by the very genuine and acute anxiety of the Muslims lest they should find themselves subjected to a perpetual Hindu-majority rule.

This feeling has become so strong and widespread amongst the Muslims that it cannot be allayed by mere paper safeguards. If there is to be internal peace in India it must be secured by measures which will assure to the Muslims a control in all matters vital to their culture, religion, and economic or other interests.

6. We therefore examined in the first instance the question of a separate and fully independent sovereign State of Pakistan as claimed by the Muslim League. Such a Pakistan would comprise two areas; one in the north-west consisting of the Provinces of the Punjab, Sind, North-West Frontier, and British Baluchistan; the other in the north-east consisting of the Provinces of Bengal and Assam. The League were prepared to consider adjustment of boundaries at a later stage, but insisted that the principle of Pakistan should first be acknowledged. The argument for a separate State of Pakistan was based, first, upon the right of the Muslim majority to decide their method of government according to their wishes, and secondly, upon the necessity to include substantial areas in which Muslims are in a minority, in order to make Pakistan administratively and economically workable.

The size of the non-Muslim minorities in a Pakistan comprising the whole of the six provinces enumerated above would be very considerable as the following figures[1] show:—

| | | *Muslim* | *Non-Muslim* |
|---|---|---|---|
| *North-western Area* | | | |
| Punjab | .. | 16,217,242 | 12,201,577 |
| North-West Frontier Province | .. | 2,788,797 | 249,270 |
| Sind | .. | 3,208,325 | 1,326,683 |
| Br. Baluchistan | .. | 438,930 | 62,701 |
| | | 22,653,294 | 13,840,231 |
| | | 62·07% | 37·93% |

[1] All population figures in this statement are from the most recent census taken in 1941.

|                       | Muslim | Non-Muslim |
|---|---|---|
| *North-eastern Area* | | |
| Bengal | .. 33,005,434 | 27,301,091 |
| Assam | .. 3,442,479 | 6,762,254 |
| | 36,447,913 | 34,063,345 |
| | 51·69% | 48·31% |

The Muslim minorities in the remainder of British India number some 20 million dispersed amongst a total population of 188 million.

These figures show that the setting up of a separate sovereign State of Pakistan on the lines claimed by the Muslim League would not solve the communal minority problem; nor can we see any justification for including within a sovereign Pakistan those districts of the Punjab and of Bengal and Assam in which the population is predominantly non-Muslim. Every argument that can be used in favour of Pakistan, can equally in our view be used in favour of the exclusion of the non-Muslim areas from Pakistan. This point would particularly affect the position of the Sikhs.

7. We therefore considered whether a smaller sovereign Pakistan confined to the Muslim majority areas alone might be a possible basis of compromise. Such a Pakistan is regarded by the Muslim League as quite impracticable because it would entail the exclusion from Pakistan of (a) the whole of the Ambala and Jullundur Divisions in the Punjab; (b) the whole of Assam except the district of Sylhet; and (c) a large part of Western Bengal, including Calcutta, in which city the Muslims form 23·6% of the population. We ourselves are also convinced that any solution which involves a radical partition of the Punjab and Bengal, as this would do, would be contrary to the wishes and interests of a very large proportion of the inhabitants of these Provinces. Bengal and the Punjab each has its own common language and a long history and tradition. Moreover, any division of the Punjab would of necessity divide the Sikhs leaving substantial bodies of Sikhs on both sides of the boundary. We have therefore been forced to the conclusion that neither a larger nor a smaller sovereign State of Pakistan would provide an acceptable solution for the communal problem.

8. Apart from the great force of the foregoing arguments there are weighty administrative, economic and military considerations. The whole of the transportation and postal and telegraph systems of India have been established on the basis of a united India. To disintegrate them would gravely injure both parts of India. The case for a united defence is even stronger. The Indian armed forces have been built up as a whole for the defence of India as a whole, and to break them in two would inflict a deadly blow on the long traditions and high degree of efficiency of the Indian Army and would entail the gravest dangers. The Indian Navy and Indian Air Force would become much less effective. The two sections of the

suggested Pakistan contain the two most vulnerable frontiers in India and for a successful defence in depth the area of Pakistan would be insufficient.

9. A further consideration of importance is the greater difficulty which the Indian States would find in associating themselves with a divided British India.

10. Finally there is the geographical fact that the two halves of the proposed Pakistan State are separated by some seven hundred miles and the communications between them both in war and peace would be dependent on the goodwill of Hindustan.

11. We are therefore unable to advise the British Government that the power which at present resides in British hands should be handed over to two entirely separate sovereign States.

12. This decision does not however blind us to the very real Muslim apprehensions that their culture and political and social life might become submerged in a purely unitary India, in which the Hindus with their greatly superior numbers must be a dominating element. To meet this the Congress have put forward a scheme under which provinces would have full autonomy subject only to a minimum of central subjects, such as foreign affairs, defence and communications.

Under this scheme provinces, if they wished to take part in economic and administrative planning on a large scale, could cede to the Centre optional subjects in addition to the compulsory ones mentioned above.

13. Such a scheme would, in our view, present considerable constitutional disadvantages and anomalies. It would be very difficult to work a central Executive and Legislature in which some Ministers, who dealt with compulsory subjects, were responsible to the whole of India while other Ministers, who dealt with optional subjects, would be responsible only to those provinces which had elected to act together in respect of such subjects. This difficulty would be accentuated in the Central Legislature, where it would be necessary to exclude certain members from speaking and voting when subjects with which their provinces were not concerned were under discussion.

Apart from the difficulty of working such a scheme, we do not consider that it would be fair to deny to other provinces, which did not desire to take the optional subjects at the Centre, the right to form themselves into a group for a similar purpose. This would indeed be no more than the exercise of their autonomous powers in a particular way.

14. Before putting forward our recommendation we turn to deal with the relationship of the Indian States to British India. It is quite clear that with the attainment of independence by British India, whether inside or outside the British Commonwealth, the relationship which has hitherto existed between the Rulers of the States and the British Crown will no longer be possible. Paramountcy can neither be retained by the British Crown

nor transferred to the new Government. This fact has been fully recognised by those whom we interviewed from the States. They have at the same time assured us that the States are ready and willing to co-operate in the new development of India. The precise form which their co-operation will take must be a matter for negotiation during the building up of the new constitutional structure, and it by no means follows that it will be identical for all the States. We have not therefore dealt with the States in the same detail as the provinces of British India in the paragraphs which follow.

15. We now indicate the nature of a solution which in our view would be just to the essential claims of all parties, and would at the same time be most likely to bring about a stable and practical form of constitution for all India.

We recommend that the constitution should take the following basic form:—

(1) There should be a Union of India, embracing both British India and the States, which should deal with the following subjects: foreign affairs, defence, and communications; and which should have the powers necessary to raise the finances required for the above subjects.

(2) The Union should have an Executive and a Legislature constituted from British-Indian and States representatives. Any question raising a major communal issue in the Legislature should require for its decision a majority of the representatives present and voting of each of the two major communities as well as a majority of all the members present and voting.

(3) All subjects other than the Union subjects and all residuary powers should vest in the Provinces.

(4) The States will retain all subjects and powers other than those ceded to the Union.

(5) Provinces should be free to form Groups with executives and legislatures, and each Group could determine the provincial subjects to be taken in common.

(6) The constitutions of the Union and of the Groups should contain a provision whereby any province could, by a majority vote of its Legislative Assembly, call for a reconsideration of the terms of the constitution after an initial period of 10 years and at 10 yearly intervals thereafter.

16. It is not our object to lay out the details of a constitution on the above lines, but to set in motion the machinery whereby a constitution can be settled by Indians for Indians.

It has been necessary however for us to make this recommendation as to the broad basis of the future constitution because it became clear to us in the course of our negotiations that not until that had been done was there any hope of getting the two major communities to join in the setting up of the constitution-making machinery.

17. We now indicate the constitution-making machinery which we

propose should be brought into being forthwith in order to enable a new constitution to be worked out.

18. In forming any Assembly to decide a new constitutional structure the first problem is to obtain as broad-based and accurate a representation of the whole population as is possible. The most satisfactory method obviously would be by election based on adult franchise; but any attempt to introduce such a step now would lead to a wholly unacceptable delay in the formulation of the new constitution. The only practicable alternative is to utilize the recently elected provincial Legislative Assemblies as the electing bodies. There are, however, two factors in their composition which make this difficult. First, the numerical strength of the provincial Legislative Assemblies do not bear the same proportion to the total population in each province. Thus, Assam with a population of 10 millions has a Legislative Assembly of 108 members, while Bengal, with a population six times as large, has an Assembly of only 250. Secondly, owing to the weightage given to minorities by the Communal Award, the strengths of the several communities in each provincial Legislative Assembly are not in proportion to their numbers in the province. Thus the number of seats reserved for Muslims in the Bengal Legislative Assembly is only 48% of the total, although they form 55% of the provincial population. After a most careful consideration of the various methods by which these inequalities might be corrected, we have come to the conclusion that the fairest and most practicable plan would be—

(*a*) to allot to each province a total number of seats proportional to its population, roughly in the ratio of one to a million, as the nearest substitute for representation by adult suffrage.

(*b*) to divide this provincial allocation of seats between the main communities in each province in proportion to their population.

(*c*) to provide that the representatives allotted to each community in a province shall be elected by the members of that community in its Legislative Assembly.

We think that for these purposes it is sufficient to recognise only three main communities in India: General, Muslim, and Sikh, the 'General' community including all persons who are not Muslims or Sikhs. As the smaller minorities would, upon the population basis, have little or no representation since they would lose the weightage which assures them seats in the provincial Legislatures, we have made the arrangements set out in paragraph 20 below to give them a full representation upon all matters of special interest to the minorities.

19. (*i*) We therefore propose that there shall be elected by each provincial Legislative Assembly the following numbers of representatives, each part of the Legislature (General, Muslim or Sikh) electing its own representatives by the method of proportional representation with the single transferable vote:—

### TABLE OF REPRESENTATION

Section A

| Province | | | General | Muslim | Total |
|---|---|---|---|---|---|
| Madras | .. | .. | 45 | 4 | 49 |
| Bombay | .. | .. | 19 | 2 | 21 |
| United Provinces | .. | .. | 47 | 8 | 55 |
| Bihar | .. | .. | 31 | 5 | 36 |
| Central Provinces | .. | .. | 16 | 1 | 17 |
| Orissa | .. | .. | 9 | 0 | 9 |
| | Total | .. | 167 | 20 | 187 |

Section B

| Province | | General | Muslim | Sikh | Total |
|---|---|---|---|---|---|
| Punjab | .. | 8 | 16 | 4 | 28 |
| North-West Frontier Province | .. | 0 | 3 | 0 | 3 |
| Sind | .. | 1 | 3 | 0 | 4 |
| | Total .. | 9 | 22 | 4 | 35 |

Section C

| Province | | | General | Muslim | Total |
|---|---|---|---|---|---|
| Bengal | .. | .. | 27 | 33 | 60 |
| Assam | .. | .. | 7 | 3 | 10 |
| | Total | .. | 34 | 36 | 70 |

Total for British India .. 292

Maximum for Indian States .. 93

Total .. 385

*Note.*—In order to represent the Chief Commissioners' Provinces there will be added to Section A the Member representing Delhi in the central Legislative Assembly, the Member representing Ajmer-Merwara in the central Legislative Assembly, and a representative to be elected by the Coorg Legislative Council.

To Section B will be added a representative of British Baluchistan.

(*ii*) It is the intention that the States should be given in the final Constituent Assembly appropriate representation which would not, on the basis of the calculations adopted for British India, exceed 93, but the method of selection will have to be determined by consultation. The States would in the preliminary stage be represented by a Negotiating Committee.

(*iii*) The representatives thus chosen shall meet at New Delhi as soon as possible.

(*iv*) A preliminary meeting will be held at which the general order of business will be decided, a Chairman and other officers elected, and an Advisory Committee (see paragraph 20 below) on the rights of citizens, minorities, and tribal and excluded areas set up. Thereafter the provincial representatives will divide up into the three sections shown under A, B and C, in the Table of Representation in sub-paragraph (*i*) of this paragraph.

(*v*) These sections shall proceed to settle the provincial Constitutions for the provinces included in each section, and shall also decide whether any Group Constitution shall be set up for those provinces and, if so, with what provincial subjects the Group should deal. Provinces shall have the power to opt out of the Groups in accordance with the provisions of sub-clause (*viii*) below.

(*vi*) The representatives of the Sections and the Indian States shall reassemble for the purpose of settling the Union Constitution.

(*vii*) In the Union Constituent Assembly resolutions varying the provisions of paragraph 15 above or raising any major communal issue shall require a majority of the representatives present and voting of each of the two major communities.

The Chairman of the Assembly shall decide which (if any) of the resolutions raise major communal issues and shall, if so requested by a majority of the representatives of either of the major communities, consult the Federal Court before giving his decision.

(*viii*) As soon as the new constitutional arrangements have come into operation, it shall be open to any province to elect to come out of any Group in which it has been placed. Such a decision shall be taken by the new legislature of the province after the first general election under the new constitution.

20. The Advisory Committee on the rights of citizens, minorities, and tribal and excluded areas should contain full representation of the interests affected, and their function will be to report to the Union Constituent Assembly upon the list of Fundamental Rights, the clauses for the protection of minorities, and a scheme for the administration of the tribal and excluded areas, and to advise whether these rights should be incorporated in the Provincial, Group, or Union constitution.

21. His Excellency the Viceroy will forthwith request the provincial Legislatures to proceed with the election of their representatives and the States to set up a Negotiating Committee. It is hoped that the process of constitution-making can proceed as rapidly as the complexities of the task permit so that the interim period may be as short as possible.

22. It will be necessary to negotiate a Treaty between the Union Constituent Assembly and the United Kingdom to provide for certain matters arising out of the transfer of power.

23. While the constitution-making proceeds, the administration of India has to be carried on. We attach the greatest importance therefore to the setting up at once of an interim Government having the support of the major political parties. It is essential during the interim period that there should be the maximum of co-operation in carrying through the difficult tasks that face the Government of India. Besides the heavy task of day-to-day administration, there is the grave danger of famine to be countered; there are decisions to be taken in many matters of post-war development which will have a far-reaching effect on India's future; and there are important international conferences in which India has to be represented. For all these purposes a Government having popular support is necessary. The Viceroy has already started discussions to this end, and hopes soon to form an interim Government in which all the portfolios, including that of War Member, will be held by Indian leaders having the full confidence of the people. The British Government, recognising the significance of the changes in the Government of India, will give the fullest measure of co-operation to the Government so formed in the accomplishment of its tasks of administration and in bringing about as rapid and smooth a transition as possible.

24. To the leaders and people of India who now have the opportunity of complete independence we would finally say this. We and our Government and countrymen hoped that it would be possible for the Indian people themselves to agree upon the method of framing the new constitution under which they will live. Despite the labours which we have shared with the Indian Parties, and the exercise of much patience and goodwill by all, this has not been possible. We therefore now lay before you proposals which, after listening to all sides and after much earnest thought, we trust will enable you to attain your independence in the shortest time and with the least danger of internal disturbance and conflict. These proposals may not, of course, completely satisfy all parties, but you will recognise with us that at this supreme moment in Indian history statesmanship demands mutual accommodation.

We ask you to consider the alternative to acceptance of these proposals. After all the efforts which we and the Indian Parties have made together for agreement, we must state that in our view there is small hope of peaceful settlement by agreement of the Indian Parties alone. The alternative would therefore be a grave danger of violence, chaos, and even civil war. The result and duration of such a disturbance cannot be foreseen; but it is certain that it would be a terrible disaster for many millions of men, women and children. This is a possibility which must be regarded with equal abhorrence by the Indian people, our own countrymen, and the world as a whole.

We therefore lay these proposals before you in the profound hope that they will be accepted and operated by you in the spirit of accommodation and goodwill in which they are offered. We appeal to all who have the future good of India at heart to extend their vision beyond their own community or interest to the interests of the whole four hundred millions of the Indian people.

We hope that the new independent India may choose to be a member of the British Commonwealth. We hope in any event that you will remain in close and friendly association with our people. But these are matters for your own free choice. Whatever that choice may be, we look forward with you to your ever increasing prosperity among the great nations of the world, and to a future even more glorious than your past.

# APPENDIX V

## The Secretary of State's Broadcast, 16 May 1946

The words which I shall speak to you are concerned with the future of a great people — the people of India. There is a passionate desire in the hearts of Indians, expressed by the leaders of all their political parties, for independence. His Majesty's Government and the British people as a whole are fully ready to accord this independence whether within or without the British Commonwealth and hope that out of it will spring a lasting and friendly association between our two peoples on a footing of complete equality.

Nearly two months ago I, as Secretary of State for India, and my two Cabinet colleagues, Sir Stafford Cripps and Mr. Alexander, were sent out by His Majesty's Government to India to assist the Viceroy in setting up in India the machinery by which Indians can devise their own constitution.

We were at once confronted with a major obstacle. The two principal parties — the Muslim League who won the great majority of the Muslim seats in the recent elections, and the Congress who won the majority of all the others — were opposed to one another as to the kind of machinery to be set up. The Muslim League claimed that British India should be divided into two completely separate sovereign states, and refused to take part in constitution-making unless this claim was conceded in advance. Congress insisted on one single united India.

During our stay in India we have tried by every means to secure such an accommodation between the parties as would enable constitution-making to proceed. Recently we were able to bring them together at Simla in a conference with ourselves, but though both sides were prepared to make substantial concessions, it was not found possible to reach complete agreement. We have therefore been compelled ourselves to seek for a solution which by securing the main objects of both parties will enable constitution-making machinery to be brought into immediate operation.

While we recognise the reality of the fear of the Muslim League that in a purely unitary India their community with its own culture and way of life might become submerged in a majority Hindu rule, we do not accept the setting up of a separate Muslim sovereign state as a solution of the communal problem. 'Pakistan', as the Muslim League would call their State, would not consist solely of Muslims; it would contain a substantial minority of other communities which would average over 40 per cent and in certain wide areas would even constitute a majority, as for instance in the city of Calcutta, where the Muslims form less than one-third of the population. Moreover the complete separation of Pakistan from the rest of India would in our view gravely endanger the defence of the whole country by splitting the army into two and by preventing that defence in depth which is essential in modern war. We therefore do not suggest the adoption of this proposal.

Our own recommendations contemplate a constitution of three tiers, at the top of which would be the Union of India with an executive and legislature empowered to deal with the essential subjects of external affairs, defence and communications and the finance necessary for these services. At the bottom would be the provinces which would have, apart from the subjects I have just named, complete autonomy. But we contemplate further that provinces will wish to unite together in groups to carry out, in common, services covering a wider area than that of a single province, and these groups may have, if they wish, legislatures and executives which in that event will be intermediate between those of the provinces and those of the Union.

On this basis, which makes it possible for the Muslims to secure the advantages of a Pakistan without incurring the dangers inherent in the division of India, we invite Indians of all parties to take part in framing a constitution. The Viceroy will accordingly summon to New Delhi representatives of British India who will be elected by the members of the provincial legislatures in such a way that as nearly as possible for each one million of the population there will be one representative, and that the proportion between the representatives of the main communities will be on the same basis.

After a preliminary meeting in common, these representatives of the provinces will divide themselves up into three sections the composition of which is laid down and which, if the provinces ultimately agree, will become the three Groups. These sections will decide upon provincial and group matters. Subsequently they will re-unite to decide upon the constitution for the Union. After the first elections under the new constitution, provinces will be free to opt out of the Group into which they have been provisionally placed. We appreciate that this machinery does not of itself give any effective representation to other than the principal minorities, and we are therefore providing for a special committee to be set up, in which the minorities will play a full part. The business of this Committee will be to formulate fundamental and minority rights and to recommend their inclusion in the constitution at the appropriate level.

So far I have said nothing about the Indian States, which comprise a third of the area of India and contain about one quarter of the whole population. These States at present are each separately governed and have individual relationships with the British Crown. There is general recognition that when British India attains independence the position of these States cannot remain unaffected, and it is anticipated that they will wish to take part in the constitution-making process and be represented in the all-India Union. It does not however lie within our province to decide these matters in advance as they will have to be the subject of negotiation with the States before action can be taken.

During the making of the constitution the administration must be carried on, and we attach therefore the greatest importance to the setting up at once of an interim Government having the support of the major political parties. The Viceroy has already started discussions to this end, and he hopes to bring them shortly to a successful issue.

During the interim period the British Government, recognising the significance of the changes in the Government of India, will give the fullest measure of co-operation to the Government so formed in the accomplishment of its tasks of administration and in bringing about as rapid and smooth a transition as possible.

The essence of statecraft is to envisage the probable course of future events, but no statesmen can be wise enough to frame a constitution which will adequately meet all the requirements of an unknown future. We may be confident therefore that the Indians on whom falls the responsibility of creating the initial constitution will give it a reasonable flexibility and will make provision for it to be revised and amended as required from time to time.

In this short talk you will not expect me to go into further details regarding our proposals, which you can read in the statement which has been released for publication this evening. But in conclusion I will repeat and emphasise what to me is the fundamental issue. The future of India and how that future is inaugurated are matters of vital importance not only to India herself but to the whole world. If a great new sovereign State can come into being in a spirit of mutual goodwill both within and without India, that of itself will be an outstanding contribution to world stability.

The Government and people of Britain are not only willing, they are anxious to play their full part in achieving this result. But the constitution for India has to be framed by Indians and worked by Indians when they have brought it into being. We appreciate to the full the difficulties which confront them in embarking on this task. We have done and we will continue to do all that lies in our power to help them to overcome these difficulties. But the responsibility and the opportunity is theirs and in their fulfilment of it we wish them Godspeed.

# APPENDIX VI

## LORD WAVELL'S BROADCAST,
### 17 MAY 1946

I speak to the people of India at the most critical hour of India's history. The statement of the Cabinet Delegation containing their recommendations has now been before you for twenty-four hours. It is a blueprint for freedom, an outline of which your representatives have to fill in the details and construct the building.

You will have studied the statement, most of you, and may perhaps already have formed your opinion on it. If you think that it shows a path to reach the summit at which you have been aiming for so long, the independence of India, I am sure you will be eager to take it. If you should have formed the view — I hope you have not — that there is no passage that way, I hope that you will study again the route indicated to you, and see whether the difficulties in the path — and we know they are formidable — cannot be surmounted by skill and patience and boldness.

I can assure you of this, that very much hard work, very much earnest study, very much anxious thought, and all the goodwill and sincerity at our command have gone to the making of these recommendations. We would much have preferred that the Indian leaders should have themselves reached agreement on the course to be followed, and we have done our best to persuade them; but it has not been found possible, in spite of concessions on both sides which at one time promised results.

These proposals put before you are obviously not those that any one of the parties would have chosen if left to itself; but I do believe that they offer a reasonable and workable basis on which to found India's future constitution. They preserve the essential unity of India which is threatened by the dispute between the two major communities; and in especial they remove the danger of the disruption of that great fellowship the Indian Army, to which India already owes so much and on whose strength, unity and efficiency her future security will depend. They offer to the Muslim community the right to direct their own essential interests, their religion, their education, their culture, their economic and other concerns in their own way and to their own best advantage. To another great community, the

Sikhs, they preserve the unity of their homeland, the Punjab, in which they have played and can still play so important and influential a part. They provide, in the Special Committee which forms a feature of the constitution-making machinery, the best chance for the smaller minorities to make their needs known and to secure protection for their interests. They seek to arrange a means for the Indian States, great and small, to enter by negotiation into the polity of a united India. They offer to India the prospect of peace — a peace from party strife, the peace so needed for all the constructive work there is to do. And they give you the opportunity of complete independence so soon as the Constituent Assembly has completed its labours.

I would like to emphasize the constructive work to be done. If you can agree to accept the proposals in the Statement as a reasonable basis on which to work out your constitution, then we are able at once to concentrate all the best efforts and abilities in India on the short-term problems that are so urgent. You know them well — the immediate danger of famine to be countered, and measures taken to provide more food for everyone in future years; the health of India to be remedied; great schemes of wider education to be initiated: roads to be built and improved; and much else to be done to raise the standard of living of the common man. There are also great schemes in hand to control India's water supplies, to extend irrigation, to provide power, to prevent floods; there are factories to be built and new industries to be started; while in the outside world India has to take her place in international bodies in which her representatives have already established a considerable reputation.

It is therefore my earnest desire that in these critical times ahead, in the interim period while the new constitution is being built, the Government of India should be in the hands of the ablest of India's leaders, men recognised as such by the Indian people, whom they will trust to further their interests and bring them to their goal.

As said in the Statement, I am charged with the responsibility to form such a Government as soon as possible, to direct the affairs of British India in the interim period. There will be no doubt in the minds of anyone, I hope, how great a step forward this will be on India's road to self-government. It will be a purely Indian Government except for its head, the Governor-General; and will include, if I can get the men I want, recognized leaders of the main Indian parties, whose influence, ability and desire to serve India are unquestioned.

Such a Government must have a profound influence and power not only in India, but also in the outside world. Some of the best ability in India, which has hitherto been spent in opposition, can be harnessed to constructive work. These men can be the architects of the new India.

No constitution and no form of government can work satisfactorily without goodwill; with goodwill and determination to succeed even an apparently illogical arrangement can be made to work. In the complex situation that faces us there are four main parties: the British; the two main parties in British India, Hindus and Muslims; and the Indian States. From all of them very considerable change of their present outlook will be required as a contribution to the general good, if this great experiment is to succeed. To make concession in ideas and principles is a hard thing and not easily palatable. It requires some greatness of mind to recognise the necessity, much greatness of spirit to make the concession. I am sure that this will not be found wanting in India, as I think you will admit that it has not been found wanting in the British people in this offer.

I wonder whether you realise that this is the greatest and most momentous experiment in government in the whole history of the world — a new constitution to control the destiny of 400,000,000 people. A grave responsibility indeed on all of us who are privileged to assist in making it.

Lastly, I must emphasise the seriousness of the choice before you. It is the choice between peaceful construction or the disorder of civil strife, between co-operation or disunity, between ordered progress or confusion. I am sure you will not hesitate in your choice for co-operation.

May I end with some words which were quoted by one great man to another at a crisis of the late war, and may well be applied to India at this crisis:

> '*Thou too, sail on, O Ship of State,*
> *Sail on, O Union, strong and great:*
> *Humanity with all its fears,*
> *With all the hopes of future years,*
> *Is hanging breathless on thy fate.*'

# APPENDIX VII

## STATEMENT BY SIR STAFFORD CRIPPS
### AT A PRESS CONFERENCE
### ON 16 MAY 1946

You have heard two broadcasts on the Statement and you have the document before you. This evening the members of the Mission wanted an opportunity to meet you to give you a few words of explanation, and to-morrow we shall be meeting you again to answer questions which you may have to put.

I will make a few remarks about the Statement while we are waiting for the Secretary of State to come from the Broadcasting studio.

The first thing I want to point out is what the Statement does *not* purport to do. Let me remind you that this is not merely the Mission's statement, that is the statement of the four signatories, but is the statement of His Majesty's Government in the United Kingdom. Now the Statement does not purport to set out a new constitution for India. It is of no use asking us, 'How do you propose to do this or that?' The answer will be, *we* don't propose to do anything as regards decision upon a constitution; that is not for us to decide.

What we have had to do is to lay down one or two broad principles of how the constitution might be constructed and recommend those as foundations to the Indian people. You will notice we use the word 'recommend' with regard to the ultimate constitutional forms with which we deal.

You may quite fairly ask, 'But why do you recommend anything; why not leave it to the Indians?' The answer is that we are most anxious to get all Indians into some constitution-making machinery as quickly as possible and the block at present is in this matter. We are therefore by this means trying to remove the block so that the constitution-making may start and progress freely and rapidly. We hope very earnestly that that will be the effect.

Now that it has been finally and absolutely decided that India is to have the complete independence she desires, whether within or without the British Commonwealth as she chooses, we are anxious that she shall have it as soon as possible, and the soonest is when there is a new constitutional structure decided upon by the Indian people.

But of course we cannot just stand by and wait till that time comes. It is bound to take some time to reach that point of completion of the new constitutional structure.

So, as you know, the Viceroy, in whose province Government-making primarily lies, has already started his talks with a view to the immediate setting up of a representative Indian Government. We hope that with the other issues out of the way on the basis of our Statement he will be able very rapidly to get that new Government representative of the main parties set up and in operation.

This matter of the interim Government is of supreme importance because of the enormous tasks facing India at the moment. It is these great tasks, and perhaps the greatest of them is to deal with the food situation, that makes it absolutely essential that we should between us arrange a smooth and efficient transition.

Nothing could be more fatal to the Indian people today in the face of dangers of famine than a breakdown of administration and communications anywhere in India, and that is why we stress as we do the vital need for co-operation between all parties and communities, including the British, in this time of transition.

So much then for the vitally important point of the interim Government. Some of you may wonder how soon this means that the British will sever their governmental connection with India — I hope that in any event we shall remain the closest friends when Indian freedom comes. Well, we certainly can't say that. Who can foretell how quickly constitutions can be hammered out? One thing is, however, absolutely certain, and this is the quicker you start the quicker you will end and the sooner we shall be able to withdraw, handing over the power to the new Governments of the Union, Provinces and, if it is so decided, of the Groups.

This brings me to what has been decided rather than recommended. It has been decided to make a start with the constitution-making right away. This does not mean a decision as to what the constitution shall finally be, that is for decision by the representatives of the Indian people. What it does mean is that the deadlock which has prevented a start on the process of constitution-making is to be removed once and for all.

The form in which we propose that the constitution-making bodies should be assembled is important for this reason. It permits of arriving at constitutions in the recommended form. It goes a little further than that in one respect. As we believe and hope that the two parties will come into this constitution-making on the bases of our recommendations, it would not be fair to either of them if the fundamental basis which we recommend could be easily departed from. So we stipulate that a departure from that basis which is laid down in paragraph 15 of the Statement should only be made if a majority of both communities agree to it. That I think is eminently fair to both parties. It does not mean that no departure can be made from the recommendations, but it does mean that the special provisions I have mentioned will apply to such resolutions in the Constituent Assembly of the Union. That is one special provision as to particular majorities; the only other is in relation to matters raising any major communal issue, when a similar rule will apply. All the rest is left to the free play of discussion and vote.

One question I am sure will occur to all of you, and that is why we have named the three sections of provinces into which the Assembly will break up to formulate the provincial and group constitutions.

There was a very good reason for this. First of all, of course, somehow or another those groups had to be formed before they could proceed to their business. There were two ways of dealing with that matter, either let the present provincial Governments opt themselves into Groups or — after seeing the constitutions produced — let the new governments, after the whole constitution-making is complete, opt themselves out if they wish. We have chosen the second alternative for two reasons. First because it follows the suggestion Congress put forward as regards the provinces and a single federation. They suggested that all the provinces should come in at the beginning but could opt out if they did not like the constitution when they had seen it. We think that this principle should apply to the groups. Second, the present legislatures are not truly representative of the whole population because of the effect of the communal award with its weightages. We have tried to get a scheme as near as possible to the full adult suffrage which would be fairest but which would take probably two years to work out — and no one believes that we could wait that length of time before starting on constitution-making. So we discard the present legislatures as decisive for the option and say let it be exercised when the first new elections have taken place, when no doubt there will be a much fuller franchise and when, if necessary, the precise issue can be raised at the election. So the three sections will formulate the provincial and group constitutions, and when that is done they work together with the States representatives to make the Union constitution. That is the final phase.

Now a word about the States. The Statement in paragraph 14 makes the position quite clear that paramountcy cannot be continued after the new constitution comes into operation, nor can it be handed over to anyone else. It isn't necessary for me to state, I am sure, that a contract or arrangement of this kind cannot be handed over to a third party without the consent of the States. They will therefore become wholly independent but they have expressed their wish to negotiate their way into the Union, and that is a matter we leave to negotiation between the States and the British-Indian parties.

There is one other important provision which I would like to stress, as it is somewhat novel in constitution-making. We were met by the difficulty of how we could deal fairly with the smaller minorities, the Tribal and the excluded areas. In any constitution-making body it would be quite impossible to give them a weightage which would secure for them any effective influence without gravely upsetting the balance between the major parties. To give them a tiny representation would be useless to them. So we decided that minorities would be dealt with really in a double way. The major minorities, such as the Hindus in Muslim provinces, and the Muslims in Hindu provinces, the Sikhs in the Punjab, and the Depressed Classes who have considerable representation in a number of provinces, would be dealt with by proportional representation in the main construction of the constitution-making bodies. But in order to give these minorities, and particularly the smaller minorities like the Indian Christians and the Anglo-Indians and also the Tribal representatives, a better opportunity of influencing minority provisions, we have made provision for the setting up by the constitution-making body of an influential advisory Commission which will take the initiative in the preparation of the list of fundamental rights, the minority protection clauses and the proposals for the administration of Tribal and excluded areas. This Commission will make its recommendations to the constitution-making body and will also suggest at which stage or stages in the constitution these provisions should be inserted, that is whether in the Union, group or provincial constitutions, or in any two or more of them.

Now, that I think gives you some picture of the main points with which we have dealt in our Statement.

There is only one other point that I want to stress before leaving the matter with you until to-morrow morning.

You will realise, I am sure, how terribly important is this moment of decision for the Indian people.

We are all agreed that we want a speedy conclusion of these matters; so far we have not been able all to agree upon how it should be brought about. We have done in this Statement what we believe to be best after two months of discussion and very hard work and in the light of all we have heard and studied. This is our firm opinion and we do not, of course, intend to start all the negotiations over again. We intend to get on with the job on the lines we have laid down. We ask the Indian people to give this Statement calm and careful consideration. I believe that the happiness of their future depends upon what they now do. If, failing their own agreement, they will accept this method that we put forward of getting on with the making of a new constitution for India, we can between us make it a smooth transition and a rapid one, but if the plan is not accepted no one can say how great will be the disturbance, or how acute and long the suffering that will be self-inflicted on the Indian people.

We are convinced that this Statement offers an honourable and peaceful method to all parties, and if they will accept it we will do all that lies in our power to help forward the constitution-making so as to arrive at the speediest possible settlement.

Let no one doubt for one moment our intentions. We have not come to India and stayed here so long and worked so hard except to carry out what has long been the policy of the British Labour Party, and that is to transfer power to the Indian people as quickly and smoothly and as co-operatively as the difficulties of the process permit.

We hope from the bottom of our hearts that the Indian people will accept the Statement in the spirit of co-operation in which it has been drawn up, and that within a week or two the process of constitution-making may begin and the interim Government may be formed.

# APPENDIX VIII

### CABINET MISSION PRESS CONFERENCE
### OF 17 MAY 1946

*Secretary of State for India*: Gentlemen, we had the pleasure and opportunity of meeting most of you last night. Sir Stafford Cripps gave you an address expounding the text of the Statement which we had just issued. We have come this morning, quite willing and, so far as I am concerned, looking forward to being put questions as to the meaning of certain words in the Statement. I should however like to make this clear, that we, the three Cabinet Ministers, are here and if you put us any veiled conundrums not as to the text of the Statement but as to something that might happen and what we would do under all sorts of hypothetical considerations, then I am not prepared to give you an answer straightaway because those are matters quite clearly which ought to be most carefully considered by the Cabinet Mission, by the Viceroy and by His Majesty's Government, with whose complete approval we issued the Statement itself. It is not therefore for us three Cabinet Ministers to enlarge upon or to add anything to the Statement which has already been issued. Having made that clear, in all sincerity and with the best of intention, I am prepared to clarify on my own responsibility and not as a complete pronouncement and enlargement of the Statement already issued, and I shall be quite happy to apply myself to any questions that you may care to ask.

*Question*: Will the Negotiating Committee mentioned on page 5 be part of the Constituent Assembly in the initial stage before the representatives of the States have been elected on an agreed basis?

*Answer*: In the preliminary meeting where all sections are meeting as one as described in sub-para (*iv*), quite clearly there will be no representatives of the States as such present, because the machinery will not have been finalised for representing the States. Therefore in that preliminary meeting, it is proposed that this Negotiating Committee shall for the moment represent the States.

*Question*: In the intervening period, will the Commander-in-Chief be subject to the British Parliament as stated by Mr. Attlee, and in the event of resistance to the terms of the award, will British forces be used to impose the award as suggested by Mr. Churchill? We take it that these decisions with regard to the composition of the groups and of the Constituent Assembly and so on are not intended to be imposed by force, but they are proposals for rejection or acceptance by Indian opinion?

*Answer:* The first point to note is that this is not an award. It is a recommendation as a certain basis of constitution and a decision to summon Indian representatives to make their own constitution, and therefore quite clearly there is no question whatever of the British enforcing an award, and under those circumstances the question of using British troops does not arise at all.

*Question:* Supposing a group decides not to come into the Union Constituent Assembly, what would be the position as far as that Group is concerned ?

*Answer:* It is purely a hypothetical question what would happen if certain provinces or groups are not willing to co-operate in proceeding with this constitutional machinery. As I said at the beginning, that is the sort of question which I cannot answer in any definite form. You cannot forejudge exactly what would be done in the event of people not co-operating. But there is every intention of proceeding with the constitution-making machinery as it is set out in this Statement, and if any group tries to put spanners in the wheel, I am not prepared at this stage to state what will be done.

*Question:* Is it not a fact that so far as membership of the Constituent Assembly is concerned, it is not by groups; but the members of the Constituent Assembly will be individuals elected, and that there is no such thing as a group deciding to join the Constituent Assembly or not; it is individuals who will be elected and who in their individual capacity will come and join the Assembly?

*Answer:* I can answer that question in the affirmative.

*Question:* Is it not a fact that the constitution-making body will be composed of individuals elected from the various provincial Legislative Assemblies and will not be composed of groups or anything else, and will Lord Pethick-Lawrence say that is a fact?

*Answer:* I do not know whether you have heard the question. As I understand it, the answer is in the affirmative.

*Question:* How do you propose to constitute the Negotiations Committee on behalf of the States? You have not indicated how that Negotiations Committee will be formed.

*Answer:* That is a matter for discussion with the States. It will presumably be for the States in the first instance to put forward a form for that Negotiations Committee, and until that is gone into, I do not think it is for us to get any further. When you get outside what is called British India and come to the States, you are dealing with bodies that are to a very large extent independent, and it is not for us in a document to say how a Negotiating Committee shall be formed.

*Question:* Consultation between whom?

*Answer:* Between all the parties concerned.

*Question:* Presumably when you deal with negotiations with the States you must mean with the autocratic rulers concerned and not with the peoples of the States.

*Answer:* The whole matter has got to be considered at the time. We are not in a position to decide this in advance, and that is why this is left vague. The object of our Statement is to deal primarily with one issue and that is the communal issue which hitherto has prevented a constitution-making body being set up at all. About the middle of page 3 it is said, 'The precise form which their co-operation (i.e. the States) will take must be a matter for negotiation during the building up of the new constitutional structure.' It by no means follows that it will be identical for all the States. We have not therefore dealt with the States in the same detail as the provinces of British India in the paragraph which follows.

*Question:* Supplementary to that, would you explain why it is that while a particular machinery is set up for the election of delegates to the Constituent Assembly from British India, no indication whatsoever is given about the representatives from the Indian States?

*Answer:* I should have thought the answer was apparent in the document itself. So far as British India is concerned, we have been discussing this very matter with representatives of the two communities. After hearing all their points of view we have come to a specific conclusion, which we have proposed in the document which we have issued. So far as the States are concerned, we are not in the same position at all, and for that reason we have proposed that the method of representation of the States shall be decided after negotiation instead of being laid down by us in a document of this kind.

*Question:* In your recommendations you have said that the constitutions of the Union and the Groups should contain a provision whereby any province could call for a reconsideration of the terms of the constitution after an initial period of ten years. Does that include the right of secession?

*Sir S. Cripps:* On page 3, para 15, sub-section 6, there is the provision that the constitutions of the Union and of the Groups should contain a provision whereby any province could by a majority vote of its Legislative Assembly call for a reconsideration of the terms of the constitution after an initial period of 10 years. The question is whether there is included in the words 'call for a reconsideration of the terms of the constitution' any right to have secession considered?

*Answer:* The answer is that if you revise the constitution, quite clearly the whole basis of the constitution can be considered again. Therefore any province can ask for a revision of the constitution as far as I can see. When that revision is undertaken, all questions in the constitution are open to re-discussion.

*Question*: Can the Constituent Assembly be regarded as sovereign in view of three points that are put forward, viz.,

1. Adult suffrage has been ruled out;
2. British troops would continue to remain on the soil;
3. The principle and the procedure of the constitution-making body have been laid down.

*Answer:* First of all it is suggested that adult suffrage is ruled out. That of course is quite untrue. Adult suffrage can, if the constitution-making body so decide, be the essential basis of the new constitution. Our friend is confusing two quite separate things. It is perfectly open to the Constituent Assembly to decide in favour of adult suffrage. What is not proposed in our Statement is that this body which is going to make the constitution shall itself be elected by adult suffrage, and the only reason why we lay that down is that otherwise you will get a delay of anything up to two years in the start of making the constitution. That was the first point.

The second point was, can the Constituent Assembly be regarded as sovereign so long as British troops remain on Indian soil? I am not quite clear what the questioner means. Of course if the constitution, as it is framed by Indians, is for complete independence outside the British Common-wealth, naturally one of the first things that will happen will be that the British troops will immediately be withdrawn, except on the possible assumption that some arrangement might be made which would be entire-ly in the hands of Indians. The normal assumption is that British troops would go. But British troops of course will remain until the constitution is made, not with the view of forcing or determining any constitution on the constitution-making body, because they are entirely free to make such a constitution as they like on this basis. Therefore I do not think the question of British troops affects the issue at all.

The third question was whether, as we had laid down certain provisions, the constitution-making body or Constituent Assembly could be regarded in any sense as sovereign. Well, we only laid these conditions down be-cause Indians did not come to an agreement among themselves. If it had been possible for the two Indian parties to come together to make a consti-tution, we should have made no stipulations of any kind. But when we got here, we found, what we suspected in advance, that a Constituent Assembly representing all parties could not be acceptable except on certain decisions taken in advance. We then asked the Indian parties whether they them-selves by agreement would lay down certain decisions which would enable the Constituent Assembly to meet together and to function, and we tried our very best to get that agreed to and we went a considerable distance towards getting agreement on that point, but we did not get all the way, and therefore only because of that we suggested this basis and we made these recommendations, because it is only on those that we felt that we could get representatives of all parties to sit together and try to draw up a constitution. But even so, I would point out to you that even that basis can be altered, but it can only be altered by a separate majority of each party who desire to do so, and the reason is this, that these representatives of different parties have agreed to meet together only on that basis. That is what we believe is the basis on which they will come together. If they do come together on that basis, it will mean that they will have accepted that basis, but they can still change it if by a majority of each party they desire to do so.

*Question:* The question is under paragraph 15, sub-para 5: the phrase ' Provinces should be free to form groups etc...' whether that means that in the initial stage provinces are free to stay out?

*Answer:* Provinces automatically come into sections A, B or C which are set out in the statement, and initially they are in the particular sections to which they are elected in the statement, and that particular section will decide whether a group shall be formed and what should be the constitution of the provinces in the section and the group. The right to opt out of the group formed by that section arises after the constitution has been framed and the first election to the Legislature has taken place under that constitution. It does not arise before that.

*Question:* Can a province, if it opts out of a certain section, go into another section?

*Answer:* If you think that out, you will see, I think, that if you gave the right to a province to opt into another section and that section did not want to receive it, it might get into an awkward situation. The answer to your question, therefore, whether a province can go into another section, is not laid down in any way and it will be open to the Constituent Assembly to deal with that point in its proper setting.

*Question:* With reference to your answer, there is to my mind a very serious lacuna regarding the exercise of the option. You say here that a province is not allowed to exercise the option of either going in or getting out of a certain group in the initial stages by the vote of its present legislature. Secondly, you say that when the provinces have gone into A, B or C sections they will be entitled as groups to vote in favour of provinces being free to form groups with executives and legislatures and each group should determine the provincial steps to be taken in common. Then the third stage arises, when a provincial legislature and executive and a group legislature and executive are formed, the provincial legislature can opt out of that group. My point is this. Supposing in such a system the grouping as such, not the province as such, decide s by a majority vote to have no provincial legislature and no provincial executive but to have a group legislature and a group executive, automatically therefore if this resolution is carried, then the option that you envisage in 3 disappears so far as that province is concerned, because that province will have no legislature of its own under the new arrangement, not by its own option but by a joint vote of the group, and therefore it will be deprived of the option of getting out, because there will be no legislature to vote at all; there will be only the group legislature. Therefore in that contingency, if there is a lacuna at all, would you give the option to the existing legislature to exercise that option in case any group decides to have no provincial legislature at all?

*Question ( as summarised by Sir S. Cripps)*: In view of the various provisions which are made as regards the provinces coming into groups and going out of groups and the powers of the groups of setting their constitutions, is it not possible that a group might settle a constitution for the group without any provincial legislature at all? In that case there would be no body to decide to opt out.

*Answer:* I do congratulate the questioner upon his great ingenuity. He has tried to imagine something arising which would be exceedingly foolish on the part of those who were responsible for it and which might conceivably lead to an impasse. All I can say in the first place with regard to that is this: that in writing down the words in our Statement we presumed, and I think we had good reason to presume, that the representatives from different parts of India who came together would be intelligent and wise people. I am not going to say for one moment that when those representatives came there and irrespective of all reason and all commonsense they wanted to tie the constitution up into such knots, so that it would not function, I certainly would not say that they could not do it, but I think on a reasonable interpretation, we may assume that will not be the case. Paragraph 15(3) says 'all subjects other than the Union subjects and all residuary powers should vest in the Provinces' and I should have thought that would rule out the possibility of a group or a section having met together and taking all the powers away from the provinces, and in my broadcast last night in which I did attempt to explain to some extent what is in this document, I distinctly pointed out, if I am right, that there would be at the top the Union legislature and executive, and at the bottom there would be the provincial legislature and executive, and I cannot imagine a group or a section taking into its head to rule out the possibility of a provincial legislature and executive. I cannot imagine that after having agreed to come into it, the first thing a province would do is to get out of it. But, as I said, the real fact is that we assumed that they are intelligent and, I am quite sure, wise human beings coming together to do something sensible and not to meet with the express purpose of tying up the constitution into knots.

*Question:* I am very glad about what you said, because I also do not envisage such a possibility. Since you have taken so much pains to leave the option there that possibility might have been envisaged. But I should be very glad if my interpretation of what you suggest is correct. You say that subjects other than the Union subjects and residuary powers should vest in the provinces. I take it, that should any such emergency arise, the very fact of this clause 3 being there will be sufficient for the provincial representatives to refuse a grouping of that kind, because that would militate, I take it from you, against clause 3.

*Answer:* I do not think we need go into it much further. If there were people so foolish as to make the mistake which our friend here suggests, I should imagine there are a sufficient number of wise and sensible people who would see that things are put right. I think that an intelligent interpretation of all the clauses and sections in this proposal would give them ample ground to do so.

*Question:* So far as Group C is concerned, it consists of Assam and Bengal, the former under a Congress ministry and the latter under a Muslim League ministry. Supposing the legislature which is Congress decides not to join that group, what would be the position?

*Answer:* This Statement puts the position thus, that these sections meet in the form in which it is intended in this Statement, and the right to opt out comes afterwards, for this reason that it is intended that the whole picture should be understood before the option is exercised. I may say to those of you who were present last night, and I expect the great bulk of you were present, Sir Stafford Cripps, if I remember aright, did deal very comprehensively with this point. Possibly you would not wish him to repeat it all over again but if it is necessary I think he will be quite willing to do so.

*Question:* Just as the provinces have the right to opt out of the groups, will they have the right to secede from the Indian Union, say within two years?

*Answer:* They will not have the right to opt out in the period of two years, but they will have a right to ask for a revision of the constitution at the end of ten years.

*Question:* There being no mention in the document of the relationship between the Union Constituent Assembly and the Group Constituent Assembly, would the Group Constituent Assembly stand in the same relationship to the Union Constituent Assembly as the Negotiating Committee of the States?

*Answer:* That is a matter of course which is entirely left open for discussion during the process of the constitution-making machinery. The fewer things we wanted to lay down we thought the better. We did not want to decide the constitution at all. We would have been glad to have made no provision about the constitution, because it is a matter for Indians to decide their constitution, not for us. The only reason why we have laid down anything at all in the nature of a basic form of the constitution is because it was brought home to us that unless we did so, the constitution-making machinery would not be set up at all, and therefore the fewer the things that we have recommended in advance, the better both from our point of view and from the point of view of India.

*Question:* I thought you had made the point clear in your earlier reply. So far as the Union Constituent Assembly is concerned the Group as such has no function. There the delegates will be in their individual capacity, and therefore the question of the relationship between the Group and the Union Constituent Assembly ought not to arise.

*Answer:* You must not confuse the constitution and the Constituent Assembly. They come as representatives to the Constituent Assembly in the form in which it is set out here, but they can make a constitution in any way they like, subject only to certain rules, and the relationship between the Group and the Union will be one of the matters which can be decided by the Constituent Assembly.

*Question:* Will this regrouping take place before or after this Constituent Assembly?

*Answer:* There is no regrouping. After the Group have decided the constitution for the Group and for the provinces within it, and after the whole constitution has been passed and after the next elections have taken place, the provinces can then opt to get out of the Group in which they have been placed.

*Question:* The Constituent Assembly will draw its representatives from the provinces. When will the grouping of provinces take place — before or after?

*Answer:* It really is all set out in this document. Para 19, sub-sections (vi) to (viii) make it perfectly clear.

*Question:* It is said that the Union should have the power necessary to raise the finances required for the above subjects. Does it mean that it will be open to the Constituent Assembly to endow the Union with all powers of taxation, including customs, income tax and other forms of taxation?

*Answer:* Under this Statement, it is left open to the Constituent Assembly to interpret the words relating to finance. But I would remind my friend that all this is subject to this one provision under para 19(vii).

*Question:* You have divided the Indian nation into three categories. General, Muslim and Sikhs. Was this done in consultation with the Parties?

*Answer:* This Statement is our own Statement, and it does not necessarily represent the opinion of anybody in India, but it is put out after we have had discussions on all these matters with different Indians and it is our intention to reach the most likely method which will be accepted by the different parties.

*Question*: Have Congress agreed to come under the term 'all other non-Muslims'?

*Answer*: We have not put this out on the basis that anybody agreed; it is our own Statement and stands on its own footing.

*Question*: May I know if the Nationalist Muslims, the Shias and others will be covered by this term 'Muslims'?

*Answer*: It is not 'Muslim League', it is 'Muslims'.

*Question*: In para 13 you have rejected the Congress suggestion to divide the subjects into 'compulsory' and 'optional'. Do you contemplate the application of some rule of uniformity of subjects as well, because under the 1935 Act, each State has the right to have its own instrument of accession.

*Answer*: We think it undesirable at this stage to predicate precisely what the position of the States will be, and in these circumstances we have not put into this document the relationship of the States after this is done. It will be a matter ultimately for the persons who go to the constitution-making body on behalf of the States to agree to the exact nature of the form in which they are in the Union of India.

*Question*: In para 14, it is said, 'It by no means follows that it will be identical for all the States.' Does that imply only during the period of negotiations, while the constitutional structure is being built up, or even afterwards?

*Answer*: I am sure the questioner appreciates the enormous difference between one State and another. For instance, in the case of Hyderabad you have a State with a very large population, and on the other hand you have very small tiny States which contain only very few people with a revenue of less than a lakh of rupees. Obviously there must be a complete difference in the approach to one State and another. If we are to go into all that in this document, if we are going to wait before all that has been settled before we go on with the constitution-making we might have to wait for a very long period. It is for that reason we have purposely left the matter over and wanted to go on with the main job.

*Question*: Would it be incumbent on every State to be represented through the Negotiating Committee or would some big States have the right to stand out and negotiate on a plane of complete equality?

*Answer*: It is not for me to decide whether particular States should be represented or not. I naturally hope that the bulk of the States would take some share in negotiating general terms on which the States should come into the constitution. We have already had indications from the States, most of the principal States and others representing large bodies of other States, that they have no desire to impede the progress of India towards self-government and independence and every one of them wants to co-operate. I am not speaking necessarily on behalf of all of them, but I believe it is the general wish of nearly all to co-operate.

*Question*: The question arises out of this, whereas certain provinces are compulsorily grouped in certain groups, are the States also necessarily grouped under the Negotiating Committee or not?

*Answer:* Our relations with the States are different from our relations with the provinces. We would have been very pleased if leaders of thought in British India, in every province, had chosen themselves, but in default of their choice, in order to get on with the constitution-making machinery, we made certain recommendations and certain means of summoning the constitution-making body for British India. We are not in the same position as regards the States, but we hope very much that they will come in and we have good ground for thinking so, but the precise method of bringing them in has not yet been decided upon.

*Question:* What would be the status of the States in the interim period? Will they be as at present under the Political Department or will they be wholly independent?

*Answer:* They remain as they are during the interim period, but obviously coming events cast their shadows before, and naturally when you are working up a new constitution things are constantly changing, and during that interim period constitution-making will go on and the States will presumably be taking their share in that constitution-making, so that the whole picture will be presumably ready at the same time.

*Question:* Is it realised that the influence of the Political Department is of such a character that it will not be helpful to the development of constitution-making?

*Answer:* I have no reason to think so. I do not think I can go beyond that.

*Question:* If the subjects of any State revolt for the establishment of self-government, will the interim central Government help the Ruler of that State to crush the revolt? Or will it help the nationalist cause?

*Answer:* I am afraid that question is outside our present discussions; it is a matter for the Crown Representative. I am not here to override the decisions of the Crown Representative or predict precisely what they will be. That is part of the normal procedure, and I should certainly not like to go into all that.

*Question:* As far as representation in the Constituent Assembly of the Indian States is concerned, is it the intention that representation should reflect the strength of the different communities, Hindus and Muslims, in the States as they would be in British India?

*Answer:* It is quite impossible to predict in advance what is going to happen in the States. As I have already indicated, of course the hope is that the representatives who come from the States will represent the opinion in those States in those forms, but what precisely will be done I cannot say. We have not reached the stage when the matter has been investigated, let alone decided.

*Question:* I was not thinking of representatives reflecting Indian States opinion as much as representatives of Hindu and Muslim population. The idea seems to be to have representation of Hindus and Muslims on a population basis in British India. I was wondering whether the same principle would be applied with regard to the population of the States? I have in mind the Hyderabad State where out of a population of 16 millions, the Muslims are only 8½ per cent. Is it the idea that representatives from Hyderabad will reflect the Hindu and Muslim population strengths in the Constituent Assembly?

*Answer:* Obviously the question is one which will be taken into account in these negotiations that you are going to initiate. I certainly cannot tell you how those negotiations are going to be decided before they even start.

*Question:* Arising out of the previous answers on the relations of Groups and Union, the position does not seem to be quite clear. It is not a hypothetical difficulty. If say, from section B which in fact means the Muslim League, a majority stood by the programme of the League and were to proclaim themselves a sovereign State, would that be possible under the constitutional arrangement, or would you prevent that, and would the subsequent relation with the Union Centre be then a matter of negotiations in the same way as between the States and the Union?

*Answer:* The questioner definitely states they will form a sovereign State outside the Union. The answer to that is, it will be prejudicial to the conditions under which all these people meet together for the purpose of making a constitution, therefore the constitution-making machinery would break down if they persisted in this. That would be contrary to the understanding on which these people are coming together. If they come together on the understanding with which we are inviting them, that presumes an honourable acceptance of the major premises, and if they were to repudiate that later on, then it would be a breach of the understanding.

*Question:* Am I right in assuming that the paramountcy of the British Crown will be enforced until such time as the three sections of the constitution-making body come to an agreement regarding the Union Centre?

*Answer:* Yes, that is quite right. Paramountcy will continue during the interim period, and when the interim period is over — which cannot be before and will be almost immediately following upon what the questioner has put — then paramountcy comes to an end.

*Question:* Arising out of the question you answered a little while ago regarding the Group B provinces not being entitled under the terms of the Statement to declare themselves sovereign States and refusing to come into the Union, would it be open to Group B provinces to take that attitude at the time of the revision after ten years? Could they then revise the present constitution and come together as a sovereign State?

*Answer:* The answer is that of course if the constitution is being revised, all sorts of proposals for its revision will be open to discussion. Whether they will be carried will be quite another question.

*Question:* Arising out of Section 22, it will be necessary to negotiate a treaty between the Union Constituent Assembly and the United Kingdom to provide for certain matters arising out of the transfer of power. I want to know whether this treaty can be freely entered into after the constitution has been formed, or after the Constituent Assembly is formed? Could you throw more light on what those certain matters arising out of the transfer of power will be and whether this treaty will be with the all-India Union, (which means also the Indian States), or with British India, and there will be separate treaties with Indian States?

*Answer:* The answer to the first question of time is quite clear. It will be when the constitution is ready. Of course it will be negotiated in the intervening period in order to prevent delay. With regard to the matters it contains I should have thought that it was obvious that there would be questions of finance and foreign relationships, and clearly any body that is becoming a sovereign state, if it is entirely outside the British Commonwealth, then a sovereign independent State will have a number of matters which it will want to settle with a country which has been so closely associated with it. It will settle those on an entirely equal footing. With regard to the third point, on the assumption that there emerges from this constitutional machinery a constitution with a Union Centre, quite clearly it will be with that Union that the treaty will have to be negotiated and not with one part of it.

*Question:* Did you consider the question of putting a time limit on the formation of these different constitutions, and further whether you could give any estimate? If you did not, what time do you think will be occupied by the various stages?

*Answer:* Of course we did consider whether we should put a time limit on this thing, and we came to the conclusion that it was not for us to decide. It entirely rests with the Indians who are going to make the constitution. The making of a constitution is a very difficult thing, and it entirely depends on how many people want to discuss it and how far there are preparations in advance. I do not think it is for us to put a time limit on what Indians are proposing to do. If Indians like to make this decision so, they can do it if they choose. In Section 19, sub-section 4, it says 'a preliminary meeting will be held in which the general business will be decided.' If Indians want to put a time limit on their labours, that is for them to decide.

As to whether we have any estimate of time, I answer, no. It depends entirely on details and how many people want to talk. I know in the House of Commons it all depends on how many people want to discuss the matter whether it can be agreed to or not. Sometimes where it looks that a question can be settled in ten minutes it takes ten hours, and where a question is expected to take ten hours it is decided in ten minutes. But there are quite a lot of very important matters which affect the whole future of India to be discussed, and quite obviously you cannot rush them beyond a point. So far as we are concerned, the quicker the thing is done the better we shall feel.

*Question:* In view of the intolerable political conditions in the Indian territory ruled by the Portuguese and the French in Pondicherry, what will be the attitude of Great Britain in view of her long-standing friendship with Portugal and France in case the Union legislature were to serve the 'Quit India' order upon them? Will you eliminate them or keep quiet?

*Answer:* It is of the essence of our scheme that foreign affairs shall be a Union subject, and that being so, it will be quite clearly for the Union Government to deal with this matter when it comes into being, and that being so I do not think we can say anything in advance in regard to it.

*Question:* During the interim period what will be the position of the India Office and presumably the Secretary of State?

*Answer:* As I said before, coming events cast their shadows before, and already I can tell you, before this statement was made, many months ago, the India Office had already been proceeding on the assumption that the time will come when great changes will be made in India and the whole position of the India Office will be altered. Naturally if this constitution-making machinery goes on, that process will be rapidly accelerated, and the India Office will be starting to make the transfers which at the end of the period will either be complete or will certainly be arranged to be wound up. You have to remember that the India Office may do a great many things you do not like. But quite apart from all that, it is an enormous administrative machine and it is going to be part of the new set-up in India. All that vast administrative machine will be at the disposal of the new constitution in India, and the transfer will have to be carried through.

Sir Stafford Cripps points out to me that I have not made it clear.

There are an immense number of files dealing with all sorts of matters which are subjects of administration. Now the new Government in India will want to have those files and they will want to be able to handle the administration of India not from scratch but to be able to carry forward the administration and that there should be no break or high hedges and difficulties. I say that transfer will not only begin from today but it has been going on for some time and it will be carried on at a greater rate when this constitutional machinery is set up and it will reach its final stage when the new Government actually comes into being.

When it came to be examined it was found that there was no point in changing the name so long as the substance of things remained. It was simpler to leave it where it was, but when the substance changes then you may be quite sure that the India Office will gradually with its apparatus be transferred to the control of the new Government.

*Question:* While the interim Government is functioning will it function as a *de facto* independent government and within that period will the India Office cease to function in fact if not in law?

*Answer:* I do not think that could be so. If you think it out carefully you could not make that change completely at the present time, but you may be perfectly sure that all that will be taken into account.

*Question:* During the interim period will the Viceroy exercise his veto in the same manner as he is entitled to exercise it now, or will it be subject to the same convention which applies in the provinces today, by mutual consent but not within the constitution, between the provincial Governor and his ministers?

*Answer:* That is a question really for the Viceroy. The Viceroy is negotiating at the present time with the various parties on the assumption that the constitution-making body is to be set up, and I do not propose to express any views on what is primarily the Viceroy's function.

*Question:* Under paragraph 19 where the table of representation is given of the number of representatives to be elected from each province, does the title 'general' include European members of the present Assembly?

*Answer:* The answer of course is Yes. You must remember that the basis now is population and in view of the small number of the European population they would not figure very largely in the result. They will take part in proportional representation in the election.

*Question:* In Bengal they have twenty-five votes. In the grouping of Bengal and Assam they will have an almost decisive influence.

*Answer:* The position is this, that when each section, General, Muslim or Sikh, as the case may be, elect their own representatives, it would not have any effect at all. They will be in the group which is electing in Bengal.

*Question:* On the question of the States, in the event of some one State or more States choosing to remain outside the Indian Union and continue their present relationship with the British Government, what happens then?

*Answer:* I cannot predict what will take place, but it seems to me to be a very difficult relationship. In paragraph 14 it is stated, 'It is quite clear that with the attainment of independence by British India, whether inside or outside the British Commonwealth, the relationship which has hitherto existed between the Rulers of the States and the British Crown will no longer be possible. Paramountcy can neither be retained by the British Crown nor transferred to the new Government. This fact has been fully recognized by those whom we interviewed from the States.' What precisely will happen under those circumstances I cannot predict, but those are the facts. That really is the answer to your question.

*Question:* Then conceivably they might remain as independent countries?

*Answer:* It may be conceivable, but of course this paragraph goes on to say: 'They have at the same time assured us that the States are ready and willing to co-operate in the new development of India. The precise form which their co-operation will take must be a matter for negotiation during the building up of the new constitutional structure.' I cannot go beyond that. The existing relationship quite clearly being altered, paramountcy does not remain. They have expressed their intention to co-operate: they are willing to negotiate.

*Question:* If you can make these mandatory recommendations for these provinces, do you want us to believe that you have no power to make similar recommendations about the States?

*Answer:* The answer is that our relationship with the provinces and States are quite different. The second answer is that we are not making mandatory provisions for the provinces at all. What we are doing is, we are endeavouring to set up a constitution-making machinery for all the provinces. If the Indians concerned had been willing to set up their own constitution-making machinery we should have said nothing about it at all. It is only with the intention of bringing them together that we have put forward this Statement. The position with regard to the States is quite different. Our relationship with the States is quite different, and the best way of securing their co-operation, we believed, was in the form in which we have set it out in this document.

*Question:* Are you aware of the discontent among the States' peoples that none of their representatives had been invited to meet the Mission?

*Answer:* There are a great many things going on in India about which a great many people are not happy. I do not think I would go beyond that. It is just for all those reasons that this matter will have to be dealt with carefully, and we thought that it would be better not to make any rigid proposals with regard to the States. I do not think it would have been in the interests either of the people in the States or the people in the provinces. I am quite satisfied that the rather vague and loose way in which we propose to deal with it is at the moment the method which is most likely to bring the results which all of us desire.

*Question:* Have you examined and excluded currency from the list of Union subjects? If so, on what grounds?

*Answer:* No. I do not think we can explain exactly whether we have considered this, that or the other question and excluded it. Currency is a question which can be discussed if necessary in the constitution-making body, if it is thought that that is a matter which can be reasonably included. If all the sections think so, there is no reason why it should not be included. We do not want to impose it. It is a matter for Indians to decide.

*Question:* If the constitution-making body decides preliminary to proceeding with their work that the British troops should be withdrawn from India, will they be withdrawn?

*Answer:* I think that is a misunderstanding of the situation. Someone must be responsible for law and order in a country. We are anxious to hand over that responsibility in so far as it remains at the earliest opportunity to a fully constituted Indian Government. There is no fully constituted Indian Government now. As a matter of fact the Indian governments in the provinces are really responsible for law and order, but the ultimate responsibility for law and order rests in the Government of India, and we are anxious to transfer that as early as possible to a properly constituted Government. When that time comes we will make that transfer.

*Question:* Do you mean to say that no law and order can be maintained in India without British troops?

*Answer:* I won't make any postulate of that kind. I would only say, in all countries the final sanction for law and order is the force of the Government, and so long as that responsibility rests with us we cannot dispense with the means which enables us to carry it through. It is not my wish that it should be used. It is our desire that, at the earliest possible moment when the new Government is set up, different arrangements should be made.

*Question:* In the interim period would Lord Wavell be able to change the constitutional position of the present Executive Council?

*Answer:* The present constitutional position of the Executive Council is laid down by statute. Quite clearly Lord Wavell cannot change that and, as I have already said, the whole constitutional machinery rests primarily with him. But as to the final statutory and legal position, that can only be changed by an Act of Parliament, and personally I think it would be unwise to start with that now when we are so very near the real final change, which is the really important thing, namely the complete transference of power from our country to an independent Indian Government.

*Question:* What will be the next stage of activity of the Cabinet Delegation?

*Answer:* The first thing is to get this plan accepted by the two main communities in India. That will be carried through as speedily as possible.

*Question:* Do you want it to be accepted by the two main communities, or parties?

*Answer:* Both.

*Question:* In Section B of para. 19 (1), in the Punjab there are sixteen Muslim seats. Will those be voted for by all the Muslims together or will they be allocated separately between the different parties amongst the Muslims?

*Answer:* They are voted for by all the Muslims together, but the election is by the method of proportional representation with the single transferable vote.

*Question:* In view of paragraph 15 (6), does it mean that the Union constitution will only be inviolable for ten years?

*Answer:* What it does mean is that the Constituent Assembly will lay down provisions enabling the constitution, and there would be a revision of the constitution. This is in accordance with what has taken place in a great many other cases in the world and there must be some provision for revision. Precisely what the conditions of revision are will be a matter for the Constituent Assembly to decide. I do not think I can go any further into that. What the basis of revision will be after a period of years and the precise terms thereof, how that revision shall be gone into, will no doubt be decided by the Constituent Assembly.

*Question:* Can the provincial assembly elect people outside its membership?

*Answer:* Yes, that is not excluded by the terms of the Statement.

*Question:* Can the representatives referred to in para. 19 (1) be from any part of India or from any legislature, or should the representatives be confined to the voters of the respective provinces only? In other words, can the representative under para. 19 (1) be any Indian citizen, or must he be from any particular category?

*Answer:* I can only go by the text of the document. 'There shall be elected by each provincial legislative assembly,' it does not say, 'from among its numbers.'

*Question:* Did you consider the desirability of appointing a boundary commission?

*Answer:* As I explained to you, all sorts of things were considered which of course do not figure in this document.

*Question:* What is the position of the Minority Commission with regard to the Constituent Assembly, and in case of a clash of opinions, whose voice will prevail?

*Answer:* You cannot appoint a minority commission assuming it is composed largely of minorities and give it absolute rights às against the main constitution-making body. We have every reason to hope that the minority committee formed of responsible people will make representations which I should have thought would be in the interest of all parties and would carry great weight with the constitution-making body.

*Question:* Is this Statement final or will you entertain suggestions made by various parties? Is this document final or is it intended starting negotiations all over again?

*Answer:* We do not propose to modify this document, because if we start modifying it in favour of one set of people, it will almost certainly be unfair to another set of people. If after discussing it all parties agree to come in and they agree to some small modifications, then I do not say we shall absolutely stick to the last word in the document. But it is not a document to be modified in favour of 'A' to the disadvantage of 'B'. I am not talking of Groups.

*Question:* Is participation in the interim Government subject to the acceptance of the proposals or is it independent?

*Answer:* Unless you have a constitutional machinery functioning I cannot see any question of interim Government. It is not an interim Government, it is a change of government, and essentially the interim Government is that which functions in the interim while the constitutional machinery is not yet in operation. That is how I interpret the term 'interim Government'.

*(Here end oral questions)*

### WRITTEN QUESTIONS

*Question:* What will be the composition of the various parties in the interim Government? What will be the percentage of Muslims?

*Answer:* As I have already explained, the question of the interim Government is not for us to decide. It is primarily a question for the Viceroy, and I do not propose to intervene in his sphere.

*Question:* Can a province opt out of a Group at the appropriate time and join another group which may be willing to take it in? For instance, could Bihar opt out of Group A and join Group B, if the latter were willing?

*Answer:* On a general point, I have already answered it.

*Question:* If after the constitution-making machinery has been set up as laid down in the Statement, the majority proceed to disregard some of the conditions and checks prescribed, who will intervene?

*Answer:* I have already answered that. The assumption is that if people accept this document and enter on the basis of it, they enter as honourable people willing to carry out the terms. Of course, if you are going to deal with dishonourable people who break their word, then we cannot proceed with any job. We proceed on the assumption that the parties who come into the scheme behave honourably.

*Question:* Is Mr. Churchill correct in suggesting that what he calls the shifting of the onus of deciding the future constitution from Indians to H.M.G. is an unfortunate step going beyond the understood purpose and mandate of the Mission?

*Answer:* There has been no shifting. If we could arrange by agreement between parties in India the basis of the constitution under which they would have to come together in the constitution-making body, nothing would have pleased us better. In default of that, we thought it our duty to make certain recommendations on the basis of which they come together. The Viceroy is prepared to summon the constitution-making body on that basis and we believe this is in accord with the wishes not only of a majority of Indians but a majority of our own people at home.

*Question:* Mr. Churchill complains that the sentence relating to States treaties and paramountcy is obscure. Can you clear up the alleged obscurity?

*Answer:* I have endeavoured to do that in answer to a great number of questions. I do not think there is any obscurity to clear up. I hope I have succeeded in clearing up all obscurities.

*Question:* What legislative steps will be required for setting up the interim Government, the creation of the new constitution and abrogation of the King's title of Emperor of India?

*Answer:* So far as the first two are concerned, no legislative steps are necessary at all. They can all be done forthwith. So far as the ultimate step is concerned, having regard to the matter of constitutional law, I could not answer off-hand. Speaking without consideration, I am not at all sure that a precise statute will be required for it. But I should not like that to be taken as final. They will of course naturally have to be accorded sanction. There has to be some definite step taken with the consent of H. M. the King. But I do not contemplate any difficulty about that at all as the present Labour Government have a considerable working majority in the House of Commons and I do not imagine that any serious difficulties will be experienced in carrying things through when they have been agreed to.

*Question:* Do you agree with Mr. Churchill when he implies that you have laboured not to gain an Empire but to cast it away?

*Answer:* I can only say this, that what we are doing is in accord with the views that have been expressed all through by really great statesmen in our country and nothing can redound more to the highest traditions of liberty which prevail in my country than if, as a result of our labours, we have in the years to come a sovereign country here in India whose relationship with ours is one of friendliness and equality in the days to come.

I hope we have satisfied your appetite for information, and I think you will agree that I have not shirked any of the issues and that I have tried my best to answer your questions.

# APPENDIX IX

### INDIAN POLICY

1. It has long been the policy of successive British Governments to work towards the realisation of self-government in India. In pursuance of this policy, an increasing measure of responsibility has been devolved on Indians, and today the civil administration and the Indian Armed Forces rely to a very large extent on Indian civilians and officers. In the constitutional field, the Acts of 1919 and 1935 passed by the British Parliament each represented a substantial transfer of political power. In 1940 the Coalition Government recognised the principle that Indians should themselves frame a new constitution for a fully autonomous India, and in the Offer of 1942 they invited them to set up a Constituent Assembly for this purpose as soon as the war was over.

2. His Majesty's Government believe this policy to have been right and in accordance with sound democratic principles. Since they came into office, they have done their utmost to carry it forward to its fulfilment. The declaration of the Prime Minister of 15 March last, which met with general approval in Parliament and the country, made it clear that it was for the Indian people themselves to choose their future status and constitution and that in the opinion of His Majesty's Government the time had come for responsibility for the government of India to pass into Indian hands.

3. The Cabinet Mission which was sent to India last year spent over three months in consultation with Indian leaders in order to help them to agree upon a method for determining the future constitution of India, so that the transfer of power might be smoothly and rapidly effected. It was only when it seemed clear, that without some initiative from the Cabinet Mission, agreement was unlikely to be reached that they put forward proposals themselves.

4. These proposals, made public in May last, envisaged that the future constitution of India should be settled by a Constituent Assembly composed

in the manner suggested therein, of representatives of all communities and interests in British India and of the Indian States.

5. Since the return of the Mission, an interim Government has been set up at the Centre composed of the political leaders of the major communities, exercising wide powers within the existing constitution. In all the provinces Indian governments responsible to legislatures are in office.

6. It is with great regret that His Majesty's Government find that there are still differences among Indian parties which are preventing the Constituent Assembly from functioning as it was intended that it should. It is of the essence of the plan that the Assembly should be fully representative.

7. His Majesty's Government desire to hand over their responsibility to authorities established by a constitution approved by all parties in India in accordance with the Cabinet Mission plan. But unfortunately there is at present no clear prospect that such a constitution and such authorities will emerge. The present state of uncertainty is fraught with danger and cannot be indefinitely prolonged. His Majesty's Government wish to make it clear that it is their definite intention to take the necessary steps to effect the transference of power to responsible Indian hands by a date not later than June 1948.

8. This great sub-continent now containing over four hundred million people has for the last century enjoyed peace and security as a part of the British Commonwealth and Empire. Continued peace and security are more than ever necessary today if the full responsibilities of economic development are to be realised and a higher standard of life attained by the Indian people.

9. His Majesty's Government are anxious to hand over their responsibilities to a Government which, resting on the sure foundation of the support of the people, is capable of maintaining peace and administering India with justice and efficiency. It is therefore essential that all parties should sink their differences in order that they may be ready to shoulder the great responsibilities which will come upon them next year.

10. After months of hard work by the Cabinet Mission a great measure of agreement was obtained as to the method by which a constitution should be worked out. This was embodied in their statements of May last. His Majesty's Government there agreed to recommend to Parliament a constitution worked out in accordance with the proposals made therein by a fully representative Constituent Assembly. But if it should appear that such a constitution will not have been worked out by a fully representative Assembly before the time mentioned in paragraph 7, His Majesty's Government will have to consider to whom the powers of the central Government in British India should be handed over, on the due date, whether as a whole to some form of central Government for British India, or in some areas to

the existing provincial Governments, or in such other way as may seem most reasonable and in the best interests of the Indian people.

11. Although the final transfer of authority may not take place until June 1948, preparatory measures must be put in hand in advance. It is important that the efficiency of the civil administration should be maintained and that the defence of India should be fully provided for. But inevitably, as the process of transfer proceeds, it will become progressively more difficult to carry out to the letter all the provisions of the Government of India Act, 1935. Legislation will be introduced in due course to give effect to the final transfer of power.

12. In regard to the Indian States, as was explicitly stated by the Cabinet Mission, His Majesty's Government do not intend to hand over their powers and obligations under paramountcy to any Government of British India. It is not intended to bring paramountcy, as a system, to a conclusion earlier than the date of the final transfer of power, but it is contemplated that for the intervening period the relations of the Crown with individual States may be adjusted by agreement.

13. His Majesty's Government will negotiate agreements in regard to matters arising out of the transfer of power with representatives of those to whom they propose to transfer power.

14. His Majesty's Government believe that British commercial and industrial interests in India can look forward to a fair field for their enterprise under the new conditions. The commercial connection between India and the United Kingdom has been long and friendly and will continue to be to their mutual advantage.

15. His Majesty's Government cannot conclude this Statement without expressing on behalf of the people of this country their goodwill and good wishes towards the people of India as they go forward to this final stage in their achievement of self-government. It will be the wish of everyone in these islands that notwithstanding constitutional changes, the association of the British and Indian peoples should not be brought to an end; and they will wish to continue to do all that is in their power to further the wellbeing of India.

### CHANGE OF VICEROY

The House will wish to know of an announcement which is being made public today. Field Marshal the Right Honourable Viscount Wavell was appointed Viceroy in 1943, after having held high military command in the Middle East, South-East Asia and India with notable distinction since the beginning of the war. It was agreed that this should be a wartime appointment. Lord Wavell has discharged this high office during this very difficult period with devotion and a high sense of duty. It has, however, seemed that the opening of a new and final phase in India is an appropriate time to terminate this war appointment. His Majesty has been pleased to approve, as successor to Lord Wavell, the appointment of Admiral the Viscount Mountbatten, who will be entrusted with the task of transferring to Indian hands responsibility for the government of British India in a manner that will best ensure the future happiness and prosperity of India. The change of office will take place during March. The House will be glad to hear that His Majesty has been pleased to approve the conferment of an earldom on Viscount Wavell.

# APPENDIX X

### INTRODUCTION

1. On 20 February 1947, His Majesty's Government announced their intention of transferring power in British India to Indian hands by June 1948. His Majesty's Government had hoped that it would be possible for the major parties to co-operate in the working-out of the Cabinet Mission Plan of 16 May 1946, and evolve for India a constitution acceptable to all concerned. This hope has not been fulfilled.

2. The majority of the representatives of the provinces of Madras, Bombay, the United Provinces, Bihar, Central Provinces and Berar, Assam, Orissa and the North-West Frontier Province, and the representatives of Delhi, Ajmer-Merwara and Coorg have already made progress in the task of evolving a new constitution. On the other hand, the Muslim League Party, including in it a majority of the representatives of Bengal, the Punjab and Sind, as also the representative of British Baluchistan, has decided not to participate in the Constituent Assembly.

3. It has always been the desire of His Majesty's Government that power should be transferred in accordance with the wishes of the Indian people themselves. This task would have been greatly facilitated if there had been agreement among the Indian political parties. In the absence of such agreement, the task of devising a method by which the wishes of the Indian people can be ascertained has devolved upon His Majesty's Government. After full consultation with political leaders in India, His Majesty's Government have decided to adopt for this purpose the plan set out below. His Majesty's Government wish to make it clear that they have no intention of attempting to frame any ultimate constitution for India; this is a matter for the Indians themselves. Nor is there anything in this plan to preclude negotiations between communities for a united India.

## THE ISSUES TO BE DECIDED

4. It is not the intention of His Majesty's Government to interrupt the work of the existing Constituent Assembly. Now that provision is made for certain provinces specified below, His Majesty's Government trust that, as a consequence of this announcement, the Muslim League representatives of those provinces, a majority of whose representatives are already participating in it, will now take their due share in its labours. At the same time, it is clear that any constitution framed by this Assembly cannot apply to those parts of the country which are unwilling to accept it. His Majesty's Government are satisfied that the procedure outlined below embodies the best practical method of ascertaining the wishes of the people of such areas on the issue whether their constitution is to be framed:—

(*a*) in the existing Constituent Assembly; or

(*b*) in a new and separate Constituent Assembly consisting of the representatives of those areas which decide not to participate in the existing Constituent Assembly.

When this has been done, it will be possible to determine the authority or authorities to whom power should be transferred.

## BENGAL AND THE PUNJAB

5. The provincial Legislative Assemblies of Bengal and the Punjab (excluding the European members) will, therefore, each be asked to meet in two parts, one representing the Muslim-majority districts and the other the rest of the Province. For the purpose of determining the population of districts, the 1941 census figures will be taken as authoritative. The Muslim-majority districts in these two provinces are set out in the Appendix to this Announcement.

6. The members of the two parts of each Legislative Assembly sitting separately will be empowered to vote whether or not the Province should be partitioned. If a simple majority of either part decides in favour of partition, division will take place and arrangements will be made accordingly.

7. Before the question as to the partition is decided, it is desirable that the representatives of each part should know in advance which Constituent Assembly the Province as a whole would join in the event of the two parts subsequently deciding to remain united. Therefore, if any member of either Legislative Assembly so demands, there shall be held a meeting of all members of the Legislative Assembly (other than Europeans) at which a decision will be taken on the issue as to which Constituent Assembly the Province as a whole would join if it were decided by the two parts to remain united.

8. In the event of partition being decided upon, each part of the Legislative Assembly will, on behalf of the areas they represent, decide which of the alternatives in paragraph 4 above to adopt.

9. For the immediate purpose of deciding on the issue of partition, the members of the Legislative Assemblies of Bengal and the Punjab will sit in two parts according to Muslim-majority districts (as laid down in the Appendix) and non-Muslim majority districts. This is only a preliminary step of a purely temporary nature, as it is evident that for the purposes of a final partition of these provinces a detailed investigation of boundary questions will be needed; and, as soon as a decision involving partition has been taken for either province, a Boundary Commission will be set up by the Governor-General, the membership and terms of reference of which will be settled in consultation with those concerned. It will be instructed to demarcate the boundaries of the two parts of the Punjab on the basis of ascertaining the contiguous majority areas of Muslims and non-Muslims. It will also be instructed to take into account other factors. Similar instructions will be given to the Bengal Boundary Commission. Until the report of a Boundary Commission has been put into effect, the provisional boundaries indicated in the Appendix will be used.

### SIND

10. The Legislative Assembly of Sind (excluding the European members) will at a special meeting also take its own decision on the alternatives in paragraph 4 above.

### NORTH-WEST FRONTIER PROVINCE

11. The position of the North-West Frontier Province is exceptional. Two of the three representatives of this Province are already participating in the existing Constituent Assembly. But it is clear, in view of its geographical situation, and other considerations, that if the whole or any part of the Punjab decides not to join the existing Constituent Assembly, it will be necessary to give the North-West Frontier Province an opportunity to reconsider its position. Accordingly, in such an event, a referendum will be made to the electors of the present Legislative Assembly in the North-West Frontier Province to choose which of the alternatives mentioned in paragraph 4 above they wish to adopt. The referendum will be held under the ægis of the Governor-General and in consultation with the provincial Government.

### BRITISH BALUCHISTAN

12. British Baluchistan has elected a member, but he has not taken his seat in the existing Constituent Assembly. In view of its geographical situation, this Province will also be given an opportunity to reconsider its position and to choose which of the alternatives in paragraph 4 above to adopt. His Excellency the Governor-General is examining how this can most appropriately be done.

## ASSAM

13. Though Assam is predominantly a non-Muslim province, the district of Sylhet which is contiguous to Bengal is predominantly Muslim. There has been a demand that, in the event of the partition of Bengal, Sylhet should be amalgamated with the Muslim part of Bengal. Accordingly, if it is decided that Bengal should be partitioned, a referendum will be held in Sylhet district under the ægis of the Governor-General and in consultation with the Assam Provincial Government to decide whether the district of Sylhet should continue to form part of the Assam Province or should be amalgamated with the new Province of Eastern Bengal, if that Province agrees. If the referendum results in favour of amalgamation with Eastern Bengal, a Boundary Commission with terms of reference similar to those for the Punjab and Bengal will be set up to demarcate the Muslim-majority areas of Sylhet district and contiguous Muslim-majority areas of adjoining districts, which will then be transferred to Eastern Bengal. The rest of the Assam Province will in any case continue to participate in the proceedings of the existing Constituent Assembly.

## REPRESENTATION IN CONSTITUENT ASSEMBLIES

14. If it is decided that Bengal and the Punjab should be partitioned, it will be necessary to hold fresh elections to choose their representatives on the scale of one for every million of population according to the principle contained in the Cabinet Mission Plan of 16 May 1946. Similar elections will also have to be held for Sylhet in the event of it being decided that this district should form part of East Bengal. The number of representatives to which each area would be entitled is as follows:—

| Province | | General | Muslims | Sikhs | Total |
|---|---|---|---|---|---|
| Sylhet District | •• | 1 | 2 | Nil | 3 |
| West Bengal | •• | 15 | 4 | Nil | 19 |
| East Bengal | •• | 12 | 29 | Nil | 41 |
| West Punjab | •• | 3 | 12 | 2 | 17 |
| East Punjab | •• | 6 | 4 | 2 | 12 |

15. In accordance with the mandates given to them, the representatives of the various areas will either join the existing Constituent Assembly or form the new Constituent Assembly.

## ADMINISTRATIVE MATTERS

16. Negotiations will have to be initiated as soon as possible on the administrative consequences of any partition that may have been decided upon :—

(a) Between the representatives of the respective successor authorities about all subjects now dealt with by the central Government, including defence, finance and communications.

(*b*) Between different successor authorities and His Majesty's Government for treaties in regard to matters arising out of the transfer of power.

(*c*) In the case of provinces that may be partitioned, as to the administration of all provincial subjects such as the division of assets and liabilities, the police and other services, the High Courts, provincial institutions, etc.

### THE TRIBES OF THE NORTH-WEST FRONTIER

17. Agreements with tribes of the North-West Frontier of India will have to be negotiated by the appropriate successor authority.

### THE STATES

18. His Majesty's Government wish to make it clear that the decisions announced above relate only to British India and that their policy towards Indian States contained in the Cabinet Mission Memorandum of 12 May 1946 remains unchanged.

### NECESSITY FOR SPEED

19. In order that the successor authorities may have time to prepare themselves to take over power, it is important that all the above processes should be completed as quickly as possible. To avoid delay, the different provinces or parts of provinces will proceed independently as far as practicable within the conditions of this Plan. The existing Constituent Assembly and the new Constituent Assembly (if formed) will proceed to frame constitutions for their respective territories: they will of course be free to frame their own rules.

### IMMEDIATE TRANSFER OF POWER

20. The major political parties have repeatedly emphasized their desire that there should be the earliest possible transfer of power in India. With this desire His Majesty's Government are in full sympathy, and they are willing to anticipate the date of June 1948, for the handing over of power by the setting up of an independent Indian Government or Governments at an even earlier date. Accordingly, as the most expeditious, and indeed the only practicable way of meeting this desire, His Majesty's Government propose to introduce legislation during the current session for the transfer of power this year on a Dominion Status basis to one or two successor authorities according to the decisions taken as a result of this announcement. This will be without prejudice to the right of the Indian Constituent Assemblies to decide in due course whether or not the part of India in respect of which they have authority will remain within the British Commonwealth.

FURTHER ANNOUNCEMENTS BY GOVERNOR-GENERAL

21. His Excellency the Governor-General will from time to time make such further announcements as may be necessary in regard to procedure or any other matters for carrying out the above arrangements.

APPENDIX

THE MUSLIM-MAJORITY DISTRICTS OF THE PUNJAB AND BENGAL
ACCORDING TO THE 1941 CENSUS

1. THE PUNJAB

*Lahore Division*—Gujranwala, Gurdaspur, Lahore, Sheikhupura, Sialkot.

*Rawalpindi Division*—Attock, Gujrat, Jhelum, Mianwali, Rawalpindi, Shahpur.

*Multan Division*—Dera Ghazi Khan, Jhang, Lyallpur, Montgomery, Multan, Muzaffargarh.

2. BENGAL

*Chittagong Division*—Chittagong, Noakhali, Tippera.

*Dacca Division*—Bakerganj, Dacca, Faridpur, Mymensingh.

*Presidency Division*—Jessore, Murshidabad, Nadia.

*Rajshahi Division*—Bogra, Dinajpur, Malda, Pabna, Rajshahi, Rangpur.

# APPENDIX XI

An Act to make provision for the setting up in India of two independent Dominions, to substitute other provisions for certain provisions of the Government of India Act, 1935, which apply outside those Dominions, and to provide for other matters consequential on or connected with the setting up of those Dominions. [18th July 1947.]

Be it enacted by the King's most Excellent Majesty, by and with the advice and consent of the Lords Spiritual and Temporal, and Commons, in this present Parliament assembled, and by the authority of the same, as follows:—

### THE NEW DOMINIONS

1. (1) As from the fifteenth day of August, nineteen hundred and forty-seven, two independent Dominions shall be set up in India, to be known respectively as India and Pakistan.

(2) The said Dominions are hereafter in this Act referred to as 'the new Dominions' and the said fifteenth day of August is hereafter in this Act referred to as 'the appointed day'.

### TERRITORIES OF THE NEW DOMINIONS

2. (1) Subject to the provisions of subsections (3) and (4) of this section, the territories of India shall be the territories under the sovereignty of his Majesty which, immediately before the appointed day, were included in British India except the territories which, under subsection (2) of this section, are to be the territories of Pakistan.

(2) Subject to the provisions of subsections (3) and (4) of this section, the territories of Pakistan shall be—

(*a*) the territories which, on the appointed day, are included in the Provinces of East Bengal and West Punjab, as constituted under the two following sections;

(*b*) the territories which, at the date of the passing of this Act, are included in the Province of Sind and the Chief Commissioner's Province of British Baluchistan; and

(*c*) if, whether before or after the passing of this Act but before the appointed day, the Governor-General declares that the majority of the valid votes cast in the referendum which, at the date of the passing of this Act, is being or has recently been held in that behalf under his authority in the North West Frontier Province are in favour of representatives of that Province taking part in the Constituent Assembly of Pakistan, the territories which, at the date of the passing of this Act, are included in that Province.

(3) Nothing in this section shall prevent any area being at any time included in or excluded from either of the new Dominions, so, however, that—

(*a*) no area not forming part of the territories specified in subsection (1) or, as the case may be, subsection (2), of this section shall be included in either Dominion without the consent of that Dominion; and

(*b*) no area which forms part of the territories specified in the said subsection (1) or, as the case may be, the said subsection (2), or which has after the appointed day been included in either Dominion, shall be excluded from that Dominion without the consent of that Dominion.

(4) Without prejudice to the generality of the provisions of subsection (3) of this section, nothing in this section shall be construed as preventing the accession of Indian States to either of the new Dominions.

## BENGAL AND ASSAM

3. (1) As from the appointed day—

(*a*) the Province of Bengal, as constituted under the Government of India Act, 1935, shall cease to exist; and

(*b*) there shall be constituted in lieu thereof two new Provinces, to be known respectively as East Bengal and West Bengal.

(2) If, whether before or after the passing of this Act, but before the appointed day, the Governor-General declares that the majority of the valid votes cast in the referendum which, at the date of the passing of this Act, is being or has recently been held in that behalf under his authority in the District of Sylhet are in favour of that District forming part of the new Province of East Bengal, then, as from that day, a part of the Province of Assam shall, in accordance with the provisions of subsection (3) of this section, form part of the new Province of East Bengal.

(3) The boundaries of the new Provinces aforesaid and, in the event mentioned in subsection (2) of this section, the boundaries after the appointed day of the Province of Assam, shall be such as may be determined, whether before or after the appointed day, by the award of a boundary commission appointed or to be appointed by the Governor-General in that behalf, but until the boundaries are so determined—

(*a*) the Bengal Districts specified in the First Schedule to this Act, together with, in the event mentioned in subsection (2) of this section, the Assam District of Sylhet, shall be treated as the territories which are to be comprised in the new Province of East Bengal;

(*b*) the remainder of the territories comprised at the date of the passing of this Act in the Province of Bengal shall be treated as the territories which are to be comprised in the new Province of West Bengal; and

(*c*) in the event mentioned in subsection (2) of this section, the District of Sylhet shall be excluded from the Province of Assam.

(4) In this section, the expression 'award' means, in relation to a boundary commission, the decisions of the chairman of that commission contained in his report to the Governor-General at the conclusion of the commission's proceedings.

### THE PUNJAB

4. (1) As from the appointed day—

(*a*) the Province of the Punjab, as constituted under the Government of India Act, 1935, shall cease to exist; and

(*b*) there shall be constituted two new Provinces, to be known respectively as West Punjab and East Punjab.

(2) The boundaries of the said new Provinces shall be such as may be determined, whether before or after the appointed day, by the award of a boundary commission appointed or to be appointed by the Governor-General in that behalf, but until the boundaries are so determined—

(*a*) the Districts specified in the Second Schedule to this Act shall be treated as the territories to be comprised in the new Province of West Punjab; and

(*b*) the remainder of the territories comprised at the date of the passing of this Act in the Province of the Punjab shall be treated as the territories which are to be comprised in the new Province of East Punjab.

(3) In this section, the expression 'award', means, in relation to a boundary commission, the decisions of the chairman of that commission contained in his report to the Governor-General at the conclusion of the commission's proceedings.

### THE GOVERNOR-GENERAL OF THE NEW DOMINIONS

5. For each of the new Dominions, there shall be a Governor-General who shall be appointed by His Majesty and shall represent His Majesty for the purposes of the government of the Dominion:

Provided that, unless and until provision to the contrary is made by a law of the Legislature of either of the new Dominions, the same person may be Governor-General of both the new Dominions.

### LEGISLATION FOR THE NEW DOMINIONS

6. (1) The Legislature of each of the new Dominions shall have full power to make laws for that Dominion, including laws having extra-territorial operation.

(2) No law and no provision of any law made by the Legislature of either of the new Dominions shall be void or inoperative on the ground that it is

repugnant to the law of England, or to the provisions of this or any existing or future Act of Parliament of the United Kingdom, or to any order, rule or regulation made under any such Act, and the powers of the Legislature of each Dominion include the power to repeal or amend any such Act, order, rule or regulation in so far as it is part of the law of the Dominion.

(3) The Governor-General of each of the new Dominions shall have full power to assent in His Majesty's name to any law of the Legislature of that Dominion and so much of any Act as relates to the disallowance of laws by His Majesty or the reservation of laws for the signification of His Majesty's pleasure thereon or the suspension of the operation of laws until the signification of His Majesty's pleasure thereon shall not apply to laws of the Legislature of either of the new Dominions.

(4) No Act of Parliament of the United Kingdom passed on or after the appointed day shall extend, or be deemed to extend, to either of the new Dominions as part of the law of that Dominion unless it is extended thereto by a law of the Legislature of the Dominion.

(5) No Order in Council made on or after the appointed day under any Act passed before the appointed day, and no order, rule or other instrument made on or after the appointed day under any such Act by any United Kingdom Minister or other authority, shall extend, or be deemed to extend, to either of the new Dominions as part of the law of that Dominion.

(6) The power referred to in subsection (1) of this section extends to the making of laws limiting for the future the powers of the Legislature of the Dominion.

CONSEQUENCES OF THE SETTING UP OF THE NEW DOMINIONS

7. (1) As from the appointed day —

(*a*) His Majesty's Government in the United Kingdom have no responsibility as respects the government of any of the territories which, immediately before that day, were included in British India;

(*b*) the suzerainty of His Majesty over the Indian States lapses, and with it, all treaties and agreements in force at the date of the passing of this Act between His Majesty and the rulers of Indian States, all functions exercisable by His Majesty at that date with respect to Indian States, all obligations of His Majesty existing at that date towards Indian States or the rulers thereof, and all powers, rights, authority or jurisdiction exercisable by His Majesty at that date in or in relation to Indian States by treaty, grant, usage, sufferance or otherwise; and

(*c*) there lapse also any treaties or agreements in force at the date of the passing of this Act between His Majesty and any persons having authority in the tribal areas, any obligations of His Majesty existing at that date to any such persons or with respect to the tribal areas, and all powers, rights, authority or jurisdiction exercisable at that date by His Majesty in or in relation to the tribal areas by treaty, grant, usage, sufferance or otherwise:

Provided that, notwithstanding anything in paragraph (*b*) or paragraph (*c*) of this subsection, effect shall, as nearly as may be, continue to be given to the provisions of any such agreement as is therein referred to which relate to customs, transit and communications, posts and telegraphs, or other like matters, until the provisions in question are denounced by the Ruler of the Indian State or person having authority in the tribal areas on the one hand, or by the Dominion or Province or other part thereof concerned on the other hand, or are superseded by subsequent agreements.

(2) The assent of the Parliament of the United Kingdom is hereby given to the omission from the Royal Style and Titles of the words 'Indiae Imperator' and the words 'Emperor of India' and to the issue by His Majesty for that purpose of His Royal Proclamation under the Great Seal of the Realm.

### TEMPORARY PROVISION AS TO GOVERNMENT OF EACH OF THE NEW DOMINIONS

8. (1) In the case of each of the new Dominions, the powers of the Legislature of the Dominion shall, for the purpose of making provision as to the constitution of the Dominion, be exercisable in the first instance by the Constituent Assembly of that Dominion, and references in this Act to the Legislature of the Dominion shall be construed accordingly.

(2) Except in so far as other provision is made by or in accordance with a law made by the Constituent Assembly of the Dominion under subsection (1) of this section, each of the new Dominions and all Provinces and other parts thereof shall be governed as nearly as may be in accordance with the Government of India Act, 1935; and the provisions of that Act, and of the Orders in Council, rules and other instruments made thereunder, shall, so far as applicable, and subject to any express provisions of this Act, and with such omissions, additions, adaptations and modifications as may be specified in orders of the Governor-General under the next succeeding section, have effect accordingly:

Provided that—

(*a*) the said provisions shall apply separately in relation to each of the new Dominions and nothing in this subsection shall be construed as continuing on or after the appointed day any Central Government or Legislature common to both the new Dominions;

(*b*) nothing in this subsection shall be construed as continuing in force on or after the appointed day any form of control by His Majesty's Government in the United Kingdom over the affairs of the new Dominions or of any Province or other part thereof;

(*c*) so much of the said provisions as requires the Governor-General or any Governor to act in his discretion or exercise his individual judgment as respects any matter shall cease to have effect as from the appointed day;

(*d*) as from the appointed day, no Provincial Bill shall be reserved under the Government of India Act, 1935, for the signification of His Majesty's pleasure, and no Provincial Act shall be disallowed by His Majesty thereunder; and

(*e*) the powers of the Federal Legislature or Indian Legislature under that Act, as in force in relation to each Dominion, shall, in the first instance, be exercisable by the Constituent Assembly of the Dominion in addition to the powers exercisable by that Assembly under subsection (1) of this section.

(3) Any provision of the Government of India Act, 1935, which, as applied to either of the new Dominions by subsection (2) of this section and the orders therein referred to, operates to limit the power of the legislature of that Dominion shall, unless and until other provision is made by or in accordance with a law made by the Constituent Assembly of the Dominion in accordance with the provisions of subsection (1) of this section, have the like effect as a law of the Legislature of the Dominion limiting for the future the powers of that Legislature.

ORDERS FOR BRINGING THIS ACT INTO FORCE

9. (1) The Governor-General shall by order make such provision as appears to him to be necessary or expedient —

(*a*) for bringing the provisions of this Act into effective operation;

(*b*) for dividing between the new Dominions, and between the new Provinces to be constituted under this Act, the powers, rights, property, duties and liabilities of the Governor-General in Council or, as the case may be, of the relevant Provinces which, under this Act, are to cease to exist;

(*c*) for making omissions from, additions to, and adaptations and modifications of, the Government of India Act, 1935, and the Orders in Council, rules and other instruments made thereunder, in their application to the separate new Dominions;

(*d*) for removing difficulties arising in connection with the transition to the provisions of this Act;

(*e*) for authorising the carrying on of the business of the Governor-General in Council between the passing of this Act and the appointed day otherwise than in accordance with the provisions in that behalf of the Ninth Schedule to the Government of India Act, 1935;

(*f*) for enabling agreements to be entered into, and other acts done, on behalf of either of the new Dominions before the appointed day;

(*g*) for authorising the continued carrying on for the time being on behalf of the new Dominions, or on behalf of any two or more of the said new Provinces, of services and activities previously carried on on behalf of British India as a whole or on behalf of the former Provinces which those new Provinces represent;

(*h*) for regulating the monetary system and any matters pertaining to the Reserve Bank of India; and

(*i*) so far as it appears necessary or expedient in connection with any of the matters aforesaid, for varying the constitution, powers or jurisdiction of any legislature, court or other authority in the new Dominions and creating new legislatures, courts or other authorities therein.

(2) The powers conferred by this section on the Governor-General shall, in relation to their respective Provinces, be exercisable also by the Governors of the Provinces which, under this Act, are to cease to exist; and those powers shall, for the purposes of the Government of India Act, 1935, be deemed to be matters as respects which the Governors are, under that Act, to exercise their individual judgment.

(3) This section shall be deemed to have had effect as from the third day of June, nineteen hundred and forty-seven, and any order of the Governor-General or any Governor made on or after that date as to any matter shall have effect accordingly, and any order made under this section may be made so as to be retrospective to any date not earlier than the said third day of June:

Provided that no person shall be deemed to be guilty of an offence by reason of so much of any such order as makes any provision thereof retrospective to any date before the making thereof.

(4) Any orders made under this section, whether before or after the appointed day, shall have effect —

(*a*) up to the appointed day, in British India;

(*b*) on and after the appointed day, in the new Dominion or Dominions concerned; and

(*c*) outside British India, or, as the case may be, outside the new Dominion or Dominions concerned, to such extent, whether before, on or after the appointed day, as a law of the Legislature of the Dominion or Dominions concerned would have on or after the appointed day,

but shall, in the case of each of the Dominions, be subject to the same powers of repeal and amendment as laws of the Legislature of that Dominion.

(5) No order shall be made under this section, by the Governor of any Province, after the appointed day, or, by the Governor-General, after the thirty-first day of March, nineteen hundred and forty-eight, or such earlier date as may be determined, in the case of either Dominion, by any law of the Legislature of that Dominion.

(6) If it appears that a part of the Province of Assam is, on the appointed day, to become part of the new Province of East Bengal, the preceding provisions of this section shall have effect as if, under this Act, the Province of Assam was to cease to exist on the appointed day and be reconstituted on that day as a new Province.

## SECRETARY OF STATE'S SERVICES, ETC.

10. (1) The provisions of this Act keeping in force provisions of the Government of India Act, 1935, shall not continue in force the provisions of that Act relating to appointments to the civil services of, and civil posts under, the Crown in India by the Secretary of State, or the provisions of that Act relating to the reservation of posts.

(2) Every person who —

(a) having been appointed by the Secretary of State, or Secretary of State in Council, to a civil service of the Crown in India continues on and after the appointed day to serve under the Government of either of the new Dominions or of any Province or part thereof; or

(b) having been appointed by His Majesty before the appointed day to be a judge of the Federal Court or of any court which is a High Court within the meaning of the Government of India Act, 1935, continues on and after the appointed day to serve as a judge in either of the new Dominions,

shall be entitled to receive from the Governments of the Dominions and Provinces or parts which he is from time to time serving or, as the case may be, which are served by the courts in which he is from time to time a judge, the same conditions of service as respects remuneration, leave and pension, and the same rights as respects disciplinary matters or, as the case may be, as respects the tenure of his office, or rights as similar thereto as changed circumstances may permit, as that person was entitled to immediately before the appointed day.

(3) Nothing in this Act shall be construed as enabling the rights and liabilities of any person with respect to the family pension funds vested in Commissioners under section two hundred and seventy-three of the Government of India Act, 1935, to be governed otherwise than by Orders in Council made (whether before or after the passing of this Act or the appointed day) by His Majesty in Council and rules made (whether before or after the passing of this Act or the appointed day) by a Secretary of State or such other Minister of the Crown as may be designated in that behalf by Order in Council under the Ministers of the Crown (Transfer of Functions) Act, 1946.

## INDIAN ARMED FORCES

11. (1) The orders to be made by the Governor-General under the preceding provisions of this Act shall make provision for the division of the Indian armed forces of His Majesty between the new Dominions, and for the command and governance of those forces until the division is completed.

(2) As from the appointed day, while any members of His Majesty's forces, other than His Majesty's Indian forces, is attached to or serving with any of His Majesty's Indian forces —

(*a*) he shall, subject to any provision to the contrary made by a law of the Legislature of the Dominion or Dominions concerned or by any order of the Governor-General under the preceding provisions of this Act, have, in relation to the Indian forces in question, the powers of command and punishment appropriate to his rank and functions; but

(*b*) nothing in any enactment in force at the date of the passing of this Act shall render him subject in any way to the law governing the Indian forces in question.

### BRITISH FORCES IN INDIA

12. (1) Nothing in this Act affects the jurisdiction or authority of His Majesty's Government in the United Kingdom, or of the Admiralty, the Army Council, or the Air Council or of any other United Kingdom authority, in relation to any of His Majesty's forces which may, on or after the appointed day, be in either of the new Dominions or elsewhere in the territories which, before the appointed day, were included in India, not being Indian forces.

(2) In its application in relation to His Majesty's military forces, other than Indian forces, the Army Act shall have effect on or after the appointed day —

(*a*) as if His Majesty's Indian forces were not included in the expressions 'the forces', 'His Majesty's forces' and 'the regular forces'; and

(*b*) subject to the further modifications specified in Parts I and II of the Third Schedule to this Act.

(3) Subject to the provisions of subsection (2) of this section, and to any provisions of any law of the Legislature of the Dominion concerned, all civil authorities in the new Dominions, and, subject as aforesaid and subject also to the provisions of the last preceding section, all service authorities in the new Dominions, shall, in those Dominions and in the other territories which were included in India before the appointed day, perform in relation to His Majesty's military forces, not being Indian forces, the same functions as were, before the appointed day, performed by them, or by the authorities corresponding to them whether by virtue of the Army Act or otherwise, and the matters for which provision is to be made by orders of the Governor-General under the preceding provisions of this Act shall include the facilitating of the withdrawal from the new Dominions and other territories aforesaid of His Majesty's military forces, not being Indian forces.

(4) The provisions of subsections (2) and (3) of this section shall apply in relation to the air forces of His Majesty, not being Indian air forces, as they apply in relation to His Majesty's military forces, subject, however, to the necessary adaptations, and, in particular, as if —

(*a*) for the references to the Army Act there were substituted references to the Air Force Act; and (*b*) for the reference to Part II of the Third Schedule to this Act there were substituted a reference to Part III of that Schedule.

NAVAL FORCES

13. (1) In the application of the Naval Discipline Act to His Majesty's naval forces, other than Indian naval forces, references to His Majesty's navy and His Majesty's ships shall not, as from the appointed day, include references to His Majesty's Indian navy or the ships thereof.

(2) In the application of the Naval Discipline Act by virtue of any law made in India before the appointed day to Indian naval forces, references to His Majesty's navy and His Majesty's ships shall, as from the appointed day, be deemed to be, and to be only, references to His Majesty's Indian navy and the ships thereof.

(3) In section ninety B of the Naval Discipline Act (which, in certain cases, subjects officers and men of the Royal Navy and Royal Marines to the law and customs of the ships and naval forces of other parts of His Majesty's dominions) the words 'or of India' shall be repealed as from the appointed day, wherever those words occur.

PROVISION AS TO THE SECRETARY OF STATE AND THE AUDITOR
OF INDIAN HOME ACCOUNTS

14. (1) A Secretary of State, or such other Minister of the Crown as may be designated in that behalf by Order in Council under the Ministers of the Crown (Transfer of Functions) Act, 1946, is hereby authorised to continue for the time being the performance, on behalf of whatever government or governments may be concerned, of functions as to the making of payments and other matters similar to the functions which, up to the appointed day, the Secretary of State was performing on behalf of governments constituted or continued under the Government of India Act, 1935.

(2) The functions referred to in subsection (1) of this section include functions as respects the management of, and the making of payments in respect of, government debt, and any enactments relating to such debt shall have effect accordingly:

Provided that nothing in this subsection shall be construed as continuing in force so much of any enactment as empowers the Secretary of State to contract sterling loans on behalf of any such Government as aforesaid or as applying to the Government of either of the new Dominions the prohibition imposed on the Governor-General in Council by section three hundred and fifteen of the Government of India Act, 1935, as respects the contracting of sterling loans.

(3) As from the appointed day, there shall not be any such advisers of the Secretary of State as are provided for by section two hundred and seventy-eight of the Government of India Act, 1935, and that section, and

any provisions of that Act which require the Secretary of State to obtain the concurrence of his advisers, are hereby repealed as from that day.

(4) The Auditor of Indian Home Accounts is hereby authorised to continue for the time being to exercise his functions as respects the accounts of the Secretary of State or any such other Minister of the Crown as is mentioned in subsection (1) of this section, both in respect of activities before, and in respect of activities after, the appointed day, in the same manner, as nearly as may be as he would have done if this Act had not passed.

LEGAL PROCEEDINGS BY AND AGAINST THE SECRETARY OF STATE

15. (1) Notwithstanding any thing in this Act, and, in particular, notwithstanding any of the provisions of the last preceding section, any provision of any enactment which, but for the passing of this Act, would authorise legal proceedings to be taken, in India or elsewhere, by or against the Secretary of State in respect of any right or liability of India or any part of India shall cease to have effect on the appointed day, and any legal proceedings pending by virtue of any such provision on the appointed day shall, by virtue of this Act, abate on the appointed day, so far as the Secretary of State is concerned.

(2) Subject to the provisions of this subsection, any legal proceedings which, but for the passing of this Act, could have been brought by or against the Secretary of State in respect of any right or liability of India, or any part of India, shall instead be brought —

(*a*) in the case of proceedings in the United Kingdom, by or against the High Commissioner;

(*b*) in the case of other proceedings, by or against such person as may be designated by order of the Governor-General under the preceding provisions of the Act or otherwise by the law of the new Dominion concerned,

and any legal proceedings by or against the Secretary of State in respect of any such right or liability as aforesaid which are pending immediately before the appointed day shall be continued by or against the High Commissioner or, as the case may be, the person designated as aforesaid:

Provided that, at any time after the appointed day, the right conferred by this subsection to bring or continue proceedings may, whether the proceedings are by, or are against, the High Commissioner or person designated as aforesaid, be withdrawn by a law of the Legislature of either of the new Dominions so far as that Dominion is concerned, as any such law may operate as respects proceedings pending at the date of the passing of the law.

(3) In this section, the expression 'the High Commissioner' means, in relation to each of the new Dominions, any such officer as may for the time being be authorised to perform in the United Kingdom, in relation to that Dominion, functions similar to those performed before the appointed day, in relation to the Governor-General in Council, by the High Commissioner referred to in section three hundred and two of the Government

of India Act, 1935; and any legal proceedings which, immediately before the appointed day, are the subject of an appeal to His Majesty in Council, or of a petition for special leave to appeal to His Majesty in Council, shall be treated for the purposes of this section as legal proceedings pending in the United Kingdom.

ADEN

16. (1) Subsections (2) to (4) of section two hundred and eighty-eight of the Government of India Act, 1935 (which confer on His Majesty power to make by Order in Council provision for the government of Aden) shall cease to have effect and the British Settlements Acts, 1887 and 1945, (which authorise His Majesty to make laws and establish institutions for British Settlements as defined in those Acts) shall apply in relation to Aden as if it were a British Settlement as so defined.

(2) Notwithstanding the repeal of the said subsections (2) to (4), the Orders in Council in force thereunder at the date of the passing of this Act shall continue in force, but the said Orders in Council, any other Orders in Council made under the Government of India Act, 1935, in so far as they apply to Aden, and any enactments applied to Aden or amended in relation to Aden by any such Orders in Council as aforesaid, may be repealed, revoked or amended under the powers of the British Settlements Acts, 1887 and 1945.

(3) Unless and until provision to the contrary is made as respects Aden under the powers of the British Settlements Acts, 1887 and 1945, or, as respects the new Dominion in question, by a law of the Legislature of that Dominion, the provisions of the said Orders in Council and enactments relating to appeals from any courts in Aden to any courts which will, after the appointed day, be in either of the new Dominions, shall continue in force in their application both to Aden and to the Dominion in question, and the last mentioned courts shall exercise their jurisdiction accordingly.

DIVORCE JURISDICTION

17. (1) No court in either of the new Dominions shall, by virtue of the Indian and Colonial Divorce Jurisdiction Acts, 1926 and 1940, have jurisdiction in or in relation to any proceedings for a decree for the dissolution of a marriage, unless those proceedings were instituted before the appointed day, but, save as aforesaid and subject to any provision to the contrary which may hereafter be made by any Act of the Parliament of the United Kingdom or by any law of the Legislature of the new Dominion concerned, all courts in the new Dominions shall have the same jurisdiction under the said Acts as they would have had if this Act had not been passed.

(2) Any rules made on or after the appointed day under subsection (4) of section one of the Indian and Colonial Divorce Jurisdiction Act, 1926, for a court in either of the new Dominions shall, instead of being

made by the Secretary of State with the concurrence of the Lord Chancellor, be made by such authority as may be determined by the law of the Dominion concerned, and so much of the said subsection and of any rules in force thereunder immediately before the appointed day as require the approval of the Lord Chancellor to the nomination for any purpose of any judges of any such court shall cease to have effect.

(3) The reference in subsection (1) of this section to proceedings for a decree for the dissolution of a marriage include references to proceedings for such a decree of presumption of death and dissolution of a marriage as is authorised by section eight of the Matrimonial Causes Act, 1937.

(4) Nothing in this section affects any court outside the new Dominions, and the power conferred by section two of the Indian and Colonial Divorce Jurisdiction Act, 1926, to apply certain provisions of that Act to other parts of His Majesty's dominions as they apply to India shall be deemed to be power to apply those provisions as they would have applied to India if this Act had not passed.

### PROVISIONS AS TO EXISTING LAWS, ETC.

18. (1) In so far as any Act of Parliament, Order in Council, order, rule, regulation or other instrument passed or made before the appointed day operates otherwise than as part of the law of British India or the new Dominions, references therein to India or British India, however worded and whether by name or not, shall, in so far as the context permits and except so far as Parliament may hereafter otherwise provide, be construed as, or as including, references to the new Dominions, taken together, or taken separately, according as the circumstances and subject matter may require:

Provided that nothing in this subsection shall be construed as continuing in operation any provision in so far as the continuance thereof as adapted by this subsection is inconsistent with any of the provisions of this Act other than this section.

(2) Subject to the provisions of subsection (1) of this section and to any other express provision of this Act, the Orders in Council made under subsection (5) of section three hundred and eleven of the Government of India Act, 1935, for adapting and modifying Acts of Parliament shall, except so far as Parliament may hereafter otherwise provide, continue in force in relation to all Acts in so far as they operate otherwise than as part of the law of British India or the new Dominions.

(3) Save as otherwise expressly provided in this Act, the law of British India and of the several parts thereof existing immediately before the appointed day shall, so far as applicable and with the necessary adaptations, continue as the law of each of the new Dominions and the several parts thereof until other provision is made by laws of the Legislature of the Dominion in question or by any other Legislature or other authority having power in that behalf.

(4) It is hereby declared that the Instruments of Instructions issued before the passing of this Act by His Majesty to the Governor-General and the Governors of Provinces lapse as from the appointed day, and nothing in this Act shall be construed as continuing in force any provision of the Government of India Act, 1935, relating to such Instruments of Instructions.

(5) As from the appointed day, so much of any enactment as requires the approval of His Majesty in Council to any rules of court shall not apply to any court in either of the new Dominions.

### INTERPRETATION, ETC.

19. (1) References in this Act to the Governor-General shall, in relation to any order to be made or other act done on or after the appointed day, be construed —

(*a*) where the order or other act concerns one only of the new Dominions, as references to the Governor-General of that Dominion;

(*b*) where the order or other act concerns both of the new Dominions and the same person is the Governor-General of both those Dominions, as references to that person; and

(*c*) in any other case, as references to the Governors-General of the new Dominions, acting jointly.

(2) References in this Act to the Governor-General shall, in relation to any order to be made or other act done before the appointed day, be construed as references to the Governor-General of India within the meaning of the Government of India Act, 1935, and so much of that or any other Act as requires references to the Governor-General to be construed as references to the Governor-General in Council shall not apply to references to the Governor-General in this Act.

(3) References in this Act to the Constituent Assembly of a Dominion shall be construed as references —

(*a*) in relation to India, to the Constituent Assembly, the first sitting whereof was held on the ninth day of December, nineteen hundred and forty-six, modified —

(*i*) by the exclusion of the members representing Bengal, the Punjab, Sind and British Baluchistan; and

(*ii*) should it appear that the North West Frontier Province will form part of Pakistan, by the exclusion of the members representing that Province; and

(*iii*) by the inclusion of members representing West Bengal and East Punjab; and

(*iv*) should it appear that, on the appointed day, a part of the Province of Assam is to form part of the new Province of East Bengal, by the exclusion of the members theretofore representing the Province of

Assam and the inclusion of members chosen to represent the remainder of that Province;

(*b*) in relation to Pakistan, to the Assembly set up or about to be set up at the date of the passing of this Act under the authority of the Governor-General as the Constituent Assembly for Pakistan:

Provided that nothing in this subsection shall be construed as affecting the extent to which representatives of the Indian States take part in either of the said Assemblies, or as preventing the filling of casual vacancies in the said Assemblies, or as preventing the participation in either of the said Assemblies, in accordance with such arrangements as may be made in that behalf, of representatives of the tribal areas on the borders of the Dominion for which that Assembly sits, and the powers of the said Assemblies shall extend and be deemed always to have extended to the making of provision for the matters specified in this proviso.

(4) In this Act, except so far as the context otherwise requires —

references to the Government of India Act, 1935, include references to any enactments amending or supplementing that Act, and, in particular references to the India (Central Government and Legislature) Act, 1946;

'India', where the reference is to a state of affairs existing before the appointed day or which would have existed but for the passing of this Act, has the meaning assigned to it by section three hundred and eleven of the Government of India Act, 1935;

'Indian forces' includes all His Majesty's Indian forces existing before the appointed day and also any forces of either of the new Dominions;

'pension' means, in relation to any person, a pension whether contributory or not, of any kind whatsoever payable to or in respect of that person and includes retired pay so payable, a gratuity so payable and any sum or sums so payable by way of the return, with or without interest thereon or other additions thereto, of subscriptions to a provident fund;

'Province' means a Governor's Province;

'remuneration' includes leave pay, allowances and the cost of any privileges or facilities provided in kind.

(5) Any power conferred by this Act to make any order includes power to revoke or vary any order previously made in the exercise of that power.

### SHORT TITLE

20. This Act may be cited as the Indian Independence Act, 1947.

### SCHEDULES
### FIRST SCHEDULE

BENGAL DISTRICTS PROVISIONALLY INCLUDED IN THE NEW PROVINCE OF EAST BENGAL

In the Chittagong Division, the districts of Chittagong, Noakhali and Tippera.

In the Dacca Division, the districts of Bakarganj, Dacca, Faridpur and Mymensingh.

In the Presidency Division, the districts of Jessore, Murshidabad and Nadia.

In the Rajshahi Division, the districts of Bogra, Dinajpur, Malda, Pabna, Rajshahi and Rangpur.

## SECOND SCHEDULE

### DISTRICTS PROVISIONALLY INCLUDED IN THE NEW PROVINCE OF WEST PUNJAB

In the Lahore Division, the districts of Gujranwala, Gurdaspur, Lahore, Sheikhupura and Sialkot.

In the Rawalpindi Division, the districts of Attock, Gujrat, Jhelum, Mianwali, Rawalpindi and Shahpur.

In the Multan Division, the districts of Dera Ghazi Khan, Jhang, Lyallpur, Montgomery, Multan and Muzaffargarh.

## THIRD SCHEDULE

### MODIFICATIONS OF ARMY ACT AND AIR FORCE ACT IN RELATION TO BRITISH FORCES

#### PART I

##### MODIFICATIONS OF ARMY ACT APPLICABLE ALSO TO AIR FORCE ACT

1. The proviso to section forty-one (which limits the jurisdiction of courts martial) shall not apply to offences committed in either of the new Dominions or in any of the other territories which were included in India before the appointed day.

2. In section forty-three (which relates to complaints), the words 'with the approval of the Governor-General of India in Council' shall be omitted.

3. In subsections (8) and (9) of section fifty-four (which, amongst other things, require certain sentences to be confirmed by the Governor-General in Council), the words 'India or', the words 'by the Governor-General, or, as the case may be' and the words 'in India, by the Governor-General, or, if he has been tried' shall be omitted.

4. In subsection (3) of section seventy-three (which provides for the nomination of officers with power to dispense with courts martial for desertion and fraudulent enlistment) the words 'with the approval of the Governor-General' shall be omitted.

5. The powers conferred by subsection (5) of section one hundred and thirty (which provides for the removal of insane persons) shall not be exercised except with the consent of the officer commanding the forces in the new Dominions.

6. In subsection (2) of section one hundred and thirty-two (which relates to rules regulating service prisons and detention barracks) the words 'and

in India for the Governor-General' and the words 'the Governor-General' shall be omitted except as respects rules made before the appointed day.

7. In the cases specified in subsection (1) of section one hundred and thirty-four, inquests shall be held in all cases in accordance with the provisions of subsection (3) of that section.

8. In section one hundred and thirty-six (which relates to deductions from pay), in subsection (1) the words 'India or' and the words 'being in the case of India a law of the Indian legislature', and the whole of subsection (2), shall be omitted.

9. In paragraph (4) of section one hundred and thirty-seven (which relates to penal stoppages from the ordinary pay of officers), the words 'or in the case of officers serving in India the Governor-General' the words 'India or' and the words 'for India or, as the case may be' shall be omitted.

10. In paragraph (12) of section one hundred and seventy-five and paragraph (11) of section one hundred and seventy-six (which apply the Act to certain members of His Majesty's Indian Forces and to certain other persons) the word 'India' shall be omitted wherever it occurs.

11. In subsection (1) of section one hundred and eighty (which provides for the punishment of misconduct by civilians in relation to courts martial) the words 'India or' shall be omitted wherever they occur.

12. In the provisions of section one hundred and eighty-three relating to the reduction in rank of non-commissioned officers, the words 'with the approval of the Governor-General' shall be omitted in both places where they occur.

## Part II

### MODIFICATIONS OF ARMY ACT

Section 184B (which regulates relations with the Indian Air Force) shall be omitted.

## Part III

### MODIFICATIONS OF AIR FORCE ACT

1. In section 179D (which relates to the attachment of officers and airmen to Indian and Burma Air Forces), the words 'by the Air Council and the Governor-General of India or, as the case may be', and the words 'India or', wherever those words occur, shall be omitted.

2. In section 184B (which regulates relations with Indian and Burma Air Forces) the words 'India or' and the words 'by the Air Council and the Governor-General of India or, as the case may be', shall be omitted.

3. Sub-paragraph (e) of paragraph (4) of section one hundred and ninety (which provides that officers of His Majesty's Indian Air Force are to be officers within the meaning of the Act) shall be omitted.

# APPENDIX XII

Congress Comments on the Draft Independence Bill, with Nehru's Corrections and Signature.

## CONGRESS C— ON THE D-B—

We have considered the Draft Bill and have
the following comments to offer:-

1. Form of Bill.-(A)We understand that in the
opinion of H.M.G. the form of the present Bill makes
it sufficiently clear that the new Dominion of India
will continue the international personality of the
existing India. But the point is so vital that all
avoidable doubt should be removed.

(b) For international purposes, the whole of India,
including British India and the Indian States, is
at present a single State. Under the Bill, two
independent Dominions are set up in British India
and the Indian States are detached from both. This
simultaneous fragmentation may create doubts as
to whether even the Dominion of India is anything
more than one of the new fragments and whether as
such it can continue to represent the old entity,
since even the two Dominions are described in the
Bill as "new Dominions". To avoid all possible
doubt *in this respect, and to preserve the continuity of the parent State for these essential purposes,* there should be two separate Bills: the first,
creating the Dominion of India to consist of the whole
of the existing India excluding the Pakistan Provinces
and such of the contiguous Indian States as may accede to
Pakistan; and the second, creating the Dominion of
Pakistan to consist of the excluded territories. *(c)* If,
owing to the time factor, it is not possible to have
two Bills at once, we would suggest that the single
Act now being passed should be divided as soon as
possible into two separate Acts, in much the same way
as the Government of Burma Act was separated from
the Government of India Act in December 1935, although

New para ¶

the two were originally passed as a single measure in August 1935. (d) We would in any case suggest the insertion of a provision in the Bill explicitly stating that the rights and obligations of India under any treaty or ~~xxxxxxxxxxxx~~ agreement with foreign States shall as from the appointed day become the rights and obligations of the Dominion of India, saving only those obligations which by their nature, can only be performed in territories outside the Dominion. Such a provision will, incidentally, contain the assurance which H.M.G. apparently desire in this behalf.

2. We now proceed to the details of the Bill in its present form.

<u>Preamble</u>.- For the reasons mentioned above, the preamble should read -

"A Bill to make provision for the establishment of the Dominion of India and the creation of a separate Dominion of Pakistan and for other matters consequential etc., etc."

<u>Clause 1(1)</u>.- For the same reasons, this sub-clause should provide that as from August 15, 1947, India shall be a Dominion and Pakistan a separate Dominion.

<u>Clause 2(1)</u>.- India should be defined to be the whole of India as under the Act of 1935 excluding Pakistan; Pakistan should be defined to be the British Indian areas mentioned in the Bill <u>plus</u> such of the contiguous Indian States as may accede thereto.

<u>Clause 2(3)</u>.- It should be made clear that "any area" in this sub-clause includes acceding Indian States. There is no specific provision in the Bill in its present form for the accession of Indian States.

Clause 3(2)(a).- We see no reason why merely because of the transfer of Sylhet to East Bengal, the present Province of Assam should cease to exist. This would merely furnish an additional argument to those who might wish to contend that the State now recognised as India ceased to exist with the separation of Pakistan. Sylhet is only one district out of about a dozen in Assam, although it has a large population. Bombay did not cease to exist as Bombay owing to the separation of Sind.

Clause 3(3).- We prefer, for the sake of finality, that the recommendations of the Boundary Commissions should be treated as an award binding on all those concerned and the orders of the Governor General, whether passed before or on or after the appointed day, should be in accordance with those recommendations. There is no need for agreement between the two Dominions in this matter.

Clause 4(2).- Same comment as on clause 3(3) above.

Clause 6(2).- The words "any existing or future Act of Parliament" may not cover the Act that is being now passed. The words should be "this Act or any existing or future Act of Parliament".

Clause 6(4).- Owing to the ambiguity of the words "as part of the law of the Dominion", a written assurance was given to the Dominion delegates at the Imperial Conference of 1930 in connection with a similar phrase then proposed to be inserted in the Statute of Westminster that it was not Parliament's intention, under the

provision in question to enact any law in relation
to the Dominions which, if enacted in relation to
a foreign State, would be inconsistent with international comity. The same object can be better
achieved by substituting for the words "unless it
is declared in the Act that the Dominion has requested
and consented to the passing thereof", which occur
in the Bill, the words "unless extended thereto by
an Act of the Legislature of the Dominion" which
occur in section 2 of the Status of the Union Act,
1934, in South Africa.

Clause 7(1)(b).- The complete wiping out of
all treaties and agreements in force at the date
of passing of the Act will create administrative
chaos of the gravest kind. Railway agreements,
customs agreements, harbour agreements, agreements
ceding criminal and civil jurisdiction, extradition
agreements, agreements connected with the administration of Posts and Telegraphs, Irrigation
agreements, agreements for the protection of
Indian States from external aggression, and more
generally, agreements relating to defence and
external affairs and a host of other agreements
will all lapse and even the existence of States
like Benares and Mysore which rest on Instruments
of Transfer from the Crown might be deprived of all
legal basis. Even the Cabinet Mission's Memorandum
of May 12, 1946, contemplated in paragraph 4 that
pending the conclusion of new agreements, existing
arrangements in all matters of common concern should
continue. Paragraph 5 of the same memorandum, after

referring to the xxxxx lapse of paramountcy and the
consequent cessation of all rights and obliga-
tions/therefrom goes on to state that the void
so created must be filled by the States entering
either into a federal relationship or into new
political arrangements with the successor government. To negotiate new agreements - some of
them multipartite - with a large number of
Indian States will be a long and laborious task.
Therefore, both to save time and trouble, instead
of individual standstill agreements, a standstill
proviso of general application to all the
States should be inserted in the Bill itself.

It may be pointed out that under the
clause as drafted, treaties and agreements
in force at the date of the passing of the Act
lapse as from "the appointed day". This seems
to imply that agreements which may be negotiated
between the passing of the Act and the appointed
day do not lapse. It may be that the intention
of the provision is that standstill agreements
should be negotiated during this intervening
period, while the paramountcy of the Crown
continues. This is borne out by the statement
in the Memorandum of May 12, 1946, that the
British Government and the Crown Representative -
i.e., the Paramount Power - will lend such
assistance as they can in negotiating such
agreements. There is, however, no intrinsic
difference between such agreements and the
agreements which the Bill seeks to terminate.
Moreover, owing to the time factor, it will not

be possible to arrive at new agreements before
the appointed day and the easiest way of achieving what was the intention of the Memorandum
of May 12, 1946, would be to insert in the
Bill itself a proviso on the following lines:-

> "Until new agreements are completed the
> existing relations and arrangements
> between His Majesty and any Indian Ruler
> in all matters of common concern shall
> continue, as between the new Dominion
> Government and the State concerned."

The proviso should be added to clause 7(1)(b)
and we would suggest that the three alternatives
mentioned below (in order of preference) be
considered in this connection:-

(1) Clause 7(1)(b) should read:-
"The suzerainty of His Majesty over the
Indian States lapses, provided that,---
(here insert the proviso mentioned above).
Under this alternative, all the words
occurring in the sub-clause except those
relating to the lapse of suzerainty go out.

(2) The sub=clause should read:-
"The suzerainty of His Majesty over the
Indian States lapses and with it all
functions exercised by His Majesty . . . .
sufferance or otherwise, provided that --
(here insert the proviso mentioned above).
Under this alternative, the words "all
treaties and agreements in force between
His Majesty and the Rulers of Indian States "
occurring in the Bill go out.

(3) The sub-clause may be retained in its
present form, but with the proviso mentioned above.

Clause 7(1)(c).- There should be a ~~proviso~~
proviso similar to that suggested in connection
with clause 7(1)(b); otherwise there is the danger
of agreements relating to the Khyber Pass, the
Bolan Pass etc. lapsing, with prejudicial consequences to the security of the country.

Clause 6(1).- Now that we have suggested
a new definition of India so as to make it
consist of existing India excluding Pakistan, a
proviso will have to be inserted under this
sub-clause on the following lines:-

This goes
after
p 3.

to above

"provided that save as otherwise provided
by or under this Act, the Legislature
of the Dominion shall exercise jurisdiction
only over the Governors' Provinces and
Chief Commissioners' Provinces or parts
thereof included in India".

**Clause 9 (5).** ~~It has been suggested~~
~~that the six months' period referred to in this~~
~~sub-clause should be extended to nine months.~~
~~We see no reason for any such extension,~~
~~particularly in view of the fact that~~ under
the modified clause 6 (2), the Legislature of
the Dominion can itself extend the period if
an extension is found necessary.

*[handwritten right margin:]* We agree to the substitution of "until 31 March 1948" for "six months from the appointed day."

*[handwritten left margin:]* up to 31 March.

**Clause 10.** We have no objection, on
the merits, to any suitable amendment, but we
consider that the security of tenure provided
for the Judges of the Federal Court and of the
High Courts in the Government of India Act 1935
is adequate.

**Clause 14.** We see no ~~particular~~ reason
why the Secretary of State should continue to
make these payments but if he does make them
the Dominion will of course provide the necessary
funds. *[handwritten:]* The High Commissioner should in future do this work. The clause is unnecessary and should be deleted.

**Clause 19 (3) (a) (iii)** We have already
pointed out that the Province of Assam should
not cease to exist merely because of the transfer
of Sylhet. Therefore this sub-clause will need
modification.

**Proviso:** ~~Instead of the proviso insert~~
~~the following as a fresh sub-clause between~~
~~sub-clause 3 and sub-clause 4 of clause 19.~~

*[handwritten:]* The proviso to Cl. 19(3) is at present vaguely worded. We consider it essential that the powers and functioning of the Constituent Assembly in respect of the making of the new constitutions should be placed beyond doubt. The C.As should have full power on their own to provide for the filling of casual vacancies and the participation in their work of representatives from Indian States and Tribal Areas.

*we would therefore suggest that Two provisos, as drafted, be dropped and in its place the following be inserted as a new sub-clause 3 A :*

"Nothing in this Act shall be construed
as detracting from the full power of
either Constituent Assembly

    (a) to frame a Constitution for India
        or Pakistan, as the case may be,

    (b) to give full effect to such Constitu-
        tion in supersession of the Constitu-
        tion previously in force,

    (c) to make provision for the filling of
        casual vacancies, and

    (d) to regulate the participation of
        representatives of the Indian States
        and of the Tribal Areas in the
        Assembly in accordance with such
        arrangements as it may make in this
        behalf."

———————

*J Nehru*
*3/7/47*

# BOOKS AND PUBLICATIONS
# CONSULTED

AMBEDKAR, B. R.: *Pakistan or the Partition of India*, 1940.
BOLITHO, HECTOR: *Jinnah — Creator of Pakistan*, 1954.
CAMPBELL-JOHNSON, ALAN: *Mission with Mountbatten*, 1951.
CHAUDHURI, B. M.: *Muslim Politics in India*, 1946.
COUPLAND, REGINALD: *The Constitutional Problem in India*, 1944.
DUNBAR, SIR GEORGE: *India and the Passing of Empire*, 1951.
FISCHER, LOUIS: *The Life of Mahatma Gandhi*, 1951.
GRAHAM POLE, D.: *India in Transition*, 1932.
KHOSLA, G. D.: *The Stern Reckoning*, n. d.
LINLITHGOW, THE MARQUESS OF: *Indian Speeches, 1936 – 43.*
LUMBY, E. W. R.: *The Transfer of Power in India*, 1954.
MAJUMDAR, R. C., RAYCHAUDHURI, H. C. AND KALIKINKAR DUTTA: *An Advanced History of India*, 1950.
MOUNTBATTEN OF BURMA, EARL: *Speeches as Viceroy and Governor-General, 1947 – 48.*
NEHRU, JAWAHARLAL: *Discovery of India*, 1946.
                                *Independence and After*, 1949.
PRASAD, RAJENDRA: *India Divided*, 1946.
RANDHAWA, M. S.: *Out of the Ashes*, 1954.
SHIVAPURI, S. N.: *The Grand Hypocrisy*, 1952.
SIMON, VISCOUNT: *Retrospect*, 1952.
SITARAMAYYA, DR PATTABHI: *History of the Indian National Congress*, 1935.
SUBRAHMANYAN, M.: *Why Cripps Failed*, 1942.
TEMPLEWOOD, VISCOUNT: *Nine Troubled Years*, 1954.
TENDULKAR, D. G.: *Mahatma: Life of Mohandas Karamchand Gandhi* (8 vols.) 1951 – 54.
*Montagu-Chelmsford Report on Indian Constitutional Reforms*, 1918.
*The Government of India Act, 1919.*
*Report of the Reforms Enquiry (Muddiman) Committee*, 1924.
*All-Parties Conference*, 1928.
*Report of the Indian Statutory (Simon) Commission.* (2 vols.), 1930.
*Indian Round Table Conference*, (Cmd. 3778).
*Report of the Joint Committee on Indian Constitutional Reform*, 1934.

*The Government of India Act, 1935.*

*India [Lord Privy Seal's (Cripps) Mission]*, (Cmd. 6350), April 1942.

*Correspondence with Mr Gandhi* (August 1942—April 1944)

*Gandhi-Jinnah Talks* (July—October 1944).

*Constitutional Proposals of the Sapru Committee*, 1945.

*India (Cabinet Mission)*, Cmd. 6821, 6829, 6835, 6861, 6862.

*The Indian Independence Act, 1947.*

*After Partition*, 1948.

*Muslim League Attack on Sikhs and Hindus in the Punjab*, 1950.

# INDEX

Abell, George, 357.

Act, Indian Naturalization, 407.

Act, of 1858 (For the Better Government of India), 3, 436.

—1861, Indian Councils, 3-4.

—1892, Indian Councils, 6.

—1909, Indian Councils, 11-12.

—1914, British Nationality & Status of Aliens, 407,

—1919, Government of India, 19-26.

—1935, Government of India, 51-4, 66, 193, 366, 381; adaptations to, 390, 393, 438.

—1939, Government of India (Amendments), 59.

—1940, India and Burma (Emergency Provisions), 86.

—1947, Indian Independence, 391, 393.

Act, Rowlatt, 27.

Act, Vernacular Press, 4-5.

Afghanistan, 389.

Aga Khan, His Highness the, 9.

Ahmed, Sir Sultan, 110, 331.

Akbar, 411.

Akram, Justice A.S.M., 401.

Alexander, A. V., 234.

Ali, Chaudhuri Mahomed, 397, 398.

Ali, Maulana Mohamed, 42.

Ali, Rashid, 109.

Allah Baksh, 83, 149.

All Parties Conference (1928), 35, 36, 37; (1943), 147, 173.

Alwar, 423.

Ambedkar, B. R., 49, 65, 123, 145, 175, 243-4.

Amery, L. S., 86, 92, 95, 102, 108, 111, 118, 137, 142, 153, 161, 169, 170-1, 172, 182-3, 184, 215.

Amritsar, 432, 433.

Anderson, Sir John, 118, 342.

Ansari, Dr. M. A., 35.

Arbitral Tribunal, 397, 398.

Asaf Ali, M., 297.

Assam, 148, 180, 229, 333, 343-4, 363, 369, 379.

Associated Chambers of Commerce, 145, 175, 225.

Atlantic Charter, 110, 111, 415.

Attlee, Clement, 118, 216, 220, 234, 235, 291; personal message to Nehru, 328; 329; Statement of February 1947, 338; 343, 351; announces June 3rd Plan, 378; 391.

Auchinleck, Sir Claude, 366, 399, 400.

August 1917 Announcement, 16-17.

August 1940 Offer, 92-4, 95, 96, 97, 100, 102.

Azad, Abul Kalam, 61, 84, 94, 96, 97, 103, 112, 123, 126, 127, 129, 130, 131, 132, 185, 189, 190, 191; addresses Simla Conference, 194-5; 196, 201, 202, 203, 204, 207, 209, 212, 221-2, 234, 235; interview with Cabinet Mission, 237-9; 247, 248, 252, 254, 255, 272, 273, 274, 275, 277, 296, 334, 385, 390.

Azad, Prithvi Singh, 244.

Azad Muslim Conference, 83.

Backward Communities, 119.

Baldwin, Stanley, 41.

Baluchistan, 37, 195, 253, 270, 271, 363, 369, 388, 390, 407.

*Bande Mataram* 56, 72.

Banerjea, Surendranath, 7, 27, 29,

Banerjee, P. N., 191, 196, 198, 200, 201, 203, 212.

Bardolai, Gopinath, 180, 229.

Bengal, partition, 6-7, 10; annulment of partition, 12, 112; 150-1, 180, 343, 347, 353, 355, 356, 368, 369, 370, 379, 383, 387, 388, 389, 396, 401, 402, 442.

Bengal Pact, 31.

Benn, Wedgwood, 38, 47, 67.

Besant, Mrs. Annie, 15, 40.

Bhabha, C. H., 297, 425, 426.